26-99

south essex college
FURTHER & HIGHER EDUCATION
Skills | Education | Careers

B

South Essex College
Thurrock Campus

D0590808

Cisco Networking Academy Program
IT Essentials I: PC Hardware and Software Companion Guide

Cisco Systems, Inc.

Cisco Networking Academy Program

Cisco Press

201 West 103rd Street

Indianapolis, Indiana 46290 USA

www.ciscopress.com

000 70092490010

Cisco Networking Academy Program
IT Essentials I: PC Hardware and Software Companion Guide

Cisco Systems, Inc.

Cisco Networking Academy Program

Course sponsored by Hewlett-Packard Company

Published by:
Cisco Press
201 West 103rd Street
Indianapolis, IN 46290 USA

Printed in the United States of America 1 2 3 4 5 6 7 8 9 0

First Printing   March 2003

Library of Congress Cataloging-in-Publication Number: 2001087347

ISBN: 1-58713-092-0

Trademark Acknowledgments

Warning and Disclaimer

This book is designed to provide information about PC hardware and software. Every effort has been made to make this book as complete and as accurate as possible, but no warranty or fitness is implied.

The information is provided on an "as is" basis. The author, Cisco Press, and Cisco Systems, Inc. shall have neither liability nor responsibility to any person or entity with respect to any loss or damages arising from the information contained in this book or from the use of the discs or programs that may accompany it.

The opinions expressed in this book belong to the author and are not necessarily those of Cisco Systems, Inc.

Feedback Information

At Cisco Press, our goal is to create in-depth technical books of the highest quality and value. Each book is crafted with care and precision, undergoing rigorous development that involves the unique expertise of members from the professional technical community.

Readers' feedback is a natural continuation of this process. If you have any comments regarding how we could improve the quality of this book, or otherwise alter it to better suit your needs, you can contact us through e-mail at networkingacademy@ciscopress.com. Please make sure to include the book title and ISBN in your message.

We greatly appreciate your assistance.

Publisher	*John Wait*
Editor-in-Chief	*John Kane*
Executive Editor	*Carl Lindholm*
Cisco Representative	*Anthony Wolfenden*
Cisco Press Program Manager	*Sonia Torres Chavez*
Cisco Marketing Communications Manager	*Tom Geitner*
Cisco Marketing Program Manager	*Edie Quiroz*
Production Manager	*Patrick Kanouse*
Development Editor	*Deborah Doorley*
Senior Project Editor	*Sheri Cain*
Copy Editor	*Progressive Information Technologies, John Edwards*
Technical Editors	*Frank Mann, David Planchard*
Assistant Editor	*Sarah Kimberly*
Cover Designer	*Louisa Adair*
Composition	*Octal Publishing, Inc.*
Indexer	*Tim Wright*

CISCO SYSTEMS

Corporate Headquarters
Cisco Systems, Inc.
170 West Tasman Drive
San Jose, CA 95134-1706
USA
http://www.cisco.com
Tel: 408 526-4000
        800 553-NETS (6387)
Fax: 408 526-4100

European Headquarters
Cisco Systems Europe
11 Rue Camille Desmoulins
92782 Issy-les-Moulineaux
Cedex 9
France
http://www-europe.cisco.com
Tel: 33 1 58 04 60 00
Fax: 33 1 58 04 61 00

Americas Headquarters
Cisco Systems, Inc.
170 West Tasman Drive
San Jose, CA 95134-1706
USA
http://www.cisco.com
Tel: 408 526-7660
Fax: 408 527-0883

Asia Pacific Headquarters
Cisco Systems Australia,
Pty., Ltd
Level 17, 99 Walker Street
North Sydney
NSW 2059 Australia
http://www.cisco.com
Tel: +61 2 8448 7100
Fax: +61 2 9957 4350

Cisco Systems has more than 200 offices in the following countries. Addresses, phone numbers, and fax numbers are listed on the Cisco Web site at www.cisco.com/go/offices

Argentina • Australia • Austria • Belgium • Brazil • Bulgaria • Canada • Chile • China • Colombia • Costa Rica • Croatia • Czech Republic • Denmark • Dubai, UAE • Finland • France • Germany • Greece • Hong Kong • Hungary • India • Indonesia • Ireland Israel • Italy • Japan • Korea • Luxembourg • Malaysia • Mexico • The Netherlands • New Zealand • Norway • Peru • Philippines Poland • Portugal • Puerto Rico • Romania • Russia • Saudi Arabia • Scotland • Singapore • Slovakia • Slovenia • South Africa • Spain Sweden • Switzerland • Taiwan • Thailand • Turkey • Ukraine • United Kingdom • United States • Venezuela • Vietnam • Zimbabwe

About the Technical Reviewers

Frank Mann is the department head of the telecommunications programs at Worcester Vocational High School in Worcester, MA. He has a Bachelor of Science degree in electrical engineering and a Master of Business Administration degree. He is an adjunct professor in the MSIT program at Clark University in Worcester, MA. Prior to entering academia, he acquired 17 years of engineering management experience in MCI's East Region's operations groups.

David Planchard is the director of corporate technology programs at Middlesex Community College in Bedford, MA. He has a Bachelor of Science degree in mechanical engineering and a Master of Science degree in management and holds the following Cisco certifications: CCNA, CCAI, CCNP. Before entering academia, he started his own semiconductor capital equipment company and spent over 19 years in the semiconductor industry in various engineering and marketing positions. He holds five U.S. and one international patent. He has published and authored numerous technical papers.

Overview

Table of Contents

Introduction

Cisco Networking Academy Program IT Essentials I: PC Hardware and Software Companion Guide supplements the online course and its corresponding classroom and laboratory instruction. The course is designed to be taken as a prerequisite to the IT Essentials II: Network Operating Systems course. This book parallels the online course to provide support for the information and skills you need to pursue a career in information technology as a PC technician or a network administrator. In addition to the CompTIA A+ certification exam objectives covered, this book provides information on Windows, UNIX, and Linux network operating systems.

This *Companion Guide* starts with the basics of technology and progresses through the assembly of a computer system. Features and functions of computer components are introduced, and then the process of preparing and installing the components is detailed in a step-by-step manner.

Once the computer system is up and running, this book explains the operating system, with an emphasis on the Disk Operating System (DOS). After learning the basics of DOS, students are introduced to the Windows 9X operating systems, including file system, file management, the Control Panel, and system tools. Windows NT/2000/XP is also discussed, as well as the differences between the installation of each operating system.

This book also goes over advanced hardware fundamentals for servers. It discusses RAID for the network server, including the different types and configuration issues. The fundamentals of networks is then introduced, which covers understanding the types of networks, adding a network interface card, and understanding the physical components of a network. Printers and their operation and maintenance are also discussed.

Information on preventive maintenance and troubleshooting for hardware, software, and the network server is detailed as is information covering careers available to IT professionals.

Hands-on experience, along with the review questions and worksheets, provides the foundation for students who will be taking the CompTIA A+ certification exam and continuing their studies in IT Essentials II: Network Operating Systems. The CD-ROM included with this book further enforces important topics, such as the floppy drive, the CD-ROM drive, the sound card, and other interactive elements.

The Goal of This Book

The goal of this book is to lay a foundation of the basic information required to build a computer and troubleshoot problems that occur. It is designed to prepare students to pass the CompTIA A+ certification exam and, when studied in conjunction with the IT Essentials II: Network Operating Systems course and its related titles, the CompTIA Server+ certification exam.

The Audience for This Book

This book is intended for students who want to pursue a career in information technology or who want to have knowledge about how a computer works, how to assemble a computer, and how to troubleshoot hardware and software issues. Students who will be seeking their A+ certification will find this book particularly useful.

This Book's Features

The features in this book facilitate an understanding of computer systems and troubleshooting system problems. The highlights of each chapter are as follows:

■ **Objectives**—Each chapter starts with a list of objectives that should be mastered by the end of the chapter. The objectives provide a reference of the concepts covered in the chapter.

■ **Figures, examples, tables, and scenarios**—This book contains figures, examples, and tables that help explain theories, concepts, commands, and setup sequences, as well as help you visualize the content covered in the chapter. In addition, specific scenarios provide real-world situations that detail problems and solutions.

■ **Chapter summaries**—At the end of each chapter is a summary of the concepts covered in the chapter. The summary provides a synopsis of the chapter and serves as a study aid.

■ **"Check Your Understanding" review questions**—Review questions are presented at the end of each chapter to serve as an assessment. In addition, the questions reinforce the concepts introduced in the chapter and help test your understanding before moving on to subsequent chapters.

■ **Skill builders**—Throughout this book are references to worksheet and lab activities found in *Cisco Networking Academy Program IT Essentials I: PC Hardware and Software Lab Companion*. These labs allow you to make a connection between theory and practice.

How This Book Is Organized

This book is divided into 13 chapters, two appendixes, and a glossary of key terms. These sections are described as follows:

■ **Chapter 1, "Information Technology Basics"**—Different computer systems, programs, and computer types are discussed in this chapter. The Windows Desktop environment is identified, and relevant computer terminology is defined. Number systems that relate to the computer industry are covered in order to perform binary, decimal, and hexadecimal conversions. The safety requirements are emphasized as are the tools used to assemble a computer.

- **Chapter 2, "How Computers Work"**—This chapter details the features and functions of computer components in preparation for the assembly process. This includes the case, power supply, motherboard, expansion slots, memory, I/O ports, SCSI disk types, and system resources. Detailed information is provided on the floppy drive, hard drive, and CD-ROM drive. In addition, the components of portable computers are discussed.

- **Chapter 3, "Assembling a Computer"**—The first step in the assembly process is gathering the components and completing the computer inventory. Preparing and installing the components are detailed in a step-by-step process. In the final steps, you review the checklist, assemble the case, and boot the system for the first time.

- **Chapter 4, "Operating System Fundamentals"**—The operating system and terminology important to the technician are explained in this chapter. The emphasis is on the Disk Operating System (DOS). You will learn the basics of DOS, the commands used, and the file structure. Additionally, memory management is detailed, along with the tools that are used to adjust and optimize memory.

- **Chapter 5, "Windows 9X Operating Systems"**—This chapter provides an in-depth discussion of Windows 9X although the focus is on Windows 98. This includes the file system, file management, the Control Panel, and system tools. It is important to understand the requirements for installing Windows 98 in order to install and troubleshoot errors that might occur.

- **Chapter 6, "Multimedia Capabilities"**—Multimedia is an important part of a computer system. This chapter covers the basic hardware required, including video cards, sound cards, CD-ROM drives, and DVD drives.

- **Chapter 7, "Windows NT/2000/XP Operating Systems"**—This chapter compares the file systems and discusses the differences between the installation of Windows 98 and Windows 2000. Topics include the Windows 2000 boot system and administrative tools.

- **Chapter 8, "Advanced Hardware Fundamentals for Servers"**—The focus of this chapter is RAID for the network server. You learn about the different types of RAID along with configuration issues. In addition, adding hardware to the server and upgrading server components are covered in detail.

- **Chapter 9, "Networking Fundamentals"**—In this chapter, you are introduced to the fundamentals of a network, including understanding the types of networks, adding a network interface card, and understanding the physical components of a network. Of importance is the OSI model, TCP/IP, and network protocols. You learn about LAN architectures and the media needed to connect to the Internet.

- **Chapter 10, "Printers and Printing"**—Printers are extremely important in a network environment. This chapter discusses the different types of printers, how they work, and the maintenance required to ensure optimal performance. In addition, you learn about print sharing and management, and how to solve printer problems.

- **Chapter 11, "Preventive Maintenance"**—A computer system and a network are kept in good working order with preventive maintenance. You learn about electrostatic discharge (ESD) and how to create an ESD-free environment. Maintaining computer components, including the keyboard, monitor, and mouse, is covered along with information on cleaning and disposing.

- **Chapter 12, "Troubleshooting PC Hardware"**—This chapter details the troubleshooting cycle and the steps to take when there is a computer problem. These steps help the technician determine and fix problems relating to the hardware box and peripheral devices.

- **Chapter 13, "Troubleshooting Software"**—Problems that are attributed to software can be complicated. In this chapter, you use system tools to troubleshoot Windows-specific problems relating to the operating system and Registry, and programs that are running on the computer.

- **Appendix A, "The Information Technology Professional"**—The careers available to an IT professional is the focus of this appendix. Career paths are detailed, including related fields, degree fields, and the fields where certification is necessary.

- **Appendix B, "Answers to Check Your Understanding Review Questions"**—This appendix lists the answers to the Check Your Understanding review questions that are included at the end of each chapter.

- **Glossary of Key Terms**—This glossary provides you with a complete list of the key terms defined in each chapter.

CompTIA Authorized Quality Curriculum

The contents of this training material were created for the CompTIA A+ Certification exam covering CompTIA certification exam objectives that were current as of December 2002.

How to Become CompTIA Certified

This training material can help you prepare for and pass a related CompTIA certification exam or exams. In order to achieve CompTIA certification, you must register for and pass a CompTIA certification exam or exams.

In order to become CompTIA certified, you must

1. Select a certification exam provider. For more information, please visit www.comptia.org/certification/general_information/test_locations.asp.

2. Register for and schedule a time to take the CompTIA certification exam(s) at a convenient location.

3. Read and sign the Candidate Agreement, which will be presented at the time of the exam(s). The text of the Candidate Agreement can be found at www.comptia.org/certification/general_information/candidate_agreement.asp.

4. Take and pass the CompTIA certification exam(s).

For more information about CompTIA's certifications, such as industry acceptance, benefits, or program news, visit www.comptia.org/certification/default.asp.

CompTIA is a nonprofit information technology (IT) trade association. CompTIA's certifications are designed by subject-matter experts from across the IT industry. Each CompTIA certification is vendor-neutral, covers multiple technologies, and requires demonstration of skills and knowledge widely sought after by the IT industry.

To contact CompTIA with any questions or comments, please call + 1 630 268 1818 or send an e-mail to questions@comptia.org.

About the CD-ROM

A CD-ROM complements this book. This CD contains three test engines consisting of A+ and Server+ questions, interactive e-Lab Activities, high-resolution PhotoZooms, and instructional video vignettes. These materials review and reinforce the content covered in this book. This CD also includes supplemental material on the Windows XP operating system and a certification map that aligns chapters to A+ certification exam objectives. Additionally, this CD provides the following:

- An easy-to-use graphical user interface
- Accurate and concise feedback
- Frequent interaction with content
- Support for guided and exploratory navigation
- Learner-direction and support
- Flexibility to learners at different levels of expertise

Objectives

Upon completion of this chapter, you will be able to perform the following tasks:

- Describe the different computer systems, programs, and computer types
- Identify and navigate the Windows desktop environment
- Use the features of Microsoft Windows, including creating shortcuts and adjusting display properties
- Define relevant computer terminology used in digital math
- Perform number conversions, including decimal, binary, and hexadecimal
- Understand the safety procedures promoted throughout the IT Essentials I course
- Identify and use the tools in the PC technician's tool kit

Chapter 1

Information Technology Basics

This chapter discusses the basics of information technology (IT) as they relate to the computer technician. It covers the different computer types used today, several software applications, and a brief overview of the Internet. You will identify the basic features of Windows and the elements of the Windows desktop.

Additionally, you learn some of the vocabulary that is important to the technician. You will also examine the methods used in number conversions, including binary to decimal, decimal to binary, and so on. An explanation of analog and digital is included as well as an introduction to algorithms.

The first priority in working with computers is safety. This chapter details safety procedures that pertain to the labs mentioned in this text and used in the workplace.

Getting Started in IT

This section includes the following topics:

- Computer systems and programs
- Computer types
- Connecting computer systems
- The birth of the Internet
- The cost of technology: more and more for less and less

Computer Systems and Programs

A *computer system*, as shown in Figure 1-1, consists of hardware and software components. *Hardware* is the physical equipment, such as the case, floppy disk drives, keyboard, monitor, cables, speakers, and printers. The term *software* describes the programs that operate the computer system. Computer software, also called programs, instructs the computer how to operate. These operations can include identifying, accessing, and processing information. Essentially, a *program* is a sequence of instructions that describe how data are to be processed. Programs vary widely, depending on the type of information that is to be accessed or generated. For example, the instructions involved in balancing a checkbook are different from those required to simulate a virtual-reality world on the Internet.

Figure 1-1 Computer System

HP DeskJet 630 Printer

HP Pavilion bg922 PC

There are two types of software: applications and operating systems. *Application software* accepts input from the user and then manipulates it to achieve a result, known as the *output*. Applications are programs designed to perform a specific function directly for the user or for another program. Examples of applications include word processors, database programs, spreadsheets, web browsers, web development tools, and graphic design tools. Computer applications are detailed later in this chapter.

An *operating system (OS)* is a program that manages all the other programs in a computer. It also provides the operating environment with the applications that access resources on the computer. OSs perform basic tasks such as recognizing input from the keyboard or mouse, sending output to the video screen or printer, keeping track of files on the drives, and controlling peripherals, such as printers and modems. The Disk Operating System (DOS), Windows 98, Windows 2000, Windows XP, Windows NT, Linux, Mac OS X, DEC VMS, and IBM OS/400 are examples of OSs.

OSs are platform-specific, which means they are designed for uses with different types of computers. For example, the Windows OS (3.1, 95, 98, 2000, XP, or NT) is designed for use with an IBM-compatible personal computer, often referred to as a PC. The

Mac OS, on the other hand, only works with Macintosh computers. PC and Macintosh are called *platforms*. A platform is the computer system on which programs can run.

Firmware is a program that is embedded in a silicon chip rather than stored on a floppy disk. Any change to either the hardware or software can cause firmware to become outdated, leading to device or system failure or even data loss. When firmware becomes outdated, the only solution is to replace it. Current firmware is *flashable*, which means that the contents can be upgraded or flashed. This concept is covered more thoroughly in a later chapter.

Computer Types

Two types of computers are detailed in this section: the mainframe, which has provided computing power for major corporations for more than 40 years, and the personal computer, which has had more impact on people and business than any other single device in history.

Mainframes

Mainframes are powerful machines that enable companies to automate manual tasks, shorten the time to market for new products, run financial models that enhanced profitability, and so on. The mainframe model consists of centralized computers, usually housed in secure, climate-controlled rooms. End users interface with the computers via *dumb terminals*. These dumb terminals are low-cost devices that usually consist of a monitor, a keyboard, and a port that communicates with the mainframe. Initially, terminals were hard wired directly to communication ports on the mainframe, and the communications were asynchronous. An illustration of a mainframe computer is shown in Figure 1-2.

A mainframe environment depends on a single computer or group of computers that can easily be centrally managed and maintained. This configuration has the additional advantage of being secure. It is secure not only because of the physical security of the computer room, but also because of the end users' minimal ability to introduce viruses into the system. Virus protection and eradication today cost companies hundreds of millions of U.S. dollars annually.

At its peak in the late 1970s and early 1980s, the mainframe (and later the minicomputer) market was dominated by IBM and Digital Equipment Corporation. These high-powered machines, however, came with high price tags. The cost of entry into the mainframe market was typically several hundred thousand to several million U.S. dollars. The minicomputer provided similar capabilities at a lower price, but minicomputer configurations were often over US$ 10,000 as well.

NOTE

Asynchronous means without respect to time. In terms of data transmission, asynchronous means that no clock or timing source is needed to keep both the sender and the receiver synchronized. Without the benefit of a clock, the sender must signal the start and stop of each character so that the receiver knows when to expect data.

Figure 1-2 A Mainframe Computer

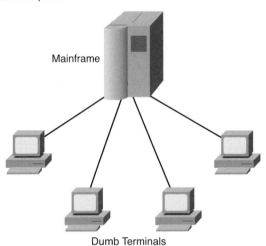

Mainframes continue to play a large role in corporate computing. It is estimated that 24 million dumb terminals are still in use worldwide. In addition, 15 million PCs are currently deployed to function primarily as mainframe terminal emulators. These dumb terminals are American Standard Code for Information Interchange (ASCII) character-based devices and are often referred to as *green screens* because many display green characters.

The term mainframe used to refer to the cabinet that housed the central processing unit (CPU); today, it refers to a large computer system. Table 1-1 lists the advantages and disadvantages of mainframes.

Table 1-1 Advantages and Disadvantages of Mainframes

Advantages	Disadvantages
Scalability (the ability to add more users as the need arises)	Character-based applications
Centralized management	Lack of vendor OS standards and interoperability in multivendor environments
Centralized backup	Expensive, with a high cost for setup, maintenance, and initial equipment
Low-cost desktop devices (dumb terminals)	Potential single point of failure (non-fault-tolerant configurations)
High level of security	Timesharing systems, that is, with the potential for a bottleneck

Personal Computers

A *personal computer (PC)* is a standalone device, which means that it is independent of all other computers, as shown in Figure 1-3. With the advent of the PC, the *graphical user interface (GUI)* gained wide introduction to users.

GUIs, (pronounced goo-ee) employ a graphics display to represent procedures and programs that can be executed by the computer. An example is the Windows desktop. These programs routinely use small pictures, called *icons*, to represent different programs. The advantage of using a GUI is that the user does not have to remember complicated commands to execute a program. The GUIs first appeared in Xerox and Apple computers. Along with the GUI, thousands of Windows-based applications were also introduced.

Figure 1-3 Personal Computer

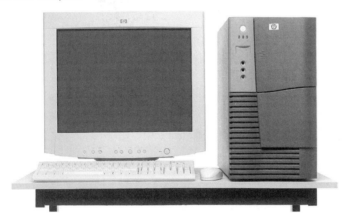

As PC technology has improved, the power of the PC has risen to the point that it can perform enterprise-level functions. The advantages and disadvantages are listed in Table 1-2.

Table 1-2 Advantages and Disadvantages of PC Computing

Advantages	Disadvantages
Standardized hardware	Desktop computers cost, on average, five times as much as dumb terminals, according to some industry estimates.
Standardized, highly interoperable operating systems	No centralized backup.
Graphical user interface	No centralized management.

continues

Table 1-2 Advantages and Disadvantages of PC Computing (Continued)

Advantages	Disadvantages
Low-cost devices (when compared to mainframes), low cost of entry	Security risks can be greater (physical, data access, and virus security risks).
Distributed computing	High management and maintenance costs, although they are generally cheaper to maintain than mainframes.
User flexibility	
High-productivity applications	

Connecting Computer Systems

The PC as a standalone device might be adequate for home use, but businesses, government offices, and schools need to exchange information and share equipment and resources. In order to do this, a method was developed to connect individual computers. This method is called *networking*. The individual computers in a network are referred to as *workstations* as illustrated in Figure 1-4.

Figure 1-4 Workstations

Workstation   Workstation   Workstation

A *network* is simply a group of computers that are connected so that their resources can be shared, as illustrated in Figure 1-5. Schools have networks. Computers used by students, teachers, and administrators are all connected. This saves the expense of having to buy peripheral equipment, such as printers, for each computer. For example, when a homework assignment is being printed in the school computer lab, the printer is being shared with all the students. It would be expensive if a school bought a printer for every computer. In addition, a network enables users to share files. If work is being done on a group project, a file can be saved to a central computer called a *server*. This file can then be accessed from any other student computer in the school.

Figure 1-5 Connecting Computer Systems

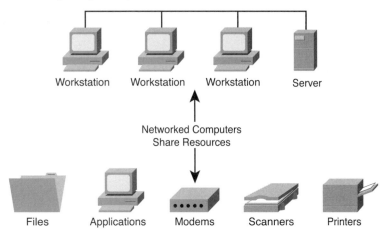

Networks are not limited to just a building or school campus. Networks can connect an entire school district or all the offices in a company. A school, for example, is connected to a main district office, as are all the other schools in a district. The Internet is the ultimate network, connecting millions of smaller networks.

Most network connections are made by cable, but wireless connections are beginning to gain popularity. Cable can carry voice, data, or both. Homes might have modems that plug into telephone jacks. The telephone line carries voice signals when the telephone is plugged into the phone jack, but carries data signals (encoded to appear as if they were voice) when the modem is connected. Other, faster connections to the Internet are available, such as Digital Subscriber Line (DSL), cable, and T1, T3, or E1 lines. In some parts of the world, Integrated Services Digital Network (ISDN) is used as well. Most of these technologies are used by businesses because of their higher cost. Some high-speed services are only available in a limited area. Improvements in communication devices and an ever-increasing demand for high-speed links, however, will mean that in the next few years, many home users should have access to these Internet connections.

The Birth of the Internet

As the Cold War between the West and the (former) Soviet Union intensified in the 1960s, the U.S. Department of Defense (DoD) recognized the need to establish communications links between major U.S. military installations. The primary motivation was to maintain communications if a nuclear war resulted in the mass destruction and breakdown of traditional communications channels. Major universities, such as the University of California and the Massachusetts Institute of Technology (MIT), were also involved in networking projects.

The DoD funded research sites throughout the U.S, and in 1968, the Advanced Research Projects Agency (ARPA) contracted with Bolt, Beranek, and Newman, Inc. (BBN), a private company, to build a network based on the packet-switching technology that had been developed for better transmission of computer data.

The 1970s: The Growth Spurt Begins

When the Advanced Research Projects Agency Network (ARPANET) project began, no one anticipated that the network would grow to the extent that it did. Throughout the 1970s, more nodes, or access points, were added, both domestically and abroad.

The 1980s: More Is Better

In 1983, the ARPANET was split, and Military Network (MILNET), which was integrated with the Defense Data Network (DDN), took 68 of the 113 existing nodes. The DDN had been created the previous year.

The *Domain Name System (DNS)* was introduced in 1984, providing a way to map "friendly" host names to Internet Protocol (IP) addresses. It was more efficient and convenient than previous methods. These methods are discussed in Chapter 9, "Networking Fundamentals." In 1984, there were more than 1000 host computers on the network.

During the last half of the 1980s, networking increased considerably. For example, the National Science Foundation (NSF) created supercomputer centers in the U.S at Princeton, the University of California, the University of Illinois, and Cornell University. The Internet Engineering Task Force (IETF) was also created during this time. By 1987, 10,000 hosts were on the network, and by 1989, that number increased to over 100,000.

The 1990s: The Net Becomes Big Business

The phenomenal growth rate of the 1980s was small compared to what came in the 1990s. ARPANET evolved into the Internet, with the U.S. government getting involved in pushing the development of the so-called information superhighway. The National Science Foundation Network (NSFNET) backbone was upgraded to T3 speed (that is,

44.736 MBps), and in 1991, this backbone sent more than 1 trillion bytes per month. The Internet Society (ISOC) was formed, and in 1992, more than 1 million hosts existed on the Internet.

The 1990s saw the explosion of commerce on the Internet. As more college students, faculty, home users, and companies of all sizes got connected, the business world recognized the opportunity to reach a large and expanding affluent market. By 1995, online advertising had caught on and online banking had arrived; you could even order a pizza over the Internet.

The last half of the last decade of the century ushered in new major developments on an almost-daily basis. Streaming audio and video, "push" technologies, and Java and ActiveX scripting took advantage of higher-performance connectivity that was available at falling prices. Domain names became big business, with particularly desirable names selling for upwards of US$ 1 million. Today, millions of sites exist on the World Wide Web, with millions of host computers participating in this great linking. The graph shown in Figure 1-6 shows the growth of the Internet.

Figure 1-6 The Exponential Growth of the Internet

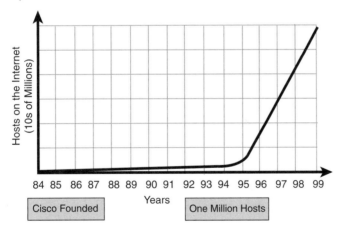

Table 1-3 shows a timeline of significant events in PC networking history.

The tremendous growth in the computer industry means exciting job possibilities. According to new projections from the U.S. Bureau of Labor Statistics, eight of the ten fastest-growing occupations will be computer-related. That means that jobs for IT technicians and computer-support personnel will just about double by the year 2010.

Table 1-3 The Exponential Growth of the Internet

Year	Event
1957	ARPA is created by the DoD.
1969	ARPANET connects the first four universities in the U.S.
1970	ALOHANET is developed by the University of Hawaii.
1973	ARPANET goes international with connections to University College in London, England, and the Royal Radar Establishment in Norway.
1974	BBN opens Telnet, the first commercial version of ARPANET.
1982	The term Internet is used for the first time.
1983	Transmission Control Protocol/Internet Protocol (TCP/IP) becomes the universal language of the Internet. ARPANET is split into ARPANET and MILNET.
1984	The number of Internet hosts exceeds 1000. Domain Name Service (DNS) is introduced.
1986	NSFNET is created (with a backbone speed of 56 KBps).
1987	The number of Internet hosts exceeds 10,000.
1988	Computer Emergency Response Team (CERT) is formed by DARPA.
1989	The number of Internet hosts exceeds 100,000.
1990	ARPANET becomes the Internet.
1991	The World Wide Web (WWW) is born.
1992	Internet Society (ISOC) is chartered. The number of Internet hosts breaks 1 million.
1993	Mosaic, the first graphics-based web browser, becomes available.
1996	The number of Internet hosts exceeds 10 million. The Internet covers the globe.
1997	The American Registry for Internet Numbers (ARIN) is established. Internet 2 comes online.
1999	The Internet 2 backbone network deploys IPv6.
2001	The number of Internet hosts exceeds 110 million.

The Cost of Technology: More and More for Less and Less

As computer and networking technologies have advanced over the past few decades, the cost of the increasingly sophisticated technology has fallen dramatically. Those falling prices are at least partially responsible for the rising popularity of connectivity solutions in the business world and in personal lives.

In the 1970s and 1980s, the PC shown in Figure 1-7, which was considered state of the art for the time, cost several thousand U.S. dollars. Online services existed, but with fees of US$ 25 or more per hour of access, only big businesses and the wealthy could afford them. PC veterans can still remember the announcement of the Prodigy bargain rate of US$ 9.95 an hour for online access. This connection was at speeds of 1200 or 2400 baud, which today would be considered unusable.

Figure 1-7 Legacy PC

Today in the U.S., for example, for less than US$ 1000, you can buy a computer system that is capable of doing much more, and doing it better and faster, than the US$ 500,000 mainframe version of 20 years ago. Internet access at speeds equivalent to T1 are available through DSL or cable modems for US$ 30 to 40 per month, and prices continue to fall. Basic Internet access at 56 kbps can be obtained for much less—sometimes even free—if you can tolerate additional on-screen advertising.

Windows Desktop Environment

This section includes the following topics:

- Starting, shutting down, and restarting Microsoft Windows
- Using Windows Explorer
- Navigating the desktop

- Working with icons
- Recognizing an application window
- Resizing a desktop window
- Switching between windows

Starting, Shutting Down, and Restarting Microsoft Windows

Basic functions include turning the computer on, which is referred to as a *cold boot*; restarting the system, which is referred to as a *warm boot*; and shutting down the system. Because most computers have both the power button and reset button on the front, it is important to know the function of each.

Turning on the PC

To turn on a PC, an external switch (or pair of switches) must be activated. The rear switch, if included, provides the physical connection between the house power (through the wall outlet) and the computer power supply. This switch has to be on prior to turning on the front switch. Most PCs will have a single switch in the front that is activated to provide power.

In most cases, the monitor will also have a power switch. This switch is usually in the front or lower-right portion of the display case. Switches can be push-on, push-off, or rocker type. They are manufactured to withstand thousands of on/off cycles, typically outlasting the PC itself.

Starting a computer is also referred to as booting the system. A cold boot is performed when the PC is turned on using the power button. At the end of this process, a single tone will sound, and the Windows desktop will be displayed.

Shutting Down the Computer

To shut down the computer, click the Start button in the lower-left corner of the Windows Taskbar, as shown in Figure 1-8, and select **Shut Down**. Alternatively, press **Ctrl-Alt-Delete**, and click **Shut Down** from the menu that displays.

Do not turn the computer off until a message displays indicating that it is safe to do so. Important data that are stored in memory while the system is running need to be written to the hard disk before turning off the computer. Newer computers will automatically turn off power when the shutdown process is complete.

NOTE

It is extremely important not to power off the computer with the power switch (until instructed to do so by Windows). Most OSs, such as Macintosh and Windows, have a specific method for turning the system off. In Windows, choose the Shut Down button from the Start menu. On a Macintosh, choose the Shut Down button from the Special menu.

Figure 1-8 Shutting Down a Computer

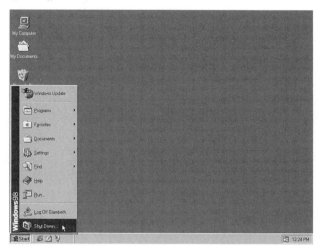

Restarting the PC

Restarting a PC that has already been powered up is referred to as a warm boot. A restart can be achieved by pressing the reset button on the front panel of the computer. Alternatively, click the Start button, choose **Shut Down**, and click **Restart** from the menu that displays. The concepts of warm boot and cold boot are discussed more thoroughly in Chapter 2, "How Computers Work."

Using Windows Explorer

The Explorer file manager in Windows 95/98/NT4/2000 provides the ability to create, copy, move, and delete files and folders. In the left window, Explorer displays the hierarchy of folders stored on the hard disk or other storage device. When you click a folder in the left Explorer window, its contents will display in the right window. Two or more instances of Explorer can be launched simultaneously in order to drag and drop items between them.

Explorer can be accessed in Windows 9x (95, 98, and Millennium), by choosing **Start, Programs, Windows Explorer** from the Windows desktop as shown in Figure 1-9. In Windows 2000/XP, choose **Start, Programs, Accessories, Windows Explorer** from the menu that displays (see Figure 1-9). Another way to open Windows Explorer in Windows 9x, 2000, and XP is to right-click **Start** and select **Explore**.

TEST TIP

Know the different ways to open Windows Explorer.

Figure 1-9 Accessing Windows Explorer in Windows 98 and Windows 2000

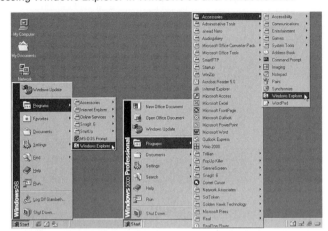

Navigating the Desktop

The main display screen in Windows is known as the *desktop*. The Windows desktop has remained consistent for most versions of Windows, including 95, 98, 98 Second Edition (SE), Millennium edition (Me), NT, and 2000. Figure 1-10 shows the desktop in Windows 98. However, some variations can be seen in older versions of Windows 95 or a special type of installation, such as that on a laptop or network, when certain features are disabled.

Figure 1-10 The Windows Desktop

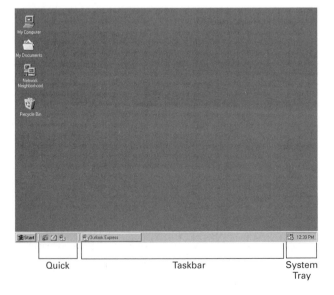

Quick   Taskbar   System
                                                    Tray

An *icon* is an image that represents an application or a capability. Typically, an icon is selectable as a shortcut to a program or file on the desktop. It can also be non-selectable, as in a company's logo on a web page.

Some of the icons on the desktop, such as My Computer, Network Neighborhood (or My Network Places), Recycle Bin, and My Documents, are *shortcuts* to their respective directories. (Directories are discussed in Chapter 4, "Operating System Fundamentals.") Other icons that might be on the desktop, such as Microsoft Word, Excel, or Adobe Photoshop, are shortcuts to those applications as well.

Double-clicking the My Computer icon gives access to all the installed drives (or computer storage components).

My Documents is a shortcut to personal, or frequently accessed files, and Network Neighborhood enables the user to see neighboring computers in a networked environment. The Recycle Bin is discussed later in this chapter (see the section, "Basic Features of Windows").

Located at the bottom of the desktop is the *Taskbar.* The Taskbar contains the Start button, quick-launch buttons, and the clock. The Start button displays the Start menu. This menu allows access to virtually every program and function on the PC. *Quick-launch buttons* are similar to desktop icons, as they are also shortcuts to applications. These quick-launch buttons are particularly useful when several applications or documents are already open, and you need a quick way to open another application. The Start menu for Windows 98 and Windows 2000 is shown in Figure 1-11.

TEST TIP

Practice navigating the desktop with both the mouse and keyboard.

Figure 1-11 The Start Menu in Windows 98 and Windows 2000

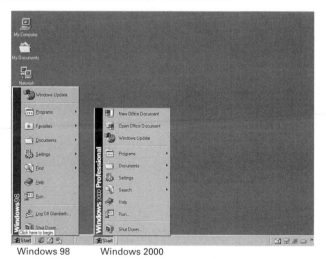

Windows 98   Windows 2000

TEST TIP

Know the different
ways to open Win-
dows Explorer.

Quick-launch buttons are on the Taskbar next to the Start button. They allow quick access to the desktop from any application as well as from Internet Explorer and Outlook Express.

Working with Icons

This section shows how to select and move desktop icons, and how to recognize basic desktop icons such as Hard Disk, Directory Tree, Directories/Folders and Files, and Recycle Bin/Wastebasket. The section also explains how to create a desktop shortcut icon or a desktop menu alias.

Creating Shortcuts (Icons)

To create a shortcut (icon), navigate to the desired program or file in Windows Explorer. Right-click the program or file, and select **Create Shortcut**. The shortcut icon will appear as the last item in the Explorer window. This icon can be moved using cut/paste or drag and drop. An icon can also be created right on the desktop. Right-click the desktop, and select **New, New Shortcut** or **Create Shortcut**. Enter the path for the program or file, and the shortcut will display.

Moving Icons

To move the created icon or another desktop icon to another position on the desktop, click it, as shown in Figure 1-12, and then drag it to the desired location. The icon becomes semitransparent while being dragged. To restore the icon to full intensity, click outside of it. If the icon does not move, disable the Auto Arrange function on the desktop. To do this, right-click an empty space of the desktop and uncheck the **Auto Arrange** selection, as shown in Figure 1-13. Shortcut icons can be created for frequently used programs such as web browsers, word processors, spreadsheets, and instant messengers.

Selecting Multiple Icons

To select several icons to move at once, hold the Ctrl key and click all the icons that are to be moved, as shown in Figure 1-14. Then, drag the group of icons to the new location and release the mouse button. Deselect the icons by clicking an empty part of the desktop.

Figure 1-12   Moving an Icon

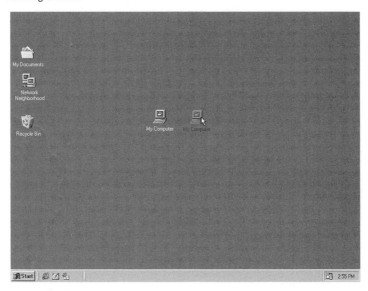

Figure 1-13   Arranging Icons

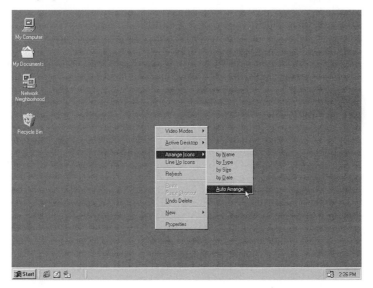

Figure 1-14 Moving Multiple Icons

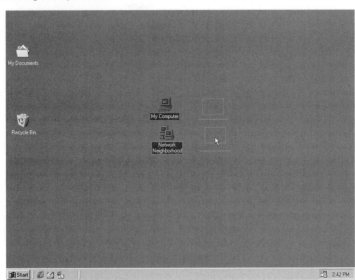

Renaming Icons

There are two ways to rename an icon. The first way is to simply click the name under the icon, as shown in Figure 1-15. Then, type in a new name, as shown in Figure 1-16. Click an empty part of the desktop to complete the action. A second way is to right-click the icon and select **Rename**.

Figure 1-15 Highlighting the Icon Name

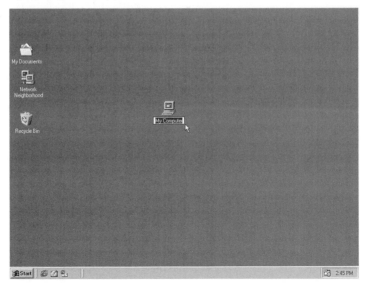

Figure 1-16 Changing the Icon Name

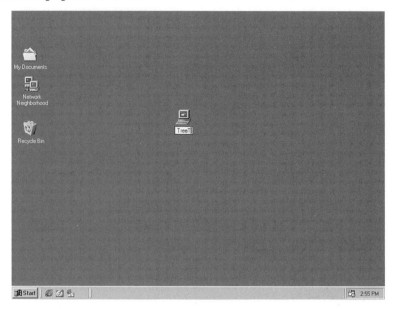

Navigating and working with the desktop is easier when you use icons. Because icons are simply shortcuts that point to programs and files, they can be copied, moved, and even deleted without affecting the program or file.

Recognizing an Application Window

Application windows typically have a title bar, Toolbar, menu bar, status bar, and scroll bar. WordPad is used here to demonstrate the features common to most Windows applications, as shown in Figure 1-17. WordPad, or Notepad on some Windows computers, is a simple word processing program located in the Start, Programs, Accessories directory of the Windows environment.

Figure 1-17 WordPad Application Window

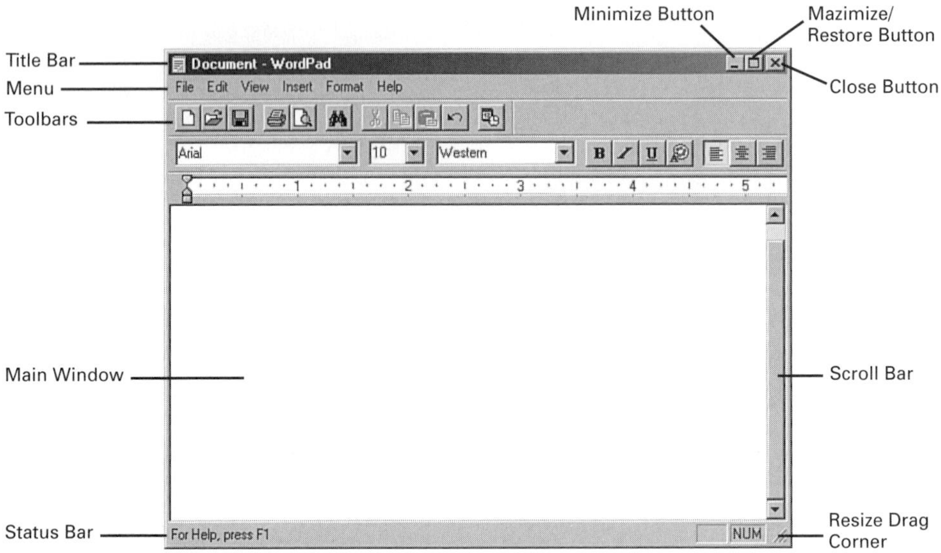

The functions of the Toolbar are easy to understand and are described in Table 1-4.

Table 1-4 Toolbar Descriptions

Toolbar	Description
Title bar	Displays the name of the document and application. In this example, it is Document – WordPad. Also located in the title bar are the Minimize, Maximize, and Exit buttons that will be discussed in this chapter.
Menu bar	Contains menus for manipulating the document, such as creating new documents, copying text, inserting images, and so on. To see the menu for each item, click a button. A drop-down menu displays.
Status bar	Located at the bottom of the window, the status bar shows information such as the page number, whether the file is being saved, how to access the Help feature, and so on.
Scroll bar	Scroll bars might appear on the right side or the bottom of the window, or both. These bars appear when the document is too large to be viewed entirely on one screen. Clicking the arrows on either end of the scroll bar moves the images or text through the window. Clicking and dragging the scroll bar moves the image or text even more quickly through a window.

Figure 1-18 shows an example of a file option on the menu bar.

Figure 1-18 File Option on the Menu Bar

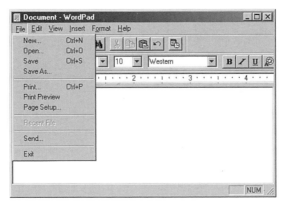

You might want to move a window to another location on the screen, particularly if there is more than one window open. Click the title bar and then drag the window to the desired position, as shown in Figure 1-19. The window will dynamically follow the cursor as if you were moving a piece of paper on a real desktop.

Figure 1-19 Moving an Application Window

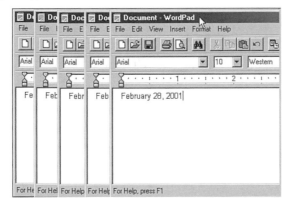

Most Windows applications have similar-looking menus and functions. Differences depend on the type of application and the version of the operating system.

Resizing a Desktop Window

Windows that display applications like WordPad can have sizes ranging from very small to full-screen. To resize a window, move the cursor to any corner or side of the application window. A double-headed arrow will appear, as shown in Figure 1-20. Click and drag the arrow to change the window size.

Figure 1-20   Double-Headed Arrows

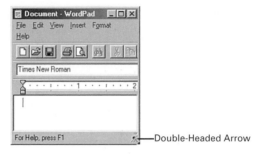

Double-Headed Arrow

There are different types of arrows, pointers, cursors, and other items can be used to navigate in Windows. Many are displayed in Figure 1-21. Go to **My Computer, Control Panel, Mouse, Pointer** to modify your cursor.

Figure 1-21   Cursor Types

Switching Between Windows

When more than one window is open, you can switch between windows by pressing **Alt-Tab**. As shown in Figure 1-22, a window pops up that indicates which applications are open. While holding down the Alt button, keep pressing Tab to find the desired window.

Figure 1-22   Switching Between Windows

Microsoft Photo Editor - [1-29.gif]

Document windows can also be selected by clicking the desired document on the desktop Taskbar, which displays at the bottom of the screen.

Basic Features of Windows

This section includes the following topics:

- Viewing a computer's basic system information
- Setting the clock and date
- Minimizing, maximizing, and exiting
- Adjusting the screen display
- Modifying desktop settings
- Adjusting audio volume
- Understanding the Start menu options: accessing more Windows features
- Using the Recycle Bin

Viewing a Computer's Basic System Information

This section discusses how to find system information in Windows 2000. It also shows how to view information such as the type of operating system, the processor type, and the type and amount of random-access memory (RAM) that is installed. This information is valuable to the PC technician for troubleshooting and for updating the system or its applications.

To view information about the system in Windows 2000, choose **Start, Programs, Accessories, System Tools, System Information** as shown in Figure 1-23.

Figure 1-23   A Nested Menu Display

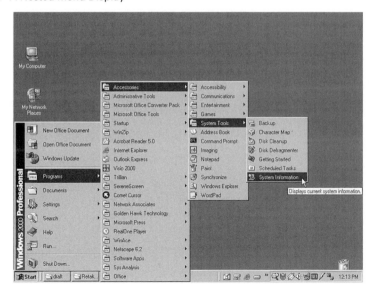

The window that opens gives the operating system (OS) name and version, the system manufacturer and model, the processor type and manufacturer, the BIOS version, and the amount of RAM (also called memory) Figure 1-24 shows the window that displays. This information can be saved as a text file by selecting **Action** from the Toolbar and choosing **Save As Text File**, as shown in Figure 1-25. Where the file is to be saved can be specified. Figure 1-26 shows the Save As box and Figure 1-27 shows the *System Info.txt* file in the directory. Double-click the file *System Info.txt*. The document opens in Notepad text editor. If the System Info.txt file is too large, Windows prompts the user to open it in WordPad instead. The contents will be similar to what is shown in Figure 1-28. The text can then be copied and pasted into a word processing program such as Microsoft Word or a spreadsheet program like Microsoft Excel, so that the information is easier to read, as shown in Figure 1-29.

Figure 1-24   System Information

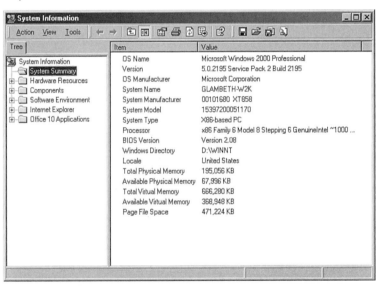

Figure 1-25 Save the System Information

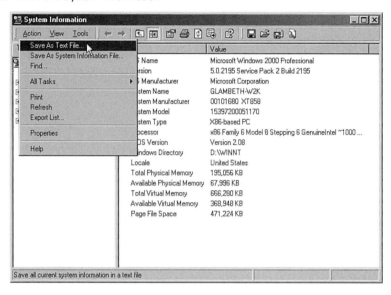

Figure 1-26 Save as a Text File: System Info.txt

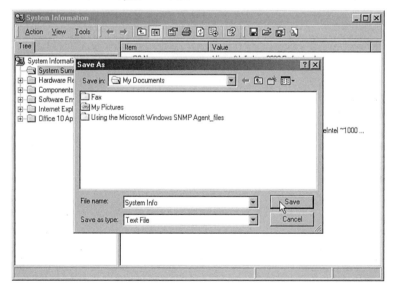

Figure 1-27   Verify Text File Saved in My Documents

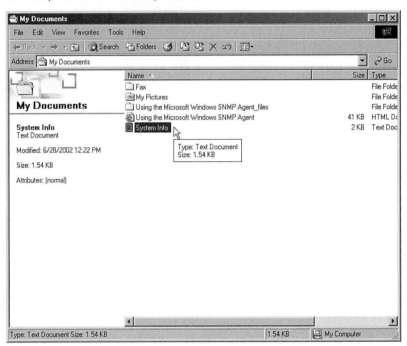

Figure 1-28   System Info.txt Displayed in Notepad

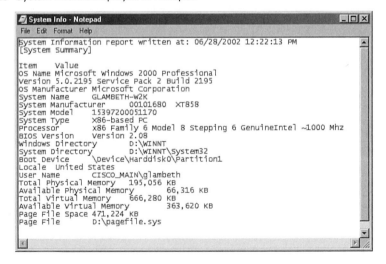

Figure 1-29 Reformatted in MS Word

```
System Information report written at: 06/28/2002 12:22:13 PM
[System Summary]

Item                          Value
OS Name                       Microsoft Windows 2000 Professional
Version                       5.0.2195 Service Pack 2 Build 2195
OS Manufacturer               Microsoft Corporation
System Name                   GLAMBETH-W2K
System Manufacturer           00101680__XT858
System Model                  15397200051170
System Type                   X86-based PC
Processor                     x86 Family 6 Model 8 Stepping 6 GenuineIntel ~1000 Mhz
BIOS Version                  Version 2.08
Windows Directory             D:\WINNT
System Directory              D:\WINNT\System32
Boot Device                   \Device\Harddisk0\Partition1
Locale                        United States
User Name                     CISCO_MAIN\glambeth
Total Physical Memory         195,056 KB
Available Physical Memory     66,316 KB
Total Virtual Memory          666,280 KB
Available Virtual Memory      363,620 KB
Page File Space               471,224 KB
Page File                     D:\pagefile.sys
```

NOTE

The preceding steps are specific to Windows 2000. These steps are slightly different when using Windows 98/Me. In 98 and Me, choose **Start, Programs, Accessories, System Tools, System Information**. Then, select from the window that displays File, Export, and provide a filename and a directory in which to save it. The system information is saved as a text file.

Setting the Clock and Date

The next few sections show how to use the Microsoft Windows graphical user interface (GUI) to modify the desktop. Items that you can change include the date and time, the volume settings for the speaker, and other desktop display options, such as background options, screen settings, screen saver options, and so on.

To adjust the date and time, double-click the clock, located on the Taskbar. A pop-up window that's similar to Figure 1-30 displays. Click the down arrow next to the month displayed to select the current month, as shown in Figure 1-31. Change the year in the same manner if needed. To adjust the date, click the desired numerical day of the month. Set the clock by entering the new time in the field and selecting AM or PM.

Figure 1-30 The System Clock, Where You Can Set the Time, Date, and the Time Zone

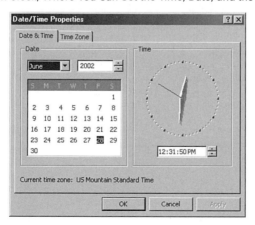

Figure 1-31 Adjusting the Month by Using a Drop-Down Menu

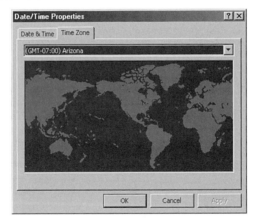

Next, click the tab labeled **Time Zone**. Figure 1-32 shows the Date/Time Properties window. Click the down arrow and choose the appropriate time zone, as shown in Figure 1-33. The clock is automatically adjusted for Daylight Savings Time changes annually.

Figure 1-32 Choosing the Time Zone

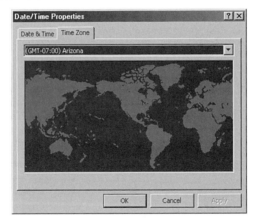

Figure 1-33 Adjusting the Time Zone Using a Drop-Down Menu

In Windows 98, the display window used to adjust the date and time properties is slightly different from that in Windows 2000. In Windows 98, the Time Zone drop-down menu is located in the main Date & Time tab. To select the time zone in Windows 98, click the Time Zone down arrow, which opens a drop-down menu, and select a time zone.

Minimizing, Maximizing, and Exiting

Most applications in Windows have three small icons in the upper-right corner of the screen that are used to minimize the screen, maximize the screen, or exit the application. Figure 1-34 shows these icons.

Figure 1-34 Minimize, Maximize/Restore, and Exit Buttons

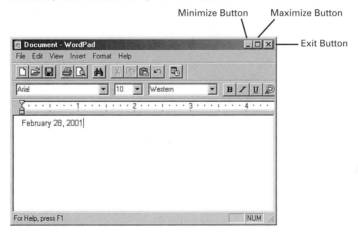

TEST TIP

The fastest way to minimize all windows quickly is to click the Show Desktop icon next to the Start button. Clicking the button again restores all windows.

By clicking the Minimize (left) button, the application is placed on the Taskbar. It is still open and can be accessed simply by clicking it in the Taskbar.

The middle button, the Maximize/Restore button, changes depending on whether the window being viewed is opened partially or fully. Click this button to make the application screen smaller or larger. The right button, marked with an *X*, closes the application.

Adjusting the Screen Display

Setting the screen resolution depends on your requirements, the application being used, and the version of Windows that is installed. Young children, older adults, and those with vision difficulties might prefer larger text and images. In addition, older video cards might not support more detailed colors or the speed of display as demanded by the most advanced computer games, graphics, design software, or video-editing tools.

To adjust the screen display, first minimize all windows that are open. Right-click an empty space on the desktop, and choose **Properties** to open the Display Properties window as shown in Figure 1-35. Alternatively, choose **Start, Settings, Control Panel, Display**.

Figure 1-35 Opening the Display Properties Window

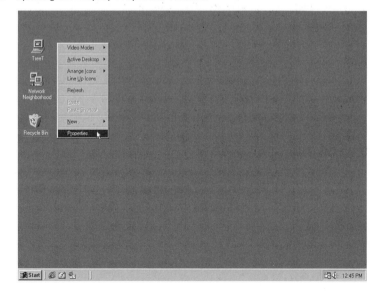

The following list details the tabs found on the Display Properties Window:

- The *Background tab*, as shown in Figure 1-36, allows users to choose what is displayed as background for the desktop. The Windows default background is a blue screen.
- The *Screen Saver tab*, as shown in Figure 1-37, permits selecting a screen saver and indicating when it should activate on the desktop. In addition, the screen saver can be set up to require a password. This tab is also used to apply the energy-saving features of the monitor.
- The *Appearance tab*, as shown in Figure 1-38, has settings that allow you to choose the size and color of the text and backgrounds for applications.
- The **Effects** tab, as shown in Figure 1-39, allows users to choose visual effects such as fade effects, large icons, and the ability to show contents while dragging windows.
- The *Web tab*, as shown in Figure 1-40 (not included in Windows 95), allows you to decide whether to show web content on the desktop.

Setting the screen display properties is a matter of preference. Individual users can set the features of the various windows as desired.

Figure 1-36 Display Properties: Background

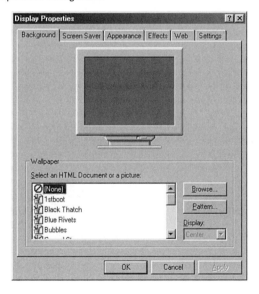

Figure 1-37 Display Properties: Screen Saver

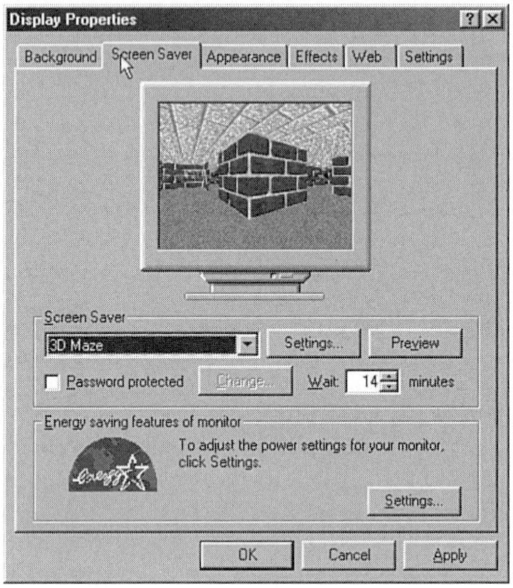

Figure 1-38 Display Properties: Appearance

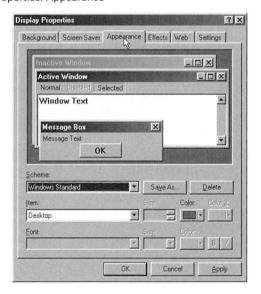

Figure 1-39 Display Properties—Effects

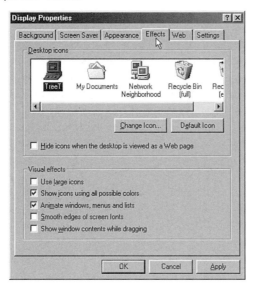

Figure 1-40 Display Properties: Web

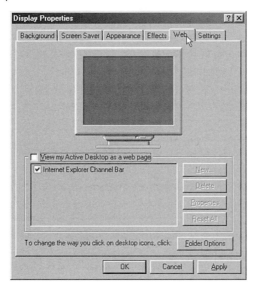

NOTE

When first installing a video card, Windows defaults to the lowest setting of 640×480 resolution and possibly even eight colors. When a video card driver is installed with software that is supplied by the manufacturer, more colors and resolutions can then be displayed. This topic is covered in more detail in Chapter 2.

Modifying Desktop Settings

To adjust the desktop settings, access the Display Properties window as explained in the previous section. In the Settings tab, adjust the number of colors and the number of pixels that are to be displayed, as shown in Figure 1-41. *Pixels* are the tiny dots that make up the light on the screen and determine the intensity of a screen image. Lower pixel values, for example, tend to display cartoon-like color images, which are grainy with few details. Higher values display more realistic color images, approaching a true value of 16.7 million colors and superb detail. After the color or number of pixels is selected, click **Apply**. The message shown in Figure 1-42 displays. Click **OK**. The message in Figure 1-43 then displays. Choose **Yes** to reconfigure the desktop. The screen display might go blank or the desktop screen might jump around, but don't worry. Windows is adjusting the desktop to match the new settings.

Figure 1-41   Changing the Color Settings

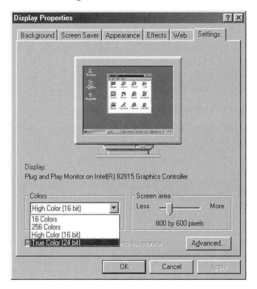

Figure 1-42   Confirm the New Settings

Figure 1-43 Accept or Reject the New Settings

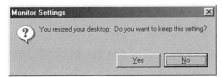

Adjusting Audio Volume

To access the volume control, click the speaker icon on the Taskbar. Audio properties can also be accessed from the Sounds and Multimedia icon in the Control Panel. Slide the bars up and down until the volume level and other audio settings are acceptable to you. The volume control screen includes a mute option that can be used to turn off the sound, as shown in Figure 1-44.

Figure 1-44 Adjusting the Volume Controls

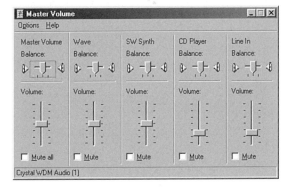

Start Menu Options: Accessing More Windows Features

The Start button is located on the Windows Taskbar in the lower-left corner of the Windows desktop. Imbedded in the Start menu are several useful Windows features. Clicking the Start button as shown in Figure 1-45 allows you to access these options.

Figure 1-45   Start Menu Options

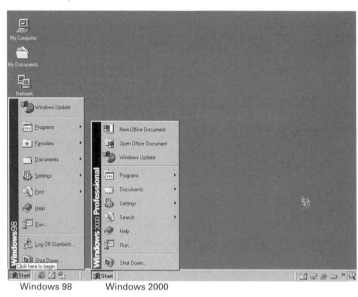

Windows 98   Windows 2000

Run

NOTE

This feature is often
used by the IT techni-
cian to access the
command editor and
to execute diagnostic
routines, such as ping.

The *Run* feature is another method of starting a program, so that you don't have to
click the program's shortcut icon on the desktop or search the list of programs within
the **Programs** directory. (The directory is discussed more thoroughly in Chapter 4.)
Access the Run feature by selecting **Start, Run**. Figure 1-46 shows the command-line
entry space into which the program name and any parameters that are needed can be
entered as in a DOS prompt window.

Figure 1-46   Run

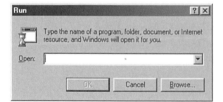

Help

The Help feature provides tips and instructions on how to use Windows, along with
an index and search function so that information can easily be found. The Help feature is easy to use, and learning to navigate it will allow you to find useful information
quickly. The following example shows you how to search for help and how to format

a floppy disk. From the Start menu, select Help. Figure 1-47 shows the Help screen that displays from the Start menu.

Figure 1-47 Windows Help

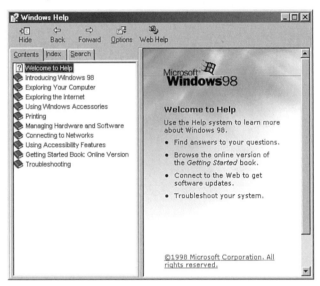

Click the Index tab as shown in Figure 1-48. Type the keyword phrase formatting disks. Click Display. The right side of the screen displays instructions on how to format a floppy disk, as shown in Figure 1-49.

Figure 1-48 Index Tab on the Help Screen

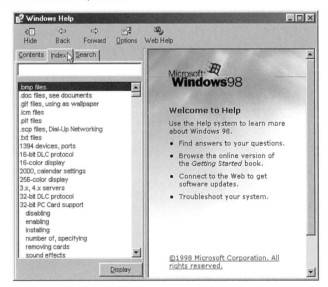

Figure 1-49 How to Format a Floppy Disk

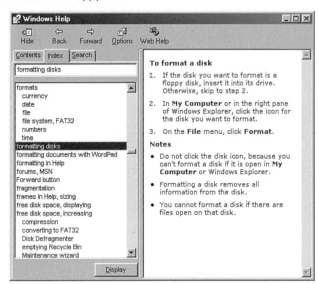

Find/Search

In Windows 95, 98, and Windows NT, the Find function is used to locate files, folders, and network connections to other computers and peripherals. In Windows 2000, Find has been renamed Search.

Documents

The *Documents* menu shows a list of the most recent documents that have been accessed or created. A shortcut method for finding documents, it is a convenient means of going back to a file that has recently been used. These documents are linked to the applications that created them, so clicking the document launches the application as well.

Programs

The Programs menu lists all the programs that are installed on the computer. To start a program, click **Start, Programs,** locate the program to be started, and click it. Shortcut icons on the desktop can be made for those programs that are used regularly.

Using the Recycle Bin

The Recycle Bin stores deleted files, folders, graphics, and web pages from the hard disk. Items remain there until you permanently delete them from the computer. These items can be undeleted, or restored, to their original location. When the Recycle Bin reaches a preset percentage of hard disk space, Windows 2000 automatically deletes enough items to accommodate only the most recently deleted files and folders. Figure 1-50 shows the recycle bin in Windows 98 and Windows 2000 with deleted files and folders.

Figure 1-50 The Recycle Bin for Windows 98 and Windows 2000

Windows 98   Windows 2000

Lab 1.3.8   Getting to Know Windows

In this lab, you navigate the Windows desktop, use the Windows Help features, resize windows, and explain the proper way to shut down the system.

Worksheet 1.3.8   Windows Navigation and Settings

This worksheet tests your knowledge of navigating in Windows and modifying desktop settings.

Overview of Software Applications

This section includes the following topics:

- Word processors
- Spreadsheets
- Databases
- Graphics applications
- Presentation applications
- Web browsers
- E-mail

Word Processors

As discussed earlier in this chapter, software applications are the programs that allow you to complete tasks, such as writing a report, keeping track of clients, drawing a company logo, displaying web pages, and writing and sending e-mail.

A *word processor* is an application that creates, edits, stores, and prints documents. Figure 1-51 shows Microsoft Word 2000 as an example of a word processor. All word processors can insert or delete text, copy, cut, paste, and define margins. Word processors that only support these features are called *text editors*. Most word processors support additional features that enable the manipulation and formation of documents in very sophisticated ways. Examples include file management, macros, spell checkers, headers and footers, merge capabilities, advanced layout features, multiple windows, and preview modes. The most popular word processors are Corel WordPerfect, Microsoft Word, and Lotus Notes.

Figure 1-51   Microsoft Word 2000

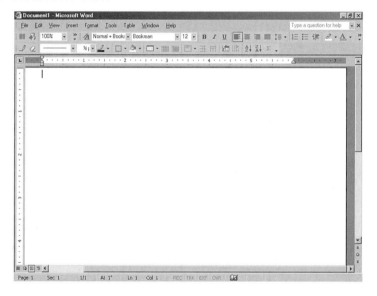

Spreadsheets

In a *spreadsheet*, data are stored in cells that are arranged in a grid. Cells are referred to by their position in this grid according to the column and row that they occupy (such as A3). The data could be a number, text, or a calculation. If cell A3 contained the value 10 and the adjacent cell (B3) contained the calculation =A3*2.54 (that is, multiply the value in A3 by 2.54), then the value 25.4 would be shown in cell B3. In other words, a value in inches in A3 is converted to centimeters in B3, since 2.54 is the conversion factor.

A range of numerical values can be calculated in this way, and it is possible to carry out large and complex calculations. Many spreadsheets have the ability to plot data in the form of graphs, bar charts, and pie charts. Microsoft Excel as shown in Figure 1-52 and Lotus 1-2-3 are examples of spreadsheet applications.

Figure 1-52 Microsoft Excel 2000

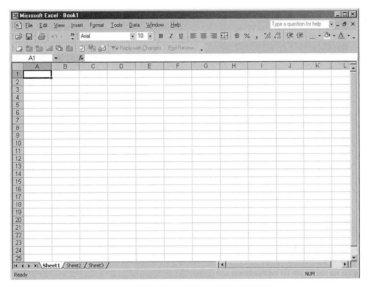

Databases

A *database* is a collection of data that is organized so that its contents can be easily accessed, managed, and updated. It is an electronic filing system. Microsoft Access as shown in Figure 1-53, Oracle Database, and FileMaker are all examples of database applications. PC databases fall into two distinct categories, flat-file and relational.

Figure 1-53 Microsoft Access 2000

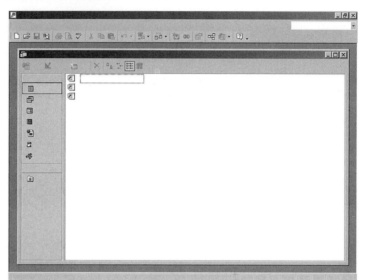

Flat-File Database

A *flat-file database* stores its information in a single table. Each column, called a *field*, contains a particular piece of information such as a first name, last name, address, or telephone number. Each row, called a *record*, contains information for a particular database item (for example, John/Smith/24 Main Street/286 555 9880). An ordinary telephone directory might be stored in this format.

Relational Database

A *relational database* is a collection of flat-file databases (or tables) that are linked through a particular relationship. For example, a bank would use a relational database to store information about its clients. There would be a table containing the names and addresses of clients, a table with detailed information about each bank account, a table with the amount in each account, a table with passwords, and so on. A unique identifier, called a *key*, which forms the relationship between records in different tables, links the information in these tables. For example, when taking money out of a cash machine, the bank card details and the password number are checked in a security table. Then the account balance table is checked to make sure that sufficient funds are available, and the transaction is stored in an account transaction table.

Relational databases are the best way to store large amounts of interrelated data. Their advantage, when compared with flat-file databases, is their ability to handle multiple relationships with a minimum of duplication of data; for example, each bank account can have many transactions (a *one-to-many relationship*). To do this in a single flat-file database would make it overwhelmingly large and inefficient. Flat-file databases are two dimensional, while relational databases have three or more dimensions.

Graphics Applications

Graphics applications are used to create or modify graphical images. The two types include (a) *object-based* or *vector-based* and (b) *bitmaps* or *raster images*. To understand the difference, imagine using one to create the letter *T*. The bitmap would represent this as if the *T* were drawn on graph paper and the corresponding squares were shaded in. A vector-based graphic would describe the *T* with geometrical elements: two rectangular shapes of the same size, one standing up and the other resting on top at its middle. The difference might seem unimportant, and the vector method might seem overly complex, but it is actually much better. The vector-based graphic can be enlarged or shrunk to any size, whereas a bitmap shows the individual "squares" if the image is enlarged. Generally, bitmaps also require much more file space than vector graphics.

There are several types of graphics programs. They can be broken down into four main categories:

- **Image editing**—The industry standard image-editing software is Adobe Photoshop. Its vast tool set makes it possible to manipulate and create raster (bitmap) images.

- **Illustration**—The most popular illustration software is Adobe Illustrator. It has a tool set similar to Photoshop, yet it creates vector-based images as opposed to raster images. Figure 1-54 shows an example of this program.

- **Animation**—Animation is the process of creating sequential images that, when played in a series, give the impression of continuous movement. There are many ways to accomplish this task. The most popular types are *frame-by-frame* and *keyframe* animation. Frame-by-frame animation involves creating each frame, while keyframe animation allows the animator to define two key points and uses the computer to calculate the in-between frames. This process is commonly called *tweening*.

- **3D graphics**—Using a simulated three-dimensional environment, geometric objects can be created, textured, painted, and animated. This geometry can have real-world scale and depth to assist in creating floor plans, model cars, or even movie special effects.

Other graphics applications find their use in multimedia, audio, and games.

Figure 1-54 Illustrator

Computer-Aided Design

Another type of application worth mentioning is computer-aided design (CAD). CAD software requires high-speed workstations or desktop computers. It is available for generic design or specialized uses, such as architectural, electrical, and mechanical projects.

More complex forms of CAD software provide solid modeling and parametric modeling capabilities, which allow objects to be created with real-world characteristics. For example, in solid modeling, objects can be sectioned (sliced down the middle) to reveal their internal structure.

Presentation Applications

Presentation applications, also known as *business graphics*, permit the organization, design, and delivery of presentations in the form of slide shows and reports. Bar charts, pie charts, graphics, and other types of images can be created based on data that are imported from spreadsheet applications. Figure 1-55 shows Microsoft PowerPoint, which is a popular presentation application.

Figure 1-55 Microsoft PowerPoint 2000

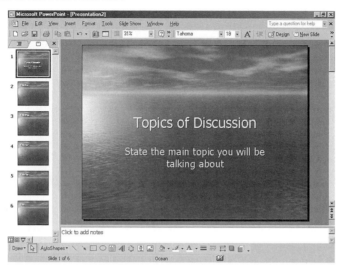

Web Browsers and E-Mail

A *web browser* is an application that is used to locate and display pages from the World Wide Web. The two most common browsers are Netscape Navigator, as shown in Figure 1-56 and Microsoft Internet Explorer as shown in Figure 1-57. These are graphical browsers, which means that they can display graphics as well as text. In addition, most modern browsers can present multimedia information, including sound and video, although they require plug-ins for some formats.

Figure 1-56 Netscape Navigator

Figure 1-57   Microsoft Internet Explorer

A *plug-in* is an auxiliary program that works with a major software package to enhance its capabilities. An example of a plug-in would be a filter that adds special effects in an imaging program such as Photoshop. Plug-ins are added to web browsers to enable them to support new types of content (audio, video, etc.). Although the term plug-in is widely used for software, it could also be used to refer to a module for hardware.

E-Mail

Electronic mail (e-mail) is the exchange of computer-stored messages by network communication. Both Netscape and Microsoft include an e-mail utility with their web browsers. Figure 1-58 shows the Netscape e-mail utility.

Figure 1-58 Netscape Navigator E-Mail Client

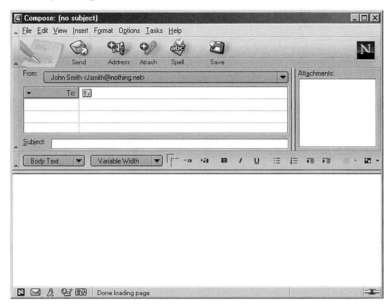

Math for a Digital Age

This section includes the following topics:

- Measurement-related terminology
- Analog and digital systems
- Boolean logic gates: AND, OR, NOT, NOR, XOR
- Decimal and binary number systems
- Decimal-to-binary conversion
- The base 16 (hexadecimal) number system
- Binary-to-hexadecimal conversion
- Hexadecimal-to-binary conversion
- Converting to any base
- Introduction to algorithms

Measurement-Related Terminology

When working in the computer industry, it is important to understand the terms that are used. Whether reading the specifications about a computer system or talking with another computer technician, there is a rather large vocabulary that you should know. The technician needs to know the following terminology:

- **Bit**—The smallest unit of data in a computer. A bit can take the value of either 1 or 0, and it is the binary format in which data are processed by computers.

- **Byte**—A unit of measure that is used to describe the size of a data file, the amount of space on a disk or other storage medium, or the amount of data being sent over a network. One byte consists of eight bits of data.

- **Nibble**—Half a byte, or four bits.

- **Kilobit (kb)**—1024 (or approximately 1000) bits.

- **Kilobits per second (kbps)**—A measure of the amount of data transferred over a connection (for example, a network connection). One kbps is a data transfer rate of approximately 1000 bits per second.

- **Kilobyte (KB)**—1024 (or approximately 1000) bytes.

- **Kilobytes per second (KBps)**—A measure of the amount of data transferred over a connection. One KBps is a data transfer rate of approximately 1000 bytes per second.

- **Megabit (Mb)**—1,048,576 (or approximately 1,000,000) bits.

- **Megabits per second (Mbps)**—A common measure of the amount of data transferred over a connection. One Mbps is a data transfer rate of approximately 1,000,000 (10^6) bits per second.

- **Megabyte (MB)**—1,048,576 (or approximately 1,000,000) bytes.

- **Megabytes per second (MBps)**—A common measure of the amount of data transferred over a connection. One MBps is a data transfer rate of approximately 1,000,000 (10^6) bytes per second.

- **Hertz (Hz)**—A unit of measure of frequency. It is the rate of change in the state or cycle in a sound wave, alternating current, or other cyclical waveform. Hertz is synonymous with cycles per second and is used to describe the speed of a computer's microprocessor.

- **Megahertz (MHz)**—One million (10^6) cycles per second. This is a common measure of the speed of a processing chip.

- **Gigahertz (GHz)**—One billion (10^9) cycles per second. This is a common measure of the speed of a processing chip.

NOTE

A common error is confusing KB with kb and MB with Mb. Note that a capital *B* indicates bytes while a lowercase *b* indicates bits. Remember to do the proper calculations when comparing transmission speeds that are measured in KB with those measured in kb. For example, modem software usually shows the connection speed in kilobits per second (for example, 45 kbps). However, popular browsers display file-download speeds in kilobytes per second. Therefore, with a 45-kbps connection, the download speed would be a maximum of 5.76 KBps.

NOTE

In practice, the download speed of a dialup connection cannot reach 45 kbps because of other factors that consume bandwidth at the same time as the download.

Analog and Digital Systems

As time goes on, the world is becoming more digital. We used to depend entirely on analog processes, machinery, and communications. The variables that characterize an analog system can have an infinite number of values. For example, the hands on an analog clock face might show an infinite number of times of the day. In digital systems, the variables that characterize them only occupy a fixed number of discrete values. In binary arithmetic, as used in modern computers, only two values are allowed: 0 and 1. Computers and cable modems are examples of digital devices. Digital devices are gradually replacing analog devices. Thirty years ago, digital watches, home computers, cable modems, electronic games, electronic car parts, and flat-screen monitors did not exist.

Can a world without computers even be imagined? Twenty years ago, it was rare for someone to have a home computer. Now computers are embedded in toys, watches, personal digital assistants (PDAs), pets (for identification), and "smart" cards (credit cards with microchips). In twenty years, it might be commonplace for doctors to treat medical conditions using digital devices embedded in the skin, swallowed by the patient, or injected into the bloodstream.

Traditional telephones transmit voice over copper wire using analog signals. When using a microphone connected to a computer and the accompanying software to talk to someone far away for free, the analog phone system between the user and the phone company is being circumvented with a digital transmission over a data network that connects the user to an Internet Service Provider (ISP). In other words, the user effectively bypasses the toll system (long-distance charges), as the ISP links on both ends are local. This is an example of how digital systems are changing lives.

The changes that happen from year to year do not seem to be very dramatic. However, if someone were to live in isolation for five years and then return to the modern world, he or she would be shocked at the drastic changes that had taken place due to digital technology. Digital devices make it easier to do everyday tasks, but they also make it harder for individuals to appreciate the effort that people used to endure to complete those same tasks. The only constant is change, and the digital age will continue to progress independently of how people feel about its impact on their lives.

The more digital the world becomes, the more important it is to understand the basic function of digital systems. How do computers work at the most fundamental level? What is going on at the core of a computer that makes it perform a certain way? The answer is that it all comes down to 0s and 1s. This chapter explores how a computer thinks. The math of the digital age—arithmetic with binary and hexadecimal numbers—is explored. It is important to have this foundation in math in order to continue in Information Technology.

NOTE

PC processors are getting faster all the time. The microprocessors used in PCs in the 1980s typically ran at less than 10 MHz (the original IBM PC was 4.77 MHz). At the beginning of 2000, PC processors approached the speed of 1 GHz and are reaching 2.3 GHz as of 2002.

Boolean Logic Gates: AND, OR, NOT, NOR, XOR

Computers are built from various types of electronic circuits. These circuits depend on what are called AND, OR, NOT, and NOR *logic gates*. These gates are characterized by how they respond to input signals. Figures 1-59, 1-60, and 1-61 show logic gates with two inputs. The X and Y represent inputs, and the F represents output. Think of 0 as representing off and 1 as representing on.

Figure 1-59 Boolean Logic Gates: AND and OR

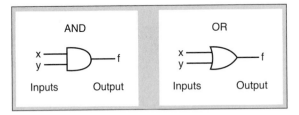

Figure 1-60 Boolean Logic Gate: NOR

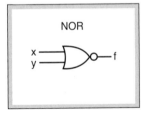

Figure 1-61 Boolean Logic Gate: NOT

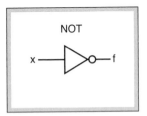

There are only three primary logic functions: AND, OR, and NOT. An *OR gate* acts as follows: If either input is on, the output is on. The *AND gate* acts as follows: If either input is off, the output is off. A *NOT gate* acts as follows: If the input is on, the output is off, and vice versa.

The *NOR gate* is a combination of the OR and NOT gates and should not be presented as a primary gate. A NOR gate acts as follows: If either input is on, the output is off.

It helps to look at the truth tables in Figure 1-62 to represent these statements in a compact form. Other logic-gate combinations or extensions such as XOR, NAND, and so on are beyond the scope of this book.

Figure 1-62 Boolean Logic Gate: Truth Tables

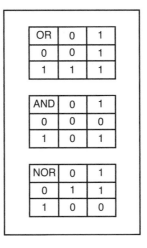

Lab 1.5.3 Boolean Operations

In this lab, you are introduced to the AND, OR, NOR, and NOT Boolean operations. You will also be able to calculate the output of combinations of Boolean operations based on input.

Decimal and Binary Number Systems

The *decimal*, or *base-10*, number system is used every day for doing math (counting change, measuring, telling time, and so on). The decimal number system uses 10 digits: 0 through 9.

The *binary*, or *base-2*, number system uses two digits to express all numerical quantities. The only digits used in the binary number system are 0 and 1. An example of a binary number is 1001110101000110100101.

One important thing to keep in mind is the role of the digit 0. Every number system uses the digit 0. However, note that whenever the digit 0 appears on the left side of a string of digits, it can be removed without changing the string value. For example, in base 10, 02947 equals 2947. In base 2, 0001001101 equals 1001101. Sometimes people include 0s on the left side of a number to emphasize places that would otherwise not be represented.

Another important concept when working with binary numbers is the *powers of numbers*. The numbers 2^0 and 2^3 are examples of values represented by powers. To describe these examples, you would say "two to the zero power" and "two to the third power." Their values are as follows: $2^0 = 1$, $2^1 = 2$, $2^2 = 2 \times 2 = 4$, and $2^3 = 2 \times 2 \times 2 = 8$. Obviously, there is a pattern here. The power is the number of 2s that need to be multiplied together. A common mistake is to confuse taking powers with simple multiplication: 2^4 is not equal to $2 \times 4 = 8$; instead it is equal to $2 \times 2 \times 2 \times 2 = 16$.

In base 10, powers of ten are used. For example, 23,605 in base 10 means:

$$(2 \times 10,000) + (3 \times 1000) + (6 \times 100) + (0 \times 10) + (5 \times 1)$$

Note that $10^0 = 1$, $10^1 = 10$, $10^2 = 100$, $10^3 = 1000$, and $10^4 = 10,000$.

It is useful to think in terms of powers of 10 (10^0, 10^1, 10^2, etc.) in relation to a decimal number. When focusing on the actual value of a decimal number, use the expanded form of the powers (1, 10, 100, and so on). It helps to keep track by using tables. In Table 1-5, see the base-10 number 23,605 as it relates to the powers of 10.

Table 1-5 The Decimal Number System

Power-of-10 representation	10^4	10^3	10^2	10^1	10^0
Decimal representation	10,000	1,000	100	10	1
Base-10 representation	2	3	6	0	5

Binary Numbers

The same method is used with binary numbers and powers of 2. Look at the binary number 10010001. Table 1-6 can be used to convert the binary number 10010001 into decimal as follows:

$$10010001 = (1 \times 128) + (0 \times 64) + (0 \times 32) + (1 \times 16) + (0 \times 8) + (0 \times 4) + (0 \times 2) + (1 \times 1)$$
$$= 128 + 16 + 1 = 145$$

CAUTION

Although $0 \times 10 = 0$, do not leave this portion out of the equation. If it is left out, the base-10 places all shift to the right, yielding the number 2365 instead of 23,605. Although a 0 within a number should never be ignored, ignoring or adding 0s to the beginning of numbers has no effect on their value. For instance, 23,605 can be expressed as 0023605.

Table 1-6 The Binary Number System

Power-of-10 representation	2^7	2^6	2^5	2^4	2^3	2^2	2^1	2^0
Decimal representation	128	64	32	16	8	4	2	1
Base-10 representation	1	0	0	1	0	0	0	1

This is one of the ways to convert a binary number into a decimal number. As an exercise, draw a similar table to convert the binary number 11111001 to the decimal number 249. Although the table method is an efficient way to convert binary numbers to decimal, there are other faster methods that can be used.

Decimal-to-Binary Conversion

There is usually more than one way to solve a math problem, and decimal-to-binary conversion is no exception. One method is explored here, but feel free to use another method if it is easier for you.

To convert a decimal number to binary, first find the biggest power of 2 that will "fit" into the decimal number. Consider the decimal number 35. Looking at Table 1-7, what is the greatest power of 2 that fits into 35? The largest number, 2^6, or 64, is too big, so place a 0 in that column.

Table 1-7 Converting the Decimal Number 35 to Binary Form

Power-of-10 representation	2^6	2^5	2^4	2^3	2^2	2^1	2^0
Decimal representation	64	32	16	8	4	2	1
Base-10 representation	0	1	0	0	0	1	1

The next largest number, 2^5, or 32, is smaller than 35. Place a 1 in that column. Now, calculate how much is left over by subtracting 32 from 35. The result is 3.

Next, determine if 16 (the next lower power of 2) fits into 3. Because it does not, a 0 is placed in that column.

The value of the next number is 8, which is larger than 3, so a 0 is placed in that column, too.

The next value is 4, which is still larger than 3, so it too receives a 0.

The next value is 2, which is smaller than 3. Because 2 fits into 3, place a 1 in that column. Now subtract 2 from 3, which results in 1.

The last number's value is 1, which fits in the remaining number. Thus, place a 1 in the last column.

The binary equivalent of the decimal number 35 is 0100011. Ignoring the first 0, the binary number can be written as 100011.

This conversion method works for any decimal number. Consider the decimal number 1 million. What's the biggest power of 2 that fits in the decimal number 1,000,000? The number $2^{19} = 524,288$ and $2^{20} = 1,048,576$, so 2^{19} is the largest power of 2 that fits into 1,000,000. Continuing with the procedure described above, determine that the decimal number 1 million is equal to the binary number 11110100001001000000.

This technique can rapidly become clumsy when dealing with very large numbers. A simpler technique is shown later in the section, "Converting to Any Base."

Lab Activity on CD-ROM

In this interactive lab, you follow the steps presented on the CD-ROM to perform a decimal-to binary-conversion and a binary-to-decimal conversion.

The Base-16 (Hexadecimal) Number System

The Base-16, or hexadecimal, number system is used frequently when working with computers, since it can be used to represent binary numbers in a more readable form. The computer performs computations in binary, but there are several instances when a computer's binary output is expressed in hexadecimal form to make the output easier to read. One way for computers and software to express hexadecimal output is by placing 0x in front of the hexadecimal number. Whenever 0x is seen, the number that follows is a hexadecimal number. For example, 0x1234 means 1234 in base 16, typically in a router-configuration register. MAC addresses can be represented in two formats, six sets of 2 as in FF.FF.FF.FF.FF.FF or three sets of 4 as in FFFF.FFFF.FFFF.

Base 16 uses 16 characters to express numerical quantities. These characters are 0, 1, 2, 3, 4, 5, 6, 7, 8, 9, A, B, C, D, E, and F. An A represents the decimal number 10, B represents 11, C represents 12, D represents 13, E represents 14, and F represents 15. Examples of hexadecimal numbers are 2A5F, 99901, FFFFFFFF, and EBACD3. A number such as B23CF (hexadecimal) equals 730,063 (decimal).

The traditional conversion between decimal and hexadecimal forms is outside the scope of this book. However, later in this chapter, some shortcuts for conversion to any base, including decimal and hexadecimal, are discussed.

Binary-to-Hexadecimal Conversion

Binary-to-hexadecimal conversion is fairly straightforward. First, observe that 1111 in binary is F in hexadecimal. Also, 11111111 in binary is FF in hexadecimal. Without going into a mathematical proof, one fact that is useful when working with these two number systems is that one hexadecimal character requires 4 bits, or 4 binary digits, to be represented in binary. Note that a bit is simply a binary digit. Used in the binary numbering system, a bit can be 0 or 1.

To convert a binary number to hexadecimal form, break down the number into groups of 4 bits at a time, starting from the right. Then convert each group of 4 bits into hexadecimal form, thus producing a hexadecimal equivalent to the original binary number, as shown in Table 1-8.

Table 1-8 Binary to Hexadecimal Conversion

Binary	Hexadecimal
0000	0
0001	1
0010	2
0011	3
0100	4
0101	5
0110	6
0111	7
1000	8
1001	9
1010	A
1011	B
1100	C
1101	D
1110	E
1111	F

Consider, for example, the binary number 11110111001100010000. Breaking it down into groups of 4 bits would equal 1111 0111 0011 0001 0000. This binary number is equivalent to F7310 in hexadecimal form (a much easier number to read).

As another example, the binary number 111101 is grouped as 11 1101 or, when "padded" with 0s, 0011 1101. Therefore, the hexadecimal equivalent is 3D.

Lab Activity on CD-ROM

In this interactive lab, you follow the steps presented on the CD-ROM to perform a binary-to-hexadecimal conversion.

Worksheet 1.5.9   Number System Exercise

Practice number conversions and increase your understanding of decimal, binary, and hexadecimal forms.

Hexadecimal-to-Binary Conversion

Converting numbers from hexadecimal to binary form is simply the reverse of the method discussed in the previous section. Take each individual hexadecimal digit and convert it to binary form; then string together the solution. However, be careful to pad each binary representation with 0s to fill four binary places for each hexadecimal digit. For example, consider the hexadecimal number FE27. F is 1111, E is 1110, 2 is 10 (or 0010), and 7 is 0111. So, in binary, the conversion is 1111 1110 0010 0111, or 1111111000100111.

Converting to Any Base

Most people already know how to do many number conversions. For example, when converting inches to yards, first divide the number of inches by 12 to get the number of feet. The remainder is the number of inches left. Next, divide the number of feet by 3 to get the number of yards. The remainder is the number of feet left. These same techniques are used for converting numbers to other bases.

If you are converting from decimal (the normal base) to octal form, base 8 (known here as the foreign base) for example, divide by 8 (the foreign base) successively and keep track of the remainders starting from the least significant remainder.

The following example converts the decimal number 1234 to octal form (the letter *R* indicates remainder):

> 1234 / 8 = 154 R 2
>
> 154 / 8 = 19 R 2
>
> 19 / 8 = 2 R 3
>
> 2 / 8 = 0 R 2

The remainders, taking the last one first, the next to the last one next, etc., provide the result of 2322 in octal form.

To convert back to decimal form, multiply a running total by 8 and add each digit successively, starting with the most significant number, as follows:

> $2 \times 8 = 16$
>
> $16 + 3 = 19$
>
> $19 \times 8 = 152$
>
> $152 + 2 = 154$
>
> $154 \times 8 = 1232$
>
> $1232 + 2 = 1234$

An easier way of achieving the same results in the above reverse conversions is by using numerical powers, as follows:

> $(2 \times 8^3) + (3 \times 8^2) + (2 \times 8^1) + (2 \times 8^0) = 1024 + 192 + 16 + 2 = 1234$

NOTE

Any number raised to the power of 0 is 1.

Using Numerical Powers to Convert

Similar techniques can be used to convert to and from any base just by dividing or multiplying by the foreign base.

However, binary is unique in that odd and even can be used to determine 1s and 0s without recording the remainders. Given the same number that we used above, 1234, you can determine the binary equivalent simply by dividing it by 2 successively. The bit is determined by the oddness and evenness of the result. If the result is even, the bit associated with it is 0. If the result is odd, the binary digit associated with it is 1.

The following shows the conversion of 1234 to a binary equivalent:

1234 is even: Record a 0 in the least significant position.

1234/2 = 617 is odd: Record a 1 in the next most significant position (10).

617/2 = 308 is even (010).

308/2 = 154 is even (0010).

154/2 = 77 is odd (10010).

77/2 = 38 is even (010010).

38/2 = 19 is odd (1010010).

19/2 = 9 is odd (11010010).

9/2 = 4 is even (011010010).

4/2 = 2 is even (0011010010).

2/2 = 1 is odd (10011010010).

With practice, the running dividend can be mastered, and you can write the binary form quickly.

Note that just as a hexadecimal digit is a group of 4 bits, an octal number is a group of 3 digits. Break down the above number into groups of 3 starting at the right, as follows:

010,011,010,010 = 2322 octal

To obtain a hexadecimal number, group by 4 bits, starting from the right, as follows:

0100,1101,0010 = 4D2 hexadecimal, or 0x4D2

This is a quick and easy method to convert to any base.

Lab Activity 1.5.9   Converting Numbers Overview

In this lab, you identify the places in binary and decimal numbers as they relate to the powers of 10 and the powers of 2. You will be able to manually convert binary and decimal numbers and describe the difference between them.

Introduction to Algorithms

An *algorithm* is a systematic description or method of exactly how to carry out a series of steps to complete a certain task. Computers use algorithms in practically every function they perform. Essentially, a software program is many algorithms pieced together into a huge set of *code*. Learning computer programming means learning how to create and implement algorithms. Many algorithms are prepackaged, so they can be used in programs, saving programmers from having to reinvent the wheel every time a program is written. The idea, especially with *object-oriented programming*, is to use existing code to build more sophisticated programs or code. Two examples are described in the following sections.

Euclidean Algorithm

One example, seen earlier in the chapter, is the *Euclidean algorithm*. This is essentially the algorithm that is used to do long division (when dividing two numbers). Other algorithm techniques include the number conversion techniques previously described. Vacuuming the carpet or sweeping the garage could both be algorithms if there is a systematic way that these tasks are carried out each time. The term does not have to be used rigidly.

Dijkstra Algorithm

A popular algorithm used by networking devices on the Internet is the *Dijkstra algorithm*. This algorithm is used to find the shortest path between a specific networking device and all other devices in its routing domain. The algorithm uses bandwidth as a means of measuring the shortest path.

Encryption Algorithm

Another common type of algorithm is an *encryption algorithm*. These algorithms are used to prevent hackers from viewing data as they pass through the Internet. One example of such an algorithm is used by 3DES (pronounced triple dez), an encryption standard used to secure connections between networking devices and hosts. Further details about 3DES are outside the scope of this text.

To summarize, algorithms are step-by-step procedures that perform a specific task. Computers use algorithms to speed and simplify procedures. Most of the algorithms used by computers are fairly complex and require some background in computer science to understand.

Laboratory Safety and Tools

This section includes the following topics:

- Basic lab safety principles
- Workspace practices that help reduce ESD potential
- When a wrist strap should not be used for grounding
- Tools of the trade
- Workspace cleaning supplies
- Workplace testing equipment
- Lab safety agreement

Basic Lab Safety Principles

In the following chapters, you will be assembling a computer. The following is list of guidelines that help create a safe, efficient work environment:

- The workspace should be large enough to accommodate the system unit, the technician's tools, the testing equipment, and the electrostatic discharge (ESD)–prevention equipment, as shown in Figure 1-63. Near the workbench, power outlets should be available to at least accommodate the system unit power and the power needs of other electrical devices.

- The ideal humidity level in the workspace should be 20–50 percent to reduce the likelihood of ESD. It is also important to control the temperature so that the workspace does not get too hot.

- The workbench should be a nonconductive surface; additionally, it should have a flat, cleanable surface.

- The workspace should be distant from areas of heavy electrical equipment or concentrations of electronics (for example, a building's HVAC or phone-system controls).

- The workspace should be free of dust. Dust can contaminate the area, causing premature damage to computer components. The work area should have a filtered air system to reduce dust and contaminants.

- Lighting should be adequate to see small details. Two different illumination forms are preferred: an adjustable lamp with a shade and fluorescent lighting.

- Extreme variations of temperature can affect computer components. Temperatures should be maintained so that they are consistent with the specifications of the components.

- Properly grounded AC electrical current is essential Figure 1-64 illustrates the components of an outlet. Power outlets should be tested with an outlet tester for proper grounding.

Figure 1-63 A Typical Workbench

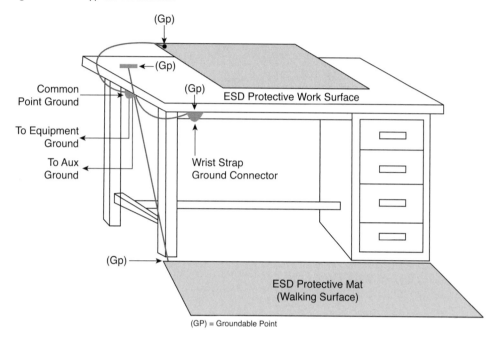

(Gp)

(Gp)

Common
Point Ground

(Gp)

ESD Protective Work Surface

To Equipment
Ground

To Aux
Ground

Wrist Strap
Ground Connector

(Gp)

ESD Protective Mat
(Walking Surface)

(GP) = Groundable Point

Figure 1-64 An AC Outlet

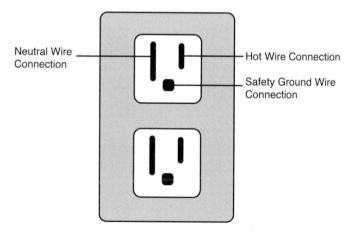

Neutral Wire
Connection

Hot Wire Connection

Safety Ground Wire
Connection

TEST TIP

Know when and how
damage from ESD
occurs.

Workspace Practices that Help Reduce ESD Potential

The workspace should be situated away from carpeted areas because carpets can cause the buildup of electrostatic charges. If distance from carpeting is not possible, the carpeted surface could be covered with a plastic antistatic mat such as that commonly used under a desk chair. Using ESD protection tools such as a wrist strap and a mat, which are commonly sold in kits, can largely eliminate this type of danger.

When working with components, lay the mat on the workspace next to or under the system case. The mat is then clipped to the case to provide a grounded surface on which parts can be placed as they are removed from the system. Always handle all components by their edges. Avoid touching pins, chips, or anything made of metal, so that the chance of producing a damaging electrostatic discharge is reduced. Reducing the potential for electrostatic discharge reduces the likelihood of damage to delicate circuits or components.

Avoid touching the computer screen for any reason while it is turned on. Even brief contact with an active screen can put an electrostatic charge in your hand that can discharge through the keyboard.

Using a Wrist Strap

A *wrist strap* is a device that is attached to the technician's wrist and clipped to the metal system chassis on which the work is being done. The wrist strap prevents ESD damage by channeling static electricity from the person to the ground.

After putting the wrist strap on, allow 15 seconds to pass before touching any sensitive electronic components with your bare hands. This pause allows the wrist strap to neutralize the static electricity that already exists on a person's body. ESD potential can also be reduced by not wearing clothing made of silk, polyester, or wool. These fabrics tend to build static charges.

A wrist strap, as shown in Figure 1-65, can only offer protection from ESD voltages carried on the body. ESD charges on clothing can still cause damage. Therefore, avoid making contact between electronic components and clothing. If static shocks are still being experienced in the workspace while working near a computer, try using a fabric softener or using an antistatic spray on your clothing. Be certain to spray clothes and **not** the computer. A wrist-grounding strap does not discharge electrostatic charges that have built up on hair, so take precautions to ensure that your hair does not rub across any of the components.

Figure 1-65 A Wrist Strap

When a Wrist Strap Should Not Be Used for Grounding

There are some exceptions to wearing a wrist strap in order to provide a safe ground. A wrist strap is never worn when working on a monitor or when working on a computer power supply. Monitors and power supplies are considered replaceable components. Only highly skilled professionals should attempt to open and repair these components.

Components inside a monitor can hold a charge for a long time, even after the monitor has been unplugged from its power source. The amount of voltage that a monitor can contain, even when turned off and unplugged, is enough to kill someone. Wearing a wrist strap can heighten the risk of contacting the monitor's dangerous electric current. The cathode ray tube (CRT) in the monitor is charged to 20,000 volts or more. This charge can last for weeks after the monitor is turned off.

WARNING

The components described here should **not** be opened, regardless of whether a wrist strap is worn, as this could expose a person to danger.

Storage of Equipment

Electronic components or circuit boards should be stored in shielded antistatic bags, which are easily recognized by a shielding characteristic—usually a silvery-sheen, transparent appearance. Shielded antistatic bags are important because they prevent static electricity from entering the bags. These bags need to be in good condition, without crinkles or holes. Even tiny openings from crinkles limits the ability of the bag to provide protection from electrostatic discharges.

When original packaging is not available, circuit boards and peripherals should be transported in a shielded antistatic bag. However, never put a shielded antistatic bag inside a PC. In addition, never plug in a motherboard while it is sitting on top of an antistatic bag. Remember that these bags are antistatic because they are partially conductive. A motherboard could easily be shorted out while starting up if several hundred pins from its components were touching the conductive bag.

If computer components are stored in plastic bins, the bins should be made of a conductive plastic. A nonconductive plastic bin tends to build up an electrostatic charge. Make a habit of touching the bins to equalize the bin charge to your body before reaching for the components in the bin. When passing components between individuals, first touch the skin of the hands before passing the component.

Tools of the Trade

Most of the tools used in the assembly process are small hand tools. They are available individually or included as part of PC tool kits that can be purchased at computer stores. If a technician is working on laptops, then a small Torx screwdriver (which does not come in all PC tool kits) is necessary. Figure 1-66 shows a typical tool set used by a technician.

Figure 1-66 A Technician's Tool Set

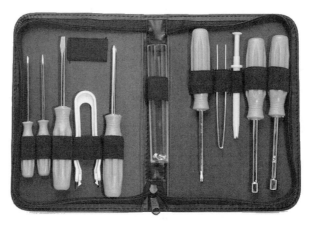

The right tools can save you time and help you avoid damage to your equipment. Tool kits range widely in size, quality, and price. PC technicians typically have the following tools:

- ESD wrist strap
- Flat-head screwdriver (large and small)
- Phillips-head screwdriver (large and small)
- Tweezers or part retriever
- Long-nosed pliers
- Wire cutters
- Chip extractor
- Hex wrench set
- Torx driver
- Nut driver (large and small)

- Three-claw component holder
- Digital multimeter
- Wrap plugs
- Small mirror
- Small dust brush
- Soft, lint-free cloth
- Cable ties
- Scissors
- Flashlight (small)
- Electric tape
- Notebook and pencil or pen

Additionally, the following materials should be on hand:

- Additional screws
- Expansion card inserts
- Drive faceplates
- Mounting kits
- Extra cables

Organizational Aids

The following are workspace organizational aids:

- A parts organizer to keep track of small parts, such as screws and connectors
- Adhesive or masking tape, to make labels that identify parts
- A small notebook, to keep track of assembly and/or troubleshooting steps
- A place for quick references and detailed troubleshooting guides
- A clipboard for paperwork

Diagnostic Software for System Repair and Maintenance

Once a computer system has been assembled, it is necessary to load the software that allows it to boot. If there are any problems in getting a new system to boot up, there is testing software available on floppy disk. The three types of disk software that should be kept in the workspace include an operating system boot disk, a virus-scanning and -repair disk, and a diagnostic software disk.

The following are commonly used software tools in PC computing:

- **Partition Magic**—Advanced drive-partitioning software
- **CheckIt**—Fault-isolation software
- **Spinrite**—A hard drive scanning tool
- **AmiDiag**—Hardware fault-isolation software
- **DiskSuite**—Hard drive defragmenting software
- **SecureCRT**—Feature-filled terminal software
- **VNC**—Remote access software
- **Norton AntiVirus**—One of the industry-leading virus-protection software

Depending on the technician's needs, information on each of these software tools can be readily downloaded from the respective manufacturer's website. It is always useful to find out what a particular software tool can do before purchasing it, to ensure that it meets the requirements of the job.

Workspace Cleaning Supplies

Although a new system will not need to be cleaned during the assembly process, over time, computer systems can gather dust and other residues. Dust particles themselves might contain chemical residues that can degrade or short-circuit chips, contact surfaces, and wire contacts. Oil from human fingers can contaminate or corrode a sensitive electrical connection. Even perspiration from skin contains chemical salts that can corrode electrical connections. This fact presents another good reason to hold all electronic boards by their edges, not where the metal contacts are located.

A computer's component surfaces need cleaning periodically, and this means more than just blowing off or vacuuming out the dust and lint. Commonly used cleaning products include spray contact cleaner, as shown in Figure 1-67, solvents, swabs, and cleaning pads. Most vendors provide guidelines for the cleaning supplies that should be used with their equipment. Be familiar with these guidelines, and stock the recommended supplies.

Spray contact cleaner is a mixture of a solvent and a lubricant. It is used to get into a very small area like a contact point. The can usually has a long thin plastic nozzle inserted into the head so that you can discharge the solution in pinpoint fashion. Spray contact cleaner is useful when removing corroded electrical contacts or loosening adapter boards with gummy connection points.

Figure 1-67 An Air Can

Solvents are used with swabs to remove residues that stick to circuit boards or contacts, especially when boards or contacts cannot be easily reached with regular cleaning pads. A reliable and frequently used solvent is isopropyl alcohol, which is commonly sold in pharmacies.

Prepackaged cleaning pads are used for open, flat, easily accessible surfaces. These types of swabs and cleaning pads can be easily obtained at any electronics supply store.

Be especially careful when using cleaning chemicals. Take measures to protect the eyes against volatile solutions. Additionally, be careful when storing volatile cleaning chemicals because they can escape from the storage container.

Workplace Testing Equipment

When assembling a computer system, it can be necessary to test electrical signals on a motherboard or its components. In addition, testing the external power environment is often necessary. A troublesome power source can cause difficulties for the plugged-in computer systems. Figure 1-68 shows a Fluke 110 Multimeter, which is used to test high-voltage devices. In addition to the outlet tester and digital multimeter, *wrap plugs* should be part of the standard equipment kept in the workspace. These plugs are also referred to as *loopback plugs*, or *loopback connectors*.

CAUTION

Do not confuse iso-propyl alcohol with rubbing alcohol. Rubbing alcohol is relatively impure and can contaminate electrical connections. Swabs that resemble typical cotton swabs, but have a foam or chamois cloth on the end, should be used together with isopropyl alcohol. Cotton swabs should not be used, as they shred and leave strands on the components.

Figure 1-68 A High-Voltage Tester

Loopback connectors test signaling ports that are located on the back of the computer. The loopback plugs are wired so that they either loop or send the signals back on themselves. These plugs are used in conjunction with suitable test software to check the integrity of computer ports.

Worksheet 1.6.6 Lab Safety Checklist

Use this worksheet to test your knowledge about the safety requirements for an IT technician's workspace.

Preventive maintenance, hardware maintenance, and software maintenance will be discussed with more detail in later chapters.

Lab Safety Agreement

The Lab Safety Agreement details the procedures to be followed when working with computers. The classroom instructor will provide a copy of the agreement for you to sign.

Because many classroom lab exercises do not use high voltages, electrical safety might not appear to be important. However, do not become complacent about electrical safety. Electricity can injure or cause death. Abide by all electrical safety procedures at all times. Read more about general safety issues in Chapter 3, "Assembling a Computer."

Before repairing any electronic device, it is important to know the hazards and the proper safety procedures. Use extreme care and follow these safety procedures at all times:

- ❏ Remove all jewelry.
- ❏ Unplug the power cord before removing or reinstalling any electrical component or circuit board, or when performing maintenance on electrical equipment.
- ❏ Do not touch any exposed circuit with power applied.
- ❏ Only have power applied when taking voltage measurements or waveforms.
- ❏ Insert test probes with one hand only. Keeping one hand behind your back or under the test bench reduces the chance of electrocution. This is referred to as the *one-hand rule.*
- ❏ Do not leave objects loose on the equipment, such as screws, nuts, or washers. They can fall into the equipment.
- ❏ Before handling or replacing integrated-circuit (IC) processors, properly ground yourself by touching the outside metal of the equipment and by using an anti-static wrist strap that is connected to the chassis. Make sure that the equipment is grounded prior to removing its case. This reduces ESD damage.
- ❏ Do not troubleshoot electronic equipment without having appropriate documentation, unless instructor approval is given.
- ❏ Never solder a connection with the power on.
- ❏ After soldering, look for possible solder splashes, cold-solder joints, or damaged insulation.
- ❏ Maintain a clean and safe work area.
- ❏ Take your time.
- ❏ Be certain about what you are going to do. If you are unsure about a procedure, ask for help.
- ❏ **If in doubt, don't touch it!**
- ❏ Other: The instructor covers fire extinguisher locations, fire evacuation procedures, safety/first aid kit locations, and emergency phone numbers in class.
- ❏ Shoes, a shirt, and long pants are required when soldering and working on equipment.

STUDENT ACKNOWLEDGMENT:

- ❏ I have read and understand this document.

Student Signature	Print Name	Date

Summary

This chapter discussed the basics of Information Technology. Some of the important concepts to retain from this chapter include the following:

- A computer system consists of hardware and software. Hardware includes the physical equipment, such as the case, the drives, the monitor, and the mouse. Computer software (or programs) includes the operating system and applications that perform specific functions for the user.

- Work with the desktop to start the system and shut it down properly. Navigate the desktop to view system information, use shortcut icons, switch between windows, set up the desktop, and recover deleted files from the Recycle Bin.

- Open programs and documents, utilize help features, search for files, and open a command line with the Run command on the Start menu.

- Understand computer terminology, and know the difference between a byte, kilobyte, and megabyte. Understand how frequency is measured, and know the difference between Hz, MHz, and GHz.

- Use the most effective method of converting number systems, including binary to decimal and back again, and binary to hexadecimal and back again. Identify the places in binary and decimal numbers, and know the value of each.

- Safety is the number-one concern when working with computer systems. The proper safety procedures must be followed to reduce the risk of ESD, which can damage computer components. Additionally, the proper safety procedures keep the IT technician safe.

The next chapter introduces you to computer theory. It discusses the various components of a computer and explains how these pieces come together to make a functional system.

Check Your Understanding

Use the following review questions to test your understanding of the concepts covered in this chapter. Answers are listed in Appendix B, "Answers to Check Your Understanding Review Questions."

1. What is the name of the method that is used to connect computers?

   A. Networking

   B. Linking

   C. Communicating

   D. Connecting

2. When was the term Internet first used?

   A. 1980

   B. 1960

   C. 1882

   D. 1982

3. What does asynchronous mean?

   A. With respect to time

   B. Consistent with time

   C. Always synchronized

   D. Without respect to time

4. How many nibbles are in 64 bits?

   A. 16

   B. 32

   C. 8

   D. 24

5. How many bytes are in 64 bits?

   A. 18

   B. 9

   C. 8

   D. 24

6. What type of numbering system is characterized by 0s and 1s?

   A. Base 4

   B. Base 10

   C. Binary

   D. Hexadecimal

7. Which numbering system is based on powers of 2?

   A. Octal

   B. Hexadecimal

   C. Binary

   D. ASCII

8. What is the decimal number 151 in binary?

   A. 10100111

   B. 10010111

   C. 10101011

   D. 10010011

9. What is the binary number 11011010 in decimal?

   A. 186

   B. 202

   C. 222

   D. 218

10. What is the binary number 10110 decimal?

    A. 28

    B. 22

    C. 24

    D. 23

11. What is the decimal number 202 in binary?

    A. 11000100

    B. 11000101

    C. 11001010

    D. 11000111

12. What is the binary number 11101100 in decimal?

    A. 234

    B. 236

    C. 262

    D. 242

13. How much time should elapse between putting on a wrist strap and touching any computer component?

    A. 15 seconds

    B. 1 minute

    C. 30 seconds

    D. None

14. How much charge (in volts) can a CRT in a monitor hold?

    A. 1000

    B. 5000

    C. 10,000

    D. 20,000 or more

15. What is the agreement that provides important safety information and should be signed before beginning lab exercises?

    A. Classroom rules

    B. Lab Safety Agreement

    C. Workspace layout

    D. Chapter summary

Key Terms

3D graphics   A three-dimensional environment.

algorithm   A systematic description or method of how a series of steps is carried out.

AND gate   If either input is off, the output is off.

animation   A tool that creates sequential images that can be played in a series displaying continuous movement.

application software   Accepts input from the user and manipulates it to achieve a result, known as output.

Application window   The window for a program that includes a title bar, tool bar, menu bar, status bar, and scroll bar.

asynchronous   Does not use a clock or timing source to keep both the sender and receiver in sync.

background tab   Adjusts the appearance of the desktop.

Base 2   Same as binary, uses two digits to express all numerical quantities.

binary   Same as Base 2, number system that uses two digits to express all numerical quantities.

bit   The smallest unit of data in a computer.

bitmaps   A type of graphical image.

business graphics   Used in presentation applications.

byte   Eight bits of data.

cold boot   Starting the computer with the power button.

Computer Aided Design (CAD)   An application that performs solid modeling.

computer system   Hardware and software components.

database   An application that organizes and manages data.

desktop   The main display screen.

Dijkstra algorithm   An algorithm used to find the shortest path between a specific networking device.

Documents menu   Displays the most recently accessed documents.

Domain Name System (DNS)   Maps host names to IP addresses.

electronic mail (e-mail)   The exchange of computer generated messages.

Encryption algorithm   An algorithm that encrypts data.

Euclidean algorithm   An algorithm essentially used to do long division.

flat-file database   Data stored in a single table.

frame-by-frame   A type of animation.

gigahertz (MHz)   1,000,000,000 cycles per second.

graphical user interface (GUI; pronounced goo-ee)   Uses a visual display to represent the procedures and programs that can be executed by the computer.

graphics applications   An application used to create or modify graphical images.

hardware   The physical equipment of a computer system.

Help feature   Provides instructions and tips on using the computer system.

hertz (Hz)   The rate of change in the state or cycle in a sound wave, alternating current, or other cyclical waveform.

icon   An image representing an application or capability.

illustration   A tool that creates and manipulates vector based images.

image editing   A tool that creates and manipulates raster or bitmap images.

key   Used in a database as a unique identifier.

keyframe   A type of animation.

kilobit (Kb)   1024 bits.

kilobit per second (Kbps)   Data transfer rate of about 1000 bits per second.

kilobyte (KB)   1024 bytes.

kilobytes per second (KBps)   A data transfer rate of about 1000 bytes per second.

logic gates   An electronic circuit that recognizes AND, OR, NOT, and NOR.

loopback plugs or connectors   A way of testing signaling ports.

mainframe   A centralized computer that allows end users to interface via "dumb terminals."

maximize the screen   Restoring the size of the display to full screen.

Megabit per second (Mbps)   Data transfer rate of about 1,000,000 bits per second.

megabyte (MB)   1,048,576 bytes.

megabyte per second (MBps)   Data transfer rate of about 1,000,000 bytes per second.

megahertz (MHz)   1,000,000 cycles per second.

minimize the screen   Reducing the size of the display window.

My Computer   Icon on the desktop that gives access to all the installed drives.

My Documents   A shortcut to personal or frequently accessed files.

Network Neighborhood   Displays neighboring computers in a networked environment.

network   A group of computers that are connected so the resources can be shared.

nibble   One half a byte, or four bits.

NOR gate   A combination of OR and NOT, if either input is on, the output is off.

NOT gate   If the input is on, the output is off, and vice versa.

object based   A type of graphical image.

object-oriented programming   A type of programming that uses algorithms.

operating system   The program that manages all the other programs in a computer.

OR gate   If either input is on, the output is on.

personal computer   A standalone device, independent of all other computers.

pixels   Tiny dots that make up the light on the screen and determine the intensity of a screen image.

powers of numbers   The number of times a number is multiplied by itself.

presentation applications   Organize, design, and deliver business presentations in the form of slide shows.

Program menu   Lists all programs installed on the computer.

program   Sequence of instructions that describe how data is to be processed.

quick-launch buttons   Shortcuts to applications.

raster image   A type of graphical image.

Recycle Bin   Stores deleted files, folders, etc until the user is ready to empty.

relational database   A collection of flat-file databases or tables.

Run feature   An alternate method of starting a program or accessing troubleshooting applications.

Screen Saver tab   Activates a screen saver on the desktop.

server   A central computer that stores resources in a network.

software   Programs used to operate the computer system.

spreadsheet   An application that manipulates numerical data.

Start button   Contains the access to programs, control panel, etc.

Start menu   Provides access to the programs and functions on the PC.

Taskbar   Contains quick launch buttons, clock, etc.

tweening   The process of defining keyframes.

vector based   A type of graphical image.

warm boot   Restarting the computer while it's running.

web browser   An application used to locate and display pages from the Internet.

word processor   An application that creates, edits, stores, and prints documents.

workstations   Individual computers in a network.

Objectives

Upon completion of this chapter, you will be able to perform the following tasks:

- Define and understand the computer's four basic functions: input, processing, output, and storage
- Understand the actions of the boot sequence that initializes and tests the system hardware
- Distinguish the features and functions of the hardware components that make the computer work
- Identify the components of portable computers as they relate to their desktop counterparts
- Understand system resources, including IRQs, DMA, and I/O

Chapter 2

How Computers Work

This chapter discusses how computers work. Starting with a system overview, you learn the boot process, including initializing and testing the system, loading the operating system (OS), and running the boot sequence required to operate the computer.

The hardware that makes up the computer is explained in detail, and illustrations are included. In addition to the components of the desktop computer, this chapter provides information relating to laptops, or portable computers.

System resources are shared between computer components and devices. Interrupt requests (IRQs), direct memory access (DMA), and input/output (I/O) addresses enable the central processing unit (CPU) to handle multiple requests.

Input, Process, Output, and Storage

As mentioned in the previous chapter, the operating system is the software that controls functionality and provides lower-level routines for applications. Most operating systems provide functions to read and write data to files. The OS then translates requests for operations on files into operations that the disk controller can carry out. The operating system helps the computer perform four basic operations, as follows:

- **Input**—Recognizing input from the keyboard or mouse.
- **Processing**—Manipulating data according to the user's instructions.
- **Output**—Sending output to the video screen or printer.
- **Storage**—Keeping track of files for use later. Examples of storage devices include floppy disks and hard drives.

The most common way to *input* data into a computer is from the keyboard, as shown in Figure 2-1. Opening a web page, an e-mail file, or a file that came from a network server are also ways to input data. After the data has been input, the computer can then *process* it. When a file is opened and the text is reformatted, the computer is processing data.

Figure 2-1 An Input Device

Processing data usually results in some kind of *output*, such as a word processor file or a spreadsheet. The most common way to output data is to send the data to the computer's monitor, as shown in Figure 2-2, or to a printer. Today, most computers have a connection to the Internet, making it common to output the data to the Internet via e-mail or as a web page.

Figure 2-2 An Output Device

Data *storage* is probably the most important of the four basic computer functions. The most common way to store a file is to save it to a hard drive. Hard drives can be thought of as large file cabinets. An operating system finds a place on the hard drive, saves the file, and remembers the file's location.

The Boot Process

This section includes the following topics:

- Initializing and testing the system hardware
- Loading the operating system and hardware configuration
- Running the boot sequence

Initializing and Testing the System Hardware

For an operating system to run, it must be loaded into the computer's random access memory (RAM). When a computer is first turned on, it launches a small program called the *bootstrap loader*, which resides in the *Basic Input Output System (BIOS)* chip or firmware. The BIOS chip is discussed later in this chapter. The term *bootstrap* comes from the phrase "picking yourself up by the bootstraps," hence the term *booting* the computer. The bootstrap's primary functions are to test the computer's hardware and to locate and load the operating system into RAM. (RAM is discussed later in this chapter.) Because the bootstrap program is built into the BIOS chip, it is also referred to as *BIOS control*. During the execution of the BIOS firmware routines, three major sets of operations are performed:

1. Power-on self-tests (POSTs) are run.

2. Initialization is done.

3. The BIOS moves the starting address and mode information into the DMA controller and then loads the master boot record (MBR).

Power-On Self-Test

To test the computer's hardware, the bootstrap program runs a program called a *power-on self-test (POST)*. In this test, the computer's CPU checks itself first and then checks the computer's system timer. The POST checks the random access memory by writing data to each RAM chip and then reading those data. Any difference indicates a problem.

If the POST finds errors, it sends a message to the computer monitor. If the POST finds errors that cannot be displayed on the monitor, it sends errors in the form of beeps.

The POST sends one beep and the screen begins to display OS loading messages after the bootstrap has determined that the computer has passed the POST. The meaning of any beep code depends on the manufacturer of the BIOS.

The three major manufacturers of BIOS chips are AMIBIOS (American Megatrends, Inc.), PhoenixBIOS (Phoenix Technologies Ltd.), and AwardBIOS (Award Software, Inc.). Award Software is now part of Phoenix Technologies, but Award Software continues to offer products and support. These manufacturers all have different beep codes, even between versions of their BIOS. It is normal to hear a single beep during the boot process, as long as the boot process does not stop. This is a code to signify that the computer is starting normally.

The POST is an important phase of the bootstrap process. Consult the manual that comes with the motherboard to learn more about the BIOS and its error beep codes, or visit the manufacturer's website.

Loading the Operating System and Hardware Configuration

The next step for the bootstrap program is to locate the OS and copy it to the computer's RAM. The bootstrap loader first checks whether the OS boot file (or boot record) is located on a floppy drive. If not, it looks for the file on the hard disk. In some cases, if the operating system is not found on either the floppy drive or the hard disk, the bootstrap loader looks for the OS on the built-in CD-ROM drive. However, the most common means of storing the OS is on the computer's hard drive. The order in which the bootstrap program searches the OS boot file can be changed in the system BIOS setup. The most common order of search is (1) floppy drive, (2) hard disk, and (3) CD-ROM drive. When the bootstrap finds the OS, it looks for a file called the *boot record*. The boot record is copied to the computer's RAM, and the bootstrap program then turns over control of the boot process to the boot record. The boot record looks for files on the hard disk that help the hard disk locate the rest of the OS. As files are located and loaded into RAM, the boot record is no longer needed. The OS that was stored on the hard disk is now in control of the boot process. Figure 2-3 demonstrates the loading of the bootstrap program.

The last step of the boot process is for the OS to find *hardware configuration files*, which are specific to the computer. If the computer has a modem or a sound card, the OS finds the configuration files (hardware drivers) and loads them.

Figure 2-3 Bootstrap Loading

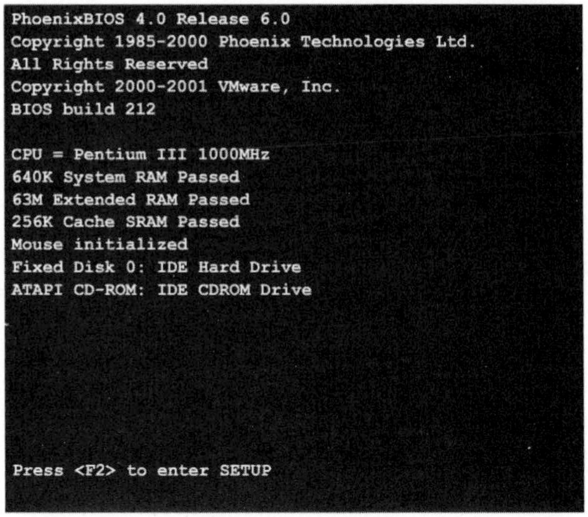

```
PhoenixBIOS 4.0 Release 6.0
Copyright 1985-2000 Phoenix Technologies Ltd.
All Rights Reserved
Copyright 2000-2001 VMware, Inc.
BIOS build 212

CPU = Pentium III 1000MHz
640K System RAM Passed
63M Extended RAM Passed
256K Cache SRAM Passed
Mouse initialized
Fixed Disk 0: IDE Hard Drive
ATAPI CD-ROM: IDE CDROM Drive




Press <F2> to enter SETUP
```

Running the Boot Sequence

The PC's boot sequence defines the set of actions as well as the sequence of the actions that take place when you start your computer from a power-off status or when you restart the PC (with the power already on). The number of events that happen in the boot process depends on the version of Windows you are running and whether it is a cold boot or a warm boot. These terms are defined as follows:

- **Warm boot**—This is performed whenever the PC is restarted or reset with the power still on. The warm boot, which is a subset of the cold boot, is accomplished in one of the following ways:
  - By choosing **Start, Shutdown, Restart**
  - By pressing the computer's reset button
  - By pressing **Ctrl-Alt-Delete** twice
- **Cold boot**—A cold boot occurs whenever the PC's power switch is turned from off to on. This type of boot involves many more events and bootstrap (BIOS) activities than the warm boot. The cold boot causes the BIOS to guide the computer's boot sequence through a series of steps that verify the system's integrity.

The exact steps in the boot process can vary depending on a number of factors that affect your computer. These include the BIOS manufacturer, the BIOS version, and your system hardware configuration. These steps, listed in the Table 2-1, represent what generally happens when you cold boot a PC.

Table 2-1 Generic Cold Boot Sequence

Step	Device	Description
1	Power supply	The power supply initializes. The chipset then waits for the Power Good signal from the power supply.
2	BIOS ROM	The processor looks for the start of the BIOS (basic input/output system) boot program at the end of the system memory, where a pointer tells it where to get the BIOS startup program.
3	POST	The BIOS performs the POST. If any fatal errors are encountered, the boot process stops.
4	Video	The BIOS looks for the video card BIOS program and executes it to initialize the video card.
5	Other BIOS	The BIOS looks for any other device BIOS, such as a hard disk BIOS, and executes it.
6	Startup screen	The BIOS displays the Startup screen.
7	Memory	The BIOS tests other system components and performs a memory count-up test.
8	Hardware	The BIOS tests the system to find the various hardware in the system. Hard disks and memory timings are configured at this time.
9	Plug and Play	The BIOS configures Plug and Play devices.
10	Configuration screen	The BIOS displays a configuration summary of the system.
11	Boot drive	The BIOS searches for a drive to boot from based on the boot sequence.
12	Boot record	The BIOS searches the first boot device in the sequence for either the master boot record (MBR) on a hard disk or the volume boot sector on a floppy disk.
13	Operating system	The BIOS begins to boot the operating system, where boot information code takes over from the BIOS code.
14	Error	If the BIOS does not find a bootable device in the boot sequence, it displays an error message and halts the system.

Hardware Components

This section includes the following topics:

- Computer cases and power supplies
- The motherboard
- The CPU: Intel and AMD processors
- BIOS, EPROM, EEPROM, and Flash ROM
- Expansion slots and bus types
- RAM and cache/COASt memory
- Monitors
- Video cards
- I/O ports: serial, parallel, PS/2, 6-pin mini-DIN, 5-pin DIN USB, and FireWire
- IDE and SCSI controllers
- Floppy drives
- Hard drives
- CD-ROM drives
- Modems
- Network interface cards (NICs)

Computer Cases and Power Supplies

The power supply and the computer case are two important parts that help determine the performance of the system. The type of motherboard used is usually determined by the type of case and power supply you have. (The power supply is usually included in the computer case.) Computer cases and power supplies are detailed in this section.

Computer Cases

The type of *case* is the first decision that is made when building a computer. The case is made up of the metal chassis (or frame) and a cover, usually constructed of metal or hard plastic. The case is the housing unit for the internal components, and it protects the components from dust and damage. The case usually comes with the *power supply*, which is needed to power the computer and the installed components. Computer cases are either *desktop* or *tower models*, as shown in Figure 2-4. The two are defined as follows:

- **Desktop model**—Sits on a desk horizontally. The monitor can be set on top of the case. This choice can be a space-saver.
- **Tower model**—Stands upright in a vertical position that allows easy placement on the floor. Mini-tower, mid-tower, and full-tower cases are available.

Figure 2-4 Desktop and Tower Models

The choice of a desktop case or tower is a matter of personal preference. However, it is important to consider the workspace before choosing a case.

Hardware components are installed in the bays of the case. The bays are placeholders for your drives so that they are neatly organized. Devices can be easily interchanged from bay to bay. Drive bays are 5-1/4 or 3-1/2 inches wide. Some bays are normally left unfilled in a new computer so the machine can be upgraded later with a ZIP drive, tape backup, or a CD-ROM burner.

Tables 2-2 and 2-3 summarize information about the different parts of a typical computer case and indicate the factors to consider when selecting a case.

Table 2-2 Typical Parts of a Computer Case

Part	Purpose
Frame	The main board and all the objects inside and outside are attached to the frame. The frame is what defines the computer's size and shape.
Cover panels	These panels attach to the frame to enclose all the parts of the PC. It is not advisable to operate the computer without the cover panels in place because they are instrumental in protecting the parts, directing airflow to cool the circuits, and containing the radio frequency interference/electromagnetic interference (RFI/ EMI) emissions of the power supply unit.
LED and button connectors	These connect the buttons and light-emitting diodes (LEDs) on the front of the case to the motherboard.
Speaker and connector	The speaker connects to the motherboard and provides a basic way to diagnose startup problems.
I/O template	This is a metal template on the back of the case that provides access holes to the motherboard peripheral connectors. On some cases, the template can be replaced to provide the correct access holes, depending on the main board connector locations and spacing.
Expansion slots	These slots are opened when an expansion card is installed on the motherboard to provide access to the card's ports or connectors.
Case fan and connector	Most modern cases provide a secondary fan at the front of the unit to draw air in to circulate over the circuits and devices in the system. The fan connects to the main board to receive power.

continues

Table 2-2 Typical Parts of a Computer Case (Continued)

Part	Purpose
5-1/4-inch drive bays	These are the large bays where a 5-1/4-inch-wide device, like a CD-ROM drive, can be installed in the case. Usually, a front plate covering the bay must be removed before the installation.
3-1/2-inch drive bays	These are the smaller bays where 3-1/2-inch-wide devices, like a floppy drive or hard disk, can be mounted. If a hard disk is installed, the metal or plastic cover plate does not need to be removed, because the disk is not removable.
Vent holes	The design of the case dictates where the appropriate vent holes are placed. The manufacturer places these holes in the best possible locations to ensure the correct airflow within the case.
Power supply mounting area	This area is for mounting the power supply unit if the case does not have one. Some cases come with a power supply already installed.
Front cover plate	This plate fits on the front of the case, providing a place for the LEDs and buttons, an air intake control, and an aesthetically pleasing look.
Feet	The feet on the bottom of the case provide stability on uneven or slick surfaces. Some cases draw air from the bottom of the case, and the feet elevate the case to ensure proper airflow.

Table 2-3 Factors to Consider in Choosing a Computer Case

Factor	Rationale
Model type	There are four main case models. One type is for desktop PCs, and three types are for tower computers. The type of motherboard you choose determines the type of case that can be used. The size and shape must match exactly.
Size	The case should have enough space for the installed components. Additionally, there should be enough space for access to the components for service and for air to move across the components to dissipate the heat.
Available space	Desktop cases allow space conservation in tight areas because the monitor can be placed on top of the unit. Tower cases can be located on or under the desk.

Table 2-3 Factors to Consider in Choosing a Computer Case (Continued)

Factor	Rationale
Number of devices	The more devices that need power in the system, the larger the power supply must be. This relates to the mounting area of the power supply in the case.
Power supply	Depending on the type of motherboard you have chosen, you must match the power rating and connection type to the power supply that you are using.
Environmental conditions	If the system will be in a dusty area, it's a good idea to purchase a case designed to reduce the amount of dust entering the system. Some cases offer easily replaceable filters for the case fan to trap dust.
Aesthetics	For some people, the appearance of the case doesn't matter. For others, it is critical. If you must have a case that is attractive and aesthetically pleasing, a number of case manufacturers do consider this.
Status display	What is going on inside the case can be important. LED indicators that are mounted on the front of the case can tell you if the system is receiving power, when the hard drive is being used, and when the computer is in standby mode.
Vents	All cases have a vent on the power supply, and some have another vent on the back to help draw air into or out of the system. Some cases are designed with more vents in the event that the system needs a way to dissipate an unusual amount of heat. This situation might occur when many devices are installed close together in the case.
Rigidity	When choosing a case, remember that the components inside are not designed to bend. The case you use should be sturdy enough to keep all the components inside from flexing.

Power Supplies

As shown in Figure 2-5, a power supply provides the needed voltage to power the various electronic circuits that make up the PC. It receives external AC power.

The power supply is contained in a metal box. Within this box, a transformer converts the current that is generated from standard outlets into voltages and current flows that the computer parts need to operate.

TEST TIP

Power supplies are rated in watts. A typical computer has a 250 to 300-watt power supply.

TEST TIP

AC stands for alternating current, which means that the current flows in one direction and then reverses its direction and repeats the process. It is the most common form of electricity generated from a power plant. The computer's power supply converts AC to direct current (DC) or other levels required for the system. DC is electrical current that travels in only one direction.

Figure 2-5   External View of a Typical Power Supply

Power Supply and Connectors

Use this interactive photo to review the parts of the power supply and power supply connectors.

A fan installed in the power supply prevents the computer and its components from overheating by maintaining airflow. It is critical that these components be kept at a consistent operating temperature to ensure their best performance. The fan is built into the power supply with openings on the backside of the case. Never block or cover the fan inlet port.

Several different types of power supplies are available, varying in size and design. The more common types are known as the AT and ATX power supply form factors. AT-type supplies are no longer used in new systems and are generally found on computers built prior to the mid-1990s. ATX is the more common type; the connectors of the two types allow you to distinguish the AT from the ATX power supply. Common PC power supplies are *switched* and *linear* power supplies.

The devices that attach to the power supply use +5V, +12V, and +3.3V DC power. Older devices (PC/XT and early AT models) use –5V and –12V DC power. The power supply must support the type of processor to be used. Each power supply comes with these specifications. Tables 2-4 and 2-5 describe the components of a typical ATX power supply and the factors required when selecting a power supply.

Table 2-4 Components of a Power Supply

Part	Description
Case and cover	Isolate the power supply from the rest of the PC and keep electromagnetic emissions inside the unit.
Power cord	Connects the unit to a receptacle to supply AC power.
Voltage selector switch	Allows the power supply to accept 110/120-volt, 60-Hz AC power (within North America) or 220/240-volt, 50-Hz AC power (outside North America). The following website offers more information: http://kropla.com/electric.htm.
Power switch	Directs power from the AC outlet to the computer.
Power converter	Converts AC to DC power for use within the PC.
Motherboard power connector	Supplies the necessary power to the motherboard.
Disk drive power connectors	Supply the necessary power to the drives, auxiliary fans, and other devices inside the case.
Fan	Circulates air inside the case to keep itself and all the electronics and devices cool.
Fuse	Protects the power supply from damage in the event of a power surge. The fuse blows when it is subjected to too much current.

Table 2-5 Factors to Consider When Selecting a Power Supply

Factor	Rationale
Wattage	In order to upgrade the PC with more equipment or faster processors, the power supply must provide enough power to the equipment without becoming overloaded.
Form factor	Depending on the type of case and motherboard selected, the power supply must adhere to the same form factor requirements as these items in order to fit inside the case and correctly power the motherboard and other devices.

continues

Table 2-5 Factors to Consider When Selecting a Power Supply (Continued)

Factor	Rationale
CPU type	Different CPUs require different voltages. For example, some AMD chips and motherboards require more power than certain Intel chips, and vice versa.
Expandability	If the power supply only has enough power to supply the current CPU, motherboard, and devices, there might not be enough power to supply any upgrade to the system.
Energy efficiency	Each power supply has an efficiency rating. The higher the rating, the lower the heat generated by the power supply when converting voltage.
Fan type and direction	The power supply must have a high-quality fan, because the fan is the primary source of airflow inside the case. Some fans can change direction to allow air to be blown directly on the CPU and to regulate the quality of the air entering the case.
Signals	Modern power supplies can be regulated by the motherboard. The main board can regulate the speed of the fan, depending on the temperature inside the case. The board can also turn off the fan to save power, and some "smart" power supplies can turn off the computer in the event of a fan failure before the components overheat.
Fault tolerance	If you have a PC that needs to be on at all times, consider using a dual power supply. If one unit fails, the other one takes over. Some designs enable a power supply to be replaced while the computer is still powered.
Line conditioning	One way to ensure that the DC voltages supplied to the PC are kept at normal levels when spikes or brownouts occur is to install a power supply that has built-in conditioning. These units ensure that the DC voltages supplied to the system remain stable, even when the incoming AC current is not.

Current

Electrical current, or current, is the flow of charges that is created when electrons move. In electrical circuits, current is caused by a flow of free electrons. When voltage (electrical pressure) is applied, and a path is present for the current, electrons move from the negative terminal (which repels them) along the path to the positive terminal (which attracts them).

Worksheet 2.3.1   PC Power Supply

Review important information relating to the power supply.

The Motherboard

This section discusses the subject of motherboard technology. Knowledge of the *motherboard*, also called the system board or main board, is crucial because the board is the nerve center of the computer system. Everything else in the system plugs into it, is controlled by it, and depends on it to communicate with other devices in the system. The system board is the largest of the printed circuit boards, and every system has one. It generally houses the CPU, controller circuitry, bus, RAM, expansion slots for additional boards, and ports for external devices. In addition, it contains the Complementary Metal-Oxide Semiconductor known as CMOS (pronounced C moss) and other Read Only Memory (ROM) BIOS chips and support chips, providing varied functionality. If the computer is a desktop type, the system board is generally located at the bottom of the computer's case. If the computer is a tower-configuration case, the system board is mounted vertically along one side. All components relating to the system connect directly to the system board. External devices such as the mouse, keyboard, or monitor would not be able to communicate with the system without the system board.

Printed circuit boards are constructed from sheets of fiberglass. These sheets are covered with sockets and various electronic parts, including different kinds of chips. A *chip* is made up of a small circuit board etched on a square of silicon, a material with the same chemical structure as common sand. Chips vary in size, but many are roughly the size of a postage stamp. A chip is also referred to as a *semiconductor* or *integrated circuit*. The individual wires and hand-soldered connectors used in older system boards are now replaced by aluminum or copper traces printed on the circuit boards. This improvement has significantly saved the amount of time spent on building a PC and has reduced the cost, both for the manufacturer and the consumer. Figure 2-6 shows the components of an ATX motherboard and how they fit together.

Interactive PhotoZoom Activity   Motherboard

Included on the CD, this PhotoZoom details the motherboard and defines the components of the motherboard.

Lab Activity 2.3.2   Motherboard Identification

Identify motherboards, remove motherboards, replace motherboards, and use the motherboard manuals to identify a number of the system's components.

Figure 2-6 An ATX Motherboard

Motherboard Form Factors

Motherboards are also referred to as *system boards* or *planar boards*. They are usually described by their form factors, which describe their physical dimensions. The two most common form factors in use today are the *Baby AT motherboard* and the *ATX motherboard*. The Baby AT motherboard is about the same size as the IBM XT motherboard. The ATX motherboard is similar to the Baby AT motherboard, except for a number of important enhancements. Most new systems come with the ATX motherboard form factor.

TEST TIP

Understand the difference between motherboard form factors.

ATX motherboard distinguishing features include the following:

- The expansion slots are parallel to the short side of the board, which allows more space for other components.
- The CPU and RAM are located next to the power supply. These components consume plenty of power, so they need direct cooling by the power supply's fan.
- ATX motherboards contain an integrated I/O port and PS/2 mouse connectors.
- ATX motherboards support 3.3V operation from an ATX power supply.

Table 2-6 provides a general summary of the motherboard form factors in use today.

Table 2-6 Motherboard Form Factors

Form Factor	Dimensions (Inches)	Notes
Baby AT	8.5×10–13	Used by older PCs but is becoming outdated
ATX	12×9.6	Most common form factor in use today
Mini-ATX	11.2×8.2	Used in newer, smaller PCs
LPX	9×11–13	Found in older PCs and uses a riser card to save space
Mini-LPX	8–9×10–11	Found in older PCs and uses a riser card to save space
NLX	8–9×10–13.6	Found in newer PCs. Setup provides easier access to components

Beyond describing motherboards according to the form factor, they are sometimes described according to the type of microprocessor interface (socket) they present. Motherboards can be described as Socket 7, Socket 370, Socket 423, Socket 478, Slot 1, and so on. Slot 1 is first-generation ATX, whereas Single Socket 370 is second-generation ATX. Sockets and slots are discussed later in this chapter in the section, "The CPU: Intel and AMD Processors."

Similarly, a motherboard can be described as *dual-processor*, as shown in Figure 2-7, or *single-processor*, as shown in Figure 2-8, depending on whether it can use only one or two processors concurrently. Although most motherboards support a single processor, some have dual processors. Because the need for processing power continues to grow, single processors are not always able to meet the demand, especially in corporate networking environments. Dual-processor boards are a welcome development because some advanced network operating systems (for example, Windows 2000) are now designed to take advantages of multiple processors.

Motherboard Components

The components found on a motherboard can vary, depending on the board's age and level of integration. Some motherboards have more or fewer chips or devices. The most common items found on a typical modern motherboard are listed in Table 2-7.

Figure 2-7 Dual-Processor Motherboard

Figure 2-8 Single-Processor Motherboard

Table 2-7 Motherboard Components

Component	Description
Chipset	A set of microcircuits that define how much RAM a motherboard can use, the type of RAM chip, the cache size and speed, the processor types and speeds, and the types of expansion slots the motherboard can accommodate.
CPU interface	The socket or slot that the CPU connects to on the motherboard.
Expansion slots	Receptacles on the motherboard that accept printed circuit boards. All computers have expansion slots that allow additional devices to be added.
Dip switches/jumpers	Used to change various aspects of how the motherboard is configured.
I/O support	Connectors for input and output devices controlled by the main board.
Internal buses	Channels for data to move between the devices attached to the system, and to the CPU and its components.
Power supply socket	The connection for the power supply that provides power to the motherboard.
BIOS chip	Provides the computer with the basic instructions to start up and check the hardware for errors.
Battery	Keeps system time and provides a way for the BIOS to remember certain settings.
RAM sockets	Connectors for inserting memory chips.

Motherboard Chipset

The *chipset* is a crucial component of the motherboard. The motherboard chipset determines the motherboard's compatibility with several other vital system components. This chipset consists of a group of microcircuits contained on several integrated chips or combined into one or two large-scale integration (VLSI) integrated chips. These chips have over 20,000 circuits.

The chipset determines the following:

- How much RAM a motherboard can use
- The type of RAM chip
- The cache size and speed

- The processor types and speed
- The types of expansion slots the motherboard can accommodate

In other words, the motherboard chipset determines motherboard performance and limitations. Although new microprocessor technologies and speed improvements tend to receive all the attention, chipset innovations are just as important.

Chipsets are produced by a number of manufacturers. Intel and AMD are major suppliers.

The CPU: Intel and AMD Processors

The *CPU* is one of the most important elements of the personal computer. On the motherboard, the CPU is contained on a single integrated circuit called the *microprocessor*. The computer cannot run without a CPU. Often referred to as the brains of a computer, the CPU contains two basic components:

- **Control unit**—The control unit instructs the rest of the computer system on how to follow a program's instructions. It directs the movement of data to and from processor memory. The control unit temporarily holds data, instructions, and processed information in its arithmetic/logic unit (see next paragraph). In addition, the control unit directs control signals between the CPU and external devices such as hard disks, main memory, I/O ports, etc.
- **Arithmetic/logic unit (ALU)**—The ALU performs both arithmetic and logical operations. Arithmetic operations are fundamental math operations like addition, subtraction, multiplication, and division. Logical operations such as AND, OR, and XOR make comparisons and decisions, and these determine how a program is executed.

The processor handles most of the operations that are required of the computer by processing instructions and sending signals out, checking for connectivity, and ensuring that operations and hardware are functioning properly. It acts as a messenger to major components such as RAM, the monitor, and disk drives. The microprocessor is connected to the rest of the computer system through three buses, including the data bus, address bus, and control bus. (Bus types are discussed in detail later in this chapter.) Many different companies produce CPUs, including Intel, AMD, and Cyrix. Intel is credited with making the first modern, silicon-based CPU chip in 1971.

Processor Socket Types

In dealing with microprocessors, terminology such as Socket 7, Socket 370, Socket 423, and Slot 1 is frequently encountered. Socket X (*X* being any numerical value) is a descriptive term for the way certain processors plug into a computer motherboard so that the processor makes contact with the motherboard's built-in circuitry or data bus. Manufacturers can have different socket types for their processors. Socket 7, mostly outdated, is the best known of the major connection variations. It is used by some generation of each of the three major processor types: Advanced Micro Devices (AMD), Intel, and Cyrix.

Socket types that contain a higher number are more current. For example, Socket 370 is more current than lower socket numbers. The progression from Socket 1 (Intel 486 processors) through Socket 423 (Intel Pentium 4 processors) has provided improved processor technology and speed. Table 2-8 summarizes the socket types and the different processors that use them. More information can be found at www.firmware.com/support/bios/pentium.htm.

Table 2-8 CPU Socket Types

Socket Type	AMD	Intel
Socket 1	AM486DX-4, Am5x86	486SX/SX2,DX,DX2,DX4, Overdrive processor
Socket 2	AM486DX-4, Am5x86	486SX/SX2,DX,DX2,DX4, Pentium Overdrive processor
Socket 3	AM486DX-4, Am5x86	486SX/SX2,DX,DX2,DX4, Pentium Overdrive Processor
Socket 4	—	Pentium 60-MHz, Pentium 66-MHz, Pentium Overdrive 120–133-MHz
Socket 5	K5	Pentium 75–133-MHz, Pentium Overdrive 125–166-MHz, Pentium Overdrive MMX 125–180-MHz, Pentium MMX 166–200-MHz
Socket 6	—	The last 486-class socket standard created by Intel. It is not used in modern motherboards.
Socket 7	K5, K6 166–300-MHz, K6-2 266–550-MHz, K6-3 400–450-MHz	Pentium 75–200-MHz, Pentium Overdrive 125–166-MHz, Pentium Overdrive MMX 125–200-MHz, Pentium MMX 166–233-MHz
Socket 8	—	Pentium Pro 150–200-MHz, Pentium II Overdrive 300–333-MHz

continues

Table 2-8 CPU Socket Types (Continued)

Socket Type	AMD	Intel
Slot 1	—	Celeron, Pentium II 233–450-MHz, Pentium III 450-MHz (and higher)
Slot 2	—	Pentium II Xeon 400–450-MHz, Pentium III Xeon 500 MHz–1-GHz
Slot A	Athlon 500-MHz–1-GHz	—
Socket 370	—	Celeron, Pentium II 233–450-MHz, Pentium III 450-MHz–1.13-GHz
Socket A	Duron 600-MHz +, Athlon 750-MHz +	—
Socket 423	—	Pentium 4 1.3-GHz +
Socket 478	—	Pentium 4 1–2.3-GHz +
Socket 603	—	Xeon 1–1.4-GHz +

Processor Slots

Slot-type processors had a brief lifespan (just about a year on the market). Intel, with its Pentium II processor, moved from the socket configuration to a processor packaged in a cartridge that fits into a slot in the motherboard. Similarly, AMD has progressed to Slot A (similar to Slot 1) and then to Socket A for its high-end Athlon and Duron processors.

Socket 7 and other socket-type processors use the *zero-insertion- force (ZIF)* socket. A ZIF socket is designed to be easily manufactured and to easily upgrade the microprocessor. A typical ZIF socket contains a lever that opens and closes, securing the microprocessor in place. Additionally, the various sockets have a differing number of pins and pin layout arrangements. Socket 7, for example, has 321 pins, and the number of pins generally increases with the socket number.

Pentium Processors

The current family of Intel Pentium microprocessors includes the Pentium II, III, 4, and Xeon. The Pentium class is the current standard for processor chips. These chips represent the second- and third-generation Intel processors. By combining memory cache with microprocessor circuitry, the Pentium supports processor speeds of 1000 MHz

(1 GHz) and higher. The combined chip covers less than 2 square inches (6 cm^2) and comprises over a million transistors.

The Pentium processors have made several improvements over their predecessor, which evolved from the Intel 80486 chip. For example, the Pentium data bus is 64 bits wide and can take in data 64 bits at a time, compared to 32 bits with the Intel 486. The Pentium has multiple caches of storage totaling as much as 2 MB, compared to the 8 KB of the Intel 80486.

Improvements in processor speeds allow the components to get data in and out of the chip faster. The processor does not become idle waiting for data or instructions, which enables the software to run faster. These components need to handle the flow of information through the processor, interpret instructions so the processor can execute them, and send the results back to the PC's memory. The manufacturer's website, www.intel.com, provides more information about the Pentium family of processors.

AMD Processors

The best-performing Advanced Micro Devices (AMD) processors are the Athlon, Thunderbird, and Duron series. They are currently the most-used microprocessors, along with the Intel Pentium IIIs, in high-end desktop systems, workstations, and servers. The AMD Athlon processor's system bus is designed for scalable multiprocessing, with the number of AMD Athlon processors in a multiprocessor system determined by chipset implementation. The manufacturer's website, www.amd.com, provides more information about the AMD family of processors.

Processor Speed Rating

CPU descriptions such as Pentium 133, Pentium 166, or Pentium 200 are well known. These numbers are specifications that indicate the maximum (reliable) operating speed at which the CPU can execute instructions. The CPU speed is not controlled by the microprocessor itself, but by an external clock located on the motherboard. The speed of the processor is determined by the frequency of the clock signal. This frequency is typically expressed in megahertz (MHz), and the higher the number, the faster the processor. Processor speeds continue to increase. Current processors operate at speeds of up to 2.3 GHz (2300 MHz).

The CPU speed and the frequency of the clock signal are not always at a one-to-one ratio. This is because the CPU can run at a much higher speed than the other chips on the motherboard. A *variable-frequency synthesizer circuit*, built into the motherboard circuit, multiplies the clock signal so that the motherboard can support several speeds of CPUs. Generally, three factors determine how much information can be processed at a given time:

- The size of the internal bus
- The size of the address bus
- The processor's speed rating

BIOS, EPROM, EEPROM, and Flash ROM

Read-only memory (ROM) chips, located on the motherboard, contain instructions that can be directly accessed by the microprocessor. Unlike RAM, ROM chips retain their contents even when the computer is powered off. ROM chip contents cannot be erased or changed by normal means. Data transfer from ROM is faster than any disk but slower than RAM. Some examples of ROM chips that can be found on the motherboard include BIOS ROM, EEPROM, and Flash ROM.

Basic Input/Output System

The instructions and data in the ROM chip that control the boot process and your computer's hardware are known as the *basic input/output system (BIOS)*, sometimes called *firmware*. The ROM chip that contains the firmware is called the ROM BIOS chip. It is also referred to as ROM BIOS, or simply BIOS, and is usually marked BIOS on the motherboard. The system BIOS is a critical part of the computer. In fact, if the CPU is considered the brains of the computer, the system BIOS is considered the heart of the system. The system BIOS determines what hard drive is installed, whether a 3-1/2-inch floppy drive is present, what kind of memory is installed, and many other important parts of the system hardware at startup. The responsibility of the BIOS is to serve as a liaison between the computer's operating system and the various hardware components that support it. These responsibilities include the following:

- Hosting the setup program for the hardware
- Testing the system in a process known as POST
- Controlling all the aspects of the boot process
- Producing audio and video error codes when a problem occurs during the POST
- Providing the computer with basic instructions to control devices in the system
- Locating any BIOS codes on expansion cards and executing them
- Locating a volume or boot sector from any drives to start the operating system
- Ensuring hardware and system compatibility

The BIOS is easy to locate because it is larger than most other chips, and it often has a shiny plastic label containing the manufacturer's name, the serial number of the chip, and the date the chip was manufactured. This information is vital when choosing an upgrade for the chip. The unique role the BIOS plays in the computer's functionality is described in Chapter 3, "Assembling a Computer."

EPROM, EEPROM, and Flash ROM

ROM is most commonly used to store system-level programs that you want to have available to the PC at all times. The most common example is the system BIOS program, which is stored in a ROM called the system BIOS ROM. Having this in a permanent ROM means it is available when the power is turned on so that the PC can use it to boot up the system. Evolving from the EEPROM chip technology, which can be erased in place, Flash ROM is less expensive and denser. The term was coined by Toshiba for its ability to be erased "in a flash." These ROM terms are defined as follows:

- **EPROM and EEPROM**—ROM chips that can be erased and reprogrammed. *Erasable programmable read-only memory (EPROM)* is a special type of programmable read-only memory (PROM) that can be erased by shining ultraviolet light through a clear window on the top of the chip. Because the ROM chip holds the instructions that enable a device to function properly, the chip must sometimes be reprogrammed or replaced when upgraded device instructions are required. Unlike EPROM, *electrically erasable programmable read-only memory (EEPROM) chips* are erased using a higher-than-normal electric voltage instead of ultraviolet light. When the system BIOS (or firmware) is contained on EEPROM, it can be upgraded (reprogrammed) by running special instructions.

- **Flash ROM**—Special EEPROM chips that have been developed as a result of advancements in EEPROM technology. Flash ROM holds the firmware, or BIOS, in most new systems. It can be reprogrammed under special software control. Upgrading the BIOS by running special software is known as *flashing*. The BIOS implemented on a Flash ROM is known as Plug and Play BIOS, and it supports Plug and Play devices. These chips retain data when the computer is powered down so information is permanently stored.

Lab Activity 2.3.4   Identify ROM and BIOS Chips

Locate and identify the ROM chip, BIOS, and BIOS manufacturer on the motherboard.

Worksheet 2.3.4   BIOS/ROM

Define BIOS, and know the difference between RAM and ROM.

Expansion Slots and Bus Types

Expansion slots, also known as *sockets*, are receptacles on the computer's mother-board that accept printed circuit boards. All computers have expansion slots that allow additional devices to be added. Video cards, I/O cards, and sound cards are examples of components that are located in expansion slots.

A motherboard can contain several types of expansion slots. The number and type of expansion slots in the computer determine future expansion possibilities. Common expansion slots include the following:

- **Industry Standard Architecture (ISA)**—A 16-bit expansion slot developed by IBM. It transfers data with the motherboard at 8 MHz. ISA slots are becoming obsolete and are being replaced by PCI slots in new systems. However, many motherboard manufacturers might still include one or two of these slots for backward compatibility with older expansion cards. In 1987, IBM introduced the 32-bit, extended ISA (EISA) bus, which accommodates the Pentium chip. EISA became fairly popular in the PC market.

- **Peripheral Component Interconnect (PCI)**—A 32-bit local bus slot developed by Intel. Because they communicate with the motherboard at 33 MHz, the PCI bus slots offer a significant improvement over ISA or EISA expansion slots. With the PCI bus, each add-on card contains information that the processor uses to auto-matically configure the card. The PCI bus is one of the three components neces-sary for Plug and Play capability. The main purpose of the PCI bus is to allow direct access to the CPU for devices such as memory and video. PCI expansion slots are the most commonly used type in motherboards today.

- **Accelerated Graphics Port (AGP)**—Developed by Intel, AGP is a dedicated high-speed bus that supports the high demands of graphical software. This slot is reserved for video adapters. This is the standard graphics port in all new systems. On AGP-equipped motherboards, a single AGP slot holds the display adapter, and the PCI slot can be used for another device. Slightly shorter than the white PCI slot, the AGP slot is usually a different color and is located about an inch beyond the PCI slot. The latest version of the accelerated graphics port, AGP-4, was introduced in 1992; it offers a 1-GB transfer rate.

Figure 2-9 shows the different slot types, while Table 2-9 summarizes some useful information on the more common slot types, as well as others that have never gained widespread use in the industry.

Figure 2-9 Expansion Slot Types

Table 2-9 Expansion Slots

Slot Type	Speed (MHz)	Data Bits	Use
ISA	4.77, 8	8, 16	Modems, 8-bit expansion cards.
MCA	10	32	This bus is now obsolete.
EISA	8	8, 16, 32	Specialty roles, mostly obsolete and being replaced by PCI slots in new systems.
VESA local	33	32, 64	Once used for faster video performance than the ISA bus, this bus has since become obsolete.
PCI	33	32, 64	Audio and video cards, networking cards, modems, SCSI adapters, and more. Not for use with serial or parallel ports.
AGP	66	32	Video adapter only.

Lab Activity 2.3.6 Identifying Computer Expansion Slots

Identify safety issues, specifications, and components relating to expansion slots. You should also be able to list the advantages and disadvantages of each expansion slot.

Worksheet 2.3.5 Expansion Slots

This worksheet reviews expansion slots, including the definition and the different types utilized.

Bus Types

All the basic components of the computer are connected by communication paths that are referred to as *buses*. The system bus is a parallel collection of conductors that carry data and control signals from one component to the other. Recall that the conductors in modern computers are actually metallic traces on the circuit board.

The major system bus types, which can be identified based on the type of information they carry, are as follows:

- **Address bus**—This is a unidirectional pathway, which means that information can only flow one way. The function of the address bus is to carry addresses generated by the CPU to the memory and I/O elements of the computer. The number of conductors in the bus determines the size of the address bus; this, in turn, determines the number of memory locations and I/O elements that the microprocessor can address.

- **Data bus**—Unlike the address bus, the data bus is a bidirectional pathway for data flow, which means that information can flow in two directions. Data can flow along the data bus from the CPU to memory during a *write* operation, and data can move from the computer memory to the CPU during a *read* operation. However, should two devices attempt to use the bus at the same time, data errors occur. Any device connected to the data bus must have the capability to temporarily put its output on hold (a floating state) when it is not involved in an operation with the processor. The data bus size, measured in bits, represents the computer's word size. Generally, the larger the bus size, the faster your system. Common data bus sizes are 8 bits or 16 bits (older systems) and 32 bits (new systems). Currently under development are 64-bit data bus systems.

- **Control bus**—Carries the control and timing signals needed to coordinate the activities of the entire computer. Control bus signals, unlike information carried by the data and address buses, are not necessarily related to each other. Some are output signals from the CPU, and others are input signals to the CPU from I/O elements of the system. Every microprocessor type generates or responds to its own set of control signals. The most common control signals in use today are as follows:

— System clock (SYSCLK)

— Memory read (MEMR)

— Memory write (MEMW)

— Read/write line (R/W line)

— I/O read (IOR)

— I/O write (IOW)

Random-Access Memory and Cache/COASt Memory

Random-access memory (RAM) is the place in a computer where the OS, applications, and data in current use are kept so that they can be quickly reached by the processor. The *cache* (pronounced *cash*) is a place to store something temporarily. For example, the files automatically requested by looking at a web page are stored on your hard disk in a cache subdirectory in your browser directory. *COASt* stands for "cache on a stick." It provides cache memory on many Pentium-based systems.

RAM

RAM is considered temporary, or volatile, memory. The contents of RAM are lost when the computer power is turned off. RAM chips on the computer hold the data and programs that the microprocessor is processing. In other words, RAM is memory that stores frequently used data for rapid retrieval by the processor. The more RAM a computer has, the more capacity the computer has to hold and process large programs and files. The amount and type of memory in the system can make a big difference in the system's performance. Some programs have more memory requirements than others. Typically, a computer running Windows 95, 98, or Me would have 64 MB RAM installed. It is common to find systems with 128 MB or 256 MB of RAM, especially if they are running newer operating systems such as Windows 2000 or other network operating systems.

Two classes of RAM are commonly used today. These classes, static RAM (SRAM) and dynamic RAM (DRAM), are defined as follows:

- **SRAM**—Relatively more expensive, but it is fast and holds data when the power is turned off for a brief period of time. This is useful in such circumstances as an unexpected loss of power. SRAM is used for cache memory.

■ **DRAM**—Inexpensive and somewhat slow, and requires an uninterrupted power supply to maintain its data. When the power is turned off, the data is lost.

RAM can be installed on the motherboard, either as a permanent fixture or in the form of small chips, referred to as SIMMs (single inline memory modules) or DIMMs (dual inline memory modules). SIMMs and DIMMs are removable cards that can be replaced with larger or smaller increments of memory. Although having more memory installed in your computer is a good thing, most system boards have limitations on the amount and type of RAM that can be added or supported. Some systems might require that only SIMMs be used, while others might require that SIMMs be installed in matched sets of two or four modules at a time. Additionally, some systems use only RAM with parity (built-in error checking) while others use nonparity RAM (having no error-checking capability).

Identifying SIMMs and DIMMs

A *SIMM* plugs into the motherboard with a 72-pin or 30-pin connector. The pins connect to the system bus, creating an electronic path through which memory data can flow to and from other system components. Two 72-pin SIMMs can be installed in a computer that supports 64-bit data flow. With a SIMM board, the pins on opposite sides of the module board are connected to each other, forming a single row of contacts, as shown in Figure 2-10.

Figure 2-10 A 72-Pin SIMM

A *DIMM* plugs into the system's memory bank using a 168-pin connector. The pins establish a connection with the system bus, creating an electronic path through which data can flow between the memory chip and other system components. A single 168-pin DIMM supports 64-bit (nonparity) and 72-bit (parity) data flow. This configuration is now being used in the latest generation of 64-bit systems. Recall that parity refers to error-checking capability built into the RAM chip to ensure data integrity. An important feature is that the pins on a DIMM board are not connected side to side (as with SIMMs); the pins form two sets of contacts, as shown in Figure 2-11.

Figure 2-11 A 168-Pin DIMM

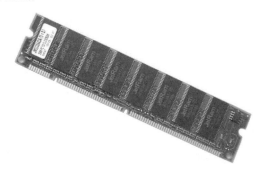

With most technologies, newer or more specialized forms of RAM are being introduced all the time. The following are some examples:

- **Video RAM (VRAM) and Windows RAM (WRAM)**—Currently the best kinds of memory for video. Both VRAM and WRAM are optimized for video cards and are designed to be *dual-ported*. This means that the chipset processor and RAMDAC chip (see the following paragraph) can access the memory at the same time. Simultaneous access greatly increases video throughput. The newest types of video cards also support the newest system RAM types, such as synchronous DRAM (SDRAM).

- **Random-access memory digital-to-analog converter (RAMDAC)**—Another specialized form of memory designed to convert digitally encoded images into analog signals for display. It is made of an SRAM component (for storing the color map) and three digital-to-analog converters, one each for the red, green, and blue electron guns.

Most other types of RAM, such as extended data out (EDO) RAM and fast page mode (FPM) RAM, are too slow for today's computing standards and are no longer used in new computers. Table 2-10 provides a summary of the different types of RAM.

Table 2-10 RAM Types, Usage, and Capabilities

Type	Usage	Capabilities	Notes
SRAM	L1 and L2 cache	Fast, does not need to be refreshed.	Large and expensive.
DRAM	Main memory, expansion cards	Smaller and less expensive than SRAM.	More complicated and slower than SRAM, this memory is considered outdated.

continues

Table 2-10 RAM Types, Usage, and Capabilities (Continued)

Type	Usage	Capabilities	Notes
FPM DRAM	Main memory, video memory	Does not need row and column for each access, does not require special support.	Slowest type of memory in modern PCs. This memory type is also considered outdated.
EDO DRAM	Main memory, video memory	One access to the memory can begin before the last one has ended.	Does not work well at 75 MHz and faster, same cost as FPM DRAM.
SDRAM	Main memory, video memory	Synchronized with system clock and can read/write in burst mode up to 100 MHz.	Supports internal interleaving, allowing one access to begin halfway through a previous one.
DDR SDRAM	Main memory, video memory	Doubles bandwidth by transferring data twice per clock cycle.	More expensive than SDRAM.
DRDRAM	Main memory, video memory	Based on a high-speed, 16-bit bus with a clock speed of 400 MHz.	Proprietary to Intel and Rambus.
SLDRAM	Main Memory, video memory	Uses a 64-bit bus running at 200 MHz, transferring data twice on each cycle.	Open standard.

Cache/COASt Memory

A cache is a specialized form of computer chip or firmware that is designed to enhance memory performance. Cache memory stores frequently used information and transfers it to the processor much faster than does RAM. Most computers have two separate memory cache levels:

- **L1 cache**—Located on the CPU
- **L2 cache**—Located between the CPU and DRAM

L1 cache is faster than L2 because L1 is located within the CPU and runs at same speed as the CPU. L1 is the first place the CPU looks for its data. If data are not found in the L1 cache, the search then continues with the L2 cache and then on to main memory (or DIMM).

L1 and L2 caches are made of SRAM chips. However, some systems use the COASt modules. These modules provide cache memory on many Pentium-based systems. The COASt module is noted for its reliability and speed because it uses the pipeline-burst cache, which is significantly faster than an SRAM cache. Some systems offer both SRAM sockets and a COASt module socket. The COASt module essentially resembles a SIMM, except that it is taller and has a different connector, as shown in Figure 2-12.

Figure 2-12 A COASt Module

Lab Activity 2.3.7   Identifying RAM and RAM Sockets

In this lab, you focus on the identification of various types of RAM and RAM sockets.

Worksheet 2.3.7   RAM and RAM Sockets

RAM and RAM sockets are reviewed in this worksheet.

Monitors

Computers are usually connected to a *display*, also called a *monitor*, as shown in Figure 2-13. Monitors are available in different types and sizes, and with various characteristics. When purchasing a new computer, the monitor might have to be purchased separately.

Figure 2-13 An HP Monitor

Understanding the characteristics of a good monitor helps you determine which type is best suited for a specific system. The following terms relate to monitors:

- **Pixels**—These are picture elements. The screen image is made of pixels (tiny dots), which are arranged in rows across the screen. Each pixel consists of three colors: red, green, and blue (RGB). Examine the screen closely to see them.

- **Dot pitch**—This is a measurement of how close the pixels are placed to each other on the screen. The finer (smaller) the dot pitch, the better the image quality. Most modern monitors have a 0.25-mm dot pitch, although some provide even-better 0.22-mm spacing.

- **Refresh rate**—The screen image is refreshed many times per second. Refresh rates are measured in hertz (Hz), which means times per second. The higher the refresh rate, the more steady the screen image. The image might look like a steady picture, but it actually flickers every time the electron beam hits the phosphor-coated pixels. Refresh rate is also called vertical frequency or vertical refresh rate.

- **Color depth**—Each pixel can display a number of different colors. The number of colors that can be displayed is called the color depth, which is measured in bits. The higher the depth, the more colors that can be produced.

- **Video RAM (VRAM)**—All video cards have some memory. How much they have determines the color-depth setting available to the monitor. The more VRAM your video card has, the more colors that can be displayed. The video card also sends out the refresh signal, thus controlling the refresh rate.

- **Resolution**—The more pixels in the screen, the better the resolution. Better resolution means a sharper image. The lowest screen resolution on modern PCs is

640×480 pixels, which is called VGA (video graphics array). Presently, SVGA (super video graphics array) and XGA (extended graphics array) have resolutions of up to 1600×1200 (see Table 2-11).

- **Screen size**—Monitor screen sizes are measured in inches, just like televisions. The most common screen sizes are 14, 15, 17, 19, and 21 inches, measured diagonally. Note that the visible area is actually smaller than the measurement size. Keep this in mind when you shop for a monitor.

- **Colors**—Most PCs display many colors on the screen. The colors are created by varying the light intensity of the three basic colors (red, green, and blue). The usual choices for graphic artists and professional photographers are 24- and 32-bit colors. For most other applications, a 16-bit color is sufficient. The following is a summary of the most commonly used color depths:

  — 256 colors (8-bit color)

  — 65,536 colors (16-bit color, also called 65K or Hi Color)

  — 16 million colors (24-bit color, also called True Color)

  — 4 billion colors (32-bit color, also called True Color)

Table 2-11 Summary of Monitor Characteristics by Type

Standard	Resolution (Pixels)	Number of Pixels	Screen Size (Inches)	Refresh Rate (Hertz)
VGA	640×480	307,200	14	60–72
SVGA	800×600	480,000	15, 17	75–85
SVGA	1024×728	786,432	17, 19	75–85
XGA	1152×864	995,328	17, 19, 21	75–85
XGA	1280×1024	1,310,720	19, 21	75–85
XGA	1600×1200	1,920,000	21	75–85

A high-quality monitor and a high-quality video card, discussed in the next section, are required for both a high resolution and a high refresh rate.

Video Cards

The *video card* or *video adapter* is the interface between the computer and monitor. The video card tells the monitor which pixels to light up, what color the pixels should be, and what intensity the color should be. The video card can be an expansion card (installed into one of the motherboard expansion slots), or it can be built into the motherboard. The display capabilities of a computer depend on both the video adapter and the monitor. A monochrome (black and white) monitor, for example, cannot display colors no matter how powerful the video adapter.

The following are key terms related to video cards:

- **Video memory**—It is important not to confuse the terms video memory and video RAM (VRAM). Video memory is a generic term that refers to memory in the computer's video system, while VRAM is a special type of memory used on video cards. Most modern video cards contain VRAM, which is a special form of DRAM that has two separate data ports. One port is dedicated to updating the image that is viewed on the computer screen, while the other port is used for changing the image data stored on the video card. Thanks to VRAM, the computer's RAM is not being used for storing displays. A 64-bit AGP video card with 4 MB of RAM should be enough for most applications, but more graphic intensive games might perform better with a video card having 32 MB or more video RAM. Some video cards even include a graphics coprocessor for performing graphics calculations. These adapters are referred to as *graphics accelerators*. A newer form of VRAM is Windows RAM (WRAM).

- **AGP port**—The Pentium II has an *accelerated graphics port (AGP)* expansion slot for installing a video card, as shown in Figure 2-14. AGP is designed exclusively for video cards. An AGP card allows game and 3D applications to store and retrieve finer, more realistic textures in system memory rather than video memory, without incurring performance problems. A significant advantage of the AGP port is that the PCI bus is relieved of handling graphics data, so that the PCI slot can concentrate on other demanding duties. AGP also doubles the PCI transfer speed.

Figure 2-14 A Typical Video Card

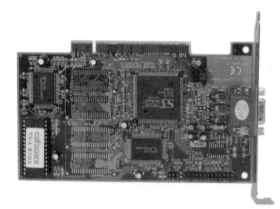

Video adapters are also known as video cards, video boards, and video display boards. At a minimum, a video card should be a PCI adapter with at least 4 MB of RAM, depending on the type of graphics to be run.

Interactive PhotoZoom Activity   Video Card and Monitor

Included on this book's CD, this PhotoZoom allows you to explore the video card and monitor, and defines the function of each component.

Lab Activity 2.3.9   Video Card Identification

Identify the video card by the markings on the card.

Worksheet 2.3.9   Video Cards

This worksheet reviews the video card and monitor.

I/O Ports: Serial, Parallel, PS/2, 6-Pin Mini-DIN, 5-Pin DIN USB, and FireWire

All peripheral devices that connect to the computer, such as printers and scanners, use connectors on the back of the computer known as I/O ports. An *I/O port* is a pathway into and out of the computer. Different types of ports on the computer serve different purposes. This section explores the various types of ports and the types of devices that use them to interface with the computer.

Serial Ports

A *serial port* can be used to connect devices that use a serial interface, such as a modem, scanner, mouse, etc. Generally, a PC can identify up to four serial ports, but the typical computer contains only two, referred to as COM1 and COM2. Serial ports are sometimes called the RS-232 ports because they use the RS-232C standard as defined by the Electronics Industry Association (EIA). Unlike the parallel port, a serial port transmits data bits one after the other (serially) over a single line. USB 2.0, the most recent version, runs at a speed of 450 Mbps.

Figure 2-15 shows a DB-9 (9-pin) connector used on most new computers for the serial ports. Older printers use a larger, 25-pin connector for the serial port interface, as shown in Figure 2-16. The mouse is sometimes used in serial port 1, called COM1, which is a 9-pin male connector. The modem is typically used in serial port 2, called COM2, which is also a 9-pin male connector. Both serial ports are located in the back of the computer system.

Figure 2-15 A 9-Pin Male Serial Connector

Figure 2-16 A 25-Pin Male Serial Connector

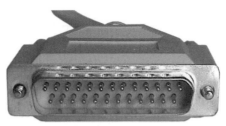

Parallel Ports

A *parallel port* is a socket on the computer that connects newer printers or other peripheral devices, such as a portable hard disk, tape backup unit, scanner, or CD-ROM drive. The parallel port contains eight lines for transmitting an entire byte (8 bits) across the eight data lines simultaneously. The parallel port interface offers 8-bit parallel data words and 9 I/O control lines at a DB-25 socket (25-pin female connector). You can find the DB-25 socket on the back of your computer unit. Figure 2-17 shows a female DB-25 parallel port. Figure 2-18 shows the 36-pin female port typically found on the printer. Parallel ports can be configured as LPT1, LPT2, or LPT3.

Figure 2-17 A DB-25 Female Parallel Port

Figure 2-18 Centronics 36-Pin Female Port

Parallel ports were originally used for printers, but today they can be used for both data input and output devices. This type of parallel port is called *bidirectional* and is often used for the rapid transmission of data over short distances. The newer, enhanced parallel ports can be converted from unidirectional to bidirectional through the CMOS setup screen. In older PCs, the parallel printer interface was located on the back of the video adapter card, on a multiple I/O card, or on a dedicated parallel printer card. Today, on Pentium system boards, the parallel port is located directly on the back plate of an I/O card, or is connected through a ribbon cable to the 25-pin connector on the back of the unit. When connecting an external device such as a printer to the computer's parallel port, avoid using a parallel cable longer than 15 feet. A shorter cable reduces the chance for errors and ensures data integrity.

PS/2 Ports, 6-Pin Mini-DIN, 5-Pin DIN

A *PS/2 keyboard* or *PS/2 mouse ports* connect your PC to its keyboard and mouse. Although both ports look identical, the mouse (green) and keyboard (purple) ports are not interchangeable. Usually, both ports are color coded or labeled to avoid confusion, as shown in Figure 2-19. The cable that connects the PS/2 keyboard or mouse uses a PS/2-type connector, also known as a 6-pin mini-DIN connector. The PS/2 (or 6-pin mini-DIN) has become popular since its introduction by IBM in 1987 with the IBM PS/2. However, the 5-pin DIN XT/AT connector-type ports and serial mice are still common. The 5-pin DIN AT connectors are typically used to connect the AT keyboard directly to the motherboard. One advantage of the PS/2 port is that a mouse might be connected to the computer without using a serial port.

Figure 2-19 PS/2 Keyboard and Mouse Ports

Universal Serial Bus

The *universal serial bus (USB)* is an external port that allows you to connect up to 127 PC peripherals, including USB keyboards, mice, printers, modems, scanners, and external disk drives (see Figure 2-20). USB is an emerging technology. The original technology offers a data transfer rate of up to 12 Mbps. The latest version, USB 2.0, can transfer data at a rate of 450 Mbps. Seven USB devices can typically be connected directly to the computer using the standard USB 4-pin connector. By using external *hubs*, a networking device that is discussed in a later chapter, each of the seven devices can be connected to the others, creating a *daisy chain* of 127 devices. USB devices can be *hot-plugged* (or *hot-swapped*). This means that they can be attached while the computer is powered up. USB devices also have Plug and Play capability.

Figure 2-20 USB Port/Connector

USB devices are classified as full-speed or low-speed based on their communication capabilities. A cable serving a full-speed device has a length limit of 5 meters (16 feet, 5 inches). Conversely, the length limit for cables used between low-speed USB devices is 3 meters (9 feet, 10 inches).

USB was introduced in the late 1990s and was not supported by Windows 95 or NT 4.0. Support for USB is one of the reasons that Windows 98 or 2000 is preferred. This port might eventually replace everything except the VGA port. Most PC USB peripherals can also be used on a Macintosh, although some lack the necessary drivers.

FireWire

FireWire is a high-speed, platform-independent communication bus that interconnects digital devices, such as digital video cameras, printers, scanners, digital cameras, and hard drives. (FireWire is shown in Figure 2-21.) It is also known as *i.LINK* or

IEEE 1394. Developed by Apple, FireWire was designed to allow peripherals to seamlessly plug into a computer. The benefits of FireWire include compatible, smaller connectors; hot-plug connection; shared memory; a single connection; backward compatibility; and speed. FireWire can support up to 63 devices using cable lengths up to 4.5 meters (14 feet). Like USB, these devices can be hot-swapped or hot-plugged.

Figure 2-21 FireWire 6-Pin Cable and Connector

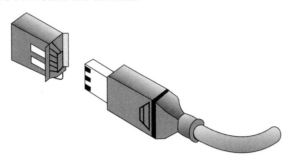

FireWire is based on a shared memory model that allows devices to directly access locations in memory instead of having to wait for information to flow in a stream. FireWire is much faster than the original version of USB, transferring data at rates up to 400 Mbps.

IDE and SCSI Controllers

The hard drive, along with other devices, can use one of two types of interface controllers to communicate with the computer. These include the integrated drive electronics (IDE) and small computer system interface [SCSI (pronounced *scuzzy*)] connections.

IDE Drive Interface Controllers

Integrated drive electronics (IDE) is a type of hardware interface that is widely used to connect hard disks, CD-ROM drives, and tape drives to a PC. IDE is popular because it is an economical way to connect peripherals. The IDE interface originally offered 40-MB capacities years ago; now, 20-GB IDE hard disks have become entry level, costing less than half a cent per megabyte.

With IDE, the controller electronics are built into the drive itself, requiring a simple circuit in the PC for connection. IDE drives were attached to earlier PCs using an IDE host adapter card. Today, two enhanced IDE (EIDE) sockets are built onto the motherboard, and each socket connects to two devices via a 40-pin ribbon cable. Starting with ATA-66 drives, the cable uses 80 wires and 39 pins. It plugs into the same socket with one pin removed.

The IDE interface is officially known as the AT attachment (ATA) specification. ATAPI (ATA packet interface) defines the IDE standard for CD-ROM drives and tape drives. ATA-2 (fast ATA) defines the faster transfer rates used in enhanced IDE. ATA-3 added interface improvements, including the ability to report potential problems.

Enhanced IDE

Enhanced IDE (EIDE) or *ATA-2* is the latest version of the IDE interface. Not confined to IDE's 528 MB of data, the EIDE interface can handle up to 8.4 GB. While IDE can support only two drives, EIDE can support up to four devices using two IDE cables that have 40 pins and a maximum length of 18 inches. Additionally, EIDE supports nondisk peripherals that follow the ATAPI protocol. The EIDE interface is often described as an AT attachment packet interface (ATAPI) or a fast AT attachment (ATA) interface. ATAPI is the protocol used by enhanced IDE devices such as IDE CD-ROM drives, IDE external tape backup drives, etc.

The EIDE/ATA-2 specification was developed in 1994 and subsequently modified to final form in 1995. The EIDE/ATA-2 specification covers the interface signals on the 18-inch, 40-pin cable connector; the drive commands issued by the BIOS; cable specifications; and drive configuration circuitry. ATA-3 added interface improvements, including the ability to report potential problems.

Each disk drive that is attached to an IDE/ATA, EIDE/ATA-2, or EIDE/ATA-3 disk controller must have a jumper set on the back of the disk drive to specify the role that the disk performs in relation to the other disk on the same channel. A single IDE or EIDE disk is usually set to the master role. If a second IDE or EIDE disk is attached to the same channel as an existing IDE or EIDE disk drive that is set to master, the second disk must be set to the slave role. In essence, the hardware on the master disk drive controls both the master and slave disk drives.

An option called *cable select (CSEL)* allows the IDE adapter to select which IDE or EIDE disk drive functions as master and which IDE or EIDE disk drive functions as slave. If both IDE and EIDE disk drives that are on a single channel are set to master, or if both are set to slave, the disk subsystem will not work.

Read drive documentation carefully because industry standards do not apply to the jumper settings for IDE or EIDE disk drives.

Ultra Drive Interface Controllers　Starting with ATA-4, either the word Ultra or the transfer rate was added to the name in various combinations. For example, at 33 Mbps, terms such as Ultra ATA, Ultra DMA, UDMA, ATA-33, DMA-33, Ultra ATA-33, and Ultra DMA-33 have been used.

Ultra ATA disk drives are typically much faster than the older ATA and ATA-2 drives. These disk drives are installed and configured the same way that ATA-2 disk drives are configured (master/slave/CSEL). However, the faster versions, ATA-66 and ATA-100, require that a special ribbon cable be used to connect the disk drives to the ATA adapter. This cable contains 80 conductors, but it still uses the same 40-pin connectors used by earlier ATA disk drives. Failure to use these special cables for these high-speed disks can result in disk system problems and possible data loss.

Sector translation and continuous technological improvements have allowed hard drives to grow larger in size. Today, typical drive sizes can reach 100 GB.

SCSI Interface Controller

The *small computer systems interface (SCSI)* controller was developed in 1979 at Shugart Associates Standard Interface (SASI). Like EIDE, SCSI devices have the controlling electronics on each of the drives. However, SCSI is a much more advanced interface controller than ATA-2/EIDE. It is ideal for high-end computers, including network servers.

SCSI devices are typically connected in series, forming a chain that is commonly referred to as a *daisy chain*, as shown in Figure 2-22. The two SCSI devices at either end of the daisy chain (external cable) must be terminated. The other devices do not need to be terminated.

Figure 2-22 An Internal and External Daisy Chain

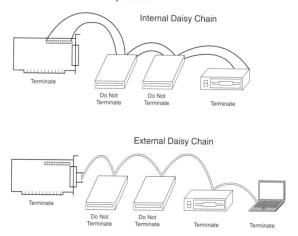

When using only an internal cable, you need to terminate the adapter card and the device at the end of the cable. Don't terminate the rest of the devices in between. If you are using both an internal and an external cable, you must terminate the devices located at the end of each cable. Don't terminate the rest of the devices, including the adapter or controller card.

Each end of the SCSI bus must be terminated. Generally, the SCSI controller itself is on one end of the SCSI bus, and it usually has onboard termination. The other end of the SCSI cable is either terminated by a resistor on the last disk drive on the chain or a physical terminator on the end of the SCSI bus.

The SCSI bus identifies each device by a SCSI ID number. Most SCSI buses can handle a total of 8 devices per channel, which are numbered from 0 through 7. (Some versions of SCSI support a total of 16 devices per channel, which are numbered 0 through 15.) Each device on a SCSI channel must have a unique SCSI ID. Such devices can include hard drives, CD-ROM drives, tape drives, scanners, and removable drives. Each SCSI device in the chain, including the SCSI controller card, is given a SCSI ID number from 0 to 7: 0 for the primary boot device (hard drive) and 7 for the SCSI controller card.

Each device on a SCSI channel must have a unique SCSI ID. SCSI ID numbers do not have to be sequential, but no two devices can have the same number.

SCSI ID numbers are generally set by jumpers on the SCSI disk drive itself. Duplication of the SCSI IDs on a SCSI channel can cause the channel to be inaccessible. If you want to be able to boot from a SCSI disk drive, give it a SCSI ID of 0 or 1.

Three types of SCSI termination are

- **Passive termination**—Cheap to implement, but should be used only for lower-speed SCSI channels with relative short cables.
- **Active termination**—Is preferred and can handle much higher speeds and longer cables.
- **Forced perfect termination (FPT)**—The best method and can be used for even the highest-speed SCSI implementation. It also is the most complex to implement and therefore the most costly. However, the extra cost results in a much more reliable system.

SCSI termination can be implemented in several ways. Because both ends of the SCSI bus must be terminated and because the SCSI adapter is going to be on one end of the SCSI bus, one termination point is on the SCSI adapter itself. This is usually done automatically with no need for additional changes to the SCSI adapter to make it terminate the SCSI bus at one end. On the other end of the SCSI bus, the last disk drive on the SCSI channel must be terminated (usually done via a jumper on the disk drive or a special terminator inserted on the last connector on the SCSI cable). It is common for low-voltage differential SCSI devices to not have the capability to terminate the SCSI bus on the device itself; you must use a special terminator inserted in the last connector on the SCSI cable.

SCSI-1, SCSI-2, and SCSI-3 disk drives can be mixed on the same SCSI channel, but this is not recommended. Mixing disk drives from different versions of SCSI can seriously impact performance of the SCSI channel.

SCSI Disk Types

Three major versions of the SCSI standard are currently available: SCSI-1, SCSI-2, and SCSI-3. Installation of SCSI devices among the three different SCSI standards is similar. The differences are mainly in the size of the SCSI connector that connect the SCSI disk drive to the SCSI cable.

Three signaling systems can be used by SCSI devices:

- Single-ended (SE)
- Differential (DIFF), also known as high-voltage differential (HVD)
- Low-voltage differential (LVD)

There is no difference in the connectors used among the three different signaling systems. To help identify the signaling system used by SCSI devices (controllers and drives), a system of symbols has been devised to identify the different signaling systems. Figure 2-23 shows the SCSI symbols displayed on SCSI devices.

Figure 2-23 SCSI Symbols

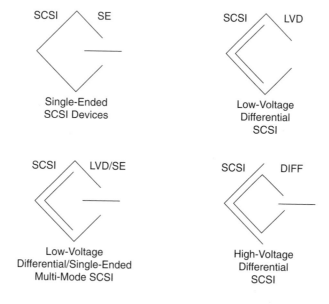

The major versions of the SCSI standard are defined as follows:

- **SCSI-1**—Originally known as just SCSI, this was used by many Apple computers in the early 1980s. By today's standards, it was rather slow. The SCSI bus ran at 5 MHz using an 8-bit data path. This allowed a data transfer rate of 5 Mbps. SCSI-1 generally supported a single channel per SCSI controller. The SCSI-1 internal cable was a ribbon cable that was attached to the disk controller by a 50-pin connector. Many early SCSI controllers used a DB-25, 25-pin connector for external SCSI devices. The termination for the SCSI-1 was usually a set of three resistors on the SCSI controller (assuming it was at the end of the SCSI bus), a set of three resistors on the last SCSI disk drive on the bus, or an actual terminator attached to the end of the SCSI bus. The maximum cable length of SCSI-1 was 6 meters.

- **SCSI-2**—SCSI-2 uses two different signaling systems, known as *single-ended interface* and *differential interface*. The two signaling systems are incompatible and cannot be mixed on the same SCSI bus. Make sure that all devices, including the SCSI-2 controller, are all using either the single-ended interface or the differential interface. Because of bus length restrictions, single-ended SCSI-2 cabling is usually found inside a server chassis. The differential interface allows for longer cable lengths and is generally found connecting the server to an external SCSI device. SCSI-2 uses the same 50-pin connector on the internal SCSI cable that is used by SCSI-1 devices.

  SCSI-2 also has a variant called wide SCSI-2, which can transfer 16 bits at a time as opposed to the 8 bits at a time used by normal SCSI-1 and normal SCSI-2. This extra bus width requires the use of a 68-pin connector. Wide SCSI-2 allows for 16 devices on the SCSI-2 channel, whereas normal SCSI-2 (also called narrow SCSI-2) and SCSI-1 only allow 8 devices on the SCSI channel.

  Another variant of SCSI-2 is fast SCSI-2, which doubles the bus speed from 5 MHz to 10 MHz. Fast SCSI-2 requires an active termination technique. Because of the increased speed, the bus length is reduced from 6 meters to 3 meters. Fast-wide SCSI-2 implementation is also available. It requires 68-pin cables, active termination, and a short cable length (3 meters), but it can transfer data at 20 MBps. SCSI-2 (narrow SCSI-2) uses 50-pin connectors on the internal SCSI-2 devices. Wide SCSI-2 uses 68-pin connectors on the internal SCSI-2 devices. Figure 2-24 shows an example of a 50-pin, 68-pin, and 80-pin (SCA) connector. The fast SCSI-2 and fast-wide SCSI-2 variants require active termination. Regular SCSI-2 and wide SCSI-2 can use passive termination, although active termination is preferred.

- **SCSI-3**—SCSI-3 is the latest standard of the SCSI family. It combines all the best features of the previous SCSI standards. It uses LVD, which features differential signaling, and supports up to 15 devices on a single cable, which can be up to 12 meters long. SCSI-3 supports three different bus speeds, known as Ultra (20-MHz), Ultra2 (40-MHz), and Ultra 3 (double-clocked 40-MHz). The three SCSI-3 bus speeds have both narrow (8-bit) and wide (16-bit) implementations.

Figure 2-24   SCSI 50-, 68-, and 80-Pin Connectors

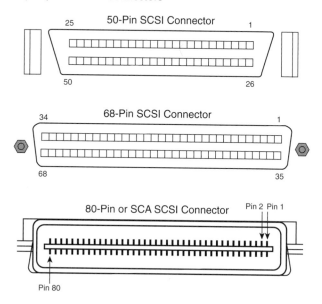

Ultra SCSI-3 and Ultra2 SCSI-3 both use 50-pin connectors. The wide variants (wide Ultra SCSI-3 and wide Ultra2 SCSI-3), as well as Ultra3 (also known as Ultra160 SCSI-3), use 68-pin connectors. All versions of SCSI-3 require active termination. Table2-12 summarizes the maximum cable lengths for various types of SCSI.

Table 2-12   SCSI Cable Lengths

SCSI Type	Maximum Cable Length (Meters)
Standard	6
Fast	3
Wide-Ultra	1.5
Low-voltage differential	12
Differential	25

Floppy Drives

A *floppy disk drive (FDD)* magnetically reads and writes information onto floppy disks, which are a form of removable storage media. Introduced in 1987, the 3-1/2-inch disks have a hard plastic exterior shell that protects the thin, flexible disk inside.

An FDD is mounted inside the system unit and is only removed for repairs or upgrades. The floppy disk, on the other hand, can be removed at the end of a computer working session. The main drawback to the floppy disk is that it only holds 1.44 MB of information; nevertheless, most PCs still have a floppy disk drive. For most text documents, such as MS Word and Excel files, 1.44 MB is plenty of space; however, for files containing rich graphical content, a floppy disk's capacity might be insufficient. The main parts of a typical floppy disk include the plastic protective case, the thin magnetic flexible disk, a sliding door, and a sliding door spring. Figure 2-25 shows a floppy disk.

Figure 2-25   A Typical Floppy Disk

Interactive PhotoZoom Activity   Floppy Drive

Included on this book's CD, this PhotoZoom defines the components of the floppy drive.

Worksheet 2.3.13   Floppy Drive Identification

This worksheet provides a review of the components of the floppy drive and how the drive works.

Hard Drives

This section discusses the computer's main storage medium, the *hard disk drive (HDD)*, and provides an overview of the hard drive's components, operations, interfaces, and specifications. An HDD, as shown in Figure 2-26, shares many physical and operational characteristics with the FDD. It has a more complex design and provides a greater speed of access. The HDD has a much larger storage capacity than the floppy disk for long-term storage. It stores programs and files, as well as the operating system. Typically, the HDD is an internal drive that cannot be removed from the computer.

Figure 2-26 A Typical Hard Disk Drive

The HDD is composed of relatively inflexible aluminum, glass platters, or disks. This inflexibility led to the name hard disk drive. The hard drive is typically not removable, which is why IBM refers to hard drives as fixed disk drives. In short, a hard disk drive is a high-volume disk storage device with fixed, high-density, rigid media.

Hard Drive Components

Figure 2-27 shows the components shared by all hard disk drives: disk platters, read/write heads, a head actuator assembly, a spindle motor, a logic/circuit board, a bezel/faceplate, configuration jumpers, and interface connectors.

Disk platters, as shown in Figure 2-28, are the media on which data is stored on the hard disk drive. A hard disk drive typically has two to ten platters. They are usually either 2-1/2 or 3-1/2 inches in diameter and are typically constructed of aluminum or a glass-ceramic composite material. They are coated with a *thin-film media* that is magnetically sensitive. The platters are double-sided, with the magnetically sensitive media on each side. Platters are stacked with spaces between them on a *hub* that holds them in position, separate from one another. The hub is also called the *spindle*.

Figure 2-27 Hard Drive Components

Figure 2-28 Hard Disk Platters

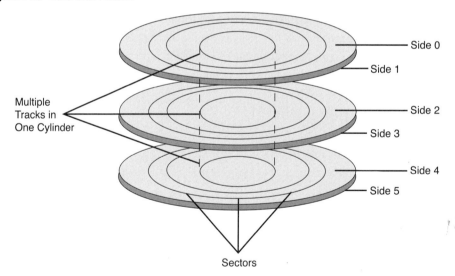

The disk platters require a *read/write head* for each side. The read/write head is used to access the media. The read/write heads are stacked, or *ganged*, on a carrier called a *rack*. Because the heads are mounted together, they move in unison across the platters with the rack. The heads are joined to the rack by arms. The arms extend from the *head actuator assembly*. The head itself is a U- or V-shaped device of electrically conductive material wrapped with wires, which cause it to be sensitive to the magnetic media of the platters.

While the read/write heads on floppy drives directly contact the media surface, those of hard disk drives float at a small distance above the surface. This is because the platters typically spin at high speeds, such as 4500 to 10,000 revolutions per minute, causing air pressure to build between them and the read/write head. The central hub (or spindle) on which the platters are mounted is spun by a *spindle motor*. No belts or gears are used to connect them to the hard disk platter spindle. Belts and gears are an added expense and tend to be noisy and can be a reliability issue.

NOTE

Users should never open a disk drive to attempt to repair it. The disks are sealed in a protective housing and should never be opened to the atmosphere. Repairs are performed in special facilities called *ultra-clean rooms* where particles, such as smoke, dust, and hair, have been removed from the air.

How the Drive Functions

The hard disk drive functions in much the same way as a floppy disk drive. The disk platters spin at a high speed while the drive heads access the media to conduct read or write operations. Understanding how the heads read and write the data structures on the platter media is critical to knowing how the drive functions.

The media on the drive platters is a layer of magnetically sensitive material. In general, modern hard disk drives use a thin film of a cobalt metal alloy laid down in several microthin layers. The magnetic particles in this media are randomly aligned when the disk is empty of data. However, as the read/write head writes to an area, it causes the particles on that track to align in a specific direction. This is done according to the direction of electric current flow in the heads. This local magnetic direction in the media is referred to as a *flux*. The current in the head can be reversed, causing a *flux reversal* (opposite magnetic orientation in the media). As the platter spins, the head lays down a *flux pattern* along the length of a track. This pattern of flux transitions on the track represents your recorded data.

Evolution of the Hard Drive and Drive Capacity

Personal computers have at least one HDD installed inside the system unit. If more storage capacity is needed, another HDD can usually be added. The capacity of the HDD is a measure of how much information it can store. This capacity is normally measured in megabytes or gigabytes. Older hard disks retained about 5 MB and used platters up to 12 inches in diameter. Today, hard disks generally use 3-1/2-inch-diameter platters for desktop computers and 2-1/2-inch-diameter platters for notebooks. These disks can hold several gigabytes. A 2-GB HDD, for example, can store close to 2,147,483,648 characters. This might sound large, but for today's applications and operating systems such as Windows 95, 98, Me, and 2000, 2 GB can be used up rather quickly, leaving little space for data storage purposes.

Some of the older hard disk interfaces used a device-level interface. These older hard disks had many problems with compatibility, data integrity, and speed. The original hard disk interface, used in the IBM PC/XT, was developed by Seagate Technologies and was referred to as modified frequency modulation (MFM). MFM used a magnetic disk encoding method with the ST-506 interface.

Run length limited (RLL) is a hard disk interface that is similar to the MFM but has a larger number of sectors. RLL is an encoding method commonly used on magnetic disks, including RLL, SCSI, IDE, and ESDI interfaces. Currently, the most common hard disk drive standards are IDE, EIDE, and SCSI.

Interactive PhotoZoom Activity   Hard Drive

Included on this book's CD, this PhotoZoom defines the components of the hard drive.

Worksheet 2.3.14   Hard Drive Identification

This worksheet provides a review of the components of the hard drive and how the drive works.

CD-ROM Drives

The CD-ROM drive's impact on modern computing makes it an important technological development. This section discusses compact disc read-only memory (CD-ROM) drives and media. The technology behind the CD-ROM drive dates back to 1978, with the introduction of the audio compact disc (CD) by the Sony and Phillips Corporations. The size of the media and the CD-ROM drive's basic design have not changed since their inception. Virtually every computer system assembled today includes a CD-ROM drive. The drive consists of a spindle, a laser that flashes onto the disc's uneven surface, a prism that deflects the laser beam, and a light-sensitive diode that reads the flashing light. Today, you have many choices of CD drives, including CD-ROM, CD-R, CD-RW, and DVD-ROM (see Table 2-13).

Table 2-13 CD Drive Types and What They Can Do

Drive Type	Name	What It Can Do
CD-ROM and CD-ROM multiread	Compact disc read-only memory	Reads CD-ROM and CD-R media.
CD-R	Compact disc recordable	Reads CD-ROM and CD-R media. Writes once on special discs named CD-R.

Table 2-13 CD Drive Types and What They Can Do (Continued)

Drive Type	Name	What It Can Do
CD-RW	Compact disc rewritable	Reads CD-ROM and CD-R media. Writes and rewrites on special discs named CD-RW.
DVD	Digital versatile disc	Reads all CD formats. Reads DVD media.

A *CD-ROM drive* is a secondary storage device that reads information stored on a compact disc. While floppy and hard disks are magnetic media, the CD-ROM is an *optical medium.* The lifespan of optical media is counted in tens of years, which makes CD-ROM a useful storage tool. CD-ROM drives can be housed inside the computer case (internal) or connected to the computer by a cable (external). CD-ROM drives are useful for installing programs, running applications that install some of the files to the hard drive, and executing the program by transferring the data from the compact disc to memory while the program is running.

Components of a CD-ROM

A *CD-ROM* is a read-only optical storage medium. The term CD-ROM can refer to both the media and the reader unit, also called a CD-ROM drive or CD. Music CDs have all but replaced cassette tapes as the medium of choice for musical recordings. The computer compact disc retains the same form factor, or physical dimensions, as its music counterpart. It is a layered disc with a polycarbonate body, approximately 4.75 inches in diameter, coated with a thin film of aluminum alloy. A plastic coating protects the disc from scratches, and data are laid on the alloy film.

The CD is usually produced, or mastered, at a factory with a laser that etches the data onto a master disc. The recording technique is a physical one rather than a magnetic one (as is the case with floppy and hard disk media.) The production laser burns *pits* into the smooth surface of the disc, leaving flat surfaces in between. The patterns of pits and *lands* represent data. After the master is produced, it is used to stamp copies. Up to 682 MB of text, audio, video, and graphical data can be written to a disc. After the copies have been made, they are then sealed for distribution. CD writers are now commonly available, providing the ability to write compact discs in a process known as *CD burning.*

The major components within a CD-ROM drive are the optical head assembly, head actuator mechanism, spindle motor, loading mechanism, connectors and jumpers, and logic board.

How the CD-ROM Drive Works

Data are stored in the form of indentations and bumps on the reflective surface of every compact disc. When data are being read, light from the laser is bounced off the pits and the lands located on the underside of the disc. Because the pits reflect less light, they are read by the CD-ROM drive as 0s. Because lands reflect more light, they are read as 1s. Together, these 1s and 0s make up the binary language that is understood by computers.

Speed, Access Time, and Transfer Rate

One specification for a CD-ROM drive is its speed, or how fast the disc spins. The faster the disc spins, the faster the data can be transferred to the computer's memory. The CD-ROM speed is indicated by a number with an *x* after it. For example, a 12-speed CD-ROM drive is labeled as 12x. The larger the number, the faster the disc can spin (see Table 2-14). Two other important specifications to consider are the *access time* and *data transfer rate*, which are defined as follows:

- **Access time**—How quickly the data you are looking for can be located.
- **Data transfer rate**—How fast the computer can transfer the information into memory.

Table 2-14 CD-ROM Drive Speed Ratings

CD-ROM Drive Rating	Data Transfer Speed	Rotational Speed (Revolutions/Minute, Outer to Inner Track)
2x	300 KBps/second	400 to 1060
4x	600 KBps/second	800 to 2120
8x	1.2 MBps/second	1600 to 4240
12x	1.8 MBps/second	2400 to 6360

Speed ratings for external CD-ROM drives vary. Check the manufacturer's documentation for more information.

Other specifications that directly or indirectly influence speed, access time, or transfer rate are seek time, cache memory, interface type, and error correction. Table 2-15 defines and/or describes each of these specifications.

Table 2-15 CD-ROM Transfer Rate Specifications

Specification	Definition/Description
Seek time	The amount of time it takes for the device to locate a piece of data.
Cache memory	Stores commonly accessed data so that the processor need not locate and retrieve it from the disc each time. The more often cache memory is used, the faster the data can be accessed because memory is much faster than the drive.
Interface type	CD-ROM drives have different interfaces. A SCSI connection is capable of much faster transfer rates than an IDE interface, for example.
Error correction	Error correction uses over 10 percent of the space on the disc to provide the ability to recover from faulty data being transferred. The more the drive must use error correction, the slower it becomes.
Access time	The amount of time it takes for the device to locate a piece of data and its latency period (the time it takes to position the laser over the desired data location). Note the difference from seek time.
Data transfer rate	The speed of data being transmitted from the CD-ROM device to the computer's main memory.

Interactive PhotoZoom Activity   CD-ROM Drive

Included on this book's CD, this PhotoZoom defines the components of a CD-ROM drive.

Worksheet 2.3.15   CD-ROM Drive Identification

This worksheet provides a review of the components of the CD-ROM drive and how the drive works.

Modems

A *modem* is the primary way to connect to the Internet with Windows 9X through a dialup networking connection. The word modem is an acronym for modulator/

demodulator. A modem is, in essence, a device that converts the digital data used by computers into analog signals that are suitable for transmission over a telephone line, and converts the analog signals back to a digital signal at the destination. A computer not connected to a network by some other means, such as a network interface card, typically has a modem card installed. A modem plugged into one of the expansion slots inside a PC is known as an *internal modem*. Such a modem usually has two connectors called registered jack type 11, more commonly called *RJ-11* jacks. One connector is for the phone line, while the other is for attaching a traditional telephone handset.

Internal modems come in the form of expansion cards, also known as modem cards. The modem card handles all the data transmission on the computer's serial port, with the help of a special chip called the universal asynchronous receiver transmitter (UART) chip. Almost every PC sold today contains a 16550 UART chip because buyers want a high-speed Internet connection. The number preceding UART, for example, 16550, represents a generational evolution of these chips, typically associated with a PC generation. The three generations of UART chip are defined as follows:

- **8250**—The original chip in XTs, this chip has only a 1-byte buffer (temporal storage for data as they are sent out bit-by-bit over a serial line such as a phone line).
- **16450**—This chip, introduced with AT systems, has a 2-byte buffer.
- **16550**—The 16550 chip, most popular with Pentium computers, has a first in, first out (FIFO) buffer that effectively eliminates data overrun. Data overrun occurs when a system port runs faster than it can be processed by the CPU.

The major difference between the UART chips is the speed at which they can enable data transmission. Notably advanced UART versions include the 16450 and 16550. The 16450 was the 16-byte improvement of the 8250, while the 16550 was a high-performance UART with an on-board 16-byte buffer.

More about modems and their role in Internet connectivity is discussed in a later chapter.

Network Interface Cards

A *network interface card (NIC)*, also known as a *network adapter*, connects a local computer to a group of other computers so they can share data and resources in a networked environment (see Figure 2-29). All network interface cards on a local-area network (LAN) are designed to use Ethernet, Token Ring, or another similar protocol to communicate with other machines on the network.

Figure 2-29 A Typical NIC

As the name implies, NICs are made in the form of expansion cards (PCI or ISA) that can be installed in one of the computer's expansion slots. The network cable plugs into the computer through the adapter card or NIC. This is possible because of a connector type known as the RJ-45 connector, shown in Figure 2-30. This connector is similar to the RJ-11 jack, discussed earlier, except that it has eight wires inside (instead of four wires for the RJ-11 phone jack). In order for two networked computers to communicate, they must be connected at the same speed and use the same Layer 2 technology. Layer 2 technology refers to the TCP/IP networking model and is discussed with greater detail in Chapter 9, "Networking Fundamentals."

Figure 2-30 An RJ-45 Plug

With the NIC, the RJ-45 jack is used with *unshielded twisted pair (UTP)* LAN cabling, while another type of connector, the *British Naval connector (BNC)*, is provided for coaxial cable connections. Network cabling (networking media), as well as NICs, are discussed in more detail in a later chapter.

Portables

This section includes the following topics:

- Why portables can be portable
- Portable hardware
- Portable computer displays
- Docking stations

Why Portables Can Be Portable

Portables incorporate the system unit, input unit, and output unit into a single, light-weight package, which unlike the towers or desktops, can be carried around by the user. Portables are also called notebook computers, laptop computers, palmtops, or personal digital assistants (PDAs), depending on their size function. This section focuses on notebook and laptop computers, but the issues discussed are common to all portables.

Producing portable computers has not been without problems. Early attempts at developing a portable computer produced heavy systems with short operating times between battery recharges. With the advancements in technology, particularly in IC (integrated circuit) and peripheral component designs, the portable now competes with desktop and tower systems in speed, power, and number of features. A typical notebook computer, such that depicted in Figure 2-31, features a video display that is larger than those typically associated with the older PC-AT desktop machines, a hard drive with a capacity in the tens of gigabytes, and a CD-ROM/DVD drive. As technology improves, notebook components are designed to use less power (via rechargeable batteries) but are at the same time more rugged. These concepts are explored further in the following sections.

Figure 2-31 A Typical Notebook Computer

Portable Hardware

Portables are built to be lightweight and to fit within a certain size or form factor. This has led to special considerations in developing the hardware components that go into a portable computer. This section explores some of these components.

Batteries

Because notebooks and other portable devices are built to be used on the road, a power outlet might not always be available. To solve this problem, batteries have been incorporated as an integrated component of portable systems.

Originally, portables used nickel cadmium (Ni-Cad) batteries (shown in Figure 2-32) that were in an external battery pack that was attached to the portable device. When first introduced, Ni-Cad batteries would only operate a device for 30–45 minutes, depending on power consumption. The operating time then increased to 45–75 minutes, depending on the screen size and the application that was open. In addition, the time to recharge these batteries could take nearly a day. Better batteries have since been developed to address these limitations and to provide a longer time of use and allow a faster recharge.

Figure 2-32   Ni-Cad Batteries

More recently, nickel metal-hydride (NiMH) and lithium-ion batteries, as shown in Figure 2-33, have been used in portable devices. These batteries are usually constructed in a plastic holder that can be easily inserted into the portable device. The batteries usually last for slightly more than two hours, depending on their size and the power consumption by the device. Also, it only takes three to five hours to recharge them, a considerably shorter time than it would take for a Ni-Cad battery.

Figure 2-33 Lithium-Ion Batteries

One drawback for portable systems is that currently no industry standards are in place for the power supplies. Therefore, a battery in one portable device might not be compatible with a different portable device.

Hard Drives

As with most components of a portable device, hard drives have been specially developed to be smaller and use less power to accommodate size and power limitations. The size of hard drives in portable devices ranges dramatically. Power issues have also been addressed with hard drives; they can be powered down when they have not been accessed for a certain amount of time.

PCMCIA Cards

The *Personal Computer Memory Card International Association (PCMCIA) card*, introduced in 1989, is a special expansion card type designed primarily to accommodate the needs of the portable computer market. Recently, the term PCMCIA has been used less often and has been replaced by the more easily spoken PC card. The three types of PCMCIA slots and cards are defined as follows:

- **Type I cards**—3.3 mm thick; used as memory expansion units.
- **Type II cards**—5 mm thick; used for any expansion device except hard drives.
- **Type III cards**—10.5 mm thick; designed to be used solely for hard drives.

Memory

Most portable computers do not use a standard type of memory. With nearly any notebook, to upgrade the memory, the owner must visit the manufacturer's website or consult the user's manual for more information. Even within the same manufacturer, memory types can vary among different products or different versions of the same product. This calls for careful research before upgrading a portable's memory.

Portable Computer Displays

Because of their compact nature and limited power supply, notebook computers and other portables use non-CRT-type displays, also referred to as flat-panel displays. Two examples of such displays are *liquid crystal displays (LCDs)* and *gas-plasma panels*. These two types of display systems are suited to the needs of portable computers for the following reasons:

- They are much lighter and more compact than CRT monitors.
- They require much less electrical energy to operate.
- Both types of display units can be operated from batteries.

The most common flat-panel displays used with most of the newer portable systems are LCDs. They have the advantage of being relatively thin, flat, and lightweight, and they require little power to operate. Additionally, these displays offer better reliability and longer life than CRT units. Figure 2-34 shows an LCD on a PDA.

Figure 2-34 A Liquid Crystal Display

The detailed electrical properties of LCDs and how they are different from the traditional CRT displays is beyond the scope of this text.

Docking Stations

A *docking station*, as shown in Figure 2-34, also called a *docking port*, is a device that allows the portable PC to operate with hardware devices associated with desktop computers. When you insert the notebook into the docking station, the extension bus in the docking station plugs into the expansion connector in the notebook. Usually, a docking station provides standard PC expansion slots so that non-notebook peripheral devices, such as network adapters, sound cards, and so on, can be used with the system. When a notebook computer is in a docking station, its normal input/output devices (display or monitor, keyboard, and pointing device) are disabled and the docking station's peripherals take over. This makes it possible for the notebook to use a collection of desktop devices, such as an AC power source, a CRT monitor, a full-sized keyboard, a mouse, a modem, and standard personal computer port connectors, which otherwise would not be available to it.

Figure 2-35 HP Omnibook Docking Station

The notebook and the docking station communicate with each other through a special docking port connector in the rear of the notebook. However, most docking stations are proprietary, which means that they can only be used with the portable they were designed to work with. Two important factors account for the proprietary nature of these products:

- The connector in the notebook must correctly align with the docking port connection in the docking station.
- The notebook unit must also fit correctly within the docking station opening.

Because no standards exist for portable systems, the chances of two different manufacturers locating the connectors in the same place or even designing the same case outline are slim.

System Resources: IRQs, DMA, and I/O Addresses

This section includes the following topics:

- What are system resources?
- Interrupt requests (IRQs).
- Direct memory access (DMA).
- Input/output (I/O) addresses.

What Are System Resources?

In the context of a computer configuration, *system resources* refer to the mechanisms used to interface, communicate, and control individual device adapters along with the serial, parallel, and mouse ports. System resources are shared among the different hardware components or devices of the computer system that need to communicate with the central processing unit.

The *central processing unit (CPU)* is a complete computation engine that is fabricated on a single chip. It not only controls the functions of the computer but also handles requests from many input and output devices. Computers appear to handle multiple requests at the same time, but in reality the CPU is only capable of handling one request at a time. System resources prevent two or more devices from communicating at the same time and also enable the CPU to identify the hardware device that is seeking its attention.

Interrupt Requests

Modern computers and operating systems owe their reliability to the organized way in which they handle internal transactions. Various hardware devices, for example, might want to tell the CPU that they have some information that is ready for transfer. The devices indicate this by making an interrupt request (IRQ). It is a general rule that IRQs cannot be shared. A device's IRQ causes the operating system to stop momentarily as the operating system asks the CPU to service the device's request. Because IRQs are so critical to the proper functioning of the system, it is important that you thoroughly understand default-device IRQ assignments (see Table 2-16).

TEST TIP

Know which device or port each IRQ is assigned to.

Table 2-16 Common IRQ Default Assignments

IRQ	Common Device or Port Assignment
0	System timer
1	Keyboard
2	Programmable interrupt controller (cascade IRQs 8–15)
3	COM2 and COM4
4	COM1 and COM3
5	Parallel port 2 (LPT2), sound card, or network card
6	Floppy disk controller
7	Parallel port 1 (LPT1) or sound card (shared)
8	Real-time clock
9	Cascade IRQ2
10	Available
11	Available
12	PS/2 mouse (available if not used)
13	Numerical processing unit (i.e., math coprocessor)
14	Primary IDE controller (i.e., hard disk controller)
15	Secondary IDE controller

What Are Cascaded IRQs?

TEST TIP

Take the time to understand IRQ cascading, because it is often confusing to many people. When source information is redirected to a destination, the destination receives cascaded information from the source.

To understand the concept of cascading IRQs, look back at how controllers worked with the XT (8088 chips), and then later, the AT (80286 and later) system board BIOS. The XT BIOS provided eight IRQ lines, that is, 0 through 7. The more advanced AT BIOS came with eight more IRQ lines, that is, 8 through 15. Although the instructions for controllers designed to work on the AT system board are usually located at IRQ9, they are typically redirected (cascaded) to IRQ2.

Therefore, if IRQ2 is being used by BIOS instructions, IRQ9 is also being used. This behavior is described as *cascading*, which simply means redirecting. In fact, cascading is also commonly referred to as *redirecting* or *vectoring*. In this instance, IRQ9 is said to be cascading, vectoring, or redirecting to IRQ2. Note that all three words refer to the same process of pointing to somewhere else.

Direct Memory Access

Direct memory access (DMA) channels allow devices to bypass the processor and directly access the computer memory. Devices with a DMA channel assignment, as a result, gain the advantage of faster data transfers. DMA channels are typically used by high-speed communication devices for transferring large amounts of data at high speeds. Examples of such devices include sound cards and some network cards, SCSI cards, disk drives, and tape backup drives.

When a device signals its intention to use the DMA channel, the DMA controller takes control of the *data bus* and *address bus* from the CPU. (Data and address buses are communication lines that bring information to the computer memory.) The CPU is effectively put in a floating state. Therefore, it is temporarily disconnected from the buses. After the transfer is complete, the DMA controller releases the data bus and address bus to the CPU, which can continue with its normal functions. One drawback of DMA use, especially with older systems, is that the CPU might be put on hold while the DMA device is working, slowing everything else in the system until the DMA transfer is complete.

As with IRQs, devices that want to make a DMA transfer are assigned a priority level. Devices with lower DMA numbers are assigned higher priority levels. It is important to understand DMA assignments, which are summarized in Table 2-17.

Table 2-17 Common DMA Default Channel Assignments

DMA Channel	Default Device	Channel Can Also Be Used For
0	Dynamic RAM memory refresh	—
1	Sound card (low DMA setting)	Network cards, SCSI adapters, parallel printing ports, and voice modems
2	Floppy disk controller	—
3	Available	Network cards, SCSI adapters, parallel printing ports, voice modems, and sound cards (low DMA setting)
4	Cascade for DMA0–3	—
5	Sound card (high DMA setting)	Network cards and SCSI adapters

continues

Table 2-17 Common DMA Default Channel Assignments (Continued)

DMA Channel	Default Device	Channel Can Also Be Used For
6	Available	Network cards and sound cards (high DMA setting)
7	Available	Network cards and sound cards (high DMA setting)

Input/Output Addresses

In addition to an IRQ, computer components also need to be assigned an input/output (I/O) port number. An *I/O port number* is a memory address where data are temporarily stored as they move in and out of the devices. The I/O address is similar to a post office box. As mail comes in, it is stored temporarily in a post office box. No two boxes can have the same number or the mail can end up in the wrong box. The same is true for I/O ports: No two devices can have the same I/O address. Table 2-18 shows I/O settings for common input and output devices.

Table 2-18 I/O Address Assignments

I/O Port Address (In Hexadecimal Form)	Typical Device or Port Assignment
000-00F, 081-09F	Direct memory access controller
010-01F, 0A0-0A1	Programmable interrupt controller
040-043	System timer
060-060, 064-064	Keyboard
061-061	PC speaker
070-071	CMOS/real-time clock
0F0-0FF	Math coprocessor
130-14F	SCSI host adapter
170-177	Secondary hard disk controller
1F0-1F7	Primary hard disk controller
200-207	Game port joystick
220-22F	Sound card
294-297	PCI bus (data communication line)

Table 2-18 I/O Address Assignments (Continued)

I/O Port Address (In Hexadecimal Form)	Typical Device or Port Assignment
278-27F	LPT2 or LPT3
2E8-2EF	COM4 serial port
2F8-2FF	COM2 serial port
376-376	PCI IDE controller
378-37F	LPT1 printer port
3E8-3EF	COM3 serial port
3F2-3F5	Floppy disk controller
3F6-3F6	PCI primary IDE controller
3F8-3EF	COM1 serial port
E000-E01F	USB host controller
E800-E87F	Fast Ethernet adapter
F000-F00F	IDE controllers

Summary

This chapter discussed the theory and operation of the various computer components. Some of the important concepts to retain from this chapter are as follows:

- The OS helps the computer perform four basic operations: input, processing, output, and storage. Entering data with a keyboard is the most common form of input. Processing is manipulating data according to the instructions. Output is the processed data on a screen or printer. Finally, storage occurs on the hard drive or floppy disk.

- The bootstrap loader is a small program located on the BIOS chip. The primary functions of the bootstrap loader are to test the computer hardware using the POST and to load the OS into RAM.

- A cold boot is the process of starting the computer from an off position and requires the system to go through the boot sequence and POST. A warm boot is restarting the already powered computer.

- You have many factors to consider when choosing a computer case. Most modern cases have the power supply installed. The motherboard that is to be used and the components to be installed are the major considerations.

- The motherboard, or system board, is the nerve center of the computer. It houses the CPU, the controller circuitry, bus, RAM, expansion slots for additional boards, and ports for external devices.

- The computer display or monitor is available in various types and sizes, and with various characteristics. Important monitor-related terms include pixels, or the tiny dots that make up the image; refresh rate, which is measured in hertz; resolution, which refers to the sharpness of the image, and screen size.

- The video card is the interface between the computer and the monitor. It determines which pixels light up, the color of the pixels, and the intensity of the pixels on the monitor. It is either installed as an expansion card or built into the motherboard.

- I/O ports are the connectors on the back of the computer that allows peripheral devices, such as printers, scanners, etc., to connect to the computer. It is important to understand the difference between the USB port, FireWire, serial port, parallel port, PS/2 port, and 5-pin DIN adapter.

- The hard drive, connected to a disk controller with a cable, and other devices use either enhanced integrated drive electronics (EIDE) or small computer system interface (SCSI) connections.

- A floppy disk drive (FDD) magnetically reads and writes information onto floppy disks, which are a form of removable storage media. A hard disk drive (HDD) shares many physical and operational characteristics with the floppy disk drive but has a more complex design and provides greater access speed. The HDD has a much larger storage capacity than the floppy for long-term storage. The hard disk drive stores your programs and files as well as the operating system. Typically, the HDD is an internal drive that cannot be removed from the computer.

■ A compact disc is a read-only optical storage medium. The term CD-ROM can refer to both the media and the reader unit, also called a CD-ROM drive or CD. Music CDs have all but replaced cassette tapes as the medium of choice for musical recordings.

■ A modem is typically an expansion card that connects a computer to the Internet with a dialup network connection. Modems come in the form of internal expansion cards also known as modem cards. The modem card handles all the data transmission through the computer's serial port, with the help of a special chip called the universal asynchronous receiver transmitter (UART) chip.

■ Portable computers, or notebooks, are built to be lightweight and are within a certain size form factor. Special components include the batteries, hard drives, and memory. The PCMCIA card (more recently called the PC card) is a special expansion card. The three types of PCMCIA slots and cards are Type I for memory expansion, Type II for devices, and Type III for hard drives.

■ System resources are shared between the different hardware components or devices of the computer system that need to communicate with the CPU. The CPU is able to handle only one request at a time. System resources identify the device and prevent two or more devices from communicating at the same time.

■ Each device is assigned an interrupt request, or IRQ, that cannot be shared. The IRQ causes a program to stop momentarily as it asks the CPU to handle the request. A cascading IRQ is an IRQ that is redirected or vectored.

■ Direct memory access (DMA) channels allow devices to bypass the processor and directly access the computer memory. Devices with a DMA channel have faster data transfers.

■ An I/O port number is a memory address where data are temporarily stored as they move into and out of the devices, much like a post office box. An I/O address can be assigned to only one device.

The next chapter discusses how to use the hardware components to assemble a working computer.

Check Your Understanding

The following are review questions for the A+ exam. Answers can be found in Appendix B, "Answers to Check Your Understanding Review Questions."

1. What performs a quick self-diagnostic check of the system hardware early in the boot sequence?

   A. The POST, which is located in the CPU

   B. The POST, which is located in ROM

   C. DOS

   D. HIMEM.SYS

2. What is the first thing that the POST routine does?

   A. Initializes the expansion slots and serial and parallel ports

   B. Resets the CPU and the program counter to F000

   C. Initializes the operating system and prepares it for execution

   D. Looks for hardware drivers for peripheral devices

3. What computer component is NOT tested by the POST routine?

   A. RAM

   B. Power supply

   C. Main board

   D. BIOS

4. During the boot process, what is the first code that is executed?

   A. CMOS

   B. BIOS

   C. RAM

   D. SIMM

5. PC power supplies use what type of power?

   A. DC current

   B. Voltage

   C. AC current

   D. Amps

6. What controls the temperature of the power supply?

A. Thermostat

B. Case cooler

C. Cooling fan

D. CPU

7. How do you prevent a power supply from overheating?

A. Turn down the air conditioner

B. Verify that the cooling vents are not blocked

C. Turn off the computer every night

D. Disconnect any device not currently in use

8. What is the main circuit board in a computer?

A. PCI board

B. Processor board

C. Memory board

D. Motherboard

9. Which of the following is not a CPU manufacturer?

A. Intel

B. Cyrex

C. Sun Microsystems

D. Advanced Micro Devices

10. When powering up, where does the microprocessor find its first code?

A. CPU

B. RAM

C. ROM

D. Cache

11. Pentium CPUs normally run what voltage type?

A. VDC

B. VAC

C. DCV

D. VRM

12. To improve CPU access time, what do you need to upgrade?

    A. Hard drive

    B. Motherboard

    C. ROM memory

    D. Cache

13. What does BIOS stand for?

    A. Beginning information organization service

    B. Basic input/output system

    C. Basic input/output service

    D. Beginning information

14. What is the advantage of using Flash ROM?

    A. BIOS can be upgraded without replacing the chip.

    B. The ROM is flashed with new programs every time the system is started.

    C. Hard drives run faster.

    D. Memory is doubled.

15. What is the typical size of a SIMM?

    A. 32 and 70 pins

    B. 30 and 70 pins

    C. 30 and 72 pins

    D. 32 and 72 pins

16. What type of connector is used for a serial port connection on a PC?

    A. DB-15, male D-shell

    B. DB-25, male D-shell

    C. DB-9, male D-shell

    D. 5-pin, male DIN

17. Why are hardware resource conflicts more likely to be IRQ related than I/O related?

    A. There are more I/O addresses than IRQs.

    B. The BIOS can't control IRQs.

    C. I/O addresses never conflict.

    D. Software corrects I/O conflicts.

18. What is a feature of EIDE?

    A. More drives

    B. SCSI connectors

    C. High-speed floppy drives

    D. ATAPI

19. What is a common failure in SCSI devices?

    A. Improper termination

    B. Bad terminator

    C. Bad device

    D. Bad host adapter

20. What type of interface has the fastest data transfer?

    A. IDE

    B. SCSI

    C. Parallel

    D. Modem

21. What is the minimum storage unit for an IDE hard drive?

    A. Cluster

    B. Cylinder

    C. Byte

    D. Sector

22. What is the typical CD-ROM interface?

    A. Parallel

    B. Serial

    C. IDE

    D. ESDI

23. What are external modems usually connected to?

    A. Parallel port

    B. NIC

    C. Serial port

    D. MIDI port

24. Which statement is true about IRQs?

   A. Devices share IRQs all the time.

   B. IRQs are stored in the Windows configuration files.

   C. After processing an IRQ, the CPU looks for others to process.

   D. Each device on a PC must have a unique IRQ.

25. What does DMA stand for?

   A. Direct memory access

   B. Direct memory availability

   C. Dual memory availability

   D. Dual memory access

Key Terms

8250 UART   A one-byte buffer (temporal storage for data as it is sent out bit-by-bit out a serial line such as a phone line).

16450 UART   A two-byte buffer.

16550 UART   A FIFO (first in, first out) buffer that effectively eliminates data overrun.

Accelerated Graphics Port (AGP)   Developed by Intel, AGP is a dedicated high-speed bus that supports the high demands of graphical software. Expansion slot for installing the video card.

access time   How quickly the data can be located.

address bus   A unidirectional pathway, which means that information can only flow one way.

Arithmetic/Logic Unit (ALU)   The ALU performs both arithmetic and logical operations.

ATA-2 disk drives   A new and improved IDE.

ATX   A type of motherboard.

Baby AT   A type of motherboard.

Basic input/output system (BIOS)   The instructions and data in the ROM chip that control the boot process and your computer's hardware.

bidirectional   A type of parallel port used for rapid transmission over short distances.

BIOS   Basic input output system.

Bootstrap Loader   A program launched when the computer is first turned on.

British Navel Connector (BNC)   A connector used with coaxial cable.

cascading   Redirecting, in regards to IRQ.

CD-ROM drive   A secondary storage device.

central processing unit (CPU)   A complete computation engine that is fabricated on a single chip. It not only controls the functions of the computer, but also handles requests from many input and output devices.

chipset   A group of microcircuits contained on several integrated chips or combined into one or two large scale integration (VLSI) integrated chips.

cold boot   The process of starting the computer from the off position.

color depth   The number of colors that can be displayed.

colors   The number of colors that can be displayed.

computer case   The metal chassis that houses the computer components.

control bus   Carries the control and timing signals needed to coordinate the activities of the entire computer.

control unit   Instructs the rest of the computer system on how to follow a program's instructions.

Data bus   A bidirectional pathway for data flow, which means that information can flow in two directions.

data transfer rate   How fast data can be transferred into memory.

desktop model   A type of case that sits horizontally.

Direct Memory Access (DMA)   Allows devices to bypass the processor and directly access the computer memory.

disk platter   A component of a hard drive, actual media on which data is stored in the hard disk drive.

display   A device to view output.

docking station or docking port   Allows the portable PC to operate with hardware devices associated with desktop computers.

dot pitch   A measurement of how close together the phosphor dots are on the screen.

DRAM   Memory that is inexpensive and somewhat slow, and requires an uninterrupted power supply to maintain the data. When the power is turned off, the data is lost.

Dual Inline Memory Modules (DIMMs)   Memory module.

Electronics Industry Association (EIA)   Develops standards for electronics used in the computer industry.

Enhanced IDE   A new and improved IDE.

EPROM and EEPROM   ROM chips that can be erased and reprogrammed.

expansion slots   Receptacles on the computer motherboard that accept printed circuit boards.

FireWire   A high-speed, platform-independent communication bus that interconnects digital devices.

Flash ROM   Special EEPROM chips that can be reprogrammed under special software control. Upgrading BIOS by running special software is known as *flashing*.

floppy disk drive (FDD)   A device that magnetically reads and writes information onto floppy diskettes.

flux   Local magnetic direction in the media.

flux reversal   Opposite magnetic orientation in the media.

flux pattern   The recorded data on a track.

ganged   A way in which disks are stacked in a hard drive.

gas-plasma panels   Display designed to be used in portable computers.

graphics accelerator   An adapter that improves video.

hard disk drive (HDD)   The computer's main storage medium.

Head Actuator Assembly   A component of the hard drive.

hub   A networking device that holds the disks together in a hard disk drive.

Industry Standard Architecture (ISA)   A 16-bit expansion slot developed by IBM. It transfers data with the motherboard at 8 MHz.

input   Recognizing data entered to the computer via a keyboard or mouse.

Integrated Drive Electronics (IDE)   A type of hardware interface widely used to connect hard disks, CD-ROMs and tape drives.

L1 cache   A specialized computer chip that enhances memory performance located on the CPU.

L2 cache   A specialized computer chip that enhances memory performance located between the CPU and DRAM.

lands   The bumps on the surface of a CD.

Liquid Crystal Display (LCD)   A display type used primarily on portable computers.

modem   Stands for modulator/demodulator, a device that converts the digital data used by computers into analog signals that is suitable for transmission over a telephone line, and converts the analog signals back to a digital signal at the destination.

modulator/demodulator   A modem.

monitor   A device to view output.

motherboard/system board   The nerve center of the computer.

network interface card (NIC)   Used to connect a local computer to a network.

optical media   The method used by a CD-ROM to read and write data.

output   The data sent from the computer to the monitor or printer.

parallel port   A socket on the computer used to connect peripheral devices that use a parallel interface.

Peripheral Component Interconnect (PCI)   A 32-bit local bus slot developed by Intel. Because they "talk" to the motherboard at 33 MHz, the PCI bus slots offer a significant improvement over ISA or EISA expansion slots.

Personal Computer Memory Card International association (PCMCI)   An expansion card type designed primarily to accommodate the needs of the portable computer.

pits   The indentations burned on a CD.

pixel   Picture elements.

portables   System unit, input unit, and output unit into a single, lightweight package.

printed circuit board   A computer component.

process   Manipulating data based on the user's instructions.

PS/2 keyboard   A type of connection used to connect a keyboard to the computer.

PS/2 mouse port   A type of connection used to connect a mouse to the computer.

random-access memory (RAM)   Computer memory that is temporary.

random-access memory digital to analog converter (RAMDAC)   A specialized form of memory designed to convert digitally encoded images into analog signals for display.

read/write head   Used to access the media in a hard disk drive.

refresh rate   The number of times the display is reenergized.

resolution   Refers to the pixels in the screen.

RJ-11 (registered jack type 11)   A connector used by the modem and the telephone.

screen size   The actual size of the display on the monitor.

SCSI 1   The original SCSI.

SCSI 1   Uses two different signaling systems, known as single-ended interface and differential interface.

SCSI-3   The latest standard of the SCSI family. It combines all the best features of the previous SCSI standards. It uses LVD, which uses differential signaling, and supports up to 15 devices on a single cable, which can be up to 12 meters long.

serial port   Used to connect devices that use a serial interface.

SIMMs (Single Inline Memory Modules)   A memory module.

small computer systems interface (SCSI)   An advanced interface controller that is ideal for high-end computers, including network servers.

spindle motor   Drives the hard disk drive.

SRAM   A memory type that is relatively more expensive, but is fast and holds data when the power is turned off for a brief period of time.

storage   An organized repository for data.

system bus   A parallel collection of conductors that carry data and control signals from one component to the other.

system resource   The mechanisms used to interface, communicate, and control individual device adapters along with the serial, parallel, and mouse ports.

thin film media   Magnetically sensitive coating in the hard drive.

tower model   A type of case that stands vertically.

Type I PCMCI card   A memory expansion unit.

Type II PCMCI card   An expansion for devices except hard drives.

Type III PCMCI card   An expansion for hard drives.

Ultra ATA disk drive   Refers to the transfer rate.

unidirectional   A type of parallel port used in older systems.

universal asynchronous receiver transmitter (UART) chip   A special chip used for data transmission through a modem.

unshielded twisted pair (UTP)   A Cable type used with the RJ-45 jack.

variable-frequency synthesizer circuit   Multiplies the clock signal so that the motherboard can support several speeds of CPUs.

video card or adapter   The interface between the computer and monitor.

video memory   The memory in the computer's video system.

video RAM   The memory utilized by the video.

warm boot   The process of restarting or resetting the computer.

Windows RAM (WRAM)   Memory for video.

Zero Insertion Force   A type of processor.

Objectives

Upon completion of this chapter, you will be able to perform the following tasks:

- Understand ESD and safety precautions that must be taken prior to assembly of the computer
- Create an inventory to ensure that the components required to assemble the computer are available
- Prepare the motherboard and its components for installation
- Install and secure the floppy drive, hard drive, and CD-ROM drive in the computer case
- Install and secure the video card in the computer case
- Perform the final steps and boot the system
- Determine the BIOS configuration and CMOS setup, and remedy POST errors

Chapter 3

Assembling a Computer

This chapter discusses computer component installation and the assembly of a computer. The chapter takes the information gained in the previous chapter and guides you through the assembly process to build a computer. Safety precautions are emphasized and reviewed in order to keep you safe and to protect expensive computer components. Upon completion, you will boot the system and explore the BIOS configuration and CMOS setup, and troubleshoot initial boot problems using POST errors.

Overview of the Assembly Process and Safety Issues

This section includes the following topics:

- Overview of general safety issues
- ESD precautions
- Process demonstration

Overview of General Safety Issues

Assembling a computer helps demystify the inner workings of a computer and is considered a milestone by IT professionals. In fact, it helps create the confidence needed to advance in the IT profession. Before beginning any assembly process, it is a good idea to review safety procedures. The following items should be taken into account when working with computers:

- Keep the work area free of clutter, and keep it clean.
- Keep food and drinks out of the work area.
- A computer monitor can store up to 25,000 volts, so avoid opening a monitor unless you are trained to do so.

- Remove all jewelry and watches.
- Make sure that the power is off and the power plug has been removed when working inside the computer.
- Never look at a laser beam. Lasers are found in optical devices such as the laser mouse and fiber cable.
- Make sure that a fire extinguisher and first aid kit are available.
- Cover sharp edges with tape when working inside the computer case.

Assembling a computer is not an inherently dangerous job, but being aware of safety procedures is a good starting point. In addition to these safety procedures, there are safety concerns with leaving the computer plugged in while working inside it.

If the computer is plugged in, there might be an unequal electric potential between a person and the computer case. The current flow is usually increased if there is a potential difference. There are 120 volts inside the case (in North America and some parts of Asia). This value can be 220 volts or more (in Europe and the rest of the world). By moving the machine when it is plugged into the power outlet, you might accidentally press the power button, creating a live machine. This creates a dangerous situation.

If the computer is unplugged and the power supply has a short to the hot line, you have a hot chassis. This creates a lethal situation, even if the computer is turned off.

To remedy these concerns, the computer should be plugged into a power strip. The power strip is then turned off along with the machine and power supply on the back of the case, removing the concern of live power while retaining the ground plug in the power cord. When the technician connects the wrist strap to the chassis, the ground connector in the power cord protects the equipment from electrostatic discharge (ESD).

The technician should also know where the power main or circuit breakers are located in case of a fire or short.

The importance of protecting the technician and the computer hardware cannot be overemphasized. The list that follows summarizes more safety measures and precautions to adhere to when assembling a computer. You can also consult the student lab safety agreement from Chapter 1, "Information Technology Basics," for more information. Recall that this is a contract that requires the technician (student) work according to the safety procedures put forth in this document.

Technicians are required to handle computer components, so it is best to take precautions to protect yourself and the computer hardware by following some basic safety procedures. The following list summarizes the safety measures and precautions to follow when assembling or working on a computer:

- Use an antistatic mat and grounding wrist strap or a grounding wrist strap only.
- Use antistatic bags to store and move computer components. Do not put more than one component in each bag, as stacking them can cause components to become loose or broken.
- Do not remove or install components while the computer is on. If you discover a mistake in wiring or component installation, turn the computer off and unplug it before replacing the cable or component.
- Ground yourself often to prevent static charges from building. Touch a piece of bare metal on the chassis or power supply.
- Work on a bare floor, if possible, as carpets can build static charges.
- Hold cards by their edges. Avoid touching chips or the edge connectors on the expansion cards.
- Do not touch chips or expansion boards with a magnetized screwdriver.
- Always turn off the computer before moving it. This is to protect the hard drive, which is always spinning when the computer is turned on.
- Keep installation/maintenance CDs and disks away from magnetic fields, heat, and cold.
- When laying components down, put them on top of an antistatic bag or mat. Never place a circuit board onto a conductive surface, especially a metal foil. The lithium and nickel cadmium (NiCad) batteries used on boards might short out.
- Do not use a pencil or metal-tipped instrument to change dip switches or touch or probe components. The graphite in the pencil is conductive and could easily cause damage.
- Do not allow anyone who is not properly grounded to touch or handle computer components. This is true even when working with a lab partner. When passing components, always touch hands first to neutralize any charges.
- Do not allow food or drinks in the work area.
- Keep the work area clean and orderly. When finished with a tool or component, put it back in its proper place.

Electrostatic Discharge Precautions

Electrostatic discharge (ESD) is more commonly referred to as static electricity. Static charges can build in your body just by walking across the room. It might not be apparent, but this buildup is usually enough to damage computer components if they are touched. A static charge of 2000 volts is enough for a person to notice; you might have experienced this when walking across a room and touching a doorknob or other metal surfaces. A static charge of only 200 volts is sufficient to damage a computer component.

ESD is probably the greatest enemy when unwrapping newly purchased computer parts and components. Always review the ESD precautions before beginning the assembly process. The following recommendations help prevent ESD-related damage:

- Keep all computer parts in antistatic bags.
- Keep the humidity at 20–30 percent.
- Use grounded mats on workbenches.
- Use grounded floor mats in work areas.
- Use wrist straps when working on computer parts, except when working on monitors.
- Periodically touch unpainted grounded metal parts of the computer to lower the body's static energy.

Remember that just because a discharge cannot be felt does not mean it cannot harm a computer component. Components can be destroyed or sustain only minor damage. The latter allows the component to function to some degree or cause intermittent errors. This type of ESD damage is the most difficult to detect. Cases, when closed properly, are designed to provide ESD protection for the components inside. The case channels ESD away from sensitive components. Basically, any component inside of the computer is susceptible to ESD. ESD becomes a threat when the case is opened and the components inside are exposed, or when the components are removed from the antistatic bags in which they are shipped.

The best way to protect against ESD is to use an antistatic mat, a grounding wrist strap, and antistatic bags. The grounding wrist strap, as shown in Figure 3-1, can be connected to the mat. The mat is in turn grounded to a wall outlet. Alternatively, the wrist strap can be clipped to the metal frame of the computer case.

Figure 3-1   A Wrist Strap

Process Demonstration

The video on the accompanying CD, "Assembling a Computer," demonstrates how a computer is assembled from beginning to the end. Note the safety procedures that are followed by the technician as the computer is assembled.

Creating a Computer Inventory

This section includes the following topics:

- Importance of an inventory
- An inventory checklist

Importance of an Inventory

When building a computer, it is important to document all components purchased. Once the computer is built and operational, it might be difficult to recall the brand of each component used, as not all expansion cards or computer parts are clearly labeled with manufacturer information. This documentation comes in handy after the packaging has been discarded or the manual or instruction sheet for a particular part cannot be found. With these details, and using the Internet, any required device drivers or other information might be found or downloaded.

You should note specific warranty information for each part bought. Make sure the specifics about installation and maintenance requirements are saved, so that warranties will be valid. Use a small secure box to hold all of the manuals and disks used in the assembly of the computer. Label the box with a name that identifies the computer with which it is associated, and store the box in a secure location. If information is needed in the future, all the documentation will be easily accessible.

In a lab environment where many students use the same kits, it is not possible to preserve the original packaging and to repackage the parts upon dismantling the computer. There should be access to the documentation for each component. In addition, an inventory checklist should be used, such as the one shown in the following section. This list ensures that all the components needed to assemble a computer are available and records important information about each of the components.

An Inventory Checklist

The first step in the computer assembly process is to get organized. In Chapter 2, "How Computers Work," all the components of the computer were introduced. Now gather those components to create an inventory checklist using the following example.

Sample Inventory Checklist

Computer Identification

Name:

Number:

Computer Case

Manufacturer:

Type (mini, mid, full, desktop):

Number of

3-1/2-inch bays:

5-1/4-inch bays:

Motherboard

Manufacturer:

Model:

Bus speed: ＿＿ MHz

Form factor:

❑ AT

❑ ATX

Chipset manufacturer:

Model:

BIOS manufacturer:

Version:

Does the CPU use a socket or a slot?

How many CPU sockets/slots exist?

How many ISA slots exist?

How many PCI slots exist?

How many EIDE connectors exist?

How many floppy connectors exist?

How many serial ports exist

How many parallel ports exist?

Is an AGP slot available?

How many USB ports exist?

How many other ports or slots exist?

What kind(s) are they?

CPU

Manufacturer:

Model:

Speed: ___ MHz

Memory

30-pin SIMMs:

72-pin SIMMs:

168-pin DIMMs:

160-pin RIMMs:

184-pin RIMMs:

Other:

How many memory slots exist?

What is the fastest type of memory supported?

What is the maximum memory supported?

Hard Drive

Manufacturer:

Model:

Size:

Number of cylinders:

Number of heads:

SPT:

Interface type:

❑ IDE

❑ SCSI

CD-ROM Drive

Manufacturer:

Model:

Speed:

Interface type:

❑ IDE

❑ SCSI

Rewritable CD-ROM Drive

Manufacturer:

Model:

Speed:

Interface type:

❑ IDE

❑ SCSI

DVD Drive

Manufacturer:

Model:

Speed:

Interface type:

❑ IDE

❑ SCSI

Floppy Disk Drive

Manufacturer:

Monitor

Manufacturer:

Model number:

Size:

Video Card

Manufacturer:

Model:

Memory: ___ MB

- ❏ ISA
- ❏ PCI
- ❏ On board
- ❏ AGP

Sound Card

Manufacturer:

Model:

- ❏ ISA
- ❏ PCI
- ❏ On board

Mouse

- ❏ PS/2
- ❏ Serial
- ❏ USB

Keyboard

Connector:

- ❏ 5-pin DIN
- ❏ 6-pin mini-DIN
- ❏ USB

Does it match the connector on the motherboard?

Power Supply

- ❏ AT
- ❏ ATX
- ❏ Other:

Power supply wattage:

Tape Backup

Manufacturer:

Model:

Scanner

Manufacturer:

Model:

Speakers

Manufacturer:

Model:

Additional information:

In addition to the checklist, it is important to save all the documentation that comes with the components. Store original documentation in Ziploc-type bags, and keep paperwork in three-ring binders. Additionally, keep a notebook and record component manufacturers' websites for later reference.

The Computer Case and Power Supply

This section includes the following topics:

- Computer cases and system units
- Desktop units
- Tower units
- Power supplies

Computer Cases and System Units

In Chapter 2, computer cases and power supplies were introduced. Issues and concerns that affect the purchasing or gathering of parts to assemble a computer are discussed in this section.

Whether buying a tower or desktop computer (to be discussed in the next sections), the case should conform to the ATX standard and have a minimum of a 250-watt power supply (300 watts is ideal.) Make sure to purchase a case that comes with a tray that allows easy access to the internal components. If frequent upgrades are intended, the case should provide enough room for expansion. Features to consider include spare drive bays, ample room to work inside the case, easily removable motherboard mounting plates, and drive racks. Additionally, verify the sturdiness of the case, because cheaper ones can be flimsy. A summary of the factors to consider in selecting a computer case is provided in Chapter 2.

A *system unit* is typically a metal and plastic case that contains the basic parts of the computer system. There are three basic system unit styles: desktops, towers, and portables. Each design offers characteristics that adapt the system for different environments. These characteristics include mounting methods for the printed circuit boards, ventilation characteristics, total drive capacity, footprint (the amount of desk space used), and portability. The desktop and tower design styles are examined in the following sections; portable system units are discussed in Chapter 2.

Desktop Units

The desktop design as shown in Figure 3-2, is one of the more familiar case styles. *Desktop units* are designed to sit horizontally on the desktop. Note that the first IBM computers—the original PC, XT, and AT designs—used this case style. Most modern desktop cases come in two sizes: slim-line and standard.

Figure 3-2 A Desktop Computer Case

The two important considerations in choosing a desktop case style for a computer are as follows:

- **Available desktop space**—Generally, this computer has to share the desktop with the monitor and other peripherals, so space must be allowed. Avoid buying the slim-line, because this design is generally small and intended for business environments. These units have little room for expansion.

- **Form factor**—Cases come in different form factors. As mentioned previously, the form factor simply describes the general layout of the computer case, the positioning of the slots in the case, and the type of motherboard the case can accommodate. The baby AT form factor, which accommodates the baby AT motherboard, has been the most popular for the past few years. However, the newest form factor, and the one most often encountered, is the ATX. It accommodates the ATX motherboard, which has integrated I/O ports, and is designed for easier access to the common components as well as for better airflow. If you are selecting a desktop case, choose the ATX form factor.

Tower Units

Tower units are usually designed to sit vertically on the floor beneath a desk. Some users in the past resorted to standing the desktop cases on their sides under the desk to provide more usable workspace on the desktop. This prompted computer makers today to develop cases that would naturally fit under the desk. In general, tower cases typically have enough bays to hold floppy drives, CD-ROM drives, tape drives, DVD drives, as well as other components. The internal design of a tower system resembles that of the desktop unit. Tower cases come in three sizes: mini-, mid-, and full-size.

NOTE

External devices can be added to mini- and mid-tower computers if there is insufficient room inside the case for an internal device. Typically, these external devices cost slightly more and use external ports.

Mini-towers and mid-towers, as shown in Figure 3-3, are shorter and less expensive than their full-size counterparts, shown in Figure 3-4. There is one major drawback to choosing the smaller towers: There is little additional space for internal add-ons or disk drives, particularly if the mini-tower is chosen.

Many easy-access schemes have been used to allow convenient access to the inside of the system case. Some towers, for example, use removable trays that allow the motherboard and I/O cards to be plugged in before being slid into the unit. Other tower cases use hinged doors on the side of the case, allowing the system and I/O boards to swing away from the chassis. Either of these features facilitates the process of assembling the computer.

Figure 3-3 Mini- and Mid-Tower Units

Finally, note that the ventilation characteristics of some tower units tend to be poor. This is because the I/O cards are mounted horizontally. When the heat generated by the boards rises (see Figure 3-4), it passes through the upper boards, which are then subjected to additional heat. Thus, most tower cases include a secondary case fan to help increase the airflow and dissipate excessive heat.

Figure 3-4 Full-Size Tower Units

Power Supplies

The power supply is one of the most important parts of the computer. The *power supply unit* provides electrical power for every component inside the system unit. In the past, it also supplied alternating current (AC) to the monitor. Some power supply units that can supply AC power can still be found. These units are identified by the existence of two power plugs at the rear.

As mentioned in the previous chapter, the computer power supply plays the critical role of converting electrical power received from a 120V AC, 60-Hz outlet (or 220V AC, 50-Hz outlet outside the United States) into other levels required by the components of the computer. The power supply unit also provides the system's ground.

In both the desktop- and tower-style case, the power supply is a shiny metal box located at the rear of the system unit. The large bundle of cables (red, yellow, black, etc.) provides power to the components of the system unit and its peripherals. Figure 3-5 shows an ATX power supply.

There are two basic types of power supplies:

- **AT**—Designed to support AT-compatible motherboards
- **ATX**—Designed according to newer ATX design specifications to support the ATX motherboard

Figure 3-5 An ATX Computer Power Supply

There are two major distinctions between the legacy AT and the new ATX power supplies. The AT power supply has two 6-pin motherboard power connectors (P8/P9), while ATX power supplies use a single 20-pin power connector (P1). In the ATX-compatible power supply, the cooling fan pulls air through the case from the front and exhausts it out the rear of the power supply unit. Conversely, the AT design pulls air in through the rear of the power supply unit and blows it directly on the AT motherboard.

Table 3-1 summarizes some important factors to consider when shopping for a power supply. Review Chapter 2 for additional information.

TEST TIP

Know the difference between the AT and the ATX power supply.

Table 3-1 Issues to Consider When Selecting a Computer Power Supply

Factor	Rationale
Wattage	To upgrade the PC with more equipment or faster processors, the power supply must provide enough power to the equipment without becoming overloaded.
Form factor	Depending on the type of case and motherboard selected, the power supply must adhere to the same form factor requirements in order to fit inside the case and correctly power the motherboard and other devices.
CPU type	Different CPUs require different voltages. For example, some AMD chips require more power than a Pentium chip.
Expandability	If the power supply only has enough power to supply the current CPU, motherboard, and devices, there might not be enough power to upgrade the system.

continues

Table 3-1 Issues to Consider When Selecting a Computer Power Supply (Continued)

Factor	Rationale
Energy efficiency	Each power supply has an efficiency rating. The higher the rating, the lower the heat generated by the power supply when converting voltage.
Fan type and direction	The power supply must have a high-quality fan. The fan is the primary source for airflow inside the case. Some fans can change direction to allow air to be blown directly on the CPU and to regulate the quality of the air entering the case. Some fans can adjust their speed to match the cooling requirements of the system.
Signals	Modern power supplies can be controlled by the motherboard. The main board can regulate the speed of the fan depending on the temperature inside the case and turn off the fan to save power, and some "smart" power supplies can turn off the computer in the event of a fan failure before the components overheat.
Fault tolerance	For a PC that needs to be on at all times, consider a dual power supply. If one of the units fails, the other one takes over immediately. Some designs enable a power supply to be replaced while the computer is powered on.
Line conditioning	One way to ensure that the DC voltages supplied to the PC are kept at normal levels during spikes or brownouts is to install a power supply that has built-in conditioning. These units ensure that the DC voltages supplied to the system remain stable, even when the AC current coming in is not. (These concerns are addressed in Chapter 11, "Preventive Maintenance.")

Levels of DC Voltage from the Power Supply

The power supply produces four different levels of well-regulated DC voltage (five in the ATX) for use by the system components. These are +5V, −5V, +12V, and −12V. In ATX power supplies, the +3.3V level is also produced and is used by the second-generation Intel Pentium processors. The integrated circuit devices on the motherboard and adapter cards use the +5V level. Table 3-2 summarizes the use of each DC voltage level produced by computer power supplies as well as the power supply form factors where these are produced. The power supply form factor indicates if those listed accommodate the voltage.

Table 3-2 DC Voltages Produced by PC Power Supplies

Voltage	Wire Color	Use	Power Supply Form Factor		
			AT	ATX	ATX v12
+12V	Yellow	Disk drive motors, fans, cooling devices, and the system bus slots	*	*	*
–12V	Blue	Some types of serial port circuits and early PROM (programmable read-only memory) chips	*	*	*
+3.3V	Orange	Most newer CPUs, some types of system memory, and AGP video cards		*	*
+5V	Red	Motherboard, baby AT and earlier CPUs, and many motherboard components	*	*	*
–5V	White	ISA bus cards and early PROMs	*	*	*
0V	Black	Ground—used to complete circuits with the other voltages	*	*	*

* DC voltage level is produced by power supply form factor.

It is important to be able to identify the uses for each voltage level and the corresponding color-coded wire. This allows you to test the wires using a multimeter to determine if there are problems with the power supply. Note that the computer power supply produces a voltage only when it has a load. In other words, some component in the machine must be running before a voltage can be found in the cable connectors that supply power to the internal components.

The voltage levels, mentioned earlier, are available for use through the motherboard's expansion slot connectors. Motherboard power connectors provide the motherboard and the individual expansion slots with up to 1 amp of current each. The power supply delivers power to the motherboard and its expansion slots through the motherboard power connectors. The ATX motherboard connector is a 20-pin (P1) keyed connector. It is keyed so that it cannot be connected incorrectly. Note that the Pentium 4–type connectors are different from the normal ATX connectors (for example, Pentium II

WARNING

Never attempt to repair a defective power supply. Capacitors inside a power supply box store electricity and can discharge through the body if touched. The capacitor holds the electricity even if the unit is turned off and disconnected from a power source. Generally, power supplies are replaced rather than repaired.

connectors). This information is typically contained in the motherboard user's manual or is automatically detected by the onboard BIOS.

Lab Activity 3.3.4   The Computer Case and Power Supply

Identify the type of computer case to be used, the form factor of the unit, and voltage selector switch on the power supply.

Worksheet 3.3.4   Power Supplies

This worksheet provides a review of the power supply and components, including voltage requirements.

Preparing the Motherboard for Installation

This section includes the following topics:

- Motherboard location map
- Motherboard configuration
- Motherboard jumpers
- Installing the CPU
- Installing the heat sink and fan
- Installing RAM

Motherboard Location Map

A *motherboard location map* shows where the major components and hardware are located on the motherboard. A motherboard map can be found in the documentation that comes with the motherboard. Typically, everything listed in the specifications section of the motherboard manual is depicted and labeled on the location map. This map is intended to help define the board layout so that components can be identified and properly installed according to the instructions listed in other sections of the manual. For example, the processor socket location might be labeled Pentium II CPU Slot 1.

The location map also provides additional information that is useful during installation and assembly. For example, as shown in Figure 3-6, the main memory is subdivided into slots, and the slots are identified and numbered in the sequence DIMM1, DIMM2, DIMM3, and DIMM4. This indicates that the DIMMs (dual inline memory modules) must be installed in the sequence indicated on the map. Study the motherboard location map before proceeding with any installation.

Figure 3-6 Motherboard Location Map

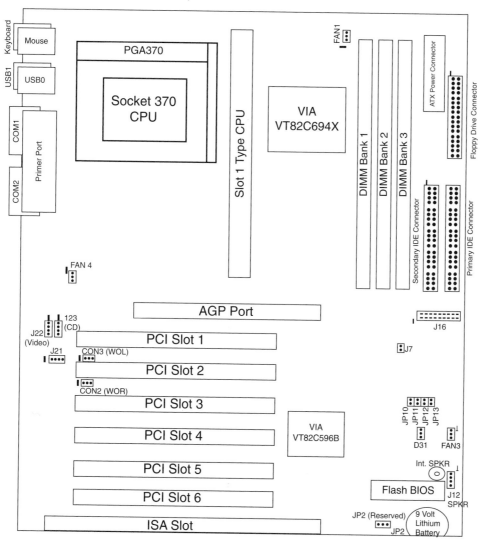

The more familiar you are with a particular motherboard, the easier it is to assemble the rest of the computer. If you are working with a lab partner, study this map with your partner.

Motherboard Configuration

Configuring the motherboard is one of the most important tasks to accomplish when preparing it for the installation of the various components. This process is also known

NOTE

The tiny 1s next to the jumper of three or more pins indicate the position of pin 1 for that jumper.

as *setting the system hardware*. Configuring the motherboard typically involves the following steps:

- Installing the CPU
- Installing the heat sink and fan
- Installing RAM
- Connecting the power supply cables to the motherboard power connectors and connecting miscellaneous connectors to the correct switches and status lights on the case front panel
- Setting the system BIOS

In the sections that follow, installation of the CPU, RAM, and heat sink/fan is discussed. The process for connecting the power supply cables to the motherboard is discussed in "Installing the Motherboard." Finally, instructions for setting the system BIOS are discussed at the end of the chapter in "Booting the System for the First Time."

Configuring the Connectors

Location maps allow the correct configuration of the motherboard for the case controls and monitor lights on the case front panel (sometimes called the *bezel* or *faceplate*). For the disk controllers, remember that a colored stripe on the data cable is pin 1. Most modern connectors are keyed by a missing pin or a blocked connector, so they cannot be fitted the wrong way. Usually, the colored wire(s) in a power cable are positive and the white or black wire(s) are ground or negative. I/O connectors generally follow industry standard conventions. You should review the motherboard manual for more information.

Configuring the BIOS

The *ROM BIOS* and *CMOS* chip contain the software that sets and records the master configuration for all components in the system, including those on the motherboard and the logic chip sets. CMOS stands for complementary metal oxide semiconductor and is pronounced *see'-moss*. The BIOS, or basic input/output system, typically has an interface that can be accessed at boot time after the initial power-on self test (POST) runs. The BIOS also sets up other components, such as the type of hard drive and CD-ROM drive, and the floppy drive settings. The BIOS interface can be keyboard driven, or it can be graphical and mouse driven. As components such as drives are replaced, memory is upgraded, or adapter boards are added, the BIOS setup needs to be updated to reflect the configuration changes and saved to the CMOS chip. The BIOS is discussed more thoroughly later in this chapter.

Configuring the Processor

The motherboard must be configured for the frequency of the installed processor. Table 3-3 shows the jumper settings for each frequency and the corresponding host bus frequency. It also provides examples of how such settings are accomplished. There are similar charts in the manual that comes with the motherboard. These settings differ for each motherboard and processor type. Typically, the motherboard manual details how the CPU and bus frequencies are related. Exercise care to ensure that the CPU being used supports both the bus speed and CPU clock speed. The fact that the motherboard is capable of all these speeds does not imply that the CPU is capable of running all variations that can be configured.

Table 3-3 A Processor Frequency Versus Host Bus Frequency Configuration Chart

Processor Frequency (MHz)	Jumpers J9C1-C	Jumpers J9C1-D	Host Bus Frequency (MHz)
233	5-6	1-2 and 4-5	66
200	5-6	1-2 and 5-6	66
166	5-6	2-3 and 5-6	66
150	4-5	2-3 and 5-6	60
133	5-6	2-3 and 4-5	66
120	4-5	2-3 and 4-5	60
100	5-6	1-2 and 4-5	66
90	4-5	1-2 and 4-5	60

CPU voltage configuration is discussed later in this chapter in the section, "Installing the CPU." In practice, when working on most new systems, motherboard configuration parameters are handled by PnP BIOS. However, it is important to know how to configure these parameters. This enables you to check the BIOS setup and ensure that everything is configured according to manufacturer's specifications.

Motherboard Jumpers

A *jumper* is a pair of prongs that are electrical contact points set into the computer motherboard or an adapter card. When you set a jumper, you place a plug on the prongs that completes, or closes, the contact. Closing or opening the circuits establishes logic levels to select functions for the operation of the board. (Data generally does not travel through these circuits.) Most jumpers relate to the CPU on newer motherboards. Figure 3-7 shows the motherboard, the jumper location, and an example of the plug used to close the contact.

Figure 3-7 Motherboard Jumpers

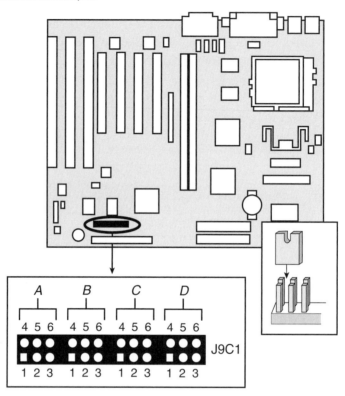

CAUTION

Do not move any of the jumpers with the power on. Always turn off the power and unplug the power cord from the computer before changing jumpers.

Typically, motherboard jumpers are configured by using a jumper to bridge a pair of pins that are to be connected (to complete a circuit) on the board. Removing or inserting jumpers on a set of pins enables or clears a given option, as specified in the motherboard manual. For all settings, it is important to closely follow the instructions found in the motherboard manual. Table 3-4 is a sample of how this information is presented. Remember that the jumper specifications for any board are provided by its manufacturer; the specifications are not necessarily the same as those found in this table.

Additional information regarding motherboard jumpers can be found at the motherboard manufacturer's website.

Table 3-4 Sample Motherboard Jumper Connectors

Function	Jumper	Jumper Number	Configuration
Processor voltage	J6M2	1-2 2-3	Standard voltage VRE (Voltage Regulator Enhanced) (default)
Password	J9C1-A	1-2 2-3	Password enabled (default) Password cleared/disabled
CMOS (NVRAM and ESCD) clear	J9C1-A	4-5 5-6	Keep (default) Clear
BIOS setup access	J9C1-B	1-2 2-3	Access enabled (default) Access denied
Reserved	J9C1-B	4-5 5-6	(Reserved) (Reserved)
Host bus frequency	J9C1-C	Check motherboard manufacturer	
Processor frequency	J9C1-D	Check motherboard manufacturer	
BIOS recovery	J8A1	1-2 2-3	Normal (default) Recovery

Additional Jumpers

Several additional jumper settings might have to be set along with the general motherboard configurations. These are summarized as follows:

- **BIOS recovery**—This jumper is for recovering BIOS data from a floppy disk in the event of a catastrophic failure. Leave this set to the default (normal operation) values. Check the technical product specifications for details.

- **Clear CMOS**—This jumper, when provided, is used to reset the CMOS settings to the default values. This procedure must be done each time the BIOS is updated.

- **Password clear**—Use this jumper, if provided, to clear the password if the password is forgotten. The default setting is usually "password enabled."

- **BIOS setup access**—This jumper enables or disables access to the setup program. The default setting is "access enabled."

- **Processor voltage**—This jumper (or jumpers), when provided, sets the output of the onboard voltage regulator. The two choices are usually standard voltage and Voltage Regulator Enhanced (VRE).

Any jumper pins that need to be removed should be saved with other spare parts. Because jumper pins can be easily lost, it is possible to disable a jumper without removing the pin by connecting the jumper to only one pin. This is known as *parking* the jumper; the procedure disables the jumper while keeping the pin from getting lost.

Installing the CPU

CAUTION

When installing a processor in the motherboard for the first time or when upgrading to a new processor, check the processor's documentation for the correct voltage setting. Operating the processor at the wrong voltage can cause unreliable performance or damage to the system components.

Microprocessor installation is not a complicated process. Most problems occur when the chip is hastily installed or installed backward, causing the chip's pins to break. It is important to handle the microprocessor with extreme care.

There are two main types of CPU interfaces: the socket type (for example, socket 7) and the slot type (for example, slot 1), as shown in Figure 3-8. For more information regarding CPU interfaces, see Chapter 2. Socket 7 has been the standard interface, although newer systems are now using different sockets. Socket 7 is the only interface used by at least one generation of Intel Pentium processors (Pentium I) as well as AMD and Cyrix chips. Older-technology processors, such as the Intel P24T, P24D, 80486DX4, 80486DX2/DX/SX-SL, and 80486DX2/DX/SX; the AMD AM486DX4/DX2/DX; and the Cyrix CX486DX2/DX/S and 5X86 processors attach to the motherboard by means of a specially designed socket, commonly called socket 3. These technologies are quite old, so it is unlikely that you will encounter them.

Slot-type interfaces use a slot similar to an expansion card. Slot 1 is the single edge contact (SEC) interface used only by the Intel Pentium II processor family. SEC is a cartridge containing the CPU and L2 cache chips. Therefore, the installation of the CPU differs depending on the processor being used and the interface type.

This text gives instructions on how to install a socket 7 chip. All the newer socket-type interfaces are derived from socket 7 and differ mainly by the number of pins they have. The latest chips, such as socket A (for AMD Athlon and Duron chips) and socket 370 (for Celeron and some Pentium II and Pentium III chips) are installed using the same basic steps as a socket 7.

Figure 3-8 The Slot 1 and Socket 7 Processors

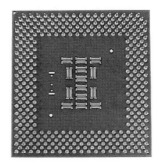

The Step-by-Step Installation of the CPU

Almost all socket 7 systems make use of the *zero-insertion-force (ZIF) socket*. To install a socket 7 or similar chip, follow this general procedure:

Step 1   Turn over the chip and inspect the pins to make sure that none are damaged (bent or broken). All pins should stick straight out.

Step 2   Orient the chip by locating pin 1 on both the chip and the socket. Notice that the chip is always marked at pin 1. The mark might be slightly different for various chips. For example, it might be a slightly notched corner, a small dot on the corner, a small mark at one of the pins under the chip, or more likely, a missing corner pin, as shown in Figure 3-9. On the socket itself, pin 1 is commonly identified by a notch on one corner, a large *1*, or an arrow on the motherboard pointing to that particular corner of the socket. As always, consult the motherboard manual for additional guidance. Align pin 1 on the chip with pin 1 on the socket for a correct installation.

Step 3 Open the ZIF socket. Shift the lever slightly away from the socket, from its default closed, level position, and raise it to the open, vertical position. Do this with care to avoid breaking the lever. If you experience a little resistance when raising the lever, this is normal. When the lever is fully raised, the top part of the ZIF socket slides over slightly.

Step 4 With the socket open, it is time to insert the processor. Aligning pin 1 according to the orientation that was determined in Step 2, insert the processor chip into the socket so that all of the pins slide into the matching holes. With any ZIF socket, the CPU pins should slide easily into the corresponding holes in the socket. Generally, the chip can only go in one way. Avoid forcing the processor into the socket, as the pins can be damaged.

Step 5 Double-check to make sure that there is no gap between the bottom of the CPU chip and the socket. If there is none, the processor chip is properly inserted.

Step 6 To secure the installed chip, simply push the lever gently back down to the closed, level position. A little resistance might be felt, but the lever and ZIF socket should close fairly easily.

Figure 3-9 The Missing Corner Pin on the CPU Chip

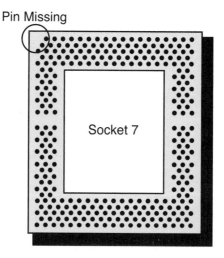

Configuring the CPU Voltage

Most motherboards are flexible enough to handle a variety of CPUs, but most CPUs are particular about the amount of voltage they can handle. Therefore, once you have installed the CPU, make sure that the right voltage is present for the proper performance of the processor. Pentium II and most current CPUs adjust automatically to the voltage, so they do not require voltage configuration. While this has been a great development, the configuration process is still necessary with older CPUs. If the proper voltage is not set, damage to the entire system could occur. With some hands-on experience, voltage configuration for any motherboard can be set. Remember to keep yourself grounded, check the CPU specifications, and follow the motherboard manual.

The information needed for setting voltage should be contained in the "Jumper Settings and Connectors" section of the processor's manual. CPU voltage varies between 1.8V and 3.5V. Dual voltage requirements accompany some CPUs. This means that two separate voltages, a core voltage and an I/O voltage, are required for these CPUs to function, as shown in Table 3-5. The AMD-K6 CPU family, for example, requires dual-voltage power for operation.

Table 3-5 Examples of CPU Dual Voltage Requirements

Operating Voltage (V)	I/O Voltage (V)	Core Voltage (V)
2.2	3.3	2.2
2.9	3.3	2.9
3.2	3.3	3.2

Installing the Heat Sink and Fan

Most of today's microprocessors can produce a lot of heat, which if not efficiently dissipated, can cause the system to operate intermittently or fail. One way to dissipate heat from processors is to use a heat sink and cooling fan. Proper installation is crucial to allow these units to perform effectively. Although the heat sink can be mounted before installing the processor chip on the motherboard, there is a risk of causing damage to the pins on the chip. Only on Pentium II processors is the fan attached before the CPU installation.

Use the following steps when installing a heat sink and fan to socket 7 and other socket-type processors:

Step 1   If the CPU fan did not come with the heat sink already attached (in most cases, it is attached), use the screws that came with the fan to attach the fan to the heat sink.

Step 2   Apply heat sink compound to the surface of the chip. Some setups use heat sink compound or thermal grease. Apply a thin layer, just enough to cover the surface of the chip. The heat sink compound application is sometimes skipped in setups where clips are used to retain the heat sink, but it is still a good idea to use the compound. The heat sink compound or thermal grease improves the contact between the CPU surface and the heat sink, thereby permitting better heat dissipation.

Step 3   Attach the heat sink. Proceed with care at this point. Place the heat sink squarely on top of the processor, and press it down gently. Most of the newer heat sinks use a set of clips on each side to hold them in place. You might need to apply slight force to bend the clips in place. In fact, if the orientation is not right, the clips are quite challenging to bend into the right position. Sometimes it takes a few attempts to get the right orientation. (This is especially true for the new AMD socket A.) In other cases, the heat sink simply wraps around the processor, with the heat sink compound being the only real attachment.

Step 4   Make sure that the heat sink maintains a good contact with the processor chip surface. Usually, when the heat sink is inserted backward, the chip surface and heat sink become staggered. If this happens, remove the heat sink, turn it around, and reattach it.

Step 5   Some heat sink compound or thermal grease might have oozed out the sides of the contact surfaces when you pressed down the heat sink. Wipe off the excess compound.

Step 6   Plug the power cord from the fan into the fan power pins provided on the motherboard, making sure to observe the proper orientation.

Processors that come with the fan and heat sink already attached to them are more convenient. These are called *boxed processors*. These processors cost a bit more but are safer to install because there is less chance of breaking the pins. These installation steps can then be skipped. Boxed processors also have better warranties than those without the fan and heat sink attached. Boxed processors are referred to as *original equipment manufacturer (OEM) processors*.

Installing RAM

Two types of memory modules are used on most PCs: *168-pin dual inline memory module (DIMM) cards* and *72-pin single inline memory module (SIMM) cards*. Figure 3-10 shows both a 168-pin DIMM and a 72-pin SIMM. DIMMs and SIMMs both share common edge connectors and fit into slots on the motherboard called RAM sockets. RAM sockets used for DIMM cards are often called DIMM sockets, while those used for SIMM cards are called SIMM sockets. When the DIMM card or SIMM card is inserted into the slot, each edge connector makes contact with a corresponding gold trace on the motherboard. Each gold line represents an individual data path. Just as the gold lines leading to the CPU make up the processor bus, these gold lines make up the memory bus. The memory bus data "highway" is used to transfer data between the RAM and the CPU. (Bus types are discussed more thoroughly in Chapter 2.) For information relating to memory modules that use other access technologies, see the note at the end of this section.

Figure 3-10 Types of Memory Modules

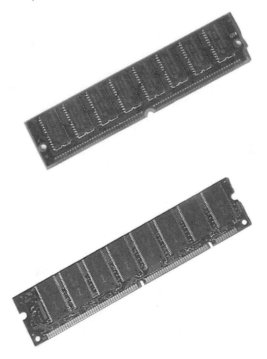

Configuring Memory

The motherboard manual usually shows the permissible combinations of DIMM types that can be installed in the system. New motherboards do not use SIMMs. The DIMM sockets on the motherboard map might be grouped into three or four banks of one slot each. Using the information provided in Figure 3-11, note that DIMM1 and DIMM2 are Bank 0 and Bank 1, and DIMM3 and DIMM4 are Bank 2 and Bank 3. Each bank can have any type of SDRAM (the most commonly used form of RAM).

Figure 3-11 Motherboard Location Map Showing Memory Banks

The memory banks should be filled in the exact combinations shown in the system board manual. For example, the manual might state that the maximum memory size is 512 MB and that the size of each DIMM can be 8 MB, 16 MB, 32 MB, 64 MB, or 128 MB. Any combination of these sizes can be used. Depending on memory needs, there might be four 128-MB DIMMs installed in the memory banks on the motherboard. Or, there might be two 128-MB DIMMs and two 64-MB DIMMs installed. When DIMM sizes are mixed on the motherboard, you must place the DIMM with the largest amount of memory in the first bank. The system automatically reads the size of the first DIMM and records it as the largest. If a smaller DIMM were put in the first bank, the system would read it as the largest and might fail to recognize or use the additional memory capacity of the DIMMs placed in the subsequent banks.

Banking with SIMM modules is slightly different. Each bank of memory for a SIMM has two sockets. You must fill the first bank before moving on to the next. Additionally, each bank must be filled with RAM modules that have the same access time and size.

Step-by-Step Installation of RAM

This procedure describes the installation of DIMMs and SIMMs. The following steps summarize the installation process:

Step 1 Decide on which slots to use, and then orient the SIMM or DIMM chip over it. Both SIMMs and DIMMs are keyed, so they can only be inserted in one way.

Step 2 Insert the DIMM straight into the slot. The SIMM is inserted at an angle of about 45 degrees.

Step 3 The memory module must be locked into place. With a SIMM, rotate it from the angled position to the vertical position. Some resistance is normal; do not force it. If difficulty is encountered, the chip might be inserted backward. Rotate it and try again. When the SIMM is vertical, the small metal or plastic clip should snap into place, securing the SIMM vertically in the memory slot.

With a DIMM, simply close the levers on either side of it. Usually, if the levers do not close, it is because the DIMM is not inserted all the way into the slot or it is installed backward. In most cases, if the DIMM is inserted properly, the levers snap into place without further action.

Step 4 Repeat Steps 1 to 3 for the rest of the memory modules. When finished, be sure that each module is well seated in the slot on both ends.

> **NOTE**
>
> When using other types of memory modules such as RIMMs (Rambus inline memory modules), other constraints must be considered. Unlike DIMMs and SIMMs, RIMMs use only the Rambus direct memory (RDRAM) chips. Some systems require that RIMMs be added in identical pairs, and others allow single RIMMs to be installed. Information on specific memory types can be found in the module manual or the motherboard manual, or at the manufacturers' websites.

Installing the Motherboard

This section discusses the following topics:

- Installing the motherboard into the case
- Attaching the LEDs, keylock, and speaker
- Connecting power supply cables to the motherboard

Installing the Motherboard into the Case

Before installing the motherboard, review the section on motherboards in Chapter 2. Make sure that the board is handled by its edges. When manipulating the board, take care not to bang it or any of the components on it. The following steps summarize the motherboard installation process:

Step 1 Position the case to allow easy access. Then, locate the holes on the motherboard and the corresponding holes on the case. Holding the board just above the case allows you to see the holes on the case and the motherboard for alignment purposes. The expansion card slots give a good indication of how the board should be oriented.

Step 2 Insert the spacers that come with the motherboard securely into the holes on the case (or mounting plate).

Step 3 Install plastic standoffs into the holes on the motherboard that line up with an eyelet (a hole that is very long and key-shaped so that you can slide something into it). Some cases do not have an eyelet and instead use only the metal spacer screws to hold the motherboard in place.

Step 4 Carefully slide the board into the case, making sure that it sits on the spacers and that all the spacers line up with an available hole on the motherboard.

Step 5 Inspect the screws to be used. It is good practice to insert plastic washers on each screw before it is installed. This prevents the metallic screws from overlapping and possibly destroying or shorting any part of the circuitry near the holes.

Step 6 Tighten the board to the case, first by hand, and then finish with a screwdriver. Make sure that the screws are not overtightened. The screws need only be tight enough to prevent the board from moving around in the case.

Step 7 Check your work, and verify the following:

- The back of the motherboard is not touching any part of the case.
- All the slots and connectors line up properly with the holes on the back of case.
- The board is securely held in place.
- When pressed at any point, the board does not bend.

These steps are very general. Some cases have additional features. After becoming familiar with assembling PCs, some of the steps can be combined or bypassed.

Attaching the LEDs, Keylock, and Speaker

NOTE

LED stands for light emitting diodes.

LEDs, the status lights, are useful in indicating whether components inside the computer are on or working. Connecting the LEDs is usually the next step of assembling a computer once the motherboard is securely installed. LEDs that could be installed include those indicating turbo operation, power on, and hard drive activity. Use the following tips when attaching the LEDs:

- **Turbo operation**—Both the turbo LED and turbo switch are now mainly legacy items, and many new computer cases might not include them. If a case does have a turbo LED, it can be connected by simply plugging it into the corresponding pins. This step can be skipped. Sometimes the turbo LED is connected to a different component, such as the SCSI adapter, where it serves as the SCSI drive activity light.

- **Power on**—On older systems, the power LED is combined with the keylock switch as one 5-pin plug. Check the labels on the motherboard for a matching connector. To connect the LEDs, just plug **the connectors** into the corresponding plug on the system board. Make sure that the LEDs are connected separately if the system provides separate plugs for each.

- **Hard drive activity**—This LED is supplied as either a 2-pin or a 4-pin plug. Occasionally, only 2 pins of the 4-pin plug provide the connectivity. Consult the user's manual for installation procedures.

The keylock and speaker are two other wire leads that are usually connected at the same time as the LEDs. They all make up a group of small connectors and plugs that need the same amount of attention to attach them. Attach the keylock switch and PC speaker as follows:

- **Keylock switch**—This switch is common in older systems. It was mainly used to prevent unauthorized individuals from booting the computer and changing the BIOS settings. These switches are rare in newer systems. As previously mentioned, most AT or older systems combine the keylock switch with the power LED as one 5-pin plug. Check the motherboard manual for additional instructions for plugging in the keylock switch.

- **PC speaker**—Most computer cases have the speaker in a 4-wire plug. Plug the speaker wire into the designated plug, making sure that it attaches to pins 1 and 4.

Additional information about connecting LED devices as well as the keylock switch and PC speaker can be found in the user's manual. Because LEDs involve very small connectors, sometimes one or two connections could be wrong. If the wrong connector is used, the LED will not light up when the computer is powered up. Simply turn off the system and readjust or switch the connectors between different plugs until all the LEDs illuminate. LEDs are polarity sensitive, and the connector might have to be reversed if they do not light up properly. Figure 3-12 shows an HP Vectra that has hard drive activity and power LEDs, and a keylock switch.

Figure 3-12 LEDs and a Keylock Switch on an HP Vectra PC

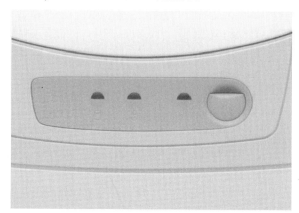

Connecting Power Supply Cables to the Motherboard

After successfully installing the motherboard in the computer case, proceed with attaching the appropriate power supply connector(s) to it. This process is easy with an ATX (boards and power supply) because there is only one connector and it is keyed to fit only one way. Take more care with the older AT systems because there are two separate but physically identical connectors that must be attached in a specific way. This topic is covered in the next section.

Use the following steps to connect the power supply cables to the motherboard:

Step 1   On an AT system, locate the two large wire leads from the power supply; these leads are labeled P8 and P9.

Step 2   Locate the large 12-pin power connector on the motherboard. This connector is usually located directly behind the keyboard connector.

Step 3   Plug the P8 and P9 wire lead connectors into the 12-pin power connector. Caution: Make sure that the black wires are in the middle and adjacent to each other. If this configuration is reversed, the motherboard is likely to be damaged when the power is turned on. You might have to apply pressure to insert the connectors. On an ATX system, there is one large 20-pin (P1) connector. It is keyed for easy installation.

Sometimes, it is helpful to delay attaching the power connector to the motherboard until all the components have been installed. This allows more maneuvering room inside the case.

Lab Activity 3.5.3   Motherboard Installation

This lab prepares you to install a motherboard. In addition, the CPU, the heat sink, and the memory will be installed.

Installing the Floppy Drive, Hard Drive, and CD-ROM Drive

This section includes the following topics:

- Attaching the floppy drive to the case
- Attaching the hard drive and CD-ROM drive to the case
- Connecting the floppy drive, hard drive, and CD-ROM drive to the system
- Connecting power cables to the floppy drive, hard drive, and CD-ROM drive

Attaching the Floppy Drive to the Case

Installing the floppy drive is a fairly simple process. Make sure that the floppy cables and power cables are long enough to reach the drive before starting. Also verify that the drive is mounted right side up. Figure 3-13 shows a floppy drive. Use the following steps to install either a 3-1/2-inch or 5-1/4-inch drive:

Step 1   Select which drive bay is to be used for the floppy drive. Remove the faceplate of that bay, and save the faceplate for future use. You might have both a 3-1/2-inch and a 5-1/4-inch bay available. Be sure to choose the correct bay for the floppy drive that is being attached. To mount a 3-1/2-inch drive into a 5-1/4-inch bay, a special bracket might be needed; this bracket is usually packaged with the new floppy drive.

Step 2   Without connecting anything, insert the drive into the chosen bay, making sure it fits properly.

Step 3   Select the proper size screws (preferably those that came with the drive). If using brackets to hold the drive in place, secure them now, or simply use the screws to attach the drive to the bay. First, tighten the screws by hand, and then use a screwdriver to secure the screws. Make sure that they are not too tight, and take care not to cross thread or strip the screws.

Step 4   Attach the power and ribbon cable to the drive. If other drives are to be installed, this step can be skipped. This provides more maneuvering room in the case, especially if there are no removable drive bays. The drive cable and power cord can then be connected after all the drives have been installed.

Step 5   Check your work.

Figure 3-13 A Floppy Disk Drive

 CD Activity   Installing the Floppy Drive, Hard Drive, and CD-ROM Drive

The video on the accompanying CD, "Installing the Floppy Drive, Hard Drive, and CD-ROM Drive," provides detailed steps for this installation process.

Attaching the Hard Drive and CD-ROM Drive to the Case

Attaching the hard drive and CD-ROM drive are basically similar. This section shows how to attach both to the case.

Before proceeding, make sure that the interface cable can reach the drive in its intended location. With IDE/ATA drives, the length of the cable is limited to 18 inches, and less in some cases. Also, make sure that the power cable reaches the drive from the power supply. Do not mount the drive upside down or backward. Verify that the label of the drive is up and that the circuit board is down.

The first step in attaching the drive is setting the jumpers. The video on the accompanying CD, "Installing the Floppy Drive, Hard Drive, and CD-ROM Drive," details the steps for this process.

TEST TIP

Know what makes a floppy drive designated as A or B, and understand how to set up the drives to function as either master or slave.

Master/Slave Jumper Settings

The designation of a hard drive or CD-ROM drive as either master or slave is generally determined by the jumper configuration, not by the order in which one drive is daisy-chained to the other. The only exception is if the drive is jumpered (set to) "cable select" and both the system and ribbon cable support cable select. In this case, master and slave are determined by the position on the data ribbon cable. Depending on how the system controls the cable, the select line on the ribbon cable determines where the master and slave need to be attached. Refer to the system manual for more information. This description applies only to the case where both drives are attached to the same IDE channel (that is, where the CD-ROM drive is set to slave). For better performance, always attach the drives to separate channels—the hard drive to the primary

IDE channel as primary master and the CD-ROM to the second IDE channel as secondary master.

It is much easier to configure these drives before installing them in the computer case. Installing them first might leave little room to set the jumpers. Before setting the jumpers, determine the types and number of drives to install. It is assumed here that there are two IDE drives, one hard drive, and one CD-ROM drive. The jumper settings are often printed on top of the drive itself. If this is not the case, consult the manual. In either case, use needle-nosed pliers or tweezers to set the jumpers. Always save spare jumpers for future use by hanging them on one pin.

NOTE

Hanging the jumper on one pin means the same as *not jumpered*—that is, no circuit configuration has been selected. This is also known as parking a jumper. Figure 3-14 illustrates some typical jumper settings on an IDE drive.

Figure 3-14 Jumper Settings on an IDE Drive

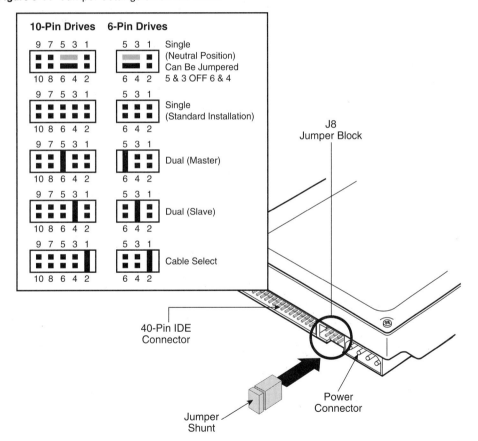

In a basic system that only has one hard drive, set the jumper to master. Some drives have another setting called *single*. This setting essentially tells the drive that it is alone on that IDE channel and works the same as the master. You should use this setting, if available, on a one-hard-drive system. The CD-ROM drive is similarly easy to configure. However, jumpers might be located in different places on each drive and might even be labeled differently. Set the CD-ROM to master if it is the only drive connected to the second IDE channel.

Attaching the Hard Drive

Technically, the hard drive can be inserted in any free bay in a computer case. However, consider the following items:

- Hard drives, especially the newer 7200- and 10,000-rpm units, can generate a lot of heat. Therefore, keep these drives as far away from other hardware as possible.
- If you need to install a drive cooler, make sure there is enough room.
- Install a hard drive away from the power supply. Poorly designed cases might provide room under the power supply to install the hard drive, but this is not a good location. Power supplies act like magnets and can damage data.
- Try to keep the hard drive near the front of the case. It then benefits from the cooling effect of the air drawn into the case through the front by the system cooling fans.

With the previous considerations in mind, use the following steps when mounting a hard drive:

Step 1 Set the hard drive jumper to master, as previously explained.

Step 2 Slide the drive into the selected drive rail of the case. Recall that you do not have to remove the faceplate in this area. Modern (ATX) cases usually provide a hard drive bay without a faceplate. If the drive is smaller than the bay, you might have to add rails or a mounting bracket to make the drive fit.

Step 3 Select the proper size screws (preferably those packaged with the drive). Screw the drive into place, making sure not to force anything. Hand tighten the screws first, and then tighten them with a screwdriver.

Step 4 Attach the ribbon cable and the power cord to the hard drive, as you did with the floppy drive. Normally, the ribbon cable goes from the primary controller of the motherboard to the drive.

The details of how to make these connections are explained later in this chapter.

Attaching the CD-ROM Drive

Installing the CD-ROM drive is similar to installing the hard drive. Remove the drive bay cover first. Then, set the CD-ROM drive jumper to master because it is to be connected to the secondary IDE channel. Now slide the drive into the bay from the front, making sure that it is flush with the front panel, and screw the drive in place.

In some computer cases, particularly the mini-towers, it can be challenging to work behind the CD-ROM drive because of its length and because it is obstructed by the power supply.

NOTE

Do not tighten the screws until the cables have been connected to the drive.

Role of the Drive Rails

As with the hard drive, the installation of the CD-ROM drive depends on the case design or type. Some cases come with drive rails to help install the hardware. Simply screw a drive rail in the correct direction to each side of the CD-ROM drive. Then, slide the CD-ROM drive into the case from the front, using the rails as a guide, until it snaps into place. Drive rails make hardware installations relatively easy.

Connecting the Floppy Drive, Hard Drive, and CD-ROM Drive to the System

The floppy drive, hard drive, and CD-ROM drive communicate with the rest of the system using ribbon cables. This section discusses the types of ribbon cables used as well as how to connect them to the various drives.

Characterizing Ribbon Cables

Ribbon cables are widely used to internally connect peripherals such as floppy drives and hard drives. These cables are rarely used outside of the system case. They are thin, flat, multiconductor cables that must be connected correctly for the component to work.

Floppy Drive Cable

The floppy drive exchanges data with the motherboard devices, including the microprocessor, via a 34-pin flat ribbon (data) cable. The ribbon cable typically connects from a 34-pin male connector at the rear of the floppy drive to a 34-pin male connector on the motherboard. The cable plugs, drive connector, and floppy controller interface are all keyed, beginning at pin 1, for proper alignment. Usually, a red stripe on the edge of the cable identifies pin 1. Figure 3-15 shows a floppy drive cable.

Figure 3-15 Pin 1 Ribbon Cable Identification

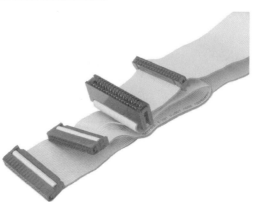

Aligning the red-stripe edge with pin 1 of the drive connector or drive controller interface assures a correct connection.

Current system BIOS versions can support up to two floppy drives on one controller via a daisy-chain cable arrangement. Cable pin-outs 10 through 16 are cross-wired between the middle drive connector and end drive connector, producing a twist that reverses the drive select (DS) configuration of the drive that is plugged into the end connector of the ribbon cable. The twist consists of seven data wires. This feature, called *cable select*, automatically configures the drive on the middle connector as drive B and the drive on the end connector as drive A. This greatly simplifies installation and configuration of the floppy drives. In this example, only one 3-1/2-inch floppy (drive A) is being used.

Hard Drive and CD-ROM Drive Cables

The hard drive and CD-ROM drive, just like the floppy drive, exchange data signals with the controller on the motherboard by means of a flat ribbon cable. The ribbon cable pin-outs and cable width depend on the type of interface. In this text, the IDE interface is used. The ribbon cable used in this case looks similar to the floppy cable previously mentioned, but the ribbon cable is wider, as shown in Figure 3-16. Pin 1 is also identified by a red edge. However, an IDE cable typically has 40 pins; it can also have two devices attached to it (like the floppy cable). In this case, however, one device must be set as the master and the other as the slave using jumpers. A second cable is called IDE 2, and it can have a master and a slave. The cable connectors and plugs, just like the floppy cable, are keyed for proper alignment.

Figure 3-16 Hard Drive Ribbon Cable

After you become familiar with ribbon cables, the floppy drive, hard drive, and CD-ROM drive, you can then connect these components to the system board.

Connecting the Floppy Drive

The following steps detail how to connect the floppy drive to the motherboard:

Step 1 Identify the appropriate ribbon cable that goes with the floppy drive. It has a seven-wire twist toward one end and is smaller in width (with 34 pins) to the 40-pin IDE ribbon cable.

Step 2 Identify pin 1, the red edge of the cable, and align this with pin 1 on the rear of the floppy drive. Gently push on the cable connector until it is fully inserted. In most cases, the connectors are keyed. If any resistance is experienced as the cable is attached, recheck the pin 1 alignment. Since this drive is being installed as drive A, be sure to use the connector that is past the twist in the cable.

Step 3 Identify the floppy controller on the system board. Consult the motherboard manual to determine this. Attach the connector on the far end of the ribbon cable to the floppy controller on the board, making sure that pin 1 is properly aligned for the cable and controller interface connectors.

Step 4 Check your work, making sure that no pin is bent or displaced.

If pin 1 has accidentally been reversed (not damaged), the drive will not work and the drive LED will stay on until the problem is corrected.

Connecting the Hard Drive and CD-ROM Drive

The following steps detail how to connect the hard drive and CD-ROM drive to the motherboard:

Step 1   Identify the two 40-pin IDE ribbon cables that go with the hard drive and CD-ROM. These are wider than the floppy cable and have no twist at one end.

Step 2   Attach one end of one cable connector to the rear of the hard drive connector, and one end of the second cable to the rear of the CD-ROM drive. You might need to slide the CD-ROM drive out a few inches to have enough access at the rear. Both cable connectors are keyed. Make sure that pin 1 is properly aligned for the cable and drive connectors. The end of the cable with the longer span is usually connected to the motherboard.

Step 3   Attach the free end of the hard drive cable to IDE controller 1, the primary IDE, on the motherboard. Attach the free end of the CD-ROM drive cable to IDE controller 2, the secondary IDE, on the motherboard. Make sure that pin 1 on each cable is aligned with pin 1 of the corresponding controller interface. Installing the hard drive and CD-ROM drive on separate IDE channels might improve performance.

Step 4   Check your work, making sure that all cable connectors are properly seated, no pins are displaced, and all pin 1s are aligned.

If the hard drive cable is attached backward, you might get error messages that make the new drive appear to be defective. If this happens, remove the hard drive cable and reinstall it.

NOTE

Pin 1 on both the hard drive and CD-ROM drive is usually located on the side closest to the power connector. Pin 1 might be labeled on the back of the hard drive. Conversely, pin 1 on the motherboard might not be properly labeled, so consult your manual to make this determination. The CD-ROM drive audio cable can remain disconnected until a sound card is installed.

Connecting Power Cables to the Floppy Drive, Hard Drive, and CD-ROM Drive

Small cable drive connectors from the power supply provide power to the floppy drive, hard drive, and CD-ROM drive. The cable connectors have a female 4-pin plug that connects to a male 4-pin connector at the rear of each drive. The pin-outs or wire scheme is color coded to identify the proper voltages of the wires.

Power Voltage Requirements

Two different power voltages are required for the proper functioning of these drives. The circuit board and the logic chips that each drive uses are designed to use +5V power. The drive motors use +12V power (see Table 3-6).

Table 3-6 Power Connector Pin-Outs

Pin No.	Signal	Wire Color
1	+5v	Red
2	Ground	Black
3	Ground	Black
4	+12v	Yellow

Connecting the Drives

Attaching the power cables to the floppy drive, hard drive, and CD-ROM drive is simple because all the connectors are keyed and therefore can only be inserted one way. The connectors should go on easily and not need to be forced. Verify that the proper connector is going to the appropriate drive as follows:

- **Floppy drive**—Identify the proper connector that goes with the 3-1/2-inch drive. These connectors are usually the smallest plugs coming out of the power supply. Push the plugs in gently. Do not rock them back and forth to secure a connection.

- **Hard drive and CD-ROM drive**—Identify the proper power connectors for these drives. These connectors are larger than those for the floppy; sometimes these power plugs are labeled P1, P2, P3, and so on. These connectors are harder to assemble, so rock them gently back and forth if needed until they snap into place.

As always, check all your work, making sure that all power plugs are properly inserted and secure.

Lab Activity 3.6.4 Floppy Drive, Hard Drive, and CD-ROM Installation

This lab prepares you to install the floppy drive, hard drive, CD-ROM drive and to attach the appropriate cables.

Video Card Installation

This section addresses the installation of the video card. The video card, as shown in Figure 3-17, is the only expansion card that needs to be installed before booting the PC for the first time. It is critical in displaying vital information needed to configure the BIOS during the initial boot process. All other cards can be installed after the computer is up and running. To learn more about the video adapter, review the relevant section in Chapter 2.

Figure 3-17 A Video Card

Install the video card using the following steps:

CAUTION

Some motherboards have built-in video. If this is the case, the video must be disabled in the CMOS to install an external video card. Built-in video that is not disabled causes a system conflict that must be resolved before the new external video card can be recognized.

Step 1   Locate an expansion slot type that matches the video card. AGP is used for newer (ATX) motherboards, whereas ISA and PCI are used for older boards.

Step 2   Remove the slot insert that corresponds to the appropriate slot on the motherboard. Some cases have punch-out inserts, whereas others have inserts that are screwed in.

Step 3   Insert the video card into the slot by aligning the pins and gently applying pressure alternately to the front and back of the board until all the pins are in place. Older ISA cards might be more difficult to insert because of their length. When pushing the card into the slot, try not to let the motherboard bend. It might be necessary to place one hand underneath to push up the board if it bends. Make sure that you are properly grounded to the case.

Step 4   When the card is in place, secure it to the case with a screw. Remember to check your work.

These general steps can also be used to install other expansion cards, such as a modem card and sound card.

If the video card is a Plug and Play type, the system will detect the new hardware and install the proper driver. If the proper driver is not detected, you should use the driver that came with the video card. Current drivers can also be downloaded from the video card manufacturer's website.

Final Steps

This section addresses the following topics:

- Fitting the case together
- Connecting the keyboard, mouse, monitor, and power cord

Fitting the Case Together

After all the components have been installed in the case, it is time to complete the PC assembly process. First, check the cable connectors. Check to make sure that all the pin-1 indicators on the cables match up with the pin-1 indicators on the sockets. Next, make sure that all the connections are snug. If a connection does not look correct, push on it gently to seat it. Do not force a connection, because the pins and circuit boards bend and break easily. No connection should be too difficult to attach. If it is, there is probably something wrong.

After all the cables are secure, make sure that all the screws are properly tightened. These screws should be secure, but not overly tight. Finally, when securing the case, make sure that no cables or wires are sticking out or are caught between the parts of the case.

All the extras, such as the sound card, modem card, and so on, can be installed later, after the initial bootup. This ensures that the basic computer is working properly before you add new hardware. Take extra time to check all work before turning on the power for the first time. The following list is a post-assembly checklist that should be used before closing the case. Make sure that everything included in the list is complete and properly done:

- ❑ All expansion cards are fully inserted in the appropriate slots.
- ❑ The CPU fan is attached to power.
- ❑ The 110/220-volt switch is properly configured.

❑ The drives are properly connected to power.

❑ The ribbon cables are attached correctly.

❑ No wires are protruding into the fans.

❑ The CPU voltage settings are correctly configured.

❑ The power switch is off and the power supply connectors are properly attached to the motherboard.

❑ All connections are sufficiently tight.

❑ All pins are properly aligned.

Close the newly assembled case before testing the computer to avoid accidental contact with the internal parts while the machine is running, since there is no grounding at this point. This situation can be hazardous for both the installer and the computer, as discussed earlier in this chapter.

Connecting the Keyboard, Mouse, Monitor, and Power Cord

The last step before turning on the power is to connect the basic input and output (I/O) devices that the computer needs to start up. These devices can be connected in any order. The following list includes instructions for connecting these devices:

■ **Connect the keyboard to the back of the case**—Older-model motherboards use a 5-pin connector, but most computers use a 6-pin PS/2 port. Sometimes, the keyboard connector and port are color coded (violet) to distinguish them from the mouse.

■ **Connect the mouse to the back of the computer**—If you are using a PS/2 mouse, its connection is usually right next to the keyboard connection. Follow any color codes (usually green) where applicable. If you have a serial mouse, plug it into the serial port. Some motherboards number the ports, and because the mouse is the first serial device in the system, plug it into serial port 1.

■ **Connect the monitor**—If the motherboard has video capabilities, the connection point is near the mouse and keyboard connections. If the motherboard has a video adapter card, plug the monitor into the connector located on that card. Because the connector is large, it normally has two screws that hold it in place. Turn in the screws until the connection is secure.

■ **Connect the main power supply**—Plug the AC power cord into the back of the power supply, and plug the other end into a wall socket. If there is a switch on the power supply, turn it on as well. This usually does not power the computer; it is just the master power switch for the power supply.

The computer is normally started using the power switch on the front of the case. The computer can now be turned on.

Booting the System for the First Time

This section addresses the following topics:

- What is BIOS?
- Entering the BIOS configuration.
- The standard CMOS setup screen.
- BIOS Features and Chipset Features setup screens.
- Power Management and Plug and Play screens.
- Integrated Peripherals and Fixed-Disk Detection screens.
- Password screens and the Load Setup Defaults screen.
- BIOS exit options.
- The startup sequence: POST errors and troubleshooting.

What Is BIOS?

BIOS stands for *basic input/output system*. The BIOS contains the program code required to control all the basic operating components of the computer system. In other words, the BIOS contains the software required to test the hardware at bootup, load the operating system, and support the transfer of data between hardware components. In this section and those that follow, the crucial role of the system BIOS is covered as it pertains to the proper functioning of a newly assembled computer. The technique for using the BIOS to configure the computer when booted for the first time is also covered.

The final step in the configuration of a new computer is the BIOS setup. Enter the BIOS setup during the boot process by following the on-screen instructions. Pressing F2, for example, accesses some versions of BIOS. Figure 3-18 shows the system entering setup after pressing F2.

The *BIOS setup* allows you to customize the computer to function optimally based on the included hardware and software profiles. The BIOS code is typically embedded in ROM (a read-only memory chip) on the motherboard, which is discussed in Chapter 2. Because the ROM chip is read-only, it cannot normally be changed. This protects the ROM from disk, RAM, or power failures that could corrupt it. Additionally, this feature ensures that the BIOS code is always available because it is required for the system to boot.

Figure 3-18 Entering the BIOS Setup

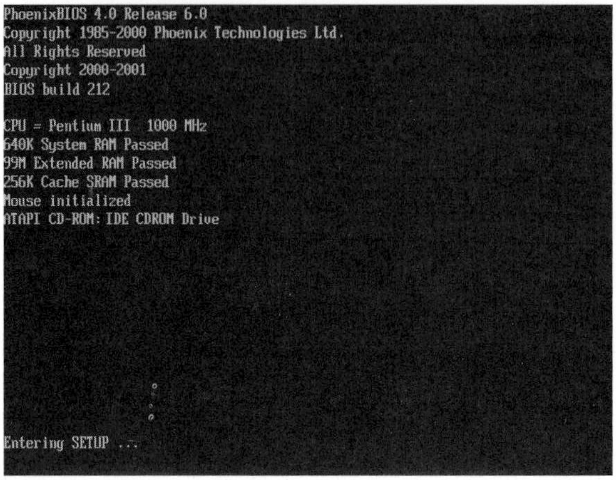

```
PhoenixBIOS 4.0 Release 6.0
Copyright 1985-2000 Phoenix Technologies Ltd.
All Rights Reserved
Copyright 2000-2001
BIOS build 212

CPU = Pentium III  1000 MHz
640K System RAM Passed
99M Extended RAM Passed
256K Cache SRAM Passed
Mouse initialized
ATAPI CD-ROM: IDE CDROM Drive




Entering SETUP ...
```

Although the BIOS cannot be changed while loaded in memory, the basic BIOS program can be updated. Newer BIOS ROM chips are of a type called *electrically erasable programmable read-only memory (EEPROM)*, also called *Flash BIOS*. Flash BIOS allows an upgrade of the BIOS software from a floppy disk provided by the manufacturer without replacing the chip. BIOS upgrades are typically used by manufacturers to fix flaws in the BIOS code, called *bugs*, and to improve system capabilities.

Evolution of the BIOS

The basic design standard of the system BIOS was originally developed by IBM Corporation for use in its XT and AT computer systems in the early 1980s. Unfortunately, the IBM BIOS only worked with IBM hardware. Therefore, other manufacturers who built clones of these systems had to guarantee compatibility of their computers with the IBM standard. By the late 1980s, a few companies had successfully developed compatible BIOSs that other manufacturers could use. The following companies have since come to dominate the BIOS market:

- Phoenix Technologies, Ltd. (Phoenix)
- American Megatrends, Inc. (AMI)
- Award Software, Inc. (Award)

NOTE

Award is now a division of Phoenix Technologies, Ltd.

Of the three manufacturers, Phoenix now concentrates primarily in the specialized laptop computer market, while AMI and Award are the chief suppliers to the modern non-IBM computer market.

The BIOS Function

The BIOS function is not complex. It initially runs basic device test programs and then seeks to configure these devices. The system BIOS and the information required to configure it are stored on a *complementary metal-oxide semiconductor (CMOS) chip*. CMOS is a battery-powered storage chip that is located on the system board. The CMOS chip has rewritable memory, since the configuration data can be changed or updated as the components or devices in the computer are changed. In essence, the CMOS allows the BIOS upgrade.

Configuration of the BIOS on a computer is called the *BIOS setup*. It is also called the *CMOS setup*, named for the chip that stores the BIOS settings. It is especially important to get the BIOS setup right the first time. Because the BIOS scans the system at boot time and compares what it finds against the settings in CMOS, the BIOS must be properly configured to avoid errors. Proper operation of the system depends on the BIOS loading the correct program code for its devices and internal components. Without the correct code and device drivers, the system either does not boot properly or works inconsistently with frequent errors.

If a system *crashes*, or fails unexpectedly, it can be restarted thanks to the BIOS. Built into the BIOS is a comprehensive self-diagnostic routine called the *power-on self-test (POST)*, which checks the internal system circuits at bootup and gives error codes. (The POST is discussed more thoroughly in Chapter 2.) After the initial circuit checks, the BIOS also checks the internal components against a known list of operating devices stored in the CMOS chip. Any problems are indicated using error codes or messages. These error messages help in diagnosing and repairing the problem. In order for the BIOS to have meaningful diagnostics and error checking, the internal components and devices of a newly assembled computer need to be properly configured in the CMOS.

Worksheet 3.9.1   What Is BIOS?

This worksheet provides a review of BIOS, including what it is and how it works.

Entering the BIOS Configuration

When setting up the computer for the first time, you must run the CMOS configuration setup utility. As mentioned in the previous section, the computer checks the CMOS to determine what types of options are installed in the system. The system's BIOS allows access to this configuration information through its CMOS setup utility. (Recall that the CMOS refers to the type of integrated circuit that is used to store the BIOS configuration.)

Simply pressing Delete during the boot sequence provides access to the BIOS on some computers. But in general, early in the startup process, the BIOS places a prompt on the display to tell the user what special key, or combination of keys, can be pressed to give access to the CMOS setup utility. Typical keys and key combinations include Esc, Del, F2, and Ctrl+Alt+Esc. Note that the keys, or key combinations, used to access the setup menus might vary from one BIOS manufacturer to another, and from one BIOS version to another.

Press the proper key or key combinations within a predetermined time to access the setup utility. If the keys are not pressed within that time, the BIOS continues the bootup process, possibly with undesirable results. The key commands stop the bootup routine and display the main menu screen of the setup utility, as shown in Figure 3-19.

NOTE

The main menu on a given computer might be different from the one shown in Figure 3-19, depending on which BIOS and version are being used.

Figure 3-19 The BIOS Main Menu

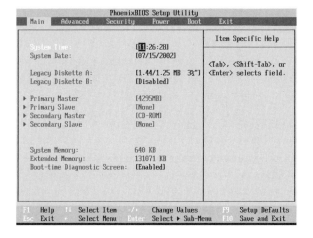

The values input through the BIOS setup are stored in the system's CMOS configuration registers. These registers are examined each time the system is booted in the future to tell the computer what types of devices are installed.

The Standard CMOS Setup Screen

The instructions regarding choices in the CMOS setup screen can be found in the corresponding section of the motherboard manual. A typical configuration setup screen is shown in Figure 3-20. Through this screen, the desired configuration values can be entered into the CMOS registers. The cursor on the screen can be moved from item to item using the keyboard's cursor control keys. The standard CMOS setup screen includes the basic operating parameters that need to be set for the system to work correctly. These BIOS features are typically universal for all PCs.

Figure 3-20 A Standard CMOS Setup Screen

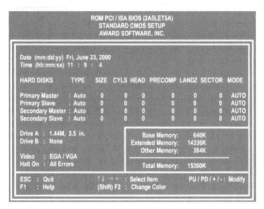

The fields available for entering configuration data that are commonly found in this screen are Date and Time, Hard Disks, Drive A, Drive B, Video, and Halt On. Each of these items is described as follows:

- **Date and Time**—These two fields are used for setting the clock that governs the settings in the operating system. The date and time are required for many types of software applications to manage data. The format required is very important. For the initial system setup, a default date is usually assigned (for example, January 1, 1980). The time is given in the 24-hour format, often referred to as military time.

- **Hard Disks**—This section contains fields that identify devices that are attached to the two IDE controllers integrated on the motherboard. IDE controllers can have up to two hard drives, or one hard drive and another IDE device such as a CD-ROM drive. Normally, one is configured as a master and the other as a slave. There can be four configuration entries: Primary Master, Primary Slave, Secondary Master, and Secondary Slave. You should normally set the drive type to Auto. This allows the BIOS to auto-detect and configure the hard drives so that this information does not have to be entered manually.

- **Drive A and Drive B**—This section identifies the types of floppy disk drives using the options available. In this instance, there is only one drive, a 3-1/2-inch, high-density, 1.44-MB floppy drive. There are no options for Drive B because a second drive was not installed.

- **Video**—This section identifies the video adapter. The choices here are very few; the default EGA/VGA has been the standard since 1990. Whether VGA, SVGA, or anything more advanced, all video adapters since 1990 support the basic VGA BIOS instructions built into the system BIOS.
- **Halt On**—This is the last user-definable field in the standard CMOS screen. The choices here allow a specific system response to errors, so that error problems can be reported before they corrupt data.

In addition, the information box in the lower-right corner of the screen has non-user-definable screens that give information about the total memory configuration of a system.

BIOS Features and Chipset Features Setup Screens

The BIOS Features setup screen, as shown in Figure 3-21, provides advanced features that control the behavior of the system. This setup screen is where the system hardware can be fine-tuned for optimal performance. The disable/enable features for advanced troubleshooting can also be used. Unless there is a good reason to change them, most of the features should be left at their default settings.

Figure 3-21 The BIOS Features Setup Screen

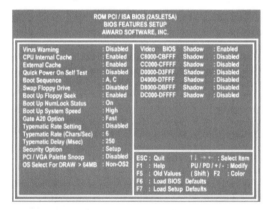

One important setup option on the BIOS features screen allows the system boot order to be specified. For example, on newer systems it is preferable to boot from the hard drive or CD-ROM drive rather than from the floppy drive, as older systems did. Table 3-7 summarizes the various boot sequence configuration options that are available.

Table 3-7 Boot Sequence Configuration Options

Boot Sequence	Description
A, C	System first searches for a master boot record on the floppy disk drive and then the hard drive.
C, A	System first searches for a master boot record on the hard disk drive and then the floppy disk drive.
C, CD-ROM, A	System first searches for a master boot record on the hard disk drive, then the CD-ROM drive, and finally the floppy disk drive.
CD-ROM, C, A	System first searches for a master boot record on the CD-ROM drive, then the hard drive, and finally the floppy disk drive.

Chipset Features Setup

Every chipset variation has a specific BIOS designed for it. Therefore, there are functions specific to the design of system boards using that chipset. The Chipset Features setup screen, as shown in Figure 3-22, allows the fine-tuning of the control parameters for the main system chipset. Recall from Chapter 2 that the chipset controls the memory, system cache, processor, and I/O buses. Because of the potentially disabling nature of these settings, the first feature set choice is Automatic Configuration, with the default set to Enabled. The default should be left at Enabled unless there is a good reason to disable automatic configuration. The remaining features (System BIOS Cacheable, Video BIOS cacheable, Memory Hole at 15m-16m, and Peer Concurrency) are not automatically configurable. BIOS and chipset features setup are covered in future labs.

Figure 3-22 The Chipset Features Setup Screen

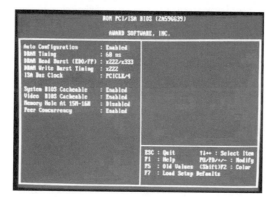

Power Management and Plug and Play Screens

As with other setup screens, the instructions governing choices in this environment can be found in the corresponding section of the motherboard manual. Use the feature settings found in the Power Management setup screen, as shown in Figure 3-23, to control the computer's optional power management for devices. These features can be enabled to control devices going into sleep or suspend mode. However, some software applications and operating systems might not deal well with components being powered down, as the software might no longer recognize such devices properly. If this is the case, the power management feature can be disabled.

Figure 3-23 The Power Management Setup Screen

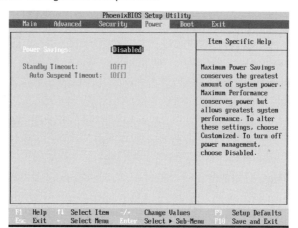

Plug and Play/PCI Configuration Setup

The Plug and Play (PnP) and the Peripheral Component Interconnect (PCI) configuration screen contains the feature settings used to control the system I/O bus, and IRQ and DMA allocation for ISA and PCI PnP devices, as shown in Figure 3-24. For PnP to work, the device/adapter to be installed, the BIOS, and the operating system must all support PnP.

One feature of particular importance in this section is the Resource Controlled By setting. When set by default to Automatic Configuration, the BIOS automatically manages the interrupts and direct memory access channels on the I/O bus for the PnP devices to avoid conflicts with any legacy (non-PnP) ISA devices. Note that IRQs or DMA must sometimes be manually designated for some nonconforming PnP expansion boards or adapter cards. In such cases, such designated resources must be removed from BIOS handling.

Figure 3-24 The PnP/PCI Configuration Screen

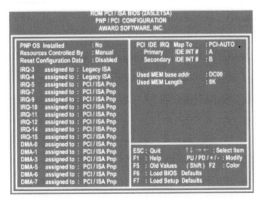

In general, the default settings should be used for this section of the BIOS setup when working on newer systems, because any manual configurations require a good knowledge of the bus devices installed. If any conflicts occur, be aware that the Reset Configuration Data feature clears this portion of the BIOS setup and returns it to defaults upon rebooting the system. Additionally, consult the system board manual before making any changes here.

Integrated Peripherals and Fixed-Disk Detection Screens

The features found in this section of the BIOS setup are used to configure the control of integrated peripheral support on the motherboard. Integrated peripherals typically include devices such as the onboard floppy and hard drive controllers, USB controller, serial ports, parallel ports, and sound card chip. An example of the Integrated Peripherals configuration screen is shown in Figure 3-25. Setting these features to Auto, when applicable, permits the BIOS to issue, for example, the appropriate IDE drive commands to determine what mode the hard drives support. This is always a recommended option. The USB controller feature is simply for enabling or disabling the controller chip for the USB ports on the motherboard.

Fixed-Disk Detection

From the standard CMOS setup screen discussed earlier, recall the "Hard Disks" feature, which had an Auto setting for automatically detecting the hard drive's geometry (number of heads, cylinders, sectors, etc.). At times, this feature does not work with certain IDE hard drives. IDE HDD auto-detection is used for such situations. It allows you to manually run the IDE auto-detection program and select the auto-detection for each drive on the controller channel. The BIOS then scans and reports drive parameters that can be accepted or rejected. Any drive parameters that are accepted are then entered into the standard CMOS setup.

Figure 3-25 The Integrated Peripherals Configuration Screen

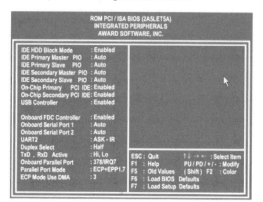

As usual, the "Reset Configuration Data" feature is an escape mode for resetting this section to defaults and returning to the last known good configuration during reboot. Instructions for configuring each feature are included in the manual that comes with the motherboard.

Password Screens and the Load Setup Defaults Screen

Passwords add security to a network system. The system administrator sets passwords for users and for the supervisor to manage the system. Figure 3-26 shows the two password screens that will be encountered in the BIOS setup:

- **User Password**—This option allows the installation of a password that must be entered before the system can boot. The option also prevents access to the BIOS, eliminating the possibility of others changing the BIOS setup on the computer. This option is particularly useful when booting up the computer for the first time. You should follow the on-screen and password instructions in the motherboard user's manual.

- **Supervisor Password**—This feature is normally found only in large institutions (corporations, school districts, etc.), where BIOS settings are standardized by computer support personnel. Once set, these BIOS setups are locked with a master password known only to the network administrator or an administrator designee. The instructions for this option can also be found in the motherboard manual.

Figure 3-26 AMIBIOS Security Options

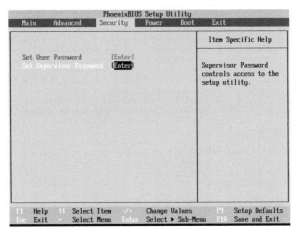

If no password is required but this screen is accidentally engaged, complete the following actions to move to the next screen:

- When prompted for a password, press Enter without entering a password.
- At the second screen labeled Password Disabled, press any key to return to the main setup screen.

Load Setup Defaults Screen

The Load Setup Defaults screen resets the BIOS setup to default settings. This feature does not affect those settings in the standard CMOS setup screen, because the defaults are the minimums required for the system to function. If you are configuring the system for the first time and you encounter problems, this method can be used to restore the system to its default settings.

Additional information regarding this feature can be found in the motherboard manual.

BIOS Exit Options

In addition to exiting BIOS, options are provided to save or discard any changes and to continue to work in the utility. Another option on the exit screen is Load System Defaults. System defaults allow the BIOS to return to the basic settings originally set by the manufacturer.

The BIOS exit options are as follows:

- **Exit Without Saving Setup**—This setup screen is used to exit the BIOS setup program without saving any modified settings made to the system.

- **Save & Exit Setup**—Use this option to exit the BIOS setup program and save your changes to the CMOS chip. Although there are shortcuts for doing this, always use this exit feature to avoid accidental loss of the setup modification entries.

When exiting and saving settings, the computer restarts according to the new configuration. The startup disk can then be inserted (DOS or Windows 98, for example); this allows the system to boot to a command prompt. The hard drive can now be partitioned in preparation for installing the operating system. Figure 3-27 shows an AMIBIOS with the available exit options.

Figure 3-27   AMIBIOS Exit Options

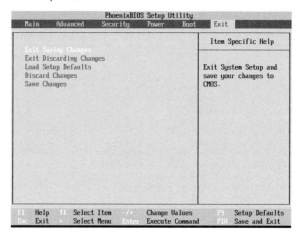

Lab Activity 3.7.1   Video Card Installation and System Booting

In this lab, you install the video card, and connect the mouse, keyboard, and monitor. Upon completion, review the checklist and boot the system.

The Startup Sequence: POST Errors and Troubleshooting

Even after careful post-assembly inspection, the first boot can still result in problems. If this happens, depending at what stage of the boot sequence the problem occurs, you might not have an opportunity to enter the BIOS menu to configure the BIOS setup. This section describes the critical role played by the POST. The POST allows the troubleshooting of many common problems.

Whenever a computer starts up, a series of tests are automatically performed to check the primary components in the system, such as the CPU, ROM, memory, and motherboard support circuitry. The routine that carries out this function is referred to as the power-on self-test. POST, as mentioned in Chapter 2, is a hardware diagnostics routine that is built into the system BIOS. The basic function of the POST routine is to make sure that all the hardware the system needs for startup is there and that everything is functioning properly before the boot process begins. The POST routine therefore ensures that the computer is ready to begin the boot sequence. The POST also provides some basic troubleshooting to determine what devices have failed or have problems initializing during this pre-startup hardware check.

POST Errors and Troubleshooting

The POST routine provides error or warning messages whenever it encounters a faulty component. POST error codes take the form of a series of beeps that identify a faulty hardware component. If everything has been installed correctly during the assembly process and the new system is functioning normally, one short beep is usually heard at the completion of the POST. If a problem is detected, a different number of beeps will be heard—sometimes in a combination of short and long tones. These are mainly BIOS-dependent codes. They vary according to BIOS manufacturer and among different BIOS versions.

The beep codes can be used to troubleshoot hardware failures that occur during the POST routine. Although the POST routine is not very thorough compared to existing disk-based diagnostics, it is a first line of defense, especially in detecting severe motherboard problems. The POST typically provides three types of output messages: audio codes (beeps), on-screen text messages, and hexadecimal numeric codes that are sent to an I/O port address.

The POST generally continues past nonfatal problems, but fatal problems cause the POST to halt the boot process. If problems occur early, before any drivers are loaded for the monitor, for example, then the POST can only signal that a problem exists using beeps. Beeps are issued through the computer's system speaker. Conversely, if the POST and the boot sequence can advance to a point where the system can use the system video to display messages, then a message can be displayed on the screen. The message indicates what problems occurred and the probable cause. These are referred to as visual error codes. These error messages are usually in the form of a numeric code, for example, 1790-Disk 0 Error.

In many instances, the BIOS manual or the manufacturer's website can be consulted for charts to help decode some of the more detailed error codes. Table 3-8 gives a summary of the major groups of visual error codes frequently encountered. Although most of the major BIOS manufacturers use many of these codes, not one uses all of these codes. Consult your manual for a specific system BIOS.

Table 3-8 Common POST Hardware Diagnostic Error Message Groups

Error Code/Range	Possible Problem
1xx	System board or BIOS
16x	CMOS, options, or time not set
2xx	Main memory
3xx	Keyboard
5xx	Color monitor
6xx	Floppy drive
17xx	Hard drive
86xx	Mouse

Problems that occur during the POST are usually caused by incorrect hardware configuration or installation. Actual hardware failure is rare. If you get a POST error, the system might have to be powered off. Unplug the system from the wall, and carefully check the assembled computer to make sure that one or all of the steps in the list that follows were properly carried out.

❑ All cables are correctly connected and secured.

❑ All drivers are properly installed.

❑ The CMOS/BIOS setup configuration settings are correct.

❑ The motherboard jumper settings are correct, if changed from the original settings.

❑ There are no device conflicts (for example, two add-in boards sharing the same IRQ).

❑ The expansion boards and disk drives are installed correctly.

❑ The power supply is set to the proper input voltage of your country or region, for example, 110–120V AC (in North America) or 220–240V AC (in Europe and other regions of the world).

❑ A keyboard, monitor, and mouse are properly attached.

❑ A bootable hard disk is properly installed.

- ❑ Your BIOS is the right version and supports the drive you have installed, and the parameters are entered correctly.
- ❑ A bootable floppy disk is in drive A, if necessary.
- ❑ All SIMMs or DIMMs are installed correctly.

Summary

This chapter discussed the steps required to assemble a computer. Some of the important concepts to retain from this chapter are as follows:

- The general safety precautions are provided to keep the technician safe and to prevent ESD damage to computer components.
- The inventory checklist provides an accounting of the components used in the assembly of a computer.
- The computer case should conform to the ATX standard, with at least a 250-watt power supply, although 300 watts is ideal. Additionally, the case should have enough space to install the components and any upgrades.
- Follow the detailed steps to prepare and install the motherboard. In addition to using spacers to keep the motherboard from touching the case, use caution when handling the motherboard.
- Refer to the motherboard manual for the jumper configuration. Jumpers establish logic levels to select functions for the operation of the motherboard. Do not move jumpers with the power on.
- Additional jumpers might have to be set for BIOS recovery, to clear the CMOS, to clear the password, and for BIOS setup access.
- The LEDs indicate that the system is getting power. The LEDs for the floppy drive, hard drive, and CD-ROM drive indicate if the devices have been installed properly.
- The floppy drive, hard drive, and CD-ROM drive are installed similarly. Make sure that the proper ribbon cables are installed and that the devices are mounted right-side up.
- The video card is the only expansion card that must be installed before booting the PC for the first time. It provides the information required to configure the BIOS during the initial boot process.
- Before booting the system for the first time, review the final checklist and double-check all work.
- Entering the BIOS/CMOS setup is required when setting up the computer for the first time. Configuration data must be entered for date, time, hard drive, drive A, drive B, video, and halt on. Additionally, advanced features that control the behavior of the system can be fine-tuned for optimal performance.

- The POST is a series of tests that are automatically performed to check the primary components in the system. One short beep is heard at the completion of the POST if everything is installed and functioning correctly. To determine the meaning of any other series of beeps that indicate a problem or error, refer to the motherboard manual.

Now that you have the computer up and running, it is important to understand the operating system. The next chapter focuses on the components and functions of the disk operating system (DOS).

Check Your Understanding

The following are review questions for the A+ exam. Answers can be found in Appendix B, "Answers to Check Your Understanding Review Questions."

1. What does ESD stand for?

    A. Electronic stasis device

    B. Electrostatic discharge

    C. Electric surge device

    D. Electronic system driver

2. How do you best prevent damaging a computer with static electricity?

    A. Always use a rubber mat as a work surface.

    B. Always touch a ground point on the chassis to discharge static.

    C. Always take off your shoes before working inside a computer.

    D. Always wear an ESD strap when working inside a computer.

3. What type of current can kill you?

    A. AC.

    B. DC.

    C. Voltage kills; current is only a measurement.

    D. AC and DC.

4. Which of the following statements describes the PC power supply?

    A. It provides AC current to the system components.

    B. It converts AC power to DC power.

    C. It connects the computer's components to a power source.

    D. It protects the computer's components against power surges.

5. What tool is used to check the power supply voltage at the P8 and P9 connections?

   A. Multiprobe

   B. Cable tester

   C. Multimeter

   D. Battery

6. What is a memory bank?

   A. The cache where memory is stored

   B. The actual slot that memory goes into

   C. The collection of all memory

   D. Virtual memory

7. What indicates the correct positioning when installing SIMMs?

   A. Missing pin

   B. Red stripe

   C. Notch on one end

   D. Red 1

8. Which method is used to install a DIMM?

   A. Line it up straight over the socket and press it in.

   B. Tilt it 45 degrees and push.

   C. Press down on the lever.

   D. Line up all metal pins and slide.

9. Which components reside in expansion slots on the motherboard?

   A. CPU, RAM, and power plugs

   B. Keyboard, mouse, and printer

   C. Network interface, sound, and SCSI cards

   D. CD-ROM, floppy, and hard drives

10. What is the purpose of expansion slots?

    A. To expand the CPU

    B. To allow the hard drive and floppy drive to communicate with the CPU

    C. To add processing power to the computer

    D. To allow the addition of optional components

11. Care should be taken when handling an expansion card. You should not touch which component(s)?

    A. Metal bracket

    B. Metal edge connectors

    C. Corners of the card

    D. Connector slots

12. Which type of expansion card is configured using software instead of jumpers?

    A. Configured cards

    B. 32-bit cards

    C. 16-bit cards

    D. Plug and Play cards

13. When connecting a ribbon cable, how is the connector installed?

    A. By connecting the black stripe to pin 1

    B. By connecting the black stripe to pin 2

    C. By connecting the red stripe to pin 1

    D. By connecting the red stripe to pin 2

14. When installing an IDE drive, which jumper settings are not a factor?

    A. Single

    B. Slave

    C. Master

    D. Secondary

15. Where do you connect an ATA CD-ROM drive in a computer with an EIDE adapter?

    A. Floppy cable.

    B. Primary IDE.

    C. Secondary IDE.

    D. You can't connect it without an ATA connector or expansion card.

16. How should the jumpers be set on your IDE CD-ROM drive when it is attached to the primary IDE adapter with your hard drive?

    A. Master

    B. Slave

    C. Remove the jumpers

    D. Auto

17. Plugging in or unplugging a keyboard with the power turned on can damage which component?

    A. Hard drive

    B. Mouse

    C. Motherboard

    D. Keyboard

18. What port does a mouse plug into?

    A. RJ-11

    B. Serial

    C. Parallel

    D. RJ-45

19. How are PCI devices configured?

    A. During DOS boot.

    B. The Internet.

    C. Windows setup.

    D. They are always self-configuring.

20. How many pins are in an IDE connector?

    A. 80

    B. 50

    C. 68

    D. 40

21. What determines the length of a SCSI cable?

    A. Number of devices

    B. Computer's speed

    C. SCSI device

    D. Thickness of the cable

22. What technique loads the system BIOS from ROM into system RAM during bootup?

    A. Fault tolerance

    B. Int19

    C. Shadowing

    D. Loading

23. Where are basic instructions for the CPU and I/O device communication located?

    A. CMOS

    B. Windows configuration files

    C. DOS

    D. BIOS

24. Which software or firmware routine is executed first during the computer boot up procedure?

    A. BIOS

    B. CMOS

    C. CONFIG.SYS

    D. WIN.INI

25. In which case should circuit boards or devices not be added or removed?

    A. Until software is installed

    B. With a grounding strap on

    C. Until the computer is not busy

    D. With power on

Key Terms

AT power supply   Designed to support AT compatible motherboards.

ATX power supply   Designed according to newer ATX design specifications to support the ATX motherboard.

available desktop space   A consideration when choosing a computer case.

Basic Input/Output System (BIOS)   Contains the program code required to control all the basic operating components of the computer system.

bezel   Faceplate.

BIOS recovery   Used for recovering BIOS data from a diskette in the event of a catastrophic failure.

BIOS setup   Provides access to configure the BIOS. Allows the customization of a computer to function optimally based on the hardware and software profiles.

BIOS setup access   Enables or disables access to the Setup program.

boxed processors   Processors that come with the fan and heat sink already attached.

bugs   Flaws in BIOS code.

CD-ROM   Secondary data storage.

clear CMOS   Used to reset the CMOS settings to the default values.

CMOS   Chip that contains software that sets and records the master configuration for all components in the system.

complementary metal-oxide semiconductor (CMOS)   A battery-powered storage chip located on the system board. The CMOS chip has rewritable memory since the configuration data can be changed or updated as the components or devices in the computer are changed.

date and time   Configuration data required for many types of software applications to manage data.

desktop   Designed to sit horizontally on the desktop.

device drivers   Program code for devices and internal components.

Drive A: and Drive B: Configuration data identifies the types of floppy disk drives using the options available.

dual in-line memory module (DIMM)   168-pin memory module.

electrically erasable programmable read-only memory (EEPROM)   Flash BIOS.

ESD discharge (ESD)   Static electricity.

faceplate   The front case panel.

Flash BIOS   Allows the upgrade of the BIOS software from a disk provided by the manufacturer without replacing the chip.

form factor   The general layout of the computer case.

halt on   Configuration data that allows a specific system response to errors.

hard disks   Configuration data that identifies devices attached to the two IDE controllers integrated on the motherboard.

hard drive   Primary data storage.

motherboard location map   Shows where the major components and hardware is located on the motherboard.

original equipment manufacturer (OEM) processors   Boxed processors.

password clear   Used to clear the password if the password is forgotten.

POST   Power-on self test is a diagnostic tool that is run when the machine boots up in order to verify and test hardware.

power supply unit   Provides electrical power for every component inside the system unit.

processor voltage   Sets the output of the onboard voltage regulator.

ROM BIOS   Chip that contains software that sets and records the master configuration for all components in the system.

setting the system hardware   The process of configuring the motherboard.

single in-line memory module (SIMM)   72-pin memory module.

Socket 7   A standard CPU interface.

standard voltage   Type of voltage.

supervisor password   On larger networks, this password restricts the computer BIOS.

system unit   A metal and plastic case that contains the basic parts of the computer system.

tower cases   Designed to sit vertically on the floor beneath a desk.

user password   Provides the option of setting a password that must be entered before the system will boot.

video   Configuration data that identifies the video adapter.

VRE   Voltage Regulator Enhanced. Motherboard jumper to select voltage.

Objectives

Upon completion of this chapter, you will be able to perform the following tasks:

- Explain the three basic elements that make up the major design components of any operating system
- Understand the components and functions of the operating system
- Modify DOS commands with switches
- Create a DOS boot disk, which is used to boot a computer to the DOS prompt
- Use system memory tools to help simplify the task of placing terminate-and-stay-resident programs into upper memory
- Resolve memory conflicts that can lead to a general protection fault

Chapter 4

Operating System Fundamentals

This chapter discusses the basics of the operating system. The operating system is the program that is in charge of running the computer. The components and functions of the operating system are detailed, and the terminology that is important to the technician is explained. The emphasis is on the Disk Operating System (DOS). You will learn the basics of DOS, the commands used, and the file structure. Additionally, you will gain an understanding of memory management and the tools used to adjust and optimize memory.

The Operating System

This section includes the following topics:

- Components of an operating system
- Operating system functions
- Operating system types—basic terminology

Components of an Operating System

An *operating system (OS)* is a software program that controls thousands of operations, provides an interface between the user and the computer, and runs applications. Basically, the OS is in charge of running the computer. Today, most computer systems are sold with a preinstalled OS. Computers that are designed for individual users (called personal computers [PCs]) have OSs that are designed for individuals running small jobs. An OS is designed to control the operations of programs such as web browsers, word processors, and e-mail software.

With the development of processor technology, computers have become capable of executing increasingly more instructions per second. These advances have made it possible to run OSs that are capable of executing many complex tasks simultaneously. When a computer needs to accommodate concurrent users and multiple jobs, information technology (IT) professionals usually turn to faster computers that have more robust OSs.

Computers that are capable of handling concurrent users and multiple jobs are often called *network servers*, or simply *servers*, as shown in Figure 4-1. The OSs installed on servers are called *network operating systems (NOSs)*. A fast computer with a NOS installed might run a large company or a large Internet site. This task involves keeping track of many users and multiple programs, as illustrated in Figure 4-2.

Figure 4-1 A Network Server

Three basic elements make up the major design components of any OS. These components are described as *modular* because each has a distinct function and can be developed separately. These components are as follows:

- **User interface**—A user interacts with the OS through the user interface. The user interface is the part of the OS that can be used to issue commands by either typing them at a command prompt or pointing and clicking the mouse on the screen of a graphical user interface (GUI).

- **Kernel**—The core of the OS, the kernel is responsible for loading and running programs or processes and managing input and output.

- **File-management system**—The OS uses the file-management system to organize and manage files. A file is a collection of data given a single logical name called a *filename*. Virtually all the information that a computer stores is in the form of a file. There are many types of files, including program files, data files, text files, and so on. An OS organizes information into files by using a *file system*. Most OSs use a hierarchical file system in which files are organized into directories in a tree structure. The beginning of the directory system is referred to as the *root directory*.

Figure 4-2 Network Server Environment

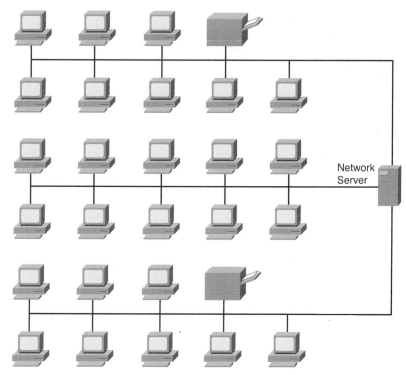

Operating System Functions

Regardless of the size or complexity of the computer or its OS, all OSs perform the same basic functions, which are described as follows:

- **File and folder management**—An OS creates a file structure on the computer's hard drive where the user's data can be stored and retrieved. When you issue a command to save a file, the OS saves it, attaches a name to it, and remembers where it put the file for future use.

- **Management of applications**—When a user requests a program, the OS locates the application and loads it into the computer's primary memory or RAM. As more programs are loaded, the OS must allocate the computer's resources.

- **Support for built-in utility programs**—The OS uses utility programs to maintain and repair itself. These programs help identify problems, locate lost files, repair damaged files, and back up data. Figure 4-3 shows the progress of the Disk Defragmenter, which can be accessed by choosing **Programs, Accessories, System Tools, Disk Defragmenter.**

Figure 4-3 Defragmenting Drive C

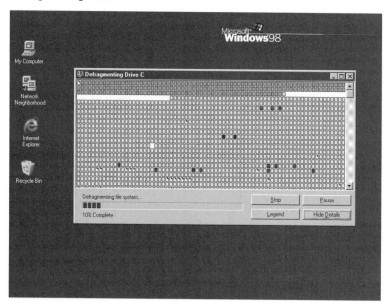

NOTE

The Windows 2000 NOS bypasses the system BIOS and controls the hardware directly.

- **Control of the computer's hardware**—The OS resides between the programs and the basic input/output system (BIOS). The BIOS was explained in previous chapters, and more discussion is provided later in this chapter. The BIOS provides the hardware control. All programs that need hardware resources must first go through the OS. The OS in turn can either access the hardware through the BIOS or through the device drivers, as shown in Figure 4-4.

All programs are written for a specific OS. Programs written for the UNIX OS do not work on a Windows-based system and vice versa. The OS relieves the programmer of having to consider hardware access when writing an application. If the OS did not communicate information between the application and the hardware, programs would have to be rewritten every time they were installed on a new computer.

Figure 4-4 Functions of the Operating System

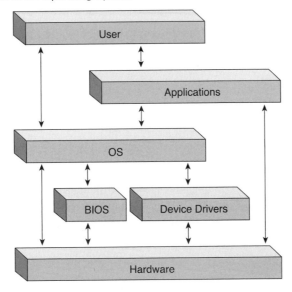

Operating System Types—Basic Terminology

To understand what an OS is capable of, it is important to understand some basic terms. The following terms are often used when comparing OSs:

- **Multiuser**—Two or more users running programs and sharing peripheral devices, such as a printer, at the same time.

- **Multitasking**—A computer's capability to run multiple applications at the same time.

- **Multiprocessing**—Allows a computer to have two or more central processing units (CPUs) that programs can share.

- **Multithreading**—The capability of a program to be broken into smaller parts that can be loaded as needed by the OS. Multithreading allows individual programs to be multitasked.

Today, most OSs are multiuser and multitasking and support multithreading. The following is a list of popular OSs:

- **Microsoft Windows 95, 98, Me**—Windows is one of today's most popular OSs. Windows is designed to run on PCs and to use an Intel-compatible CPU. Windows-based PCs use a GUI as the interface between the computer and the user. The Windows 98 desktop is shown in Figure 4-5. These Windows OSs are designed to be run and maintained by a single user.

- **Microsoft Windows NT, 2000, XP**—These OSs are designed to support multiple (concurrent) users and to run several applications simultaneously. Windows NT, 2000, and XP have incorporated many networking features.

- **Macintosh operating system**—The first Macintosh computers, which became available in January 1984, were designed to be user friendly compared to the existing DOS computers. The latest release of the Macintosh operating system, System X, is highly functional and is based on UNIX as its core technology. The Apple iMac desktop is shown in Figure 4-6.

- **UNIX**—This is one of the oldest OSs, dating back to the late 1960s. UNIX has always been popular with computer professionals, who are responsible for running and maintaining computer networks. UNIX-based computers from IBM, Hewlett-Packard (HP), and Sun Microsystems have helped run the Internet from its inception. There are many different versions of UNIX today. One of the most recent is the popular Linux. Figure 4-7 shows the startup screen for Linux as distributed by Red Hat. The Linux OS is not within the scope of this course.

Figure 4-5 The Windows 98 Desktop

Windows, Sun, and Macintosh OSs are *proprietary*, meaning that they must be purchased. On the other hand, Linux can be copied freely and has recently gained acceptance with IT professionals. As UNIX-run computers have become more powerful and GUIs more common, Linux has gained in popularity with individual users. OSs are constantly under development. As new ones become available, older versions are no longer supported.

Figure 4-6 The iMac Desktop

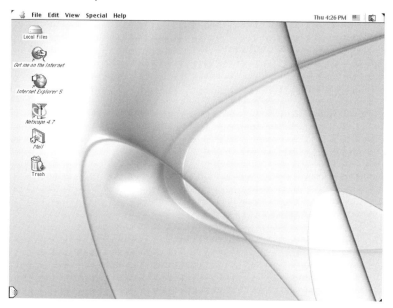

Figure 4-7 Red Hat Linux

Worksheet 4.1.3   Operating System Fundamentals

This worksheet is an overview of the operating system.

Disk Operating System

This section includes the following topics:

- What is DOS, and why learn about it?
- The DOS file structure
- An overview of basic DOS commands
- Creating a DOS boot disk
- Booting the system with a DOS disk
- DOS configuration files
- Editing system configuration files using SYSEDIT.EXE

What Is DOS, and Why Learn About It?

In 1981, Microsoft developed DOS, also called MS-DOS, for the IBM personal computer. Windows 98 and Windows 2000 both support DOS commands in order to address compatibility issues related to older applications. Simply put, *DOS* is a collection of programs and commands used to control the overall computer operation in a disk-based system. Figure 4-8 shows an example of a DOS prompt. DOS is made up of the following sections:

- **Boot files**—These files are used during the boot process (that is, startup).
- **File-management files**—These files enable the system to manage the data that it holds in a system of files and folders.
- **Utility files**—These files enable the user to manage system resources, troubleshoot the system, and configure the system settings.

Figure 4-8 A DOS Prompt

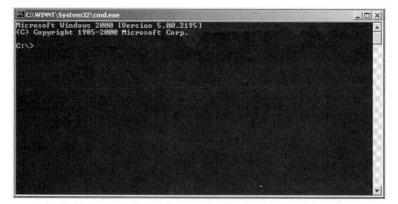

DOS programs usually work in the background, permitting the user to input characters from the keyboard, to define a file structure for storing records on the disk, and to output data to a printer or monitor. Basically, DOS is responsible for finding and organizing data and applications on the disk.

The introduction of OSs having a GUI, such as Microsoft Windows, has made DOS mostly obsolete. However, DOS continues to play a significant role in many areas, including programming, running older applications, and installing the Windows OS, especially on older computers. All generations of Windows support DOS commands for backward compatibility with older applications. It is important to understand the basics of DOS before proceeding with a Windows OS installation.

Basic Elements of DOS

DOS is useful as a troubleshooting aid when Windows does not boot. DOS allows you to access the hard drive without the GUI and provides the ability to run troubleshooting or diagnostic programs. Remember the following basic items when working with DOS:

- DOS is a command-line OS; it is not user friendly. The best way to learn DOS is to use it.
- DOS can only run one program at a time. It does not support multitasking.
- DOS can only run small programs and has memory limitations.
- DOS is an essential tool for IT professionals and is used extensively for troubleshooting.

To access DOS from Windows, choose **Start, Run, Command**. A window then opens to allow you to enter commands.

The DOS File Structure

To understand basic DOS commands, first look at the structure of the disk. Programs and data are stored on a disk similar to the way that a filing cabinet is organized. These programs and data are stored the same way a document would be filed in a folder in a file cabinet. In DOS, these documents are called *files* and are grouped together in *directories*. Directories are much like the folders in a file cabinet. This process organizes the files and directories for easier retrieval and use. Directories can be nested inside other directories, just like a folder might be placed inside another folder. Nested directories are referred to as *subdirectories*. Directories became known as folders in the Windows OS.

What Is a File?

A *file* is a block of logically related data, given a single name and treated as a single unit, such as a program, a document, drawings or other illustrations, sound components, and so on. A record is kept of the location of every directory, subdirectory, and file found on a disk. This record is stored in a table called the *file allocation table (FAT)*. *FAT32*, an improved version of FAT that allows more efficient use of disk space for storing files, was introduced in Win 95 OSR 2. (The similarities and differences between these file systems are discussed in Chapter 7, "Windows NT/2000/XP Operating Systems.")

Files are referred to by *filenames*. In DOS, filenames can be up to eight characters long with an extension of three characters. The extension is separated from the main portion of the filename by a period, and the extension identifies the type of file. An example of a DOS filename is mynotes.txt. In this example, the txt extension indicates a basic text file.

In DOS, all files have *attributes*, which are a set of parameters that describe a file. Given a file's attributes, you can determine the nature of the file. Common attributes for DOS files are as follows:

- **Hidden file**—The user cannot see this type of file with a standard search in a DOS environment.
- **Read-only file**—The user can open and read this type of file but cannot write or modify it.
- **Archive file**—This is a backup copy of a file.
- **System file**—This file is needed by DOS for a successful bootup.

NOTE

Hiding a file does not make it immune to changes or access.

The use of hidden files keeps them from being seen and tampered with by unauthorized users. Hiding a file makes it invisible in a standard DOS directory listing; the file can only be seen with a special command. To see a hidden file, use the following command at the DOS prompt:

C:\>DIR /AH

Directory Structures and Organization

Hard drives are organized into directories and subdirectories. The main directory is known as the *root directory*. All other directories, if they exist, then radiate (branch out) from the root directory, similar to the branches of a tree. In MS-DOS, a graphical representation of the disk drive's directory organization is called a *directory tree*, as shown in Figure 4-9. It is important to have a basic understanding of how DOS organizes disks before you install a version of Windows.

Figure 4-9 A DOS Directory Tree

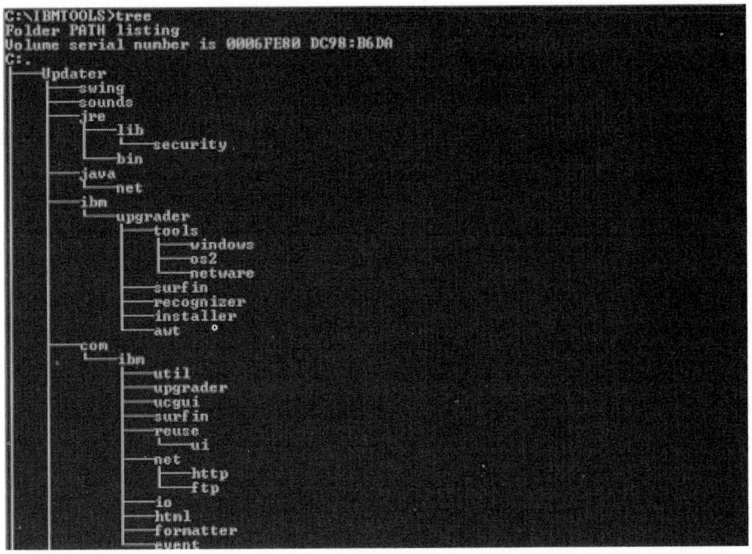

```
C:\IBMTOOLS>tree
Folder PATH listing
Volume serial number is 0006FE80 DC98:B6DA
C:.
├───Updater
│   ├───swing
│   ├───sounds
│   ├───jre
│   │   ├───lib
│   │   │   └───security
│   │   └───bin
│   ├───java
│   │   └───net
│   ├───ibm
│   │   └───upgrader
│   │       └───tools
│   │           ├───windows
│   │           ├───os2
│   │           └───netware
│   ├───surfin
│   ├───recognizer
│   ├───installer
│   └───awt
├───com
│   └───ibm
│       ├───util
│       ├───upgrader
│       ├───ucgui
│       ├───surfin
│       ├───reuse
│       │   └───ui
│       ├───net
│       │   ├───http
│       │   └───ftp
│       ├───io
│       ├───html
│       ├───formatter
│       └───event
```

Locating a file requires knowledge of three things: the drive, directory, and subdirectory in which the file is found. The primary hard drive in most computer systems is labeled C. Each hard disk in the computer can be considered a *file cabinet* or *root*. The root of the C drive is represented by C:\. Any files or directories within the root are represented by the root, followed by the name of the file or directory (for example, C:\FILEDIR). A directory or file located within that directory is represented by that directory, followed by a backslash, followed by the name of the file or subdirectory (for example, C:\FILEDIR\FILE.EXE). In MS-DOS, the format for specifying the path to a file is as follows:

C:\directory\subdirectory\subdirectory\filename

The components of this path are as follows:

- C:\ specifies the C disk drive of the computer.
- The backslash (\) after each item signifies the presence of a directory or subdirectory. The first backslash indicates the root directory, which is present on all DOS disks.
- The filename, found at the end of the path, is located in the last-named subdirectory.

An Overview of Basic DOS Commands

A *DOS command* is an instruction that DOS executes from the command line. A variety of internal commands, such as DIR and COPY, are built into the command.com file and are always available as long as DOS is running. Many external commands, such as FORMAT and XCOPY, are individual programs that reside in the DOS directory.

Internal Versus External DOS Commands

DOS contains two types of commands: those built into the OS (internal) and those that must be executed from a file (external). Basic commands are generally internal, and more advanced commands are usually external. *External commands* are stored on disk for future use. *Internal commands*, located in the command.com file, are loaded into memory during the bootup process. Examples of internal and external commands are discussed later in this chapter.

What Is a Command Line?

Normally, the OS provides the system's user interface. In DOS, the main user interface is the command line. The *command line* is the space immediately following the DOS prompt (C:\>). C:\ represents the hard disk drive root directory, and > is known as the prompt. All DOS commands are typed to the right of the prompt and are executed by pressing Enter. All DOS functions can be typed and executed from the command line. For example, to view all system files in the C directory, you would type C:\>DIR *.SYS.

Commonly Used DOS Commands and Switches

DOS commands are used to tell DOS to perform specific tasks. Placing one or more software switches at the end of the basic command can modify many of the DOS commands. *Switches* are options that can be added to a command that modify the output of that command. A switch is added to the command by adding a space, a forward slash (/), and a single letter. An example is as follows:

    C:\>DIR /W

In this example, /W is the switch. This switch modifies the DIR command by presenting the screen output information in a wide format, that is, across the screen. The rest of this section focuses on commonly used DOS commands and the switches that go with them. The commands described in the following list are helpful when doing various OS installations, including Windows:

- **ATTRIB**—Used to display, set, or remove one or more of the four attributes—read-only, archive, system, and hidden—that can be assigned to files and directories. ATTRIB is an external DOS command. A plus or minus sign used in the ATTRIB command sets or clears an attribute, respectively. The format of the ATTRIB command is as follows:

   ATTRIB [+ or –][variable] [directory\filename] /[switch]

   The following variables can be used with the ATTRIB command:
   — R—Indicates a read-only file
   — A—Indicates an archive file
   — S—Indicates a system file
   — H—Indicates a hidden file

- **DEL**—This command deletes named files. The DEL and ERASE commands are synonymous. The commonly used switch, /P, prompts the user for confirmation before deleting each file. The format of the DEL command is as follows:

   DEL [directory\filename] /[switch]

- **EDIT**—This external command allows the user to view, create, or modify a file. The format of the EDIT command is as follows:

   EDIT [directory\filename] /[switch]

   The following switches are commonly used with the EDIT command:
   — /B—Forces monochrome mode.
   — /H—Displays the maximum number of lines possible for the hardware.
   — /R—Loads file(s) in read-only mode.
   — [file]—Specifies initial files(s) to load. Wildcards and multiple file specs can be given.

- **FORMAT**—This external command is used to erase all the information from a floppy disk or hard drive. The FORMAT command will be used in a future lab to prepare the hard drive for installing the Windows OS. A typical FORMAT command is as follows:

   FORMAT [directory\filename] /[switch]

   The following switches are commonly used with the FORMAT command:
   — /Q—Performs a quick format but does not clear the FAT. File recovery is possible when a quick format has been performed.

— /S—Copies system files to the formatted disk.

— /U—Performs an unconditional format. All previous data, including the FAT, are permanently erased.

■ **FDISK**—This external command allows the user to delete and/or create partitions on the hard disk drive. The FDISK command is commonly used to prepare the hard drive for installing the Windows OS. This command is entered at the command prompt as follows:

FDISK /[switch]

A commonly used switch, /STATUS, displays partition information when used with the FDISK command.

■ **SCANDISK**—This command is a DOS program that is designed to detect and repair errors on a hard drive or floppy disk. The SCANDISK command is entered at the command prompt as follows:

SCANDISK /[switch]

Switches commonly used with the SCANDISK command are as follows:

— ALL—Checks and repairs all local drives at once.

— CHECKONLY—Checks the drive for errors but does not make repairs.

■ **AUTOFIX**—Automatically fixes errors. Saves lost clusters by default as files in the drive's root directory.

■ **MEM**—This external command is used to display a table that shows how memory (RAM) is currently allocated. The MEM command is entered at the command prompt as follows:

MEM /[switch]

Switches commonly used with the MEM command are as follows:

— C—Lists the programs that are currently loaded into memory and shows how much conventional and upper memory each program is using.

— D—Lists the programs and internal drivers that are currently loaded into memory.

— F—Lists the free areas of conventional and upper memory (which are discussed later in this chapter in "Memory Types").

— P—Pauses after each screen of information.

■ **COPY**—This command is commonly used to copy one or more files from one location to another. The COPY command can also be used to create new files. By copying from the keyboard console (COPY CON:) to the screen, files can be created and then saved to a disk. Switches commonly used with the COPY command are as follows:

- — /Y—Replaces existing files without providing a confirmation prompt.
- — /–Y—Displays a confirmation prompt before overwriting (copying over) existing files.
- — /A—Copies ASCII files. Applies to the filename preceding it and to all following filenames.
- — /B—Copies binary files. Applies to the filename preceding it and to all following filenames.
- — /V—Checks the copy to make sure that a file was copied correctly. If the copy cannot be verified, the program displays an error message.

- **MORE**—Displays output one screen at a time. The MORE command is entered at the command prompt as follows:

  MORE [filename]

The CD, MKDIR, RMDIR, and DELTREE commands are slightly different than those previously discussed because they do not use switches. A brief description of these commands is as follows:

- **CD**—Changes or displays the current directory on the specified drive
- **MKDIR (or MD)**—Creates a new directory
- **DELTREE**—Deletes (erases) a directory, including all files and subdirectories that are in it

Table 4-1 summarizes the most commonly used DOS commands.

Table 4-1 Common Internal and External DOS Commands

Command Name	Type	Function
DIR	Internal	Displays the contents of a directory
CD	Internal	Changes to a specified directory
MD	Internal	Creates a new directory
RD	Internal	Removes a directory
DEL	Internal	Deletes a file
REN	Internal	Renames a file

continues

Table 4-1 Common Internal and External DOS Commands (Continued)

Command Name	Type	Function
SET	Internal	Displays the contents of the environment variables
MEM	External	Displays memory properties
COPY	External	Copies a file
TYPE	Internal	Displays the contents of a text file
FDISK	External	Partitions fixed disks
TIME	Internal	Sets the system time
DATE	Internal	Sets the system date
CHKDSK	External	Displays the status of a disk
DISKCOPY	External	Copies one floppy disk to another
EDIT	External	Opens a file for editing
FORMAT	External	Formats a disk
PRINT	Internal	Prints a text document or displays the contents of the print queue
ATTRIB	External	Changes the attributes of a file
.	Internal	Wildcards representing all files

TEST TIP

Be able to perform DOS operations and know the commands that are most commonly used.

Lab Activity 4.2.3   Basic DOS Commands

In this lab, you navigate the DOS command line and perform basic file management tasks.

Worksheet 4.2.3   DOS Commands

This worksheet provides a review of DOS commands used to navigate in the CLI.

Creating a DOS Boot Disk

Sometimes, things do not go as expected and the computer will not boot. To troubleshoot this problem, you need an alternate way of starting the system. A DOS boot disk is a great tool to use to perform this task. One of the most useful functions of a DOS boot disk is to boot a newly assembled computer before installing the OS. A DOS boot disk, as shown in Figure 4-10, is a floppy disk that contains the following system files:

- COMMAND.COM
- IO.SYS
- MSDOS.SYS

Figure 4-10   Contents of a DOS Boot Disk

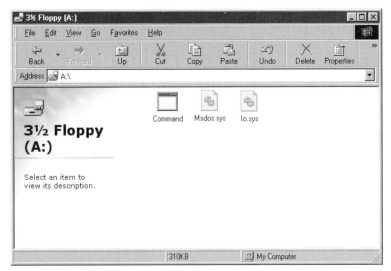

NOTE

The DOS boot disk might also contain a file called drvspace.bin. This file is only necessary to read the drive if the drive has been compressed. Without this file, you cannot access the data on a compressed drive.

It is also a good idea to place diagnostic programs on this disk. To create a boot disk, perform the following steps (this process assumes that DOS is installed on the hard disk):

Step 1   Start the computer.

Step 2   Insert a blank floppy disk in the floppy drive.

Step 3   At the command prompt, type **FORMAT A: /S** and press Enter.

Step 4   If the disk is already formatted, type **SYS A:** and press Enter.

Lab Activity 4.2.4   Creating a DOS Boot Disk

In this lab, you review the necessary files for making a floppy disk bootable and the commands necessary to create a boot disk.

Booting the System with a DOS Disk

A *DOS boot disk* is used to boot a computer to the DOS prompt. The first section of a DOS disk contains the boot sector. The *boot sector* contains information about how the disk is organized. Sometimes, it contains a small optional master boot record that can access a larger, more powerful bootstrap loader program, which is located in the root directory.

In most cases, the master boot record is found at sector 1, head 0, and track 0 of the first logical hard drive (or in this case, the boot disk). The *master boot record (MBR)* is the required boot record on any disks that are created as boot or system disks. If a boot disk possesses the master boot record, it can boot up the hardware system to the OS. A disk that can boot a system to the OS is called a *bootable disk* or a *system disk*. This disk must contain the three system files mentioned in the previous section. Having a boot disk greatly facilitates the process of preparing a hard drive and installing the OS.

Booting the System

To boot your system, insert a bootable disk in the floppy disk drive and turn on the computer. The BIOS executes the bootstrap program (a small BIOS program that initiates and controls much of the bootup routine) to move the master boot record into RAM and then begins the process of loading the OS. Typically, if the system performs a standard DOS boot, it should print the DATE and TIME prompts on the monitor, followed by the DOS command-line prompt (A:\). This indicates that DOS is operational and that the A floppy drive (which contains the boot disk) is the currently active drive.

The following list summarizes the chain of events that culminates in the display of the DOS command line when a system boots with a DOS boot disk:

1. The BIOS performs INT19, searching for a master boot record.

2. The primary bootstrap loader moves the master boot record into main memory.

3. The system executes the secondary bootstrap loader from the master boot record.

4. The bootstrap loader program looks at the partition table to find the active partition and then checks the root directory of the active partition for the files io.sys and msdos.sys.

5. The secondary bootstrap loader moves io.sys and msdos.sys into main memory.

6. The file io.sys executes the msdos.sys file to load file-management functions.

7. The file io.sys looks for the config.sys file.

8. If config.sys is found, io.sys reconfigures the system in a three-step process: device, install, and shell.

9. The file io.sys executes the command.com file.

10. The file command.com looks for the autoexec.bat file.

11. If command.com finds autoexec.bat, command.com executes that file.

12. If there is no autoexec.bat file, command.com displays the TIME and DATE prompts, and finally, the command-line prompt is displayed.

DOS Configuration Files

In the MS-DOS operating system, there are two special configuration files: config.sys and autoexec.bat. These important files can be included in the DOS bootup process. These files play a crucial role in optimizing the system for operations of particular functions or with different options.

As the system moves through the steps in the boot procedure, the BIOS first checks the root directory of the boot disk for the config.sys file. Next, it searches for the command.com interpreter, and finally, it looks in the root directory again for the autoexec.bat file. Both autoexec.bat and config.sys can play significant roles in optimizing the system's memory (as discussed later in this chapter) and disk-drive usage. The order of file execution in the bootup process can be summarized as follows:

1. io.sys

2. msdos.sys

3. config.sys

4. command.com

5. autoexec.bat

This is also the order in which config.sys, autoexec.bat, and the other important files involved in the MS-DOS boot process are loaded and executed. Figure 4-11 illustrates the bootup process.

In Windows 9X, config.sys is primarily needed to install real-mode device drivers for those devices that might not be supported by Windows 9X's 32-bit device drivers. Real mode is discussed later in this chapter in "Real-Mode Versus Protected-Mode Memory Addressing."

TEST TIP

Remember the files involved with the DOS bootup process and the order of their execution.

Figure 4-11 The Bootup Process

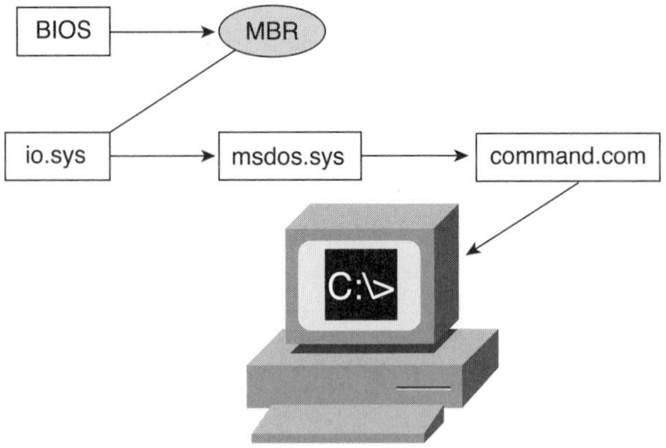
BIOS
MBR
io.sys
msdos.sys
command.com
C:\>

The config.sys File

The *config.sys* file resides in the root directory and is used to load drivers and change settings at startup. Installation programs often modify config.sys to customize the computer for their own use. The config.sys file in most versions of Windows 9X is empty, waiting for any changes that the user might want to add to the system. In the migration from DOS to Windows 9X, most of the values formerly located in config.sys have been moved to io.sys. To override the values in io.sys, enter the appropriate statements in config.sys, including the values. The file io.sys is also used to run memory managers, which are detailed later in this chapter.

TEST TIP

Know the function keys that can be used during the boot process.

During the boot process, while the MS-DOS message "Starting DOS" is shown onscreen, the following special function keys are available to alter config.sys. There is also an option to access autoexec.bat:

- **F5 (also the left Shift key)**—Skips config.sys (including autoexec.bat, if this option is chosen)
- F8—Proceeds through config.sys (and autoexec.bat, if needed) one step at a time, waiting for confirmation from the user

The autoexec.bat File

The *autoexec.bat* file contains DOS commands that are automatically carried out when DOS is loaded into the system. Examples of commands normally located in the autoexec.bat file are as follows:

- **DATE**—Causes DOS to prompt the user for the date.
- **TIME**—Causes DOS to prompt the user for the date and time.
- **PROMPT=PG**—Causes the active drive and directory path to be displayed on the command line.

- **SET TEMP=C:\TEMP**—Sets up a temporary data-holding area in the TEMP directory.

- **PATH=C:\;C:\DOS;C:\MOUSE**—Creates a specific set of paths that DOS uses to search for executable (.com, .exe, and .bat) files. In this example, DOS searches first for executable files in the root directory (C:\), followed by the DOS directory (C:\DOS), and finally in the MOUSE directory (C:\MOUSE).

- **DOSKEY**—Loads the DOSKEY program into memory.

- **SMARTDRV.EXE 2048 1024**—Configures the system for a 1-MB disk cache in DOS and a 2-MB cache in Windows.

- **CD**—Causes the DOS default directory to change to the root directory.

- **DIR**—Causes a DOS DIR command to be performed automatically.

TEST TIP

It is important to know which commands are normally located in the autoexec.bat file.

Editing System Configuration Files Using sysedit.exe

The sysedit.exe file is a standard text editor that is used to edit system configuration files such as config.sys and autoexec.bat. Additionally, this utility can be used to edit the set of Windows initialization files (text files) generally referred to as ini files. The ini files, created when Windows 3.*X* was added to the structure of DOS, have since been carried in later versions of Windows (Windows 9*X*) in the WINDOWS directory, for backward compatibility. Common examples are win.ini and system.ini. The config.sys and autoexec.bat files are found at the root directory (C:\). To access these configuration files in Windows 95, for example, choose **Start, Run**, and type **sysedit**. Figure 4-12 shows the files accessed in several cascaded Windows.

Figure 4-12 Accessing Configuration Files in Windows

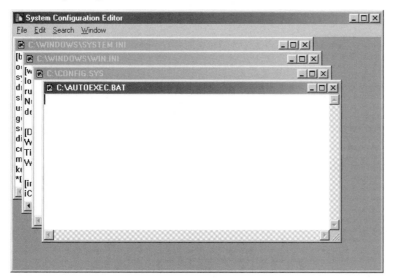

These files can also be edited in MS-DOS by typing **EDIT CONFIG.SYS** or **EDIT AUTOEXEC.BAT** at the DOS prompt.

Worksheet 4.2.7   DOS

This worksheet provides a review of DOS in a true/false format.

Memory Management

This section includes the following topics:

- Memory types
- Memory-management tools: adjusting and optimizing system memory
- Other types of memory
- Memory conflicts: general protection faults
- Real-mode versus protected-mode memory addressing

Memory Types

The OS that runs the computer uses two main types of memory: *random-access memory (RAM)*, also known as system memory and physical memory, and *virtual memory*. The four categories of system memory in the OS are conventional, upper/expanded, high, and extended memory. In addition to the terms dynamic random access memory (DRAM) and read-only memory (ROM), discussed in previous chapters, it is important to understand how memory is divided into its logical types.

The logical divisions or categories of memory are the result of MS-DOS and early microprocessors, and are associated with the early IBM PC, having been designed to address a maximum of 1 MB of memory. This 1 MB was further split into two pieces: the first 640 KB for the user and OS, and the upper (second) 384 KB for the BIOS and utilities. Windows 9*X*, because it is basically built on an MS-DOS foundation, supports the different types of physical memory specifications that result from the design of the original IBM PC and its many descendants. These physical memory specifications are discussed in this section, while virtual memory is discussed in a later section, "Other Types of Memory." Figure 4-13 illustrates the allocation of physical memory.

Figure 4-13 Physical Memory Allocation

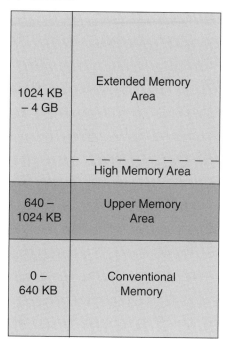

1024 KB – 4 GB	Extended Memory Area
	High Memory Area
640 – 1024 KB	Upper Memory Area
0 – 640 KB	Conventional Memory

Conventional Memory

Conventional memory, also known as *base memory*, includes all memory addresses between 0 and 640 KB. This is the area where MS-DOS programs normally run. In older DOS machines, this is the only memory available for running the OS files, application programs, memory-resident routines, and device drivers. Memory-resident routines include terminate-and-stay-resident (TSR) programs such as mouse and CD-ROM drivers. Figure 4-14 illustrates the allocation of conventional memory.

Upper Memory/Expanded Memory

Upper memory, also known as *reserved memory*, includes memory addresses that fall between 640 KB and 1024 KB (1 MB). This memory follows conventional memory and has a size of 384 KB. Upper memory is available in the form of *upper memory blocks (UMBs)*. Programs that run in upper memory include the system BIOS, Plug and Play BIOS, video BIOS, and video RAM. Depending on the system, between 96 KB and 160 KB of this memory space is not used by hardware. These addresses are only available if an appropriate memory manager, such as emm386.exe, is installed during the startup process. Figure 4-15 illustrates the allocation of upper memory/ expanded memory.

Figure 4-14 Conventional Memory Allocation

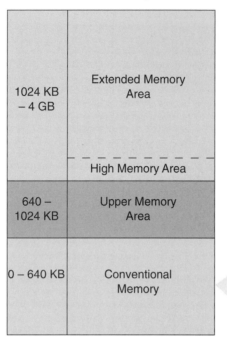

1024 KB – 4 GB	Extended Memory Area
	High Memory Area
640 – 1024 KB	Upper Memory Area
0 – 640 KB	Conventional Memory

- Base Memory
- First 640 KB of Memory
- MS-DOS Programs
- Memory Resident Routines
    - TSRs

Figure 4-15 Upper Memory/Expanded Memory Allocation

1024 KB – 4 GB	Extended Memory Area
	High Memory Area
640 – 1024 KB	Upper Memory Area
0 – 640 KB	Conventional Memory

- Reserved Memory
- Next 384 KB of Memory
- Available as UMBs
- Programs That Run Here
    - System BIOS
    - Plug-n-Play BIOS
    - Video BIOS
    - Other Applications
- Controlled By EMM386.EXE

Closely related to upper memory is another memory area known as *expanded memory*, also called the *expanded memory specification (EMS)*. This is memory that can be accessed in pages (16 KB pieces) from a 64 KB page frame, established in unused UMBs. As mentioned earlier, the primary device driver that allows the use of the EMS is emm386.exe. This program frees conventional memory by allowing unused portions of the reserved memory area to be used for DOS drivers and memory-resident routines.

Extended Memory

With the advent of the Intel 80286 microprocessor and its protected operating mode, the user could access physical memory locations beyond the 1 MB limit of the 8088/8086 chip. Memory above this address is generally referred to as *extended memory*, also called the *extended memory specification (XMS)*. XMS is the primary memory area used by Windows 9X. A device driver that is loaded by the OS controls this memory area. Windows 9X loads the XMS driver called himem.sys during startup. Once loaded, himem.sys makes extended memory available to the Windows 9X and other compatible MS-DOS programs. Figure 4-16 illustrates the allocation of extended memory.

Figure 4-16 Extended Memory Allocation

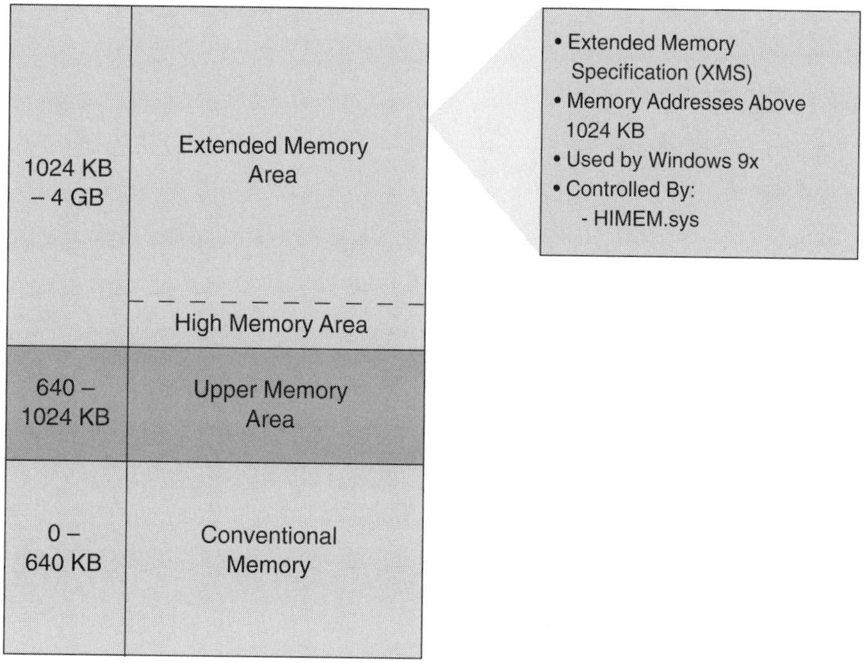

High Memory

As previously mentioned, after the XMS driver is loaded, extended memory becomes available to the OS. When this happens, the first 64 KB of extended memory is called the high memory area (HMA). Typically, the XMS driver (himem.sys) activates the DOS=HIGH option, enabling it to copy the MS-DOS kernel used by Windows 9X into the HMA. Therefore, DOS uses the HMA, and by so doing, frees more conventional memory for use by applications. Figure 4-17 illustrates the allocation of high memory.

Figure 4-17 High Memory Allocation

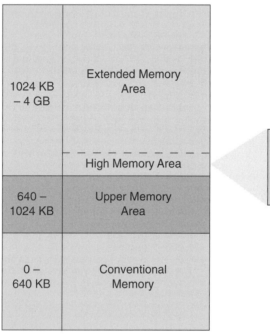

Memory-Management Tools: Adjusting and Optimizing System Memory

Several tools can be used to manage and optimize system memory. Some of these tools and their uses are explained as follows:

- EMM386.EXE—This memory manager emulates expanded memory and thus makes upper memory available for use by the OS. It can be used as follows:
  - To add MS-DOS TSR utilities into UMBs, include the following line in config.sys:

    DEVICE=C: \WINDOWS\EMM386.EXE NOEMS

The NOEMS (No Expanded Memory) option tells the OS not to convert extended memory to expanded memory. This is shown in Figure 4-18. The file io.sys adds the following statement to the memory configuration to make UMBs available to MS-DOS TSRs:

DOS=UMB

Figure 4-18 Adding MS-DOS TSR Utilities into UMBs

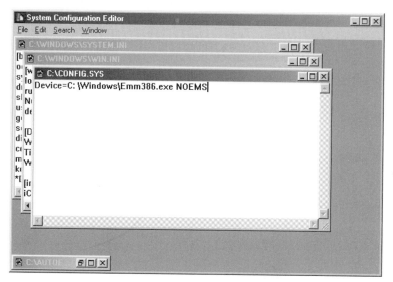

— To add MS-DOS applications needing access to EMS memory, include the following statement in config.sys:

DEVICE=C: \WINDOWS\EMM386.EXE RAM

This statement, shown in Figure 4-19, converts XMS memory space to a common pool of XMS/EMS memory that is available to both Windows 9X and DOS applications. Note that again the DOS=UMB statement is added by io.sys to make unused UMBs available to MS-DOS TSRs.

- HIMEM.SYS—Load this device driver to convert memory starting at 1 MB available as extended memory. The driver is loaded from config.sys. The syntax for this command is as follows:

DEVICE=C: \DOS\HIMEM.SYS

- DOS=HIGH—This option is added in config.sys to tell the OS to move a portion of itself (such as the MS-DOS kernel) into the HMA. This command is usually combined with DOS=UMB to create a UMB using the following syntax:

DOS=HIGH, UMB

■ DEVICEHIGH/LOADHIGH—DEVICEHIGH (used in config.sys) and LOADHIGH (used in autoexec.bat) both put upper memory blocks to use, once himem.sys and emm386.exe have been loaded. To load a mouse driver into upper memory, for example, use the following syntax:

DEVICEHIGH=C: \DOS\MOUSE.SYS

Figure 4-19 Adding an MS-DOS Application with Access to EMS Memory

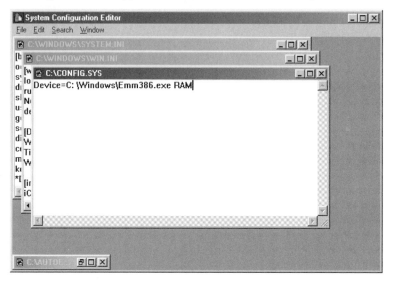

Other system memory tools include MEMMAKER, included with DOS 6.0, to help simplify the task of placing TSRs into upper memory. Use this utility to make the needed entries in config.sys and autoexec.bat.

Other Types of Memory

Other types of memory are outside the physical or system memory discussed in the preceding sections. Two examples of these are the virtual memory and the RAM drive.

Virtual Memory: Swap File or Page File on Disk

The term *virtual memory* is used to describe memory that isn't what it appears to be; hard disk drive space is manipulated to seem like RAM. The combination of virtual memory and installed physical memory gives the appearance of more memory than is actually installed in the system. Virtual memory is the basis of multitasking in Windows 9X. Without virtual memory, it would be almost impossible to run most of today's software. Windows 3.X and 9X implement virtual memory in files called *swap files*. Software called the *memory manager* or *memory management unit (MMU)* creates virtual memory by swapping files between RAM and the hard disk drive, as illustrated in Figure 4-20. This memory-management technique is how more total memory is created for the system applications to use.

NOTE

Because the hard drive is slower than RAM, an overall reduction in speed is encountered with virtual memory operations. In fact, virtual memory is the slowest of any memory model.

Figure 4-20 How Virtual Memory Operates

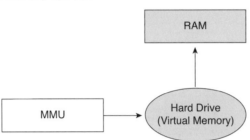

It is difficult to think of any OS since Windows 3X (Windows 9X, Windows NT/2000/XP, UNIX, or Linux) does not use some form of virtual memory operations. In older OSs, there was often a permanent swap file, having an extension of par. Today, most OSs use temporary swap files with an swp extension. A permanent swap file is always present and is a constant size. A temporary swap file is created when Windows starts and has a variable size. Control of Windows 95 (also Windows 98 and Me) virtual memory operations is established through the Control Panel's System Performance tab, as shown in Figure 4-21.

Figure 4-21 System Performance in the Control Panel

Clicking the Virtual Memory button produces the Virtual Memory options screen. The default and recommended setting is "Let Windows manage my virtual memory settings," as shown in Figure 4-22.

Figure 4-22   Controlling Windows' Virtual Memory

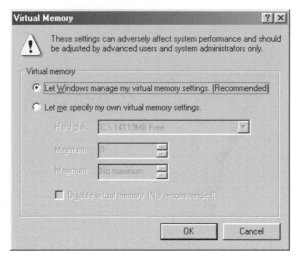

The Windows 95 swap file is called win386.swp. It is dynamically assigned and varies in size. The Windows 2000 swap file (or page file) is pagefile.sys. This file, created when Windows 2000 is installed, has a default size that is typically 1.5 times the amount of RAM installed in the system.

RAM Drive

Setting aside a portion of RAM to emulate a drive can create a *RAM drive*. For example, on a machine that has a hard drive partitioned into drives C and D, a RAM drive of 4 MB (4096 KB) can be created as the E drive with the following command:

    DEVICE=C: \DOS\RAMDRIVE.SYS 4096

This command is entered in config.sys. The RAM drive becomes the next available alphabetical letter and can be any size up to the amount of RAM installed on the computer. Because data stored on the RAM drive exists only in RAM, these data are cleared on each reboot. This is obviously not a good place to store data files.

Memory Conflicts: General Protection Faults

Several things can cause a memory conflict (for example, two memory managers running at the same time, such as those from a third party and those supplied with

MS-DOS). Many diagnostic tools can be used to remedy such problems, including the Microsoft Diagnostics (MSD) utility.

Memory conflicts can lead to a condition called a *general protection fault (GPF)*. Figure 4-23 shows an example of a GPF, also commonly known as the "blue screen of death." The GPF indicates that an error has occurred and provides the choices that are available to the user. Usually, the best choice is to restart the system.

Figure 4-23 A General Protection Fault (GPF)

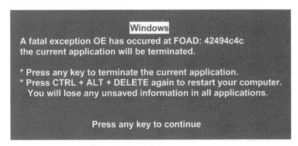

A GPF is a carryover from the 16-bit Windows 3.*X* era, where Win 16 applications are run. A GPF typically occurs when an application attempts to violate the system integrity in one of the following ways:

- Tries to use a memory address or space taken by another application
- Tries to interact with a failing hardware driver
- Tries to have direct access to the system hardware

Other conflicting situations arise when, at any given time, more than one memory-resident routine (such as TSRs) is attempting to access the same upper memory space (address). A GPF is usually manifested by a nonresponsive system or application(s) that were running. Figure 4-24 shows the error message that is generated when a GPF occurs. The use of diagnostic utilities, mentioned earlier, is necessary to remedy these conflicts. If the conflicting applications are found, one way of resolving the problem is to reassign different memory areas by using the various memory-management and -optimization tools described earlier in this chapter.

Real-Mode Versus Protected-Mode Memory Addressing

The concepts of real- and protected-mode memory addressing come up frequently in discussions of memory that is located above conventional memory (that is, all memory above 1024 KB).

Figure 4-24   A Sample GPF Error Message

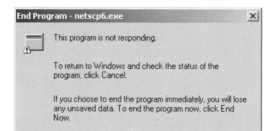

Real Mode

Real-mode memory addressing means that software, such as DOS or its applications, can address only 1024 KB (1 MB) of RAM. In other words, running in *real mode* means that the microprocessor chip addresses the first 1024 bytes of conventional memory by assigning real addresses to real locations in memory. An 80286 system running in real mode, for example, acts essentially the same as an 8088/86 system and can run older software with no modifications.

Protected Mode

The counterpart to real-mode memory addressing is *protected-mode memory addressing*. Unlike real mode, protected mode in theory allows one program to fail without bringing down the system. The theory behind *protected-mode* is that what happens in one area of memory has no effect on other programs. When running in protected mode, a program is limited to its own memory space allocation, but it can access memory above 1 MB. The 80286 chip could address up to 16 MB of memory, but software could use the chip to access even more memory. However, before programs that run concurrently are truly safe from one another's actions, the microprocessor (along with other system chips) requires an OS that can work to provide that protection. Just about every OS other than DOS runs in protected mode.

Summary

This chapter discussed the basics of the OS, the program that controls thousands of operations, provides an interface between the user and the computer, and runs applications. Some of the important concepts to retain from this chapter are as follows:

- The three elements that make up the OS include the user interface, kernel, and file-management system.

- Multiusers means the OS is capable of running programs and sharing devices for two or more users. Multitasking means that the OS can handle multiple applications. An OS is multiprocessing if it can support a computer with two or more CPUs that programs can share. Multithreading is the capability of a program to be broken into smaller parts that can be loaded as needed by the OS.

- The GUI is what makes Windows one of the most popular OSs. It is the GUI that makes the computer easier to use than the previous DOS environment.

- DOS is primarily responsible for finding and organizing data and applications on the hard drive. The sections that make up DOS include boot files, file-management files, and utility files.

- DOS is a useful troubleshooting tool when Windows will not load. Understanding the DOS command line and common commands and switches enables the technician to access the hard drive and run diagnostic programs.

- The boot disk is used to boot the computer to the DOS prompt. The boot disk must include the following system files: command.com, io.sys, and msdos.sys. In addition, diagnostic tools are added for troubleshooting.

- Two configuration files are used to optimize the system in DOS: config.sys and autoexec.bat. The config.sys file resides in the root directory and is used to load drivers and change settings at startup. The autoexec.bat file contains DOS commands that are automatically carried out when DOS is loaded into the system.

- The two main types of memory are system memory, also known as physical memory, and virtual memory. System memory includes four categories in the OS: conventional, upper/expanded, high, and extended. It is important to understand how system memory is divided into logical types. Virtual memory is memory that is not what it appears to be. The combination of virtual memory and installed physical memory gives the appearance of more memory than is actually in the system.

- Memory conflicts occur when two memory managers running at the same time collide. Memory conflicts can lead to a GPF, which typically occurs when an application attempts to violate the system integrity.

The next chapter goes beyond the DOS operating system to explain the Windows operating system. You will gain an understanding of how the Windows file structure and file-management system work, and the steps required to install Windows.

Check Your Understanding

The following are review questions for the A+ exam. Answers can be found in Appendix B, "Answers to Check Your Understanding Review Questions."

1. What is the definition of an operating system?

   A. Software that executes other software

   B. An interface between a user and software

   C. A software program that controls thousands of operations, provides an interface between the user and the computer, and runs applications

   D. Software that is manipulated by hardware

2. Which of the following is not a valid OS?

   A. DOS

   B. Windows

   C. LAN

   D. UNIX

3. What does DOS stand for?

   A. Disk Operating Sectors

   B. Disk Operating System

   C. Disk Operating Services

   D. Disk Organizing Software

4. What is the maximum length of a DOS filename?

   A. 8 characters with an extension of 3 characters

   B. 12 characters; the extension is optional

   C. 16 characters with an extension of 4 characters

   D. 32 characters with an extension of 3 characters

5. What three files are necessary on a DOS boot disk?

   A. autoexec.bat, io.sys, command.com

   B. io.sys, command.com, system.ini

   C. io.sys, msdos.sys, command.com

   D. win.ini, system.ini, command.com

6. Where is the statement LOADHI or LH used?

   A. config.sys

   B. autoexec.bat

   C. system.ini

   D. msdos.sys

7. What does the DOS command MEM show?

   A. Memory updates

   B. Memory properties

   C. Microsoft enhanced memory

   D. DOS memory installed

8. Which of the following is an external DOS command?

   A. DIR

   B. HELP

   C. COPY

   D. CLS

9. Which of the following is an internal DOS command?

   A. GRAPHICS

   B. UNERASE

   C. DISKCOPY

   D. DIR

10. How do you show all the system files within a directory?

    A. DIR *.SYS

    B. DIR SYS

    C. DIR SYS /ALL

    D. DIR *.SYS /ALL

11. An ini file usually contains what type of information?

    A. The locations of files used by the operating system

    B. The names and locations of startup files

    C. User instructions

    D. Parameter information about a program

12. What does the DEVICE= statement mean in config.sys?

    A. It identifies the devices on the computer.

    B. It sets up the driver configuration.

    C. It tells the operating system what drivers are running.

    D. It loads a device driver.

13. What is in conventional memory loaded right above DOS?

    A. Command interpreter

    B. Device drivers

    C. config.sys

    D. msdos.sys

14. What is the memory address from 0 to 640 KB called?

    A. Common memory

    B. Basic memory

    C. Usable memory

    D. Conventional memory

15. What is extended memory?

    A. All memory above 640 KB

    B. Memory between 640 KB and 1024 KB

    C. All memory below 640 KB

    D. All memory after 1024 KB

16. What is the first 64 KB of extended memory called?

   A. XMS

   B. UMB

   C. HMA

   D. Conventional

17. What is virtual memory?

   A. Swapping memory in and out of the high memory area

   B. Simulating RAM by using a file on the hard drive

   C. Paging memory between conventional memory and the HMA

   D. Using extended memory to simulate expanded memory

18. If the himem.sys file is corrupt or missing, what will happen?

   A. Windows will start in Safe mode.

   B. Windows will load but applications will not run.

   C. Windows 98 will load but will not use more than 640 KB.

   D. Windows 98 will not load.

19. What program is used to find and repair lost clusters?

   A. SCANDISK

   B. DEFRAG

   C. MSD

   D. DOS

20. Which program is used to set up a partition on a hard drive?

   A. PARTITION

   B. FDISK

   C. FORMAT

   D. DISKPART

21. What file should not be edited by the user?

   A. config.sys

   B. win.ini

   C. autoexec.bat

   D. himem.sys

22. Why would a read-only attribute be applied to a file?

A. So it cannot be changed

B. So it can only be read by DOS

C. So changes can be tracked

D. So the user knows it is a system file

23. How do you step through the startup files when DOS starts?

A. Press F5.

B. Press F6.

C. Press F8.

D. Press Shift-F5.

Key Terms

/A   Switch added to the COPY command to copy ASCII files.

/ALL   Switch added to the SCANDISK command to check and repair all local drives at once.

archive   A backup copy of files.

ATTRIB   Command used to display, set, or remove one or more attributes.

attributes   A set of parameters that describe a file.

autoexec.bat   Configuration file used by the operating system. It contains a group of DOS commands that are automatically carried out when DOS is loaded into the system.

/AUTOFIX   Switch added to the SCANDISK command to fix errors without further input.

/B   Switch added to the COPY command to copy binary files.

bootable disk   A disk created to boot the computer to the operating system for troubleshooting purposes. It contains the three required system files. Also known as a system disk.

boot files   Used to start the system.

boot sector   Contains information about how the disk is organized.

/C   Switch added to the MEM command to list programs currently loaded into memory. It shows how much conventional and upper memory each program is using.

C drive   The label for the first hard drive in a computer system.

CD   DOS command that changes or displays the current directory on a specific drive.

/CHECKONLY   Switch added to the SCANDISK command to check for errors but not make repairs.

command line   The main user interface in DOS.

config.sys   Configuration file used by the operating system. It loads drivers and changes settings at startup.

conventional memory   Includes all memory addresses between 0 and 640 KB. It is also known as base memory.

COPY   Used to copy one or more files from one location to another.

/D   Switch added to the MEM command to list the programs and internal drivers that are currently loaded into memory.

DATE   Command in autoexec.bat that causes DOS to prompt the user for the date.

DEL   Command that removes named files.

DELTREE   DOS command that removes a directory, including all files and subdirectories.

DEVICEHIGH/LOADHIGH   Puts upper memory blocks into use once himem.sys and emm386.exe have been loaded.

DIR   Command in autoexec.bat that causes a DOS DIR command to be performed automatically.

directories   A group of files stored in DOS.

directory tree   A graphical representation of a disk drive's directory organization.

DOS boot disk   Used to boot a computer to the DOS prompt.

DOS command   An instruction that is executed from a command line.

DOS (Disk Operating System)   A collection of programs and commands used to control the overall computer operation in a disk-based system.

DOS=HIGH   Option included in config.sys to tell the operating system to move a portion of itself to the high memory area.

DOSKEY   Command in autoexec.bat that loads the DOSKEY program into memory.

EDIT   Command used to view or modify files.

emm386.exe   Memory manager that emulates expanded memory and makes upper memory available for use by the operating system.

expanded memory   Memory closely related to upper memory.

expanded memory specification (EMS)   Memory accessed in pages (16 KB pieces) from a 64 KB page frame, established in unused UMBs.

extended memory   Memory above 1 MB.

extended memory specification (XMS)   Primary memory area used by Windows 9X.

external command   A command that must be executed from a file.

/F   Switch added to the MEM command to list the free areas of conventional and upper memory.

F5   Skips config.sys, including autoexec.bat files.

F8   Proceeds through the config.sys files (and autoexec.bat if needed), waiting for confirmation from the user.

FAT32   An improved version of FAT that was introduced in Windows 98.

FDISK   An external DOS command used to delete and/or create partitions on the hard drive.

file   A block of logically related data given a single name and treated as a single unit.

file allocation table (FAT)   A table of records that includes the location of every directory, subdirectory, and file on the hard drive.

file cabinet   The hard drive in a computer where files are stored.

file-management files   Enable the system to manage data.

file-management system   Used by the operating system to organize and manage files.

filename   The logical name given to a collection of data.

FORMAT   Command that erases all information from a computer disk or hard drive.

general protection fault (GPF)   Memory conflict.

hidden file   An attribute that hides files. Primarily used to hide important files that should not be changed.

himem.sys   Device driver that converts memory starting at 1 MB available as extended memory.

internal command   A command that is built into the operating system.

kernel   The core of the operating system that loads and runs programs or processes and manages input and output.

Macintosh   Designed to be user friendly, based on the UNIX core technology.

master boot record (MBR)   The required boot record on any disks that are created as boot or system disks.

MEM   An external DOS command used to display a table showing how RAM is currently allocated.

MEMMAKER   System memory tool used to simplify the task of placing TSRs into upper memory.

Microsoft Windows NT/2000/XP   Operating systems designed to support multiple users and to run multiple applications simultaneously.

MKDIR   DOS command that creates a new directory or subdirectory.

MORE   DOS command that displays output one screen at a time.

multiprocessing   Allows a computer to have two or more CPUs that programs share.

multitasking   The computer's ability to run multiple applications at the same time.

multithreading   The capability of a program to be broken into smaller parts that can be loaded as needed by the operating system.

multiuser   The ability for two or more users to run programs and share resources.

network operating system (NOS)   An operating system that enables the server to track multiple users and programs.

network servers (also know as servers)   Computers that are capable of handling multiple users and multiple jobs.

operating system   A program that controls thousands of operations, provides an interface between the user and the computer, and runs applications.

/P   Switch added to the MEM command to pause at each screen of information.

PATH=C:\;C:\DOS;C:\Mouse   Command in autoexec.bat that creates a specific set of paths that DOS uses to search for executable files.

physical memory (also known as system memory)   Memory that is divided into four categories: conventional, upper/expanded, high, and extended.

PROMPT-PG   Command in autoexec.bat that causes the active drive and directory path to be displayed on the command line.

protected mode   An area of memory that has no effect on other programs.

protected-mode memory addressing   Allows one program to fail without bringing down the rest of the system.

/Q   Switch added to the FORMAT command to perform a quick format; it does not clear the FAT.

RAM drive   Setting aside a portion of RAM to emulate a drive.

read-only   An attribute that allows a file to be opened but not changed.

real mode   Refers to the microprocessor chip that addresses the first 1024 KB of conventional memory by assigning real addresses to real locations in memory.

real-mode memory addressing   Software, such as DOS, that can address only the first 1024 KB of memory.

RMDIR   DOS command that removes a directory or subdirectory.

root   The top level of a directory.

root directory   The file system's main directory.

/S   Switch added to the FORMAT command to copy system files.

SCANDISK   DOS program designed to detect and repair errors on the hard drive or floppy drive.

SET TEMP C:\TEMP   Command in autoexec.bat that sets up a temporary data-holding area in the TEMP directory.

SMARTDRV.EXE 2048 1024   Command in autoexec.bat that configures the system for a 1 MB disk cache in DOS and a 2 MB cache in Windows.

/STATUS   Switch added to the FDISK command to display partition information.

subdirectories   A directory within a directory in DOS.

swap files   Implementing virtual memory by swapping files between RAM and the hard disk drive.

switch   An operation added to a command to modify the output.

sysedit.exe   Text editor used to edit system configuration files.

system disk   A disk created to boot the computer to the operating system for trouble-shooting purposes. It contains the three required system files. Also known as a boot disk.

system file   A file required by DOS to boot up.

TIME   Command in autoexec.bat that causes DOS to prompt the user for the time and date.

/U   Switch added to the FORMAT command to perform an unconditional format.

UNIX   Used primarily to run and maintain computer networks.

upper memory blocks (UMBs)   Allocated memory in upper memory.

upper memory/expanded memory   Also known as reserved memory. It includes memory addresses between 640 KB and 1024 KB (1 MB).

user interface   The part of the operating system that is used to issue commands.

utility files   Enable the user to manage system resources, troubleshoot the system, and configure the system settings.

utility program   Used to maintain and repair the operating system.

/V   Switch added to the COPY command to verify the action.

virtual memory   Manipulating hard disk space to provide more memory than is actually installed.

/Y   Switch added to the COPY command to replace existing files without a confirmation prompt.

/–Y   Switch added to the COPY command to display a confirmation prompt before overwriting an existing file.

Objectives

Upon completion of this chapter, you will be able to perform the following tasks:

- Manage and organize the drives and files in Windows
- Use the tools provided in the Windows Control Panel
- Understand the Registry and the tools available
- Format and partition a hard drive
- Prepare the hard drive and install the Windows operating system
- Troubleshoot the Windows installation with the tips and tricks used by professional technicians

Chapter 5

Windows 9*X* Operating Systems

Introduction

Windows 9*X* refers to Windows 95, Windows 95 OEM Service Release 2 (OSR2), Windows 98, and Windows Me collectively. In this chapter, you learn about the Windows file structure and how the file-management system works. This chapter provides information on the Registry and the system tools that are used to manage the information contained in the operating system. Preparing a hard drive and then installing an operating system are covered in detail as is troubleshooting the system.

The Windows 9*X* File Structure and File-Management System

This section includes the following topics:

- Naming files in Windows
- Using directories and folders
- Using a text-editing application to create a file
- Copying, moving, and creating shortcuts: Windows Explorer
- Viewing document details
- Recognizing file types in Windows
- Selecting, copying, and moving files
- Searching for a file, folder, or directory
- Make backup copies of files on a floppy disk
- Using the Recycle Bin

Naming Files in Windows

It is important to understand how the Windows file structure and file-management system work. This chapter provides information on directories, Windows Explorer, drive letters, filenames, and valid characters.

A *directory* and a *folder* are equivalent terms for the same concept—a place to store information. Prior to the introduction of Windows, files were stored in directories and subdirectories utilizing a tree structure. While this structure still exists in the graphical Windows environment, the terminology has changed from directories to folders. A *subfolder* is simply a folder within a folder. Figure 5-1 shows the folders on drive C. Similarly, *files* are now referred to as *documents*. These terms are now used somewhat interchangeably (files, directories, and folders are discussed more thoroughly in a later section).

Figure 5-1 Folders on Drive C

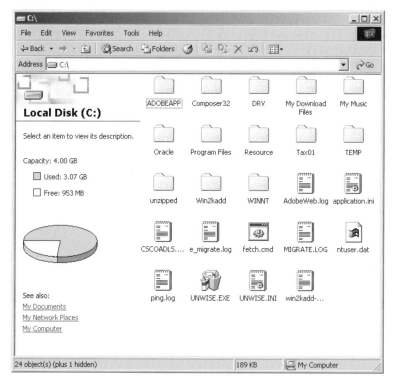

Windows 3.1 and DOS filenames are limited to eight characters plus a three-letter suffix called an extension (this DOS format is referred to as an 8+3 format). Windows 98 and later versions of Windows allow filenames of up to 255 characters in length. Folder names follow the same length rules as filenames.

Never use any of the following characters in filenames or folder names, because each is associated with a special function that executes a command from a prompt:

/ \ ; : * ? " < >

If these characters are used, a warning is displayed, prompting the user to rename a file, as shown in Figure 5-2. Allowable filename characters include all other characters and numbers that are available on a standard keyboard.

Figure 5-2 Invalid Filename Error Message

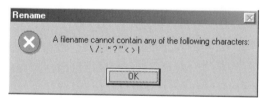

TEST TIP

Know what characters can be used when naming files in Windows.

Uppercase characters are treated the same as lowercase characters in Windows. A file named BOB.TXT is considered the same as a file named bob.txt. However, this is not true on the Internet, which uses UNIX servers. UNIX treats filenames more uniquely, so BOB.TXT is different from bob.txt.

Drive Letters

Drive letters use the 26 letters of the alphabet followed by a colon. The letters A: and B: are reserved for floppy drives, C: refers to the first (or only) hard drive or drive partition, D: is used for a subsequent hard drive or partition (if present), and E: represents the CD-ROM or DVD-ROM drive. In this example, if only one hard drive were present, the CD-ROM or DVD-ROM drive would be represented by D:.

The *My Computer* window lists all the hard drives, floppy drives, CD-ROM drives, DVD-ROM drives, and network drives that are part of the computer or that can be accessed over a network, as shown in Figure 5-3. Use caution when making drive letter assignments because many DOS and Windows programs make references to a specific drive letter.

Figure 5-3 The My Computer Window

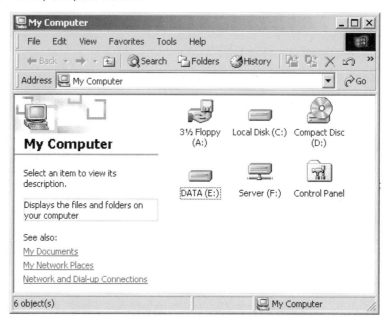

In Windows 98, in addition to each drive being assigned a drive letter, the drive can optionally be assigned a name called a *drive label*. The drive label can be up to 11 characters in length.

Using Directories and Folders

It is important to know how Windows manages files. In this section, you learn about the Windows basic directory structure and file-management system.

To understand files, folders, and subfolders, imagine a tree. The trunk is the starting place or the main part of the tree. When dealing with files and folders, the trunk or main starting place is the root directory or root folder. Branches of the tree are folders. These folders connect to the trunk. Minor branches attach to these major branches as subfolders are inside (attached) to folders. Leaves attach to the major and minor branches just like files attach to (are inside of) folders and subfolders. A Windows utility application called Windows Explorer represents this concept of a tree and branches in the Windows file-management (directory) structure.

Windows Explorer displays the *file management* as a hierarchical structure of files, folders, and drives on a computer as shown in Figure 5-4. To open Explorer, choose **Start, Programs, Windows Explorer.** Alternatively, right-click the Start button and choose Explore from the pop-up menu. There are three main parts to this window: the area at the top known as the *title bar*, the pane on the left labeled Folders, and the pane on the right that contains filenames and possibly file details such as size and type.

NOTE

The best way to understand the Windows Explorer is to open it and practice viewing folders and files. Click the plus sign to display contents, and click the minus sign to collapse the folders. Also, try the different view options, and notice the information that each provides.

Figure 5-4 Windows Explorer

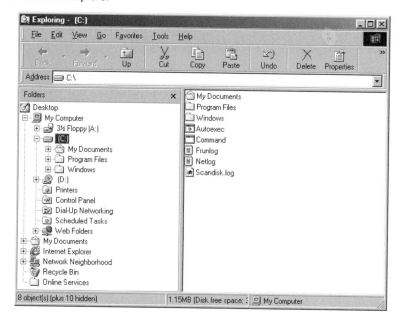

These files can be viewed in different modes by selecting the View icon on the title bar, as shown in Figure 5-5.

The Details mode gives the most information about each file, but other modes can simplify the viewing by providing just the name of the file, as in the List view.

Folders that contain subfolders have a plus sign beside that folder. Click the plus sign to view subfolders. Click a specific folder in the left pane and the folder contents (files and possible subfolders) appear in the right pane. Click the plus sign to view all the files and folders. Notice that this action causes the plus sign to become a minus sign. Click the minus sign to collapse the subfolders back into the folder.

Figure 5-5 The View Option in Windows Explorer

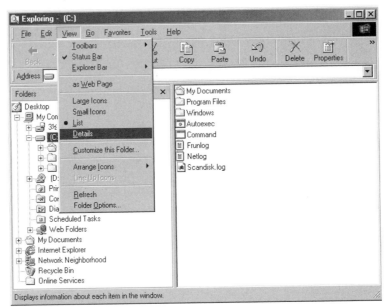

File management is done to organize a computer. Just as a desk or a room can become messy with many items scattered around, so can the files on a computer. Folders allow you to store your files in a logical and neat manner.

Creating a New Folder

To make a new folder, use the scroll bar between the left and right panes, and in the left pane, locate and click the desktop. The *desktop* is the area of the screen that appears when Windows 98 boots. The desktop allows easy access to Windows 98 files, folders, hardware devices, applications, and possibly the Internet or other computers. With the desktop highlighted, move the cursor to the right pane and right-click a blank area. Choose **New, Folder**, as shown in Figure 5-6.

As you create the folder, the rename mode is shown by the highlighted words New Folder. Simply start typing the folder name, and the changes appear on the screen. Press Enter or simply click a blank screen area when finished typing. Remember, a folder name can have up to 255 characters and must use valid characters. To rename the folder later, click the folder once to highlight it and press F2. The name highlights, and you can type the new name. In Figure 5-7, the folder is given the name Projects.

Figure 5-6 Creating a New Folder in Windows

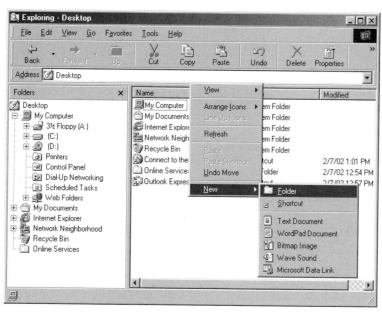

Figure 5-7 Renaming a Folder

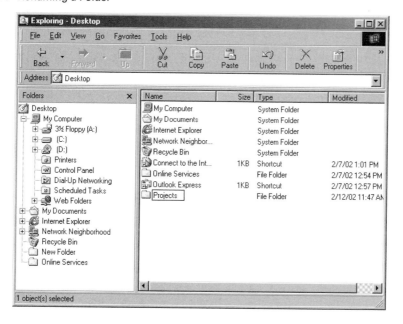

Worksheet 5.1.10   Windows Files and Folders

This worksheet reviews the information necessary to understand Windows files and folders.

Using a Text-Editing Application to Create a File

In this section, a file (document) is created using WordPad to demonstrate the process of saving a file and then moving it. This document is created by typing the steps needed to wash a car, as shown in Figure 5-8.

Figure 5-8   Car Wash Steps in WordPad

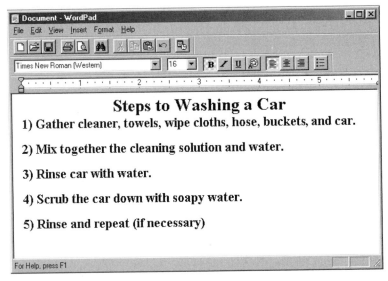

The document can be saved in rich text format (RTF) to the desktop by selecting Save As from the File menu, as shown in Figure 5-9, and entering the filename Car Wash Steps.doc, as shown in Figure 5-10.

Figure 5-9 Saving the Document

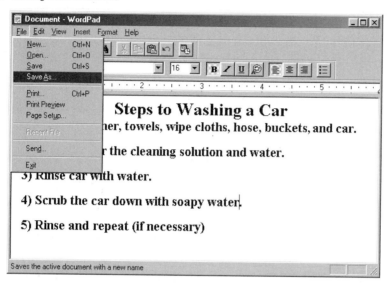

Figure 5-10 Save As Information

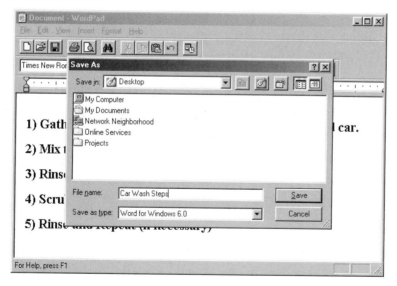

Additionally, the file can be changed from RTF to the Word for Windows format by clicking the Save As option from the File menu. Use the following steps:

Step 1   Choose **File, Save As.**

Step 2   In the Save as Type text box, choose **Rich Text Format** as shown in Figure 5-11.

Step 3   Click **Save.**

Figure 5-11   Saving as a Rich Text Format (RTF) Document

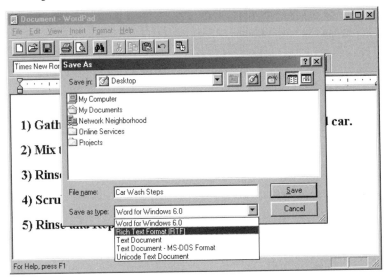

Now, open Windows Explorer, as shown in Figure 5-12. In the left pane, click the desktop. Desktop items then display in the right pane.

To view the full name of the file, as in Figure 5-13, move the cursor to the file properties bar between the Name and Size columns. Note that a double-headed arrow appears. Double-click between Name and Size. The filename region then self-adjusts, displaying the full name of every file.

Figure 5-12 Car Wash Steps Document in Windows Explorer

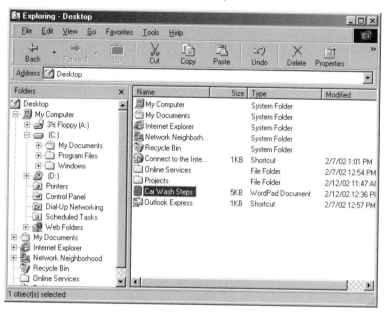

Figure 5-13 Expanding the Filename Column

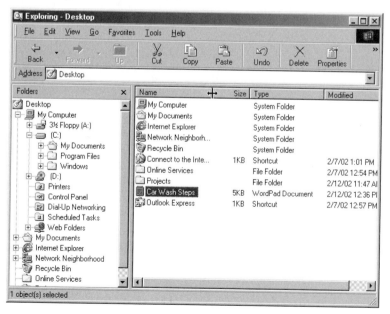

You can move Car Wash Steps.doc to the Projects folder using one of the following methods:

1. On the desktop, click and hold the mouse button while dragging the file to the Projects folder; the file becomes semitransparent until it disappears into the Projects folder, as shown in Figure 5-14.

Figure 5-14 Moving a Desktop Item into a Folder

2. In Windows Explorer, drag the file to the Projects folder, as shown in Figure 5-15.

Figure 5-15 Moving a Windows Explorer File into a Folder

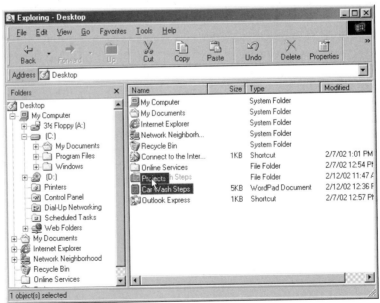

3. Cut the file from the desktop, and paste it to the Projects folder. Right-click the file, and select Cut from the pop-up menu. Move the cursor to the Projects folder, right-click an empty area, and select Paste from the pop-up menu. The results are shown in Figure 5-16.

Figure 5-16 Verifying the Recently Moved Document

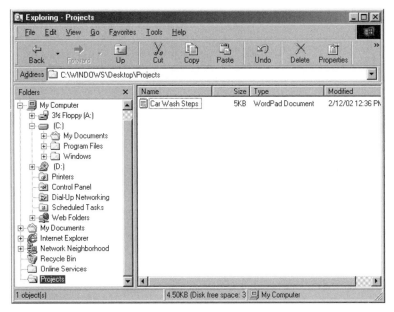

Copying, Moving, and Creating Shortcuts: Windows Explorer

Another folder can be created inside the previous folder and files or documents copied into this folder. Figure 5-17 shows the options that are available by right-clicking an item. Copying, moving, and creating shortcuts are described in the following list:

- **Copy** makes a duplicate of the file and puts it into the newly created folder. You now have two files, one file inside the new folder and one file outside the new folder. Both files have the same name; this is permitted as long as the files are not in the same folder with the same attributes.

- **Move** relocates the original file to the new folder.

- **Create Shortcut** makes a link from where the file currently resides to the desktop or other folder. If you click a shortcut, the original document opens from its original location (not from the shortcut location).

Figure 5-17   Options Available When You Right-Click an Item

 Lab Activity 5.1.6   Change File Views in Windows

Upon completion of this lab, you will be able to change the file view based on the information needed or preference.

Viewing Document Details

File details or *document details* in Windows are the same as *file attributes* in MS-DOS. The right pane in Windows Explorer provides the details of the directory, folders, and files, as shown in Figure 5-18. Details include the creation or last-modified date of a file or folder, the type of item (folder, MS Word document, MS Excel spreadsheet, etc.), and file size.

Figure 5-18 Viewing File Attributes

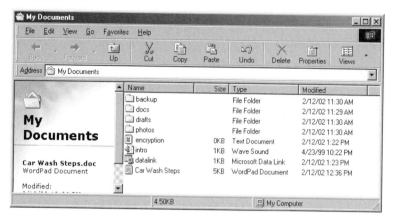

Many users include the date that the file was last opened in the document filename to track the latest versions. You can also indicate versions by adding numbers or "ver 1" to filenames. The author's name or organization can also be useful in filenames, especially if others share the documents.

Recognizing File Types in Windows

This section discusses how to recognize the most widely used types of files in a directory/folder (for example, word processing, spreadsheet, database, presentation, RTF, and image files). The main parameter used, previously mentioned in this chapter, is the file extension.

The *file extensions* shown in Table 5-1 describe the file format or type of application that is associated with the file.

Table 5-1 File Extensions and Their Descriptions

File Extension	Description
doc	Microsoft Word or WordPad
xls	Microsoft Excel
dbf or dat	Database
txt	ASCII text with no formatting
exe, com, bat	Executable file

continues

Table 5-1 File Extensions and Their Descriptions (Continued)

File Extension	Description
sys	DOS or Windows driver
dll	Windows dynamic link library
htm or html	Internet hypertext markup language (web page)
ini	Windows or other configuration file
rtf	Rich text format
wks, wk1	Lotus 1-2-3 spreadsheet
bmp	Bitmap
jpeg	Joint Photographic Experts Group
mpg	Moving Pictures Group
gif	Graphic interchange format
tif	Tagged image format
ppt	PowerPoint
wav, mp3	Sound
log, bat	Log or batch file

Lab Activity 5.1.7   Text Editing and File Management

In this lab, you create a file in Notepad, save it to the hard drive, and create a folder on a floppy disk.

Selecting, Copying, and Moving Files

This section details how to select a file individually or as part of a group. Copying files and pasting files within directories/folders to make duplicate copies are also explained.

To select a file, right-click it, and select Copy from the pop-up menu, as shown in Figure 5-19. Go to the location where it is to be pasted.

Figure 5-19 The Copy Option

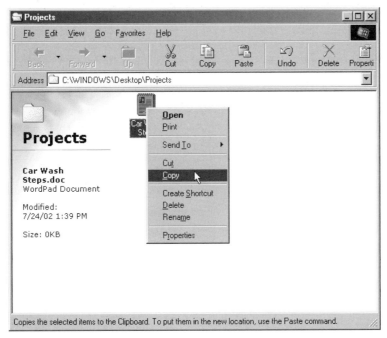

Right-click a blank area of Explorer's right pane, and choose Paste, as shown in Figure 5-20. A duplicate copy of that file is now available.

To select several files (even discontinuous ones), hold Ctrl while clicking the filenames. The files are then highlighted. To deselect a file, continue holding Ctrl and click the file to be deselected.

To highlight all files, select Edit from the toolbar menu, and then choose Select All. To deselect all the files, press Esc. Once these files are highlighted, they can be moved, copied, deleted, or opened simultaneously.

Searching for a File, Folder, or Directory

To find a file or folder, choose **Start, Find** (or **Start, Search** in Windows 2000), as shown in Figure 5-21. Next, choose Files or Folders, and type in the name or part of the name of the file, as shown in Figure 5-22. An efficient search means looking for a file or folder using a part of the name that is unique. In this example, choosing Wash, Car Wash, or Steps helps you narrow the search to just a few files. Windows then searches for files or folders that contain that word, as shown in Figure 5-23. You can also sort by date created or modified, or by type of file. Double-click the file to open it.

NOTE

Use the following shortcut to reach files or folders: Press the Windows key, press **f** for Find, and press **f** again for Files and Folders.

Figure 5-20 The Paste Option

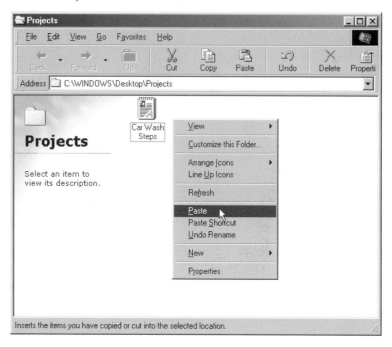

Figure 5-21 Search for Files or Folders

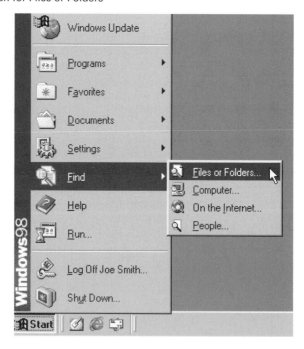

Figure 5-22 Enter a Unique Part of the Name "Wash"

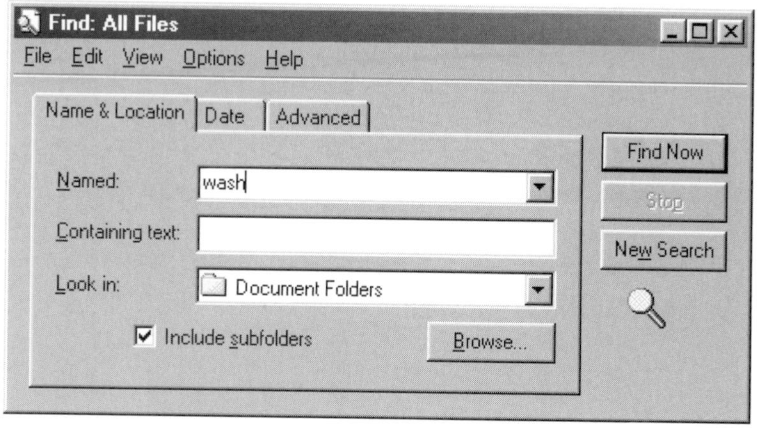

Figure 5-23 Search Results

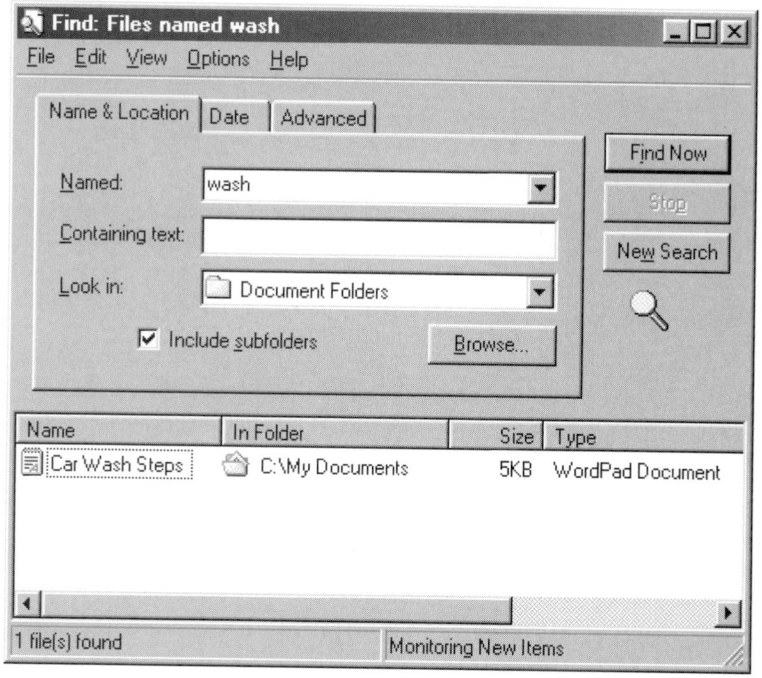

In addition to indicating the text you are searching for, it is important to indicate where the search should occur. The system can search the entire hard drive, the desktop, or specific folders.

Make Backup Copies of Files on a Floppy Disk

To copy a file or folder to a floppy disk, right-click the file and choose Send To 3-1/2 Floppy. You can also drag and drop selected files to the drive A icon, as shown in Figure 5-24.

Figure 5-24   Sending a File to a Floppy Disk

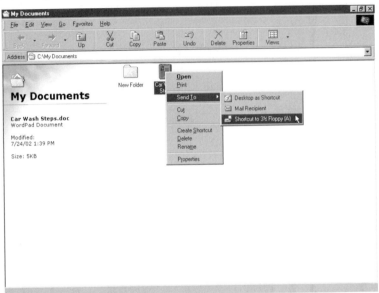

Using the Recycle Bin

The *Recycle Bin* can be used to temporarily delete or permanently delete files from the computer. Until the Recycle Bin is emptied, the files remain on the hard drive. Before the Recycle Bin is emptied, files can be restored (or undeleted) to their original folder(s). In Windows 98, 10 percent of the hard drive is set aside for the recycle bin by default.

Double-clicking the Recycle Bin icon on the desktop opens a window that shows the files that have been deleted. Right-click a filename, and then select Delete from the shortcut menu, as shown in Figure 5-25, to clear the file from the Recycle Bin.

Right-click a filename, and then select Restore from the pop-up menu, as shown in Figure 5-26, to restore the file to the hard drive.

rmanently Deleting a File

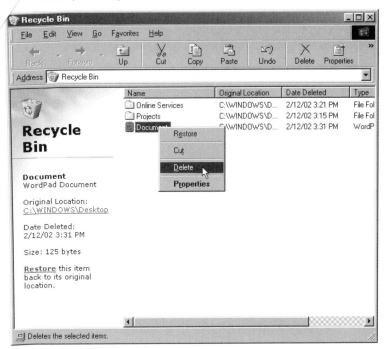

Figure 5-26 Restoring a File

Right-click the file to view Document Properties. The window that opens displays the file's original folder, as shown in Figure 5-27.

Figure 5-27 Original File Properties

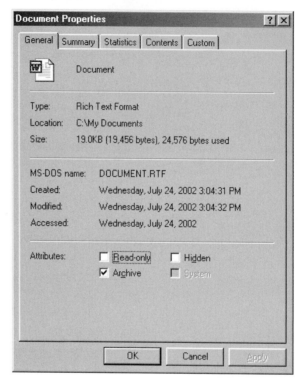

A Recycle Bin that is not empty, but has at least one file or folder is shown in Figure 5-28. Right-clicking this Recycle Bin brings up the menu shown in Figure 5-29. Select Empty Recycle Bin to permanently remove all the Recycle Bin contents.

Figure 5-28 Recycle Bin

Figure 5-29 Right-Click to Empty the Recycle Bin

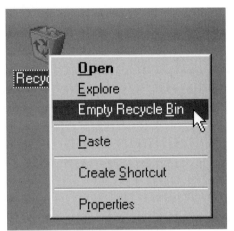

Files and folders can be viewed in the Recycle Bin the same way as they are viewed in Windows Explorer. Before permanently deleting a file, verify that it is the correct file to be removed by choosing **View, Details**.

Windows Management with the Control Panel

This section includes the following topics:

- Using the System Properties applet
- Using a printer
- Adding and removing programs
- Adding and removing hardware
- Adjusting the display and sounds

Using the System Properties Window

One of the most useful tools in the Windows Control Panel is the System Properties window. This tool can be accessed from within the Control Panel by choosing **Start, Settings, Control Panel, System**. The System Properties window includes a series of tabs. The default is the General tab, as shown in Figure 5-30, which lists information relating to the system. This information includes the operating system version, the licensee of the operating system, and system specifics such as processor type and the amount of memory.

Figure 5-30 The General Tab

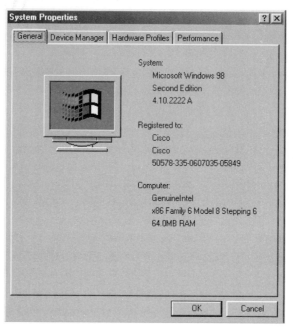

The next tab is the Device Manager, as shown in Figure 5-31. Device Manager provides a list of all the hardware within the system and allows the user to view which system resources are being used. It can also be used to update device drivers, disable or enable devices, and change resource settings.

The third tab is the Hardware Profiles tab, as shown in Figure 5-32. Hardware Profiles allows the user to have different hardware configurations for the same operating system. Most users do not need to set up hardware profiles; however, a laptop user might have one profile for the system when it is docked and one when it is not docked.

Finally, the fourth tab is the Performance tab, as shown in Figure 5-33. This tab displays information about the system's performance statistics and allows access to virtual memory and file system settings.

Figure 5-31 The Device Manager Tab

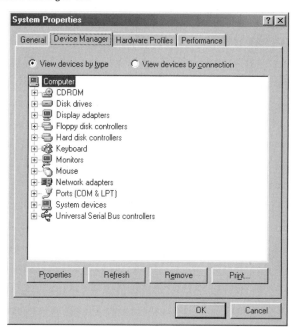

Figure 5-32 The Hardware Profiles Tab

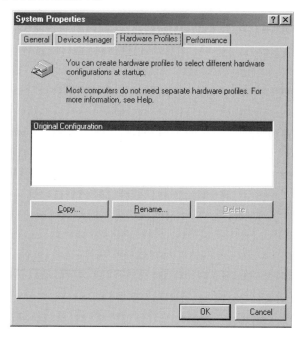

Figure 5-33 The Performance Tab

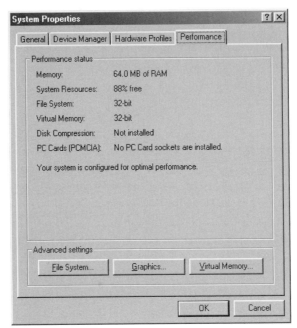

Using a Printer

This section provides information on how to send a file to a printer that has already been installed, how to change the default printer, and how to view the progress of a print job.

To send an open document to an installed printer, choose **File, Print**, as shown in Figure 5-34.

The printer window opens and allows you to select the following options: print the entire document, print the current page or a range of pages, choose the number of copies, modify the layout, or alter the characteristics of the printer output. See Figure 5-35.

Figure 5-34 The Document File Menu

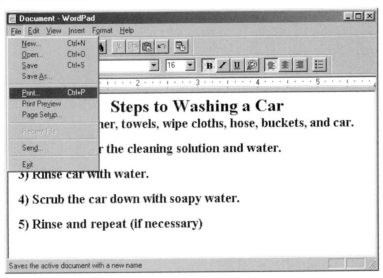

Figure 5-35 Print Options

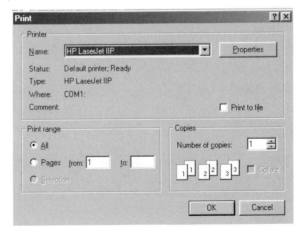

Adding a Printer

The Add Printer wizard is used when a new printer is purchased or an additional network printer needs to be added. To add a printer, choose **Start, Settings, Printers**. The following steps detail how to add a printer:

Step 1   Select the Add Printer option, as shown in Figure 5-36.

Figure 5-36   Adding a Printer

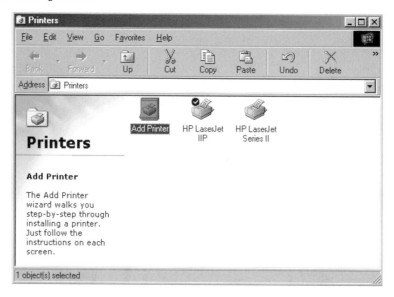

Step 2   The Add Printer wizard displays, as shown in Figure 5-37. Click Next to start the wizard, and follow the screen commands to add the printer.

Figure 5-37   The Add Printer Wizard

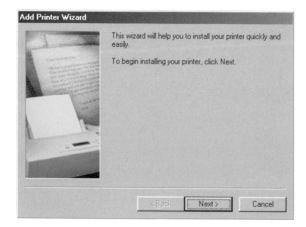

Step 3   The first option is to select a local or network printer, as shown in Figure 5-38. Click the Next button.

Figure 5-38   Choose a Local or Network Printer

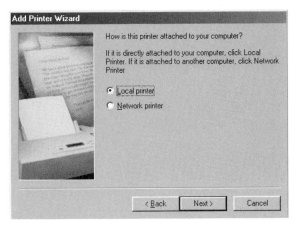

Step 4   Find the manufacturer and printer model from the displayed list, as shown in Figure 5-39. Click the Next button.

Figure 5-39   Select the Printer Manufacturer

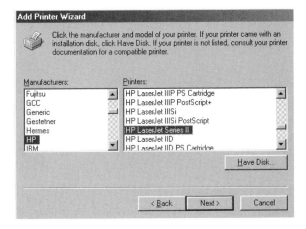

Step 5   Choose whether you want to keep the existing driver or replace the driver, as shown in Figure 5-40. Click the Next button.

Figure 5-40 Keep or Replace the Printer Driver

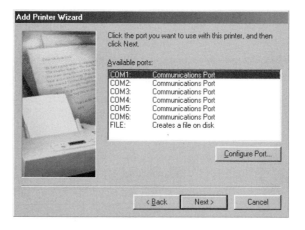

Step 6   Select the printer port. The LPT1 port is the default port, as shown in Figure 5-41. Click the Next button.

Figure 5-41 Choose the Printer Port

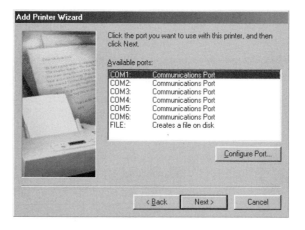

Step 7   Enter a name for the new printer, as shown in Figure 5-42. Use the printer's model name, or choose a custom name, such as Tim's printer or Floor2West, especially if many printers are being used on the network or in your office. You must also indicate whether this is the default printer for Windows-based programs. Click the Next button.

Figure 5-42 Name the Printer

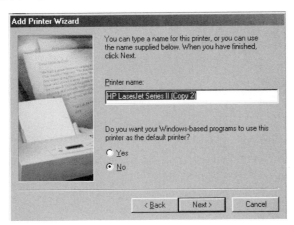

Step 8 The next screen suggests that you print a test page. This demonstrates if the printer is connected correctly and whether the correct drivers are installed. Choose Yes, and then click the Finish button (see Figure 5-43).

Figure 5-43 Print a Test Page

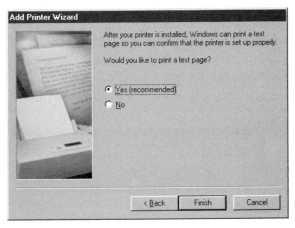

If the printer was added successfully, an icon displays in the Printer window. The icon has a checkmark next to it if the printer is set as the default (see Figure 5-44).

Figure 5-44 The Newly Added Printer

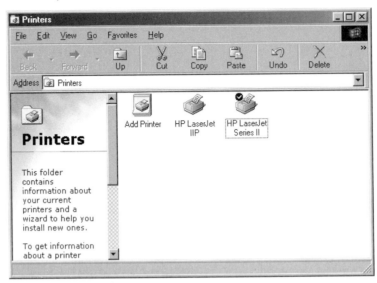

Changing the Default Printer

The system automatically prints to the default printer. Networks usually have several printers to choose from, and users can select a different printer from an application. But selecting a different printer does not change the default printer. To make this change, right-click the new default printer. Select Set as Default, as shown in Figure 5-45. The checkmark now appears next to the new default printer.

Figure 5-45 Changing the Default Printer

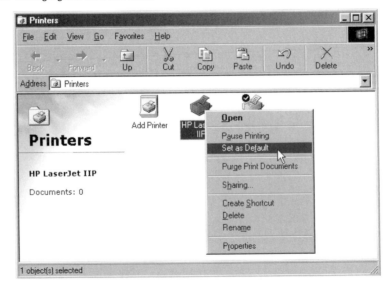

Viewing the Progress of a Print Job

The desktop Print Manager displays the print job as it starts, is in progress, and finishes. The Print Manager can be accessed by double-clicking the printer icon on the desktop Taskbar. It can also be accessed by choosing **Start, Settings, Printers,** as shown in Figure 5-46. Double-click the printer; the current jobs are as shown in Figure 5-47. Figure 5-48 shows the options that are available in the Printer menu. These options include Pause Printing, Purge Print Documents, and Printer Properties.

NOTE

If a printer malfunctions, delete the print job(s) within Print Manager. This is especially helpful if the printer jams.

Figure 5-46 Accessing Print Manager

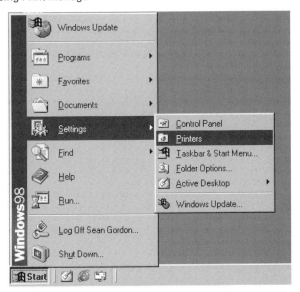

Figure 5-47 Accessing Current Print Jobs

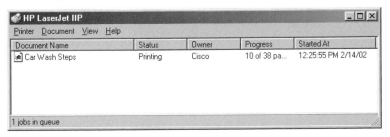

Figure 5-48 Printer Options

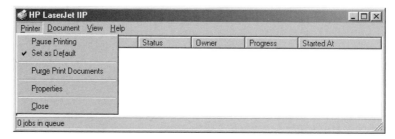

Figure 5-49 shows a document that is experiencing an error in printing. A pop-up window appears, indicating the nature of the problem, as shown in Figure 5-50.

Figure 5-49 Print Error

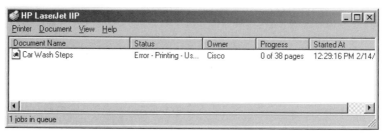

Figure 5-50 Error Message

If the wrong document is being printed or the document is too long, it can be deleted from the print queue. Highlight the document, and select **Document, Cancel**, as shown in Figure 5-51. The Print Manager indicates that the document is being deleted, as shown in Figure 5-52.

Figure 5-51 Canceling a Print Job

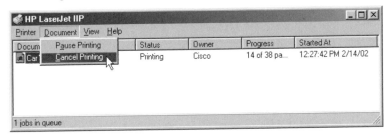

Figure 5-52 Deleting the Document

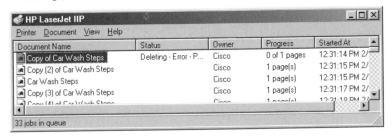

Worksheet 5.2.2 Managing Printers

This worksheet reviews the process of managing printers including setting up new printers.

Adding and Removing Programs

Another important tool in the Control Panel is the Add/Remove Programs utility, shown in Figure 5-53. This utility is used to remove installed programs, to install Windows-specific components that were not installed initially, and to create a Windows startup disk. When you uninstall a program, it is better to use the Add/Remove Programs utility than to manually delete the program's directory and files. This ensures that the uninstalled application is removed from the system together with all its associated components.

Figure 5-53 The Add/Remove Programs Utility

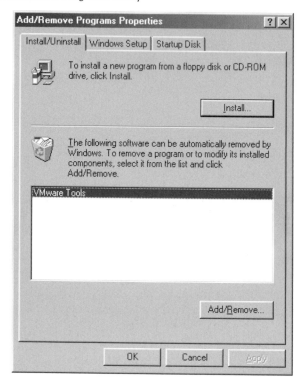

Adding and Removing Hardware

The Add/Remove Hardware utility in the Control Panel is an easy-to-use tool that automates the process of adding and removing hardware in the system. This utility, as shown in Figure 5-54, searches the computer for new hardware and installs the appropriate drivers. If the appropriate driver is not found automatically, the utility allows you to manually select the type of device from a list and then installs drivers from a specific location.

Adjusting the Display and Sounds

Two tools that are useful when changing the appearance and sounds of Windows are the Display utility and the Sounds utility. The Display utility, shown in Figure 5-55, can be accessed either by selecting it in the Control Panel or by right-clicking the desktop and selecting Properties. This allows the user to select a screensaver, change the background color, and change the look and feel of Windows as well as change display resolution settings.

Figure 5-54 The Add/Remove Hardware Utility

Figure 5-55 The Display Utility

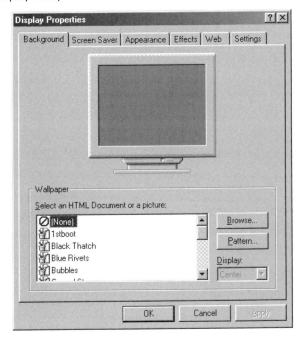

The Sounds utility, shown in Figure 5-56, allows the user to choose which sounds are played for different system events, such as when the computer is booted or shut down. Themes can also be used to coordinate the background, the look and feel of Windows, and the sounds so they all blend to create a uniform environment.

Figure 5-56   The Sounds Utility

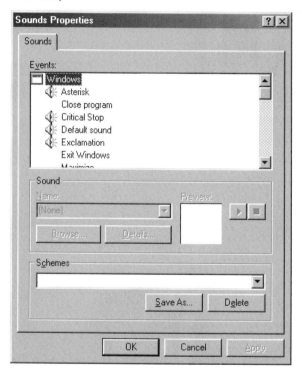

System Tools

This section includes the following topics:

- Understanding the Registry
- Using REGEDIT and SCANREG
- Understanding MSCONFIG, the Startup menu, and Safe mode
- Using WSCRIPT, HWINFO, and ASD

Understanding the Registry

The *Registry* is a hierarchical database used to manage the information needed by the Windows operating system. Older versions of Windows stored system and user data in ini files, which were usually scattered across multiple directories and could easily be edited by programs or the end user. The Registry takes all those files and stores them in a considerably more secure location.

The Registry is made up of two files: system.dat and user.dat. The system.dat file contains information about the hardware in the system. The user.dat file contains user-specific information. Windows 98 can still use the system.ini and win.ini files to run applications designed for Windows 3.X. More recently, since the release of Windows 98, the Registry consists of three files: system.dat, user.dat, and policy.pol (see Figure 5-57). The function of system.dat and user.dat remains the same. The Registry is more thoroughly discussed in a later chapter.

Figure 5-57 Windows 98 Registry Files

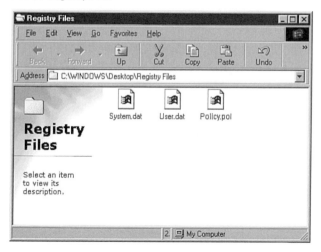

Using REGEDIT and SCANREG

Because the Registry is a hierarchical database, it can be viewed by using the regedit.exe utility, known as the Registry Editor (see Figure 5-58). The Registry Editor displays the Registry in a format that is similar to that of Windows Explorer. The file scanreg.exe can be used with any Windows 9X operating system to back up or repair the system's Registry.

Figure 5-58 The Registry Editor

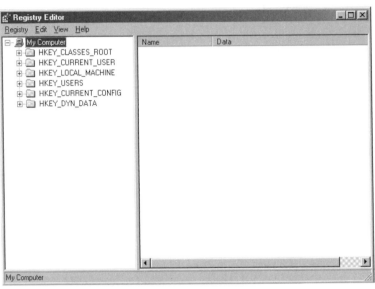

Understanding MSCONFIG, the Startup Menu, and Safe Mode

The file msconfig.exe is an excellent tool for users of Windows 98 and Me. It is not included in Windows 95. Shown in Figure 5-59, msconfig.exe allows the user to control how the system is started by giving quick access to important Windows configuration/ initialization files, including config.sys, autoexec.bat, system.ini, and win.ini. MSCONFIG also allows the user to select what programs are loaded automatically when the computer is booted.

When the operating system is loaded, it checks the Startup menu in config.sys for programs that are listed and initializes those programs automatically upon startup.

This utility can also be used to help troubleshoot problems that occur during the boot process. Another startup method that can be used in the troubleshooting process is Safe mode. Safe mode allows the user to load Windows without specific device drivers or allocated resources. Only the basic user interface and generic drivers are loaded so that the system is operable. For more information on Safe mode, see Chapter 13, "Troubleshooting Software."

CAUTION

Required system files are listed in the Startup menu and should not be removed. Only advanced users should edit these files.

TEST TIP

Know the difference between Safe mode and Normal mode.

Figure 5-59 The System Configuration Utility

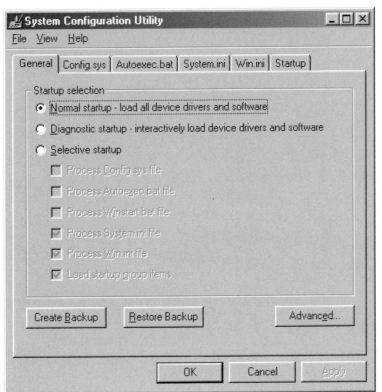

Using WSCRIPT, HWINFO, and ASD

The wscript.exe command allows configuration of the properties related to the Windows scripting host, as shown in Figure 5-60. The Windows scripting host allows scripts to be easily run within the operating system.

The hwinfo.exe file is a utility that provides a detailed collection of information about the computer, as shown in Figure 5-61. If the proper switches are not used, this command does not provide the desired results. The /UI switch is used when running this program to provide a detailed list of information about the computer.

Figure 5-60 The wscript.exe Command

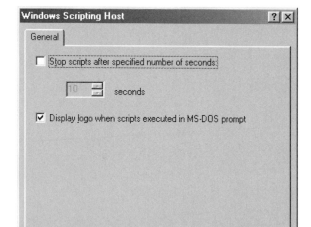

Figure 5-61 The hwinfo.exe File

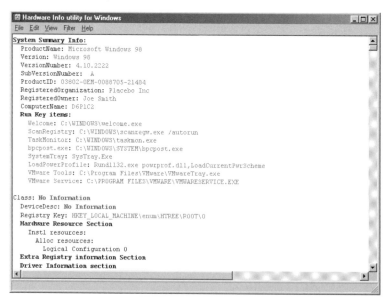

The asd.exe file is used to skip a driver when the operating system fails during bootup. This troubleshooting utility should be used when a problem with a driver cannot be solved by booting into Safe mode.

Preparing a Hard Drive for Installing the Operating System

This section includes the following topics:

- Partitioning a hard drive: primary and extended partitions, and logical drives.
- Formatting a hard drive: tracks, sectors, clusters, and cylinders.

Partitioning a Hard Drive: Primary and Extended Partitions, and Logical Drives

When a new hard drive is installed, it is blank. There are no spaces where files and folders can be stored. To create those spaces, a hard drive must first be divided into logical sections. These sections are called *partitions*. The partitioning process creates spaces of contiguous sectors on the hard drive. Each partition can receive a file system for an operating system. Without a file system, the partition is useless.

Primary and Extended Partitions

Typically with DOS, when the hard drive is divided into more than one partition, the first partition is referred to as the *primary partition*, while the second is called the *extended partition*. DOS and Windows refer to these drives with letters, such as C or D. The primary partition is usually the *active partition*, that is, the partition that DOS refers to during the bootup process. Figure 5-62 illustrates a hard drive divided into primary and extended DOS partitions with logical drives.

DOS can have up to four separate primary partitions, three primary and one extended partition, two primary and one extended partition, or just one primary and one extended partition on one hard drive, depending on the user's needs. DOS can have up to four separate partitions on a hard disk. The extended partition uses the free hard disk space and is normally assigned all the available space outside the primary partition(s). DOS can only address a maximum of 2 GB of hard disk space when using FAT16. FAT32 increased the limit to 2 terabytes (TB) of hard disk space. FAT is discussed later in this chapter.

NOTE

Only the primary partition on a hard drive can be designated as active, or bootable. DOS and Windows 95/98 can only manage one primary partition per hard drive. Conversely, Windows NT/2000 (as well as some third-party disk-management utilities) can be used to manage multiple primary partitions on a hard drive. A primary partition cannot be subdivided into smaller units.

Figure 5-62 Primary and Extended DOS Partitions

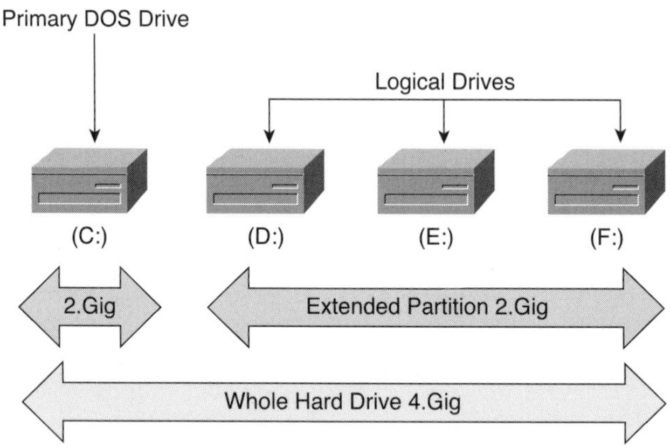

Primary DOS Drive

Logical Drives

(C:)   (D:)   (E:)   (F:)

2.Gig   Extended Partition 2.Gig

Whole Hard Drive 4.Gig

Lab Activity 5.4.2   Hard Drive Preparation Using FDISK and FORMAT

In this lab, you partition the hard drive into two drives, and install the three system files onto the hard drive to make it a bootable drive.

Logical Drives

When a hard drive is partitioned and includes an extended partition, the extended partition uses all the free hard disk space not included in the primary partition(s). There can be only one extended partition per disk, but unlike the primary partition, the extended partition can be subdivided into multiple (up to 23) sections called *logical drives*. Having multiple logical drives inside the extended partition provides the following advantages:

- Allows rapid retrieval of information.
- Permits multiple operating systems, such as MS-DOS and Windows 98, to be installed on the same computer, provided that both drives have the same file system or file allocation table (FAT). FAT is detailed later in this chapter.
- Provides physically separate information for organizational and security reasons.

By creating a second logical drive on the hard disk when it is formatted, another complete file-tracking structure is created on the hard drive. The operating system sees this new structure as a new disk. Therefore, a unique drive letter is assigned to it, as previously mentioned.

FDISK, Boot Sector, and Partition Table

FDISK is the partitioning program for MS-DOS, Windows 9X (95, 98, and Me), UNIX, and Linux. When partitioning a hard drive, FDISK creates the disk's *boot sector*. Typically, the boot sector is the first area on each logical DOS disk, or partition. When formatting the hard drive, the information needed to boot the operating system is recorded in the boot sector. During the partitioning process, FDISK also establishes partition information. On a drive that has been partitioned, the partition information is in the form of a special table, called the *partition table*. The partition table is located in the boot sector at the beginning of the disk. Three critical types of information reside in the partition table:

- The location and starting point of each logical drive on the disk.
- Information on which partition is marked active.
- The location of the master boot record (MBR). (The master boot record is contained only on bootable disks.)

The location of the partition table at the beginning of the disk is significant in that this is the point where the system looks for bootup information.

Formatting a Hard Drive: Tracks, Sectors, Clusters, and Cylinders

After partitioning the drive, you must prepare it to store data. This process is called *formatting*. Formatting a hard drive creates magnetic *tracks* in concentric circles on the disk surface. These tracks are then broken into segments of 512 bytes called *sectors*. The tracks of the disk are numbered, beginning with 00 from the outer edge of the disk and moving inward. (In the computer world, numbering begins at 0 instead of 1.) The number of tracks per disk depends on the type of disk and the drive in use. The combination of two or more sectors on a single track is called a *cluster*. A cluster is sometimes called a *block*. The size of each cluster depends on the size of the hard disk and the version of DOS in use.

A cluster is the minimum unit DOS can use to store a file. This means that even if a file is only 1 byte long, an entire cluster is still used to store the file. The number of tracks and sectors and, therefore, the number of clusters that can be created on a disk's surface by formatting it, determine the disk's capacity.

Finally, in a hard disk drive where several disks are stacked and rotate on a common spindle, all the tracks having the same number are referred to collectively as a *cylinder*. Figure 5-63 shows a detailed view of the hard drive.

NOTE

Each sector on a DOS disk holds 512 bytes. However, files can be any length. Therefore, a single file might occupy several sectors on the disk. On floppy disks, common cluster sizes are 1 or 2 sectors long. With hard disks, the cluster size can vary from 1 to 16 sectors in length, depending on the type of disk.

Figure 5-63 Tracks, Sectors, and the Cylinder on Hard Disk Platters

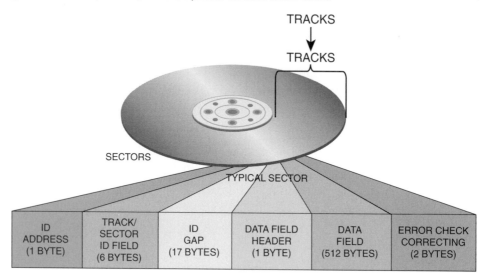

File Allocation Table

During formatting, a special file, called the *file allocation table (FAT)* is created and located in the disk's sector 0. FAT is a reference table that the operating system uses to locate files on the disk. Newer DOS versions provide additional protection by storing a second (identical) copy of the original FAT that was created during formatting at another location. The first copy is the normal working copy, while the second FAT is used as a backup measure in case the contents of the first FAT become corrupted. Under normal circumstances, the contents of either copy of the FAT are hidden.

The original FAT associated with DOS was called FAT16 (16-bit), and since then, other versions have been introduced. VFAT is the version that came with the original version of Windows 95. FAT32 (32-bit), a more efficient form of FAT, was released with Windows 95 Service Release 2 (commonly known as OSR2), Windows 98, and Windows Me (collectively called Windows 9X). Only DOS and the 16-bit Windows 3.X still use FAT16. When written as "FAT," with no number associated with it, it is understood to be FAT16. When a hard drive is formatted for installation of DOS, the FAT is created. When the disk is formatted for the installation of Windows 9X, FAT32 is created as the file system in the disk partition where the Windows 9X operating system is to be installed.

A built-in program such as cvt1.exe, or other third-party utilities such as Partition Magic, can be used to convert FAT16 to FAT32, without destroying the data in the disk partition. However, you cannot convert a FAT32 partition back to a FAT16 partition. FAT16,

FAT32, and other file systems, including NTFS, are discussed more thoroughly in Chapter 7, "Windows NT/2000/XP Operating Systems."

Low-Level and High-Level Formatting

You need to understand two important concepts about formatting a hard drive. These include low-level formatting and high-level formatting, which are described as follows:

- **Low-level formatting routine**—Marks off the disk into sectors and cylinders and defines their placement on the disk. IDE and SCSI, which are system-level drive types, normally come with the low-level format already performed at the factory. Some SCSI devices might still require a low-level format, but you should never do a low-level format on an IDE hard drive unless it has failed.

- **High-level formatting routine**—Performed by the FORMAT command in MS-DOS. This procedure creates logical structures on the disk that tell the system what files are on the disk and where they can be found. When using MS-DOS or a Windows 9X boot system (containing the FORMAT command) to format the hard drive, the process creates a blank FAT and root directory structure on the disk. Perform a high-level format when preparing the hard drive for installation of the operating system.

When using a Windows 98 bootable disk containing the FORMAT command to format a hard drive, enter the following syntax at the DOS command prompt:

A:\>FORMAT C:

C is the hard drive, A is the floppy boot disk drive, and A:\> is the DOS command prompt.

Typing a space and the switch /S after the drive letter designation in the command formats the hard drive and transfers the system files, making it bootable. The syntax at the DOS command prompt is as follows:

A:\>FORMAT C: /S

Worksheet 5.4.2   Hard Drive Preparation

This worksheet is a review of the steps required to prepare a hard drive for installation of the operating system.

Installing Windows 9X

This section includes the following topics:

- Overview of Windows 9X versions
- Requirements for installing Windows 98
- Understanding the steps of a Windows 98 installation
- Windows 98 setup options
- Installing a Windows upgrade

Overview of Windows 9X Versions

Before discussing the installation procedure in detail, it is useful to understand the various Windows 9X versions and how they relate to each other. This section gives a basic summary of Windows' evolution, from the departure from DOS (a command-line operating system) to the creation of the graphical user interface (GUI)–based Windows operating system.

Windows has been through many revisions. Windows 9X refers to all releases of the Microsoft Windows operating systems from Windows 95 through Windows Me. The original version started with a basic GUI. Prior to the major release of Windows 3.1, Windows went through several revisions to reach the polished look that now resides on many computers.

Windows 3.1, released in April 1992, was more stable compared to earlier versions and included scalable TrueType fonts. This version became one of the most popular operating systems from its release until the mid-1990s. One of its main limitations was that it relied on DOS to run. It therefore had all the Windows initialization files (ini files), mentioned earlier in this chapter, built into the basic DOS structure to enable Windows 3.X to start up.

By the end of 1993, Microsoft released Windows for Workgroups, version 3.11. This was the first version with integrated networking and workgroup capabilities. Features included e-mail utilities, group task scheduling, file and printer sharing, and calendar management. It offered improved NetWare and Windows NT compatibility and improved stability. Although networking was integrated, it was hard to use and still operated on top of DOS.

Windows 95 was released in August 1995 with many features and benefits over previous versions. This was the first version of Windows that could be defined as a true operating system; it did not require DOS to be loaded prior to installing Windows. This release has also been regarded as more user friendly than previous versions, thus mainstreaming PCs to new PC users. Windows 95 also introduced long-filename support, advanced networking features, and Plug and Play capabilities. Some limitations of this version include higher system requirements, a longer learning curve due to the new look and feel, and inconsistency with PnP features.

The following year, Microsoft released Windows 95 OSR2. This newer version included several bug fixes as well as improvements to various embedded features. It now included the Internet Explorer 3.0 web browser and supported the new and more efficient 32-bit file-management system called FAT32 and the universal serial bus (USB). This release of Windows had one major limitation: It was only available to manufacturers and resellers. Therefore, most end users did not get a chance to see the improvements unless they purchased a new PC.

In June 1998, Windows 98 was released. This version included Internet Explorer 4 and improved support for USB. It supported newer technologies, such as advanced configuration and power interface (ACPI) power management. Despite many improvements, the major limitation of Windows 98 is a lack of stability. However, in May 1999, Windows 98 Second Edition (SE) was released. Including year-2000 (Y2K) updates, better USB support, the latest version of Internet Explorer, and several other updates, this version of Windows was the most functional to date. Although Windows 98 lacks complete stability, it is still regarded by many technicians as the most stable version of Win 9X.

In September 2000, Microsoft released Windows Millennium Edition (Me). This version includes enhanced multimedia capabilities and improved Internet support, and is the last version of Windows to run on the Win 9X kernel. (A significant component of the operating system, this kernel is memory resident and is responsible for process, task, disk, and memory management.) Windows Me exhibits poor stability compared to Windows 98 SE.

The latest addition to the consumer-level operating systems is Windows XP Home Edition, boasting a 32-bit kernel based on the NT kernel and providing more stability than any of the Win 9X versions. However, there are compatibility issues with older software and hardware in addition to the higher system requirements needed to run this operating system.

As Microsoft continues to develop and release newer versions of Windows, end users should look forward to new features and more stability. However, as with any new operating system technologies, some limitations and lapses should be expected. Figure 5-64 is a timeline that summarizes the various releases of the Windows operating system.

Figure 5-64 Windows Operating System Release Timeline

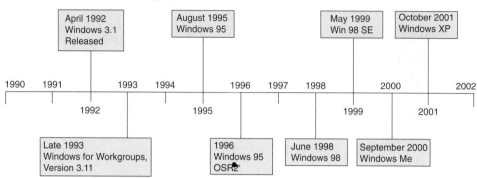

Requirements for Installing Windows 98

To install Windows 98, the following minimum hardware platform is required:

- An 80486DX/66 MHz or faster processor, operating with at least 16 MB of RAM, is necessary. A level of 32 MB of RAM is recommended, and 64 MB is preferred if the system can support it.

- The system must have a keyboard, a mouse, and a 16-color VGA monitor or better (SVGA is recommended).

- The system's hard drive must have 255–355 MB of free space available to install the full version of Windows 98 on a FAT16 drive or 175–255 MB of free space for installation on a FAT32 drive.

- An upgrade from Windows 95 requires about 195 MB of free hard disk space, but this can range from 120–255 MB, depending on the options that are installed.

- Sometimes, a modem is required to download device driver upgrades from the Internet. The minimum speed required is 14.4 kbps. (A 28.8 kbps modem or faster is recommended.)

- A 3-1/2-inch high-density floppy disk drive and a CD-ROM drive (32X is recommended) are required.

Table 5-2 Requirements for Installing Windows 98

Type of Install	Processor	Memory	Hard Drive Space	Floppy Disk Drive	Video Resolution	Modem
Upgrade from Windows 95	486DX 66-MHz or faster (Pentium CPU recommended)	16 MB (24 MB recommended)	195 MB (120–295 MB, depending on the options installed)	Yes	VGA or higher (16-bit or 24-bit color SVGA recommended)	14.4-kbps required for Internet access (28.8-kbps or faster recommended)
Full install on a FAT16 drive	486DX 66-MHz or faster (Pentium CPU recommended)	16 MB (24 MB recommended)	225 MB (165–355 MB, depending on the options installed)	Yes	VGA or higher (16-bit or 24-bit color SVGA recommended)	14.4-kbps required for Internet access (28.8-kbps or faster recommended)
Full install on a FAT32 drive	486DX 66-MHz or faster (Pentium CPU recommended)	16 MB (32 MB recommended)	175 MB (140–255 MB, depending on the options installed)	Yes	VGA or higher (16-bit or 24-bit color SVGA recommended)	14.4-kbps required for Internet access (28.8-kbps or faster recommended)

Understanding the Steps of a Windows 98 Installation

This section explains the installation procedure. Once the installation starts, most of the steps are automated through a built-in utility called Setup. An understanding of each stage of the installation or setup process is useful when performing an installation, using the Lab bundle that accompanies this chapter or at home. The steps of the installation procedure are divided into four phases, as described in the following sections.

Phase 1: Preparing to Run Windows 98 Setup

During this phase, Windows Setup performs a number of actions, which prepare the Windows 98 Setup wizard to guide the user through the installation process. The following actions are included:

- A setuplog.txt file is created in the drive's root directory.
- The source and destination drive locations for the Windows 98 files that are to be installed are identified, as shown in Figure 5-65.
- A minimal Windows 98 setup cabinet file, called mini.cab, is copied to a special directory that Setup creates at the root directory. This directory is called wininst0.400.
- The major setup files, precopy1.cab and precopy2.cab, are extracted to the wininst0.400 directory.

Figure 5-65 Selecting the Directory to Install Windows 98

Phase 2: Collecting Computer Information

After the setup files have been copied to the hard drive, the Setup wizard displays the licensing agreement. Read this agreement, become familiar with the terms and conditions of using the software, accept the agreement, and proceed. Setup asks the user to enter the product key. The product key is found on the software's certificate of authority (which verifies product authenticity) or on the back of the CD case. When the product registration is completed, Setup gathers the following critical information about the system:

- Determines a directory into which Windows 98 installation files need to be moved.
- Verifies that there is enough space on the selected drive to hold the Windows 98 installation files and the temporary files that are required to complete the procedure.
- Determines the type of installation desired (typical, portable, compact, or custom). Typical is aimed at the general user, whereas custom is for specialized technical purposes. Table 5-3 summarizes the installation options.

Table 5-3 Windows 98 Setup Options

Setup Option	Result
Typical	Setup installs all the components that are usually installed with Windows 98. Most users should select this option.
Portable	Setup installs the options required for portable (laptop) computers.
Compact	This option uses the smallest amount of hard disk space to install Windows 98. For example, you would perform a compact installation if your hard disk has little free space. Setup then installs no optional components. If you later want to use an optional component, such as games or WebTV for Windows, you can install it. To install an optional component after Setup is completed, select Add/Remove Programs in the Control Panel.
Custom	This option allows you to choose which Windows 98 components are installed. If you do not select a custom installation, Setup installs only those components that are selected by default. If you know that you are going to need certain components, select a custom installation and ensure that those components are included during Setup. Pan-European users should choose this option to select the required regional settings and keyboard layout for their locale.

- Creates company names and usernames. For a personal computer, the username is all that is required.
- Identifies the Windows 98 components that you want Setup to install.

- Adds the computer's network identification. A network ID can be entered here, even though the system might not be in a networked environment.
- Identifies the Internet location from which the system can receive regional update information. This is important for the system to function with a proper date and time for the local time zone.

When Setup has gathered all the installation information, it prompts the user to create an emergency startup disk. Follow the on-screen instructions to create this disk. Setup then begins the installation process for Windows 98. Figure 5-66 shows the Setup wizard ready to start copying files.

Figure 5-66 Copying Windows 98 Files

Phase 3: Copying Windows 98 Files and Restarting the Computer

Most of this phase of the setup is automated. It begins with the Start Copying Windows Files dialog box. Because this phase is automated, no input is required from the installer.

Once Setup has copied the Windows 98 files to their proper locations, it displays a prompt for the user to restart the system. The system restarts automatically if no entry is detected within 15 seconds.

Phase 4: Setting Up Hardware and Finalizing Settings

The system should restart automatically, and Setup finalizes the installation process based on the type of installation you selected in Phase 3. The following items are installed:

- Contents of the Start Menu
- Settings for DOS programs

- Control Panel
- Application start functions
- Windows 98 help functions
- Time zone information
- System configuration information

Setup automatically restarts the computer, once again, upon completion of these steps. Log on at the prompt (if any logon information was entered). Setup then establishes a system driver database, updates your system settings, establishes personalized system options, and displays the Welcome to Windows 98 dialog box. If Windows detects any new hardware such as video card, a window displays "New hardware detected." Windows finds stock hardware drivers and automatically installs these drivers for the hardware. At this point, the Windows 98 desktop displays and the setup process is complete.

Windows 98 Setup Options

There are two options for installing Windows 98:

- Installing directly from the CD by booting the system from the CD-ROM drive
- Copying all the files from the CD to the hard drive and then performing an internal installation from the hard drive

There are some merits to running the internal installation.

Running Windows 98 Setup from the Hard Drive

During a Windows 98 installation, installers sometimes experience problems with the Windows CD or the CD-ROM drive. The problems can usually be avoided, and the overall installation process can go faster, by copying the files to the hard drive. Use the following steps:

Step 1   Verify that there is at least 200 MB of extra disk space to store the Windows setup and cab files.

Step 2   Create a floppy boot disk that contains drivers for the CD-ROM drive. Insert the floppy disk in the computer, and turn on the unit. When prompted, select the option to boot the system with CD-ROM support, and wait for it to boot to the DOS prompt.

Step 3   From the DOS prompt, create a directory called SETUP98 to store the setup files. Type **MD C:\SETUP98** (where C is the letter assigned to the hard drive) at the DOS prompt.

NOTE

Any drivers that Windows automatically installs are stock drivers. If you experience problems with a certain hardware device, you might need an updated device driver. The best source of up-to-date drivers is the installation CD or floppy disk that came with your hardware. For even more current drivers, check the hardware manufacturer's website and download the appropriate driver.

Step 4   Copy all the files from the SETUP98 directory on the Windows CD to the corresponding directory on the hard drive. Type the following command at the DOS prompt:

COPY D:\SETUP98*.* C:\SETUP98

This assumes the usual configuration where the hard drive is labeled C and the CD-ROM drive is referred to as D.

Step 5   Change back to the SETUP98 directory on the hard drive to start the installation. Type **CD SETUP98**, press Enter, type **SETUP**, and press Enter. This starts the Windows 98 Setup process.

Copying the setup files to the hard drive and then performing the operating system installation provide certain advantages for the following reasons:

- The installation goes much faster. With current-technology drives, the hard drive is always faster than a CD-ROM drive.

- When later adding new hardware or Windows software, you might be prompted to provide the Windows setup files. Having the files on the hard drive allows you to simply point to the SETUP98 directory. You don't have to search for your Windows CD.

- If you frequently need to perform a complete format, you can create two partitions on the one drive, one for Windows and a smaller partition for the Windows setup files. In this way, it is easy to format only one partition and quickly perform the setup from the smaller partition.

Running Windows 98 Setup from DOS

It might be necessary to run the Windows 98 setup procedure from DOS if you have problems during the installation process. Follow these steps to set up Windows 98 from DOS:

Step 1   Create a bootable floppy disk with CD-ROM drivers.

Step 2   Insert the bootable disk, and turn on the computer. When prompted, select the option to boot with CD-ROM support. Allow the system to boot to the DOS prompt.

Step 3   From the command line, change to the CD-ROM drive. To do this, type D and press Enter. (Here, D is the CD-ROM drive letter.)

Step 4   Initiate the setup process. Type **CD WIN98**, press Enter, type **SETUP**, and press Enter. This procedure starts the Windows setup process.

Lab Activity 5.5.5   Windows OS Installation

Upon completion of this lab, you install the Windows operating system.

Installing Windows 98 on a New Unit and Using SCANDISK

To install Windows 98 on a new or reformatted hard disk, you must boot the system from the Windows CD or run setup.exe from the DOS prompt.

When the installation is initiated from the DOS prompt, the Windows 98 setup program runs a real-mode version (looking at all files) of the SCANDISK utility on the drive. This requires that the CD-ROM or network driver be present and loaded. SCANDISK performs a complete check (of the FAT, directory, and files) on the drive and creates a SCANDISK log file. If errors are detected, the program displays an error message. This log file can be accessed through SCANDISK's View Log screen. After the SCANDISK inspection is complete, the setup program initializes the system and begins copying installation files to the drive.

Installing a Windows Upgrade

Windows 95 users can upgrade to Windows 98 for added features and usability. Installing the upgrade is an easy procedure. To retain your Windows 95 settings, such as the background and user files, run the Windows 98 setup program from within Windows 95.

Upgrading Windows 95 to Windows 98

Typically, inserting the installation CD into the CD-ROM drive initiates the setup program. However, if the program needs to be started manually, navigate to the CD-ROM drive using Windows Explorer and double-click the setup.exe file on the root directory of the installation CD. This should start the setup program, which guides you through the installation process.

Although the upgrade might go smoothly, there could be problems with the upgraded Windows 98. If the user does not need to retain any information or settings on his or her computer, the best choice is to do a clean installation. But erasing previous settings is not recommended. However, if you back up all your data prior to installing the new operating system, you will later be able to retrieve any data you saved as well as have a clean install.

CAUTION

Be aware that a Windows 2000 upgrade can be uninstalled only once on a given system.

Upgrading Windows 98 to Windows 2000

The upgrade from Windows 98 to Windows 2000 is straightforward. There are two ways to start the upgrade from within Windows 98: Use the installation CD's autoplay feature or manually run the setup.exe program. Once the setup program has begun, follow the on-screen prompts and instructions to install the upgrade.

Troubleshooting the Installation Process

This section includes the following topics:

- Using systematic troubleshooting techniques and finding help
- Understanding Windows 98 setup errors
- Using the System Properties window
- Adding software drivers
- Making an emergency startup disk
- Uninstalling Windows 98

Using Systematic Troubleshooting Techniques and Finding Help

Knowing the various tips and tricks in troubleshooting, a Windows installation can make the difference between a good technician and an excellent technician. This section discusses some common problems that occur in the Windows operating system installation and how to solve them. The discussion is limited to problems related to the Windows operating system installation. General troubleshooting is discussed more thoroughly in later chapters.

General Troubleshooting Concepts

In general, when troubleshooting any microprocessor-based equipment such as the PC, it is good practice to begin from the outside of the system and move inward. Proceed systematically in the following manner:

1. Start the system in a logical order to see what symptoms are produced.
2. Isolate the problem as being either software or hardware related.
3. After determining the nature of the problem, isolate it to a particular section of the hardware or software.
4. Determine the appropriate solution, implement the solution, and verify that the problem is solved.
5. Document the problem and solution for future reference.

Most successful troubleshooting results from careful observation combined with deductive reasoning and an organized approach to solving problems.

The First Boot Process Hangs for No Apparent Reason

Problems can occur when installing the Windows operating system and restarting the computer. The correct action to take depends on whether the system is a newly assembled computer or a previously functioning machine. This section assumes that you are installing Windows 98 in completing the computer-assembly process. (See Chapter 3, "Assembling a Computer.")

If, after installing the operating system, you do not achieve a successful boot, you do not see a screen display, or the keyboard does not respond, first attempt to restart the machine using the reset button. Also try to restart the computer using a Windows 98 startup disk, if one is available. If the problem persists, turn the power off and perform the following checks:

- Does the CPU cooling fan run? If not, check that the power cable is plugged into the motherboard, that the power cable is plugged into the surge suppressor, and that the surge suppressor is turned on.
- Is the cable properly connected to the hard drive?
- Is the monitor cable connected to the video adapter card?
- Is the boot sequence in the CMOS set up to search drive A first?
- Do the lights on the keyboard flash during the POST?
- Does the floppy drive light illuminate during the boot process?
- Are the contrast and brightness controls on the monitor turned up enough to see the display?
- Are all DIMMs correctly seated in their sockets? If a RAM chip is not correctly seated, a typical symptom would be a blank monitor screen.
- Are all expansion cards correctly seated?
- Is the CPU installed properly and seated correctly? If the CPU is not well seated, you will see no display on the screen.
- Is there a power connector attached to the floppy drive, hard drive, CD-ROM drive, and motherboard?
- Is the keyboard connected to the motherboard?

Some Handy Windows 98 Help Tools, Tips, and Tricks

Basic setup troubleshooting tools are built into Windows or are available as third-party software; these tools can be useful when installing the operating system. Several of these tools are discussed in the following list:

- **Safe mode/Device Manager**—If Windows 98 becomes unavailable, shut off the computer, wait 30 seconds, and then turn it back on. During this process, listen for a beep or wait for a few seconds. Then press and hold the left Ctrl key. This opens the Windows 98 Startup menu. From the list of options, choose Safe Mode. In this mode, Windows loads only the basic devices it needs to run. Figure 5-67 displays the Safe Mode dialog box, which describes the function of Safe mode. Once in Windows Safe mode, check the Device Manager to ensure that there are no conflicts with any devices in the system.

Figure 5-67 The Safe Mode Dialog Box

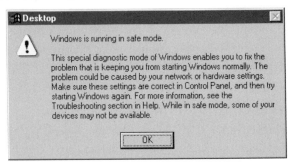

- **SCANDISK/DEFRAG**—Run SCANDISK, as shown in Figure 5-68. If any errors are found, run DEFRAG. The DEFRAG program locates bad sectors on the disk and attempts to fix them. Figure 5-69 shows the DEFRAG dialog box. It allows you to select the specific drive or drives to be examined. DEFRAG works to pull together different pieces of the same file that are scattered throughout the disk so the files can be read more easily by the system. SCANDISK only checks the surface of the disk and the files, and informs you of any errors found. As a rule, you should run SCANDISK before running DEFRAG.

Figure 5-68 Running SCANDISK

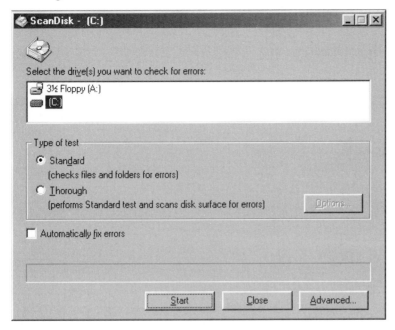

Figure 5-69 The DEFRAG Dialog Box

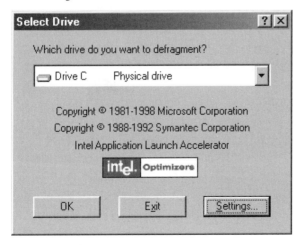

- **Virus scan**—In Windows, a virus scanner checks all the hard drives for viruses. If viruses are detected, clean the disk to eliminate them. If the errors persist, check online help resources for additional help with DOS, Windows, hardware, and software.

- **FDISK/MBR**—This is one of the undocumented MS-DOS commands that is available. MBR stands for master boot record. Basically, it is the hard drive's table of contents. One common problem when the computer does not boot is that the MBR has been corrupted. Type **FDISK/MBR** at the DOS prompt to rebuild this crucial operating system boot record.

Understanding Windows 98 Setup Errors

Setup errors are probably the most important problems to deal with. Understanding the error codes that are generated by the operating system can save a lot of time when troubleshooting Windows installation problems. In this section, the more frequent setup errors are summarized, the errors are interpreted, and solutions are presented. Common error messages are as follows:

- **Not enough disk space**—Delete unnecessary files on the hard drive. If this doesn't work, do a clean install, that is, reformat the drive and reinstall the operating system.

- **Not enough memory**—The system lacks sufficient conventional memory to continue the installation. Conventional memory is the total memory available for copying and moving files. The solution is to install more RAM; a minimum of 32 MB of RAM is recommended for a Windows 98 system.

- **Setup has detected that an earlier version of setupx.dll or neti.dll is in use**—Most likely, applications are open during the installation. Choose either the option to replace the file and continue, or cancel and close all running applications. If the error message is repeated, install Windows 98 from DOS; use the DOS boot disk that you created earlier.

- **Cab file error messages**—The computer might be infected by a virus, have insufficient conventional memory, or have a hardware problem (especially with the CD). A clean-install setup can eliminate problems related to a virus or low conventional memory. Have any defective CDs cleaned or replaced. Another remedy is to attempt to copy the cab files to the hard drive and run setup from there.

- **Unrecoverable setup error. Setup cannot continue on this system configuration. Click OK to quit Setup**—With this message, the best course of action is to try installing Windows 98 from DOS. Use the previously created DOS boot disk to boot to the DOS prompt.

- **Setup cannot create files on the startup drive and cannot set up Windows 98. There might be too many files in the root directory of the startup drive, or the startup drive letter could have been remapped (SU0018)**—The root directory of a drive holds a maximum of 512 files and/or folders. In this situation, move or delete some files to allow setup to continue, and restart Setup.

- **Setup cannot write to the Temporary Directory**—This error message indicates that there is insufficient room in the TEMP directory. Delete all the files from C:\WINDOWS\TEMP. This is the same as the TEMP directory specified in AUTOEXEC.BAT by the line TEMP=.

- **SU0011**—The computer is password-protected. Remove the password, usually in the BIOS setup, and restart Windows 98 Setup.

Only a few of the errors that might be experienced when installing Windows 98 have been covered in this section. For specific errors or to learn more about setup errors, refer to the setup.txt file that is on your Windows installation CD.

Using the System Properties Window

Access the System Properties window by choosing **Start, Settings, Control Panel, System**. This window has four tabs within it; these tabs are described as follows:

- **General**—General information about the system is shown here. This information includes the version of Windows 98 installed, total RAM, type of CPU, percentage of system resources used, etc. The type of information can vary, depending on the computer manufacturer. Figure 5-70 shows general information for a system running Windows 98.

Figure 5-70 The General Tab

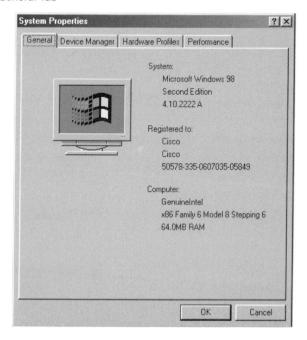

- **Device Manager**—This tab displays the hardware that is installed and the status of these devices, as shown in Figure 5-71. Devices can be viewed by type or connection. Device Manager provides options to view the properties of the devices listed, refresh the list to review any changes that have been made, remove a device, and print a summary of devices.

Figure 5-71 The Device Manager Tab

- **Hardware Profiles**—Most PCs have no need for different hardware profiles. However, a laptop used at different locations, such as at home and at work, might need different profiles. The Hardware Profiles option allows various hardware configuration profiles to be created and then selected when the system boots, as shown in Figure 5-72.
- **Performance**—This tab shows details that indicate if your system is configured for optimal performance, as shown in Figure 5-73. Advanced settings can be edited for the file system, graphics, and virtual memory.

Figure 5-72 The Hardware Profiles Tab

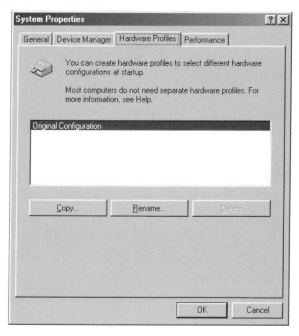

Figure 5-73 The Performance Tab

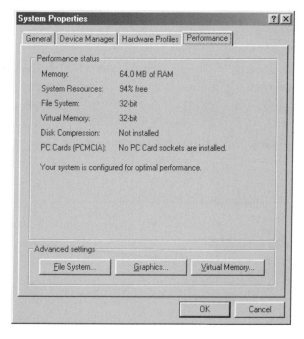

Identifying Special Icon Symbols Using the Device Manager

The Device Manager, included with Windows 98, allows the user to manage, view, and change computer resources. The Device Manager provides a graphical representation of the devices configured in the system. This utility is used to identify installed ports, update device drivers, and change I/O settings on your computer. It can also be used to manually isolate hardware and configuration conflicts. The Device Manager allows you to examine problem devices and see where the conflict might be occurring. To view the icons in the Device Manager, right-click My Computer and select Properties.

From the Device Manager menu, you can determine whether there are problems with installed devices on the system. Within a given device, three types of problem indicators are shown: an exclamation point, a red X, or the words "Other device."

- **An exclamation point inside a yellow circle appears**—Indicates that one device is experiencing a direct hardware conflict with another device.

- **A red X at the device's icon appears**—Indicates that the device has been disabled or removed, or that Windows is unable to locate the device.

- **"Other Device" appears in place of the device's icon**—Indicates that Windows cannot recognize the device being installed. In most cases, the drivers have not been installed or uninstalled, or the device is not working right and the driver needs to be upgraded.

The Device Manager Properties window provides tabs to access general information, device settings, device driver information, and device resources requirements and usage. The system resources can also be viewed in the Device Manager. Typically, if hardware conflicts exist (for example, two devices are assigned the same IRQ), click the offending device in the listing. Make sure that the selected device is the current device in the computer. Also, examine the other conflicting device to make sure that the same device has not been installed twice.

Lab Activity 5.6.1   Troubleshooting 101

Use the basic troubleshooting skills and the systematic approach to problem solving.

Adding Software Drivers

Device drivers give today's PCs the ability to add a wide variety of devices to the system. A *device driver* is specially designed software that enables the computer to "see" the hardware or devices that are installed in the system. Such devices include CD-ROM drives, the hard drive, expansion cards, and external devices, such as a mouse, keyboard, etc. Sometimes, all the problems following an installation of Windows are simply linked to the absence of the appropriate device drivers.

The device driver not only allows the basic system to recognize the presence of a device, but it also enables the system to work (or interface) with the device. Although the process of installing devices/equipment and their drivers in a PC has become increasingly easy, the technician must still be able to install all necessary drivers. There are generally two ways to install a device driver in the computer:

- **Auto-detect the device and install the driver from Windows 98's stock drivers—** The new card or device should first be installed in the system before this procedure is run. Take advantage of the Windows 98 driver installation wizard to auto-detect and install the hardware device as shown in Figure 5-74. The wizard is designed to show a series of screens that guide the user through hardware setup steps. Normally, the first user-selectable screen option is to use the AutoDetect function. Figure 5-75 shows the screen that displays that starts the search for new hardware. Once the AutoDetect option is selected, a hardware detection progress indicator bar at the bottom of the monitor appears. When the operation is complete, the wizard indicates which hardware has been found as shown in Figure 5-76. Once hardware has been found, the wizard searches for the driver software to install to complete the process. However, if the wizard does not detect the hardware, attempt to locate the device in the wizard's list of supported devices.

Figure 5-74 The Add New Hardware Wizard

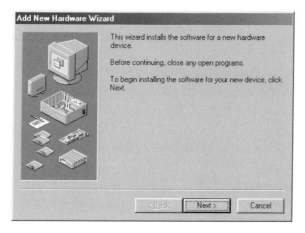

Figure 5-75 Add New Hardware Wizard Automatic Search

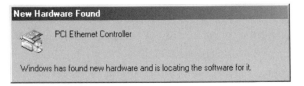

Figure 5-76 Add New Hardware Wizard: Hardware Found

Lab Activity 5.6.4 Installing a Driver

Install the driver for a roller-ball mouse. The same process is used when installing any new device in your system.

- **Use the OEM installation disk or CD**—The original equipment manufacturer (OEM) is the vendor responsible for the final packaging of computer hardware, including the necessary drivers. The only other option when installing hardware devices is to obtain an OEM floppy disk or CD for the device that has the drivers. Unfortunately, some driver disks do not have an autostart function. You can proceed in two ways:
  - Click the Have Disk button, and supply the file's location to complete the installation process.

— Boot the system to the C prompt. Use the **CD** command if necessary to change to the directory where the new driver is located. Type **SETUP** at the command line to initiate the driver installation. Follow the on-screen instructions.

— The readme.txt file contains important information and can be found on the floppy disk or CD.

The main advantage of using the OEM driver disk is that the driver is likely to be relatively current. Using AutoDetect and installing using Windows 98 stock drivers can sometimes lead to device malfunction or low performance. Stock drivers (prepackaged with the Windows 98 installation CD) might be outdated relative to the current version of the device being installed. When the driver installation is complete, the system must be rebooted to make the new changes take effect in Windows 98. After every hardware installation, it is important to update device drivers to ensure maximum performance.

Making an Emergency Startup Disk

A Windows 98 *emergency startup disk*, also called a *startup disk*, is essential if the system crashes or hangs upon startup, or when the Windows 98 setup fails before completion. The Windows 98 setup is easier with a Windows 98 startup disk. This section provides an overview of the Windows 98 startup disk, and how to make one.

A Windows boot disk, also called a startup disk, is simply a floppy disk that allows the user to boot, or start up, the computer without having to access the hard drive. A typical Windows boot disk contains all the necessary files that the operating system needs to start. The boot disk is a handy tool that no Windows user should be without. The boot disk created in Windows 98 includes a generic CD-ROM driver. In fact, it includes both a generic IDE/ATAPI driver and a generic SCSI driver.

The Windows 98 startup disk can be used to boot the system to a command prompt (not the Windows desktop) to troubleshoot the failure. Additionally, if a hard drive fails or the MBR is attacked by a virus, the startup disk can help recover from the failure. If important operating system files are accidentally deleted or become corrupt, a startup disk can help resolve the problem. If you need to reformat the hard drive or reinstall Windows 98, you need to have the startup (boot) disk.

NOTE

A boot disk created in Windows 98 can be used to boot a Windows 95 machine. However, the Windows 98 startup disk provides CD-ROM support that is not available with the Windows 95 startup disk.

Creating a Windows 98 Startup Disk

A Windows 98 startup disk can be created in two ways. The first way is to insert a blank floppy disk in the computer when prompted during the installation process. (Refer to the section, "Understanding the Steps of a Windows 98 Installation.") Figures 5-77 and 5-78 show the dialog boxes that are displayed while installing Windows 98.

Figure 5-77 Creating a Startup Disk During a Windows 98 Installation

Figure 5-78 Insert a Blank Floppy Disk

The second way is to create the startup disk after the operating system is already installed and running. The Windows Startup Disk tab is used to create a startup disk, as follows:

Step 1 Choose **Start, Settings, Control Panel,** as shown in Figure 5-79.

Step 2 From the Control Panel window, double-click Add/Remove Programs. Once this window is open, click the Startup Disk tab and click Create Disk, as shown in Figure 5-80.

Step 3 When prompted, insert the Windows 98 CD into your CD-ROM drive and place a floppy disk into the floppy drive. The system then prompts you when the disk is complete.

Figure 5-79 Accessing the Control Panel

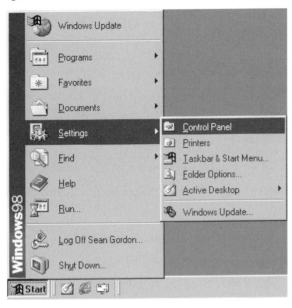

Figure 5-80 Creating a Startup Disk

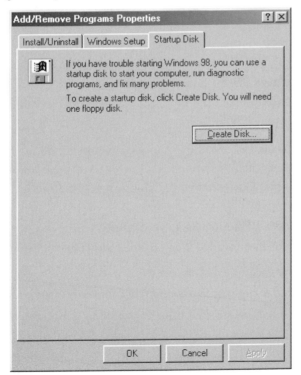

In addition to the critical operating system files that are copied to the floppy startup disk, three important troubleshooting disk utilities are also included: scandisk.exe, fdisk.exe, and format.exe.

Lab Activity 5.6.5 Create a Startup Disk

Create a Windows 9X startup disk that can boot the computer for trouble-shooting purposes.

Worksheet 5.6.6 Troubleshooting the Windows Installation

This worksheet reviews of the troubleshooting techniques used by the IT technician.

Uninstalling Windows 98

Sometimes, it is necessary to remove the Windows operating system from the computer. The uninstall procedure allows the system to return to a previous version of Windows. In some instances, uninstalling Windows 98 is the only solution left when an attempted upgrade fails, especially if no system backup was done before trying to upgrade. Otherwise, formatting the hard drive, a process that wipes the disk clean, causes you to lose all your data. In fact, uninstalling Windows is usually referred to as a solution of last resort.

When Can Windows 98 Be Uninstalled?

Windows 98 can be uninstalled if both of the following two conditions exist:

- You upgraded from a previous version of Windows, for example, Windows 95.
- The "Save uninstall information" option was selected during the Windows 98 setup. Note that when this option is selected, Setup creates the winundo.dat and winundo.ini files, which contain the uninstall information.

When Can Windows 98 Not Be Uninstalled?

Windows 98 cannot be uninstalled if any of the following conditions exist:

- The conditions mentioned in the previous section are not met.
- The winundo.dat and winundo.ini files become corrupted or deleted.
- The hard disk was compressed prior to installing Windows 98.
- The hard disk was compressed or converted to FAT32 after Windows 98 was installed.

The Step-by-Step Process of Uninstalling Windows 98

To uninstall Windows 98, follow these steps if all the previous conditions have been met:

Step 1   Choose **Start, Settings, Control Panel.**

Step 2   In the Control Panel window, double-click Add/Remove Programs.

Step 3   From the Add/Remove Programs menu, choose Uninstall Windows 98, click Add/Remove, and click Yes when prompted.

Step 4   At this point, SCANDISK checks the hard disk drive for errors. Allow SCANDISK do this by clicking Yes when prompted.

Step 5   When prompted to continue the uninstall, choose Yes and follow the on-screen instructions to uninstall Windows 98.

The requirements and options for uninstalling other versions of Windows differ from the steps mentioned here but the process is similar. Understanding these steps helps the technician troubleshoot problems that occur. Installing Windows 2000 is covered in Chapter 7.

CAUTION

Uninstalling Windows 98 is a drastic course of action and should be the last course of action. There could be many side effects, such as the malfunctioning of applications that were installed after the original installation of Windows 98.

Summary

This chapter discussed the Windows operating system. Important concepts to retain from this chapter are as follows:

- Windows uses a hierarchical structure or tree view of files, folders, and drives. DOS allowed filenames of up to eight characters with an extension of three characters. Windows allows filenames up to 255 characters long. Illegal filename characters are as follows:

  / \ ; : * ? " < >

- Drive letters use the 26 letters of the alphabet. Within Windows Explorer, the drives and folders can be expanded by clicking the plus sign. Files can be moved and copied between drives and folders. Use the Recycle Bin to recover files that have been accidentally deleted.

- The Control Panel provides access to the system properties, printers, add/remove hardware, add/remove software, and display options.

- The system Registry is a hierarchical database that is an efficient way to manage the operating system. It includes the user.dat file, which contains user-specific information, and system.dat, which contains hardware- and computer-specific settings.

- Preparing the hard drive for installing the operating system includes partitioning the drive. The partitioning process creates spaces of contiguous sectors on the hard drive. If more than one partition is created, one partition must be the primary, and the second is known as the extended. DOS can have up to four partitions on a hard drive.

- The requirements for installing or upgrading Windows are basically the same. A new installation requires more preparation for the hard drive. Do not stop any installation before it indicates that it is complete.

- Knowing the different tips and tricks can help a technician when troubleshooting is required. It is important to follow the steps and to work from the outside in.

The next chapter discusses the multimedia capabilities of the PC. You will gain an understanding of the basics of multimedia presentations and learn how to install the various devices used to play and record sounds and images.

Check Your Understanding

The following are review questions for the A+ exam. Answers can be found in Appendix B, "Answers to Check Your Understanding Review Questions."

1. What does Windows Explorer display?

    A. System resources available

    B. The date and time

    C. The hierarchical structure of files, folders, and drives

    D. The progress of the installation process

2. What is the first thing that needs to be done with a new hard drive?

    A. FDISK

    B. FORMAT

    C. SCANDISK

    D. DEFRAG

3. What is the second thing that needs to be done with a new hard drive?

    A. FDISK

    B. FORMAT

    C. SCANDISK

    D. DEFRAG

4. In Windows 98, what utilities are used to set up the hard drive?

    A. SCANDISK and NEWDRIVE

    B. SCANDISK and FDISK

    C. FDISK and FORMAT

    D. SCANDISK and FORMAT

5. What is another name for the active partition?

    A. Bootable partition

    B. Usable partition

    C. First partition

    D. Logical partition

6. How many logical drives can be created by FDISK on an EIDE drive?

   A. 4

   B. 8

   C. 16

   D. 24

7. What section of the hard drive stores the location of the operating system?

   A. Boot sector

   B. system.ini

   C. Boot cylinder

   D. Boot track

8. What is the lowest version of DOS that will allow the installation of Windows 98?

   A. 3.2.

   B. 3.

   C. An existing operating system is only required when using the upgrade version.

   D. It is not necessary to have an operating system installed.

9. What is the first thing you should try if the computer will not boot after installing the operating system?

   A. Reinstall the operating system

   B. Restart the computer

   C. Reinstall the hard drive

   D. Flash the CPU

10. Is it possible to upgrade a Windows 98 computer to Windows NT?

   A. Yes

   B. No

   C. Only if you have 64 MB of memory

   D. Only if you have 32 MB of memory

11. What does SCANDISK do?

    A. Removes viruses from the hard drive

    B. Erases temporary files from the hard drive

    C. Erases bad clusters

    D. Marks bad clusters

12. What program is used to edit the Registry?

    A. EDIT

    B. REGISTRY

    C. SYSEDIT

    D. REGEDIT

13. What should you do if the Windows 98 installation procedure fails?

    A. Remove any hardware listed in the error.txt file

    B. Restart the computer using Safe mode

    C. Remove any hardware listed in the fault.txt file

    D. Use a clean boot disk to start the computer

14. What does the io.sys file do in Windows 98?

    A. Loads the basic device drivers and sets the basic system headings

    B. Tells the operating system which hardware the user has access to

    C. Controls the video system of the computer

    D. Tells the operating system which software the user has access to

15. Where in Windows 98 can you remove or view devices and their properties?

    A. Control Panel, Devices

    B. Control Panel, System, Device Manager

    C. System, Devices

    D. Start, Devices

16. In Windows 98, how do you make an emergency startup disk?

    A. Start, Programs, Startup, Bootdisk

    B. Control Panel, Add/Remove Programs, Startup Disk tab, Create Disk

    C. Start, Programs, Add/Remove Programs, Startup Disk tab, Create Disk

    D. Double-click My Computer and choose Add/Remove Programs, Startup Disk tab, Create Disk

17. How do you restore a file if you delete it from the Windows 98 desktop?

    A. Start, Control Panel, Undelete

    B. Start, Programs, Undelete

    C. Open the Recycle Bin

    D. Open My Computer

18. By default, how much hard drive space is set aside for the Recycle Bin in Windows 98?

    A. 10%

    B. 20%

    C. 30%

    D. 40%

19. How can you view the version of Windows that is currently installed?

    A. Start, Help, About

    B. Right-click My Computer and choose Properties

    C. Right-click My Computer and choose Version

    D. Start, Help, Version

20. How do you view the file or folder properties in Windows 98?

    A. Click the icon and select Properties

    B. Right-click the icon and select Properties

    C. Drop the icon on the Taskbar

    D. Choose Start, Properties and then enter the name of the object

21. How do you locate an object in Windows 98?

    A. Start, Settings, Find

    B. Open My Computer and choose Settings, Find

    C. Start, Help, Find

    D. Start, Find

22. What character cannot be used when naming a DOS file?

    A. ~ (tilde)

    B. > (greater than sign)

    C. - (dash)

    D. _ (underscore)

23. If a printer is changed in DOS, what must be done?

    A. Change the DOS printer driver.

    B. Change each application printer driver.

    C. Change the printer in the CMOS.

    D. DOS will find the printer driver automatically.

24. What does creating a shortcut in Windows 98 allow the user to do?

    A. Find shortcuts more easily

    B. Execute applications more easily

    C. Have quick access to executable files

    D. Make use of the desktop

25. Windows 98 does not support which types of applications?

    A. DOS programs

    B. UNIX programs

    C. 16-bit Windows programs

    D. 32-bit Windows programs

Key Terms

Add Print wizard   Used to install a new printer on the system.

Add/Remove Hardware   Used to install and remove hardware on the computer.

Add/Remove Programs   Used to install and remove programs on the computer.

asd.exe   Used to skip a driver when the operating system fails during bootup.

block   Same as a cluster.

boot sector   The first area on each logical drive.

cluster   A combination of two or more sectors.

copy   Makes a duplicate of a document or file and puts it on the clipboard. The document can then be pasted to another location.

Create Shortcut   Creates a link to a file or application.

cylinder   All the tracks on a hard disk with the same number.

desktop   The area of the screen that Windows boots to.

Details mode   The view option that provides the most details of a file.

Device Manager   Displays a list of all the hardware installed on the system.

directory   A place to store data in the Windows file-management system.

Display utility   Allows the user to adjust the way the computer screen looks.

document details   Attributes.

drive letter   Distinguishes the drives in Windows.

extended partition   Second partition on the hard drive.

FDISK   Partitioning program.

FDISK /MBR   DOS command that helps to rebuild the operating system boot record on the drive.

file allocation table (FAT)   The reference table that the operating system uses to locate files on the hard disk.

file extensions   Describe the file format or the type of application used to create a file.

file management   The hierarchical structure of files, folders, and drives in Windows.

folder   A place to store data in the Windows file-management system.

formatting   Preparing a hard drive to store data.

Hardware Profiles   Allows the user to set up different hardware configurations for the same operating system.

high-level format routine   Creates the logical structure on the drive that tells the system what files are on the disk and where they can be found.

hwinfo.exe   A utility that provides a detailed collection of information about the computer.

logical drives   Sections that the partition can be divided into.

low-level format routine   Marks off the disk into sectors and cylinders, and defines their placement on the disk.

move   Relocates a file or document to a new location.

msconfig.exe   Allows the user to control how the system is started.

My Computer window   Displays the drives on the computer.

Partition table   Partition information created by FDISK.

performance   Displays information about the system.

primary partition   First partition on the hard drive.

Recycle Bin   A repository that holds deleted files, folders, etc.

regedit.exe   Displays the Registry in a hierarchical format.

Registry   A hierarchical database for the information used by the Windows operating system.

Safe mode/Device Manager   Troubleshooting options used to check whether problems are related to device conflicts.

SCANDISK   Utility that performs a complete check on the drive.

SCANDISK/DEFRAG   SCANDISK can locate errors, while DEFRAG pulls together different pieces of the same file scattered throughout the disk so the file can be more easily read by the system.

scanreg.exe   Used to back up or repair the system's Registry.

sector   Unit of storage (512 bytes) within a track.

Sounds utility   Allows the user to adjust the system sounds.

system.dat   A file that contains information about the hardware in the system.

System Properties   A tool in the Windows Control Panel that displays information relating to the system.

tracks   Magnetic area created by formatting the hard drive.

user.dat   A file that contains user-specific information.

virus scan   Checks all hard drives for viruses.

Windows 98 Setup wizard   Guides the user through the installation process.

Windows Explorer   A Windows utility that represents the file-management structure.

wscript.exe   Allows configuration of the properties relating to the Windows scripting host.

Objectives

Upon completion of this chapter, you will be able to perform the following tasks:

- Understand the hardware requirements for multimedia
- Install or upgrade the video and sound cards
- Configure video capture boards
- Uninstall hardware components and remove associated drivers
- Install and configure CD-ROM and DVD drives
- Understand the differences between recordable and rewritable CDs and DVDs

Chapter 6

Multimedia Capabilities

Introduction

This chapter discusses the multimedia capabilities of the PC. Multimedia presentations go beyond text and images to include video, animation, live situations, audience interaction, and sound. You will learn about the basic hardware, including video cards and computer displays, as well as the media file formats used in multimedia. This chapter provides information on how to install or upgrade video and sound cards, including how to configure drivers and software. CD-ROM and DVD drives are detailed, providing an overview of how they work and the advantages of each, especially in terms of multimedia production.

PC Multimedia Overview

This section includes the following topics:

- Basic hardware required for multimedia upgrades
- The video adapter
- Characterizing computer displays
- Sound cards and speaker systems
- Common media file formats used in multimedia applications
- MPEG hardware versus software

Basic Hardware Required for Multimedia Upgrades

Most modern computer systems come equipped with the capability to display and create multimedia. The ability to use different types of multimedia is as much a part of the modern PC as an Internet connection. This chapter discusses the hardware and software required to run modern presentation media on the PC.

Multimedia is a term that is typically used to mean the combination of text, sound, and/or motion video. Figure 6-1 is an example of a video in the Windows Media Player.

Figure 6-1 Windows Media Player

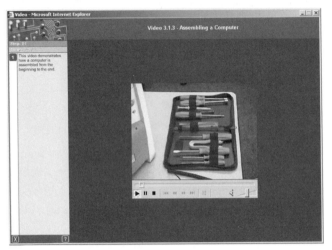

Multimedia has been described as the addition of animated images, as in an animated gif file on the web, but typically it means one of the following:

- Text and sound
- Text, sound, and still or animated graphic images
- Text, sound, and video images
- Video and sound
- Multiple display areas, images, or presentations shown concurrently
- In live situations, the use of speakers or actors and props together with sound, images, and motion video

Multimedia is distinguished from traditional motion pictures or movies both by the scale of the production (multimedia is usually smaller and less expensive) and by the addition of audience participation or *interactive multimedia*. Interactive elements can include voice commands, mouse manipulation, text entry, touch screen, video capture of the user, and live participation (as in live presentations).

Multimedia presentations are more complex than simple text-and-image presentations and are generally more expensive. Multimedia presentations can be included in many contexts, including the web, CD-ROMs, and so on. Basic development costs of a packaged multimedia production with video for commercial presentation (for example, at trade shows) can reach US$ 1000 per minute of presentation time. Multimedia software can develop presentations at considerably less expense than standard video productions, with the flexibility to distribute on the web or on CD.

PC Requirements to Run Multimedia

The types of computer hardware and software necessary to develop multimedia on the PC vary. The minimum hardware requirements include a monitor, video accelerator card, and sound adapter card with attached speakers. The following components provide visual and sound output:

- A microphone connected to a plug on the sound adapter card to input sound.
- CD-ROMs and DVD players are common PC components for input and output of multimedia.
- A connection to the Internet through a network interface card or a modem provides multimedia input to the system. Audio and video streaming is popular.
- Digital still pictures and video cameras are often connected through standard computer ports or through special card adapters.
- A video capture card, a special adapter card that samples and converts the images and sounds, can provide television and radio recordings and images.
- MPEG hardware and web-based movie players to play movies.
- Specialized hardware is required to play computer games on CD or DVD.

Video Adapter

A *video adapter* (also called a *display adapter* or *video board*) is an integrated circuit card in a computer or, in some cases, a monitor that provides digital-to-analog conversion, video RAM, and a video controller so that data can be sent to a computer's display. Figures 6-2 and 6-3 show the front and side view, respectively, of the video adapter.

Today, almost all displays and video adapters adhere to the *video graphics array (VGA)* standard. VGA is how data are passed between the computer and the display. VGA is responsible for the frame refresh rates, defined in hertz, and the number and width of horizontal lines; this amounts to specifying the resolution of the pixels that are created. VGA supports four different resolution settings and two related image refresh rates.

In addition to VGA, most displays adhere to one or more standards set by the *Video Electronics Standards Association (VESA)* which defines how software can determine the capability of a display. It also identifies resolution settings beyond those of VGA. These resolutions include 800×600, 1024×768, 1280×1024, and 1600×1200 pixels.

Figure 6-2 Video Adapter—Front View

Figure 6-3 Video Adapter—Side View

What Is a Display?

A *display* or *monitor* is a computer output surface and projecting mechanism that shows text and often graphic images, using a cathode ray tube (CRT), liquid crystal display (LCD), light-emitting diode (LED), gas plasma display, or other image-projection technology. The display is usually considered to include the screen or projection surface and the device that produces the information on the screen. In some computers, the display is packaged in a separate unit called a monitor. Figure 6-4 shows a typical flat-panel monitor.

In other computers, the display is integrated into a unit with the processor and other parts of the computer. Some sources make the distinction that the monitor includes other signal-handling devices that feed and control the display or projection device. However, there is no distinction when all these parts become integrated into a total unit, as in the case of notebook computers. A *video display terminal (VDT)* or *video display unit (VDU)* typically refers to a terminal with a display and a keyboard.

Figure 6-4 HP 15-Inch Flat-Panel Monitor

Most computer monitors use analog signals to display the image. This requirement and the need to continually refresh the displayed image mean that the computer also needs a display or video adapter. The *video adapter* takes the digital data sent by application programs, stores the data in video random-access memory (video RAM), and converts the data to analog format for the display-scanning mechanism using a digital-to-analog converter (DAC).

Characterizing Computer Displays

Computer video displays can be described according to the following characteristics:

- Color capability
- Sharpness and viewability
- Size of the screen
- Projection technology

Color Capability

Today, most desktop displays provide color. Older notebook and smaller computers sometimes have a less expensive monochrome display. The video displays can usually operate in one of several display modes that determine how many bits are used to describe color and how many colors can be displayed. A display that can operate in *super VGA (SVGA) mode* can display up to 16,777,216 colors because it can process a 24-bit-long description of a pixel.

The number of bits used to describe a pixel is known as its *bit-depth*. The 24-bit bit-depth is also known as *true color*. It allows eight bits for each of the three additive primary colors: red, green, and blue. Although humans cannot distinguish that many colors, the 24-bit system is necessary for graphic designers because it allocates 1 byte for each color. The VGA mode is the lowest common denominator of display modes. Depending on the resolution setting, this mode can provide up to 256 colors. Table 6-1 shows the relationship between bit-depth and the number of colors that can be produced.

Table 6-1 Display Bit-Depth

Bit-Depth	Number of Colors
1	2 (monochrome)
2	4 (CGA)
4	16 (EGA)
8	256 (VGA)
16	65,536 (high color, XGA)
24	16,777,216 (true color, SVGA)
32	16,777,216 (true color + alpha channel)

Sharpness and Viewability

The physical limitation on the potential sharpness of a screen image is the dot pitch. *Dot pitch* is the size of an individual beam that gets through to light up a point of phosphor on the screen. This beam can be round or a vertical, slot-shaped rectangle depending on the display technology, as shown in Figure 6-5. Displays typically come with a dot pitch of .28 mm (.28 millimeters) or smaller. Dot pitch is the diagonal distance between same-color phosphor dots. The smaller the dot pitch, the greater the potential image sharpness.

The *sharpness* of a display image is measured in dots per inch (dpi). The number of dots per inch is determined by a combination of the screen resolution (that is, how many pixels are projected on the screen horizontally and vertically) and the physical screen size. The same resolution spread out over a larger screen offers reduced sharpness. On the other hand, a high-resolution setting on a smaller surface produces a sharper image, but text becomes harder to read.

Figure 6-5 Dot Pitch Explanation

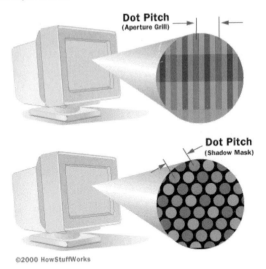

©2000 HowStuffWorks

Viewability is the ability to see the screen image from different angles (as opposed to directly facing it). Displays with CRTs generally provide good viewability from fairly wide viewing angles. Flat-panel displays, including those using light-emitting diodes and liquid crystal display technology, are often harder to see at wider viewing angles.

Size of the Screen

On desktop computers, the display screen width-to-height ratio, known as the *aspect ratio*, is generally standardized at 4 to 3 (usually indicated as 4:3). Screen sizes are measured diagonally, in either millimeters or inches, from one corner to the opposite corner. Common desktop screen sizes are 15-, 17-, and 19-inch. Notebook screen sizes are somewhat smaller.

Projection Technology

Most displays use *CRT technology*, which is similar to that used in most television sets. This technology requires a certain distance from the beam projection device to the screen in order to function. Using other technologies, displays can be much thinner and are known as flat-panel displays. Flat-panel display technologies include *LED*, *LCD*, and *gas plasma*. LED and gas plasma displays work by lighting up display screen positions based on the voltages at different grid intersections. LCDs work by blocking light rather than creating it. LCDs require far less energy than LED and gas plasma technologies and are currently the primary technology for notebook and other mobile computers.

Displays generally handle data input as character maps, or bitmaps. In character-mapping mode, a display has a preallocated amount of pixel space for each character. In bitmap mode, the display receives an exact representation of the screen image that is to be projected in the form of a sequence of bits that describe the color values for specific x and y coordinates, starting from a given location on the screen. Displays that handle bitmaps are also known as *all-points addressable displays*.

Sound Cards and Speaker Systems

Typically, the output of the sound card requires additional amplification if external speakers are used. Figure 6-6 shows external speakers that can be attached to the sound card. The amplification circuitry is normally included in the external speaker units. Power for older speakers was derived from batteries housed in the speaker cabinets or from a small AC power converter. Most sound cards today have the capability of directly driving low-power headphones. The system's internal speaker can also produce audio output, or the sound can be amplified through external audio amplifier systems for applications such as Surround Sound.

Figure 6-6 External Computer Speakers

Common Media File Formats in Multimedia Applications

To date, two common data-compression standards are used with digitized video. These are the *Joint Photographic Experts Group (JPEG)* and the *Moving Picture Experts Group (MPEG)* compression standards.

Other Compression Standards

Another data-compression method used with PCs is the *Indeo* compression standard, developed by Intel. Indeo is similar to the MPEG standard, in that it was designed to be a distribution format. It was primarily intended to play back compressed video files from the smallest-possible file size. Later versions of this standard include the MPEG compression method.

Another compression/decompression standard supported by Video for Windows is *Cinepak*. This standard uses an audio-visual interface (AVI) file format to produce 40:1 compression ratios and 30-frames-per-second capture rates, at 320×200 resolution. Windows 95 supports several different compression techniques. These include Cinepak, two versions of Indeo, an RLE format, and the Video 1 format. Figure 6-7 shows how data compression works.

Figure 6-7 How Data Compression Works

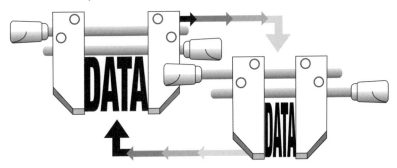

MPEG Hardware Versus Software

Although JPEG provides enough compression to allow single-frame digitized images to fit on disk drives, it soon became apparent that full-motion pictures were going to need much greater compression to be useful with current technology. Therefore, the MPEG format was developed to provide compression ratios up to 200:1, with high-quality video and audio.

As with JPEG, MPEG removes redundant picture information from individual scenes. However, instead of simply removing redundant information from within a single frame, the MPEG compression scheme removes redundant information from consecutive scenes. In addition, the MPEG methodology compresses only key objects within a frame, every 15th frame. Between these key frames, only the information that changes from frame to frame is recorded.

The MPEG standard includes specifications for audio compression and decompression in both MPEG1 and MPEG2. *MPEG1* supports a near-CD-quality stereo output, at data rates between 128 kbps and 256 kbps. The *MPEG2* specification supports CD-quality Surround Sound (four-channel) output. Table 6-2 shows the different MPEG standards.

Table 6-2 MPEG Standards

	MPEG1	**MPEG2**	**MPEG4**
Compression	320×280 full-motion video	720×480 full-motion video	Full-motion video
Application	Interactive multimedia/broadcast TV	Broadcast TV, video on demand	Interactive multimedia
Data rate	1.5 Mbps	4–80 Mbps	≥64 kbps

Worksheet 6.1.6   Multimedia Devices

This worksheet provides a review of multimedia devices and their functions.

Upgrading Video with a Video Acceleration Board

This section includes the following topics:

- Understanding PCI and AGP types
- Using all-in-one cards
- Installing and configuring the video card driver and software
- Understanding RAMDAC and video memory
- Flashing the video board with BIOS updates

Understanding PCI and AGP Types

Newer Pentium systems include an advanced *accelerated graphics port (AGP)* interface for video graphics. The AGP interface is a variation of the PCI bus design that has been modified to handle the intense data throughput associated with three-dimensional graphics. (Refer to Chapter 2, "How Computers Work," for a review of the PCI bus.) Figure 6-8 shows the AGP interface on the motherboard.

Figure 6-8 Accelerated Graphics Port (AGP) Interface

The AGP specification was introduced by Intel to provide a 32-bit video channel that runs at 66 MHz in basic 1X video mode. The standard also supports two high-speed modes that include a 2X (533-MBps) and a 4X (1.07-GBps) mode.

The AGP standard provides a direct channel between the AGP graphic controller and the computer system's main memory, instead of using the expansion buses for video data. This removes the video data traffic from the PCI buses. The speed provided by this direct link permits video data to be stored in system RAM instead of in special video memory.

The system board typically has a single slot that is supported by a Pentium/AGP-compliant chipset. System boards designed for portable systems and single-board systems can incorporate the AGP function directly into the board without using a slot connector.

Using All-In-One Cards

Video capture software is used to capture frames of television video and convert them to digital formats that can be processed by the system. Graphics packages can be used to manipulate the contents of the video after it has been converted to digital formats that the computer can handle. One of the popular file formats for video is the Microsoft AVI format.

Video capture cards are responsible for converting video signals from different sources to digital signals that can be manipulated by the computer. As in the audio conversion process, the video card samples the incoming video signal by feeding it through an *analog-to-digital (A-to-D) converter*. Figure 6-9 shows the audio signal going in as analog and coming out as digital.

Figure 6-9 Analog-to-Digital Conversion Example

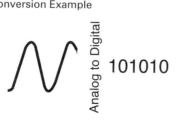

One of the jobs of the video capture card is to convert the YUV format (described in the following note) into an RGB (red-green-blue) VGA-compatible signal. YUV is a video encoding format that is different than RGB. With YUV, an encoding circuit samples the incoming analog signal and then performs an operation known as color space conversion on it. *Color space conversion* is the process of converting the YUV signal into the RGB format that is acceptable to the VGA card screen memory. The resolution of a studio-quality TV signal is delivered in two interlaced screens at a rate of 60 fields per second. The encoder converts this signal scheme into a 640×480 image (in VGA mode), delivered to the screen in a single, non-interlaced signal at a rate of 30 frames per second or higher.

In addition to changing the format, the capture card also scales the image to fit in the defined video window on the monitor's screen. The capture card's video signal processor adjusts the image to the correct size by interpolating (adding or removing) adjacent pixels as necessary. The encoder samples the analog signal at a rate of 27 MBps. This value becomes important when you realize that, at this rate, a 500-MB hard drive would be filled in 18.5 seconds. To make the digitized video manageable and useful to the digital computer system, the signal must be compressed into smaller files.

Installing and Configuring the Video Card Driver and Software

After the video card has been installed and the monitor has been connected to the video card and plugged into the power outlet, you must install the correct drivers for the video card. The Windows 9*X* operating systems should detect the video card, start the system with basic VGA video drivers, and ask you if you want to install the manufacturer's video drivers.

The Windows 2000 operating system is even more proactive. It detects the new video card, tells you that it has found the new card, and then automatically loads the card's video drivers. The only time that you might need to be directly involved with the system's video drivers is when Plug and Play fails or when the video card is not recognized by the operating system.

NOTE

YUV is the color model used for encoding video. *Y* is the luminosity of the black and white signal. *U* and *V* are color difference signals. *U* is red minus *Y* (R – Y), and *V* is blue minus *Y* (B – Y). To display YUV data on a computer screen, the data must be converted into RGB format through color space conversion (described previously). YUV is used because it reduces storage space requirements and saves transmission bandwidth compared to RGB.

 Lab Activity 6.2.3 Upgrading the Video Accelerator

Install a video card with advanced capabilities such as 3D, more memory, or AGP. Also, remove any old video drivers and install new ones.

 Video 6.2.3 Replacing a Video Card

This video shows you how to replace a video card.

Understanding RAMDAC and Video Memory

The display information stored and manipulated in the video memory is in the standard binary format of 1s and 0s. These binary patterns control the resolution and color of each pixel on the video display screen. However, monitors are analog, not digital, devices. In order for the monitor to work, the digital information in the video memory must be translated into analog form for export to the monitor screen. This is the role of the *random-access memory digital-to-analog converter (RAMDAC)* chip.

The RAMDAC chip reads the video memory contents, converts it to analog form, and sends it over a cable to the video monitor. The quality of this chip impacts the quality of the image, speed of the refresh rate, and maximum resolution capability. *Refresh rate* refers to the number of times per second that the video display screen can be redrawn.

Video Memory

The video chipset relies on video memory to render the requested image. The basic element of every video image is a dot (or pixel). Many dots comprise what you see displayed on the monitor. Every dot has a location reserved in video memory. The maximum number of dots that be displayed relates to the resolution.

Resolution is commonly expressed as a pair of numbers. Each pair of numbers represents the maximum possible number of dots on a horizontal axis and the maximum possible number of dots on a vertical axis. The basic VGA resolution of 640×480 means that there are 640 possible dots on the horizontal axis and 480 possible dots on the vertical axis. Enhanced VGA has a resolution of 800×600 dots. Super VGA has a resolution of 1024×768 dots. From these examples, you can see that higher resolutions require more memory to draw the image. However, the higher the resolution, the sharper and clearer the image. Figure 6-10 illustrates how resolution can affect the visual quality of an image.

Figure 6-10 Quality Improves as Resolution Increases

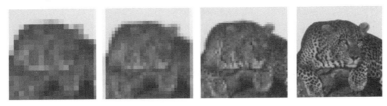

When an image is displayed in color (or grayscale), a certain number of bits must be assigned per dot (per pixel) to achieve a given color depth or possible number of colors. The more bits assigned, the more colors that can be presented.

To see how video memory impacts the execution of graphics applications, return to the previous example. Again imagine that you are using a graphics application to draw a box on the monitor screen. When the system CPU issues a series of commands to draw a box, it issues commands to the video processor chip to draw the box.

Flashing the Video Board with BIOS Updates

Although the CPU issues instructions to the video card about what to draw, the CPU does not tell the video card how to draw. How the image is to be displayed is the responsibility of the video BIOS. The *video BIOS* provides the set of video functions that can be used by the software to access the video hardware. The video BIOS allows software to interface with the video chipset in much the same way as the system BIOS does for the motherboard chipset. When SVGA technology became an industry norm, incompatibilities in the different video BIOS implementations led to the development of a standardized BIOS.

 Worksheet 6.2.5 Video Accelerators

This worksheet provides a review of information relating to video accelerators.

Adding Audio Capabilities with a Sound Card

This section includes the following topics:

- Understanding sound card operation
- Understanding USB, PCI, and built-in sound
- Removing or disabling outdated sound cards
- Installing sound cards
- Connecting a CD-ROM or DVD-ROM drive to the sound card
- Installing and configuring the sound card driver and software
- Connecting MIDI and external-audio sources

Understanding Sound Card Operation

Audio is an integral component of the multimedia experience and is a standard feature on personal computers. Educational and recreational software uses sound effects to heighten the experience. Musicians use a computer's audio capabilities to create songs. Visually impaired users can have the computer "read" information to them. The applications for computer audio are endless, but for a PC to have audio capabilities, it must have a sound card installed.

A *sound card* is a device (either in the form of an expansion card or a chipset) that allows the computer to handle audio information. Figure 6-11 shows a typical sound card.

Figure 6-11 Sound Card

The basic responsibility of a sound card is the input, processing, and output of audio information as detailed in the following list:

- **Input**—Sound cards can capture audio information from many different sources. These sources include microphones and CD players.
- **Processing**—The processing capability of a sound card allows it to convert audio information in different formats as well as to add effects to the sound data.
- **Output**—Simple sound card output devices include headphones and speakers, while more sophisticated devices consist of Surround Sound digital theater systems, digital audio tape (DAT) and CD recorders, and other musical devices.

Basic Components of a Sound Card

Even though many types of sound cards are available for different applications, every sound card has the following basic components:

- **Processor**—The digital signal processor (DSP) is a chip (or set of chips) that is the brain of the sound card. The DSP handles the basic instructions that drive the sound card as well as the routing of audio information. The DSP can also act as the synthesizer, or music generator.

- **Converters**—Digital-to-analog converters (DACs) and analog-to-digital converters (ADCs) are used in the input and output process. Most audio information recorded from outside the computer (unless in a digital format) must pass through the ADC, while data being output to the speakers uses the services of the DAC.

- **Memory**—More advanced sound cards use memory to store samples from musical instruments and to hold instructions for musical instrument digital interface (MIDI) devices. This memory is usually in the form of read-only memory (ROM), flash memory, or NVRAM and can often be upgraded or expanded.

- **Ports**—Sound cards can have multiple internal and external ports for connecting to input and output devices. Also known as jacks or interfaces, these ports expand the functionality of a sound card.

Sound Production and Quality

Sound cards produce audio (synthesize) using three distinct methods: *frequency modulation (FM)*, *wavetable*, and *MIDI*. Sound cards that use FM synthesis use programming to create waveforms that best match the instrument that is playing. These sounds are easy to produce but are unrealistic. Wavetable sound cards use digitized samples of real instruments to reproduce audio. These samples are stored within the card's memory, which usually contains an entire orchestra of musical instruments. MIDI is a combination of hardware and software that allows the sound card to control musical instruments and use these instruments to output the audio. If an external instrument is not available, the sound card can use its MIDI synthesizer to play the encoded music.

The quality of a sound card is determined by its bit-depth, sampling rate, and feature set, which are defined as follows:

- **Bit-depth**—Refers to the sample size and bus size of the sound card. In general, the larger the sample size, the higher the quality of the sound reproduced. A 32-bit sample holds a much greater amount of information about an instrument than does an 8-bit sample. Also, a 32-bit sound card can move data at faster than an 8-bit or 16-bit card.

- **Sample rate**—The rate at which the card can record audio information. This rate is measured in kHz—thousands of cycles per second. Essentially, this indicates how many samples of a sound are captured per second. CD-quality audio uses 44-kHz sampling. Today's sound cards are capable of sampling at 128 kHz and beyond. Remember, the larger the sample rate, the larger the digital file that is created. Figure 6-12 shows an audio sample rate at 44 kHz.

- **Feature set**—Can also determine the quality of the sound card. All sound cards include the basics of a processor, converters, memory, and input/output ports, but other features can include 3D audio coprocessors, device controllers, and digital output options. The 3D audio coprocessors produce spatial audio in multispeaker systems. This type of output is used to immerse the user in a world of sound and is popular with computer games.

Sound cards can also act as device controllers that have built-in SCSIRAID (detailed in a later chapter, it increases performance and provides fault tolerance), or FireWire.

Many higher-end sound cards also offer digital output ports such as Toslink (a fiber-optic connector) and coaxial to allow connection to home theatre systems.

Figure 6-12 Audio Sample Rate at 44 kHz

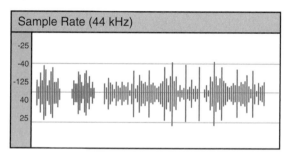

NOTE

Small Computer System Interface (SCSI) is a hardware interface that allows for the connection of up to 15 peripheral devices to a single board. Redundant Array of Inexpensive Disks (RAID) increases performance and provide fault tolerance. It is detailed in a later chapter. FireWire, also known as IEEE 1394, is a high-speed serial bus developed by Apple and Texas Instruments that allows for the connection of up to 63 devices.

Understanding USB, PCI, and Built-In Sound

Audio is created through either USB sound, PCI sound cards, or built-in sound chipsets found on the motherboard. Each of these methods has advantages and disadvantages, as described in the following sections.

USB Sound

The *universal serial bus (USB)* is a hot-swappable interface that can be used to connect many different types of peripherals to a PC. One such popular peripheral is a USB speaker system. These speaker systems allow the USB port to act as a sound card. Plug and Play is a major benefit of USB sound. There is no need for other configurations once the audio device is plugged into the interface. USB is also a standard for all Windows operating systems since 1996. One advantage with USB sound is that the PC generates all the information necessary to create sounds and music. The speakers then perform the digital-to-analog conversion. The drawback of USB sound is that it requires processing power to create audio, and this can hamper the performance of the computer. The effect is minimal in newer PCs.

NOTE

A *hot-swappable interface* allows peripherals to be changed while the system is operating. Microphones and headphones are examples of hot-swappable components.

To operate, USB speaker systems require only the speakers, a USB cable, and a USB port, as shown in Figure 6-13. The prices on these devices can vary from US$ 40 to US$ 400.

Figure 6-13 USB Port

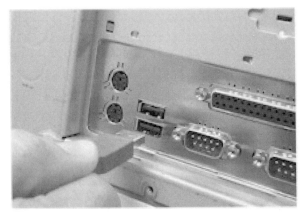

PCI Sound Cards

A *peripheral component interconnect (PCI)* sound card is an adapter card with an audio processor that connects to the motherboard using a PCI slot. These cards use the PCI 32-/64-bit bus to input and output audio information. An advantage of the onboard audio processor is that it uses this information to create the audio, bypassing the computer's processor and freeing precious CPU cycles. PCI sound cards usually have multiple ports for connecting to other audio peripherals. External ports include speaker outputs, microphone inputs, and digital connectors. Internal interfaces are used to connect directly to CD-ROM and DVD drives. A disadvantage is that a PCI sound card, like any other adapter card, requires the use of an empty PCI slot and uses some of the computer's resources.

NOTE

PCI sound cards come in many different varieties and from a variety of manufacturers. Most PCI sound cards use IRQ5 as well as multiple memory ranges.

Built-In Sound

Many motherboard manufacturers integrate both video and audio options into their products. The *built-in sound* has an audio processor located on a motherboard in the form of a single chip (or chipset). In this manner, built-in sound has the advantages of both USB and PCI sound options. Because it is built in, the setup is as simple as that for a USB sound card. Because it uses an audio processor like a PCI sound card, the computer's CPU does not process the audio information. Motherboards with built-in sound also include the common audio ports for speakers and a microphone, as shown Figure 6-14.

Figure 6-14 Motherboard with Built-In Sound

One benefit of built-in sound is that the price of the complete package is less expensive than USB and PCI sound. A separate sound card does not need to be purchased. The major drawback of built-in sound is that it is difficult (and sometimes impossible) to upgrade the audio capabilities. Upgrading built-in sound usually requires disabling the audio system and installing a PCI sound card.

Removing or Disabling Outdated Sound Cards

A common upgrade for today's PCs is the addition of a newer sound card. Before adding a more capable sound card, older sound cards should be removed. Built-in sound chipsets should be disabled. Removing or disabling outdated sound cards frees resources such as IRQs and expansion slots.

Use the proper uninstall procedures to remove hardware, related software, specific drivers, and files that could slow the system and to free resources.

Uninstalling the Card in Windows

In Windows, use the Device Manager to uninstall hardware. Open the Device Manager, and find and expand the hardware category to be removed (usually Sound, Video, and Game Controllers). Select the sound card, and choose Remove. This begins the uninstall process and might prompt the user for a floppy disk or CD. The following steps are used to remove a sound card:

Step 1   Choose **Start, Control Panel, System Properties, Device Manager.**

Step 2   Highlight the device to be removed. In this example, it is the Sound Blaster sound card, as shown in Figure 6-15.

Figure 6-15 System Properties—Device Manager Showing the Sound Card

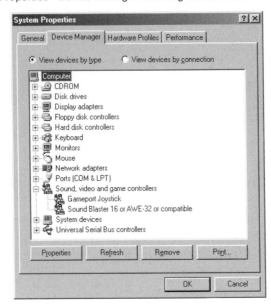

Step 3 Click the **Remove** button. A confirmation screen displays, as shown in Figure 6-16.

Figure 6-16 Confirming Device Removal

Step 4 Click **OK** to complete the process. Figure 6-17 shows the Device Manager, and the sound card is no longer listed.

To uninstall software and driver information, use the Add/Remove Programs section of the Windows Control Panel. When the uninstall is complete, the computer should be shut down so that the outdated sound card can be removed. If the computer is restarted before the sound card is removed, the operating system might detect it and reinstall the drivers.

Figure 6-17 Sound Card No Longer Listed

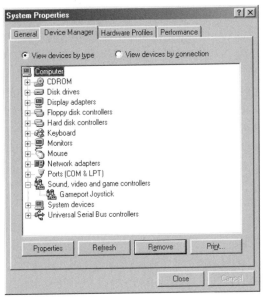

Disabling an outdated sound card or built-in sound is similar to the uninstall process. To disable a sound card or built-in sound, open the Device Manager and choose to view the properties of the sound card. Within the Properties window, choose to disable the card. This is different than removing the card because the sound card and its drivers and files are not removed. This can free resources and allow you to try other sound cards to ensure compatibility. Also, a disabled sound card can easily be re-enabled. Disabling built-in sound often requires making a change in the computer's BIOS. Typically, a setting is available to allow enabling or disabling of onboard audio. Built-in sound must be disabled within the BIOS and the operating system.

Removal of Outdated Card

The removal of a sound card follows the same basic steps as the removal of any piece of hardware from the computer. Once the computer is powered off and the power cable is removed, the case can be opened. While working inside the case, you should wear an antistatic wrist strap. After the sound card is located, all interconnecting cables should be removed. These cables include external cables (to speakers, microphones, etc.) and internal cables (to the CD-ROM drive, DVD-ROM drive, internal speaker, etc.). After removing the screw that holds the sound card in place, use both hands to firmly grasp the card and gently rock it so that it can be pulled from the slot. Once removed, the card should be placed in a static-free bag for protection. Replace the case cover and power cord, and boot the computer to ensure that the process has been done correctly.

Installing Sound Cards

Installing a sound card is similar to installing any other adapter card. See the user's guide to determine what hardware configuration settings should be made before inserting the card into the system. You should also run a diagnostic program to check the system's available resources before configuring the card. USB and built-in sound chipsets are part of an integrated motherboard and do not require installation. PCI sound cards must be physically installed, and internal connections made and configured before use. Before beginning the installation process, be sure that you have the proper tools. A screwdriver or socket set might be required to open the computer's case and to remove slot covers. Also required is an antistatic wrist strap, which should be worn at all times while handling cards and working inside the computer.

The first step in installing a sound card is to make sure that the PC has no power and that all external devices are disconnected. Next, remove the cover from the computer's case. A can of compressed air can be used to remove any dust that has built up inside of the case. Locate an available PCI slot to accommodate the sound card, and remove the corresponding slot cover, making sure to save the screw that connects the cover to the frame. While wearing the antistatic wrist strap, align the tabs on the bottom side of the sound card with the open PCI slot, and firmly press the card into the slot, keeping even pressure along the side of the card. After ensuring a snug fit, replace the cover slot screw to secure the sound card to the frame. This stabilizes the sound card and provides the proper grounding.

Connecting a CD-ROM or DVD-ROM Drive to the Sound Card

After installing the sound card, the next step is to connect any internal components and cables to the sound card. A common connection is cabling the CD-ROM or DVD-ROM drive to the sound card to produce digital audio. All CD-ROM drives have an analog audio out connector for connecting to a sound card. This four-wire connection uses the CD-ROM's digital-to-analog (D/A) converter to pass two-channel analog audio to the sound card for output through connected speakers. These connectors are labeled as analog audio out and keyed on both the CD-ROM drive and sound card to ensure the correct type of connection.

Most DVD-ROM drives (as well as some newer CD-ROM drives) offer a digital audio out connection. A DVD is capable of audio streams containing multiple channels. A multispeaker sound card can separate these channels and output them using the correct speakers to create a Surround Sound environment. The two-wire digital audio connectors are labeled and keyed on both the drive and sound card to ensure proper connection. After making one or more connections between the sound card and a drive, you must configure the connection using the sound card's setup application.

Installing and Configuring the Sound Card Driver and Software

To complete the sound card installation process, the correct sound card drivers and any other audio-related applications must be installed. A sound card driver is the software that allows the computer's operating system to communicate with the hardware. It is important that the driver being installed matches the particular sound card as well as the installed operating system. Faulty drivers can cause distorted audio output or no audio output, or can adversely affect the performance of a computer.

After installing the sound card, start the computer, and Windows will begin to install a driver for the hardware. Following the notification of new hardware detected, the operating system prompts the user for a floppy disk or CD, supplied by the manufacturer, that contains the sound card's driver; the OS then continues the installation process. Updated device drivers can also be downloaded from the sound card manufacturer's website.

You can also manually install a driver. After the sound card is installed, the driver can be installed, changed, or updated by using the Device Manager. In Device Manager, select the sound card and view its properties, as shown in Figures 6-18 and 6-19. Check the driver version to ensure that the most current one is installed. Figure 6-20 shows the driver files that are available to install.

Figure 6-18 Device Properties—General Tab

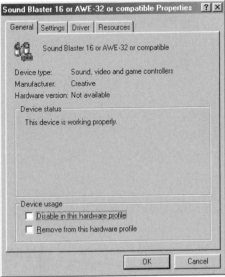

Figure 6-19 Driver Details

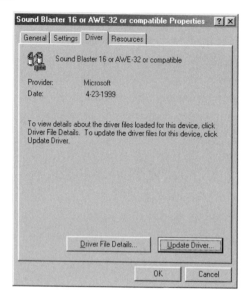

Figure 6-20 Available Driver Files

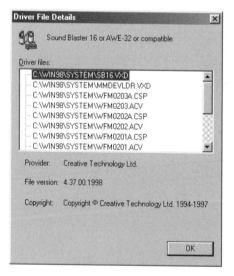

A sound card driver can also be installed by using the software that accompanies the sound card. Most sound card manufacturers include a floppy disk or CD with their product. The disk or CD typically contains different drivers for the sound card, other audio applications, and an installation program for the drivers and applications. Running the installation program allows the user to choose the proper sound card driver as well as to install any audio applications. These applications can include music players and generators, audio capture utilities, speech-recognition programs, and volume/tone controls.

Provided that the sound card is properly configured and the software configuration matches, the sound card and speakers need to be checked out. Most of these checks are simple. For example, check to see that the speakers are plugged into the speaker port. It is common for the speakers to be mistakenly plugged into the card's MIC (microphone) port. Likewise, if the sound card does not record sound, make sure that the microphone is installed in the proper jack (not the speaker jack) and that it is turned on. Check the amount of disk space on the drive to ensure that there is enough space to hold the files being installed.

Video 6.3.4   Installing a Sound Card

This video shows you how to install a sound card.

Lab Activity 6.3.4   Sound Card Installation

Install a sound card, attach the speakers and microphone, and then install the proper drivers. When the installation is complete, test the installation by playing sounds on the computer.

Worksheet 6.3.3   Sound Cards

In this worksheet, you review your understanding of how sound cards work.

Connecting MIDI and External-Audio Sources

Sound cards are used not only for audio output but also for recording audio from a variety of external sources. Common external-audio source connections include the following:

- **MIDI port**—MIDI is an industry-standard interface that is used to connect musical devices. The basic MIDI devices are controllers and generators. Musicians often use MIDI-enabled computers to control and sequence music generators, such as drum machines and synthesizers. Most sound cards have a MIDI/joystick combination port. This is commonly a female DB-15 port on the face of the sound card. A MIDI cable is used to connect one or more devices to the sound card. Special software is required to use the MIDI functions of a sound card and is usually included as part of the software package.

NOTE

Ogg Vorbis is a new audio compression format that is free, open, and unpatented. It is roughly comparable to other formats used to store and play digital music, such as mp3, vqf, aac.

- **Microphone-in port**—Microphones can be connected to a sound card using the female 3.5-mm minijack port on the face of the sound card. This provides the user with the ability to capture his or her voice using a recording application on the computer. Inputting audio through the microphone-in port requires the sound card to use its analog-to-digital (A/D) converter. Some common digital audio formats include wav and mp3 files, and Ogg Vorbis.

- **Line-in port**—The line-in port on a sound card has the same physical characteristics as the microphone-in port (a female 3.5-mm minijack) but the two ports are used for different types of sources. The microphone-in port is to be used with non-amplified sources. The line-in port is used to capture audio from amplified or powered sources, such as cassette players, DAT players, external CD players, and other devices with line-out options. As with the microphone-in port, the line-in port requires the use of the sound card's A/D converter.

- **Digital-in port**—With the popularity of digital audio sources (such as CD, mini-disk, DVD, and DAT players), sound card manufacturers are adding external digital audio source capture components. Most digital-in ports use the Sony Phillips digital interface (SPDIF). SPDIF is outlined in the red book audio standard for digital audio recording. The digital-in port on a sound card usually has one of the following configurations:

  — **Toslink**—A fiber-optic port developed by Toshiba

  — **Coaxial**—An RCA jack

  — **Minijack**—A female 3.5-mm port that is physically the same as the microphone-in and line-in ports

The major advantage of using the digital-in option is that there is no analog-to-digital conversion necessary to capture the audio information. Digital audio capture produces the best possible sound reproduction.

Although the connectivity options for sound cards vary greatly from the professional level to consumer grade, Figure 6-21 shows the ports on a typical sound card.

Figure 6-21 Sound Card Ports

Overview of CDs and DVDs

This section include the following topics:

- CDs and CD-ROM drives
- Recording CDs with CD-R and CD-RW drives
- Digital audio extraction
- DVD players
- Recordable DVDs
- CD recording formats
- DVD layering and formats

CDs and CD-ROM Drives

Compact discs (CDs) are a popular type of removable media whose initial use was for digital audio. However, they are rapidly expanding into the world of personal computer data storage. The success of CDs can be attributed to their storage capacity, ruggedness, and price. Due to the widespread acceptance of this media format, CD-ROM drives are standard devices on most personal computers.

CDs are 120 mm in diameter and 1.2 mm thick, and they can store up to 800 MB of information, as shown in Figure 6-22. They are comprised of a layer of polycarbonate plastic, a layer of reflective metal, and a coat of lacquer. CDs are optical media as opposed to floppy disks, hard disks, and Zip disks, which are magnetic media.

Figure 6-22 A Compact Disc

A CD-ROM drive is comprised of four major components: the drive motor, laser assembly, tracking mechanism, and communication circuits. The *drive motor* spins the CD-ROM at the proper speed so that the laser assembly can read the information. The *laser assembly* consists of a laser and a lens. This laser assembly reads the CD-ROM as it spins. The *tracking mechanism* is a motor and drive system that moves the lens into the correct position to access a specific area of the CD-ROM. Finally, the *communication circuits* are used to send the information read from the CD-ROM to the computer using the configured bus.

CD-ROM Drive Categories

CD-ROM drives are categorized into three areas. The case type refers to an internal or external CD-ROM drive. The bus type refers to the way the drive communicates, while the read speed is how fast the CD-ROM drive communicates with the CPU.

CD-ROM Drive Case Type

CD-ROM drives can be mounted internally in the computer or as an external drive:

- Internally mounted drives are common with today's computers. These drives draw their power from the power supply and are usually connected to the computer bus through a ribbon cable.
- External drives are enclosed in a case and have their own power supplies. They connect either directly to an external port on the computer (such as USB, FireWire, or parallel) or to a controller (usually SCSI) that is installed in one of the computer's expansion slots.

Bus Communication

A *bus* is the communications pipeline between a computer and the peripherals that are installed. Common internal connections include IDE and SCSI. Most motherboards have built-in IDE controllers and automatically recognize that a CD-ROM drive has been installed. IDE communication cables are 40-pin ribbon cables that connect to the drive and the motherboard. While some motherboards offer built-in SCSI solutions, most applications require a SCSI adapter to be purchased and installed separately. There are many varieties of SCSI and assorted cabling types.

Speed Ratings

A *CD-ROM drive read speed* indicates the rate at which information can be pulled from the CD and sent to the communications bus. In general, the higher the read speed rating on a CD-ROM drive, the faster the drive. The read speed of a CD-ROM drive is measured in multiples of 150 KB and denoted by a numeral followed by an X. A drive rated at 1X has a read speed of 150 KB per second (or 1 times 150 KB). A drive rated at 10X has a read speed of 1500 KB per second. Data that streams from a CD (such as full-motion video) can require read speeds of 12X or higher. Also, a CD-ROM drive read speed is not always uniform. A drive rated at 16X might only be able to achieve that rate near the center of the CD while only achieving a 8X rate at the outer tracks.

Installing and Configuring an IDE CD-ROM Drive

Installing and configuring an internal IDE CD-ROM drive is similar to installing an internal IDE hard drive. The CD-ROM drive needs to be connected to a 40-pin IDE cable, which is then connected to the IDE controller. The drive is usually keyed so that the cable will only connect one way, but it is important to ensure that pin 1 on the cable matches with pin 1 on the drive. An internal CD-ROM drive uses a standard Molex power connector, which supplies 12 volts to other devices inside a PC.

Next, the CD-ROM drive must be set to its proper operating status: master, slave, or single drive. A CD-ROM drive should be set as a master drive only if it is the fastest drive on that particular IDE cable. Most CD-ROM drives have a digital audio cable that connects directly to the sound card. A CD-ROM drive containing a DAC allows music to be played through the computer's speakers without requiring overhead processing. Finally, certain CD-ROM drives require the installation of a software driver to work properly. For further information on the step-by-step installation of IDE drives, refer to Chapter 3, "Assembling a Computer."

PhotoZoom Activity   CD-ROM Drive

This PhotoZoom, located on the accompanying CD, describes in detail the parts that make up a CD-ROM drive.

Recording CDs with CD-R and CD-RW Drives

CD recorders, often referred to as *CD burners*, are becoming standard equipment on personal computers. CD recorders allow users to create, or burn, their own CDs containing music, data, video, or any combination thereof. Users can now create their own compilation of audio CDs, make backup copies of software, make backups of their critical data, and create video CDs (VCDs) that can be played in standalone DVD players. The low cost of the drive and media coupled with the generous capacity of a CD have made owning a CD recorder desirable. Figure 6-23 shows a CD-R drive on the PC.

Figure 6-23 CD-R Drive

Currently, two major types of CD recorders exist: CD-R and CD-RW. These are described as follows:

- **CD-R (compact disc–recordable)**—The first of the two technologies conceived. Commercially produced CDs, whether they contain audio or other types of data, are pressed in great volume. This pressing technique produces the land and pit areas of the CD that the laser assembly reads.

  CD-R technology uses a different strategy for writing information to a CD. CD-R media adds a layer of dye between the aluminum and plastic layers. This layer of dye is translucent and allows light to shine through to the aluminum layer that reflects the light. When a CD-R drive writes information to the CD-R media, a laser is used to burn areas of the dye to create opaque, non-reflective spots. When the recorded CD-R is read, the laser assembly receives reflections from only the translucent areas of dye. This reflective/non-reflective surface easily translates into bits of data.

  To accomplish the job of reading and writing CDs, CD-R drives use two lasers: a read laser and a write laser. The speed at which a CD-R can burn a CD uses the same "number times" convention as a traditional CD-ROM drive. A CD-R drive that can write at 3000 KB per second is shown as having a 20X (or 20 times 150 KB) write speed. A drive listed as 24X/40X has a write speed of 24X and a read speed of 40X. One downside of CD-R media is that it cannot be rewritten.

- **CD-RW (compact disc–rewritable)**—Like CD-R drives, CD-RW drives require the use of a special type of disc. The CD-RW disc is compatible with other CD and CD-R reading drives and the CD-R can be read by a CD-RW drive. CD-RW media includes a phase-change compound layer between the aluminum and plastic layers. This compound is a special mix of chemical elements that can change physical states at certain temperatures and remain in those states indefinitely. The compound begins in a translucent crystalline state that allows light to pass through to the reflective aluminum layer. When the CD-RW's write laser burns information to the disc, certain areas of the phase-change compound are melted by superheating and are held in that phase by rapid cooling. These melted areas are opaque and non-reflective.

What makes CD-RW drives unique is that they include a third laser, an eraser laser. The eraser laser is used to slowly reheat melted areas of the phase-change compound into the crystalline state. This is what allows the rewriting of CDs. Similar to CD-R drives, CD-RW drives are rated by the speed at which they write, rewrite, and read information. A CD-RW drive listed as 24X/12X/40X has a write speed of 24X, a rewrite speed of 12X, and a read speed of 40X.

Copyright Issues

It is the responsibility of the PC technician to know the copyright or licensing limitations of CDs. There are instances when it is necessary to make a copy of a CD. One example is the need to keep backup copies of original installation CDs. Become familiar with the copyright or licensing agreements associated with the purchase of CDs to avoid violating copyright laws.

Digital Audio Extraction

The availability and relatively low cost of CD recorders and recordable media have put custom compilation of audio CDs within the reach of many users. Since the inception of audio CDs, users have wanted to create custom CDs while keeping the quality of the music that digital recording provides. Digital audio extraction makes this possible.

Digital audio extraction (DAE), also known as *ripping*, is the process of copying audio from a CD to another medium while keeping the audio in its original digital state. Most users use DAE techniques to move tracks (songs) from an audio CD to a computer's hard drive and then to a recordable CD. Keeping the song in a digital format greatly reduces the chances of audio discrepancies.

When a CD player/drive plays a Red Book CD (audio format CD), the drive performs a digital-to-analog conversion in real time so that the audio can be played through speakers. Before digital audio extraction, this audio had to be rerecorded and redigitized if a user decided to put the song on a recordable CD. This digital-to-analog-to-digital conversion was time consuming, and unwanted noise was usually introduced. Depending on the quality of the CD-ROM drive, computer hardware, and software used, digital audio extraction can make nearly flawless digital copies of songs in a fraction of the time required by the previous technology.

Copying a song from a Red Book CD (the Red Book is discussed later in this chapter) is much different than copying a file from a CD. Songs are stored in tracks on the CD, and drives read these tracks as they spin under the laser assembly. Because the audio information is streamed to the drive, special digital audio extraction software must be used. This software reads the raw information of a track as it is streamed and collects the information into a wav file. This wav file can then be played on a computer or recopied to a recordable CD, along with other songs, to create a custom audio CD.

When DAE is used to create wav files on a computer, these files are uncompressed and can be quite large. Other audio formats, such as mp3 and Ogg Vorbis, compress these raw files considerably with minimal loss of song quality.

DVD Players

The *digital versatile disc (DVD)* is newer technology that builds on the strengths of CDs. DVDs share the same physical size a CDs, as shown in Figure 6-24, but the DVD can store much more information. DVDs are used for movies and audio files as well as data files. Depending on the layering and whether the DVD is single- or double-sided, a DVD can store nearly 20 times more information than a CD. DVDs are able to store more information because they provide a greater area for data storage, use a higher-density recording technique, and can access multiple layers within the media.

Figure 6-24 A Digital Versatile Disc (DVD)

NOTE

You might have heard of the term *Easter Egg*. Here, it refers to an amusing tidbit that is hidden on the DVD. An Easter Egg could be hidden in computer software, movies, music, art, books, or even your watch. There are thousands of them, and they can be quite entertaining if you know where to look for them. Easter Eggs have become popular with DVDs. Check out some of the Easter Egg websites, and see what you can find on your next DVD.

The two major markets for DVD players are the home entertainment market and the computer DVD drive market. Many consumers have a DVD player as a component in their home theater setup. This is because movies recorded on DVD media are digital reproductions with vivid colors and theater-style Surround Sound, and often contain other movie-related extras. Because the movie is recorded in a digital format, the quality of the movie nearly matches that of the original film. Unlike VHS tapes, the quality of a DVD never deteriorates. Home DVD players also offer various audio options featuring multiple audio channels, including Dolby Surround, Dolby Digital 5.1, and DTS. Also, many studios include deleted scenes, information on how the movie was made, commentaries, and previews of other titles on their DVDs.

Computer *DVD drives* can also play movies and music as well as read data discs. Software manufacturers are beginning to offer their products on DVDs. These manufacturers can now place their entire program on a single DVD instead of using multiple lower-capacity CDs. Another benefit of DVD drives is that they are backward compatible with CDs. A DVD drive can read DVDs and CDs, while a CD-ROM drive can only read CDs.

DVD players and drives are similar in their design to CD-ROM drives. DVD players are comprised of a drive motor for spinning the disc, a laser assembly for reading the DVD, a tracking mechanism for moving the laser assembly into the desired area, and communication circuits for moving the data to their destination. Other optional components include decoders. All home DVD players and some computer DVD drives have an MPEG2 decoder for decompressing the video data into a format that can be shown on a television screen or monitor. Some DVD players and drives also contain audio decoders for either Dolby Digital 5.1 or DTS audio streams. These decoders decompress the audio data and separate the information into the proper discrete channels. DVD players and drives that do not contain these decoders can use other hardware (or software) to accomplish the decoding.

The laser used in a DVD player is different from lasers used in CD-ROM drives. A DVD player's laser must be able to focus on different layers of the media. While a single-layer DVD has only a single reflective layer of material, a dual-layered disc contains a semitransparent layer over top of a reflective layer. The laser must be able to distinguish between the two by focusing on the correct layer of material that contains the desired data.

When installing a DVD drive, follow the steps for installing a CD-ROM drive, including all safety procedures, as detailed in Chapter 3. Slide the drive into an open bay, connect the communication cable (usually a 40-pin IDE ribbon cable), connect the power supply, configure the drive's jumpers, and connect any necessary audio cables. DVD drives usually have connectors for analog audio out as well as digital audio out cables. Finally, install the device driver and check the operation by restarting the computer.

Recordable DVDs

Consumer demand for more removable storage options has prompted the industry to develop methods of recording DVDs. Currently, there are four different methods of DVD recording. Each of these technologies is vying to be the standard for recording DVDs; the technologies are described as follows:

- **DVD-R (DVD–recordable)**—Similar to CD-R technology in that it allows the media to be written only once. This method, most often used for DVD authoring, is not practical for consumers due to the price of the drives (US$ 2000 or more) and media (US$ 20 per disc). Even though price is a drawback for this technology, compatibility is not. Most DVD-ROM drives and standalone players can read DVD-R discs. DVD-R discs can hold 4.7 GB of data per side.

- **DVD-RAM (DVD–random–access memory)**—Allows users to write and overwrite discs 100,000 times. DVD-RAM uses phase-change technology similar to CD-RW drives and stores 4.7 GB of information on each side of the disc. DVD-RAM drives are priced below US$ 1000, with media costs of US$ 15 per disc. Compatibility is an issue with DVD-RAM drives; most of these drives require the use of a cartridge-based disc while recording.

- **DVD-RW (DVD–rewritable)**—Designed to address compatibility and rerecording issues. Geared more toward general use than authoring, DVD-RW uses a "caddyless" system and allows users to rewrite information on the media up to 1000 times. The media is compatible with most DVD-ROM drives and standalone players on the market today. The drive uses a sequential recording technology that is designed primarily for streaming media. A DVD-RW drive is capable of writing 4.7 GB of information to each side of a disc.

- **DVD+RW**—The latest DVD recording technology, DVD+RW, is backed by many major corporations. As with DVD-RW, the technology is compatible with existing hardware, and discs are easily written to multiple times. The major advantage of DVD+RW is the ability to use a variable bit rate when encoding certain types of media (such as streaming video). The major industry backing of this format, coupled with the affordability of the drive (less than US$ 600), should cause DVD+RW to be the standard DVD recording format in the near future.

CD Recording Formats

Phillips and Sony developed the format standard for audio CDs in the early 1980s. When manufacturers realized the potential for using CDs to store information for computers, they developed even more formats to ensure compatibility when recording CDs. There are two major types of CD formats: logical standards and physical standards. Each is described in the following sections.

Logical Standards

A *logical standard* defines the way information is stored on the media. CDs and other computer-accessed discs use a series of tracks and sectors (also called frames on CDs) to store the data on the disc. A CD's logical standard determines its file system structure. Currently, ISO 9660 (also referred to as the High Sierra standard) is the industry standard format. CDs created using the ISO 9660 format can be accessed by most current platforms and operating systems.

Other formats exist, such as Rock Ridge (for UNIX), HFS (for Macs), and Hybrid HFS/ISO, but ISO 9660 is internationally accepted as the current standard. Two formats that improve upon ISO 9660 include JOLIET and UDF. JOLIET is Microsoft's version of ISO 9660 that extends the maximum number of characters in a filename from 8 to 64. The universal disc format (UDF) is an emerging standard that is built on ISO 9660 and specifically designed for data storage.

Physical Standards

Physical standards define where the information is placed on a CD. Most formats fall within the "color books." When Phillips and Sony completed the format for the audio CD, the formatting rules were published in a book with a red cover. This format quickly became known as the Red Book format and is the basis of the naming conventions for the other color book formats. Table 6-3 describes these recording formats.

Table 6-3 CD Recording Formats

Format	Description
Red Book	Also known as CD-DA (compact disc–digital audio), this format defines an audio CD. It specifies how songs are placed in tracks on the disc.
Yellow Book	The Yellow Book was developed early on as the initial format for data. This format allows data to be written as files instead of as streaming information.
Green Book	In 1986, Phillips created the Green Book format for its new CD-I (interactive) discs. This format was specially designed to synchronize audio and video data for multimedia applications.
Orange Book	The 1990 Orange Book standard defines the physical format for recordable CDs. The standard is subdivided into three parts. Part 1 deals with magneto-optical (MO) devices, part 2 handles write-once (WO) drives, and part 3 addresses rewritable (RW) drives.
White Book	This standard addresses the method of recording MPEG1 audio, video, and still graphics on a video CD (VCD). These discs require a specialized player or software to access them as the information is compressed to a great degree.
Blue Book	The Blue Book standard specifies the format of enhanced CDs (E-CDs). E-CDs are stamped multisession discs that feature Red Book audio and Yellow Book multimedia data on a single disc.

DVD Layering and Formats

Even though DVD and CD media share the same physical size, DVDs offer a far greater storage capacity through the use of a higher-density data-storing technique and through the use of layering. DVD layering is the process in which the read laser of a drive is able to focus at different layers inside the disc. A dual-layered disc has an equivalent of close to twice the surface area of a regular disc, and a dual-layered, double-sided disc has almost four times the surface area on which to store data. Currently, there are three types of DVDs and four physical formats.

The three DVD types are DVD-ROM, DVD-Video, and DVD-Audio. *DVD-ROM* is designed to store computer files. *DVD-Video* is the format used by standalone DVD players for movies and extras. *DVD-Audio* is a newer format that includes multiple-channel audio with many options.

DVD physical formats define the structure of the disc and the areas to which data are recorded. DVD 5 is a single-sided, single-layer DVD with a storage capacity of 4.7 GB. DVD 9 is a single-sided, dual-layered DVD with a capacity of 8.5 GB. DVD 10 is a double-sided, single-layer-per-side DVD with a capacity of 9.4 GB. Finally, DVD 18 is a double-sided, dual-layer-per-side disc with a capacity of 17 GB. Table 6-4 shows a comparison of the different DVD formats.

Table 6-4   DVD Characteristics

DVD Format	Number of Sides	Layers Per Side	Capacity (GB)	Length (Hours)
5	1	1	4.7	2
9	1	2	8.5	4
10	2	1	9.4	4.5
18	2	2	17	8

 Worksheet 6.4.7   CD and DVD Terminology

In this worksheet, you review the terminology used in CD and DVD technology.

Digitizing Video

This section includes the following topics:

- Understanding hardware and software video capture
- Installing and configuring a video capture board

Understanding Hardware and Software Video Capture

Depending on the compression methods used, a video clip can be played back from the Windows AVI structure or through the video capture card. This is a major consideration when creating a presentation that includes a video component. Will the user's computer have a compatible video digitizer card installed, or will the video clip be played through the Windows multimedia extensions?

Sources for video capture normally include VCRs and camcorders. Some capture cards include an RF (radio frequency) demodulator and a TV tuner so that video can be captured from a television broadcast signal or a cable TV input.

The output from these video-producing devices tends to be composite TV or analog S-video signals. A *video decoder circuit* is used to convert the analog signal into a stream of digital signals. However, these are not the RGB digital signals useful to the VGA card. The characteristics of the decoded TV signal are defined in television industry terms as YUV, which was discussed previously in this chapter.

The digitized output from the A/D converter is applied to a video compression *application-specific integrated circuit (ASIC)*, a compression chip that reduces the size of the file by removing redundant information from consecutive frames. This reduction is necessary due to the extremely large size of typical digitized video files. Video-compression schemes can reduce the size of a video file by a ratio of up to 200:1. As the sections of video are compressed, the reduced files can be applied to the system's RAM or they can be routed directly to the hard drive. The audio signal is not compressed, but it is synchronized to the video signal so that the audio signal is heard at the right time when the video is run.

When the digitized video is recalled for output purposes, the file is reapplied to the compression chip, which restores the redundant information to the frames. The output from the compression chip is applied to the D/A portion of the video-processing circuitry. The analog signals are reconverted into the proper VGA format and are applied to the video-out connector at the back plate of the card.

Installing and Configuring a Video Capture Board

To prepare the hardware configuration jumpers (or switches) for operation, refer to manufacturer's documentation included with the card. The card's factory default settings usually work well, but you should examine the system's installed devices for address and IRQ conflicts.

Install the video capture card in one of the computer's adapter slots. As with any other adapter card, this requires you to remove the outer cover of the system unit. Inside the unit, remove the cover of a compatible expansion slot. Many capture cards are full-length cards, so make sure that the slot can handle the physical dimensions of the card. Make sure that the expansion slot type is compatible with the capture card's edge connector.

Connect the capture card to the VGA card as directed by the manufacturer's installation guide. Some VGA cards use an edge connector that is built into the top of the card.

Install any antennas that must be connected to the card for the intended application. These include a TV antenna, a coaxial cable from the television, and/or an FM radio antenna. Connect the video-in cables to the audio and video source(s) being used for input, and connect the audio cable to the audio source(s). In this case, there is a stereo audio-in (left/right) provision and two possible sources for video in.

The audio and video connections are typically made with standard RCA cables and connectors. Connect the VGA monitor's signal cable to the capture card's VGA-out connector. The video signal passes through the capture card and is looped to the VGA card. This means that the screen image can be present on the monitor and the video screen simultaneously. A VGA loopback cable is connected between the capture card's loopback input and the VGA card's RGB-out connector.

If all the hardware and software configuration settings are correct but capture problems occur, you must troubleshoot the video capture-related hardware. In most systems, this involves a TV signal source (such as a VCR or camcorder), the cabling, the capture card, and the video card.

Most capture card software provides a preview window that enables the user to view the video coming from the video source. If the source is visible in this window, the video source and the video-in cabling can be eliminated as sources of problems. However, simply being able to see the video in the window does not mean that the card will capture video.

If the video is present in the window, and the video source and cabling are correct, the hardware and software configurations should be checked closely. Check the capture software's setup for video buffer settings. Typical video buffer settings are D0000h, D800h, E000h, and E800h. If necessary, try different settings. Add a DEVICE= statement to the config.sys file that corresponds to the new setting for the video buffer. An example follows:

```
DEVICE=PATH\EMM386.EXE X=D000h-D700h
```

Finally, reinstall and reconfigure the capture software if problems continue.

If the signal from the video source is not present in the preview window, make certain that the video source is turned on. Check the video-in cable to make sure that it is properly connected to the video-out jack of the video source and plugged into the correct video-source input on the capture card. Check the capture card's I/O address setup closely as well as its setting in the capture software. Check the video capture software to make sure that the correct video source setting is selected. While in the software settings, check the video type selected, and make sure that the video is set for the NTSC standard (in the U.S.) or the corresponding video standard used in the country or region of operation.

Summary

This chapter discussed multimedia technology and the required hardware and software. Some of the important concepts to retain from this chapter are as follows:

- To produce multimedia using the PC, there are certain requirements and installation procedures for the specific hardware. The hardware includes the video adapter, sound card, and CD-ROM/R/RW and DVD drives.

- The characteristics of the computer display or monitor include the color capabilities, the sharpness/viewability, and projection technology. The number of bits used to describe a pixel is known as its bit-depth. The 24-bit bit-depth is known as true color.

- Video card types and installation, RAMDAC and video memory were presented. Video capture cards are responsible for converting video signals from different sources into a digital signal that can be manipulated by the computer.

- Sound card types and installation, the basic components of the sound card, and the methods sound cards use to produce audio were discussed. The basic functions of the sound card are input, processing, and output. The quality of the sound card is determined by its audio bit-depth, sampling rate, and feature set.

- CD drives are categorized by the type of case and the bus type. The CD-ROM drive read speed determines the rate at which information can be pulled from the CD and sent to the communications bus.

- Currently, CD drives can read data, record data, and rewrite data to a previously recorded CD. Although a CD drive cannot read a DVD, a DVD drive can read data from a CD. In addition, the laser used in a DVD is different, because it must be able to focus for single-layer and dual-layer DVDs.

The next chapter details the Windows NT, 2000, and XP operating systems. It covers the differences between these operating systems and the Windows 9X operating systems.

Check Your Understanding

The following are review questions for the A+ exam. Answers can be found in Appendix B, "Answers to Check Your Understanding Review Questions."

1. What does VGA stand for?

    A. Video Graphic Association

    B. Video gradient array

    C. Video graphic array

    D. Video graphic arrangement

2. VGA describes how data are passed between which two components?

   A. Computer and the display

   B. Display and the CD

   C. Display and the sound card

   D. Video card and the CPU

3. The number of bits used to describe a pixel is known as what?

   A. Bit-resolution

   B. Bit-display

   C. Bit-technology

   D. Bit-depth

4. The sharpness of a display image is measured in what units?

   A. Dots per inch

   B. Pixels per inch

   C. Resolutions

   D. Dot pitch

5. What is the resolution of super VGA?

   A. 640×480

   B. 1024×768

   C. 800×900

   D. 800×600

6. What are the basic functions of a sound card?

   A. Input, processing, and output

   B. Input, output, and display

   C. Processing, display, and format

   D. Display, input, and format

7. What is the major drawback of USB sound?

   A. Not compatible with Windows 98.

   B. Additional configurations are complicated.

   C. Processing power required hampers performance.

   D. Speaker system allows the USB port to act as a sound card.

8. What is required to upgrade built-in sound?

   A. Simple software

   B. Disabling the built-in sound

   C. Replacing the motherboard

   D. Built-in sound cannot be upgraded

9. What is used to select the sound card and view its properties?

   A. Settings, Control Panel, System Properties, Device Manager

   B. Settings, Control Panel, Sounds

   C. Settings, Control Panel, Add/Remove Hardware

   D. Explorer, Sounds

10. What does MIDI stand for?

    A. Multiple instrument digital interface

    B. Musical internal digital industry

    C. Musical instrument digital interface

    D. Musical instrument direct interface

11. CDs are considered to be what type of media?

    A. Magnetic

    B. Metal

    C. Laser

    D. Optical

12. How many methods of DVD recording are currently available?

    A. 5

    B. 3

    C. 4

    D. 2

13. What does a CD's logical standard determine?

    A. Its file system structure

    B. The amount of data that can be stored

    C. The type of platform

    D. The operating system

14. What is the physical format that defines an audio CD and specifies how songs are placed in tracks on the disc?

  A. Yellow Book

  B. Red Book

  C. Blue Book

  D. White Book

15. What is the physical format of a recordable CD that is divided into three parts?

  A. Green Book

  B. White Book

  C. Red Book

  D. Orange Book

16. What is the standard that addresses the method of recording MPEG1 audio, video, and still graphics on a video CD (VCD)?

  A. Blue Book

  B. White Book

  C. Yellow Book

  D. Green Book

17. What is DVD 5?

  A. A single-sided, single-layer DVD with a storage capacity of 4.7 GB

  B. A single-sided, single-layer DVD with a storage capacity of 5 GB

  C. A double-sided, double-layer DVD with a storage capacity of 4.7 GB

  D. A double-sided, single-layer DVD with a storage capacity of 5 GB

18. What is the storage capacity, in GB, of a DVD 18?

  A. 18

  B. 180

  C. 17

  D. 15

19. What does the Y in YUV refer to?

  A. The luminance of the signal color

  B. The connection port

  C. The color component of the signal

  D. The yellow part of the display

20. How much throughput, in KBps, is required for full-motion video?

    A. 56

    B. 128

    C. 384

    D. 768

Key Terms

advanced accelerated graphics port (AGP)   Designed to handle the intense data throughput associated with three-dimensional graphics.

all-points addressable displays   Displays that handle bitmaps.

application-specific integrated circuit (ASIC)   A compression chip that reduces the size of a file by removing redundant information from consecutive frames.

aspect ratio   The display screen width relative to its height.

bit-depth   The number of bits used to describe a pixel.

bit-depth for sound   The sample size and bus size of the sound card.

built-in sound   An audio processor that is located on the motherboard.

bus   The communication pipeline between a computer and its peripherals.

cathode ray tube (CRT)   A type of computer display that requires a certain distance from the beam-projection device to the screen.

CD-R   Compact disc–recordable. The CD media that can be recorded using a CD recorder.

CD recorder   Also referred to as CD burner. Allows CD media to be recorded with data, audio, or any combination.

CD-ROM   Compact disc read-only memory. Removable media for audio and data.

CD-ROM drive read speed   Determines the rate at which information can be pulled from the CD and sent to the communications bus.

CD-RW   Compact disc–rewritable. CD media that can be recorded multiple times.

Cinepak   A compression/decompression standard supported by Video for Windows.

coaxial   Digital configuration that uses an RCA jack.

color space conversion   The process of converting the YUV signal into the RGB format that is acceptable to the VGA card screen memory.

communication circuit   Used to send the information read from the CD to the computer using the configured bus.

converter   Converts data for sound.

digital audio extraction (DAE)   The process of copying audio from a CD to another medium while keeping the audio in its original digital state.

Digital versatile disc (DVD)   Removable media used primarily for movie and data storage.

digital-in port   An interface used to capture digital audio.

display   A computer output surface and projecting mechanism that shows text and graphic images.

display adapter   *See* video adapter.

dot pitch   The size of an individual beam that gets through to light up a point of a phosphor on the screen.

dots per inch (dpi)   How the actual sharpness of a display image is measured.

drive motor   Spins the CD up to the proper speed so that the laser can read the data.

DVD-Audio   New format that includes multiple-channel audio.

DVD drive   Computer drive that can play/read DVDs. A DVD drive can read CDs and DVDs, while a CD drive can only read CDs.

DVD physical formats   Define the structure of the disc and the area where the data are recorded.

DVD-R   A DVD drive that allows a DVD to be written to once.

DVD-RAM   Uses random-access memory to enable users to record DVDs multiple times.

DVD-ROM   Designed for storing computer files.

DVD-RW   Drive that allows the media to be recorded multiple times.

DVD+RW   Similar to DVD-RW; uses variable bit-rate when encoding.

DVD-Video   Format used by standalone DVD players for movies and extras.

external speakers   Output devices for the sound card.

feature set   Additional features that include 3D audio coprocessors, device controllers, and digital output options.

Frequency Modulation (FM) sound card   Uses programming to create waveforms that best match the instrument that is playing.

gas plasma   A type of computer display that works by lighting up display screen positions based on the voltages at different grid intersections.

Hot-swappable peripherals   Peripherals that can be changed while the system is running.

Indeo   Data compression method developed by Intel.

input   As it relates to the sound card, it is the process of capturing sound from microphones, CD players, DAT players, and MIDI devices.

Joint Photographic Experts Group (JPEG)   A compression standard used with digitized video.

laser assembly   Consists of a laser and a lens that reads the CD as it spins.

light-emitting diode (LED)   A type of computer display that works by lighting up display screen positions based on the voltages at different grid intersections.

line-in port   An interface used to capture audio from amplified or powered sources such as external stereos.

liquid crystal display (LCD)   A type of computer display that works by blocking light rather than creating it.

logical standards   Define the way information is stored on the media.

microphone-in port   An interface used to connect a microphone for sound to the PC.

microsoft audio visual interface (AVI)   A popular file format for video.

MIDI port   A standard interface used to connect musical devices.

minijack   Configuration for the digital-in port that is physically the same as the microphone-in and line-in ports.

monitor   *See* display.

Moving Picture Experts Group (MPEG)   A compression standard used with digitized video.

multimedia   The combination of text, sound, and/or motion video.

musical instrument digital interface (MIDI)   A combination of hardware and software that allows the sound card to control musical instruments and use these instruments to output the audio.

peripheral component interconnect (PCI)   An adapter card with an audio processor that connects to the motherboard.

physical standards   Define where the information is placed on the media.

random-access memory digital-to-analog converter (RAMDAC)   The firmware that translates the digital information into analog form for export to the monitor screen.

ripping   The process of digital audio extraction.

sampling rate   The rate at which the sound card can record audio information.

sound card   Device that allows the computer to handle audio information.

sound card memory   Stores samples and hold instructions for MIDI devices.

sound card output   Produces sound for devices such as headphones.

sound card ports   Internal and external ports for connecting to input and output devices.

sound card processing   The capability to convert audio information into different formats.

sound card processor   Handles the basic instructions that drive the sound card as well as the routing of audio information.

Super VGA (SVGA) monitor   A monitor that can display up to 16,777,216 colors because it can process a 24-bit-long description of a pixel.

Toslink   A fiber-optic port developed by Toshiba for the digital-in port.

tracking mechanism   A motor and drive system that moves the lens into the correct position to access a specific area of a CD.

true color   Also known as 24-bit bit-depth, it allows eight bits for each of the three additive primary colors: red, green, and blue.

universal serial bus (USB)   A hot-swappable interface used to connect peripherals such as the USB speaker system.

video adapter   Also called a display adapter or video board. An integrated circuit card in a computer or in some cases, a monitor that provides digital-to-analog conversion.

Video BIOS   Provides the set of video functions that can be used by the software to access the video hardware.

video board   *See* video adapter.

video capture card   Converts video signals from different sources into digital signals that can be manipulated by the computer.

video capture software   Used to capture frames of television video and convert them into digital formats that can be processed by the system.

video decoder circuit   Used to convert the analog signal into a stream of digital signals.

video display terminal (VDT)   A terminal with a display and a keyboard.

video display unit (VDU)   *See* video display terminal.

Video Electronics Standards Association (VESA)   Defines how software can determine the capability of a display.

video graphics array (VGA)   How data are passed between the computer and the display.

viewability   The ability to see the screen image from different angles.

visual graphics array (VGA)   The lowest common denominator of display modes.

wavetable sound card   Uses digitized samples of instruments to reproduce audio.

YUV   The color model used for encoding video. *Y* is the luminosity of the black and white signal. *U* and *V* are color difference signals. *U* is red minus Y (R – Y), and *V* is blue minus Y (B – Y).

Objectives

Upon completion of this chapter, you will be able to perform the following tasks:

- Understand the advantages and disadvantages of the different file systems used in Windows

- Apply the added security features of Windows 2000, such as setting permissions and encrypting folders and files

- Understand the Windows 2000 boot process and how it differs from that of Windows 98

- Identify the main components of the Windows 2000 Registry and the purpose of the Registry subtrees

- Create an ERD for Windows 2000 and utilize the Recovery Console

- Install or upgrade from Windows 98 to Windows 2000 and understand the concerns of using FAT32 or NTFS

Chapter 7

Windows NT/2000/XP Operating Systems

Introduction

This chapter explores the differences between the Windows NT/2000/XP operating systems and the Windows 9X operating systems. Some considerations include where the operating system is to be used, the type of file system, and security issues. You will learn the administrative tools that are specific to Windows NT/2000/XP. Additionally, the requirements for installing or upgrading to the Windows 2000 operating system and the special requirements of this OS are discussed.

Windows 9X Contrasts

This section includes the following topics:

- NTFS versus FAT
- Security and permissions
- Windows 2000 boot process
- Plug and Play/drivers

Windows NT File System Versus File Allocation Table

The Windows NT/2000 operating systems and, most recently, the Windows XP operating system have some obvious differences compared to the Windows 9X operating systems. Many differences are behind the scenes, but they are important concepts to understand in order to fully grasp the different environments that these operating systems are used in. For example, you must consider whether the operating system is to be used for office or home and whether the computer is to be part of a network. Security issues must be taken into account as well as the types of programs that are to be run on the operating system. All these factors determine whether to choose the 9X or the Windows NT, 2000, or XP operating system. When comparing these operating systems, you must understand the differences between the Windows NT file system (NTFS) and the file allocation table (FAT) file systems.

The main purpose of any file system is to store and retrieve data from the computer hard disk. How the data are organized, optimized, and retrieved is determined by the file system on the hard drive. Hard drives store information on platters, which are metal and coated with a magnetic substance. How exactly are the data organized on those little platters? The organization is achieved with file systems.

DOS/Windows is the most widely used operating system in the United States and many other parts of the world. For the most part, the file system used by DOS and Windows has become the standard. Understanding the original FAT and how it evolved into the current NTFS is important to the IT technician.

The Original FAT File System

The original FAT file system was invented by Bill Gates in 1976. The main purpose for developing this file system was to store programs and data on floppy disks. The *file allocation table (FAT)* file system is a database that keeps track of every file on the hard disk. The first company to incorporate the FAT file system design was Intel, which used it for an early version of an operating system for its 8086 chip. After buying the rights to this operating system, Bill Gates rewrote it and created the first version of DOS.

The *Windows NT file system (NTFS)*, first introduced in Windows NT, offers many advantages to the end user. In short, the NTFS file system utilizes more administration tools and offers security advantages that are not available in the FAT file system. A system administrator should be familiar with the differences between the NTFS and FAT file systems. There are three different file systems used in the Windows operating system environment—FAT16, FAT32, and NTFS; each of these is described in the following sections. Also described is HPFS, a file system that is no longer used but was important in earlier versions of Windows.

FAT16 File System

The *FAT 16 file system* (the 16 refers to 16-bit) is used for most hard drives with DOS, Windows 3.X, and the first version of Windows 95. Certain characteristics distinguish the FAT16 from the FAT32 file systems. First, the original FAT directory structure (before Windows NT and Windows 95) limits filenames to eight characters with a three-letter extension (as discussed in previous chapters). For example, the filename command.com has seven characters and the three-letter extension; therefore, it is a valid filename according to the FAT16 file structure regulations. The FAT structure also maintains a set of attributes for each file. These include S, which stands for a system dataset; H, which means that the file is hidden in the directory display; A, which indicates that the file will be archived the next time the disk is backed up; and R, which makes the file read-only. The file system also places a date and time stamp on the file when it was last changed.

The FAT file system is simple and reliable. If the computer crashes (stall or does not respond) in the middle of an update, it does not lose any data. Without using a lot of memory, the FAT file system does many administrative input/output (I/O) tasks to areas of the partition. This ability gives the FAT file system a true advantage. However, as a result of this capability, a file can become fragmented into small pieces, thus reducing performance. However, the FAT file system includes optimization tools to prevent this fragmentation from occurring.

FAT File System Utilities

Two important optimization tools that the FAT16 file system uses are the CHKDSK and SCANDISK utilities. These utilities can be used when the operating system crashes. When this happens, data are not be lost. A FAT file system might have removed disk area from the chain of free space but might not yet have assigned this area to any permanent new dataset. The CHKDSK and SCANDISK utilities examine the FAT16 table to determine the status of every record on the disk. These utilities then find the records that are not part of any dataset and return them to the free-space chain, thereby keeping the file system running at an optimal level.

If CHKDSK or SCANDISK finds unallocated sectors on the disk, the user is asked whether these sectors should be changed to files. If you were not creating a new file when the computer crashed and then ran this utility, answer no to this prompt, and the unallocated space is recycled as free space. However, if you were creating a new file and the system crashed, and the data that were lost are extremely valuable, you should answer yes when prompted to create a new file. Then the recovered file scraps can be scanned for lost information.

Sectors and Clusters

The concept behind the FAT16 file system, and what differentiates it from the FAT32 and NTFS file systems, is the way that the files are arranged and stored on the hard disk to maximize space, and more importantly, the size of the partitions that the FAT16 file system can use. The FAT16 file system can only recognize partitions up to 2 GB (2048 MB) in size.

Files are stored in *clusters*. Under this system, the hard disk is divided into 512-byte pieces called *sectors*. The sectors are then grouped into larger pieces called *clusters*. Each cluster can hold only one file. The computer assigns these clusters with a specific location to make it easy for the computer to find them. The size of the clusters is determined by the size of the partitions made on the hard disk. Table 7-1 shows the cluster sizes with the FAT16 file system, according to the size of the partition that was chosen.

Table 7-1 FAT16 Partition Cluster Sizes

FAT16 Partition Size (MB)	Cluster Size (KB)
17–32	2
33–256	4
257–512	8
513–1024	16
1025–2048	32

FAT32 File System

It is important to note that the *FAT32 file system* is still based on the original FAT file system and works in a similar fashion in order to remain compatible with existing programs, networks, and device drivers. As the technology of computers and hard drives improved, the FAT16 file system was no longer an efficient means of storing and organizing data on a hard drive. Also, the FAT16 file system was no longer an efficient means of storing files on a hard disk that was larger than 2 GB. For example, if a hard drive were larger than 2 GB and only one or two partitions were needed, the FAT16 file system would not work because FAT16 is only capable of dealing with partitions up to 2 GB. The FAT32 file system solved this problem; it was designed to support hard drives up to 2048 GB in size. The FAT32 file system also solved the problem of limited cluster size. Table 7-2 shows the cluster sizes that are available with the FAT32 file system, according to the size of the partition chosen.

Table 7-2 FAT32 Partition Cluster Sizes

FAT32 Partition Size	Cluster Size
< 260 MB	512 bytes (0.5 KB)
260 MB–8 GB	4 KB
8–16 GB	8 KB

Table 7-2 FAT32 Partition Cluster Sizes (Continued)

FAT32 Partition Size	Cluster Size
16–32 GB	16 KB
32–2048 GB	32 KB

With the FAT32 file system, data on the hard disk can be stored in a much more efficient manner. With the previous FAT16 version, a 2 GB partition, with its cluster sizes of 32 KB, wasted a lot of space because only one file could be stored in one cluster at a time. For example, with FAT16, if a file were only 1 KB, by using 32 KB clusters, the other 31 KB of space would be wasted. Conversely the FAT32 file system allows a 4 KB cluster with a 2 GB partition, thereby reducing the amount of wasted space. Table 7-3 shows the utilization of disk space with different cluster sizes. This utilization, combined with the ability to recognize partitions larger than 2 GB, made the FAT32 file system an obvious evolution of the DOS file system.

Table 7-3 Utilization of Disk Space

Disk Size	Cluster Size	Efficiency (%)
> 260 MB	4 KB	96.6
> 8 GB	8 KB	92.9
> 60 GB	16 KB	85.8
> 2 TB	32 KB	73.8

Added FAT32 Features

The many added features and advantages that came with the new FAT32 file system, when compared with FAT16, are important. As processor speeds and hard disk size advanced, it became evident that the reliability of FAT16 was insufficient. FAT32 has many advanced features that make it a reliable file system.

In the FAT16 file system, the root directory can be located only at the beginning of the hard disk. This poses problems if this part of the hard disk becomes damaged. If this were to happen, the hard disk would become unusable. With the FAT32 file system, the root directory can be located anywhere on the hard disk. This is useful because, if the section of the hard disk containing the root directory were to become damaged, the root directory could be moved to another section of the hard disk, and the damaged portion of the hard disk could be repaired.

Another benefit of FAT32 is its ability to use both the default and original copies of the FAT. Both FAT16 and FAT32 file systems maintain two copies of the FAT (the default and backup copy), but only FAT32 can use the backup copy as well as the default copy. This means that if a FAT becomes corrupted or fails, and the FAT32 file system is being used, the backup copy can be used until the default copy can be repaired. FAT16 can only use the default copy to run the operating system. This means that if the FAT16 file system becomes damaged or fails, the system will crash and become unusable.

These added features of FAT32 not only make disk space usage more efficient and reliable, they also improve the performance of the operating system. Applications respond at least 50 percent faster with FAT32 while using fewer system resources.

NT File System

The *Windows NT file system (NTFS)* was designed to be capable of managing global and enterprise-level operating systems. NTFS supports all Windows NT/2000/XP operating systems. Keep in mind that the FAT file system can still be used in the Windows NT/2000/XP operating system environments. However, the user does not have access to the full features of the operating systems when the FAT file system be used. NTFS4 was first deployed with the Windows NT operating system. When Windows NT was released, the NT file system was simply referred to as NTFS. However, with the latest releases of Windows 2000 and Windows XP, the NT file system has been improved, and many new features have been added.

The original version of NTFS that was released with Windows NT is now referred to as NTFS4. The latest version of the NT file system is now referred to as NTFS5. NTFS4 provides folder- and directory-level access only. With NTFS4, the administrator cannot control what users can do to individual files. Compared to NTFS5, NTFS4 does not have the ability to control file-level access. NTFS5, which was included with the release of Windows 2000, can control individual file access as well as provide additional security that NTFS4 could not. NTFS5 also includes *disk quotas*, which provide the system administrator with the ability to assign limits to the amount of hard disk space that users are allowed to occupy on a server or workstation.

The NT file system was developed because the FAT16 and FAT32 file systems were limited in their capabilities to provide the advanced features that are necessary when implementing an enterprise-level operating system. The NT file system provides support for added features like file and directory security by using *discretionary-access control lists (DACLs)* and *system-access control lists (SACLs)*, both of which can perform operations on a file and monitor events that trigger the logging of actions performed on a file. In addition, NTFS allows the administrator to set local permissions on files and folders that specify which groups and users have access to these files and folders. This includes setting the level of access that is permitted. NTFS file and folder permissions apply both to users working at the computer where the file is stored and to those accessing the file over a network when the file is in a shared folder. With NTFS, share rights can also be set that operate on shared folders in combination with file and folder permissions. FAT only supports share rights. Figure 7-1 shows the attributes that can be set in the Filename Properties dialog box.

Figure 7-1 The Filename Properties Dialog Box

NTFS provides added support to more efficiently recognize and address large hard disks and volumes that exceed the size limitations of a FAT16 or FAT32 file system.

In fact, the NT file system was designed so that it will be able to map disks up to sizes that might not be seen in the next 20 years. Table 7-4 shows the partition size and the associated cluster sizes.

Table 7-4 NTFS Partition Cluster Sizes

NTFS Partition Size (MB)	Default Cluster Size
512 or less	512 bytes
513–1024	1 KB
1025–2048	2 KB
2049–4096	4 KB

continues

Table 7-4 NTFS Partition Cluster Sizes (Continued)

NTFS Partition Size (MB)	Default Cluster Size
4097–8192	8 KB
8,193–16,384	32 KB
32,728 or more	64 KB

Note: These are defaults; you can choose any of them, depending on your application needs.

Another area where the FAT file system fails is in its ability to recognize filenames in a language other than English. This is because the FAT file system uses the ASCII 8-bit character set for its filename and directory name scheme. NTFS employs the Unicode 16-bit character set for its name scheme, which allows NTFS users anywhere in the world to manage files using their native language. (A 16-bit character set has a greater ability to accommodate a native alphabet/language than would an 8-bit character set.)

The Windows NT/2000/XP operating systems were designed to appeal to the corporate and business market. Features like security and the ability to access large volumes of data are a necessity to large corporations. NTFS has built-in transactional logging, so that whenever a modification is about to take place to the file system, NTFS makes a note of the modification in a special log file. If the system crashes, NTFS can examine the log file and use it to restore the disk with minimal data loss. Called *fault tolerance*, this is another important feature to the corporate and business community, because these users often deal with files that are critical from cost and time standpoints. FAT has no provision for fault tolerance. If a system crashes while creating or updating files or directories, the FAT on-disk structures can become corrupted. This can result in the loss of valuable data that is being modified as well as a general corruption of the drive. This risk is unacceptable for the Windows NT/2000/XP target market.

High-Performance File System

The *high-performance file system (HPFS)* is a seldom-used and obscure type of file system. It is worth mentioning only because the OS/2 software that uses this file system is still in use today. Microsoft used this file system with its Windows NT 3.51 operating system but stopped using this file system when it launched Windows NT 4.0.

The HPFS directory structure was the same as the FAT file system but allowed filenames of up to 254 characters in length. The FAT16 file system is limited to the 8.3 naming system (eight characters followed by a three-letter extension). Another aspect of HPFS was its ability to map hard disks up to 8 GB instead of 2 GB. Also, HPFS used physical sectors instead of clusters as the unit of management on the hard disk. Overall system performance increased as a result of this file system, but the file system lacked the necessary tools and security that NTFS would provide.

Table 7-5 summarizes the concept and evolution of the file system, from the original FAT16 introduced with DOS to the newer NTFS5, introduced with Windows 2000. Other file systems used today by other popular operating systems, such as Novel NetWare, Linux, and so on, are not within the scope of this text.

Table 7-5 File System Timeline

File System	OS That File System Was Introduced With	Year Introduced	Other OSs That Use It
FAT16	DOS	1981	Win 3.X, Win 9X/Me, Win 2000/XP
HPFS	OS/2	1989	Win NT 3.51
NTFS4	Win NT 4.0	1994	Win 2000/XP
FAT32	Win 98	1998	Win 2000/XP, Win Me
NTFS5	Win 2000	2000	Win XP

Security and Permissions

Another area in which the Windows 9X environment contrasts with the much more robust Windows NT/2000/XP environment is in the security and permissions features provided. As long as NTFS is used, Windows NT/2000/XP has enhanced system security features like file encryption and the ability to set permissions on files as well as directories or folders.

Permissions

File and directory *permissions* are used to specify which users and groups can gain access to files and folders and what they can do with the contents of these files or folders. Assigning permissions on files and directories is an excellent means of providing security and is effective whether the file or directory is being accessed over a network or from a local computer. However, the permissions that are assigned for directories are different from those assigned for files. Table 7-6 and 7-7 show the different types of permissions that can be set on folders and files.

NOTE

The feature shown in Tables 7-6 and 7-7 are only available in the Windows NT/2000/XP operating systems if NTFS is used.

Table 7-6 Folder Permissions

Folder Permission	Allows the User To
Read	See files and subfolders in the folder and view folder ownership, permissions, and attributes.
Write	Create new files and subfolders within the folder, change folder attributes, and view folder ownership and permissions.
List folder contents	See the names of files and subfolders in the folder.
Read and execute	Move through folders to reach other files and folders, even if the user does not have permission for those folders, and perform actions permitted by the Read permission and the List folder contents permission.
Modify	Delete the folder, plus perform actions permitted by the Write permission and the Read and execute permission.
Full control	Change permissions, take ownership, and delete subfolders and files, plus perform actions permitted by all other NTFS folder permissions.
No access	Prohibit unauthorized access to files or folders.

Table 7-7 File Permissions

File Permission	Allows the User To
Read	Read the file and view file attributes, ownership, and permissions.
Write	Overwrite the file, change file attributes, and view file ownership and permissions.
Read and execute	Run applications, plus perform the actions permitted by the Read permission.
Modify	Modify and delete the file, plus perform the actions permitted by the Write permission and the Read and execute permission.
Full control	Change permissions and take ownership, plus perform the actions permitted by all other NTFS file permissions.

Lab Activity 7.1.2   Assigning Permissions in Windows 2000

In this lab, you create a folder and assign the proper permissions. (This lab requires a system running Windows 2000 with NTFS.)

Access Control Lists

It is easy to lose track of who has what rights to certain files and folders when assigning permissions. This is especially true for an administrator who deals with networks that have hundreds or thousands of users. The *access control list (ACL)* is a tool that provides the administrator with a list of files that a user has access to as well as the type of access that he or she has been granted. For every file and folder in an NTFS volume, there is an ACL. For example, if a user wants to gain access to a resource, the ACL must contain an entry. This entry is called an *access control entry (ACE)*. This entry must allow the access that is requested; otherwise the user cannot access the specified file or folder.

Encryption

Another security feature included with the Windows 2000/XP operating systems is *encryption*. Microsoft provides a specific file system for encryption called the *encrypting file system (EFS)*. This provides administrators with the means to apply encryption to a file or folder that only the person who encrypted the file can view. The administrator can specify the users who can view the file as well.

The EFS is an integrated service that runs on the operating system. This means that it is easy for an administrator to manage, and it is transparent to the file owner. However, other users can be granted access to the file if they are assigned a *public key*. This allows the user to work with the file. Anyone without the public key is denied access to the file.

The administrator should encrypt folders and not individual files. Once the folder has encryption enabled, any files placed in the folder also become encrypted. This makes keeping track of the encrypted folders much easier. To encrypt a folder, click the General tab in the Properties dialog box for the folder. In the General tab, click the Advanced button and then select Encrypt Contents to Secure Data.

Compression

Microsoft has included a *compression* tool that enables space to be saved by compressing files and folders. After compressing a file or folder, it takes up less space on the Windows 2000/XP volume. This determines the *compression state* of the file: either compressed or uncompressed.

Compressing files and folders provides added disk space. However, NTFS allocates disk space based on the uncompressed file size. When a user tries to copy a compressed file to a volume that might have enough space for the compressed file (but not enough space for the uncompressed file), an error message appears, stating that there is insufficient disk space to copy the file.

NOTE

If a compressed file must be accessed, the user can do so without having to first uncompress the file. When a user attempts to open a compressed file, the operating system automatically uncompresses it and then recompresses it when work is finished and the file is closed.

NOTE

A file or folder can be either compressed or encrypted, but not both.

As with encrypting a file or folder, the same recommendation follows about compressing the folder first and then adding files to it after compression. To set the compression state of a folder or file, right-click the folder or file in Windows Explorer. Click Properties, and then click the Advanced button. In the Advanced Attributes dialog box, select Compress Contents to Save Disk Space. Click OK, and then click Apply in the Properties dialog box. Compression today is finding less importance because drives are getting larger and drive costs are getting lower.

Windows 2000 Boot Process

The boot process for Windows 2000 is different from that for Windows 9X. The Windows 2000 boot process uses additional files and extra steps because of the added features it offers, such as the security and logon features. In addition, many of the features that are supported in Windows 98, like specific device drivers, or VxDs, for example, are not supported by the Windows NT/2000 operating system. A *VxD* is a special type of device driver that has direct access to the operating system kernel. This allows the driver to interact with system and hardware resources at a low level while taking up few system resources.

NOTE

The boot process referred to in this chapter is an Intel-based system. The boot process is slightly different on non-Intel-based systems because ntldr is not needed. On these systems, the file osloader.exe performs this function. The ntdetect.com file is not needed on non-Intel–based systems as well, because that function is performed during the POST, and the information gathered from the POST is given to ntoskrnl.exe through osloader.exe. From that point on, Intel-based and non-Intel-based systems boot the same way.

Windows 2000 goes through a series of steps as it boots the computer. If everything is working properly, the user does not get involved in the details of the process. However, when troubleshooting boot problems, it is helpful to understand how the boot process works. The Windows 2000 boot process occurs in five stages, as follows:

1. The preboot sequence
2. The boot sequence
3. The kernel load
4. The kernel initialization
5. The logon process

Learning about the boot process and the files that are used in the stages of this process helps you to effectively troubleshoot problems with the operating system.

Certain files are required to complete a successful boot. Before looking at the details of the boot process, you should understand these files and know where they are located. Table 7-8 shows the files that are used in the Windows 2000 boot process.

Table 7-8 Windows 2000 Boot Files

Boot File	Location
ntldr	Root of the active partition (C:\)
boot.ini	Root of the active partition (C:\)
bootsect.dos (only if dual booting)	Root of the active partition (C:\)
ntdetect.com	Root of the active partition (C:\)
ntbootdd.sys	Root of the active partition (C:\)
ntoskrnl.exe	C:\WINNT\SYSTEM32
hal.dll	C:\WINNT\SYSTEM32
SYSTEM Registry key	C:\WINNT\SYSTEM32\CONFIG
Device drivers	C:\WINNT\SYSTEM32\DRIVERS

Step 1: Preboot Sequence

The first step in the boot process after the power is turned on to the computer is the *power-on self-test (POST)*. This is one step that Windows 2000 and Windows 9X have in common (see Chapters 2, 11, and 12). Every computer, regardless of its operating system, runs a POST. During the POST, a computer test its memory and verifies that it has all the necessary hardware, such as a keyboard, mouse, and so on. After the computer completes the POST, it allows other adapter cards to run their own POSTs (an example is a SCSI card). After the POST routine is complete, the computer locates a boot device and loads the *master boot record (MBR)* into memory, which in turn locates the active partition and loads it into memory. The MBR allows programs such as the disk operating system to load into RAM. Up to this point, the computer hardware has played an important role, and if it is not functioning properly, the operating system will not load. The computer now loads and initializes the ntldr file, which is the operating system loader, and begins to load the operating system.

Step 2: Boot Sequence

After the computer loads ntldr, the boot sequence begins to gather information about hardware and drivers. The ntldr file is the key component of this step. This file in turn uses the following files: ntdetect.com, boot.ini, and bootsect.dos. The bootsect.dos file is only used in the event that the computer is set up to dual-boot. One major function provided by ntldr is that it switches the processor into 32-bit flat memory mode. Until this point, the computer is running in real mode, just like the 8086/8088 CPUs. (Real mode is discussed in Chapter 4, "Operating System Fundamentals.")

Next, ntldr starts the file system, either FAT or NTFS, so that it can read the files from the disk. The ntldr file now reads the boot.ini file to enable the display of the boot menu on the screen. This is where the user can select which operating system to load if the computer is set to dual-boot. If an operating system other than Windows 2000 is selected, ntldr then loads the bootsect.dos file and passes control, which then boots the other OS. If Windows 2000 is selected or if the computer is not dual-booting, ntldr runs ntdetect.com, which gathers information about the computer hardware. In this step, you can press F8 for troubleshooting and advanced startup options. The file ntdetect.com detects the following hardware components:

- Computer ID
- Bus/adapter type
- Keyboard
- COM ports
- Parallel ports
- Floppy disk drive(s)
- SCSI adapters
- Mouse/pointing devices
- Floating-point coprocessor
- Video adapters

After ntdetect.com collects the hardware information, ntldr loads ntoskrnl.exe and passes that information.

Step 3: Kernel Load

The kernel load phase begins with ntoskrnl.exe loading, along with the hal.dll file. At this point, ntldr still plays a role in the boot process. The ntldr file also reads the SYSTEM Registry key into memory and selects the hardware configuration that is stored in the Registry. The ntldr loads the configuration needed for the computer to boot. At this point of the boot process, you can select which hardware profile to load, provided there is more than one profile to choose from. Next, any device drivers that have a start value of 0x0 are loaded from the Registry by ntldr. Now, all the files have been loaded into memory.

Step 4: Kernel Initialization

The initial kernel load phase is now complete, and the kernel begins to initialize. This means that the kernel is recognizing everything that was previously loaded so that ntldr can now give control to the operating system kernel. The operating system can now begin the final stages of loading. The *graphical user interface (GUI)* is now seen displaying a status bar that indicates the GUI is loading. Four additional steps now take place:

1. **The hardware key is created**—After the kernel completes the initialization process, it uses the information collected during the hardware detection phase to create the Registry key HKEY_LOCAL_MACHINE\HARDWARE. This **key** contains all the information about the hardware that is located on the computer motherboard as well as the interrupts that are used by the hardware devices.

2. **The clone control set is created**—The kernel references the Registry subkey HKEY_LOCAL_MACHINE\SYSTEM\Select and then creates a clone (or copy) of the Current Control Set value in the Registry. The computer then uses this clone to maintain an identical copy of the data used to configure the computer, so this Registry value does not reflect changes made during the startup process.

3. **Device drivers are loaded and initialized**—During this step, the kernel first initializes the low-level device drivers that were loaded in the kernel load phase of the boot process. Now the kernel must scan the Registry subkey HKEY_LOCAL_MACHINE\SYSTEM\CurrentControlSet\Services for device drivers with a value of 0x1. This device driver value indicates at what point in the process the driver is to load. This is the same for the device driver value in the kernel load phase.

4. **Services are started**—The final step is starting the Session Manager. The Session Manager is started when the smss.exe file is loaded. The Session Manager is responsible for loading the programs in its BootExecute Registry entry. The Session Manager also loads the required subsystems, which start the winlogon.exe file. This file starts the local security administration (lsass.exe) file, and the Ctrl-Alt-Delete window appears. The Service Controller (screg.exe) checks the Registry for services with a start value of 0x2 and loads them. Services with start values of 0x3 are started manually, and services with start values of 0x4 are disabled.

> **NOTE**
>
> The 0x in front of a number indicates that it is a hexadecimal number. For more information on hexadecimal numbers, see Chapter 1, "Information Technology Basics."

Step 5: Logon

The logon screen begins the final step in the bootup process. However, a boot is not considered completed or successful until a user logs on. After the user logs on, the clone of the Current Control Set value from the fourth item, in Step 4, is copied to the Last Known Good control set value in the Registry. This is a safety measure that the OS performs so that a user can reboot the computer if the boot process becomes corrupt. An example would be if a bad device driver gets loaded and does not allow the user to log on. Selecting "Last Known Good" control set during startup loads the last successful boot configuration that was saved without this bad device driver, allowing the user to log on.

Plug and Play/Drivers

It has become increasingly easy to add many devices to modern computers to expand their capabilities with the advances made in Plug and Play technology. As the administrator adds more devices and expansion cards, he or she often deals with resource conflicts that result from so many different nonstandard devices on the market. Dealing with these issues can be a time-consuming task.

In an attempt to resolve this ongoing problem, the *Plug and Play* (*PnP*) specification was developed. The goal of PnP is to create a computer whose hardware and software work together to automatically configure devices and assign resources, while allowing hardware changes and additions without the need for large-scale resource assignment tweaking. As the name suggests, the goal is to be able to just plug in a new device and immediately be able to use it, without complicated setup procedures. The PnP concept was first introduced with Windows 95, and with the release of the latest operating systems, PnP technology has advanced a great deal. Windows NT 4.0 does not support PnP; only Windows XP, Windows 2000, Windows Me, Windows 98, Windows 95 OSR2, and Windows 95 support this feature.

Device Drivers

Device drivers are programs that tell the operating system how to control specific devices. These device drivers act as an interface between the operating system and a device that allows them to recognize and communicate with each other. The Windows 2000/XP operating systems come with a large driver database already installed. This makes it easier to install many nonstandard devices. Having this driver database preloaded into the operating system facilitates the PnP capabilities of the operating system. For example, if a device or expansion card is attached to the computer and the OS has the driver in its database, then the OS automatically installs the device without any configuration from the user. Windows 98 comes with an installed driver database, but later operating system releases from Microsoft contain the most recent drivers as well as the updated drivers that are needed for the new operating systems.

System Tools

This section includes the following topics:

- Administrative tools
- The Windows 2000 Registry
- Startup menu and Safe mode
- The emergency repair disk and Recovery Console for Windows 2000

Administrative Tools

The Administrative Tools utility is a feature that is unique to the Windows NT/2000/XP operating systems. The *Administrative Tools* utility is a powerful system tool that enables the administrator to control everything related to the local computer. From this utility, permission to log on to the computer can be controlled by creating Local User accounts. The Disk Management utility allows the administrator to control and manipulate the computer hard drives.

A Services tab is also available. This tab that can start or stop any program that is running on the computer. This Services feature is helpful when troubleshooting problems with the system. Again, one of the main features of the Windows NT/2000/XP environment is security. The Administrative Tools utility includes a *Local Security Policy*, which enables the administrator to choose additional security options that allow control over user rights and audit policies to control the environment on the local computer.

Local Users

In the Windows 9X environment, there is no option to have a local user. Anyone who turns on the computer has access to it. There is no way to keep track of who is using the computer or who is allowed to use the computer. Because the target market of the Windows NT/2000/XP operating systems was the corporate and business community, there was a need to make the logon process secure. The ability to have *local users* was created; these local users became the only users that could log on to the computer.

A Local User account must first be created on the local computer before that user can log on. This allows the administrator to restrict access to other users. However, this feature only works on computers that are not part of a domain. Local user accounts essentially allow users to log on and gain access to resources only on the computer where the local user account was created. This account is created only in a specific computer security database and does not replicate the local user account information on any other computer that is networked to that computer.

 Lab Activity 7.2.1   Creating User Accounts in Windows 2000

In this lab, you create users and groups and assign the necessary properties. (This lab requires a system running Windows 2000 with NTFS.)

Disk Management

One task of an administrator is to constantly maintain and manage the hard drive storage. Whether dealing with user desktops or servers, the administrator must know how to effectively manage storage space in the Windows NT/2000/XP operating system environment. Proper *disk management* enables administrators to keep hard drives in the best working condition and to maximize them for optimal free space. For example, if free space is available on the hard disk, the disk must be partitioned and formatted so that data can be stored on that part of the disk. In addition, if there is more than one hard disk, each disk also must be partitioned and formatted so that it can store data. Whether configuring the remaining free space on a hard disk on which Windows 2000 was installed or setting up a new hard disk, the administrator needs to be aware of the tasks that are involved. To access Disk Management, right click My Computer and select Manage, as shown in Figure 7-2.

Figure 7-2 Accessing Computer Management

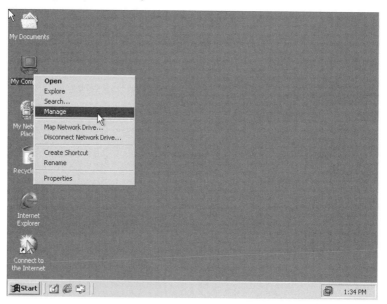

Two types of disks are available in Windows 2000 and XP, *basic disks* and *dynamic disks*. A system with one disk must be either basic or dynamic, because both types cannot be used on the same physical disk. However, if the system has more than one disk, then one can be made basic and the other dynamic.

Basic Disks

A *basic disk* is a physical disk that contains primary partitions, extended partitions, or logical drives. Basic disks can also contain spanned volumes (volume sets), mirrored volumes (mirror sets), striped volumes (stripe sets), and RAID-5 volumes (stripe sets with parity) created using Windows NT 4.0 or earlier. A basic disk can contain up to four primary partitions, or up to three primary partitions and one extended partition.

NOTE

A partition is a portion of the disk that functions as a physically separate unit of storage. This allows the separation of different types of information, such as user data on one partition and applications on another.

The operating system treat these partitions on a single hard drive as separate drives, depending on how many partitions exist. A basic disk can contain primary partitions, extended partitions, and logical drives. If a second hard disk is added to the system, the computer first recognizes it as a basic disk, the default in Windows 2000 and XP. All new disks added are basic disks unless they are converted to dynamic disks. *Basic disk storage* is typically referred to as the industry standard, and all versions of MS-DOS and Microsoft Windows support basic storage. Figure 7-3 shows a basic disk in Windows 2000 Disk Management.

Figure 7-3 Basic Disk in Computer Management

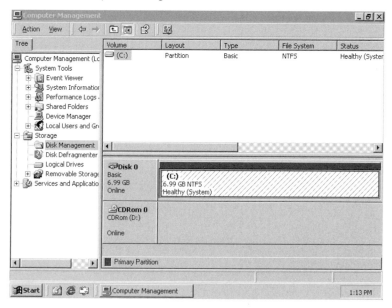

Dynamic Disks

For an operating system to support basic disks, the Disk Management tool is not needed. All the Windows operating systems that have come before Windows NT, 2000, and XP used basic disk storage as the standard. However, when dealing with the size and amount of hard drives that corporations and businesses use today, basic disk storage is no longer efficient.

One of the main reasons of having the Disk Management utility is to create *multidisk volumes.* When using *dynamic disk storage*, multidisk volumes are referred to as hard disk space. This is because the hard drives are no longer dealt with as if they are one complete disk divided by partitions, but rather are considered as multidisk volumes. These multidisk volumes are often comprised of many disks. Drives can span across

NOTE

Windows 2000 Professional does not support the mirrored and RAID-5 fault-tolerant volumes. Only the Windows 2000 Server supports these types of volumes.

these disks to give better use of the available disk space by allowing areas of unallocated space on different disks to be combined. Multidisk volumes can also improve disk performance by allowing more than one drive to read and write data.

The main difference between basic and dynamic disks is that dynamic disk volumes can be created and expanded to include new disks and storage space while the operating system is running. This makes dynamic disk management easier than creating partitions. Finally, multidisk volumes allow the use of RAID-5 technology to make volumes fault tolerant. RAID (redundant array of inexpensive disks) is discussed in a later chapter. To use any of these multidisk structures in Windows 2000, dynamic disks must be used.

Dynamic Disk Volumes

The administrator can use the Upgrade to Dynamic Disk command to convert a basic disk to a dynamic disk and then decide which type of volume to create. The following steps show the process of upgrading a basic disk to a dynamic disk:

Step 1   Open the Computer Management screen, as shown in Figure 7-4.

Step 2   Expand the Storage folder, and select Disk Management, as shown in Figure 7-5.

Step 3   Right-click the disk you want to upgrade. Figure 7-6 shows the options that display. Be sure to right-click the disk and not the partition. Then select the Upgrade to Dynamic Disk option.

Step 4   The Upgrade to Dynamic Disk window displays, as shown in Figure 7-7.

Step 5   Select the disk to upgrade, as shown in Figure 7-8, and click OK.

Step 6   Figure 7-9 shows the window that displays to confirm your selection. Choose Upgrade.

NOTE

After the upgrade is complete, a dynamic disk cannot be changed back to a basic disk.

Step 7   Figure 7-10 shows the next confirmation screen. Press OK to reboot and complete the dynamic disk upgrade.

Step 8   After the system reboots, open the Computer Management window to confirm that the disk has been upgraded. Figure 7-11 shows the upgraded disk.

Figure 7-4 The Computer Management Screen

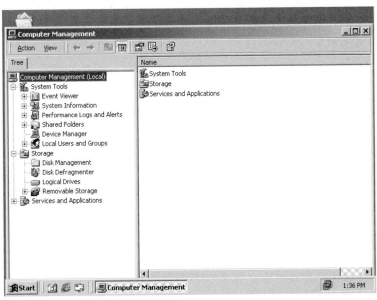

Figure 7-5 Select Disk Management in the Storage Folder

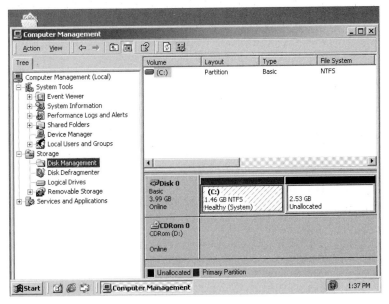

Figure 7-6 Option to Upgrade

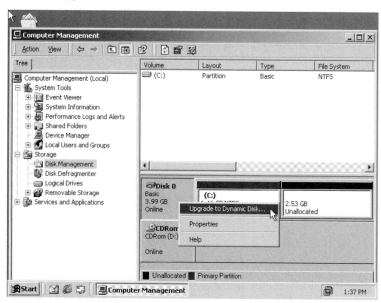

Figure 7-7 The Upgrade to Dynamic Disk Window

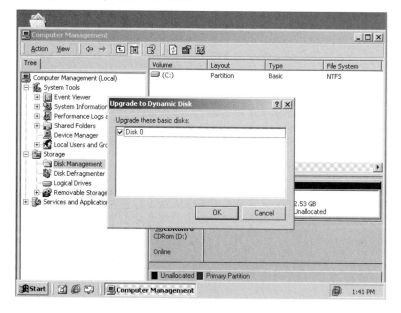

Figure 7-8 Select the Disk to Upgrade

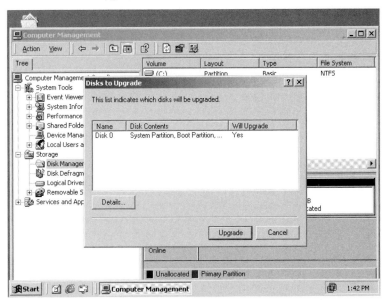

Figure 7-9 Confirm Upgrade

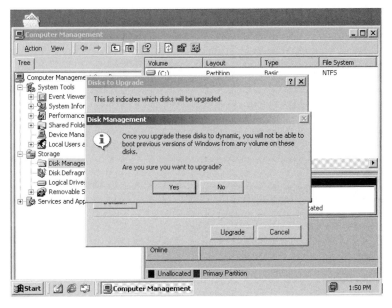

Figure 7-10 Reboot to Complete the Upgrade

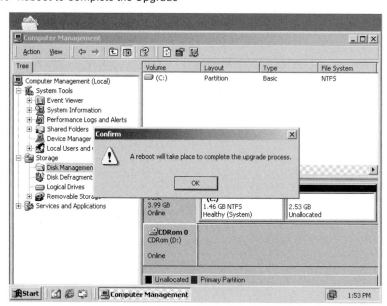

Figure 7-11 Basic Disk Converted to Dynamic Disk

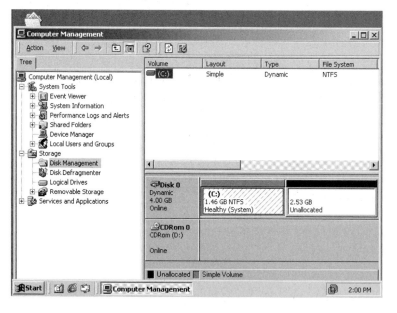

The type of volume created depends on the needs for storage space. It also depends on how crucial the data stored on that space are and if those volumes need to have a backup plan.

The types of volumes that can be created with Windows 2000 professional are *simple*, *stripped*, and *spanned volumes*, as described in the following list. There are also mirrored and RAID-5 volumes as well, but these types of volumes can only be created with the Windows 2000 Server operating system. The various volumes are described as follows:

- **Simple volume**—This volume acts as a basic disk that contains disk space from a complete single disk and is not fault tolerant.
- **Stripped volume**—Also known as RAID-0, a stripped volume combines up to 32 areas of free space from multiple hard disks into one logical volume. This volume is used to optimize performance by allowing data to be written to all the disks at the same rate. This volume is not fault tolerant; if one disk in the volume fails, all the data are lost.
- **Spanned volume**—This volume includes disk space from multiple disks. There can be up to 32 disks in a spanned volume. In a spanned volume, the operating system writes data to the first disk until it is full and then continues to write data to the proceeding disks for as many disks as are included in the volume. A spanned volume is not fault tolerant. If any disk in a spanned volume fails, the data in the entire volume are lost.
- **Mirrored volume**—This volume contains two identical copies of a simple volume that stores the same data on two separate hard drives. Mirrored volumes provide fault tolerance in the event of hard disk failure. If one disk fails, it can be replaced with a new one, and all the data are backed up on the other disk.
- **RAID-5 volume**—A RAID-5 volume consists of three or more parts of one or more drives, or three or more entire drives. Again, users can have up to 32 disks. In this volume, data are written to all drives in equal amounts to improve performance. Each drive contains parity information, which holds copies of the data that are being written to the other two disks. This enables fault tolerance because, if one of the drives should fail, the remaining two disks re-create the data automatically without having to shut down the server. After the failed hard drive gets replaced, the data get restored to the new drive. This is known as *stripping with parity*. RAID is discussed in detail in Chapter 9, "Networking Fundamentals."

The Services section of the Administrative Tools utility is useful for troubleshooting problems with the computer. This tab lists all the services that are running on a computer and allows the administrator to start or stop any of the services that are running.

For example, if files are being copied from one computer to another computer or hard drive and an antivirus program is installed in one system, the Services function can be used to stop the antivirus program. This allows the files to be copied faster because they do not have to be scanned by the antivirus program.

Local Security Policy

The *Local Security Policy* is a function of the Administrative Tools utility that allows the administrator to select additional security options. Nearly 40 security options are available to increase the security on a computer, as shown in Figure 7-12. One option, for example, is to set the number of days after which the user is prompted to change his or her password. Double-click Prompt User to Change Password before Expiration. Figure 7-13 shows the window that displays. The administrator can increase or decrease the number of days after which the system prompts the user to change the password. As indicated, domain-level policies override local security policies.

Figure 7-12   Local Security Policy

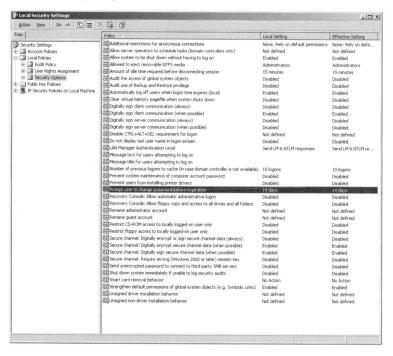

Figure 7-13 Local Security Policy Setting

The Windows 2000 Registry

Microsoft Windows 2000 stores hardware and software settings centrally in a hierarchical database called the Registry. The Registry for the Windows 2000 and XP operating systems replaces many of the ini, sys, and com files that are used in earlier versions of Windows. The Registry acts as a backbone to the operating system and provides appropriate initialization information to start applications and load components, such as device drivers and network protocols, which are explained earlier in the section, "Windows 2000 Boot Process." The Registry Editor, shown in Figure 7-14, can be used to access the Windows 2000 Registry.

Figure 7-14 The Windows 2000 Registry Editor

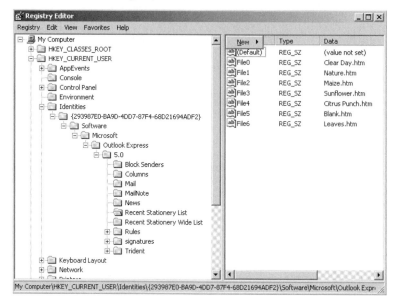

Purpose of the Registry

The Registry is a database of configuration settings in Windows 95/98/NT/2000. The main components of the Registry include the hardware installed on the computer, including the central processing unit (CPU), bus type, pointing device or mouse, and keyboard; device drivers; installed applications; and network adapter card settings. The Registry, which contains a vast amount of data, is critical to the system operation. The Registry is structured to provide a secure set of records about the components that control the operating system. These components read, update, and modify data stored in the Registry. Six main components access the Registry and store data; these components are described as follows:

- **Device drivers**—The Registry sets the configuration settings for the system device drivers. Information is written to the Registry when device drivers are updated or referenced.

- **Setup programs**—When new applications or new hardware is installed in a computer system, a setup program is run to add new configuration data to the Registry. The setup programs also scan the Registry to verify that components have been installed.

- **User profiles**—Windows NT, 2000, and XP create user profiles that maintain specific settings for all the users that log on to the computer. These settings are first changed in the Registry and then made in the user profile. The file ntuser.dat holds the user profile information.

- **Windows NT kernel**—The Registry plays an important role during the boot process. The Windows NT kernel (ntoskrnl.exe) loads the correct device drivers in the proper order.

- **ntdetect.com**—The ntdetect.com file and its role in the boot process were explained in a previous section of this chapter. Only Intel-based systems use this file to detect hardware that is installed in a system. The data that collected during the hardware detection phase are stored in this file.

- **Hardware profiles**—Windows NT, 2000, and XP have the capability to have two or more profiles in which the administrator can decide which hardware either loads or does not load. These hardware profile configurations are stored in the Registry.

Registry Subtrees

Navigating and editing the Registry can be done manually using the regedt32.exe file. When REGEDT32 is typed in the command line, an interface is displayed showing the *Registry subtrees* window, which allows a search through all the Registry values. An example of a Registry subtree is shown in Figure 7-15.

Figure 7-15 A Windows Registry Subtree

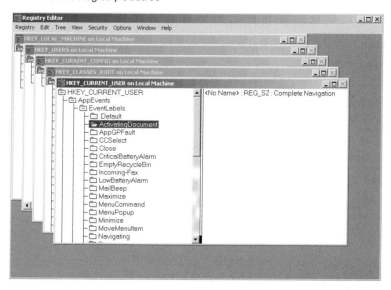

Becoming familiar with these subtrees and understanding their purpose help you to troubleshoot and maintain the computer. A key for every process that is running on a system can be found here. The following five subtrees, which contain the subtree keys, are displayed in the Registry Editor window:

- **HKEY_USERS**—Contains the system default settings used to control user profiles and environments, such as desktop settings, Windows environment, and custom software settings. Figure 7-16 shows an example of the HKEY_USERS screen.

Figure 7-16 The HKEY_USERS Screen

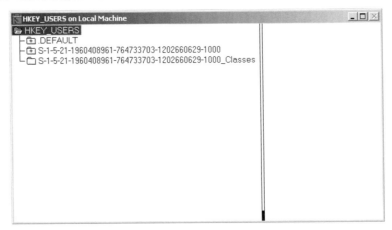

- **HKEY_CURRENT_CONFIG**—Contains data on the active hardware profile that is selected during the boot process. This information is used to configure settings such as the device drivers to load and display the resolution to use. Figure 7-17 shows an example of the HKEY_CURRENT_CONFIG screen.

Figure 7-17 The HKEY_CURRENT_CONFIG Screen

- **HKEY_CLASSES_ROOT**—This subtree contains configuration data of all the software that is installed on the computer. Figure 7-18 shows an example of the HKEY_CLASSES_ROOT screen.

Figure 7-18 The HKEY_CLASSES_ROOT Screen

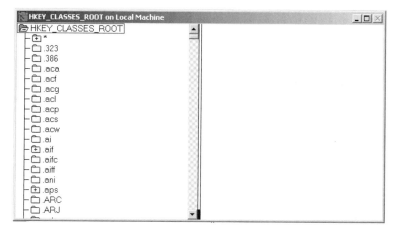

- **HKEY_CURRENT_USER**—Contains data about the user that is currently logged on to the computer. This key retrieves a copy of each user account that is used to log on to the computer and stores it in the Registry. Figure 7-19 shows an example of the HKEY_CURRENT_USER screen.

Figure 7-19 The HKEY_CURRENT_USER Screen

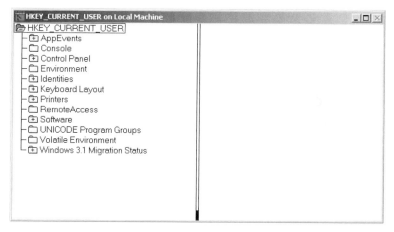

- **HKEY_LOCAL_MACHINE**—Contains all configuration data for the local computer, including hardware and operating system data such as bus type, system memory, device drivers, and startup control data. Applications, device drivers, and the operating system use these data to set the computer configuration. The data in this subtree remain constant regardless of the user. Figure 7-20 shows an example of the HKEY_LOCAL_MACHINE screen.

Figure 7-20 The HKEY_LOCAL_MACHINE Screen

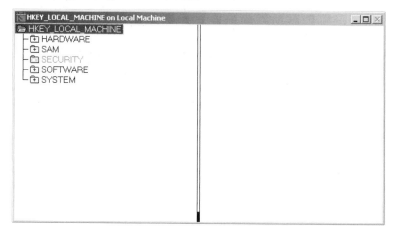

Startup Menu and Safe Mode

The Windows NT/2000/XP operating system *Startup menus* are unique security features that are not found in the Windows 9X operating system environment. The Windows NT/2000/XP operating systems must go through a multistep process to get to the Startup menu.

One advanced startup feature that is available for troubleshooting purposes is *Safe mode* startup. If the computer does not start normally, use the Safe mode advanced startup option. Enter Safe mode by pressing F8 during the operating system selection phase. This displays a screen with advanced options for booting Windows 2000, as shown in Figure 7-21. If Safe mode is selected, Windows 2000 loads and uses only basic files and drivers, including the mouse, VGA monitor, keyboard, mass storage, and default system services but no network connections. (This is similar to the Windows 9X Safe mode.) With Windows 2000, it is easy to recognize that you are working in Safe mode, because the screen background is black and the term Safe Mode appears in each corner of the screen.

Figure 7-21 Windows 98 Startup Menu

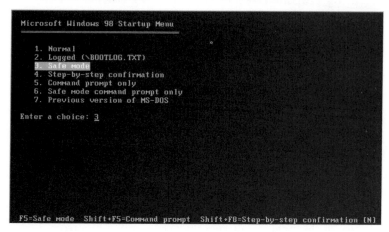

When you press F8, you have several Safe mode selection options. Figure 7-22 shows the options available when using the Safe mode startup feature. One option is Safe Mode with Networking, which is identical to Safe mode except that it adds the drivers and services necessary to enable networking to function when the computer is restarted. Another Safe mode option is Safe Mode with Command Prompt, which is the same as Safe mode except that when the computer restarts, it displays a command prompt.

Figure 7-22 Booting into Safe Mode in Windows 2000

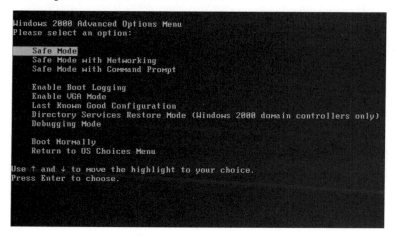

The Emergency Repair Disk and Recovery Console for Windows 2000

The system administrator might encounter computers whose operating systems have become corrupt, cannot function properly, or do not boot. Usually, a critical file or program has been deleted or changed so that the operating system no longer recognizes it. In Windows 2000, an emergency repair disk (ERD) can be created or the Recovery Console feature can be used. These options help fix boot problems by repairing files or copying new files that have been corrupted so that the hard drive does not have to be reformatted.

Emergency Repair Disk

The *emergency repair disk (ERD)* allows the reinstallation of any service packs that were loaded since the original installation. ERD also copies files from the CD-ROM of the corrupted files on the hard disk. If the file system becomes corrupt and cannot start, an ERD can provide a solution. If a service pack was applied since the original installation, it must be reinstalled because the files that are copied will be original installation files taken from the Windows CD.

Creating an Emergency Repair Disk

To create an emergency repair disk, follow these steps:

Step 1   Run the Backup program by choosing **Start, Programs, Accessories, System Tools, Backup.** The Windows 2000 Backup and Recovery Tool is shown in Figure 7-23.

Step 2   On the Welcome tab, click the Emergency Repair Disk button. A window displays, as shown in Figure 7-24.

Step 3   Insert a blank formatted 3-1/2-inch floppy disk in drive A.

Step 4   Check the box labeled Also Backup The Registry To The Repair Directory.

Step 5   Click OK.

Step 6   Remove the disk and label it Emergency Repair Disk with the current date.

Figure 7-23 The Windows 2000 Backup and Recovery Tool

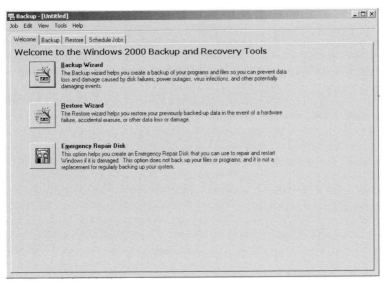

Figure 7-24 The Emergency Repair Disk Window

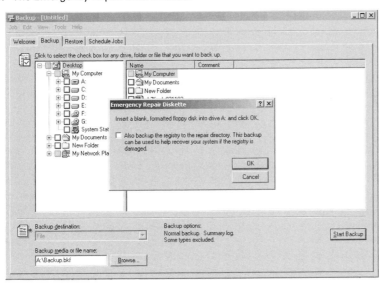

Using an Emergency Repair Disk

There are two ways that you can use the ERD. If the system supports a bootable CD-ROM drive, insert the Windows 2000 CD and boot from the CD. If the system does not support a bootable CD-ROM drive, insert Windows 2000 Setup disk 1 and restart the computer. You are then prompted to insert Setup disk 2 and Setup disk 3.

Regardless of whether you are using a CD or a floppy disk, the following steps are used to run the ERD:

1. Press Enter when asked whether you want to install Windows 2000.

2. Press R to use the ERD.

3. When presented with a fast or manual option, press F to select the Fast option.

4. Press Enter to use the ERD.

5. Insert the ERD, and press Enter.

6. After the files are repaired, reboot the operating system.

 Lab Activity 7.2.4   Creating an Emergency Repair Disk in Windows 2000

In this lab, you create and use an ERD. (This lab requires a system running Windows 2000 with NTFS.)

Recovery Console

The Windows 2000 *Recovery Console* is a command-line interface that can be used to perform a variety of troubleshooting and recovery tasks, including starting and stopping services, reading and writing data on a local drive (including drives that are formatted with the NT file system), and formatting hard disks. After the Recovery Console starts, you can enter commands to remove, replace, or copy corrupt files.

There are several ways to start the Recovery Console. The first is to insert the Windows 2000 CD into the CD-ROM drive and wait for the Microsoft Windows 2000 CD dialog box to open. If it opens, close it. If it does not open, choose **Start, Run** and type **cmd**. This brings up a command prompt window, where the administrator can change to the drive letter of the CD-ROM drive, change to the I386 folder, and run the winnt32 command by typing the following:

WINNT32 /CMDCONS

After the Recovery Console is installed, it can be accessed from the Please Select Operating System To Start menu. The Recovery Console can also be accessed by selecting the option to use the Windows 2000 setup disks or CD when prompted.

Overview of the Installation Process

This section includes the following topics:

- Differences between Windows 2000 and 9X installations
- Hardware requirements for Windows 2000
- Windows 2000 features

Differences Between Windows 2000 and 9X Installations

This chapter has explored the many differences between the Windows 9X and Windows 2000 environments. These differences exist primarily because the operating systems serve different functions and are intended for use in different environments. It should come as no surprise to learn that the installation processes of Windows 9X and 2000 are different as well. Again, these differences are due to the added security and file system features that are available with Windows 2000. Figure 7-25 shows the Windows 2000 startup screen.

Figure 7-25 The Windows 2000 Startup Screen

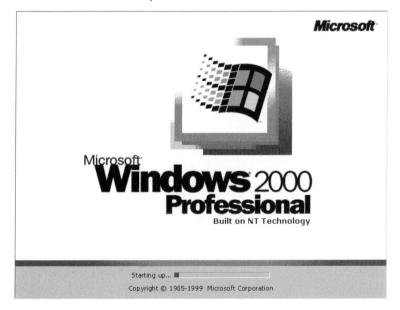

Hardware Requirements for Windows 2000

The first major difference between the Windows 2000 and 9X installation processes that the system administrator or technician encounters is the hardware requirements for the two operating systems. Windows 2000 is a more robust operating system and

NOTE

This chapter refers to "system administrator" more often than to "technician" because Windows 2000 is more likely to run in a networked environment. Here, the system administrator handles most problems that occur.

has many more features than the 9X operating system. Therefore, Windows 2000 requires a more powerful computer and advanced hardware.

The Windows 9X OS requires an 80486 66-MHz system with at least 16 MB of RAM. The system should also have a modem and a 16-color VGA monitor. The hard drive needs to have 120 to 355 MB of free space to install Windows 98. (Windows 9X installation is more thoroughly discussed in Chapter 5, "Windows 9X Operating Systems.") To install and run Windows 2000, the computer system requires a substantial hardware upgrade. This is discussed later in this chapter in "Requirements for Installing Windows 2000."

Partitioning and Formatting

It is important to become familiar with partitioning and formatting when performing operating system installations. *Partitioning and formatting* prepare the hard drive for the operating system installation. When installing one of the Windows 9X operating systems, the hard drive must be partitioned with the FDISK utility, as shown in Figure 7-26, or with a third-party utility like Partition Magic. You then insert the installation CD and install the operating system. Hard drive partitioning for a Windows 9X installation is more thoroughly discussed in Chapter 5.

Figure 7-26 FDISK Options

Windows 2000 provides an easy way to prepare the hard drive for OS installation. The administrator can take an unformatted, unpartitioned hard drive and begin installing Windows 2000. While going through the setup process, the administrator is prompted to select which partition the operating system is to be installed on. If no partitions exist, they can be created by the Setup program. The administrator is then prompted to format the partition if it has just been created, or a partition can be reformatted if one is already exists.

Device Drivers

Device drivers play an important role in both Windows 9X and 2000. If the computer does not have the proper device drivers, the system cannot run. Device drivers are an area in which Windows 2000 has a definite advantage. You must have a different set of drivers, depending on whether you are installing Windows 9X or 2000. This is because the internal structure of the two operating systems is different.

The main advantage of Windows 2000, when compared with Windows 9X, is the *hardware abstraction layer (HAL)*. The HAL is a library of hardware drivers that communicate between the operating system and the hardware that is installed on the system. The HAL enables Windows 2000 to work with different types of processors from different manufacturers. This feature frees Windows 2000 from interacting with the hardware, as it does in Windows 9X. Instead, the HAL controls all direct access for system hardware operations, providing the operating system with expanded hardware compatibility. The HAL is what makes Windows 2000 a network operating system (NOS) compared to Windows 9X, which is not.

Windows 2000 Features

While installing Windows 2000, you will find several other features that are not found in the Windows 9X installation process. When installing Windows 2000, one option is whether to add the computer to a domain or workgroup, as shown in Figure 7-27. If the computer is to be added to the domain, an account for the computer must be made in the domain. Another important feature of Windows 2000 installations is the *client access license (CAL)*. The CAL gives client computers the right to connect to computers running Windows 2000 Server so that the client computers can connect to network services, shared folders, and print resources.

Figure 7-27 Adding the Computer to a Domain or Workgroup

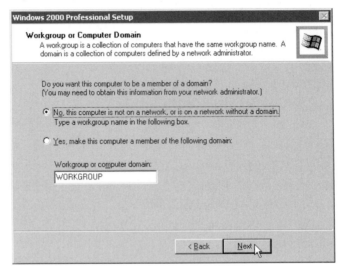

Installing Windows 2000

This section includes the following topics:

- Requirements for installing Windows 2000
- Steps for installing Windows 2000
- Setup options in Windows 2000

Requirements for Installing Windows 2000

Before installing Windows 2000, check to make sure that the hardware is capable of running the OS. Microsoft recommends verifying the following minimum requirements prior to installing the operating system:

- A Pentium-class processor
- 64 MB of RAM
- 2 GB of hard drive or partition space
- A VGA monitor
- A CD-ROM drive capable of reading at a 12X or higher
- A network card

Microsoft has a tool called the *hardware compatibility list (HCL)* that can be used before installing Windows 2000 to verify that the hardware will accept the OS. Microsoft provides drivers for only those devices that are included on this list. Using hardware that is not listed on the HCL might cause problems during and after installation. This HCL can be viewed by opening the hcl.txt file in the Support folder on the Windows 2000 Professional CD, as shown in Figure 7-28.

Figure 7-28　The HCL in WordPad

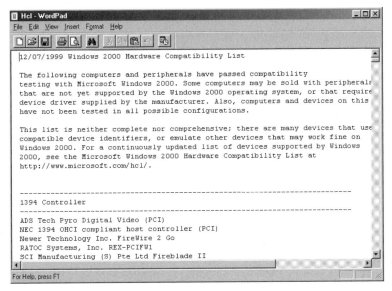

Steps for Installing Windows 2000

There are four main steps in the Windows 2000 installation process. The installation begins when the Setup program runs. This prepares the hard disk and copies files. Setup then runs a wizard that provides informational pages, which are used to complete the rest of the installation. The following list summarizes the Windows 2000 installation process:

1. Running the Setup program

2. Using the Setup wizard

3. Installing Windows networking

4. Completing the Setup program

Running the Setup Program

The first step of the installation process is to prepare the hard drive for the other stages of installation by copying the files that are needed to run the Setup wizard, which is the second step. At this point, the text portion of the setup is seen. The Windows 2000 installation can be started by either using the setup boot disks or by booting from the CD. If the setup boot disks are chosen, insert the first disk into the computer and turn it on. Follow the steps to insert the other three disks to begin copying the files.

Using the Windows 2000 Professional CD is much easier. After booting from the CD, a minimal version of Windows 2000 is copied to memory; this version is used to start the Setup program. This is where the text-based portion of Setup starts. The administrator must first read and accept the licensing agreement. Choose to delete a partition, if necessary, to reconfigure the hard disk partitions. Create and format a new partition in which to install Windows 2000, or reformat an existing partition.

After deciding on a partition for the operating system, select either the FAT or NTFS as the type of file system. Setup then formats the partition with the file system selected. After the partition is formatted, the Setup program copies the necessary files to the hard disk and saves the configuration information. Setup then automatically restarts the computer and starts the Windows 2000 Setup wizard. By default, the Windows 2000 operating system files are installed in the C:\WINNT folder. Figures 7-29 to 7-33 demonstrate the steps performed by the Setup program.

Figure 7-29 The Welcome to Setup Screen

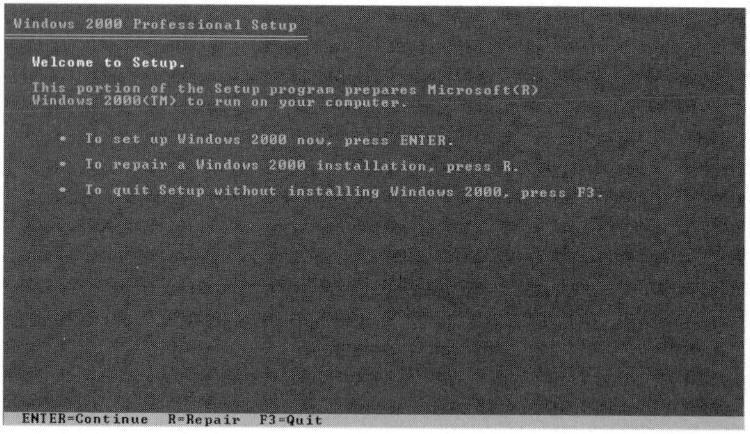

Figure 7-30 The Windows 2000 Licensing Agreement

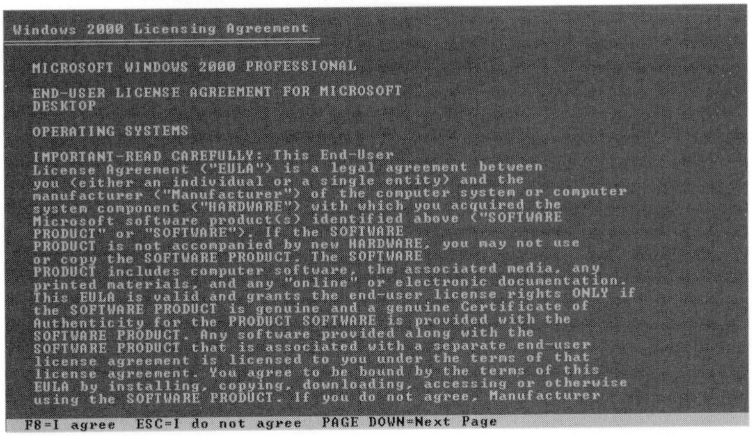

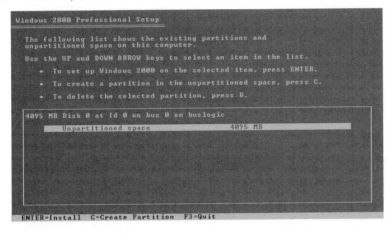

Figure 7-31 Partition Options

Figure 7-32 Formatting the Partition

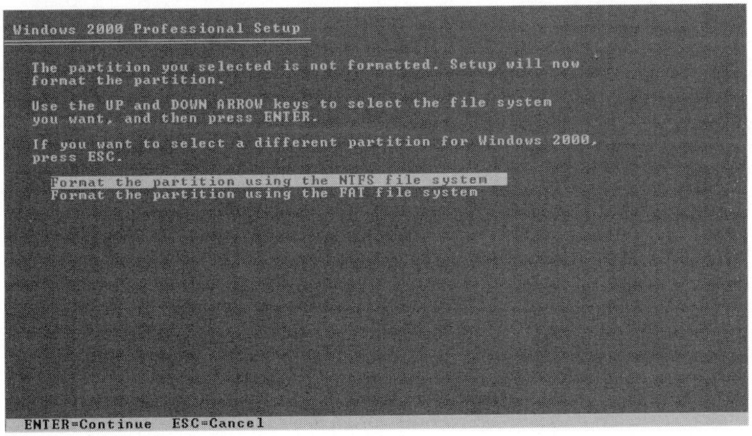

Figure 7-33 Setup Copies Files

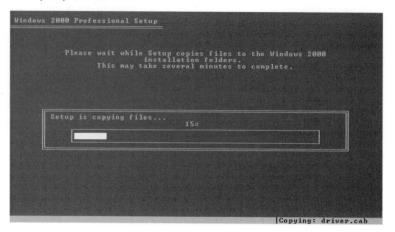

Using the Setup Wizard

The Setup wizard begins the installation process and prompts the administrator through the next stage of the installation. The wizard gathers information about the administrator, the organization, and the computer. This step installs the security features and configures the system devices. The administrator is then prompted through a series of setup screens in which the Windows 2000 Setup wizard asks for the following information:

- **Regional settings**—Windows 2000 was designed to be a global operating system. Information designed to customize language, locale, and keyboard settings must be entered. Windows 2000 can be configured to use multiple languages and regional settings.

- **Name and organization**—Enter the name of the person who is to be the computer user and the organization to which the copy of Windows 2000 Professional is licensed.

- **Product key**—Microsoft ships every copy of Windows 2000 with a 25-character product key; this is usually located on the back of the CD case.

- **Computer name**—When connecting the computer to a network, each computer on the network needs to have a unique name. Enter a computer name that is no longer than 15 characters. The Windows 2000 Setup wizard displays a default name, using the organization name that was entered earlier, but this can be changed.

- **Password for the administrator account**—Windows 2000 has the capability of having different profiles for the users of that computer. There is also a built-in administrator account that includes privileges to make any changes to the computer. At this point, the administrator must supply the password for that administrator account.

- **Modem dialing information**—Because today's networks use high-speed local-area networks (LANs) and network cards, this option first depends on whether a modem is being used. Most laptops continue to use a modem, so it might be necessary to enter information here. Select the country or region where the computer is located. This is often already completed, based on the selected regional setting. The area (or city) of the computer's location, as well as the phone number for a dialup connection, must also be entered. Finally, select whether the phone system uses tone or pulse dialing.

- **Date and time settings**—The correct date and time, as well as the time zone in which the computer is to be run, must be specified. Indicate if Windows 2000 should automatically adjust the computer clock for daylight saving time.

Figures 7-34 to 7-38 demonstrate the steps involved in the Setup wizard.

Figure 7-34 Enter Regional Settings

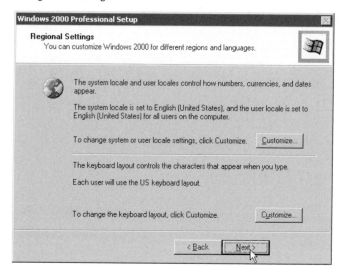

Figure 7-35 Personalize the Software

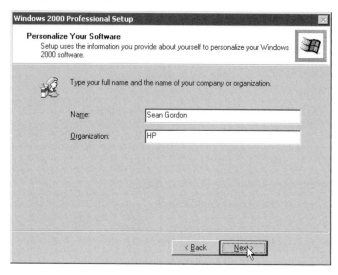

Figure 7-36 Enter the Product Key

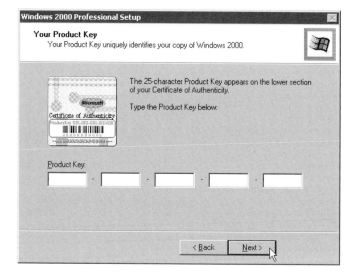

Figure 7-37 Enter the Computer Name and Set the Administrator Password

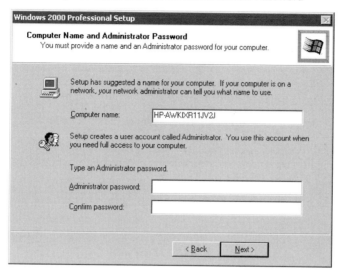

Figure 7-38 Enter Date and Time Settings

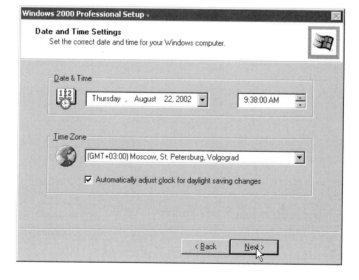

Installing Windows Networking

Windows 2000 was designed to be a network operating system. Configuring the network settings is a major step in the installation process. After gathering information about the computer, the Windows 2000 Setup program automatically installs the network software.

Windows 2000 Professional installs networking components using the following steps:

Step 1   **Detect network adapter cards.** The operating system first needs to detect the network cards. If none are installed, this step is skipped.

Step 2   **Install networking components.** Certain files must be installed to allow the computer to connect to other computers, networks, and the Internet. The Setup program next prompts the administrator to choose whether to use typical settings or customized settings to configure the networking components. If Typical is chosen, the system installs the default settings. By choosing Customized, the administrator can enter information that is specific to a company's network.

For example, Client for Microsoft Networks allows the computer to gain access to network resources. File and Printer Sharing for Microsoft Networks allows other computers to gain access to file and print resources on the computer. TCP/IP protocol is the default networking protocol that allows a computer to communicate over LANs and wide-area networks (WANs). At this stage, other clients, services, and network protocols, such as NetBIOS enhanced user interface (NetBEUI), AppleTalk, and NWLink IPX/SPX/NetBIOS-compatible transport, can be installed if the network requires them.

Step 3   **Join a workgroup or domain.** The administrator must now decide whether the computer is to be part of a domain or workgroup. If a computer account is created in the domain for the computer during the installation, the Windows 2000 Setup wizard prompts the administrator for the name and password to join the domain.

Step 4   **Install components.** The networking components that have just been selected are installed and configured.

Figures 7-39 to 7-42 demonstrate the steps involved in installing network components.

Figure 7-39 Installing Network Components

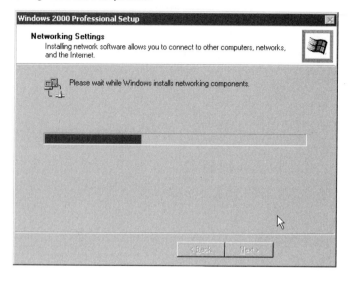

Figure 7-40 Network Settings

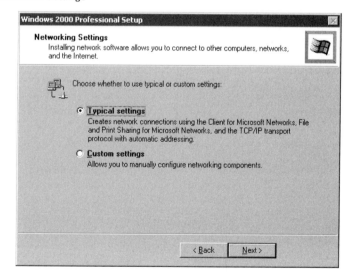

Figure 7-41 Workgroup or Computer Domain Settings

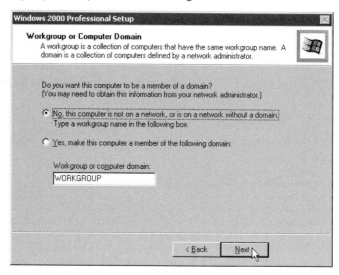

Figure 7-42 Installing Windows 2000 Components

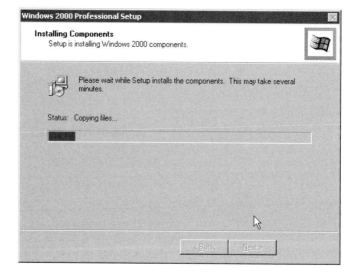

Completing the Setup Program

After the networking components are installed, the Setup wizard copies additional files to configure Windows 2000 Professional. There are four steps in the final stage of the installation process, as shown in Figures 7-43 to 7-46. The Setup program automatically performs the following items:

- **Installs Start menu items**—Shortcut items that appear on the Start menu are installed.
- **Registers components**—Windows 2000 begins to apply the configuration settings that were specified in the Setup wizard.
- **Saves the configuration**—After the configuration settings are applied, they are saved to the hard drive so that they are used every time the computer is started.
- **Removes temporary files**—During the OS installation, many files are copied to the hard disk to run the installation. When the installation is complete, these files are no longer needed. The Setup wizard automatically deletes these files. After this step is complete, the computer automatically restarts. The administrator can then log on to finish the installation procedure.

Figure 7-47 shows the completion of the Windows 2000 installation.

Figure 7-43 Performing Final Tasks, Install Start Menu Items

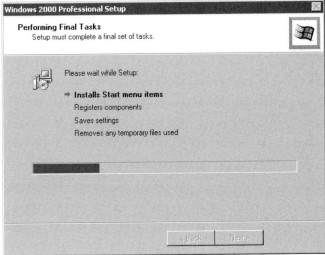

Figure 7-44 Performing Final Tasks, Register Components

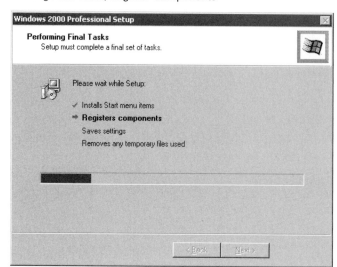

Figure 7-45 Performing Final Tasks, Save Settings

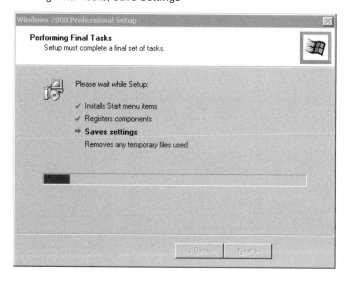

Figure 7-46 Performing Final Tasks, Remove Temporary Files

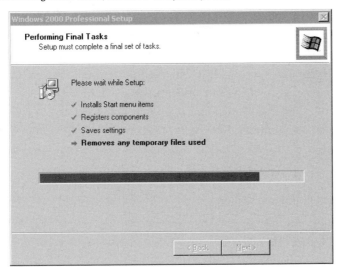

Figure 7-47 Completing the Windows 2000 Installation

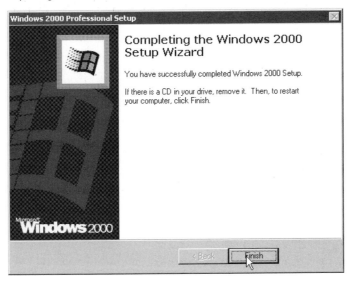

Setup Options in Windows 2000

The installation steps described in the previous section are for the default or Typical installation. However, other setup options are available in Windows 2000. The Portable installation option installs the options that are needed for a laptop computer. Another setup option is a Compact installation. This option should be used when installing Windows 2000 on a computer with a limited amount of hard drive space. The last setup option is the Custom installation. This should be chosen if the user wants custom settings for the device configurations. Select this type of installation if non–Plug and Play adapter cards or hardware devices are used. Table 7-9 shows the Windows 2000 setup options.

Table 7-9 Windows 2000 Setup Options

Setup Option	Result
Typical	Setup installs all the components that are usually installed with Windows 2000. Most users should select this option.
Portable	Setup installs the options that are generally required for laptop computers.
Compact	This is the smallest possible installation of Windows 2000. For example, you should perform a Compact installation if your hard disk has little free space. Setup then installs no optional components. If you later want to use an optional component, such as games or WebTV for Windows, you must install it. To install an optional component after Setup is completed, use Add/Remove Programs in the Control Panel.
Custom	Setup allows you to choose which optional components are installed. If you do not select a Custom installation, Setup installs only the optional components that are selected by default. If you know you are going to need certain Windows components, you should select a Custom installation and ensure that those components are included during Setup. Pan-European users should choose this option to select the required regional settings and keyboard layout for their locale.

Lab Activity 7.3.1 Installation Demonstration of Windows 2000

In this lab, you learn the proper procedures for installing Windows 2000.

Special Installations

This section includes the following topics:

- Upgrading from Windows NT 4.0 to Windows 2000
- Upgrading from Windows 9X to Windows 2000
- Dual-booting Windows 9X and Windows 2000

Upgrading from Windows NT 4.0 to Windows 2000

Upgrading a computer from Windows NT 4.0 to Windows 2000 is an easier process than doing a new installation of Windows 2000; this upgrade is similar to the upgrade process for computers running Windows 9X.

Microsoft has planned for the situation when a large corporation needs to upgrade its computers. During the upgrade, those computers that are still running Windows NT 4.0 will be able to connect to and communicate with the Windows 2000 computers. During the upgrade process, the Windows 2000 Setup utility replaces the existing files with Windows 2000 files. However, the existing applications and settings are saved. Be sure to verify that the computers meet the hardware compatibility requirements for the upgrade to Windows 2000. Run the HCL tool to determine if a computer meets these requirements.

Upgrade from Windows NT 4.0 to Windows 2000 by using the following steps:

Step 1   Insert the Windows 2000 CD in the CD-ROM drive.

Step 2   Choose **Start, Run**.

Step 3   In the Run dialog box, type **D:\I386\WINNT32** (where D is the drive letter for the CD-ROM drive) and then press Enter. The Welcome to the Windows 2000 Setup Wizard note appears.

Step 4   Select Upgrade to Windows 2000 (Recommended), and then click Next. The License Agreement page appears.

Step 5   Read the license agreement, and then click I Accept This Agreement.

Step 6   Click Next.

Step 7   The Upgrading to the Windows 2000 NT File System page appears.

Step 8   Click Yes, Upgrade My Drive, and then click Next.

Step 9   The Copying Installation Files page appears.

Step 10   The Restarting the Computer page appears, and the computer restarts.

After the computer restarts, the upgrade process should continue without the need for any further user intervention.

Upgrading from Windows 9*X* to Windows 2000

The process for upgrading Windows 9X to Windows 2000 is similar to the process of upgrading Windows NT 4.0 to Windows 2000. Use the HCL tool to make sure that the computers that are to be upgraded will work with Windows 2000.

If the computer passes the hardware compatibility test, run the Windows 2000 Setup program to start the upgrade to Windows 2000. Use the following steps:

Step 1   Choose **Start, Run** and type **winnt32.exe** at the command prompt.

Step 2   Accept the license agreement.

Step 3   If the computer is already a member of a domain, a computer account in that domain must be created. Windows 95 and Windows 98 clients do not require a computer account; Windows 2000 Professional clients do.

Step 4   Provide upgrade packs for any applications that need them. These packs update software so it works with Windows 2000. Upgrade packs are available from the software manufacturer and can be found on the Internet. During the upgrade process, users have the option of visiting the Windows Compatibility website to find the latest product updates and compatibility information.

Step 5   You are prompted to upgrade to NTFS. Select this option unless the client computer will be dual-booting operating systems, because FAT16 and FAT32 cannot recognize NTFS.

Step 6   The Windows 2000 Compatibility tool runs, generating a report. If the report shows that the computer is Windows 2000 compatible, continue with the upgrade. If the report shows that the computer is incompatible with Windows 2000, terminate the upgrade process and remove or upgrade the incompatible hardware or software before continuing.

At this point, the upgrade should finish without further user intervention. After the upgrade is complete, the password for the local computer administrator account must be entered.

If the computer is Windows 2000 compatible, it is now upgraded and is a member of the domain. Figures 7-48 to 7-59 demonstrate the process of upgrading Windows 9X to Windows 2000.

Figure 7-48 Upgrading from Windows 98 to Windows 2000

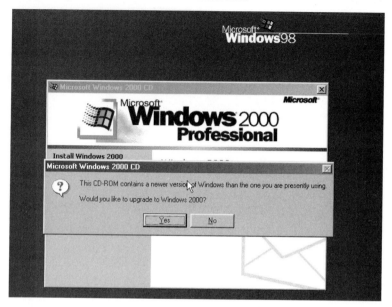

Figure 7-49 Upgrade Options

Figure 7-50   Windows 2000 License Agreement

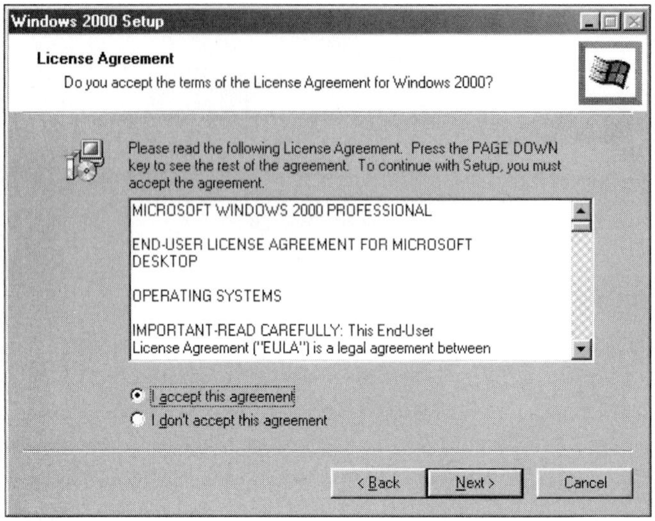

Figure 7-51   Windows 2000 Product Key

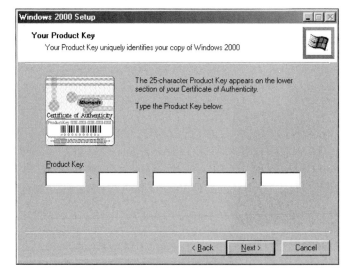

Figure 7-52   Preparing to Upgrade to Windows 2000

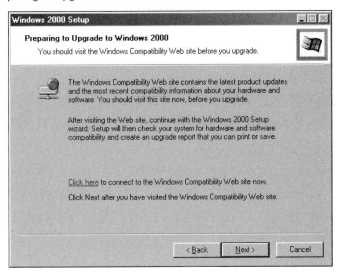

Figure 7-53   Upgrade Packs

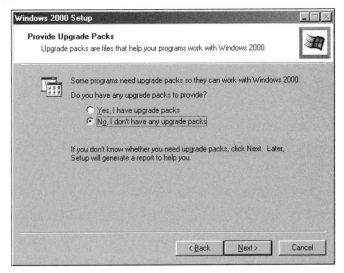

Figure 7-54 Converting an Existing FAT Partition to NTFS

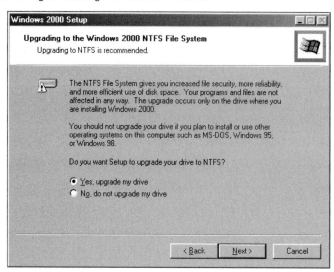

Figure 7-55 Loading Information File

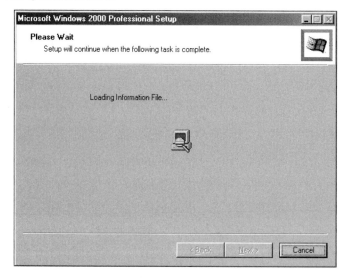

Figure 7-56 Prepares an Upgrade Report

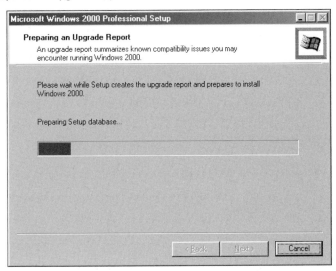

Figure 7-57 Displays the Upgrade Report

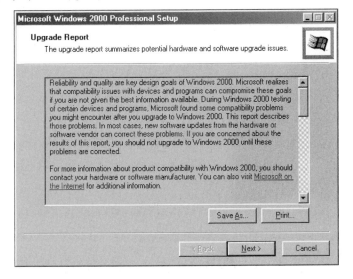

Figure 7-58 Ready to Install Windows 2000

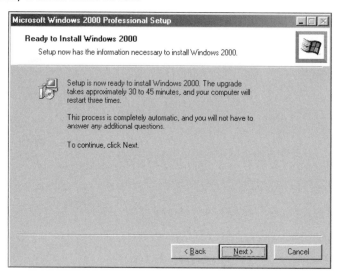

Figure 7-59 Restarting the Computer

The system must be restarted for the installation process to complete. After the system reboots, the installation process proceeds through a typical Windows 2000 installation, as previously discussed.

Dual-Booting Windows 9X and Windows 2000

Windows 2000 can be set up to *dual-boot* with Windows 98. This option provides the choice to boot into either a Windows 2000 or a Windows 98 environment. If the computer system is to be dual-booted, a menu offers a choice of operating systems to use during startup. To dual-boot the system, do a fresh installation of Windows 98 before installing Windows 2000. Figure 7-60 shows a Startup screen that has options for booting into two different operating systems.

Figure 7-60 Dual-Boot Options

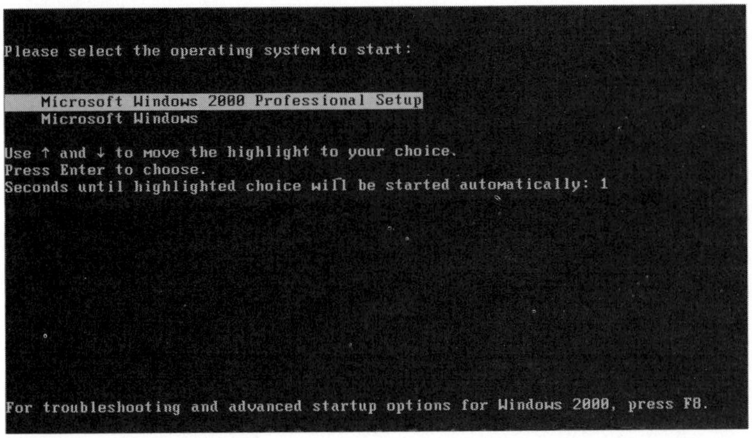

NOTE

If the system is set up to dual-boot, none of the applications that are installed in one operating system partition can be used in the second partition. If the same application needs to be used in both operating systems, the application must be installed twice, once for each operating system.

In this example, the Microsoft Windows 2000 Professional Setup option starts Windows 2000 and the Microsoft Windows option starts Windows 98.

If the two operating systems have incompatible file systems, two separate partitions can be created, and the operating systems can be installed on each partition. Alternatively, logical drives can be created, and the two operating systems can be installed on the separate logical drives. However, if the hard drive is formatted with NTFS, the Windows 98 operating system cannot read files in the Windows 2000 NTFS partition. Microsoft recommends that if the computer is set up to dual-boot with Windows 98 and Windows 2000, both partitions should be formatted with the FAT file system. Windows 2000 can operate with the FAT file system, and files in the other partition can be read.

Summary

This chapter discussed the Windows NT/2000/XP operating systems. The important concepts to retain from this chapter are as follows:

- The differences between Windows NT/2000/XP and Windows 9X are primarily in the added features in Windows NT/2000/XP that provide security for the system. Assigning permissions is made easy with the use of the ACL. Encryption allows administrators to specify who has access to folders and files.

- The FAT32 file system solved some problems of FAT16. FAT32 supports hard drives up to 2048 GB, whereas FAT16 only supported sizes up to 2 GB. FAT32 also solved the problem of limited cluster size. FAT32 changed the way the root directory is located on the hard drive and has the ability to use both the default and original copy of the file allocation table should one become corrupt.

- NTFS solved even more of the limitations of FAT16 and FAT32. NTFS was designed as an enterprise-level operating system with features that provide directory and file security. In addition, NTFS can recognize and address large hard disks and volumes more efficiently than FAT16 or FAT32.

- The Windows 2000 boot process is more involved than the Windows 9X boot process because of the added features when NTFS is utilized as the file system. The five boot stages include the preboot sequence, boot sequence, kernel load, kernel initialization, and logon process.

- The Administrative Tools utility used in the Windows NT/2000/XP operating systems allows the administrator to set up local security policies and assign permissions to users. Disk management allows the management of hard drive storage and provides the option to set up basic disks or dynamic disks.

- The Windows 2000 Registry is comprised of the six main components that access the Registry and store data. These are device drivers, setup programs, user profiles, Windows NT kernel, ntdetect.com, and hardware profiles. Within the Registry are subtrees that provide a key for every process that is running on a system. These subtrees are useful for maintenance and troubleshooting.

- Safe mode is a security feature in Windows NT/2000/XP that loads only basic files and drivers. It is a troubleshooting tool that is accessed during the bootup process by pressing F8. Safe Mode with Networking and Safe Mode with Command Prompt can also be used.

- An emergency repair disk (ERD) or the Recovery Console can help fix problems caused when an operating system becomes corrupt. The ERD copies the original installation files from the CD. The Recovery Console is a command-line interface that allows troubleshooting and recovery tasks.

- Understanding the Setup wizard and knowing the steps required to install or upgrade Windows 2000 in a network environment facilitate troubleshooting. When upgrading to Windows 2000, the HCL is used to address hardware issues before installation of the OS.

The next chapter details advanced hardware fundamentals for servers. It focuses on the network server, RAID technology, memory considerations, and server upgrades.

Check Your Understanding

1. Why is a system attribute applied to a file?

   A. So it cannot be changed or deleted

   B. So it can only be read by DOS

   C. So changes to the file can be tracked

   D. So that the user knows it is a system file

2. What file system limits filenames to eight characters?

   A. FAT 32

   B. FAT 16

   C. NTFS

   D. HPFS

3. What is the largest hard drive that the FAT 32 file system can support?

   A. 2048 GB

   B. 512 Mb

   C. 640 MB

   D. 20 GB

4. Which file system is capable of managing global and enterprise-level operating systems?

   A. FAT

   B. FAT 32

   C. NTFS

   D. HPFS

5. Which file system is used by OS/2?

   A. FAT

   B. FAT 32

   C. NTFS

   D. HPFS

6. Which of the following is an advanced startup feature used for troubleshooting?

   A. Recovery mode

   B. Safe mode

   C. Command mode

   D. Help mode

7. Which of the following describes the ability to restore a disk to a consistent state with minimal data loss?

   A. Fault tolerance

   B. Disk recovery system

   C. Disk tolerance

   D. Fault recovery

8. What is the Windows Registry?

   A. A database for file storage

   B. A driver used when booting up

   C. A database of configuration settings

   D. A database of users

9. What does POST stand for?

   A. Preoperating system test

   B. Power of system test

   C. Preoperation self test

   D. Power-on self test

10. What does Plug and Play do?

   A. Eliminates the need to manually configure jumpers on the hardware

   B. Allows the user to plug and unplug hardware connected to the computer

   C. Loads hardware drivers for system components

   D. Configures BIOS information

11. Which of the following is a tool that provides a list of files that a user has access to?

    A. User access list

    B. Administrator access list

    C. Access control list

    D. Access control directory

12. Users can gain access to an encrypted file if they are assigned which of the following?

    A. Public key

    B. Password

    C. De-encryption code

    D. Administrator key

13. The ntldr file uses which of the following files?

    A. ntdetect.ini, boot.ini, bootsect.ini

    B. ntdetect.com, boot.sys, bootsect.ini

    C. ntdetect.sys, boot.sys, bootsect.sys

    D. ntdetect.com, boot.ini, bootsect.dos

14. What is a portion of a disk that functions as a physically separate unit of storage?

    A. Partition

    B. Slave drive

    C. Cluster

    D. Sector

15. Which of the following provides a secure set of records about the components that control the OS?

    A. BIOS

    B. Registry

    C. ini files

    D. System log

16. What is a library of hardware drivers that communicate between the OS and the hardware that is installed on the system?

    A. Hardware abstraction layer

    B. Hardware detail report

    C. Library detail report

    D. Library report layer

17. What is a tool, used before installing Windows 2000, that verifies that the hardware will work?

    A. Hardware compatibility report

    B. Hardware comparison list

    C. Hardware compatibility list

    D. Windows hardware report

18. What is the Windows Compact installation option used for?

    A. A computer with a limited amount of hard drive space

    B. A computer with a small tower case

    C. Installations that need to be done quickly

    D. Temporary installations

19. Which of the Windows NT/2000/XP system tools enables the administrator to control everything related to the local computer?

    A. Local tools

    B. Administrative tools

    C. User tools

    D. Account tools

20. Setting up the computer to boot to Windows 2000 or Windows 98 is known as what?

    A. Double-boot

    B. Multi-boot

    C. Dual-boot

    D. Semi-boot

Key Terms

access control entry (ACE)   An entry to the ACL.

access control list (ACL)   A list managed by the administrator that displays files a user has access to and the type of access that has been granted.

administrative tools   Utility that enables the administrator to control the computer system.

basic disk   A physical disk that contains the primary partition, extended partition, or logical drive.

basic disk storage   Industry standard for all versions of Windows.

compression   A tool that compresses or makes a file or folder smaller.

Compression state   Describes whether a file is compressed or uncompressed.

Device driver   Program that tells the operating system how to control specific devices.

disk management   The process of optimizing disk space.

disk quotas   Provide the ability to assign limits to the amount of hard disk space that users are allocated.

dual-boot   An option that provides the choice to boot the system to either Windows 2000 or Windows 98 if both are installed.

dynamic disk storage   A method of data storage using the hard drive(s) to create multi-disk volumes.

emergency repair disk (ERD)   Disk used to restore the operating system.

encryption   A security feature that applies a coding to a file so that only authorized users can view the file.

encryption file system (EFS)   The means to apply encryption.

FAT 16 file system   Used with DOS, Windows 3.1, and the first version of Windows 95.

FAT 32 file system   Evolved from FAT 16 and supports drives up to 2048 GB in size.

fault tolerance   The ability to restore a disk to a consistent state with minimal data loss.

file allocation table (FAT)   A database that keeps track of every file on the hard disk.

hardware abstraction layer (HAL)   A library of hardware drivers that communicate between the operating system and the hardware that is installed.

hardware compatibility list (HCL)   A tool used to verify that hardware is compatible with the operating system.

hardware profiles   Windows NT, 2000, and XP can support two or more hardware profile configurations in the Registry.

HKEY_CLASSES_ROOT   Contains configuration data of the software installed on the computer.

HKEY_CURRENT_CONFIG   Contains data on the active hardware profiles selected during the boot process.

HKEY_CURRENT_USERS   Contains data about the user that is currently logged on to the computer.

HKEY_LOCAL_MACHINE   Contains configuration data for the local computer.

HKEY_USERS   Default settings used to control individual user profiles and environments.

HPFS (high-performance file system)   Older file system used with Windows NT 3.51.

local security policy   The options selected to ensure a secure computer network.

local users   An account created that allows a user access to the network.

master boot record (MBR)   Allows programs such as DOS to load into RAM.

mirrored volume   Contains two identical copies of a simple volume that stores the same data on two separate hard drives.

ntdetect.com   Used by Intel-based systems to detect hardware that is installed in a system.

NTFS (NT file system)   Designed to manage global and enterprise-level operating systems.

partitioning and formatting   Prepare the hard drive for the installation of an operating system.

permissions   File and directory permissions used to specify which users and groups can gain access to files and folders.

power-on self-test (POST)   A diagnostic test of memory and hardware when the system is powered up.

Plug and Play (PnP)   Automatically configures devices and assigns resources for new hardware.

public key   Provides access to encrypted files.

RAID-5 volume   Consists of three or more parts of one or more drives or three or more entire drives.

Recovery Console   Command-line interface used for troubleshooting purposes.

Registry subtrees   The hierarchical structure of the Registry.

Safe mode   Advanced feature used for troubleshooting purposes.

Setup program   The program that is run to add new configuration data to the Registry.

simple volume   A basic disk that contains disk space from a complete single disk and is not fault tolerant.

spanned volume   Includes disk space from multiple disks (up to 32 disks). It is not fault tolerant.

Startup menu   Unique security feature in the Windows 9X operating system. A multistep process is used to get to the Startup menu.

stripped volume   Also known as RAID-0. Combines areas of free space from multiple hard disks, up to 32, into one logical volume. It is not fault tolerant.

user profiles   Specific settings for all the users that log on to the computer.

Windows NT kernel   Loads the correct device drivers in the proper order.

Objectives

Upon completion of this chapter, you will be able to perform the following tasks:

- Install and configure hard drives in a RAID array, and understand external peripherals, external drive subsystems, and processors for a server
- Upgrade adapters, internal and external devices, system monitoring agents, and service tools as they relate to a server
- Increase memory to improve network server performance
- Document the configuration for upgrading and troubleshooting purposes

Chapter 8

Advanced Hardware Fundamentals for Servers

Introduction

A network server is the center of a network environment. This makes the server a critical component for users to access files, e-mail, programs, printers, etc. Because of this, fault tolerance is important for a network server. *Fault tolerance* is the ability for a system to continue working when a hardware failure occurs. One method used to provide fault tolerance is RAID technology. This chapter focuses on RAID technology and discusses memory upgrades, configuration of external disk subsystems, and external CD-ROM systems.

Network Server Overview

This section includes the following topics:

- Network servers
- RAID
- RAID controllers
- Hardware RAID versus software RAID
- Hardware-based RAID configuration

Network Servers

A *network server* is a computer system in a network that is shared by multiple users. Servers come in all sizes, from x86-based PCs to IBM mainframes. A server can have a keyboard, monitor, and mouse directly attached, or one keyboard, monitor, and mouse can connect to any number of servers through a KVM switch (see the following note). Servers can also be accessed through a network connection.

The term *server* can refer to both the hardware and software (the entire computer system) or just the software that performs the service. For example, the e-mail server can refer to the e-mail server software in a system that also runs other applications, or it can refer to a computer that is dedicated only to the e-mail server application.

RAID

Redundant array of inexpensive disks (RAID) is designed to allow some fault tolerance to prevent loss of data in the event of a disk drive failure on a network server. A disk drive is a mechanical device, and therefore it can fail at any time. RAID accomplishes fault tolerance, or redundancy, through *disk drive storing parity*, or storing the same information on two different disk drives.

RAID level 1 uses duplication of the data to provide fault tolerance. RAID levels 3, 4, and 5 use parity information that is calculated from the bit patterns of the data being written to the RAID array to provide fault tolerance. When a disk drive fails in RAID 3, 4, or 5, the parity information can be used, along with the data on the remaining disk drives in the array, to calculate the data that were on the disk drive that failed. This allows the disk subsystem and the network server to keep functioning, albeit at a slower rate due to the calculations required to re-create the missing data. RAID level 2 is the oddball RAID in that it does not use duplication or parity to provide fault tolerance. Instead, RAID 2 uses a special hamming code (defined later in the section, "RAID 2").

Computer technicians disagree about the meaning of the RAID acronym. There is disagreement about how many levels of RAID are defined, whether the *I* in RAID stands for inexpensive or independent, and whether the *A* stands for array or arrays. You will find RAID 6, 7, 10, 50, 53, and others mentioned in many vendors' literature. This chapter focuses on the types of RAID that are most often used in a network environment.

RAID was defined in 1987 in the paper "A Case for Redundant Arrays of Inexpensive Disks (RAID)," written by David A. Patterson, Garth A. Gibson, and Randy H. Katz at the University of California, Berkeley. The paper defined five levels of RAID (1, 2, 3, 4, and 5) and offered the RAID solution as an alternative to SLED (single large expensive disk).

Recently, the phrase "redundant array of independent disks" has become common, substituting the word independent for inexpensive.

RAID 0

RAID 0 was not defined in the 1987 Berkeley paper. In fact, it is technically not RAID, because it provides no redundancy. *RAID 0* is just an array (or group) of disk drives used as a single disk. The data are written in chunks or stripes to all the disk drives in the array. This improves disk input/output performance in that several chunks of data can be written or read simultaneously. If a disk drive in the RAID 0 array fails, all data in the RAID 0 array are lost. RAID 0 is also often called *disk striping without parity*. Figure 8-1 shows an illustration of RAID 0.

Figure 8-1 RAID 0

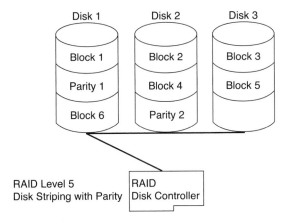

RAID 1

RAID 1 requires a minimum of two disk drives to implement. (All other RAID levels, except level 0, require at least three disk drives.) *RAID 1* writes all data to two separate locations. To store 20 GB of data using RAID 1, two 20-GB disk drives are required. This results in a 50 percent loss of storage capacity.

RAID 1 can be implemented in two ways: disk mirroring and disk duplexing. In *disk mirroring*, the two disk drives are connected to the same disk controller. The only problem with disk mirroring is that if the disk controller fails, there is no access to the mirrored data. Figure 8-2 shows a diagram of disk mirroring. To eliminate this single point of failure, use disk duplexing rather than disk mirroring.

Lab Activity on CD-ROM

In this lab, you follow the steps presented on the CD-ROM to configure RAID 1 mirroring on your PC.

In *disk duplexing*, each disk drive in the mirrored set is connected to a different disk controller. This eliminates the single point of failure in disk mirroring. The only additional cost is that of the additional disk controller. Figure 8-3 shows a diagram of disk duplexing.

Figure 8-2 RAID 1 (Disk Mirroring)

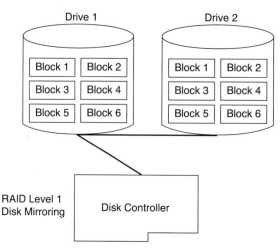

Figure 8-3 RAID 1 (Disk Duplexing)

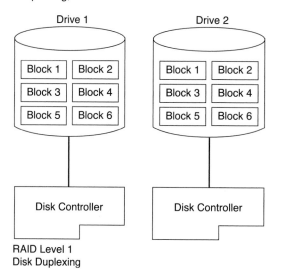

RAID 2

RAID 2 uses a hamming code to create an error correcting code (ECC) for all data to be stored on the RAID 2 array. The *error correcting code (ECC)* can detect and correct single-bit errors and detect double-bit errors. The ECC must be read and decoded each time that data are read from the disk. RAID 2 is difficult and expensive to implement and has a high overhead (for example, 3 parity bits for each 4 data bits).

RAID 2 has no commercial usage due to its expense and difficulty of implementation. It requires a minimum of three disk drives to implement.

RAID 3

RAID 3 uses bit-level parity with a single-parity disk to provide fault tolerance of data stored on the RAID 3 array in the event of failure of a single disk drive in the array. RAID 3 requires that all the disk drives in the array be synchronized. The bits of data and the parity information calculated from the data are written to all the disk drives in the array simultaneously. RAID 3 requires a minimum of three disk drives to create the array.

RAID 4

RAID 4 uses block-level parity with a single-parity disk to provide fault tolerance to the RAID 4 array in the event of failure of a single disk drive in the array. In a RAID 4 array, data and the parity information calculated from the data are written to the disk drives in blocks. There is no need for the disk drives to be synchronized, and the disk drives can be accessed independently. A minimum of three disk drives are required to create the array. The disadvantage of using RAID 4 is that the parity drive is accessed on every write operation to the RAID array. This causes heavy utilization of the parity drive, which will probably fail before the other drives in the array.

RAID 5

RAID 5 uses block-level parity but spreads the parity information among all the disk drives in the disk array. This eliminates the parity drive failure common in RAID 4 systems. The loss of storage capacity in RAID 5 systems is equivalent to the storage capacity of one of the disk drives. If you have three 10-GB disk drives in a RAID 5 array, the storage capacity of the array is 20 GB (a loss of 33 percent). As another example, if you have seven 10-GB disk drives in a RAID 5 array, the storage capacity of the array is 60 GB (a loss of 16.67 percent). Figure 8-4 shows a diagram of RAID 5.

RAID 0/1

RAID 0/1, also known as RAID 0+1 or RAID 10, is the preferred RAID array. It provides the performance of RAID 0 and the redundancy of RAID 1. RAID 0/1 requires at least four disk drives to implement. In RAID 0/1, two RAID 0 stripe sets are used (to provide high input/output performance), and these stripe sets are mirrored (to provide fault tolerance). Figure 8-5 shows a diagram of RAID 0/1.

Figure 8-4 RAID 5 (Disk Striping With Parity)

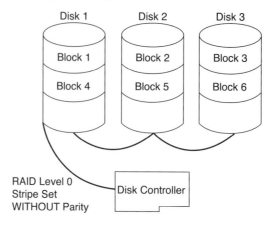

Figure 8-5 RAID 0/1 (Mirrored Stripe Set Without Parity)

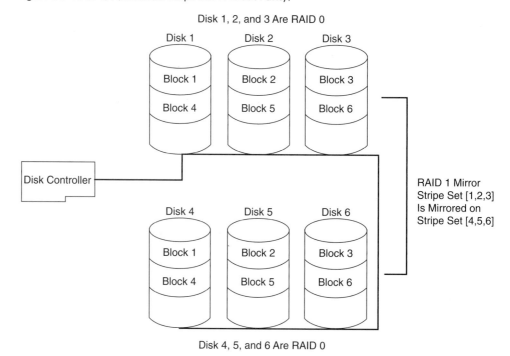

RAID Controllers

RAID controllers are specialized disk controllers that use either ATA or SCSI technologies. ATA RAID controllers are limited in the number of disks that can be attached due to ATA channel limitations. A maximum of two channels with a maximum of two disk drives per channel (for a total of four disk drives) can be attached. SCSI RAID controllers have multiple channels. (Two channels are common; RAID controllers with three, four, and five channels are available.) RAID controllers are generally expensive due to their sophistication.

RAID controllers often have an onboard memory cache ranging in size from 4 MB to 256 MB. This onboard memory cache often has a battery backup system to prevent data loss in the event of a sudden power loss to the network server. This is critical because data written from the system memory to the RAID controller are first written to the onboard cache; it could be several seconds before the data are written to the disk. Without the battery backup for the RAID controller, the onboard memory cache could prevent the data on the disk drive from being updated.

The memory cache on the RAID controller can be configured as read cache, write cache, or a combination of both. The read cache improves the read performance. The write cache allows the processor to continue with other tasks, instead of waiting for the data to be written to the disk. Figure 8-6 shows the RAID controller and the disk arrays.

Figure 8-6 The RAID Controller and Disk Arrays

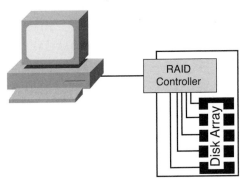

The following features should be considered when evaluating RAID controllers:

- Number of channels
- Speed of channels
- Onboard cache (read, write, or combination and battery backup option)
- Fast host adapter (PCI)
- Bus width (16-bit, 32-bit, or 64-bit)

NOTE

When using the Windows 2000 version of RAID, the hard drive must be converted to a dynamic disk before the RAID options are available to implement.

Hardware RAID Versus Software RAID

RAID is usually implemented using a RAID disk controller. However, RAID disk controllers are expensive. RAID can also be implemented in software by several network operating systems, including Novell NetWare, Microsoft Windows NT, and Microsoft Windows 2000.

Software RAID systems usually support RAID 0, 1, and 5. Software RAID is usually implemented at the disk partition level rather than at the physical disk (entire disk) level (as in hardware RAID). The drawback to software RAID is that it requires the network server processor to perform the work that is usually done by the RAID controller in hardware RAID. RAID 5 implemented in software requires the processor to calculate all the parity information when writing data to the RAID 5 disk array. RAID 1 implemented in software puts a minimal load on the network server processor.

When RAID 5 is implemented in software, the files on the RAID array are not available until the network server operating system is running. This means that the operating system cannot be stored on, and therefore cannot boot from, a RAID 5 system implemented in software. This is not an issue when a RAID 5 system is implemented using hardware.

TEST TIP

Understand the difference between hardware and software RAID.

Software-based RAID has one advantage over hardware-based RAID. In software-based RAID, the RAID implementation can be based on disk partitions rather than entire disk drives. For example, you could use three 10-GB partitions on three different disk drives to create a software RAID 5 array. Space could be available in different partitions on each of these disk drives, and this space could be used for some other purpose. In nearly all cases, hardware-based RAID is better than software-based RAID; however, having RAID implemented in software is much better than having no disk fault tolerance.

Lab Activity 8.1.2   Basic Disk to Dynamic Disk Conversion

RAID dynamic disk. In this lab, you convert a hard drive from a basic disk to a dynamic disk in order to configure RAID 0 striping on your PC.

Lab Activity on CD-ROM

In this lab, you follow the steps presented on the CD-ROM to configure RAID 0 striping on your PC.

Hardware-Based RAID Configuration

Network servers that contain a RAID controller must have the RAID system configured before the network operating system can be installed. Configuration of the RAID system consists of selecting physical disk drives and grouping them together into one of the available RAID configurations (usually RAID 1 or RAID 5). The network hardware vendor or the RAID hardware vendor usually supplies software to help configure the RAID system. The disk drives of the RAID system can be internal to the network server chassis or can be external, in a separate enclosure.

As previously discussed, RAID is used to provide fault tolerance in case of a disk drive failure in the network server. *Hardware-based RAID* means that the disk drives in the network server have RAID implemented by a special disk controller, the RAID controller. Some network operating systems can implement software-based RAID at the expense of additional load on the network server processor. Most RAID controllers are designed to use SCSI disk drives. However, at least one disk controller manufacturer makes a RAID controller that uses EIDE/ATA-2 disk drives. The RAID disk controller has its own processor to implement the RAID configuration, thus relieving the network server processor of this task.

The configuration of the RAID controller in the network server is accomplished by software that is provided by the network server (or RAID controller) vendor. Although vendor-specific, all the software works basically the same way. It enables you to view the disk drives that are attached to the RAID controller. You select the disk drives that you want to utilize and specify the version of RAID that you want to implement using the selected disk drives. The software then prepares the disk drives to implement the RAID solution. For example, you can pick two physical disk drives and tell the RAID configuration software to use these two drives to implement a RAID 1 (mirroring) solution. The RAID controller would tell the network server operating system that there is a single logical disk drive. (In reality, the RAID controller is reading from and writing to two physical disk drives.)

In another example, you could select five physical disk drives and tell the RAID configuration software to use these five drives to implement RAID 5 (disk striping with parity). The RAID controller would tell the network server operating system that there is a single logical disk drive. (In actuality, the RAID controller is reading and writing data in blocks across all five disk drives in the RAID 5 disk array.)

In yet another example, you could select the same five physical disk drives and tell the RAID configuration software to use these disk drives to implement RAID 5

TEST TIP

The Server+ exam will ask questions regarding general RAID configurations and test your general understanding of RAID.

(disk striping with parity). Furthermore, the single logical disk drive could be split into two partitions by the RAID configuration software. The network operating system would see two logical disk drives (one on each partition). (In reality, the RAID controller is reading and writing data in blocks across all five disk drives in the RAID 5 disk array.)

Figure 8-7 shows an example of how a RAID controller manages disk drives and shows the logical disk drive to the network server operating system.

Figure 8-7 RAID Controller Disk Drive Presentation

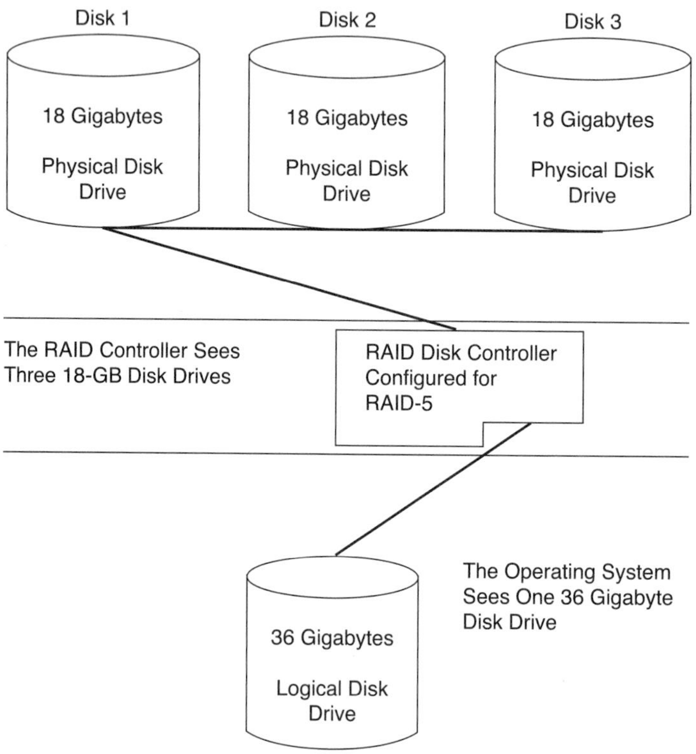

RAID 0 Configuration

RAID 0 is known as *disk striping* (specifically, it is a stripe set without parity). RAID 0 is not fault tolerant, but it is used to improve disk input/output performance. RAID 0 should not be used in a production server environment. However, RAID 0 is often used in a high-powered workstation to improve disk input/output performance by reading and writing files in blocks to several disks simultaneously as opposed to reading and writing a file sequentially to a single disk drive. You need at least two disk drives to implement RAID 0. Figure 8-8 shows an example of a RAID 0 implementation. For example, two 18-GB disk drives configured to implement RAID 0 have a storage capacity of 36 GB.

Figure 8-8 RAID 0 (Disk Striping Without Parity)

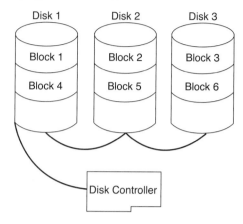

RAID 1 Configuration (Mirroring)

RAID 1 has two different implementations, disk mirroring and disk duplexing. In disk mirroring, everything written to one disk is also written to a second disk. Reading can be performed from either disk. Because data are duplicated on two different disk drives, the failure of one disk drive does not represent a catastrophe but merely an inconvenience. The network server keeps running using the single working disk drive. When time permits, the defective disk drive can be replaced, and the data on the working disk drive can be copied to the replacement, thus recreating the mirror. A minimum of two disk drives are required to implement RAID 1. In disk mirroring, both disk drives are attached to the same disk controller. The disk overhead for RAID 1 is 50 percent. The disk controller represents a single point of failure for mirrored disk drives. Figure 8-9 shows an example of a RAID 1 (mirroring) implementation.

RAID 1 Configuration (Duplexing)

Disk duplexing eliminates the single point of failure that exists in disk mirroring. This is done by adding another disk controller and configuring the RAID system to duplicate data on disk drives that are attached to two different disk controllers. There is generally no significant performance difference between disk mirroring and disk duplexing. You are just adding further redundancy in the form of a second controller. The overhead of RAID 1 (mirroring or duplexing) is 50 percent. Figure 8-10 shows an example of a RAID 1 (duplexing) implementation.

Figure 8-9 RAID 1 (Disk Mirroring)

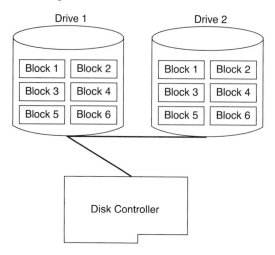

Figure 8-10 RAID 1 (Disk Duplexing)

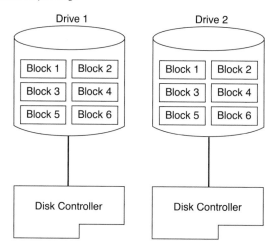

RAID 5 Configuration

RAID 5 uses a more complicated scheme to provide fault tolerance in the case of a single disk failure. A previous section provides an in-depth discussion of RAID 5.

RAID 5 requires a minimum of three disk drives to implement. The disk drives that comprise a RAID 5 solution are often referred to as a *RAID 5 array*. The failure of a single disk drive does not cause the network server to fail. The missing information that was on the failed disk can be recreated on the fly using the information on the remaining disks. The failed disk drive should be replaced as quickly as possible. RAID

5 cannot survive the failure of a second disk drive after one disk drive has failed. Because of this fact, some RAID systems allow the configuration of a hot spare disk drive. A *hot spare disk drive* is powered up and running, but contains no data; it is waiting for a drive in the disk array to fail so that it can be used.

When a disk drive in the RAID array fails, the RAID system starts rebuilding the data that were on the failed drive on the hot spare disk drive. This hot spare methodology minimizes the amount of time it takes to get the RAID array rebuilt and minimizes the amount of time that the RAID system is vulnerable to a second drive failure. Figure 8-11 shows an example of a RAID 5 implementation.

Figure 8-11 RAID 5 (Disk Striping With Parity)

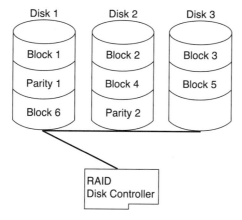

RAID 5 is more efficient than the other RAID levels in that the overhead is $(1/n) \times 100$, where n is the number of disk drives in the RAID 5 array. You essentially lose the capacity of one of the disk drives in the RAID 5 array. This space is used to store the parity information. (In reality, the parity information is stored across all the drives in the RAID 5 array.)

The total storage capacity of the RAID 5 array is $(n-1) \times c$, where c is the capacity of each of the disk drives.

RAID 0/1 Configuration

RAID 0/1 (sometimes called RAID 0+1 or RAID 10) involves mirroring (or duplexing) two RAID 0 arrays. This yields the fault tolerance of RAID 1 and the input/output speed of RAID 0. RAID 0/1 requires a minimum of four disk drives to implement. Figure 8-12 shows an example of a RAID 0/1 implementation.

Figure 8-12 RAID 0/1 (Mirrored Stripe Sets Without Parity)

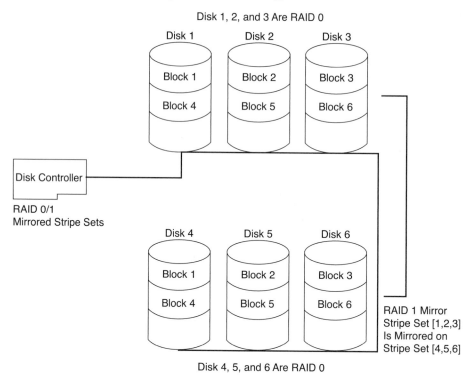

Worksheet 8.1.3 RAID

In this worksheet, you review the information on RAID and identify the different types of RAID.

Configuring External Peripherals

This section discusses the following topics:

- Understanding external disk subsystems
- Configuring an external disk subsystem
- Configuring an external CD-ROM system

Understanding External Disk Subsystems

External disk subsystems are necessary when the amount of disk storage cannot be accommodated by the disk drive bays that are internal to the network server chassis.

These external disk subsystems can be either SCSI or fibre channel. Generally, fibre channel–based systems can support many more disk drives than a SCSI-based external system. External CD-ROM systems are generally used to implement CD-ROM libraries, which can accommodate a large number of CD-ROM drives and make them available to client computers on the network. The network servers that implement CD-ROM libraries are often called *CD-ROM servers*.

Configuring an External Disk Subsystem

Even though server-class computers often have many empty bays that are designed to hold disk drives, it is often necessary to have disk drives that are external to the server chassis. An external disk subsystem can consist of a single disk drive in its own chassis with its own power supply. On the high end, an external disk subsystem chassis might have 100 or more disk drives in it.

The simple external disk subsystem that contains only a few disk drives could be attached to the external port of a SCSI or RAID controller. The external disk drives would then function in the same way as internal disk drives.

Some large external disk subsystems have a built-in RAID mechanism. These large systems are often configured separately from the disk controller in the network server to which they are to be attached.

You can often configure large external disk subsystems to be shared by more than one network server. This is one way to implement a high-availability server solution.

To connect the external disk subsystem to the network server, you could use a standard external SCSI cable or fibre channel.

Generally, fibre channel–based external disk systems can handle a large number of disk drives. In all cases, be sure to turn on the power switch of the external disk subsystem before starting up the network server.

Configuring an External CD-ROM System

External CD-ROM systems are often referred to as a *CD-ROM library*. Imagine a tower chassis with 7, 14, 21, or more CD-ROM drives. Having these CD-ROM drives attached to a network server means that it is possible to share all these CD-ROM drives and the CDs that they contain with all users on the network. The process of attaching that many CD-ROM drives to a single network server is straightforward.

Part of the SCSI standard is a little-used feature called a *logical unit number (LUN)*. Although LUNs are defined in the SCSI standards, they are seldom used (except on large groups of CD-ROM drives). A LUN enables you to assign sub-SCSI IDs to a

NOTE

Fibre channel can be configured point to point, through a switched topology or in an arbitrated loop (FC-AL), with or without a hub, which can connect up to 127 nodes. Fibre channel supports transmission rates up to 2.12 GBps in each direction, and speeds up to 4.25 GBps are expected in the future.

TEST TIP

Know how to configure external peripherals, such as external subsystems and CD-ROM systems.

single SCSI ID. This means that you could have seven CD-ROM drives, all with the SCSI ID of 5, each having a different LUN (1 through 7), all on the same SCSI channel. Therefore, on a single SCSI channel with SCSI IDs of 1 through 7, you could have seven LUNs for each SCSI ID, for a total of 49 CD-ROM drives on a single SCSI channel. To configure the external CD-ROM system, follow the manufacturer's installation and configuration instructions. Be sure that the external CD-ROM system is powered up before starting up the network server.

Adding Hardware to a Server

Processor upgrades fall into two general categories: replacing an existing processor with a faster processor and adding a processor to a multiprocessor-capable network server. This section covers the following topics:

- Replacing a single processor with a faster processor
- Installing additional processors
- Upgrading the operating system for multiple processors
- Adding hard drives
- Adding memory

Replacing a Single Processor with a Faster Processor

Determining whether a processor in a network server can be replaced with a faster processor depends on several factors, the most important of which is whether the motherboard in the network server can support a processor with a faster clock speed. Other factors include the physical package that the existing processor uses and whether a faster processor is available that utilizes that physical package (or form factor). You can obtain this important upgrade information from the manufacturer of the network server's motherboard. Check the motherboard manufacturer's website to determine whether you can upgrade the processor to a faster processor. Next, determine whether a faster processor is available in a form factor that is compatible with the existing processor. Upgrading to a faster processor might also require you to upgrade the BIOS on the system board. Use the following steps when performing a single-processor upgrade:

Step 1 Follow the upgrade checklist.

Step 2 Upgrade the system BIOS.

Step 3 Open the network server chassis [following electrostatic discharge (ESD) safety practices].

Step 4   Remove the current processor.

Step 5   Insert the new processor.

Step 6   Close the network server chassis.

Step 7   Verify that the new processor is recognized by the network server hardware and the network operating system.

Installing Additional Processors

To add another processor to a multiprocessor-capable network server, the new processor must meet the following criteria:

- Be the same model of processor (Pentium, Pentium Pro, Pentium II, Pentium II Xeon, Pentium III, Pentium III Xeon, Pentium 4, and so on) as the existing processor
- Have the same clock speed
- Have the same level 2 (L2) cache size
- Match the stepping within one version ($N+1$)

Determining what processor is currently in your network server is straightforward. Intel provides information on all of its processors at its website. The company also offers a utility that detects and identifies the Intel processor that is currently in your network server.

The Intel processor identification utility is available in two versions: one that operates under the Windows operating system and one that runs from a bootable DOS floppy disk. The Windows version of the Intel identification utility can be downloaded from the following website:

> http://support.intel.com/support/processors/tools/frequencyid/freqid.htm

Figure 8-13 shows sample output from the Windows version of the Intel identification program.

You can download the bootable floppy disk version of the Intel identification utility from the following website:

> http://support.intel.com/support/processors/tools/frequencyid/bootable.htm

Figure 8-14 shows sample output from the bootable floppy disk version of the Intel identification program.

Figure 8-13 Intel Identification Program (Windows Version)

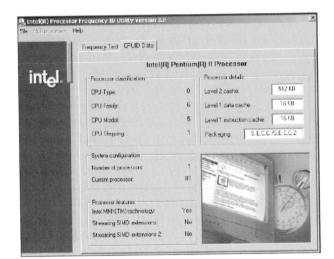

Figure 8-14 Intel Identification Program (DOS Version)

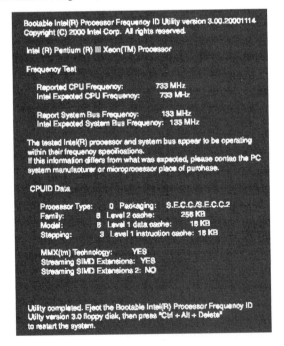

You can find a description of the Intel identification program, along with installation instructions, at the following website:

http://support.intel.com/support/processors/tools/frequencyid/download.htm

You also can identify the current processor by a tag on the processor itself. This tag contains a 5-digit spec number that starts with the letter *S*. You can use the spec number from the processor label and the following Intel websites to identify the processor that is currently in your network server:

- Pentium: http://developer.intel.com/design/pentium/qit/
- Pentium Pro: http://developer.intel.com/design/pro/qit/index.htm
- Pentium II: http://support.intel.com/support/processors/sspec/p2p.htm
- Pentium II Xeon: http://support.intel.com/support/processors/sspec/p2xp.htm
- Pentium III: http://support.intel.com/support/processors/sspec/p3p.htm
- Pentium III Xeon: http://support.intel.com/support/processors/sspec/p3xp.htm
- Pentium 4: http://support.intel.com/supprt/processors/sspec/p4p.htm

The processor that you are adding to the network server should come with installation instructions. However, you can also obtain Intel processor installation manuals at the following website:

http://support.intel.com/support/processors/manuals/

Use the following steps when adding a processor to a network server:

Step 1 Follow the upgrade checklist.

Step 2 Open the network server chassis (following ESD safety practices).

Step 3 Insert the new processor(s).

Step 4 Close the network server chassis.

Step 5 Upgrade the system BIOS.

Step 6 Upgrade the operating system to recognize multiple processors.

Step 7 Verify that the new processor is recognized by the network server hardware and the network operating system.

Upgrading the Operating System for Multiple Processors

A network server's operating system often does not recognize that an additional processor has been installed on the server. The following sections detail how to remedy this situation.

Windows NT Server 4

If your original installation of Windows NT Server 4 was on a network server with a single processor, the hardware abstraction layer (HAL) on the network server must be updated for the network server to recognize and use multiple processors. To upgrade Windows NT 4 to a multiprocessor HAL, use the uptomp.exe utility file that is available in the Microsoft Windows NT 4 Server Resource Kit.

For information about the processors recognized by the current version of Microsoft Windows NT Server 4, open a command prompt window and type **SET**. This command prints a list of all the current environment variables. Look for the variable Number_of_processors to see how many processors Windows NT Server 4 recognizes.

Windows 2000 Server

If your original installation of Windows 2000 Server was on a network server with a single processor, the HAL on the network server must be updated for the network server to recognize and use multiple processors. To install support for multiple processors in Windows 2000 Server, follow the procedure in Step by Step 4.3 (from Microsoft Knowledge Base Article Q234558).

Use the following steps to activate multiple processor support in Windows 2000 Server:

Step 1   Choose **Start, Settings, Control Panel,** and click System.

Step 2   Click the Hardware tab, and select Device Manager.

Step 3   Double-click to expand the Computer branch. Note the type of support that you currently have.

Step 4   Double-click the computer type that is listed under the Computer branch, select the Drivers tab, select Update Driver, and click Next.

Step 5   Click Display a List of Known Drivers for This Device, and then click Show All Hardware of This Device Class.

Step 6   Click the appropriate computer type (one that matches your current type, except for multiple CPUs), click Next, and click Finish.

For information about the processors recognized by the current version of Microsoft Windows 2000 Server, open a command prompt window and type **SET**. This command prints a list of all the current environment variables. Look for the variable Number_of_processors to see how many processors Windows 2000 Server recognizes.

Novell NetWare 5

If your original installation of Novell NetWare 5 was on a network server with a single processor, you must make several changes in the configuration of the server for it to recognize and use multiple processors. To upgrade Novell NetWare 5 so that it recognizes the additional processor, follow these steps:

Step 1   Load NWCONFIG | Multi CPU Options | Select a Platform Support Module.

Step 2   Restart the network server after NWCONFIG modifies the startup.ncf and autoexec.ncf files.

For information about the processors recognized by the current version of Novell NetWare 5, type **DISPLAY PROCESSORS** on the NetWare console.

Red Hat Linux

For Red Hat Linux (and other versions of Linux) to recognize multiple processors, the Linux kernel must be rebuilt. Make sure that the main Makefile (/usr/src/linux/Makefile) contains the following line:

    SMP=1

Rebuild the Linux kernel using the normal methods. For information about the processors that are recognized by the current version of Linux, type **cat /proc/cpuinfo** at the command prompt.

Worksheet 8.4.3   Adding Processors

This worksheet reviews the steps required to add a processor for a server.

Adding Hard Drives

Disk drive upgrades come in two varieties: adding disk drives to an existing network server and replacing existing disk drives with larger or faster disk drives. Upgrades to disk drives have the most potential of any upgrade to destroy data. Before attempting a disk drive upgrade, make sure that you have one, and preferably two, verified full backups of the data on the disk drives.

Upgrading ATA Hard Disk Drives

This section shows you how to upgrade ATA hard disk drives. For brevity, the term ATA is used to refer to IDE/ATA, EIDE/ATA-2, and Ultra ATA hard disk drives. The process is the same for all versions of ATA disk drives.

Upgrades to ATA disk drives generally fall into two categories: adding disk drives and replacing existing disk drives with faster or larger disk drives.

Adding ATA disk drives to an existing ATA disk subsystem is relatively straightforward. ATA disk controllers generally have two channels to which ATA devices (disk drives, CD-ROM drives, and so on) can be attached. Each channel consists of a ribbon cable that can be up to 18 inches long, to which a maximum of two disk drives can be attached. One end of the channel is attached to the ATA disk controller, which can be built into the system board. The channel (a 40-conductor ribbon cable) usually has two 40-pin connectors attached to it. These 40-pin connectors are used to attach ATA disk drives to the ATA channel.

The ATA channels are usually labeled primary and secondary so that the system can distinguish between them. When only a single disk drive is attached to the ATA disk controller, you can attach a second disk drive in either of the two following ways:

- Attach the second disk drive to the same ribbon cable as the existing disk drive using the second 40-pin connector on the ribbon cable. In this case, one disk drive must be set to the master ATA disk role, and the other must be set to the slave ATA disk role. Alternatively, you could set cable select (CSEL) for both disk drives.
- Attach the second disk drive to the secondary ATA channel using a second ribbon cable for the ATA controller. Set this single drive to either the single drive or master ATA disk role, depending on the manufacturer's instructions for configuring a single disk drive on an ATA channel.

By putting the second ATA disk drive on the secondary channel, thus having one ATA disk drive on each ATA channel, you can enhance the performance of the disk subsystem.

A system BIOS upgrade might be required when upgrading from small ATA disk drives to large ATA disk drives. See the section, "Upgrading Adapter BIOS or Firmware" later in this chapter for details on how to upgrade the system BIOS. Older system BIOSs might not be able to address all the space on large ATA disk drives. The definition of large has changed over the years. Various definitions have been 504 MB, 1 GB, 2 GB, 4 GB, and 8.4 GB. Many of these barriers to ATA have been overcome by newer or improved BIOSs.

Disk drives are characterized by their rotational speed. Common rotational speeds are 5400 rpm, 7200 rpm, and 10,000 rpm. Generally, the higher the rotational speed, the faster the disk can access data. Upgrading from slow disk drives to faster disk drives involves a complete replacement of the disk drives.

Changing from IDE/ATA/EIDE/ATA-2 Disk Drives to SCSI Disk Drives

There is no upgrade path from IDE/ATA/EIDE/ATA-2 disk drives to SCSI disk drives. To change from IDE/ATA/EIDE/ATA-2 disk drives to SCSI disk drives, you must remove all the IDE/ATA/EIDE/ATA-2 disk drives, remove or disable the built-in IDE/EIDE controller, and install a SCSI bus controller and SCSI disk drives.

Upgrading to SCSI Hard Disk Drives

Upgrades to SCSI disk drives fall into two categories:

1. Adding SCSI disks to an existing SCSI channel

2. Replacing existing SCSI disks with disk drives that have a higher rotational speed

The SCSI disk drive in the upgrade should match the existing SCSI disk in SCSI level (1, 2, or 3), type (normal or wide), and signaling system (SE, LVD, or differential).

Adding SCSI Hard Disk Drives

Adding SCSI disk drives to an existing SCSI channel is a simple process. To guarantee the success of the addition, however, the server administrator or hardware specialist must review the documentation of the SCSI bus. You need to know the SCSI IDs of the existing disk drives and where the SCSI bus is terminated. For internal SCSI devices, you also need to determine whether any SCSI connectors are available on the SCSI bus ribbon cable. If no SCSI connectors are available, obtain a new SCSI ribbon cable with the correct number of connectors. Set the SCSI ID of the new disk drive to a SCSI ID that is not already in use on the SCSI bus. You might also have to move the SCSI terminator; remember that the SCSI bus must be terminated at both ends.

External SCSI devices are usually connected to the SCSI channel in a daisy-chain manner. Adding an external SCSI device involves picking a SCSI ID that is not currently in use on the SCSI channel and adding the SCSI device into the daisy chain. Exceeding the SCSI cable length is the biggest problem encountered when adding an external SCSI device. The second most common problem is improper termination of both ends of the SCSI bus.

Replacing SCSI Hard Disk Drives

To replace an existing SCSI hard disk, remove the old SCSI hard disk and check the SCSI ID. Set the SCSI ID on the new SCSI hard disk to match the SCSI ID of the SCSI disk drive that was removed, and install the new SCSI hard disk. If the SCSI disk to be replaced uses an SCA connector, you can remove the old SCSI disk drive and insert the new SCSI disk drive in its place. SCA connectors automatically set the SCSI ID of the SCSI disk drive.

NOTE

To boot from a SCSI disk drive, the BIOS on the SCSI bus controller must be enabled, and the SCSI ID of the boot disk must be set to 0.

Adding Drives to a RAID Array

Adding drives to a SCSI-based RAID array is no different from adding drives to a SCSI channel, except that after the disk drives are added to the array, you must use the RAID configuration utility to add the disk drives to the RAID array.

New Drives in a Separate Array

If you configure the newly installed disk drives as a separate array from the existing array, the data on the existing disk array will be unaffected.

For example, if you have an existing RAID 5 array consisting of three disk drives and you install two new disk drives that you want to configure as a RAID 1 array, the original RAID 5 array will not be affected. No data will be lost on the original array. After installing the two new disk drives, use the array configuration utility to initialize the two new disk drives and configure them as a RAID 1 array. The RAID controller then has two separate RAID arrays configured: the original RAID 5 array, consisting of three disk drives, and the new RAID 1 array, consisting of two disk drives.

New Drives in an Existing Array

If you want the newly installed SCSI disk drives to become part of an existing RAID array, you must initialize all the disk drives in the array, including the existing drives. As a result, you will lose data on the existing disk drives.

For example, if you have an existing RAID 5 array consisting of three disk drives and you install two new disk drives that you want to configure into a RAID 5 array using all five disk drives, you must initialize all five disk drives. You can then combine the five disk drives into a single RAID 5 array using all five disk drives. However, the data that were on the original RAID 5 array (with the three disk drives) will be destroyed in the process and must be reloaded from your backup source. The RAID controller will have a single RAID 5 array consisting of five disk drives.

Adding Memory

Generally, you cannot have too much memory in a server. However, there are a few exceptions. You can only put as much memory in the network server as it was designed to use. There is always a maximum amount of memory that can be supported by the processors and/or the control chipsets of the motherboard of the network server. Also, you cannot have more memory than the network server operating system can utilize. You must keep both of these exceptions in mind when considering a memory upgrade to a network server.

Check Existing Memory

Before adding memory to a network server, verify the current memory configuration. The documentation for configuring the network server should have all the details for memory configuration. However, when this information is not readily available, you need to determine it. The most reliable way to check the existing memory configuration is to open the chassis of the network server. You need answers to the following questions:

- How many memory slots are in the network server?
- How many memory slots are empty and available for additional memory to be installed?
- What is the size (in megabytes) and speed of the current memory modules?
- What type of memory module [single inline memory module (SIMM), dual inline memory module (DIMM), Rambus inline memory module (RIMM), buffered, unbuffered, or registered] is currently installed?
- What type of memory module (EDO, DRAM, SDRAM, or RDRAM) is used in the network server?
- What error-detection method (parity, nonparity, ECC, or non-ECC) is used in the memory module?

Answer these questions by reviewing the documentation that shipped with the network server. You might also find this information in the log that was kept as part of the installation process.

Checking Memory Upgrade Feasibility

Before attempting a memory upgrade, first determine whether the network server hardware can support the amount of memory that you want to add to the network server. Some system board control chipsets limit the amount of memory that can be utilized in the network server. Limitations might also apply to the maximum size of a memory module that you can place into a single memory slot. The best source of information about how much memory can be installed in a particular network server is the documentation that came with the server or the network server vendor's website.

You also should verify that the network server operating system supports the amount of memory that you plan to install. Check the network server operating system vendor's website for the maximum memory supported.

NOTE

You might have to remove the existing memory modules and replace them with larger memory modules to achieve the total amount of memory required. For example, if the network server has only four memory slots and two of them are occupied by 64-MB memory modules and you want to achieve a total of 512 MB (which requires four 128-MB modules), you must remove the two 64-MB memory modules.

Checking Memory Upgrade Compatibility

After verifying the items discussed in the previous sections, check the network server vendor's hardware compatibility list to make sure that the vendor has certified the memory that you have selected.

One other important consideration is the metal plating on the leads of the memory module. Two common metals, tin and gold, are used on the memory module leads and the connectors in the memory slots. Both metals work fine. However, never mix the two metals (for example, gold on the memory module and tin in the connector or vice versa). This mismatching of metals causes corrosion at the contact points and results in a bad connection over time. This bad connection causes memory errors.

Installing Additional Memory

After determining the feasibility of the memory upgrade and the compatibility of the memory with the network server, the last step is to install the additional memory. Be sure to install the memory according to the manufacturer's instructions. Remember that the memory modules might have to be installed in pairs or groups of four. Most network servers have SIMMs, DIMMs, or RIMMs.

Figure 8-15 shows a diagram of a SIMM installation. Figure 8-16 shows a diagram of DIMM and RIMM installations.

NOTE

RIMM is commonly believed to stand for "Rambus inline memory module." Rambus licenses its memory designs to semiconductor companies, which manufacture the chips. Kingston Technology has trademarked the term RIMM and uses only that term.

RIMM installation differs only slightly from DIMM installation. All memory module slots designed to use RIMMs must be populated. If a RIMM is not installed in a slot, a continuity module, which contains no memory, must be installed in that slot. Adding a RIMM involves removing a continuity module and replacing it with a RIMM. Failure to have continuity modules in the memory slots not occupied by RIMMs can result in a network server that does not power up.

Figure 8-15 SIMM Installation

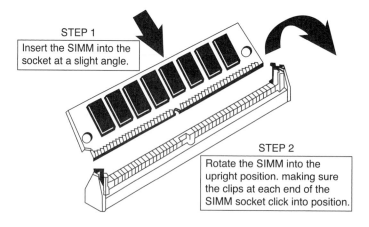

STEP 1
Insert the SIMM into the socket at a slight angle.

STEP 2
Rotate the SIMM into the upright position. making sure the clips at each end of the SIMM socket click into position.

Figure 8-16 DIMM/RIMM Installation

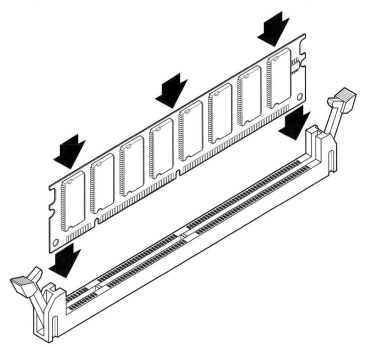

While performing a memory upgrade, be sure to follow the upgrade checklist.

Upgrading Server Components

Adapter upgrades also fall into several categories: upgrading components on the adapter, such as memory; upgrading the BIOS or firmware on the adapter; and replacing the adapter with a newer, faster, or more powerful adapter. This section covers the following topics:

- Upgrading adapter memory
- Upgrading adapter BIOS or firmware
- Replacing an adapter
- Upgrading peripheral devices
- Upgrading system-monitoring agents
- Upgrading service tools
- Documenting the configuration

Upgrading Adapter Memory

Network server adapters often have onboard memory that you can upgrade. Follow the adapter manufacturer's instructions to perform the memory upgrade. The following adapters use onboard memory:

- **Video adapter**—Uses memory to store the image that is displayed on the monitor. More memory on the video adapter allows higher resolution and/or more colors to be supported on the video monitor.

- **SCSI adapter**—Uses onboard memory as a buffer or cache between the SCSI disk drives and the network server's memory. All read and write operations actually occur in the buffer rather than on the disk drive. The larger the onboard memory buffer, the faster the information can be supplied to the network server.

- **RAID controller**—Uses onboard memory in much the same way that a SCSI adapter uses memory—as a buffer. One major difference between the two is that the onboard memory on a RAID controller is often backed up by an onboard battery. This prevents the loss of data that are in the buffer if the network server loses power unexpectedly.

Upgrading Adapter BIOS or Firmware

Upgrading the BIOS or firmware on an adapter is similar to upgrading the system BIOS. Although the upgrade steps are vendor specific, they are generally as follows:

Step 1   Locate the latest BIOS or firmware on the adapter vendor's website.

Step 2   Download the BIOS or firmware upgrade, and follow the vendor's instructions to install the upgrade.

Replacing an Adapter

You generally replace adapters after they fail. The replacement procedure generally uses the following steps:

Step 1   Power down the network server.

Step 2   Remove the defective adapter.

Step 3   Install the new adapter.

Step 4   Power up the network server.

Obviously, this process requires that the network server be taken out of operation. This results in downtime and lost productivity. However, a recent technology known as *PCI hot plug* (or *PCI hot swap*) enables you to replace, upgrade, or add an adapter without powering down the network server. PCI hot plug has three capabilities:

- **Hot replacement**—Removing a failed PCI adapter and inserting an identical adapter into the same slot while the network server is operational
- **Hot upgrade**—Replacing an existing adapter with an upgraded adapter while the network server is running
- **Hot expansion**—Installing a new adapter into a previously empty slot while the network server is running

For PCI hot plug to work, the network server hardware, the adapter drivers, and the network server operating system must be PCI hot plug aware. The network server hardware allows power to be removed from individual PCI slots and allows adapters to be removed and inserted without the use of a screwdriver. On a PCI bus that supports hot plug, a slot release lever replaces the use of a screw to secure the adapter in the PCI slot.

The following steps detail how to use a PCI hot plug to add an adapter:

Step 1   Open the network server chassis.

Step 2   Open the slot release lever on an available PCI slot. This removes power from the selected PCI slot.

Step 3   Install the adapter into the selected PCI slot.

Step 4   Attach any necessary cables to the adapter.

Step 5   Close the slot release lever to secure the adapter in the PCI slot.

Step 6   Press the PCI hot plug button. This reapplies power to the PCI slot.

Step 7   The network server operating system locates and loads the appropriate device drivers for the adapter or prompts the installer for the location of the appropriate device drivers.

Step 8   Close the server chassis.

Worksheet 8.5.3   Adapters

This worksheet reviews the information learned network server adapters.

Upgrading Peripheral Devices

A *peripheral device* is any device that is not part of the core computer system (processor, memory, or data bus). Peripheral devices can be either internal or external to the network server chassis.

Internal peripherals include components such as hard disk drives, CD-ROM drives, floppy disk drives, and network interface cards (NICs). Upgrading disk drives (EIDE and SCSI) is covered in the section, "Adding Hard Drives," earlier in this chapter.

Replacing, upgrading, or adding internal peripherals, such as a CD-ROM drive, DVD-ROM drive, Zip drive, tape drive, or NIC, requires you to shut down the network server. To install the drives, follow the manufacturer's installation instructions. To install the NIC, follow the manufacturer's installation instructions after you have identified an empty PCI slot for the card. Be sure to download the latest drivers for the NIC from the NIC vendor's website.

Some network servers have peer PCI buses, and the data load should be balanced among the buses. This requires some knowledge of which PCI slots are on which PCI bus as well as the data load placed on the PCI bus by the adapters currently on each PCI bus.

If the adapters are not Plug and Play compatible, you might have to configure the adapters with an interrupt (IRQ), a direct memory access (DMA) channel, or an input/output (I/O) address. The IRQ, DMA, and I/O address cannot conflict with any adapter already installed in the network server. As with all upgrades, be sure to follow the upgrade checklist.

External peripherals are devices that are external to the network server chassis (such as a printer, modem, monitor, keyboard, or mouse). External devices might be hot swappable (for example, printers and monitors). Other external devices might require you to shut down the network server before they can be upgraded. Follow the manufacturer's installation instructions for external peripherals. As with all upgrades, be sure to follow the upgrade checklist.

Upgrading System-Monitoring Agents

System-monitoring agents are software specific to the network server (and supplied by the network vendor). These agents are generally installed, at the installer's option, when using the vendor-supplied operating system installation-assistance software. As the network server vendor releases newer versions of the system-monitoring agents, you must upgrade the system-monitoring agents. Because the agents are extremely vendor specific, you must follow the vendor's installation instructions to upgrade the system-monitoring agents. In some cases, the agents can predict the impending failure of network server components (such as the processor, memory, or hard disk drives).

System-monitoring agents monitor various aspects of the network server (such as configuration, mass storage, network interface card, system utilization, thermal conditions, and operating system status). The agents typically use standard protocols such as HTTP, SNMP, and DMI to report information to a management console. The management console can be a standard web browser (for example, Netscape Communicator or MS

Internet Explorer), a vendor-supplied management console (for example, Compaq's Insight Manager), or a third-party network-management console (such as Hewlett-Packard's OpenView).

As with all upgrades, be sure to follow the upgrade checklist.

Upgrading Service Tools

Because of the unique nature of network servers compared to standard desktop computers, a variety of service tools are needed to configure, troubleshoot, and maintain the network servers. These service tools are software that is installed on the network server during the installation and configuration processes.

Network server vendors often release new versions of these tools to fix bugs, add new features, or add support for new hardware to the utilities.

Some service tools are part of the network operating system. Updates to these service tools are available from the network server operating system vendor. These updated tools are generally available on either CDs supplied by the network server vendor or as downloads from the vendor's website. After you have access to the updated tools, follow the vendor's installation instructions to install the updated tools on the network server. As with any upgrade, follow the upgrade checklist. Upgrading service tools is generally a software operation.

Upgrading the utilities on the diagnostic partition, which is only available at network server boot time, usually requires you to shut down the network server. This means that you need to schedule downtime to upgrade the software utilities on the diagnostic partition.

Most service tools fall into one of the following general categories:

- **Diagnostic tools**—Several sets of utilities can be categorized as diagnostic tools. Some diagnostic tools might be installed on the diagnostic partition and be specific to the network server. Other diagnostic tools comprise part of the network server operating system. Third-party diagnostic tools are also available.
- **EISA configuration utility**—On network servers that have an EISA bus, the EISA configuration utility enables you to configure the components of the network server. EISA is not Plug and Play compatible, and adapters installed in the network server must have a configuration file loaded from a disk to allow configuration of the adapter. The EISA configuration utility is used while the network operating system is not loaded.

- **Diagnostic partition utilities**—The utilities in the diagnostic partition enable you to view and change the configuration of the hardware components in the network server without the server operating system being loaded. This enables you to troubleshoot nonfunctioning hardware components.
- **Server support utilities**—These utilities (for example, backup software and anti-virus software) play a vital role in support of the network server.

Documenting the Configuration

A crucial part of being a good administrator is documenting problems and the procedures used to fix them. Having good documentation provides reduced troubleshooting time the next time a similar problem occurs.

TEST TIP

Documentation is a part of the upgrading and troubleshooting process. Be able to explain the documentation process and why it is so important.

As you install, configure, or fix the server, record each step of your success or failure. The server also keeps logs, which are stored on the hard disk and can become rather large. Depending on the amount of hard disk space you have delegated to the log files, you might have to print or archive these files to backup media. The files should be periodically removed to make room for more recent log files.

Document the following items during and after the server is installed and configured:

- Network operating system version.
- Update level for the network operating system.
- RAID configuration.
- Server name.
- Antivirus software and version.
- Backup software and version.
- Network address for each NIC.
- Location and size of swap file(s).
- SNMP community name.
- System-monitoring agents installed.
- System BIOS version.
- Server baseline measurements.
- Amount of memory, including the size and type of each memory module and which memory slot it occupies. Also record the number of available (empty) memory slots.
- Number of SCSI or RAID controllers.
- SCSI channel, ID, and size and the speed of each SCSI disk drive.
- SCSI ID of the tape backup system.
- SCSI ID of the CD-ROM/DVD-ROM drive.

Summary

This chapter discussed advanced hardware fundamentals for servers. Some of the important concepts to retain from this chapter are as follows:

- Fault tolerance is the ability for a system to continue when a hardware failure occurs. Fault tolerance is critical in a network server that provides users the ability to share files, programs, printers, etc.

- RAID stands for redundant array of inexpensive disks. It is designed to provide fault tolerance in the event of a disk drive failure on a network server.

- RAID 1 requires two disk drives. All other RAID levels (except RAID 0) require at least three disk drives. There are two ways to implement RAID 1: through disk mirroring or disk duplexing.

- RAID is typically implemented using a RAID disk controller but can also be implemented in software. Software RAID is implemented at the disk partition level, supporting RAID 0, 1, and 5. Hardware RAID is implemented on the physical disk, providing more reliable fault tolerance.

- External disk subsystems are added when the amount of disk storage cannot be accommodated by internal disk drives. Simple external disk subsystems with only a few disk drives function the same way that internal disk drives function. Large subsystems can have built-in RAID mechanisms and are often configured separately from the network server.

- Upgrading the processor or installing an additional processor can improve the performance of the server. Before proceeding, verify that the motherboard can accommodate the upgrade or can support multiple processors. Check the motherboard manual or the motherboard manufacturer's website.

- Disk drive upgrades can be accomplished by adding to the existing drives or by replacing drives with larger and faster drives.

- Increasing memory on your server improves performance, but processors have a maximum amount of memory that they can support. Check the feasibility and compatibility of adding new memory to the existing server before proceeding.

- System-monitoring agents and service tools should be updated regularly. System-monitoring agents monitor configuration, mass storage, the NIC, system utilization, thermal conditions, and the operating system status. Service tools maintain the system and for troubleshooting purposes.

- A network administrator must document the configuration of the network server. Service logs and other log files provide valuable data when troubleshooting the system should problems reoccur. Make sure that information is detailed and current.

The next chapter introduces you to PC networking. It discusses the types of networks, the components of a network, and how to connect to the Internet.

Check Your Understanding

The following are review questions for the A+ exam. Answers can be found in Appendix B, "Answers to Check Your Understanding Review Questions."

1. Which RAID level provides improved disk input/output but provides no redundancy?

   A. RAID 0

   B. RAID 1

   C. RAID 3

   D. RAID 5

2. Which RAID level provides redundancy at the expense of 50 percent of the disk storage capacity?

   A. RAID 0

   B. RAID 1

   C. RAID 3

   D. RAID 5

3. Which of the following RAID levels provides fault tolerance using parity information and requires a minimum of three disk drives?

   A. RAID 0 and RAID 1

   B. RAID 4 and RAID 5

   C. RAID 1, RAID 4, and RAID 5

   D. RAID 0 and RAID 4

4. You have a group of six 36-GB disk drives that you want to configure as a RAID 5 array. After you have configured the RAID array with the six disk drives, what is the storage capacity, in GB, of the single logical drive that is created by the RAID array?

   A. 216

   B. 180

   C. 108

   D. 36

5. Which of the following technologies allows a network server to run more programs than it can fit into its physical RAM?

   A. RAID 1

   B. RAID 5

   C. Virtual memory

   D. Backup software

6. Which of the following software packages are not normally installed on a network server to support its operation?

   A. Antivirus software

   B. Backup software

   C. UPS monitoring software

   D. Spreadsheet software

7. Which RAID level does not provide fault tolerance?

   A. RAID 0

   B. RAID 1

   C. RAID 5

   D. RAID 10

8. After installing a second processor in a network server, the network server boots up, and the second processor is detected by the system BIOS. However, the network server operating system does not recognize the second processor. How do you correct the situation?

   A. Double the amount of memory in the network server

   B. Configure the system BIOS to report both processors to the network operating system

   C. Upgrade the network operating system to recognize the additional processor

   D. Upgrade the processor software drivers to the latest version

9. What environment variable in Windows NT and Windows 2000 is set to the number of processors in the network server?

   A. Number_of_processors

   B. NoProcs

   C. NumbProc

   D. Processors

10. Which of the following must be the same on the existing processor and the processor that is to be added to a multiprocessor-capable network server?

   A. Level 2 cache and processor clock speed

   B. Date of manufacture and spec number

   C. Level 2 cache and date of manufacture

   D. Processor clock speed and spec number

11. Which memory technology requires a continuity module to be inserted into all empty memory module slots in a network server?

   A. SIMMs

   B. SIPPs

   C. RIMMs

   D. DIMMs

12. A network server has a single EIDE disk drive configured as a master. You want to add a second EIDE disk drive to the same channel. How must the second drive be configured for both disk drives to work correctly?

   A. Master

   B. Slave

   C. CSEL

   D. Secondary

13. How do you upgrade an EIDE disk subsystem to a SCSI subsystem?

   A. Remove all EIDE disk drives, cables, and controllers. Add the SCSI controller, cables, and disk drives.

   B. Remove the EIDE controller and replace it with a SCSI controller, using existing cables and disk drives.

   C. Remove the EIDE controller, add the SCSI controller, and change the drive electronics from EIDE to SCSI.

   D. Remove the EIDE disk drives, install the SCSI disk drives, and attach the SCSI disk drives to the EIDE controller.

14. Which of the following adapters usually contain onboard memory that can be upgraded?

   A. Sound card and RAID controller

   B. Video adapter, sound card, and RAID controller

C. Video adapter, RAID controller, and SCSI controller

D. Sound card only

15. In what version of Windows must the hard drive be converted to a dynamic disk before the RAID options are available to implement?

A. Windows 98

B. Windows 2000

C. Windows NT

D. Windows XP

16. What problem are you most likely to encounter when adding external SCSI disk drives to a SCSI bus?

A. No available SCSI IDs

B. Exceeding the SCSI channel cable length

C. Slow performance

D. Heat

17. What are the proper combinations for installing memory modules into memory slots?

A. Gold leads on memory modules, tin contacts in memory slots and tin leads on memory modules, gold contacts in memory slots

B. Gold leads on memory modules, tin contacts in memory slots only

C. Tin leads on memory modules, gold contacts in memory slots only

D. Gold leads on memory modules, gold contacts in memory slots and tin leads on memory modules, tin contacts in memory slots

18. Which of the following limits the amount of memory that can be utilized in a network server?

A. The control chipset on the network server motherboard

B. The speed of the processor(s) in the network server

C. The speed of the PCI bus

D. The width of the data bus

19. What is the process of replacing a SCSI disk drive with a SCA connector?

A. Remove the old SCSI disk drive and insert the new SCSI disk drive.

B. Remove the old SCSI disk drive and note its SCSI ID. Set the SCSI ID on the new SCSI disk drive to the same SCSI ID and insert the new SCSI disk drive.

C. Remove the old SCSI disk drive and note its SCSI ID. Set the SCSI ID on the new SCSI disk drive to be different from the SCSI ID of the old disk drive. Insert the new SCSI disk drive.

D. Remove the old SCSI disk drive. Set the new SCSI disk drive to CSEL. Insert the new SCSI disk drive.

Key Terms

CD-ROM library   Multiple CD-ROM drives in a tower attached to a network that can be accessed by all the users on a network.

diagnostic partition utility   Enables the troubleshooting of nonfunctioning hardware components.

diagnostic tools   Utilities used to monitor the network server.

disk duplexing   Refers to a mirrored set where each disk is connected to a different disk controller.

disk mirroring   Refers to two disk drives connected to the same disk controller.

disk stripping   Also known as RAID 0, it is not fault tolerant but is used to improve disk input/output performance.

EISA configuration utility   Enables the configuration of the components of the network server.

error correcting code (ECC)   Detects and corrects single-bit errors and detects double-bit errors. It is read and decoded each time data are read from the disk.

external peripheral   A device that is external to the network server.

hardware-based RAID   Implements RAID using a hardware device called a RAID controller.

hot expansion   Installing a new adapter in an empty slot while the server remains operational.

hot replacement   Replacing an existing adapter while the server remains operational.

hot upgrade   Upgrading an existing adapter while the server remains operational.

logical unit number (LUN)   A seldom-used SCSI standard that allows sub-SCSI IDs to a single SCSI ID, allowing one SCSI channel to support multiple CDs.

network server   A computer that is shared by multiple users.

peripheral device   Any device that is not part of the core computer system.

RAID (redundant array of inexpensive disks)   Provides fault tolerance to prevent loss of data in the event of a disk drive failure on a network server.

RAID controller   A specialized controller used in a RAID array.

RAID controller onboard memory   Used as a buffer and often backed up with an onboard battery.

RAID 0/1   Also known as RAID 0+1 and RAID 10, it provides the performance of RAID 0 and the redundancy of RAID 1. It requires at least four drives to implement.

RAID 0   An array or group of disk drives used as a single disk. Data are written in chunks or stripes to all the drives in the array.

RAID 1   Requires at least two disk drives and writes data to two separate locations.

RAID 2   Requires a minimum of three disk drives and uses a hamming code to create an ECC for all data.

RAID 3   Requires a minimum of three synchronized disk drives and uses bit-level parity with a single-parity disk for fault tolerance.

RAID 4   Requires a minimum of three disk drives that do not need to be synchronized because data are written to the drives in blocks.

RAID 5   Requires a minimum of three disk drives and uses block-level parity, but unlike RAID 4, it spreads the parity information among all the drives in the array.

SCSI adapter onboard memory   Uses onboard memory as a buffer or cache between the SCSI disk drives and the network server memory.

server support utilities   Used for backup and virus protection in support of the network server.

system-monitoring agent   Vendor-specific software that monitors various aspects of the network server such as configuration, mass storage, the NIC, etc.

video adapter onboard memory   Uses memory to store the image that is displayed on the monitor.

Objectives

Upon completion of this chapter, you will be able to perform the following tasks:

- Provide administrative duties to maintain and adapt a computer network
- Select a network interface card and know the considerations regarding the type of network, media, and system bus
- Understand network topology and the overall structure of a computer or communication system known as the architecture
- Define protocols and the OSI model
- Compare the TCP/IP model and the OSI model
- View configuration information and troubleshoot problems
- Understand synchronous and asynchronous serial transmissions

Chapter 9

Networking Fundamentals

Introduction

By definition, a computer network has two or more devices that are linked for the purpose of sharing information and resources. This chapter provides you with an overview of how networks work and share services. The types of networks that are detailed in this chapter include peer-to-peer, client/server, LAN, and WAN. Additionally, the difference between a circuit-switched and a packet-switched network is explained as is the topology of the network. You will learn how to add the network interface card, add the physical components of a network, and install important troubleshooting utilities.

Introduction to PC Networking

This section includes the following topics:

- Defining a computer network
- File, print, and application services
- Mail services
- Directory and name services
- The Internet
- Network administration
- Simplex, half-duplex, and full-duplex transmission

Defining a Computer Network

A *network* is a connected system of objects or people. The most common example of a network is the telephone system, which is widely known as the *public switched telephone network (PSTN)*. The PSTN allows people in virtually every corner of the world to communicate with anyone who has access to a telephone.

In a similar fashion, a computer network allows users to communicate with other users on the same network by transmitting data on the cables that are used to connect the computers. A *computer network*, as illustrated in Figure 9-1, is defined as having two or more devices (such as workstations, printers, or servers) that are linked for the purpose of sharing information or resources, or both. The link can be made through a variety of copper or fiber-optic cables, or it can be a wireless connection that uses radio signals, infrared (laser) technology, or satellite transmission. The information and resources shared on a network can include data files, application programs, printers, modems, and other hardware devices. Computer networks are used in businesses, schools, government agencies, and some homes.

Figure 9-1 A Computer Network

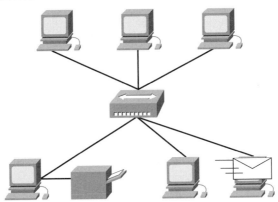

Networks are multilayered objects. A network consists of many overlapping systems, such as cabling schemes, addressing schemes, or applications. The layers work together to transmit and receive data. The *open systems interconnection (OSI)* model, which was created to define these multiple layers, is illustrated in Figure 9-2.

Figure 9-2 OSI Model

Application
Presentation
Session
Transport
Network
Data Link
Physical

The OSI model and the different ways in which computers can be networked to share resources are discussed later in this chapter.

File, Print, and Application Services

Computer networks offer file and print services, as shown in Figure 9-3. The need to share information is an important part of the development of computer networks. In networks, different computers take on specialized roles or functions. Once they are connected, one or more computers in the network can function as network file servers. The *server* is a repository for files that can be accessed and shared across the network by many users. This avoids duplication, conserves resources, and allows the management and control of key information. Network administrators can grant or restrict access to files. They also regularly copy the files to backup systems in case of problems or failures.

Figure 9-3 File, Print, and Application Services

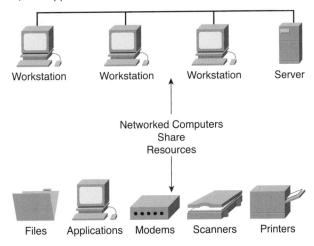

Workstation   Workstation   Workstation   Server

Networked Computers
Share
Resources

Files   Applications   Modems   Scanners   Printers

Network file services make collaboration in the development of documents and projects possible. Each member of a project team can make contributions to a document or project, through a shared network file service. In addition, network file services can enable the timely distribution of key files to a group of users who have an interest in that information. Finally, many people who are geographically separated can share games and entertainment.

In addition to sharing computer files, networks enable users to share printing devices. *Network print services* can make a high-speed printer accessible to many users. This printer operates as if it was directly attached to the individual computers. The network can send requests from many users to a central print server, where these requests are processed. Multiple printer servers, each offering a different quality of output, can be implemented according to the requirements of users. Under administrative control, users can select the service they need for a particular job. In this way, networks provide a more efficient use of expensive printing devices without duplication. Figure 9-4 illustrates one system requesting print services on the network.

Figure 9-4 Network Print Services

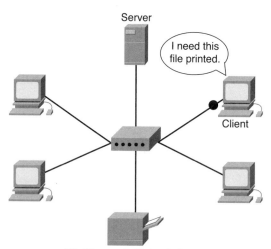

File Storage to Network Server

All network operating systems offer file and print services. Sharing information, collaborating on projects, and providing access to input and output devices are common services of computer networks. In addition to sharing information and special devices, applications such as word processing programs can be installed on a network server. Users can run the shared applications from a server without using space on their local hard disks for the program files.

The software vendors' licensing agreement might require the purchase of additional licenses for each workstation that uses a network application, even though only one copy is actually installed on the network server and all users are accessing that same copy.

Mail Services

From their earliest days, computer networks have enabled users to communicate by *electronic mail (e-mail)*. E-mail services work like the postal system, with one computer taking on the function of "post office." The user's e-mail account operates like a post office box, where mail is held for the user until it is picked up over the network by an e-mail client program running in the user's system. Figure 9-5 illustrates this concept. The e-mail is sent from the client computer to the server, which acts as the post office. The server then sends the e-mail message to the e-mail address.

Figure 9-5 Mail Services

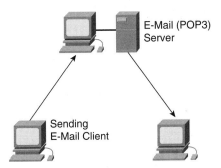

An e-mail address consists of two parts and is used like the post office uses an address on an envelope. Consider the example user@cisco.com, where user is the individual to whom the e-mail is addressed. The username is used for identification once the e-mail arrives at the appropriate server. The at sign (@) indicates that the address directly follows. In this case, the e-mail is to be sent to Cisco.com. E-mail applications such as Microsoft Mail, Eudora, Netscape Mail, and Pegasus can be different, but they can all recognize the standard e-mail format. E-mail continues to be the single most widely used function of computer networks in many parts of the world.

E-mail works as a store-and-forward application. Mail messages (and the identifying information—sender, receiver, and time stamp) are stored on an e-mail server (post office box) until the recipient retrieves his or her mail. Typically, e-mail messages are short communications. Current e-mail systems also allow users to attach different types of files (documents, pictures, and movies) to their messages. These attachments can also be retrieved, or *downloaded*, along with the e-mail message. In this way, e-mail services are similar to file transfer services on the network.

E-mail systems have evolved together with networking technology. The rapid growth of the Internet has allowed more people to connect online. This allows for immediate communication among network users. The store-and-forward nature of e-mail systems does not require that the recipient be online when the e-mail is sent; the recipient can pick up the e-mail at a later time. In addition to e-mail, the Internet has spawned a variety of *instant messaging systems* that allow network users to chat without delay. This capability, referred to as *real-time chat*, is used when two or more users are connected to the network at the same time.

Directory and Name Services

Another important benefit of networks is their ability to find resources and devices wherever they are located. To enable users and systems on the network to find the services they require, computer networks make use of *directories* and *name services*. Figure 9-6 illustrates the network device mappings that allow a specific file to be located. Similar to the telephone directory, the network assigns a name to users, services, and devices so that they can be identified and accessed. Knowing the name of a service on the network enables users to contact that service without having to know its physical location. In fact, the physical location of a service can change, and users can still find the service or device if they know its name.

Figure 9-6 Network Device Mappings

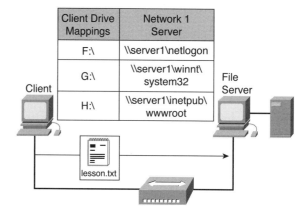

Client Drive Mappings	Network 1 Server
F:\	\\server1\netlogon
G:\	\\server1\winnt\ system32
H:\	\\server1\inetpub\ wwwroot

Directory and name services make a network easier to use. People work more efficiently when they have names for services and other entities. Network directory and name services can translate those names into the addresses that are used to communicate with the desired service. After the initial setup of the directory or name service, this translation takes place transparently. In addition to their easy use, these services also make the network more flexible. Network designers and administrators can locate or move file, print, and other services with the assurance that users can still locate them by name.

The Internet

The *Internet* is a worldwide public network of networks, interconnecting thousands of smaller networks to form one large "web" of communication. Many private networks, some with thousands of users, connect to the Internet by using the services of *Internet service providers (ISPs)*. These linkages enable long-distance access to network services for information and device sharing.

TEST TIP

An ISP is a facility that enables users to connect to the Internet. For example, users sign up with and dial in to an ISP. It is through the ISP that users are connected to the Internet.

The Internet functions like a highway to facilitate exchange between geographically separated users, organizations, and branches of companies. Figure 9-7 shows the highway analogy to explain bandwidth, network devices, and packets.

Figure 9-7 Highway Analogy

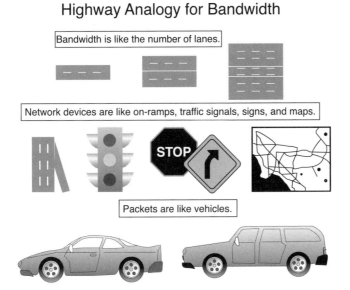

The phrase *information superhighway* describes the benefit of the Internet to business and private communications. The Internet breaks down barriers of time and space, enabling the sharing of information around the globe almost instantaneously. See Figure 9-8.

Figure 9-8 Worldwide Network

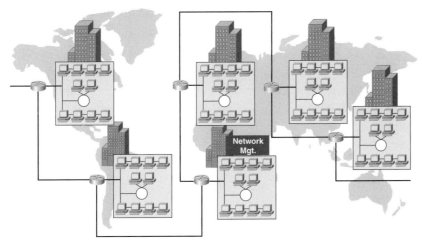

Network Administration

As businesses and individuals become more dependent on computer networks for their daily activities, these networks must function to deliver the services that users expect. Even after engineers have completed the design and installation of a new network, the network requires attention and management to deliver a consistent level of service to its users. Computer networks are dynamic; they change and grow in response to new technologies and user requirements.

The ongoing task of *network administration* is to maintain and adapt the network to changing conditions. This task is assigned to network administrators and support personnel. Network administrator responsibilities include

- Setting up new user accounts and services
- Monitoring network performance
- Repairing network failures

Administrators often rely on the skills of specialized support personnel to locate the sources of network problems and repair them efficiently. As networks grow, administrators must ensure that network availability is maintained while the network evolves to include new equipment and features. Network administrators must be skilled in the use of a wide range of tools on a variety of different types of devices and systems.

As they evaluate new technologies and requirements, administrators must measure the benefits of the new features against the issues, costs, and problems that these items can introduce to the network.

Simplex, Half-Duplex, and Full-Duplex Transmission

A *data channel*, over which a signal is sent, can operate in one of three ways: simplex, half-duplex, or full-duplex (often just called duplex). The distinction describes the way the signal can travel.

Simplex Transmission

Simplex transmission is a single, one-way baseband transmission. As the name implies, simplex transmission is simple. It is also called unidirectional because the signal travels in only one direction. An example of simplex transmission is the signal that is sent from the cable TV station to your home television. Figure 9-9 illustrates this transmission type.

Figure 9-9 Simplex Transmission

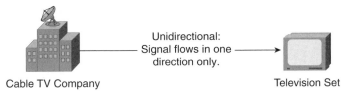

Cable TV Company

Unidirectional:
Signal flows in one
direction only.

Television Set

Contemporary applications for simplex circuits, although rare, include remote station printers, card readers, and a few alarm or security systems (for fire and smoke). This type of transmission is not frequently used because it is not practical. The only advantage of simplex transmission is that it is inexpensive.

Half-Duplex Transmission

Half-duplex transmission is an improvement over simplex transmission because the data traffic can travel in both directions. Unfortunately, the road is not wide enough to accommodate bidirectional signals simultaneously. This means that only one side can transmit at a time, as shown in Figure 9-13. Two-way radios, such as Citizens Band (CB) and police/emergency communications mobile radios, work with half-duplex transmissions. When pressing the button on the microphone to transmit, nothing being said on the other end can be heard. If people at both ends try to talk at the same time, neither transmission gets through.

NOTE

Modems are half-duplex devices. They can send and receive, but not at the same time. However, it is possible to create a full-duplex modem connection with two telephone lines and two modems.

Figure 9-10 Half-Duplex Transmission

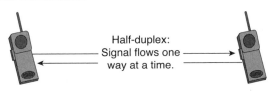

Half-duplex:
Signal flows one
way at a time.

Full-Duplex Transmission

Full-duplex transmission operates like a two-way, two-lane street. Traffic can travel in both directions at the same time, as shown in Figure 9-11.

Figure 9-11 Full-Duplex Transmission

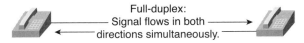

Full-duplex:
Signal flows in both
directions simultaneously.

A land-based telephone conversation is an example of full-duplex communication. Both parties can talk at the same time and hear at the same time, much like a face-to-face conversation.

Full-duplex networking technology increases performance because data can be sent and received at the same time. DSL (described later), two-way cable modem, and other broadband technologies operate in full-duplex mode. For example, with DSL, users can download data to their computer at the same time they are sending a voice message over the phone line.

Types of Networks

This section includes the following topics:

- Overview
- Peer-to-peer networks
- Client/server networks
- Local-area networks
- Wide-area networks

Overview

By using local-area network and wide-area network technologies, many computers are interconnected to provide services to their users. In providing services, networked computers take on different roles or functions in relation to each other. Some types of applications require computers to function as equal partners. Other types distribute work so that one computer functions to serve a number of others in an unequal relationship. In either case, two computers typically communicate with each other by using *request/response protocols*. One computer issues a request for a service, and a second computer receives and responds to that request. The requester takes on the role of a client, and the responder takes on the role of a server.

Peer-to-Peer Networks

In a *peer-to-peer network*, the networked computers act as equal partners, or peers, to each other. As peers, each computer can take on the client function or the server function alternately, as shown in Figure 9-12. For example, at one time computer A might make a request for a file from computer B, which responds by serving the file to computer A. Computer A functions as the client, while B functions as the server. At a later time, computers A and B can reverse roles. Computers A and B stand in a reciprocal, or peer, relationship to each other.

Figure 9-12 A Peer-to-Peer Network

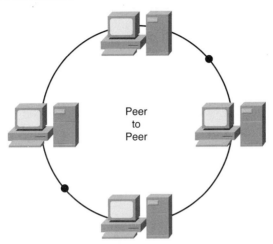

In a peer-to-peer network, users control their own resources. They might decide to share certain files with other users and could require passwords before they allow others to access their resources. Because users make these decisions, there is no central point of control or administration in the network. In addition, users must back up their own systems to be able to recover from data loss in case of failures. When a computer acts as a server, the user of that machine might experience reduced performance as the machine serves the requests made by other systems.

Peer-to-peer networks are relatively easy to install and operate. No additional equipment is necessary beyond a suitable operating system in each computer. Because users control their own resources, no dedicated administrators are needed. A peer-to-peer network works well with a small number of computers, perhaps ten or fewer.

As networks grow larger, peer-to-peer relationships become increasingly difficult to coordinate. They do not scale well, because their efficiency decreases rapidly as the number of computers on the network increases. Because individual users control access to the resources on their computers, security can be difficult to maintain. Client/server networks address these limitations.

Client/Server Networks

In a *client/server network* arrangement, network services are located in a dedicated computer whose only function is to respond to the requests of clients. The server contains the file, print, application, security, and other services in a central computer that is continuously available to respond to client requests. Most network operating systems adopt the form of client/server relationships. Typically, desktop computers function as clients, and one or more computers with additional processing power, memory, and specialized software function as servers.

Servers are designed to handle requests from many clients simultaneously. Before a client can access the server's resources, the client must identify itself and be authorized to use the resource. This is usually done by assigning each user an account name and password. A specialized authentication server acts as an entry point, guarding access to the network, and verifies this account information. By centralizing user accounts, security, and access control, server-based networks simplify the work of network administration. Figure 9-13 illustrates a client/server network.

Figure 9-13 A Client/Server Network

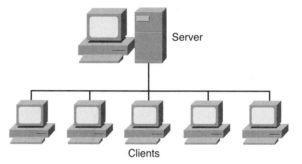

Server

Clients

The concentration of network resources, such as files, printers, and applications, on servers also makes the data they generate easier to back up and maintain. Rather than having these resources spread across individual machines, they can be located on specialized, dedicated servers for easier access. Most client/server systems also include facilities for enhancing the network by adding new services that extend the usefulness of the network.

The distribution of functions in client/server networks brings substantial advantages but also incurs some costs. Although the aggregation of resources on server systems brings greater security, simpler access, and coordinated control, the server introduces a single point of failure into the network. Without an operational server, the network cannot function. Additionally, servers require a trained, expert staff to administer and maintain them, which increases the expense of running the network. Server systems require additional hardware and specialized software that substantially adds to the cost.

Local-Area Networks

A *local-area network (LAN)* can connect many computers in a relatively small geographical area such as a home, an office, or a campus, as shown in Figure 9-14. The network allows users to access high-bandwidth media, as is found on the Internet, and allows users to share devices such as printers.

Figure 9-14 A Local-Area Network

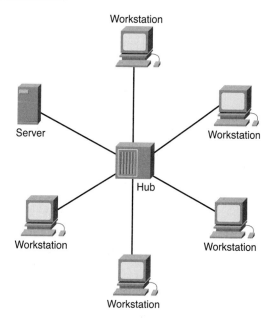

A LAN connects each computer to each of the others by using a separate communications channel. A direct connection from one computer to another is called a *point-to-point link*. If the network were designed using point-to-point links, the number of links would grow rapidly as new computers were added to the network. For each new computer, the network would need a new separate connection to each of the other computers. This approach would be costly and difficult to manage.

Starting in the late 1960s and early 1970s, network engineers designed a form of network that enabled many computers in a small area to share a single communications channel by taking turns using it. These LANs now connect more computers than any other type of network. By allowing the computers to share a communications channel, LANs greatly reduce the cost of the network. For economic and technical reasons, point-to-point links over longer distances are then used to connect computers and networks in separate cities or even across continents.

The general shape or layout of a LAN is called its *topology*. Topology defines the structure of the network. This includes the physical topology, which is the layout of the wire or media, and the logical topology, which is how the media are accessed by the hosts. Figure 9-15 illustrates physical topologies, which are discussed later in this chapter.

Figure 9-15 Physical Topologies

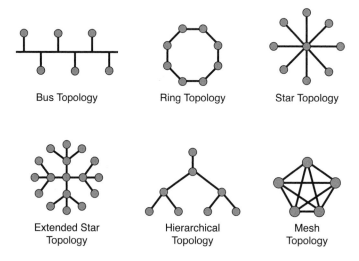

When all the computers connect to a central point, the network takes on a *star topology*. An alternate topology connects the computers in a closed loop. Here, the cable is run from one computer to the next and then from the second to its neighbor until the last one is connected back to the first. This forms a *ring topology*. A third topology, called a *bus*, attaches each computer into a single, long cable. Each topology has its benefits and drawbacks. Today, most LANs are designed using some form of star topology, although ring and bus layouts are still used in some installations.

Regardless of the layout, or topology, of the network, all LANs require the networked computers to share the communications channel that connects them. The communications channel that they share is called the *medium*. The medium is typically a cable that carries electrical signals through copper, or it can be a fiber-optic cable, which carries light signals through purified glass or plastic. In the case of wireless networks, the computers can use antennas to broadcast radio signals to each other. In all cases, the computers on a LAN share the medium by taking turns using it.

On a LAN, the rules for coordinating the use of the medium are called *media access control (MAC)*. Because there are many computers on the network but only one of them can use the medium at a time, there must be rules for deciding how they take turns sharing the network. The data link layer provides reliable transit of data across a physical link by using the MAC address. If there are conflicts when more than one computer is contending for the medium, the rules ensure resolution of the conflict. In later sections of this chapter, the major types of LANs are reviewed, including the rules for sharing the medium.

Wide-Area Networks

For economic and technical reasons, LANs are not suitable for communications over long distances. On a LAN, the computers must coordinate their use of the network, and this coordination takes time. Over long distances with greater delay in communication, the computers would take more time coordinating the use of the shared medium and less time sending data messages. In addition, the costs of providing high-speed media over long distances are much greater than in the case of LANs. For these reasons, wide-area network (WAN) technologies differ from those of LANs.

A *wide-area network (WAN)*, as the name implies, is designed to work over a larger area than a LAN. Figure 9-16 illustrates the individual LANs that are able to communicate using a WAN.

Figure 9-16 A Wide-Area Network

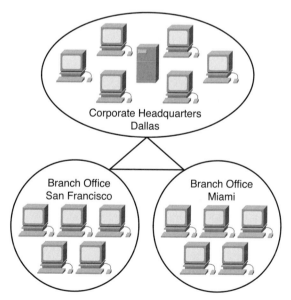

A WAN uses point-to-point or point-to-multipoint, serial communications lines. Point-to-point lines connect only two locations, one on each side of the line. Point-to-multipoint lines connect one location on one side of the line to multiple locations on the other side. They are called *serial lines* because the bits of information are transmitted one after another in a series, like cars traveling on a single-lane highway, as shown in Figure 9-17.

Figure 9-17 A Serial Transmission

The following are some of the more common WAN technologies:

- Modems: circuit switch.
- ISDN (integrated services digital network): circuit switch.
- DSL (digital subscriber line).
- Frame Relay: packet switch.
- ATM (asynchronous transfer mode).
- The T (U.S.) and E (Europe) carrier series: T1, E1, T3, E3, etc.
- SONET (synchronous optical network).

Typically, individuals and companies do not build their own WAN connections. Government regulations only allow utility companies to install lines on public property. Therefore, wide-area connections make use of the communications facilities put in place by the utility companies, called *common carriers*, such as the telephone company.

Connections across WAN lines can be temporary or permanent. Telephone, or dialup, lines, for example, might make a temporary connection to a remote network from a computer in a home or small office. In this case, the home or office computer makes a phone call to a computer on the boundary of the remote network. The telephone company provides the connection, or circuit, that is used for the duration of the call. After data are transmitted, the line is disconnected, just as it is for an ordinary voice call. If a company wants to transmit data at any time without having to connect and disconnect the line each time, the company can rent a permanent line or circuit from the common carrier. These leased lines are constantly available and operate at higher speeds than temporary dialup connections.

In both temporary and permanent cases, computers that connect over wide-area circuits must use special devices called modems or CSU/DSU (see the following note) at each end of the connection.

Modem devices are required because the electrical signals that carry digital computer data must be transformed, or modulated, before they can be transmitted on telephone lines. On the transmitting end of the connection, a modem (modulator-demodulator) transforms computer signals into phone signals. On the receiving end, the transformation is reversed from phone to computer signals. The modem is only one means of connecting computers or similar devices so that they can communicate over long distances. Other much faster technologies include ISDN, frame relay, ATM, and so on.

In general, WANs typically connect fewer computers than do LANs and normally operate at lower speeds than LANs. WANs, however, provide the means for connecting single computers and many LANs over large distances. Thus, WANs enable networks to span whole countries, and even the globe.

Circuit-Switched Versus Packet-Switched Networks

The public telephone system, sometimes referred to as *plain old telephone service (POTS)*, is a *circuit-switched communications network*. When a telephone call is placed in this type of network, only one physical path is used between the telephones for the duration of that call. This pathway, called a *circuit*, is maintained for the exclusive use of the call, until the connection is ended and the telephone is hung up. Figure 9-18 illustrates this concept with one route on the map. It is the only way to get from one place to another.

Figure 9-18 Circuit-Switched Networks

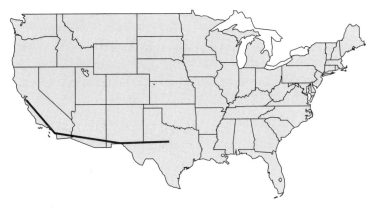

NOTE

A *channel service unit (CSU)/digital (or data) service unit (DSU)* is a pair of communications devices that connect an in-house line to an external digital circuit (T1, DDS, etc.). It is similar to a modem, but connects a digital circuit rather than an analog one.

If the same number is called from the same location at a later time, the path would probably be different. The circuit is created by a series of switches that use currently available network paths to set up the call end-to-end. This explains why callers can get a clear connection one day and noise and static on another. This demonstrates that a circuit-switched connection is *end-to-end* or *point-to-point*.

Conversely, in a packet-switched network, each packet of data can take a different route, and no dedicated pathway or circuit is established. The different routes that are shown on the map in Figure 9-19 illustrate this concept. When transferring data, such as a word processing file, from one computer to another using a packet-switched network, each packet (bundle of data) can take a different route. Although all the data arrive at the same destination, they do not all travel the same path to get there. This is the case with a dedicated path or circuit. Internet traffic uses packet-switching technology.

Figure 9-19 Packet-Switched Networks

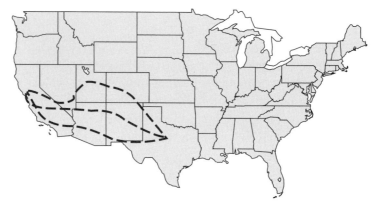

The difference between circuit and packet switching can be compared to the different ways in which a large group of people traveling from Dallas to San Francisco can reach their destination. For example, *circuit switching* is similar to loading the entire group on a bus, train, or airplane. The route is plotted out, and the whole group travels over that same route.

Packet switching is comparable to people traveling in their own automobiles. The group is broken down into individual components just as the data communication is broken into packets. Some travelers can take interstate highways, and others can use back roads. Some can drive straight through, and others can take a more roundabout path. Eventually, they all end up at the same destination. The group is rejoined, just as packets are reassembled at the endpoint of the communication.

Worksheet 9.2.5   Types of Networks

This worksheet reviews the types of networks discussed in the previous sections.

Adding a Network Interface Card

This section includes the following topics:

- What is a network interface card?
- Setting the IP address.
- DHCP servers.
- Default gateway.
- Domain name system.

What Is a Network Interface Card?

A *network interface card (NIC)*, as shown in Figure 9-20, is a device that plugs into a motherboard and provides ports for the network cable connections. It is the computer's interface with the LAN. The NIC communicates with the network through serial connections and communicates with the computer through parallel connections.

Figure 9-20   A Network Interface Card

There are several important issues to consider when selecting a NIC for use on a network:

- **The type of network**—NICs are designed for Ethernet LANs, Token Ring, FDDI, and so on. An Ethernet NIC does not work with Token Ring and vice versa.

■ **The type of media**—The type of port or connector that the NIC provides determines the specific media type, such as twisted-pair, coaxial, fiber-optic, or wireless.

■ **The type of system bus**—The type of NIC determines the system bus. A PCI slot is faster than ISA. It is recommend that PCI be used with FDDI cards because an ISA bus will not handle the required speed.

A NIC is installed in the computer in an expansion slot. NICs require an IRQ, an I/O address, and memory space for the operating system drivers in order to perform their function. New NICs are Plug and Play compatible, making the installation an easy process. Once the card is installed and the computer is turned on, the system automatically finds the new hardware, installs the driver, and sets the IRQ, I/O address, and memory space. Refer to the manufacturer's documentation or website for troubleshooting help.

Lab Activity 9.3.1   NIC Installation

In this lab, the NIC is installed into a PC. It is also configured for an IP address.

Setting the Internet Protocol Address

In a TCP/IP-based LAN, PCs use an *Internet protocol (IP) address* to identify each other. These addresses allow computers that are attached to the network to locate each other. An IP address is a 32-bit binary number. This binary number is divided into four groups of eight bits known as *octets*, each of which is represented by a decimal number in the range of 0 to 255. The octets are separated by decimal points. The combination 190.100.5.54 is an example of an IP address. This type of address is described as a *dotted decimal representation*. Each device on the network that has an IP address is known as a *host* or *node*.

A secondary dotted decimal number, known as the *subnet mask*, always accompanies an IP address. The dotted decimal number 255.255.0.0 is a subnet mask. The subnet mask is used by network computers to determine whether a particular host IP address is local (on the same network segment) or remote (on another segment).

IP addresses for hosts on a LAN can be assigned in two ways:

1. Manually assigned by the network administrator. Figure 9-21 shows the TCP/IP Properties dialog box in Windows set up to manually assign IP addresses.

2. Assigned by a DHCP server. Figure 9-22 shows the TCP/IP Properties dialog box in Windows set up to automatically assign IP addresses. (DHCP servers are discussed in the next section.)

Figure 9-21   Manually Entering an IP Address

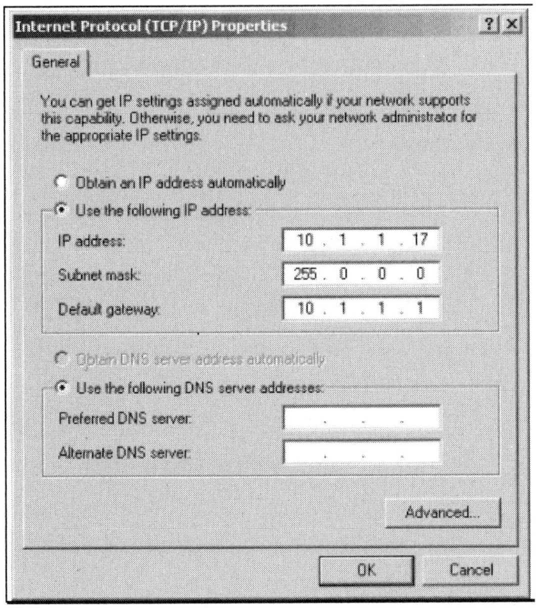

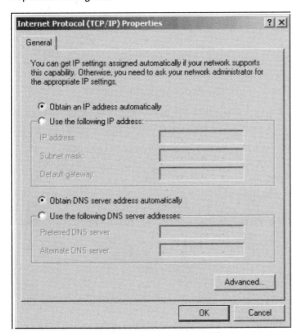

Figure 9-22   TCP/IP Properties Dialog Box

The following address settings or configurations are required (whether manually set or automatically set) to connect with the network:

- An IP address
- A subnet mask
- A default gateway address

If there are more than a few computers, manually configuring TCP/IP addresses for every host on the network can be time-consuming. This also requires the network administrator who is assigning the address to understand IP addressing and to know how to choose a valid address for the particular network. The IP address that is entered is unique for each host and resides in the computer driver software for the NIC. TCP/IP addressing is not within the scope of this text.

Dynamic Host Configuration Protocol Servers

The most common and efficient way for computers on a large network to obtain an IP address is through a *dynamic host configuration protocol (DHCP)* server. DHCP is a software utility that is designed to assign IP addresses to PCs. The computer running the software is known as a DHCP server. DHCP servers hand the IP addresses and TCP/IP configuration information to computers that are configured as DHCP clients. This dynamic process eliminates the need for manual IP address assignments. However, any devices requiring a static, or permanent, IP address must still have their IP address assigned manually.

When the DHCP server receives a request from a host, it selects IP address information from a set of predefined addresses that are stored in its database. Once the server has selected the IP information, it offers these values to the requesting device on the network. If the device accepts the offer, the DHCP server then leases the IP information to the device for a specific period of time. Figure 9-23 illustrates a DHCP operation as the client makes a request of the server, and the server responds.

Figure 9-23 DHCP Operation

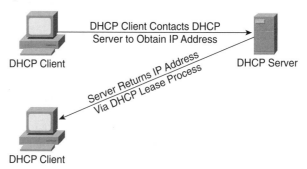

The DHCP server can hand out the following IP address information to hosts that are starting up on the network:

- An IP address
- A subnet mask
- A default gateway
- Optional values, such as a domain name system server address

The use of this system simplifies the administration of a network because the software keeps track of IP addresses. Automatically configuring TCP/IP also reduces the possibility of assigning duplicate IP addresses or invalid IP addresses. For a computer on the network to take advantage of the DHCP server services, it must be able to identify the server on the local network. This is accomplished by choosing to obtain an IP address automatically on the client's software through the computer's TCP/IP Properties dialog box. In other cases, an operating system feature called *automatic private IP addressing (APIPA)* enables a computer to assign itself an address if it is unable to contact a DHCP server.

Lab Activity 9.3.3   Configuring the NIC to Work with a DHCP Server

Upon completion of this lab, the NIC will be configured to utilize DHCP.

Default Gateway

A computer located on one network segment that is trying to talk to another computer on a different segment (that is, across the router) sends the data through a *default gateway*. The default gateway is the near-side interface of the router, that is, the interface on the router to which the local computer's network segment or wire is attached. In order for each computer to recognize its default gateway, the corresponding near-side router interface IP address must be entered in the host TCP/IP Properties dialog box. This information is stored on the NIC.

Domain Name System

If a LAN is large or is connected to the Internet, it is often difficult to remember the numeric addresses (IP addresses) of hosts. Most hosts are identified on the Internet by friendly computer names known as domain names. The *Domain Name System (DNS)* is used to translate computer names, such as cisco.com, to their corresponding unique IP address. The DNS software runs on a computer acting as a network server for handling the address translations. DNS software can be hosted on the network itself or by an ISP. Address translations are used each time the Internet is accessed. The process of translating names to addresses is known as *name resolution*. Figure 9-24 illustrates how the DNS server resolves the post office name of an e-mail address.

Figure 9-24 DNS Functions

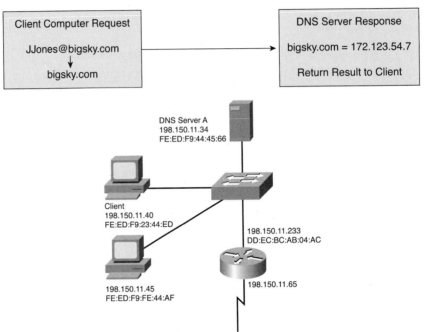

The DNS server keeps records that map computer (host) names and their corresponding IP addresses. These record types are all combined in the DNS table. When a host name needs to be translated to its IP address, the client contacts the DNS server. A hierarchy of DNS servers exists on the Internet, with different servers maintaining DNS information for their own areas of authority, called *zones*. If the DNS server consulted by a computer does not have an IP mapping for the host name sought, it passes the query to another DNS server until the information is obtained.

The DNS is not an absolute requirement to communicate on the Internet, but without it, all communications must use IP addresses instead of host names. It is much easier to remember cisco.com than 198.133.219.25.

In order for the computers on the LAN to access and make use of the DNS services, the DNS server IP address, as well as the IP address/subnet mask, must be entered into the TCP/IP Properties dialog box.

Physical Components of a Network

This section includes the following topics:

- Network topologies
- Physical versus logical topology
- Networking media
- Common networking devices
- Server components

Network Topologies

The *network topology* defines the way in which computers, printers, and other devices are connected. A network topology describes the layout of the wire and devices as well as the paths used by data transmissions. The topology greatly influences how the network functions.

The following sections discuss the different types of topologies, including bus, star, extended star, ring, mesh, and hybrid. The physical and logical topologies of a network are also discussed.

Bus Topology

All the devices on a bus topology, commonly referred to as a linear bus, are connected by a single cable. Figure 9-25 illustrates the bus topology. This cable proceeds from one computer to the next like a bus line going through a city. The main cable segment must end with a terminator that absorbs the signal when it reaches the end of the line or wire. If there is no terminator, the electrical signal representing the data bounces back at the end of the wire, causing errors in the network. Only one packet of data can be transmitted at a time. If multiple packets are transmitted, they collide and must be resent. A bus topology with many hosts can be slow due to these collisions. This topology is rarely used and would only be suitable for a home office or small business with a few hosts.

Figure 9-25 The Bus Topology

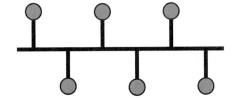

Star Topology

The star topology is the most commonly used architecture in Ethernet LANs. Figure 9-26 illustrates the star topology. When installed, the star topology resembles spokes in a bicycle wheel. The topology is made up of a central connection point that is a device such as a hub, switch, or router, where all the cabling segments meet. Each host in the network is connected to the central device with its own cable.

Figure 9-26 The Star Topology

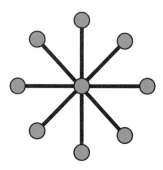

A star topology costs more to implement than the bus topology. This is because more cable is used and a central device, such as a hub, switch, or router, is needed. However, the advantages of a star topology are worth the additional costs. Because each host is connected to the central device with its own wire, if there is a problem with that cable, only that host is affected. The rest of the network is operational. This benefit is extremely important. It is the reason why virtually every newly designed network has this topology.

When a star network is expanded to include an additional networking device that is connected to the main networking device, this arrangement is called an *extended star topology*. Figure 9-27 illustrates an extended star topology. Larger networks, like those of corporations or schools, use the extended star topology. When used with network devices that filter frames or packets, such as bridges, switches, and routers, this topology significantly reduces the traffic on the wires by sending packets only to the wires of the destination host.

Figure 9-27 An Extended Star Topology

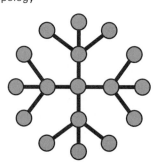

Ring Topology

As the name implies, in the ring topology, hosts are connected in the form of a ring or circle. Unlike the bus topology, the ring topology has no beginning and no end that needs to be terminated. Data are transmitted differently than with the bus or star topology. A frame travels around the ring, stopping at each node. If a node wants to transmit data, the node adds the data as well as the destination address to the frame. The frame then continues around the ring until it finds the destination node, which takes the data out of the frame. The advantage of using this type of method is that there are no collisions of data packets.

There are two types of rings, which are described as follows:

- **Single-ring**—All the devices on the network share a single cable, and the data travel in one direction only. Each device waits its turn to send data over the network, as illustrated in Figure 9-28. An example is the Token Ring topology.

Figure 9-28 A Single-Ring Topology

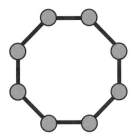

- **Dual-ring**—The dual-ring topology, as illustrated in Figure 9-29, allows data to be sent in both directions, although only one ring is used at a time. This creates redundancy (fault tolerance), meaning that in the event of a failure of one ring, data are still able to be transmitted on the other ring. An example of a dual-ring topology is the fiber distributed data interface (FDDI).

Figure 9-29 A Dual-Ring Topology

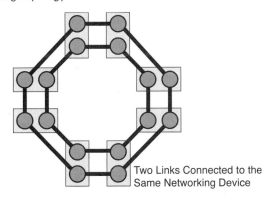

Two Links Connected to the
Same Networking Device

The most common implementation of the ring topology is in Token Ring networks. The 802.5 standard is the Token Ring access method used. FDDI is a technology that is similar to Token Ring, but FDDI uses light instead of electricity to transmit data. It uses the dual-ring topology.

Mesh Topology

The mesh topology connects all devices (nodes) to each other for redundancy and fault tolerance, as shown in Figure 9-30. This topology is used in WANs to interconnect LANs and for mission-critical networks such as those used by governments. Implementing the mesh topology is expensive and difficult.

Figure 9-30 The Mesh Topology

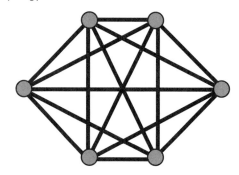

Hybrid Topology

The hybrid topology combines more than one type of topology. When a bus line joins two hubs of different topologies, this configuration is called a *star bus*. Businesses or schools that have several buildings, known as campuses, sometimes use this topology. The bus line is used to transfer the data between the star topologies.

Physical Versus Logical Topology

Networks have both a physical and logical topology, which are described as follows:

- **Physical topology**—Refers to the layout of the devices and media. Physical topologies are shown in Figure 9-31.

■ **Logical topology**—Refers to the paths that signals travel from one point on the network to another, that is, the way in which data access media and transmit packets across them.

Figure 9-31 Physical Topologies

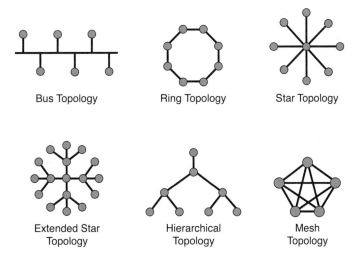

These two terminologies can be somewhat confusing; in this instance, the word logical has nothing to do with the way that the network appears to be functioning. The physical and logical topologies of a network can be the same. For example, in a network that is physically shaped as a linear bus, the data travel in a straight line from one computer to the next. Hence, it has both a bus physical topology and a bus logical topology.

A network can also have different physical and logical topologies. For example, a physical topology in the shape of a star, where cable segments can connect all computers to a central hub, can have a logical ring topology. Remember that in a ring, the data travel from one computer to the next. That is because inside the hub, the wiring connections are such that the signal travels in a circle from one port to the next, creating a *logical ring*. The way data travel in a network cannot always be predicted by simply observing the network's physical layout.

Consider Ethernet and Token Ring. Token Ring uses a logical ring topology in either a physical ring or physical star. Ethernet uses a logical bus topology in either a physical bus or physical star.

All the topologies discussed here can be both physical and logical, except that no logical star topology exists.

Networking Media

Networking media is the means by which signals (data) are sent from one computer to another (either by cable or wireless means). There are a wide variety of networking media in the marketplace. This section discusses some of the available media types, including two that use copper (coaxial and twisted-pair), one that uses glass (fiber-optic), and one that uses waves (wireless) to transmit data.

Coaxial Cable

Coaxial cable is a copper-cored cable surrounded by a heavy shielding, as shown in Figure 9-32. It is used to connect computers in a network. There are several types of coaxial cable, including thicknet, thinnet, RG-59 (standard cable for cable TV), and RG-6 (used in video distribution). Thicknet is large in diameter, rigid, and thus difficult to install. In addition, the maximum transmission rate is only 50 Mbps, significantly less than twisted-pair or fiber-optic, and its maximum run is 500 meters. A thinner version, known as thinnet or cheapernet, is occasionally used in Ethernet networks. Thinnet has the same transmission rate as thicknet.

Figure 9-32 Coaxial Cable

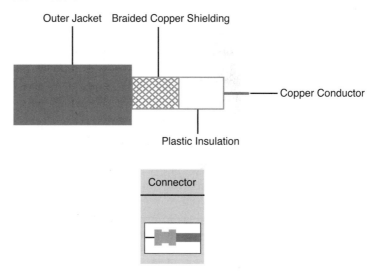

Twisted-Pair Cable

Twisted-pair is a type of cabling that is used for telephone communications and most modern Ethernet networks. A pair of wires forms a circuit that can transmit data. The pairs are twisted to provide protection against crosstalk, the noise generated by adjacent pairs. Pairs of copper wires that are encased in color-coded plastic insulation are twisted together. All the twisted-pairs are then protected inside an outer jacket. There are two types of twisted-pairs, shielded twisted-pair and unshielded twisted-pair. There are also categories of twisted-pair wiring:

- **Shielded twisted-pair (STP) cable**—This cable combines the techniques of cancellation and the twisting of wires with shielding. Each pair of wires is wrapped in metallic foil to further shield the wires from noise. The four pairs of wires are then wrapped in an overall metallic braid or foil. STP reduces electrical noise from within the cable (crosstalk) and from outside the cable (EMI and RFI). Figure 9-33 illustrates the STP cable.

- **Unshielded twisted-pair (UTP) cable**—This cable is used in a variety of networks. It has two or four pairs of wires. This type of cable relies solely on the cancellation effect produced by the twisted wire pairs to limit signal degradation caused by electromagnetic interference (EMI) and radio frequency interference (RFI). UTP is the most commonly used cabling in Ethernet networks. Figure 9-34 illustrates the UTP cable.

Figure 9-33 STP Cable

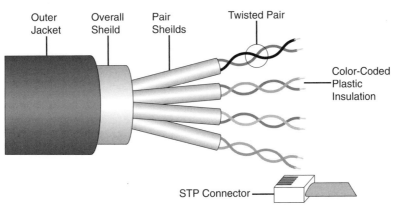

Although STP prevents interference better than UTP, STP cable is more expensive and difficult to install. In addition, the metallic shielding must be grounded at both ends. If improperly grounded, the shield acts like an antenna, picking up unwanted signals. STP cable is primarily used outside North America.

Figure 9-34 UTP Cable

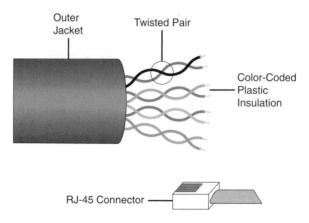

Category Rating

UTP comes in several categories that are based on the number of wires and number of twists in those wires. Category 3 is the wiring used for telephone connections. It has four pairs of wires and a maximum data rate of 16 Mbps. Category 5 and Category 5e are currently the most common Ethernet cables used. They have four pairs of wires with a maximum data rate of 100 Mbps. Category 5e has more twists per foot than Category 5 wiring. These extra twists further prevent interference from outside sources and from the other wires within the cable. Table 9-1 summarizes the common category cables and transmission speeds.

Table 9-1 UTP Category Rating

UTP Category	Number of Wire Pairs	Transmission Rate	Common Use
1	1	Voice grade (telephone only)	Not commonly used
2	4	Up to 1.544 Mbps (IEEE 802.5)	4-Mbps Token Ring
3	4 (3 twists per foot of cable length)	Up to 10 Mbps (IEEE 802.3)	Voice and 10-Mbps Ethernet

Table 9-1 UTP Category Rating (Continued)

UTP Category	Number of Wire Pairs	Transmission Rate	Common Use
4	4	Up to 16 Mbps (IEEE 802.5)	10-Mbps Ethernet and 16-Mbps Token Ring
5	4	Up to 1000 Mbps (1000 Base T)	100-Mbps Ethernet and 155-Mbps ATM

The latest design is Category 6, which has not yet been ratified by cabling industry organizations. Category 6 is similar to Category 5/5e except that a plastic divider separates the pairs of wires to prevent crosstalk. The pairs also have more twists than does Category 5e cable.

RS-232 Standard

RS-232 is a standard for serial transmission between computers and other devices (modems, mice, etc.). The standard supports a point-to-point connection over a single copper wire, so only two devices can be connected. Virtually every computer has one RS-232 serial port. Modems, monitors, mice, and serial printers are designed to connect to the RS-232 port. This port is also used to connect modems to telephones. There are two types of RS-232 connectors, a 25-pin (DB-25) and a 9-pin (DB-9) connector. The RS-232 standard has several limitations. The signaling rates are limited to 20 kbps. The rate is limited because the potential for crosstalk between signal lines in the cable is high.

RS-232 is still the most common standard for serial communication. Both RS-422 and RS-423, which are expected to replace RS-232 in the future, support higher data rates and have greater immunity to electrical interference.

Fiber-Optic Cable

Fiber-optic cable is a networking medium capable of conducting modulated light transmissions. Figure 9-35 shows an example of fiber-optic cable. To modulate light is to manipulate it so that it travels in a way that it transmits data. Fiber-optic refers to cabling that has a core of strands of glass or plastic (instead of copper) through which light pulses carry signals. Fiber-optic cable does not carry electrical impulses, as do other forms of networking media that use copper wire. Instead, signals that represent data are converted into beams of light.

Figure 9-35 Fiber-Optic Cable

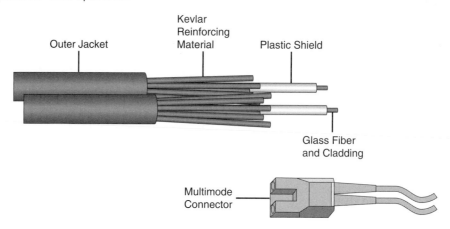

Figure 9-36 illustrates how data are transmitted in the form of light. Fiber has many advantages over copper in terms of transmission bandwidth and signal integrity over distance. However, fiber is more difficult to work with and is more expensive than copper cabling. The connectors are expensive as is the labor that is necessary to terminate the ends of the cables.

Figure 9-36 Fiber Transmits Data in the Form of Light

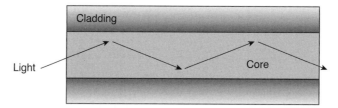

Wireless Networks

If the cost of running cables is too high or computers need to be movable without being tethered to cables, a *wireless network* is an alternative method of connecting a LAN. Wireless networks use radio frequency (RF), laser, infrared (IR), and satellites/microwaves to carry signals from one computer to another without a cable connection. Wireless signals are electromagnetic waves that travel through the air. No physical medium is necessary for wireless signals, making them a versatile way to build a network.

Common Networking Devices

Networking devices are used to connect computers and peripheral devices so that they can communicate. These devices include hubs, bridges, and switches, as detailed in the following sections.

Hubs

A *hub* is a device that is used to extend an Ethernet wire to allow more devices to communicate with each other. When using a hub, the network topology changes from a linear bus, where each device plugs directly into the wire, to a star topology. Figure 9-37 shows an example of a Cisco hub.

Figure 9-37 A Cisco Hub

Data arriving over the cables to a hub port are electrically repeated on all the other ports that are connected to the same Ethernet LAN, except for the port on which the data were received. Sometimes hubs are called *concentrators*, because they serve as a central connection point for an Ethernet LAN. Hubs are most commonly used in Ethernet 10BaseT or 100BaseT networks, although other network architectures use them. Figure 9-38 illustrates how computers are connected to the hub.

Figure 9-38 Computers Attached to a Hub

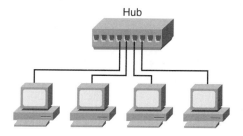

Bridges and Switches

Bridges connect network segments. The functionality of the bridge resides in its ability to make intelligent decisions about whether to pass signals on to the next segment of a network. When a bridge sees a frame (data being sent from one computer to another) on the network, it looks at the destination address and compares it to the forwarding table to determine whether to filter, flood (send to everyone), or copy the frame onto another segment. Figure 9-39 shows a Cisco bridge.

Figure 9-39 A Cisco Bridge

A *switch* is sometimes described as a multiport bridge. While a typical bridge might have just two ports (linking two systems on the same network), the switch has several ports, depending on how many network segments are to be linked, as shown in Figure 9-40. A switch is a more sophisticated device than a bridge, although the function of a switch is deceptively simple: choosing a port to forward data to its destination. Ethernet switches are becoming popular connectivity solutions because, like bridges, they increase network performance (in speed and bandwidth).

Figure 9-40 A Switch

Routers

Routers are the most sophisticated internetworking devices discussed so far. They are slower than bridges and switches, but make "smart" decisions on how to route (or send) packets received on one port to a network on another port. Each port to which a network segment is attached is described as a *router interface*. Routers can be computers with special network software installed on them, or they can be other devices built by network equipment manufacturers. Routers contain tables of network addresses along with optimal destination routes to other networks. A Cisco router is shown in Figure 9-41.

Figure 9-41 The Cisco 2600 Series Router

Server Components

Server components are those components that are used exclusively with the network server. End users depend on the server to provide the services required. To keep the server running at its optimal performance, a higher level of preventive maintenance must be maintained.

Video Controller

A video controller does not need to support high video resolutions on the network server. A video controller that can support 1024×768 resolution and 64,000 colors should be sufficient for most network servers.

Video Monitor

A video monitor for a network server should support 800×600 or higher for video resolution. A large video monitor (a 21-inch display) is useful on a network server. An LCD could also be used. If the video monitor is going to be installed in a server rack, the video monitor must be small enough to fit into the rack. The maximum size for a video monitor that is to be installed in a server rack is about 15 inches.

Keyboard Video Monitor (KVM) Switch

A *keyboard/video/monitor (KVM) switch* is a common component in a network server rack. With multiple network servers installed in a single equipment rack, it makes sense to have a single keyboard, video display, and mouse that can be switched among the network servers. A rack-mountable KVM switch usually fits within one rack unit and provides the capability to share the keyboard, video display, and mouse among the network servers in the rack.

CD-ROM/DVD-ROM Drive

Most server hardware includes either a CD-ROM or DVD-ROM drive. This is usually required for operating system and other software installation.

Floppy Drive

A floppy disk drive is often required on a network server to load some hardware drivers and to perform flash BIOS upgrades.

Universal Bus Controller

The universal serial bus (USB) is an external bus standard that supports data transfer rates up to 12 Mbps. One USB port can have up to 127 devices connected to it. On a network server, the types of devices that you might attach to a USB port include a USB mouse, a USB modem, a USB keyboard, or a USB monitoring cable for a UPS. A USB bus supports PnP technology and devices that can be hot-plugged. (Hot-plugged devices can be attached to and unattached from the USB bus without powering down the network server.) To use a USB port on a network server, the network operating system must have the capability to recognize and have drivers for the USB port. Version 2.0 of the USB standard allows data transmission rates up to 480 Mbps.

FireWire (IEEE 1394)

The IEEE 1394 standard (known as FireWire by Apple Computer) is an external serial bus that uses the SCSI-3 standards for communications. Data transfer rates of up to 400 Mbps are achievable using the IEEE 1394 standard. A single IEEE 1394 bus can have up to 63 devices attached to it. The IEEE 1394 standards support PnP technology and hot-plugging, much like the USB standard.

Modem

A modem or multiple modems might need to be installed in the network server. For example, a remote access server would need one or more modems to support dial-in access to the network. To implement a fax server, one or more fax modems (which differ from data modems) must be installed in the network server.

Redundant NIC

Having a *redundant NIC* in the network server allows the network server to keep communicating over the network even if a NIC fails. This is usually accomplished by having two identical NICs in the server, only one of which is communicating over the network. A special software driver for the redundant NICs constantly monitors the network communications and, if the software driver determines that the NIC currently being used has failed, the driver automatically switches to the other NIC.

Cooling Fan

Keeping the inside of the server chassis relatively cool is of major importance. If components inside the server chassis get too hot, they often fail. Server hardware has cooling fans to keep air circulating around the components. If you have only one cooling fan and it fails, the inside of the server chassis will overheat and the server will fail. Many hardware manufacturers provide the ability to add a redundant cooling fan, which is hot-swappable in the case of a cooling fan failure.

Cooling fans should also be placed in the network server rack to provide adequate ventilation for the network devices. Most network servers that are designed to be rack mounted are designed to have a flow of air from the front of the rack to the back. The front and rear doors of the rack are often perforated to provide ventilation.

Power Supply

Server hardware can have multiple hot-swappable power supplies for redundancy. Having two or even three power supplies allows the power supplies to balance the electrical load. If one power supply fails, the other power supply can handle the entire electrical load. The failed power supply can be replaced without taking the network server offline.

Server Rack

To conserve space in the server room, network servers can be purchased in a chassis that can be installed in a standard 19-inch equipment rack.

Electronic Industry Association Rack Unit

The Electronic Industry Association (EIA) has specified that the standard vertical rack unit is 1.75 inches. Server rack height is then specified in rack units. For example, a 42U rack is 73.5 inches (42×1.75) high.

Rack Layout

The layout of the components in the rack is important. Generally the rack-mounted UPSs are installed on the bottom of the rack due to their weight. A rack-mounted keyboard should be at the proper height to allow comfortable typing. The rack-mounted display adapter should be at eye level. Most manufacturers of network server racks provide software to aid in creating a layout of the devices in the network rack.

Rack-Mounted Keyboard/Trackball/Monitor/LCD Panel

Rack-mounted keyboards or keyboard/trackball combinations that fit into a drawer that slides into the rack are available. One keyboard can be attached to a rack-mounted KVM switch so that it can control all the network servers in the rack. The keyboard drawer is usually two rack units high.

There are several options for the video display to be used in a rack. A standard 15-inch CRT video display can be installed on a shelf in the rack. A monitor larger than 15 inches is usually too large to fit into a rack.

Different keyboard/LCD combinations are available for racks. The LCD folds down and slides into the rack when not in use. The keyboard/LCD combination is only two rack units high.

Cable Management

With several network servers and other devices in a rack, the management of the various cables becomes critical. Also, devices that are installed in a rack can generally be pulled out of the rack for service, much like a drawer can be pulled out from a cabinet. Pulling the network server out of the rack without disconnecting all the attached cables (LAN, power, video, mouse, keyboard, and so on) is accomplished by hinged cable management arms that are attached to the network server on one end and to the rack on the other.

Security

The network server should have side panels (which are usually optional) and front and rear doors that are lockable to provide security for the network devices that are installed in the rack.

LAN Architectures

This section includes the following topics:

- Ethernet
- Token Ring
- Fiber distributed data interface

Ethernet

The Ethernet architecture is now the most popular type of LAN architecture. *Architecture* refers to the overall structure of a computer or communication system. It determines the capabilities and limitations of the system. The *Ethernet architecture* is based on the IEEE 802.3 standard. The IEEE 802.3 standard specifies that a network implements the carrier sense multiple access with collision detection (CSMA/CD) access control method. CSMA/CD uses baseband transmission over coaxial or twisted-pair cable that is laid out in a bus topology (a linear or star bus). Standard transfer rates are 10 Mbps or 100 Mbps, but new standards provide for gigabit Ethernet, which is capable of attaining speeds up to 1 Gbps over fiber-optic cable or other high-speed media.

10BaseT

Currently, *10BaseT* is one of the most popular Ethernet implementations. It uses a star topology. The 10 stands for the common transmission speed, 10 Mbps. Base indicates baseband mode, and the *T* specifies twisted-pair cabling. The term *Ethernet cable* is used to describe the UTP cabling that is generally used in this architecture. STP cabling can also be used. The 10BaseT implementation and its cousin, 100BaseX, make networks that are easy to set up and expand.

Advantages of 10BaseT

Networks based on the 10BaseT specifications are relatively inexpensive. Although a hub is required to connect more than two computers, small hubs are available at a low cost. The 10BaseT network cards are inexpensive and widely available.

Twisted-pair cabling, especially the UTP most commonly used, is thin, flexible, and easier to work with than coaxial cable. The twisted-pair cabling uses modular RJ-45 plugs and jacks, so it is literally a snap to connect the cable to the NIC or hub.

Another big advantage of 10BaseT is its ability to be upgraded. By definition, a 10BaseT network runs at 10 Mbps. However, by using Category 5 cable or above and 10/100 Mbps dual-speed NICs, an upgrade to 100 Mbps can be achieved by simply replacing the hubs.

Disadvantages of 10BaseT

The maximum length for a 10BaseT segment (without repeaters) is 100 meters (about 328 feet). The UTP cable used in such a network is more vulnerable to EMI and attenuation than other cable types. Finally, the extra cost of a hub might not be feasible. Table 9-2 summarizes the advantages and disadvantages of 10BaseT.

Table 9-2 Advantages and Disadvantages of 10BaseT

Advantages	Disadvantages
Relatively inexpensive.	The maximum length for a segment (without repeaters) is 100 meters (about 328 feet).
Twisted-pair cabling is thin, flexible, and easier to work with than coaxial cable.	More susceptible to EMI and attenuation than other cable types.
Easy to upgrade.	Additional cost of a hub might not be feasible.

The high bandwidth demands of many modern applications, such as live videoconferencing and streaming audio, have created a need for speed. Many networks require more throughput than is possible with 10-Mbps Ethernet. This is where 100BaseX, also called *Fast Ethernet*, comes into play.

100BaseX

The *100BaseX* implementation is the next evolution of 10BaseT and is available in several different varieties. It can be implemented over four-pair Category 3, 4, or 5 UTP (100BaseT) cabling. It can also be implemented over two-pair Category 5 UTP or STP (100BaseTX) cabling, or as Ethernet over two-strand fiber-optic cable (100BaseFX).

Advantages of 100BaseX

Regardless of the implementation, the big advantage of 100BaseX is its high-speed performance. At 100 Mbps, transfer rates are 10 times that of 10Base2/10Base5 (both outdated technologies) and 10BaseT.

Because it uses twisted-pair cabling, 100BaseX also shares the same advantages enjoyed by 10BaseT. These include low cost, flexibility, and ease of implementation and expansion.

Disadvantages of 100BaseX

The 100BaseX implementation shares the disadvantages that are inherent to the twisted-pair cabling of 10BaseT, such as susceptibility to EMI and attenuation. The 100-Mbps NICs and hubs are generally more expensive than those designed for 10-Mbps networks, but prices have dropped as 100BaseX has gained in popularity. Fiber-optic cable remains an expensive cabling option, not so much because of the cost of the cable itself but because of the training and expertise required to install it.

Table 9-3 summarizes the advantages and disadvantages of 100BaseX.

Table 9-3 Advantages and Disadvantages of 100BaseX

Advantages	Disadvantages
High-speed performance	Susceptible to EMI and attenuation
Low cost	100-Mbps NICs and hubs are generally more expensive
Flexibility	Requires better-trained installers and technicians
Ease of implementation and expansion	

1000BaseT

If 100BaseX is known as Fast Ethernet, 1000BaseT must be considered a speed demon; its common nickname is *Gigabit Ethernet*. Although not yet widely used in production networks, this *1000BaseT* architecture supports data transfer rates of up to 1 Gbps, which is remarkably fast. Gigabit Ethernet is, for the most part, a LAN architecture, although its implementation over fiber-optic cable makes it suitable for metropolitan-area networks (MANs).

Advantages of 1000BaseT

The greatest advantage of 1000BaseT is performance. At 1 Gbps, it is 10 times as fast as Fast Ethernet and 100 times as fast as standard Ethernet. This makes it possible to implement bandwidth-intensive applications, such as live video, throughout an intranet.

Disadvantages of 1000BaseT

The main disadvantages associated with 1000BaseT are those common to all UTP networks, as detailed in the sections on 10BaseT and 100BaseT.

Table 9-4 summarizes the advantages and disadvantages of 1000BaseT.

Table 9-4 Advantages and Disadvantages of 1000BaseT

Advantages	Disadvantages
The greatest advantage of 1000BaseT is performance. At 1 Gbps, it is 10 times as fast as Fast Ethernet and 100 times as fast as standard Ethernet.	The main disadvantages associated with 1000BaseT are those common to all UTP networks, as detailed in the sections on 10BaseT and 100BaseT.
Can be used to implement bandwidth-intensive audio and video applications.	

Token Ring

IBM originally developed *Token Ring* as reliable network architecture based on the token-passing access control method. Token Ring is often integrated with IBM mainframe systems, such as the AS400. It was intended to be used with PCs and mainframes, and it works well with Systems Network Architecture (SNA), which is the IBM architecture used for connecting to mainframe networks.

The Token Ring standards are defined in IEEE 802.5. This is a prime example of an architecture whose physical topology is different from its logical topology. The Token Ring topology is referred to as a star-wired ring because the outer appearance of the network design is a star. The computers connect to a central hub, called a multistation access unit (MSAU). Inside the device, however, the wiring forms a circular data path, creating a logical ring. Figure 9-42 shows the Token Ring topology implemented on a network.

Token Ring is so named because of its logical topology and its media access control method of token-passing. The transfer rate for Token Ring can be either 4 Mbps or 16 Mbps.

Token Ring is a baseband architecture that uses digital signaling. In that way, it resembles Ethernet, but the communication process is different in many respects. Token Ring is an active topology. As the signal travels around the circle to each network card, the signal is regenerated before being sent on its way.

In an Ethernet network, all computers are created physically equal. At the software level, some can act as servers and control network accounts and access, but the servers communicate physically on the network in the same way as the clients.

Figure 9-42 Token Ring Topology Implementation

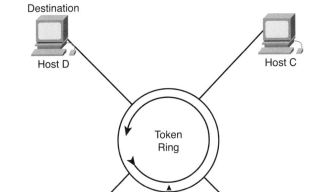

The Monitor of the Ring

In a Token Ring network, the first computer that comes online becomes the "hall monitor" and must keep track of how many times each frame circles the ring. The first computer has the responsibility of ensuring that only one token is out on the network at a time.

The monitor computer periodically sends a signal called a *beacon*, which circulates around the ring. Each computer on the network looks for the beacon. If a computer does not receive the beacon from its nearest active upstream neighbor (NAUN) when expected, that computer puts a message on the network that notifies the monitoring computer that the beacon was not received, along with its own address and that of the NAUN that failed to send when expected. In most cases, this causes an automatic reconfiguration that restores communications.

Data Transfer

A Token Ring network uses a *token* (that is, a special signal) to control access to the cable. A token is initially generated when the first computer on the network comes online. When a computer wants to transmit, it waits for and then takes control of the token when it comes its way. The token can travel in either direction around the ring but only in one direction at a time. The hardware configuration determines the direction of travel.

Fiber Distributed Data Interface

The *fiber distributed data interface (FDDI)* is a type of Token Ring network. Its implementation and topology differ from the IBM Token Ring LAN architecture, which is governed by IEEE 802.5. FDDI is often used for MANs or larger LANs, such as those connecting several buildings in an office complex or campus. MANs typically span a metro area.

As its name implies, FDDI runs on fiber-optic cable and thus combines high-speed performance with the advantages of the token-passing ring topology. FDDI runs at 100 Mbps, and its topology is a dual ring. The outer ring is called the primary ring, and the inner ring is called the secondary ring.

Normally, traffic flows only on the primary ring. If the primary ring fails, the data automatically flow onto the secondary ring in the opposite direction. When this occurs, the network is said to be in a wrapped state. This provides fault tolerance for the link. Figures 9-43 and 9-44 illustrate how FDDI works.

Figure 9-43 FDDI

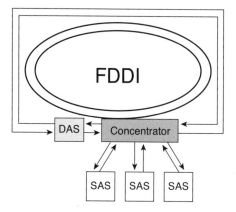

Computers on an FDDI network are divided into two classes, as follows:

- **Class A**—Computers connected to the cables of both rings
- **Class B**—Computers connected to only one ring

An FDDI dual ring supports a maximum of 500 nodes per ring. The total distance of each length of the cable ring is 100 kilometers, or 62 miles. A repeater (a device that regenerates signals) is needed every 2 kilometers, which is why FDDI is not considered to be a WAN link.

Figure 9-44 FDDI With a Break in the Cable

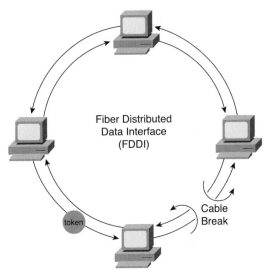

The specifications described so far refer to an FDDI that is implemented over fiber-optic cable. It is also possible to use the FDDI technology with copper cabling. This is called *copper distributed data interface (CDDI)*. The maximum distances for CDDI are considerably lower than those for FDDI.

Advantages of FDDI

FDDI combines the advantages of token-passing on the ring topology with the high speed of fiber-optic transmission. The dual-ring topology provides redundancy and fault tolerance. The fiber-optic cable is not susceptible to EMI and noise, and it is more secure than copper wiring. FDDI can send data for greater distances between repeaters than can Ethernet and traditional Token Ring.

Disadvantages of FDDI

As always, high speed and reliability come with a price. FDDI is relatively expensive to implement, and the distance limitations, though less restrictive than those of other LAN links, make it unsuitable for true WAN communications.

Worksheet 9.4.2 Network Topology

In this worksheet, you review the different topologies in a network environment.

Networking Protocols and the OSI Model

This section includes the following topics:

- OSI model overview
- What is a protocol?
- Transmission control protocol/Internet protocol
- Sequenced packet exchange/internetwork packet exchange
- NetBEUI
- AppleTalk

Open Systems Interconnection Model Overview

The *Open Systems Interconnection (OSI)* reference model is an industry standard framework that is used to divide the functions of networking into seven distinct layers. It is one of the most commonly used teaching and reference tools in networking today. The *International Organization for Standardization (ISO)* (not to be confused with OSI) developed the OSI model in the 1980s.

The seven layers of the OSI reference model are shown in Figure 9-45. Each layer provides specific services to the layers above and below it in order for the network to work effectively. At the top of the model is the *application* interface (layer), which enables the smooth usage of applications such as word processors and web browsers. At the bottom is the *physical* side of the network. The physical side includes the cabling (discussed earlier in this chapter), hubs, and other networking hardware.

Figure 9-45 The OSI Model

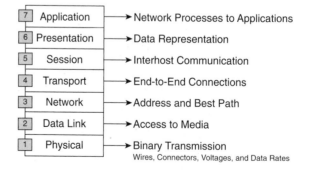

How Does the OSI Model Work?

A message begins at the top application layer and moves down the OSI layers to the bottom physical layer. One example would be a sent e-mail message. Figure 9-46 shows the progression of the e-mail as it descends and information or headers are added. A header is layer-specific information that explains what functions the layer carried out.

Figure 9-46 An E-Mail Message

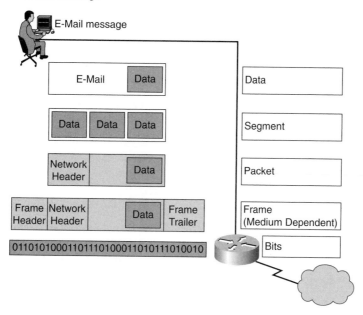

Figure 9-47 illustrates the layers of the OSI model that the e-mail goes through.

Figure 9-47 OSI Layers of an E-Mail Message

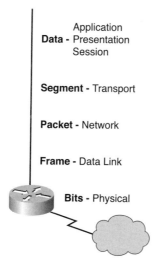

Conversely, at the receiving end, headers are striped from the message as it travels up the corresponding layers and arrives at its destination. The process of data being encapsulated on the sending end and data being deencapsulated on the receiving end is the function of the OSI model.

Communication across the layers of the reference model is achieved because of special networking software programs called protocols. Protocols are discussed in the following sections. The OSI model was intended to be used for developing networking protocols. However, most of the protocols now used on LANs do not necessarily respond exactly to these layers. Some protocols fall neatly within the boundaries between these layers, while others overlap or provide services that overlap or span several layers. This explains the meaning of "reference" as it is used in conjunction with the OSI reference model. Table 9-5 summarizes the functions of each layer, the type of data that it handles, and the type of hardware that can work at that layer.

Table 9-5 OSI Model Layers and Their Functions

Layer Number	Layer Name	PDU	Mnemonic	Purpose
7	Application	Data	All	Provides network services to application processes (such as e-mail, ftp, and telnet).
6	Presentation	Data	People	Ensures that data are readable by the receiving system. Deals with data representation.
5	Session	Data	Seem	Establishes, manages, and terminates sessions between applications.
4	Transport	Segment	To	Handles information flow control, fault detection and recovery, and data transport reliability.
3	Network	Packet	Need	Provides connectivity and path selection between two end systems.
2	Data link	Frame	Data	Provides the reliable transfer of data across media using physical addressing and the network topology.
1	Physical	Bits	Processing	Consists of voltages, wires, and connectors.

The following sections discuss examples of the networking protocols mentioned in this section.

What Is a Protocol?

A *protocol* is a controlled sequence of messages that are exchanged between two or more systems to accomplish a given task. Protocol specifications define this sequence together with the format or layout of the messages that are exchanged. In coordinating the work between systems, protocols use control structures in each system that operate like a set of interlocking gears. This occurs so that computers can precisely track the protocols' points as they move through the sequence of exchanges.

Timing is crucial to network operation. Protocols require messages to arrive within certain time intervals, so systems maintain one or more timers during protocol execution. The systems also take alternative actions if the network does not meet the timing rules. To do their work, many protocols depend on the operation of other protocols in the group or suite of protocols. Protocol functions include the following:

- Identifying errors
- Applying compression techniques

In addition, protocol functions decide on how to announce sent and received data and how to address data. How the data are to be sent is also decided by the protocol.

Transmission Control Protocol/Internet Protocol

The *transmission control protocol/Internet protocol (TCP/IP)* suite of protocols has become the dominant standard for internetworking. Originally defined by researchers in the U.S. Department of Defense, TCP/IP represents a set of public standards that specify how packets of information are exchanged between computers over one or more networks.

The TCP/IP protocol suite includes a number of major protocols, and each performs a specific function. Figure 9-48 demonstrates the relationship between the OSI model and the TCP/IP protocol.

Figure 9-48 OSI Model Versus TCP/IP Protocol

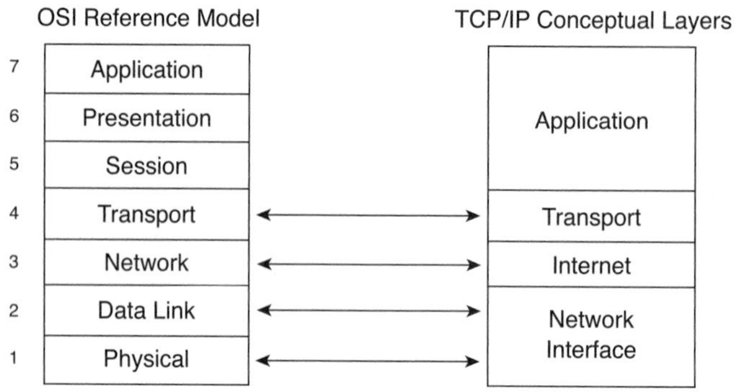

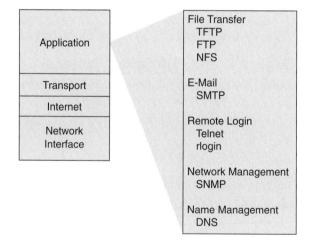

Application Protocols

The application layer is the fourth layer in the TCP/IP model. It provides the starting point for any communication session. An overview of the TCP/IP application layer is shown in Figure 9-49.

Figure 9-49 TCP/IP Application Layer

The following list details the protocols and other services used by the application layer:

- **Hypertext transfer protocol (HTTP)**—Governs how files such as text, graphics, sounds, and video are exchanged on the Internet or World Wide Web (WWW). HTTP is an application layer protocol. The Internet Engineering Task Force

(IETF) developed the standards for HTTP. HTTP 1.1 is the current version. As its name implies, HTTP is used to exchange hypertext files. These files can include links to other files. A web server runs an HTTP service or daemon (a program that services HTTP requests). These requests are transmitted by HTTP client software, which is another name for a web browser.

- **Hypertext markup language (HTML)**—A page description language. Web designers use it to indicate to web browser software how the page should look. HTML includes tags to indicate boldface type, italic type, line breaks, paragraph breaks, hyperlinks, insertion of tables, etc.

- **Telnet**—Enables terminal access to local or remote systems. The telnet application is used to access remote devices for configuration, control, and troubleshooting.

- **File transfer protocol (FTP)**—An application that provides services for file transfer and manipulation. FTP uses the session layer to allow multiple simultaneous connections to remote file systems.

- **Simple mail transport protocol (SMTP)**—Provides messaging services over TCP/IP and supports most Internet e-mail programs.

- **Domain Name System (DNS)**—Provides access to name servers where network names are translated to the addresses used by Layer 3 network protocols. DNS greatly simplifies network usage by end users.

Transport Protocols

The transport layer is the third layer in the TCP/IP model. It provides an end-to-end management of the communications session. An overview of the TCP/IP transport layer is shown in Figure 9-50.

Figure 9-50 The TCP/IP Transport Layer

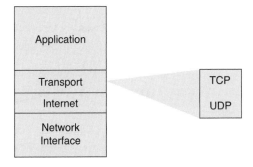

The following list details the protocols used by the transport layer:

- **Transmission control protocol (TCP)**—The primary Internet protocol for the reliable delivery of data. TCP includes facilities for end-to-end connection establishment, for error detection and recovery, and for metering the rate of data flow into the network. Many standard applications, such as e-mail, web browsing, file transfer, and telnet, depend on the services of TCP. TCP identifies the application that is using it by a port number.

- **User datagram protocol (UDP)**—Offers a connectionless service to applications. UDP uses lower overhead than TCP and can tolerate a level of data loss. Network management applications, network file systems, and simple file transports use UDP. Like TCP, UDP identifies applications by port number.

Network Protocols

The Internet layer is the second layer in the TCP/IP model. It provides internetworking for the communications session. An overview of the TCP/IP Internet layer is shown in Figure 9-51.

Figure 9-51 The TCP/IP Internet Layer

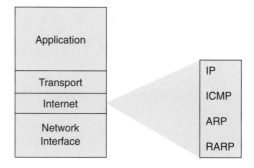

The following list details the protocols used by the Internet layer:

- **Internet Protocol (IP)**—Provides source and destination addressing and, in conjunction with routing protocols, packet forwarding from one network to another toward a destination.

- **Internet Control Message Protocol (ICMP)**—Used for network testing and troubleshooting. It enables diagnostic and error messages. ICMP echo messages are used by the ping application to determine if a remote device is reachable. (Ping is discussed in a later section.)

- **Routing Information Protocol (RIP)**—Operates between router devices to discover paths between networks. In an intranet, routers depend on a routing protocol to build and maintain information about how to forward packets toward the destination. RIP chooses routes based on the distance, or "hop count."
- **Address Resolution Protocol (ARP)**—Used to discover the local address (MAC address) of a station on the network when its IP address is known. End stations as well as routers use ARP to discover local addresses.

Sequenced Packet Exchange/Internetwork Packet Exchange

Sequenced packet exchange/internetwork packet exchange (SPX/IPX) is the protocol suite employed originally by Novell Corporation's network operating system, NetWare. SPX/IPX delivers functions similar to those included in TCP/IP. To enable desktop client systems to access NetWare services, Novell deployed a set of application, transport, and network protocols. Although NetWare client/server systems are not tied to particular hardware platforms, the native (or original) NetWare protocols remained proprietary. Unlike TCP/IP, the Novell SPX/IPX protocol suite remained the property of one company. As a result of the market pressure to move to an industry-standard way of building networks, SPX/IPX has fallen out of favor among customers. In its current releases, Novell supports the TCP/IP suite. However, a large installed base of NetWare networks continues to use SPX/IPX.

Common examples of some of the protocol elements included in the Novell SPX/IPX protocol suite include the following:

- Service advertising protocol
- Novell routing information protocol (Novell RIP)
- Netware core protocol (NCP)
- Get nearest server (GNS)
- Netware link services protocol (NLSP)

A detailed discussion of the role and functions played by these protocol elements in networking and internetworking is not within the scope of this text.

NetBIOS Extended User Interface

NetBIOS extended user interface (NetBEUI) is a protocol used primarily on small Windows NT networks. It was used earlier as the default networking protocol in Windows 3.11 (Windows for Workgroups) and LAN Manager. NetBEUI has a small overhead but cannot be routed or used by routers to communicate on a large network.

NetBEUI is a simple protocol that lacks many of the features that enable protocol suites, such as TCP/IP, to be used on networks of almost any size.

Although NetBEUI cannot be used in building large networks or connecting several networks, it is suitable for small peer-to-peer networks, in which a few computers are directly connected to each other. It can be used in conjunction with another routable protocol such as TCP/IP. This gives the network administrator the advantages of NetBEUI's high performance within the local network and the capability to communicate beyond the LAN over TCP/IP.

AppleTalk

AppleTalk is a protocol suite to network Macintosh computers; it is comprised of a comprehensive set of protocols that span the seven layers of the OSI reference model. AppleTalk protocols were designed to run over the major LAN types, notably Ethernet and Token Ring, as well as Apple's own LAN physical topology, LocalTalk.

Examples of AppleTalk protocol include the following:

- AppleTalk filing protocol (AFP)
- AppleTalk data stream protocol (ADSP)
- Zone information protocol (ZIP)
- AppleTalk session protocol (ASP)
- Printer access protocol (PAP)

A detailed discussion of these protocol elements is not within the scope of this text.

Like Novell, Apple Computer also developed its own proprietary protocol suite to network Macintosh computers. Like Novell, many customers continue to use AppleTalk to connect their systems. But just as other companies have transitioned to the use of TCP/IP, Apple now fully supports the public networking protocol standards.

 Worksheet 9.6.5 OSI Model, TCP/IP, Protocols

This worksheet reviews the important information provided in the previous sections.

TCP/IP Utilities

TCP/IP is a complex collection of protocols. Most vendors implement the suite to include a variety of utilities for viewing configuration information and troubleshooting problems. In the next sections, the following common TCP/IP utilities are explored:

- Packet Internet groper
- Address resolution protocol, reverse address resolution protocol, and NSLOOKUP
- NETSTAT and TPCON
- NBTSTAT
- IP configuration utilities
- Route-tracing utilities

Utilities that perform the same function(s) can be given different names by different vendors. How these utilities are used in software troubleshooting is discussed in a later chapter.

Packet Internet Groper

Packet Internet groper (ping) is a simple but highly useful command-line utility that is included in most implementations of TCP/IP. Ping can be used with either the host name or the IP address to test IP connectivity. Ping works by sending an ICMP echo request to the destination computer. The receiving computer then sends back an ICMP echo reply message.

It is also possible to use ping to find the IP address of a host when the name is known. If the ping apple.com command is typed, as shown in Figure 9-52, the IP address from which the reply is returned is displayed.

Figure 9-52 The Ping Utility

```
Information Returned in Response to a ping of apple.com

c:\>ping apple.com
Pinging apple.com [17.254.3.183] with 32 bytes of data:
Reply from 17.254.3.183: bytes=32 time=430ms TTL=90
Reply from 17.254.3.183: bytes=32 time=371ms TTL=90
Reply from 17.254.3.183: bytes=32 time=370ms TTL=90
Reply from 17.254.3.183: bytes=32 time=371ms TTL=90

Ping statistics for 17.254.3.183:
    Packets: Sent = 4, Received = 4, Lost = 0 <0% loss.,
Approximate round trip times in milli-seconds:
    Minimum = 370ms, Maximum = 430ms, Average = 385ms
```

Lab Activity 9.7.2   Troubleshooting the NIC

Use the **ping** command to test the connectivity and to troubleshoot problems based on the results.

Address Resolution Protocol, Reverse Address Resolution Protocol, and NSLOOKUP

Address resolution protocol (ARP) is the means by which networked computers map IP addresses to physical hardware (MAC) addresses that are recognized in a local network. ARP builds and maintains a table called the ARP cache, which contains these mappings (the IP address and MAC address). The ARP cache is the means by which a correlation is maintained between each MAC address and its corresponding IP address. ARP provides the protocol rules for making this correlation and provides address conversion in both directions.

The following switches can be used with the ARP command:

- **ARP -a:** Displays the cache
- **ARP -s:** Adds a permanent IP-to-MAC mapping
- **ARP -d:** Deletes an entry from the ARP cache

Other switches are included with vendor-specific implementations of ARP.

Reverse Address Resolution Protocol

Machines that do not know their IP addresses use *reverse address resolution protocol (RARP)* to obtain IP address information based on the physical or MAC address. RARP provides the rules by which the physical machine in a LAN can request its IP address from a gateway server ARP table or cache. A *gateway server* is a computer or router that is configured to receive information from computers in the local network and send the information to computers in remote locations such as the Internet or other areas in a large internetwork.

> **NOTE**
>
> ARP maps IP-to-MAC addresses. RARP is the reverse of ARP; it maps MAC-to-IP addresses.

NSLOOKUP

Another utility, *NSLOOKUP*, returns the IP address for a given host name. It can also find the host name for a specified IP address. For example, entering cisco.com would deliver 198.133.219.25, Cisco's IP address. Entering 198.133.219.25 would deliver Cisco.com.

NETSTAT and TPCON

It is often useful to view network statistics. The *NETSTAT* command is used in Windows and UNIX/Linux to display TCP/IP connection and protocol information. Novell uses the *TPCON* NetWare Loadable Module (NLM) to accomplish this.

The NETSTAT command provides a list of connections that are currently active. NETSTAT statistics can be useful in troubleshooting TCP/IP connectivity problems. Figure 9-53 shows the information available in summary (-s switch) mode. These error reports are especially helpful in diagnosing hardware and routing problems.

Figure 9-53 The NETSTAT Command

The netstat Command is Used to View Connection Information.

```
c:>netstat
Active Connections
   Proto  Local Address     Foreign Address                  State
   TCP    DS2000:3301       msgr-ns18.hotmail.com:1863       ESTABLISHED
   TCP    DS2000:3450       constellation.tacteam.net:3389   ESTABLISHED
   TCP    DS2000:3860       ultra1.dallas.net:pop3           TIME_WAIT
   TCP    DS2000:3861       aux153.plano.net:pop3            TIME_WAIT
```

NBTSTAT

The Microsoft TCP/IP stacks included in Windows operating systems provide the *NBTSTAT* utility, which is used to display NetBIOS information. Figure 9-54 shows the syntax and switches that are available with the NBTSTAT command.

Figure 9-54 The NBTSTAT Command—Syntax and Switches

```
Type nbtstat at the Command Line for a Display of the Syntax and a List of Available Switches.

c:\>nbtstat

Displays protocol statistics and current TCP/IP connections using NBT
(NetBIOS over TCP/IP).
NBTSTAT [ [-a RemoteName] [-A IP address] [-c] [-n]
        [-r] [-R] [-RR] [-s] [-S] [interval] ]
  -a    (adapter status) Lists the remote machine's name table given
its name
  -A    (Adapter status) Lists the remote machine's name table given
its
                         IP address.
  -c    (cache)          Lists NBT's cache of remote [machine] names
and their IP
 addresses
  -n    (names)          Lists local NetBIOS names.
  -r    (resolved)       Lists names resolved by broadcast and via WINS
  -R    (Reload)         Purges and reloads the remote cache name table
  -S    (Sessions)       Lists sessions table with the destination IP
addresses
  -s    (sessions)       Lists sessions table converting destination IP
                         addresses to computer NETBIOS names.
  -RR   (ReleaseRefresh) Sends Name Release packets to WINs and then,
starts Refresh

  RemoteName   Remote host machine name.
  IP address   Dotted decimal representation of the IP address.
  interval     Redisplays selected statistics, pausing interval
               seconds between each display. Press Ctrl+C to stop
               redisplaying statistics.
```

IP Configuration Utilities

TCP/IP configuration information can be displayed using the following utilities, which depend on the operating system being used:

- **IPCONFIG**—Windows NT and Windows 2000 (command-line), as shown in Figure 9-55.

Figure 9-55   The IPCONFIG Command

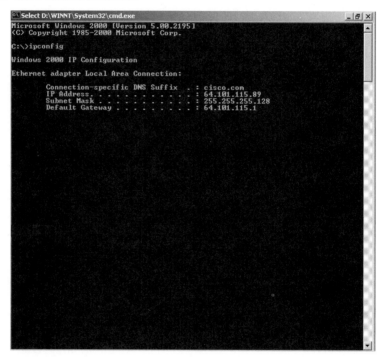

- **WINIPCFG**—Windows 95, 98, and 2000 (GUI), as shown in Figure 9-56.

Figure 9-56   The WINIPCFG Command

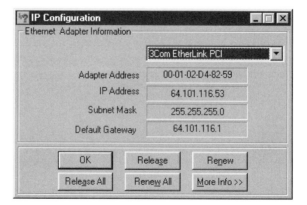

- **CONFIG**—NetWare (server console).
- **IFCONFIG**—UNIX and Linux (command-line), as shown in Figure 9-57.

Figure 9-57 Linux IFCONFIG Output

```
[root@jesselinux root]# ifconfig
eth0      Link encap:Ethernet  HWaddr
00:00:86:48:3E:85
          inet addr:64.101.115.124
Bcast:255.255.255.255 Mask:255.255.255.128
          UP BROADCAST NOTRAILERS RUNNING
MTU:1500  Metric:1
          RX packets:50156 errors:0 dropped:0
overruns:0 frame:0
          TX packets:4687 errors:0 dropped:0
overruns:0 carrier:0 collisions:0
          RX bytes:9440811 (9.0 Mb)   TX
bytes:465497 (454.5 Kb)

lo        Link encap:Local Loopback
          inet addr:127.0.0.1  Mask:255.0.0.0
          UP LOOPBACK RUNNING   MTU:16436
Metric:1
          RX packets:62 errors:0 dropped:0
overruns:0 frame:0
          TX packets:62 errors:0 dropped:0
overruns:0 carrier:0 collisions:0
          RX bytes:3604 (3.5 Kb)  TX bytes:3604
(3.5 Kb)

[root@jesselinux root]#
```

The configuration utilities can provide a wealth of information including the currently used IP address, MAC address, subnet mask, and default gateway. The utilities can show the addresses of DNS and WINS servers, DHCP information, and services enabled. A variety of switches are available, depending on the vendor and specific utility.

Route-Tracing Utilities

It is often useful to trace the route that a packet takes on its journey from source computer to destination host. TCP/IP stacks include a route-tracing utility that enables users to identify the routers through which the message passes. The following options depend on the operating system used:

- **TRACERT**—Windows, as shown in Figure 9-58
- **IPTRACE**—NetWare NLM
- **TRACEROUTE**—UNIX/Linux, as shown in Figure 9-59

Figure 9-58 The TRACERT Command

```
Microsoft(R) Windows DOS

(C)Copyright Microsoft Corp 1990-1999.

C:\>tracert www.hp.com

Tracing route to www.hp.com [192.6.234.8] over a
maximum of 30 hops:

1   <10 ms    <10 ms    <10 ms  phx2-00-
gw1.cisco.com [187.101.115.2]

2   31 ms     31 ms     32 ms  sjce-dirty-
gw1.cisco.com [115.107.240.197]

3   31 ms     16 ms     31 ms  barrnet-
gw.cisco.com [90.107.239.54]

4   31 ms     31 ms     32 ms  12.127.200.81

5   31 ms     31 ms     31 ms  gbr3-
p80.la2ca.ip.att.net [12.122.2.250]

6   31 ms     47 ms     47 ms  ggr1-
p360.la2ca.ip.att.net [12.123.28.129]

7   31 ms     47 ms     31 ms  lax-brdr-
01.inet.qwest.net [205.171.1.129]

8   31 ms     47 ms     32 ms  lax-core-
01.inet.qwest.net [205.171.19.37]

9   78 ms     109 ms    94 ms  iah-core-
01.inet.qwest.net [205.171.5.161]

10  94 ms     93 ms     94 ms  tpa-core-
02.inet.qwest.net [205.171.5.105]
```

Figure 9-59 Linux TRACEROUTE Output

```
[root@jesselinux root]# traceroute www.hp.com
traceroute: Warning: www.hp.com has multiple
addresses; using
192.151.53.86
traceroute to www.hp.com (12.151.53.86), 30 hops max,
38 byte packets
 1  phx2-00-gw1.cisco.com (164.101.115.2)  1.324 ms
0.365 ms  0.324 ms
 2  phoenix-az1-gw1.cisco.com (130.96.9.148)  0.926
ms  1.281 ms  0.808
 3  barrnet-gw.cisco.com (112.107.239.10)  26.881 ms
27.665 ms  25.962ms
 4  p3-3.paloalto-cr2.bbnplanet.net (1.0.26.13)
28.122 ms  27.434 ms 31.414 ms
 5  p7-1.paloalto-nbr2.bbnplanet.net (4.0.6.77)
30.598 ms  34.473 ms 28.098 ms
 6  p1-0.paix-bil.bbnplanet.net (4.0.6.102)  40.875
ms  28.635 ms 31.398 ms
 7  p6-0.snjpcal-br1.bbnplanet.net (4.24.7.61)  34.213
ms  28.424 ms 28.076 ms
 8  p9-0.1sanca2-br1.bbnplanet.net (4.24.5.57)  57.374
ms  45.787 ms 35.040 ms
 9  p15-0.1sanca2-br2.bbnplanet.net (4.24.5.46)
35.730 ms  38.266 ms 36.341 ms
10 p9-0.crtntx1-br2.bbnplanet.net (4.24.5.62)  72.408
ms  71.467 ms 71.645 ms
11  so-2-1-0.atlngal-br2.bbnplanet.net (4.0.5.130)
95.908 ms  95.166 ms  96.349 ms
12  so-7-0-0.atlngal-br1.bbnplanet.net (4.24.10.33)
96.946 ms  95.263ms  98.567 ms
13  p2-0.atlngal-cr5.bbnplanet.net (4.24.7.226)
96.514 ms  96.395 ms 108.542 ms
14  p5-1-0.hpatlanta.bbnplanet.net (4.24.172.54)
102.712 ms  112.919ms 109.904 ms
[root@jesselinux root]#
```

All three of these utilities, (TRACERT, IPTRACE, and TRACEROUTE) can be used to trace a packet. The determining factor is the operating system or software environment.

Connecting to the Internet

This section includes the following topics:

- Synchronous and asynchronous serial lines
- Modems
- Dialup networking, modem standards, and AT commands
- ISPs and Internet backbone providers
- Digital subscriber lines
- Cable modems
- Cable modem versus DSL Internet technologies

Synchronous and Asynchronous Serial Lines

Serial lines that are established over serial cabling connect to one of a computer's standard RS-232 communication (COM) ports. Serial transmission sends data one bit at a time (previously illustrated with a car on a one-lane highway). Analog or digital signals depend on changes in the state (modulations) to represent the binary data. To correctly interpret the signals, the receiving network device must know precisely when to measure the signal. Therefore, timing becomes important in networking. In fact, the biggest problem with sending data over serial lines is keeping the transmitted data bit timing coordinated. Two techniques are used to provide proper timing for serial transfers:

- **Synchronous serial transmission**—Data bits are sent together with a synchronizing clock pulse, as shown in Figure 9-60. In this transmission method, a built-in timing mechanism coordinates the clocks of the sending and receiving devices. This is known as *guaranteed state change synchronization*, the most commonly used type of synchronous transmission method.

Figure 9-60 Synchronous Serial Transmission

Synchronous Transmission

x y z a b c d e f g h i j k l m

- **Asynchronous serial transmission**—Data bits are sent without a synchronizing clock pulse. This transmission method uses a start bit at the beginning of each message. Asynchronous serial transmission is illustrated in Figure 9-61. The spaces in between the data indicate the start and stop bits. When the receiving device gets the start bit, it can synchronize its internal clock with the sender's clock.

Figure 9-61 Asynchronous Serial Transmission

Asynchronous Transmission

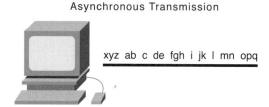

PC serial ports and most analog modems use the asynchronous communication method, while digital modems (also called terminal adapters) and LAN adapters use the synchronous method. The industry standard for the serial line interface is the Electronic Industries Association (EIA) RS-232C.

PC and modem makers have developed single-chip devices that perform all the functions that are necessary for serial transfers to occur. These devices are called *universal asynchronous receiver/transmitters (UART)*. The synchronous devices are known as *universal synchronous/asynchronous receiver/transmitters (USART)* and can handle both synchronous and asynchronous transmissions.

Modems

The *modem* is an electronic device that is used for computer communications through telephone lines. It allows data transfer between one computer and another. These UARTs convert byte-oriented data to serial bit streams. Blocks of data are handled by software. Internal modems combine a UART and a modem onboard. The modems convert digital data to analog signals and analog signals back to digital data. The term modem derives from the device's function. The process of converting analog signals to digital and back again is called modulation/demodulation (hence the term modem). Modem-based transmission is remarkably accurate, despite the fact that telephone lines can be quite noisy.

The following list details the four main types of modems:

- **Expansion cards**—These are the most common type. These cards plug into the motherboard expansion slots (ISA or PCI) and are called internal modems, as shown in Figure 9-62.

- **PCMCIA cards**—These modems are a variation of modems that are designed for easy installation in notebook computers. Also known as PC cards, they look like credit cards and are small and portable, as shown in Figure 9-63.

- **External modems**—These can be used with any computer. They plug into a serial port (COM1 or COM2) on the back of the computer. External modems, such as the cable modem shown in Figure 9-64, are typically used for high-speed connections.

- **Built-in modems**—These are used in some notebook computers.

Figure 9-62 A Typical Expansion Card Modem

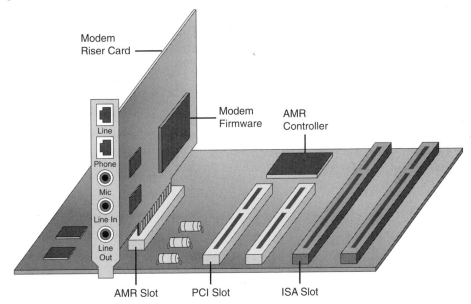

Figure 9-63 A Typical PCMCIA Card Modem

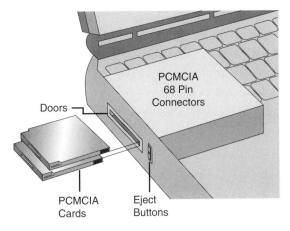

Figure 9-64 A Cisco Cable Modem

Internal modems simply plug into one of the expansion slots on the motherboard. These internal modem varieties, therefore, do not take up extra space on the desktop. They usually cost slightly less than modems that are externally plugged into the computer. You might have to set jumpers to select the IRQ and I/O addresses for these modems. No configuration is needed for a Plug and Play (PnP) modem, which is installed on a motherboard that supports PnP. A modem that is to use a serial (COM) port that is not yet in use must be configured. Additionally, the software drivers that come with the modem must be installed for the modem to work properly.

External modems are typically a bit more expensive than the internal varieties. Plugging them into one of the serial ports connects them to the computer. The computer case does not have to be opened. Newer USB modems are plugged into a USB port or hub. An external modem uses the IRQ and I/O address that are assigned to that serial port. A status light on the modem indicates whether the modem is online. Software must be installed for the external modem to work properly.

In most current modem types, a phone line is plugged into a standard RJ-11 telephone jack. Other modem types and devices, such as cable modem and DSL, are discussed in a later section.

Dialup Networking, Modem Standards, and AT Commands

When computers use the public telephone system or network to communicate, it is called *dialup networking (DUN)*. Computers are able to connect to the phone network using modems. Modems communicate with each other using audio tone signals; this means that they are able to duplicate the dialing characteristics of a telephone. If a computer is running Windows 95 or a later version and a modem is being used to connect to a LAN or WAN, DUN establishes the connection. DUN creates a point-to-point protocol (PPP) connection between the two computers over a phone line. In this process, PPP causes the modem to act like a network interface card. PPP is the WAN protocol that transports the networking protocol (TCP/IP, IPX/SPX, or NetBEUI) over the telephone line to allow network activity between the connected PCs.

The modem must operate in two of the following states to enable DUN:

- **Local command state**—The modem is offline. It receives commands and provides status information to the host computer to which the modem is installed.
- **Online state**—In this state, the modem is transferring data between the host machine and a remote computer through the telephone system.

Three activities occur during the local command and online states. These include dialing, data exchange, and answering. The modem would normally shift between the two states if, for example, the system tells it to go online and dial out to another unit, or if the modem receives an incoming call.

After the line connection has been established, a *handshake sequence* takes place between the two modems and the computers. This is a flurry of short events that take place between the two systems to establish the readiness of the two modems and their computers to engage in data exchange. Dialup modems send data over the serial telephone line in the form of an analog signal. Analog signals can be drawn as waves because they change gradually and continuously.

Recall that digital communications are based on binary format. In this system, the digital signals represent 1s and 0s. These signals must be converted to a waveform (analog) to travel across telephone lines. The signals are reconverted to digital form (1s and 0s) by the receiving modem so that the receiving computer can understand the data.

The outcome of the handshake and the negotiation between the sending and receiving devices is the establishment of a common modulation that is supported by both computers. This completes the process of a session negotiation so that effective data exchange can occur.

Other devices often determine the data transfer speed. As previously mentioned, small single-chip devices run the COM port to which an external modem is attached. These are the UART chips. The type of UART chip installed determines the top speed at which devices can communicate using the port. Current UART 16450 and 16550 chips enable speeds of up to 115,200 bps, and the 16650 chip supports a transmission rate of 230,400 bps.

AT Commands

All modems require software to control the communication session. The set of commands that most modem software uses is known as the *Hayes-compatible command set*. The command set is named after the Hayes Microcomputer Products Company, which first defined them. The Hayes command set is based on a group of instructions that always begins with a set of attention characters (AT), followed by the command characters. Because these attention characters are an important part of a Hayes command, the command set is usually referred to as the *AT command set.*

AT commands are modem-control commands. The AT command set is used to issue dial, hangup, reset, and other instructions to the modem. Most modem user manuals contain a complete listing of the AT command set. Table 9-6 shows a summary of the most commonly used AT commands. Note that the standard Hayes-compatible code to dial is ATDxxxxxxx. There are usually no spaces in an AT string. If a space is inserted, most modems ignore it. The "x" signifies the number dialed. There will be 7 digits for a local call, and 11 digits for a long-distance call (1 + the area code + phone number). A *W* indicates that the modem will wait; for example, when dialing a 9 for an outside line so a tone is established before proceeding. A *T* is added to signify tone dialing, and a *P* is added for pulse.

Table 9-6 Commonly Used Modem (AT) Control Commands

AT Command	Function
AT	Attention code that precedes all modem action commands
ATDPxxxxxxx	Dial the phone number, xxxxxxx, using pulse dialing
ATDTxxxxxxx	Dial the phone number, xxxxxxx, using tone dialing
ATA	Answer the phone immediately
ATHO	Hang up the phone immediately
ATZ	Reset the modem to its power-up settings
ATF	Reset modem parameters and settings to the factory defaults
AT+++	Break the signal, change from data mode to command mode

ISPs and Internet Backbone Providers

An ISP is required to surf the Internet. The connection to the Internet is tiered. This means that the ISP might link to a larger regional ISP, which in turn might connect to one of a number of nationwide computer centers. Therefore, by browsing the Internet, one can benefit from hundreds or even thousands of computers that are networked. This provides access to documents, music downloads, and videos from all over the world.

When connecting to an ISP, the computer becomes a remote client on the ISP's local network. It is amazing how far the Internet has gone toward turning the world into a global village. At the onset of the Internet era, a local computer or LAN had to have a direct connection to the Internet backbone; this was not affordable for individuals and smaller companies. New technologies have since led to easier and cheaper ways of building networks.

ISPs now play a critical role in providing Internet access to most homes and businesses in the United States. ISPs use more expensive and complex equipment to establish a point of presence (POP), or access point, on the Internet. They either lease the dedicated high-speed lines from a telephone company or, in the case of large ISPs, install their own lines. Note that a small, local ISP might not link directly to the Internet backbone. Instead, the small ISP might go through a larger regional ISP that is directly connected.

Internet Infrastructure Example

The current U.S. Internet infrastructure consists of a commercial backbone and a high-speed service known as the *very high speed backbone network service (vBNS)*. The vBNS connects five supercomputer networks across the country and is also used for scientific purposes (see Table 9-7). The commercial backbone is an internetwork of commercially operated networks. In the United States, for example, several companies provide the commercial backbone:

- Cable & Wireless USA
- Sprint
- AT&T
- BBN Planet

Table 9-7 vBNS Supercomputer Networks

Supercomputer Center	National Location
National Partnership for an Advanced Computational Infrastructure (NPACI)	San Diego, California
National Center for Atmospheric Research	Boulder, Colorado
National Center for Supercomputing Applications (NCSA)	Urbana, Illinois
Pittsburgh Supercomputing Center	Pittsburgh, Pennsylvania
Cornell Theory Center	Ithaca, New York

ISPs connect to the commercial networks. Usually the backbone, providers, and ISPs enter into agreements (called *peering agreements*) that allow them to carry each other's network traffic. In the United States, much of the physical cabling is still owned by the regional Bell operating companies (RBOCs). These companies then lease the cabling to the ISPs. The provider networks connect with T1, T3, OC-3 lines (in North America), or E1 lines (in Europe and most other parts of the world).

An ISP that cannot connect directly to the national backbone is charged a fee to connect to a regional provider (see Table 9-8) that links to the national backbone through a network access point (NAP). A NAP, which provides data switching, is the point at which access providers are interconnected (see Table 9-9). However, not all Internet traffic goes through NAPs. Some ISPs that are in the same geographic area make their own interconnections and peering agreements. A metropolitan area exchange (MAE) is the point where ISPs connect to each other and traffic is switched between them. MAE EAST (located in the Washington, DC, area) and MAE WEST (located in Silicon Valley, CA) are the first-tier MAEs in the United States.

Regional providers are instrumental in allowing small ISPs to connect to the national Internet backbone.

Table 9-8 Regional Providers

Regional Provider	Region Covered
NEARNET and NYSERNet	Northeastern United States
BARRNet	North-central California
MIDnet	Central United States
CICnet	Midwestern United States
SURAnet	Southeastern United States
Westnet	Western United States

Table 9-9 Network Access Point Details

Network Access Point (NAP) Location	Operating Company
Washington, DC	WorldCom
New York	Sprint
San Francisco	Pacific Bell
Chicago	Ameritech

In other countries or regions of the world where the Internet infrastructure has fully developed and matured, the structural organization is similar to that of the U.S. However, for smaller regions or countries having a smaller or developing infrastructure, there are fewer access layers than in the U.S.

Digital Subscriber Lines

A *digital subscriber line (DSL)* is an always-on technology. This means there is no need to dial up each time you want to connect to the Internet. DSL is a relatively new technology that is currently being offered by phone companies as an add-on service over existing copper wire or phone lines.

DSL comes in several varieties, as follows:

- **Asymmetric DSL (ADSL)**—Currently, the most common implementation. It has speeds that vary from 384 kbps to more than 6 Mbps downstream. The upstream speed is typically lower.
- **High data rate DSL (HDSL)**—Provides bandwidth of 768 kbps in both directions.
- **Symmetric DSL (SDSL)**—Provides the same speed, up to 3 Mbps, for uploads and downloads.
- **Very high data rate DSL (VDSL)**—Capable of bandwidths of 13 to 52 Mbps.
- **Integrated services digital network (ISDN) DSL (IDSL)**—DSL over ISDN lines. With a top speed of 144 kbps, it is available in areas that do not qualify for other DSL implementations.

Table 9-10 summarizes the different varieties of DSL. The generic term for DSL, including all its implementations, is *xDSL*.

Table 9-10 DSL Types

DSL Variety	Average Speeds	Pros	Cons
ADSL	Downstream speeds of 384 kbps to 6 Mbps, upstream speeds slower.	Most widely implemented of all the current DSL varieties. Relatively inexpensive.	Much slower upstream speed. Installed only within 17,500 feet of a telco central office.
SDSL	Up to 3 Mbps for both upstream and downstream.	Same upstream and downstream data speeds.	Generally more expensive and less widely available than ADSL.

continues

Table 9-10 DSL Types (Continued)

DSL Variety	Average Speeds	Pros	Cons
IDSL	144 kbps for both upstream and downstream.	Can be installed in many locations where other DSL varieties are not available due to distance.	Considerably lower speed and more expensive than ADSL.
HDSL	768 kbps for both upstream and downstream.	Generally faster than IDSL and some implementations of ADSL.	Not widely available.
VDSL	13–52 Mbps for both upstream and downstream.	Extremely high speed for multimedia such as live audio and video.	Most expensive DSL type, not widely available.

Transfer rates are often broken down into upstream and downstream rates. *Upstream* is the process of transferring data from the end user to the server. *Downstream* is the process of transferring data from the server to the end user. For example, when a user submits his or her username and password to gain access to e-mail, he is uploading, or transferring, that data upstream to the e-mail server. When the contents of the mailbox are displayed on the web browser, that data are downloaded, or transferred, downstream, to the computer.

ADSL is currently the most commonly used DSL technology. Its high downstream speed, typically 1.5 Mbps, works in its favor, because most Internet users spend the majority of their time doing tasks that require a lot of downloading (for example, checking e-mail and surfing the web). The slower upload rate does not work well when hosting a web server or FTP server, both of which involve upload-intensive Internet activities.

ADSL uses a technology called *frequency-division multiplexing (FDM)* to split bandwidth in order to create multiple channels. Other DSL implementations use another technique known as *echo cancellation*, which is more efficient but also more expensive. Either way, this ability to create multiple channels is the reason that a DSL user can be surfing the Internet while at the same time using the telephone to call a friend. The advantages and disadvantages of cable modems are discussed in the next section.

Cable Modems

A *cable modem* acts like a LAN interface by connecting a computer to the Internet. The cable modem connects a computer to the cable company's network through the same coaxial cabling that feeds cable TV (CATV) signals to a television set. Generally, cable modems are designed to provide Internet access only, whereas analog modems or ISDN adapters allow dial-in to any service provider or service in a remote access server. With a cable modem, the cable company must be used as the ISP.

The cable modem service is also an always-on technology, similar to DSL. A standard cable modem has two connections. One port is connected to the TV outlet, and the other is connected to the subscriber's PC. The cable modem then communicates over the cable network to a device called a *cable modem termination system (CMTS)*. The speed of the cable modem depends on traffic levels and how the overall network is set up. Although the server being contacted is at a remote location, cable modem access is more like a direct LAN connection than remote access. A dialup connection might be required for data upload using the local phone line. This is because the cable company's infrastructure is still one-way. In such a case, a phone jack is built into the cable modem.

Cable modems are capable of receiving and processing multimedia content at 30 Mbps, which is hundreds of times faster than a normal telephone dialup connection to the Internet. In reality, though, subscribers can expect to download information at speeds of 0.5 to 1.5 Mbps because the bandwidth is shared by a number of other users in the neighborhood. The modem receives digitally altered signals. A demodulator is built into the modem and, if it is a two-way modem, a burst modulator is used for transmitting data upstream.

Cable modems are available as internal and external units. Most internal cable modems are in the form of PCI cards. An external cable modem is a small box with a coaxial CATV cable connection. A splitter is typically used to divide the signal between the TV and the cable modem. The box is connected to an Ethernet card in the computer through UTP Ethernet. External USB devices might also be available to connect the modem to the computer USB port without requiring an Ethernet card.

There is currently no standard for cable modems in the cable access industry. As a result, there are many competing proprietary products. Cable service, speed, reliability, setup, and configurations can vary significantly from one cable company to another. Currently, the most common cable modem manufacturers are Cisco Systems, 3Com, Com21, Bay Networks, Motorola, RCA, Toshiba, and Terayon.

Cable Modem Versus DSL Internet Technologies

When comparing cable modem and DSL Internet technologies, both have their pros and cons. DSL service can be added incrementally in an area. This means that the service provider can start up with a handful of clients and upgrade the bandwidth as the number of subscribers grows. DSL is also backward compatible with analog voice and makes good use of the existing local loop. This means that little needs to be done to use the cable service simultaneously with normal phone service. However, DSL suffers from distance limitations. Most DSL service offerings currently require the customer to be within 18,000 feet of the provider's central office location. Additionally, the longer and older loops present problems, and the best form of voice support is still being debated. Also, the upstream (upload) speed is usually considerably lower than the downstream (download) speed.

In contrast, cable modem technology presents plenty of relatively inexpensive bandwidth. In fact, the downstream and upstream Internet channels are seen as just another premium TV channel by the system. This is a major advantage, especially when hosting a web server or FTP server, which involves upload-intensive Internet tasks. The use of fiber [hybrid-fiber-coaxial (HFC)] greatly reduces some of the service shortcomings that are initially encountered with this technology. Unfortunately, the cabling infrastructure that is needed to support cable modem technology has been slow to be upgraded; therefore, most homes in the United States cannot use this technology. Upgrading is a big investment, particularly for small providers.

The advantages and disadvantages of these two Internet technologies are summarized in Tables 9-11 and 9-12.

Table 9-11 Advantages and Disadvantages of DSL

Advantages	Disadvantages
Offers speeds up to and exceeding those of T-1, at a fraction of the cost.	The availability of DSL is presently limited, with service for most varieties only possible in areas that fall within a specified number of feet from the telephone company central office.
Service can be added incrementally as more users subscribe.	The telephone company central office that is servicing the location must have DSL equipment installed.
Both voice and data can be transmitted over the same line at the same time.	The best form of voice support is still being debated.

Table 9-11 Advantages and Disadvantages of DSL (Continued)

Advantages	Disadvantages
Offers always-on technology. Users do not need to dial up each time they wish to connect to the Internet.	
Backward-compatible with conventional analog phones.	

Table 9-12 Advantages and Disadvantages of Cable Modems

Advantages	Disadvantages
Existing cable TV systems offer plenty of bandwidth for both upstream and downstream traffic.	Almost always requires an overhaul of the existing cable infrastructure, and is expensive for smaller providers.
Cable TV infrastructure upgrade with HFC has addressed many of the existing service bottlenecks.	Because it is a shared media structure, less bandwidth is available as more users come on the network.

 Worksheet 9.8.7   Connecting to the Internet

This worksheet reviews the terms and devices used to connect to the Internet.

Connecting to the Internet presents the IT technician with new challenges. Users always want the fastest connection, so the technician must understand how the Internet works and know the connection options that are available.

Summary

This chapter discussed network fundamentals. Important concepts to retain from this chapter are as follows:

- A network is a connected system of objects or people. The most common example of a network is the telephone system. A computer network is defined as having two or more devices (such as workstations, printers, or servers) that are linked for the purpose of sharing information, resources, or both.

- A data channel can send a signal using simplex, half-duplex, or full-duplex transmission. Full-duplex networking technology increases performance, because data can be sent and received at the same time. DSL, two-way cable modem, and other broadband technologies operate in full-duplex mode.

- A peer-to-peer network is easy to install, and no additional equipment or dedicated administrator is required. Users control their own resources, and the network works best with a small number of computers. A client/server network uses a dedicated system that functions as the server, that is, it responds to requests made by users or clients connected to the network.

- A local-area network (LAN) uses a direct connection from one computer to another called a point-to-point link. A LAN is suitable for a small area such as a home, building, or school. A wide-area network (WAN) uses point-to-point or point-to-multipoint, serial communications lines to communicate over greater distances.

- A network interface card (NIC) is a device that plugs into a motherboard and provides ports for the network cable connections. It is the computer's interface with the LAN. When choosing a NIC, it is important to consider the type of network, media, and system bus. PCI should be used with FDDI cards because an ISA bus cannot handle the required speed.

- The network topology defines the way in which computers, printers, and other devices are connected. Physical topology describes the layout of the wires and devices as well as the paths used by data transmissions. Logical topology is the path that signals travel from one point to another. Topologies include bus, star, ring, and mesh.

- Networking media can be defined as the means by which signals (data) are sent from one computer to another (either by cable or wireless means). The media types discussed include two that use copper (coaxial and twisted-pair), one that uses glass (fiber-optic), and one that uses microwaves (wireless) to transmit data.

- Networking devices are used to connect computers and peripheral devices so that they can communicate. These include hubs, bridges, and switches. The type of device implemented depends on the type of network in use.

- Server components are specific to the network server. The peripheral devices, such as the monitor, CD-ROM drive, and floppy drive, are not any different, except that a higher level of preventive maintenance must be maintained to keep the server running at peak performance.

- Ethernet architecture is now the most popular type of LAN architecture. Architecture refers to the overall structure of a computer or communication system. It determines the capabilities and limitations of the system. The Ethernet architecture is based on the IEEE 802.3 standard. This standard specifies that a network implements the carrier sense multiple access with collision detection (CSMA/CD) access control method.

- The open systems interconnection (OSI) reference model is an industry-standard framework that is used to divide the functions of networking into seven distinct layers. These include application, presentation, session, transport, network, data link, and physical. It is important to understand the purpose of each layer.

- The transmission control protocol/Internet protocol (TCP/IP) suite of protocols has become the dominant standard for internetworking. TCP/IP represents a set of public standards that specify how packets of information are exchanged between computers over one or more networks.

- In synchronous serial transmission, data bits are sent together with a synchronizing clock pulse. In this transmission method, a built-in timing mechanism coordinates the clocks of the sending and receiving devices. This is known as guaranteed state change synchronization. This is the most commonly used type of synchronous transmission method.

- In asynchronous serial transmission, data bits are sent without a synchronizing clock pulse. This transmission method uses a start bit at the beginning of each message. When the receiving device gets the start bit, it can synchronize its internal clock with the sender's clock.

- The modem is an electronic device that is used for computer communications through telephone lines. It allows data transfer between one computer and another. The UARTs convert byte-oriented data to serial bit streams. All modems require software to control the communication session. The set of commands that most modem software uses is known as the Hayes-compatible command set.

In the next chapter, you will learn about printers and printing. It includes an overview, buying a printer, connecting and sharing printers, managing print jobs, and dealing with paper problems.

Check Your Understanding

The following are review questions for the A+ exam. Answers can be found in Appendix B, "Answers to Check Your Understanding Review Questions."

1. What is the name of the largest network of computers in the world?

    A. DoD

    B. The World Wide Web

    C. The Internet

    D. Microsoft

2. When was the Internet developed?

    A. Late 1950

    B. Late 1960

    C. Late 1970

    D. Late 1980

3. What is the term for three computers sharing communications?

    A. Operating system

    B. Network

    C. Remote connection

    D. Sharing violation

4. How do you share a resource on the network in Windows 98 using Windows Explorer?

    A. Highlight the desired item and then right-click and select Explore

    B. Highlight the desired item and then right-click and select Open

    C. Highlight the desired item and then right-click and select Network

    D. Highlight the desired item and then right-click and select Sharing

5. What is the problem if other computers on the network cannot see files or printers on your computer?

    A. They didn't enable file and print sharing

    B. Your network settings are incorrect

    C. Their network settings are incorrect

    D. You didn't enable file and print sharing

6. To set up remote administration, which object would you select?

   A. RAS

   B. Passwords

   C. Dialup networking

   D. NAT

7. If you upgrade your LAN to use TCP/IP, what problem does this create?

   A. It requires large amounts of memory and lacks speed

   B. It takes up more hard disk space

   C. None

   D. It will not function unless it is the first and only protocol installed

8. Which of the following is not a basic network architecture?

   A. Extended star

   B. Ring

   C. Extended ring

   D. Star

9. What does NIC stand for?

   A. No information current

   B. Network interface card

   C. Network Internet community

   D. Network Isolation Committee

10. What does DNS provide?

   A. 16-bit addresses

   B. Unique alphanumeric addresses

   C. 32-bit addresses

   D. Web browsers

11. When using a hub, the network topology changes from a linear bus to what?

   A. It does not change

   B. Star

   C. Extended star

   D. Extended bus

12. What is the name of the standard Internet addressing scheme that creates the linkage between international subnetworks?

    A. Internet address

    B. IP address

    C. Web address

    D. MAC address

13. If you are using a Token Ring network, when does each station transmit?

    A. When no other stations are using the network

    B. Only when that station has been given transmission time

    C. Only when the station processes the token

    D. Only when another station on the network permits

14. How is a KVM switch is used?

    A. At an end user's computer

    B. With network servers

    C. With the server that connects to the Internet

    D. To manage printers

15. What is the name of a cable with a braided copper shield around it and only a single conductor?

    A. UTP

    B. STP

    C. FDDI

    D. Coaxial

16. In a twisted-pair network, what type of conductor is used?

    A. 100Base2

    B. 10Base2

    C. 10BaseT

    D. 10BaseFL

17. What should you do if you ping an IP address and cannot get a response?

    A. Use the TRACERT command

    B. Use the MSD command

    C. Try a different IP address

    D. Ask the site when it will be running

18. How many layers does the OSI reference model have?

   A. Six

   B. Seven

   C. Eight

   D. Nine

19. Which layer of the OSI model describes the cable and how it is attached?

   A. Network

   B. Transport

   C. Data link

   D. Physical

20. Which layer of the OSI model is responsible for establishing a unique network address?

   A. Network

   B. Transport

   C. Data link

   D. Physical

21. Which layer of the OSI model is responsible for the accuracy of the data transmission?

   A. Presentation

   B. Data link

   C. Session

   D. Transport

22. Which layer of the OSI model translates data into an appropriate transmission format?

   A. Application

   B. Network

   C. Presentation

   D. Data link

23. To receive access to the Internet, which network protocol is required?

    A. TCP/IP

    B. ISP

    C. IPX/SPX

    D. DNS

24. Which of the following dialup protocols has the fastest connections?

    A. SLIP

    B. PPP

    C. TCP

    D. IP

25. To receive a direct connection to the Internet, what is required?

    A. At least two routers between the local network and the Internet

    B. Only a bridge between the local network and the Internet

    C. Only a hub between the local network and the Internet

    D. Only one router between the local network and the Internet

Key Terms

10BaseT   The most popular Ethernet using the star topology with a transmission speed of 10 Mbps.

100BaseX   The evolution of 10BaseT. It is available in different varieties based on the type of cabling used.

*1000Base*T   Supports data transfer rates of 1 Gbps.

-a   Switch used with the ARP command that displays the cache.

-s   Switch used with the ARP command that adds a permanent IP-to-MAC mapping.

-d   Switch used with the ARP command that deletes an entry from the ARP cache.

address resolution protocol (ARP)   The means by which networked computers map Internet protocol (IP) addresses to physical hardware (MAC) addresses that are recognized in a local network.

AppleTalk   A protocol suite to network Macintosh computers, comprised of a comprehensive set of protocols that span the seven layers of the OSI reference model. AppleTalk protocols were designed to run over the major LAN types, notably Ethernet and Token Ring, as well as over Apple's LAN physical topology, LocalTalk.

application layer   The fourth layer in the TCP/IP model. It is the starting point for communication sessions.

architecture   The overall structure of a computer or communication system.

ARP cache   ARP builds and maintains a table called the ARP cache, which contains these mappings (IP address to MAC address). The ARP cache is the means by which a correlation is maintained between each MAC address and its corresponding IP address.

asymmetric DSL (ADSL)   Currently the most common implementation of DSL. It has speeds of 384 kbps to more than 6 Mbps downstream. The upstream speed is typically lower.

asynchronous serial transmission   Data bits are sent without a synchronizing clock pulse. This transmission method uses a start bit at the beginning of each message. When the receiving device gets the start bit, it can synchronize its internal clock with the sender's clock.

AT commands   Modem control commands.

automatic private IP addressing (APIPA)   An operating system feature that enables a computer to assign itself an address if it is unable to contact a DHCP server.

bridge   Connects network segments.

built-in modem   Used in some notebook computers.

bus topology   Connects all devices on a single cable.

cable modem   Acts like a LAN interface by connecting a computer to the Internet. The cable modem connects a computer to the cable company's network through the same coaxial cabling that feeds cable TV (CATV) signals to a television set.

CONFIG   A configuration utility used in NetWare (server console) to access IP address, MAC address, subnet mask, and default gateway.

dynamic host configuration protocol (DHCP)   A software utility that automatically assigns IP addresses in a large network.

carrier sense multiple access/collision detection (CSMA/CD)   The LAN access method used in Ethernet. A device checks to see if the network is quiet (senses the carrier). If not, it waits a random amount of time before retrying. If the network is quiet and two devices access the line at the same time, their signals collide. When a collision is detected, both devices back off and wait a random amount of time before retrying.

Category 3   Primarily used in telephone connections.

Category 5   Four pairs of wires with a maximum data rate of 100 Mbps.

Category 5e   Provides more twists per foot than Category 5.

Category 6   Not yet ratified by the cabling industry. It has a plastic divider that separates the pairs of wires, preventing crosstalk.

circuit   The pathway that a data transmission takes.

circuit-switched communications network   Developed for use primarily by the telephone, it provides one physical path that is used for the duration of the transmission.

client/server network   A network where services are located in a dedicated computer that responds to client (or user) requests.

coaxial cable   Copper-cored cable surrounded by a heavy shielding.

computer network   Two or more devices, such as workstations printers, or servers, that are linked for the purpose of sharing information, resources, or both.

copper distributed data interface (CDDI)   The FDDI technology with copper cabling.

data channel   The path over which a signal is sent.

default gateway   The route used so that a computer on one segment can communicate with a computer on another segment.

dialup networking (DUN)   When computers use the public telephone system or network to communicate. The modem must operate in the local command state or online state to enable DUN.

digital subscriber line (DSL)   An always-on technology used to connect to the Internet.

directories and name services   Make it possible for users to find people and services on a computer network.

Domain Name System (DNS)   Translates computer names into IP addresses.

downstream   The process of transferring data from the server to the end user.

electronic mail (e-mail)   The ability for users to communicate over a computer network.

end-to-end   Refers to the pathway that is currently available for a telephone, for example. It is a temporary path.

Ethernet architecture   Based on the IEEE 802.3 standard that specifies that a network implement CSMA/CD.

expansion cards   Most common type of card. They plug into the motherboard expansion slots (ISA or PCI). Also called internal modems.

extended star topology   A star topology expanded to include additional networking devices.

external modem   Used with any computer, it plugs into a serial port (COM1 or COM2) on the back of the computer. External modems are typically used for high-speed connections such as the cable modem.

Fast Ethernet   100BaseX.

FDDI Class A   Computers connected to the cables of both rings.

FDDI Class B   Computers connected to only one ring.

Fiber Distributed Data Interface (FDDI)   A type of Token Ring used in larger LANs or MANs.

fiber-optic cable   Conducts modulated light to transmit data.

file transfer protocol (FTP)   An application that provides services for file transfer and manipulation.

full duplex   Data transmission that can go two ways at the same time. An Internet connection using a DSL is an example.

Gigabit Ethernet   1000BaseT.

half-duplex transmission   Data transmission that can go two ways but not at the same time. A telephone and two-way radio are examples.

Hayes-compatible command set   Set of commands that most modem software uses. They are named after the Hayes Microcomputer Products Company, which first defined them.

high data rate DSL (HDSL)   Provides a bandwidth of 768 kbps in both directions.

hub   A device used to extend an Ethernet wire to allow more devices to communicate with each other.

hybrid topology   A combination of one or more topologies.

HyperText Markup Language (HTML)   Page description language.

Hypertext Transfer Protocol (HTTP)   Governs how files are exchanged on the Internet.

ICMP echo request/reply   Ping works by sending an ICMP echo request to the destination computer. The receiving computer then sends back an ICMP echo reply message.

IEEE   Institute of Electrical and Electronics Engineers, based in New York (www.ieee.org). A membership organization that sets standards for computers and communications.

IFCONFIG   A configuration utility used in UNIX and Linux (command-line) to access IP address, MAC address, subnet mask, and default gateway.

information superhighway   The benefit of the Internet to business and private communications.

instant messaging (IM) services   The ability for users to communicate in real time, or without delay, over a computer network.

internal modem   Plugs into one of the expansion slots on the motherboard. No configuration is needed for a Plug and Play (PnP) modem, which is installed on a motherboard that supports PnP.

International Organization for Standardization (ISO)   Developed the OSI model in the 1980s.

Internet   A worldwide public network forming one large web of communication.

Internet Control Message Protocol (ICMP)   Used for network testing and troubleshooting. It enables diagnostic and error messages. ICMP echo messages are used by the ping application to test if a remote device is reachable.

Internet Protocol (IP)   Provides source and destination addressing and, in conjunction with routing protocols, packet forwarding from one network to another toward a destination.

Internet service provider (ISP)   A private network that enables users to connect to the Internet.

IPCONFIG   A configuration utility used in Windows NT and Windows 2000 (command-line) to access IP address, MAC address, subnet mask, and default gateway.

IPTRACE   A configuration utility used in NetWare NLM to trace packets on a network.

ISDN DSL (IDSL)   Has a top speed of 144 kbps but is available only in areas that do not qualify for other DSL implementations. IDSL is DSL running over ISDN lines.

keyboard/video/monitor (KVM) switch   A switch that allows a single keyboard, video display, and mouse to be used with all network servers.

local-area network (LAN)   A communication network that covers a small geographical area.

local command state   The modem is offline. It receives commands and provides status information to the host computer to which the modem is installed.

logical topology   The paths that signals travel from one point on a network to another.

medium   The communication channel or cable that enables computers to communicate over the network.

mesh topology   Interconnects devices providing redundancy and fault tolerance.

metropolitan-area network (MAN)   A network that spans an area larger than a local area network typically implemented with fiber-optic cable.

modem   An electronic device that is used for computer communications through telephone lines.

name resolution   The process of name translation.

NBTSTAT   Used by Windows to display NetBIOS information.

NetBIOS extended user interface (NetBEUI)   A protocol used primarily on small Windows NT networks. NetBEUI is a simple protocol that lacks many of the features that enable protocol suites such as TCP/IP to be used on networks of almost any size.

NETSTAT   A command that is used in Windows and UNIX/Linux to display TCP/IP connection and protocol information.

network   A connected system of objects or people.

network access point (NAP)   The point at which access providers are interconnected.

network administration   The task of network administrators to maintain and upgrade a private network.

network file services   Allow documents to be shared over a network to facilitate the development of a project.

network interface card (NIC)   The computer's interface with the LAN.

network media   The means by which signals are sent from one computer to another (either cable or wireless).

network print services   Make printers available to many users.

network protocols   The second layer in TCP/IP model. It provides internetworking for the communications session.

network topology   The way computers, printers, and other devices are connected.

NSLOOKUP   Returns the IP address for a given host name. It can also find the host name for a specified IP address.

octets   Four groups of eight bits.

online state   In this state, the modem is transferring data between the host machine and a remote computer through the telephone system.

Open Systems Interconnection (OSI)   A model that was created to define the multiple layers of a network.

packet-switched communications network   Individual packets of data take an available route. The route does not have to be dedicated, as in circuit-switched communications.

PCMCIA card   A variation of modems that is designed for easy installation in notebook computers. Also known as PC cards, they look like credit cards and are small and portable.

peer-to-peer network   A network where computers act as equal partners.

physical topology   The layout of the devices and media.

ping   A simple but highly useful command-line utility that is included in most implementations of TCP/IP. Ping can be used with either the host name or the IP address to test IP connectivity.

point-to-point   Same as end-to-end.

POTS   Plain old telephone service.

protocol   A controlled sequence of messages that are exchanged between two or more systems to accomplish a given task.

public switched telephone network (PSTN)   The telephone system that allows people in every corner of the world to communicate with anyone who has access to a telephone. It is the most common example of a network.

Redundant NIC   In a network server, it serves as a backup NIC.

Reverse Address Resolution Protocol (RARP)   A protocol used to obtain IP address information based on the physical or MAC address.

ring topology   Common in Ethernet LANs, this topology connects devices in the shape of a ring. Ring topology can be single-ring, where data travel in one direction, and dual-ring, which allows data to be sent bidirectionally.

router   A networking device that makes decisions on how to send data packets.

Routing Information Protocol (RIP)   Operates between router devices to discover paths between networks. In an intranet, routers depend on a routing protocol to build and maintain information about how to forward packets toward the destination. RIP chooses routes based on the distance or "hop count."

RS-232   A standard for serial transmissions between computers and other devices.

sequenced packet exchange/internetwork packet exchange (SPX/IPX)   The protocol suite originally employed by Novell Corporation's network operating system, NetWare. It delivers functions similar to those included in TCP/IP.

server   A repository for files that can be accessed and shared across a network by many users.

shielded twisted-pair (STP)   A pair of wires that forms a circuit that can transmit data. The wires are wrapped in metallic foil to shield them from noise.

Simple Mail Transport Protocol (SMTP)   Includes messaging services of TCP/IP and supports most Internet e-mail programs.

simplex transmission   A single, one-way data transmission.

star topology   Common in Ethernet LANs, it is made up of a central connection point (hub, etc.) where all cabling segments meet.

subnet mask   The second group of numbers in an IP address.

switch   Also know as a multiport bridge.

Symmetric DSL (SDSL)   Provides the same speed, up to 3 Mbps, for uploads and downloads.

Synchronous serial transmission   Data bits are sent together with a synchronizing clock pulse. In this transmission method, a built-in timing mechanism coordinates the clocks of the sending and receiving devices.

TCP/IP utilities   Most vendors implement the suite to include a variety of utilities for viewing configuration information and for troubleshooting problems.

Telnet   Enables terminal access to local or remote systems.

token   A special signal.

Token Ring   Based on the token-passing access control method.

topology   The structure of a network. It includes the physical topology, that is, the layout of the media (or wire), and the logical topology, which is how the media are accessed by the hosts.

TPCON   Novell uses the NLM to display TCP/IP connection and protocol information.

TRACEROUTE   A configuration utility used in UNIX/Linux to trace packets on a network.

TRACERT   A configuration utility used in Windows to trace packets on a network.

Transmission Control Protocol (TCP)   The primary Internet protocol for the reliable delivery of data. TCP includes facilities for end-to-end connection establishment, for error detection and recovery, and for metering the rate of data flow into the network.

Transmission Control Protocol/Internet Protocol (TCP/IP)   A suite of protocols that has become the dominant standard for internetworking.

transport layer   The third layer in the TCP/IP model. It provides end-to-end management of the communication session.

twisted pair   A pair of wires that forms a circuit that can transmit data.

universal asynchronous receiver/transmitter (UART)   This type of chip determines the top speed at which devices can communicate using the port. It handles both synchronous and asynchronous transmissions.

unshielded twisted-pair (UTP)   A twisted pair of wires that relies on the cancellation effect to limit signal degradation.

upstream   The process of transferring data from the end user to the server.

user datagram protocol (UDP)   Offers a connectionless service to applications. UDP uses lower overhead than TCP and can tolerate a level of data loss.

very high data rate DSL (VDSL)   Capable of bandwidths of 13–52 Mbps.

very high speed backbone network service (vBNS)   The current U.S. Internet infrastructure that consists of a commercial backbone and a high-speed service.

wide-area network (WAN)   A communication network that covers a large geographical area.

WINIPCFG   A configuration utility used in Windows 95, 98, and 2000 (graphical interface) to access IP address, MAC address, subnet mask, and default gateway.

zones   A server's area of authority.

Objectives

Upon completion of this chapter, you will be able to perform the following tasks:

- Understand the basic types of printers used with the PC
- Define the major components of popular printer types and know how they work
- Know how different types of printers operate and understand the process they use to place images on paper
- Define the items to consider when buying a printer
- Troubleshoot printer problems and replace defective components
- Install various types of printers on a personal computer
- Understand the different types of printer connections and their configurations
- Know the appropriate safety measures when servicing printers

Chapter 10

Printers and Printing

Introduction

This chapter provides detailed information regarding printers and printing. You gain an understanding of how the different printers operate, what to consider when purchasing a printer, and how to connect printers to a PC or a network. Print management, including utilizing the queue and configuring printer options, is covered. Additionally, you learn how to troubleshoot basic printer problems such as paper jams.

Understanding Printers and Printing

This section includes the following topics:

- Printer overview
- Understanding dot matrix printer operation
- Understanding ink jet printer operation
- Understanding laser printer operation

Printer Overview

Printers are a vital part of modern PC systems. The need for hard copies of computer and online documents is no less important today than when the paperless revolution began several years ago. Today's computer technician must be able to understand the operation of various types of printers in order to install, maintain, and troubleshoot printer problems.

The most popular types of printers in use today are electrophotographic-type laser printers and sprayed ink jet printers, as shown in Figure 10-1. Older impact-type dot matrix printers are still used in many offices and homes, but it is becoming difficult to find replacement parts for these older units.

Figure 10-1 Laser and Ink Jet Printers

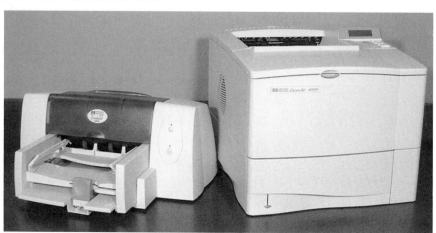

Printers are connected to personal computers with serial, parallel, USB, FireWire, and network cable connections. Wireless types of connections include infrared and radio wave technology.

Printer drivers are software that must be installed on the PC so that the printer can communicate and coordinate the printing process. Printer drivers vary according to printer type, manufacturer, and model.

In this section, the operation of the various printers is explained.

Understanding Dot Matrix Printer Operation

The *dot matrix printer*, as shown in Figure 10-2, belongs to a printer class called *impact printers*. In this type, the print head impacts a printer tape or inked ribbon to cause characters to be formed on paper.

Figure 10-2 Dot Matrix Printer

In the dot matrix printer, the impact occurs as the print head fires pins (or print wires) at an ink ribbon; the pins then contact the paper and leave a mark. The print head, the assembly that contains the pins, moves from left to right across the paper, one line at a time, creating letters out of the circular dots of ink that impact the paper. (Many dot matrix printers also print bidirectionally, which increases the speed.) Coils of wires form electromagnets that are called *solenoids*. The solenoids are energized, thus causing the pins to move forward and strike the ribbon.

The number of pins in dot matrix printer indicates the quality of the print. Common printers are 9-pin, 24-pin, and 48-pin designs. The highest quality of print that can be produced by the dot matrix printer is referred to as *NLQ*, which stands for near letter quality. The speed at which the dot matrix printer can operate is measured in characters per second (cps).

The type of paper that is most often used with the dot matrix printer is *continuous-feed paper*. This paper has perforations between each sheet and perforated strips on the side. The pin feeders and tractor feeders are used to feed the paper and to prevent skewing or shifting. Sheet feeders that print one page at a time were added to some of the higher-quality printers used in offices. A large roller, called the *platen*, applies pressure to keep the paper from slipping. If a multiple-copy paper is used, the platen gap can be adjusted for the thickness of the paper.

Once the least expensive printer, dot matrix printers are now rare and somewhat expensive because they serve a small market that requires multiple-copy stationery.

Understanding Ink Jet Printer Operation

Color ink jet printers are the most popular type of printer in home use today. This is because of their low cost and moderate print quality. The ink jet printer, as shown in Figure 10-3, uses liquid ink-filled cartridges that force out and spray ink particles at the page through tiny holes called nozzles. Although ink jet printers usually print one page at a time, they are still faster than the dot matrix printer.

The ink jet printer sprays tiny dots of ink at the page by applying pressure that is caused by electricity or an electrical charge. Pressure inside the ink reservoir of the cartridge is less than the outside pressure until the electricity is applied, and then the pressure increases. This internal pressure causes small dots of ink to be forced out through the nozzles. Figure 10-4 shows the components of a typical ink jet printer.

Figure 10-3 An HP DeskJet Color Ink Jet Printer

Figure 10-4 Components of an Ink Jet Printer

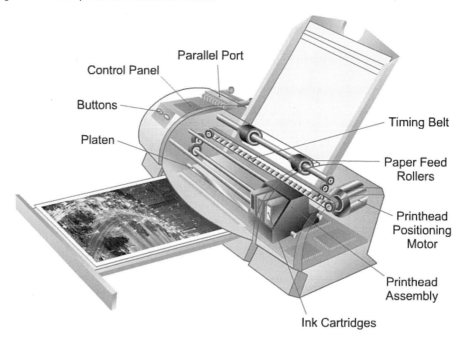

Ink jet printers have two kinds of print heads. One popular brand of ink jet printer uses a thermal-shock print head. It has a heating element that surrounds each nozzle and, when heated by an electrical current, the heat causes the ink to expand. When the ink expands, it is ejected through the nozzle.

Another popular brand of ink jet printer operates based on electrostatic charges. When the deflection plates are electrically charged, the size and shape of the nozzle change, causing the plate to act like a pump. This pumping action forces ink through the nozzle to the paper. These print heads are called *piezoelectric print heads*.

Ink jet printers are designed to use plain paper, but they can also be used with specific ink jet paper when high-quality print or photographs are required.

When the ink jet print operation is complete and the paper exits the printer, the ink is often still wet. Touching it immediately can smear the ink and smudge the printout. Most inks dry in 10 to 15 seconds.

The quality of print for an ink jet printer is measured in dots per inch (dpi), and the print speed is measured in pages per minute (ppm).

Understanding Laser Printer Operation

Today, the *laser printer* is the printer of choice, especially in office settings, because of its high resolution, superior operation, and speed. However, its internal operation is more complex than other types of printers. Figure 10-5 shows a laser printer that can accommodate different paper sizes and can collate paper for large projects.

TEST TIP

Know the components of a laser printer and the steps required to print a page.

Figure 10-5 HP LaserJet 8150dn with Accessories

As is the case with photocopiers, static electricity is the primary principle in the operation of a laser printer. This is the same static electricity that causes lightning or other oppositely charged particles to attract each other. This attraction is used to temporally hold small dry ink particles, called *toner*, to a statically charged image on an electrophotographic drum. A laser beam is used to draw this image.

Figure 10-6 illustrates the components of a laser printer. The central part of the laser printer is its *electrophotographic drum.* The drum is a metal cylinder that is coated with a light-sensitive insulating material. When a beam of laser light strikes the drum, the drum becomes a conductor at the point where the light hits it. As the drum rotates, the laser beam draws an electrostatic image on the drum called the image. The *latent image,* that is, the undeveloped image, is passed by a supply of dry ink, or toner, that is attracted to it. The drum turns and brings this image in contact with the paper, which attracts the toner from the drum. The paper is then passed through a fuser, which is made up of hot rollers that melt the toner into the paper.

Figure 10-6 The Components of a Laser Printer

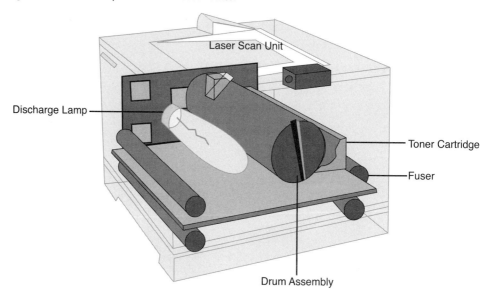

This laser printing process is completed in six steps, which are detailed as follows:

Step 1 Cleaning—When an image has been deposited on the paper and the drum has separated from the paper, any remaining toner must be removed from the drum. One method uses a blade to scrape all excess toner from the drum. Other printers use an AC voltage on a wire that removes the charge from the drum surface and allows the excess toner to fall away from the drum. The excess toner is stored in a used toner container that can be emptied and/or discarded.

Step 2 Conditioning—This step involves removing the old latent image from the drum and clearing or conditioning the drum for a new latent image. Placing a special wire, grid, or roller that is charged to about –6000V DC uniformly across the surface of the drum accomplishes this. This charged wire or grid is referred to as the *primary corona*. Some printers provide this charge by using a conditioning roller. The charge impressed on the surface of the drum is –600 to –1000V DC.

Step 3   Writing—This process involves scanning the photosensitive drum with the laser beam. Every portion of the drum that is exposed to the light has its surface charge reduced to about –100V DC. This electrical charge has a lower negative charge than the remainder of the drum. As the drum turns, an invisible latent image is created on the drum. Figure 10-7 illustrates the various voltage transitions involved with creating a printed page in the laser printing process.

WARNING

The voltage device that is used to erase the drum, called the *primary corona wire or grid*, or the conditioning roller, is dangerous. This voltage runs as high as –6000V. Only certified technicians should work on the unit to make sure that it is properly discharged.

Figure 10-7 Laser Printing Voltage Transitions

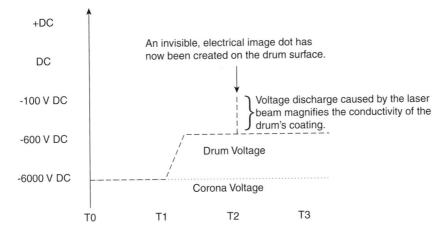

Step 4   Developing—This is the step where the toner is applied to the latent image. Inside the toner unit is developer particles made up of magnetic materials. These particles are coated with a plastic-like material. A triboelectric charge on the developer particles causes them to attract toner. The toner, as a result, is charged to about –200V DC, which causes it to be attracted to the more positive (–100V DC) areas of the photosensitive drum, but repelled by the more negative (–600V DC) areas. Typically, a cylinder within the toner unit releases toner so it can fall against a control blade or developer blade as the developer rollers travel. Also known as the restricting blade, the control blade keeps toner from pouring onto the drum. Instead, the control blade holds the toner at a microscopic distance from the drum, and toner leaps from it to the drum, where the toner is attracted by the more positively charged latent image.

Step 5 Transferring—In this step, the toner attached to the latent image is transferred to the paper. The transfer, or *secondary corona*, places a positive charge on the paper (remember that the drum was negatively charged) so that it attracts the negative toner image from the drum to the paper. The image is now on the paper and is held in place by the positive charge.

Step 6 Fusing—The toner particles on the paper are only there because of the charge that is present. They are kept in place permanently by the *fusing process*. In this process, the printing paper is rolled between a heated roller and a pressure roller. As the paper rolls, the top fuser roller is heated to about 350°F. This melts the plastic, which is mixed with the carbon black to make toner, into the paper. This operation is called *fixing* by some manufacturers. After the fusing operation is complete, the paper is moved to the output tray as a printed page.

A good way to memorize the order of the laser printing steps is to use the first letter of each word to create a mnemonic: Continuous Care Will Delay Trouble Forever. The steps are shown graphically in Figure 10-8.

Figure 10-8 The Six Steps of the Laser Printing Process

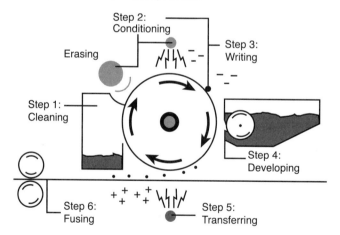

Buying a Printer

This section includes the following topics:

- Print capacity and speed
- Print quality and resolution
- Reliability
- Cost of ownership
- Laser versus ink jet printers

Print Capacity and Speed

Speed and capacity are important factors in printing; they are especially important if the printer is to be used in an office environment. Having an understanding of the capacity and speed of printers is critical in selecting the right printer.

Printer capacity and speed are important factors in the overall decision of buying a printer. If speed is an important consideration, lower-end ink jet printers are not a good choice. Ink jet printers generally print text at 2 to 6 pages per minute; printing a page of graphics can take several minutes. Compare this with color lasers; some can print at 16 pages per minute and send out the first page in about 10 seconds.

Personal laser printers are sufficient for printing an average of 200 pages per week. These low-end printers cost US$ 200 and up. Personal printers can print up to 8 pages per minute (ppm). They generally would also meet the needs of small businesses. If an average of 1000 pages per week is needed, a *workgroup printer* is required. Typically, a workgroup printer can print up to 24 ppm and can cost US$ 1000–6000. Finally, higher-capacity printing jobs would require a *production printer*. A production printer is needed for printing 50,000 or more pages per week. These printers can be expensive and are mostly used by commercial publishers. These units cost about US$ 100,000 but they can print up to 700 ppm and are capable of printing 24 hours a day, 7 days a week.

Print Quality and Resolution

Both ink jet and color laser printers can produce professional-quality photos. However, all ink jets are not made equal. Not all are capable of professional-quality printing. Generally, the higher-end ink jets provide the best quality. Certain ink jet printers are specially designed to produce top-quality photos, but these units tend to perform poorly when printing text. Print quality is a factor of the printer's resolution capabilities that is discussed in a later section.

Resolution

A printer's *print resolution* refers to the number of dots the print head is capable of applying per inch when forming an image. For most modern laser printers, the standard resolution is 600 dots per inch (dpi). This resolution is sufficient for everyday printing, including small desktop publishing jobs. However, the high-end production printer, mentioned in the previous section, might have a resolution of 2400 dpi. It is possible to find some laser printers that still use a resolution of 300 dpi. Note that this low resolution can cause jagged lines to appear on the outer edge of an image.

The printer resolution is an important factor to consider when buying a printer or when recommending the purchase of one. Always check the resolution to see how many dots per inch the printer can provide; higher numbers indicate better image quality. In this process, the standard resolution of 600×600 is more than adequate for most printing, except for photo-quality. Additionally, determine if the printer offers a range of resolutions, so the user can choose different resolutions for different printing jobs.

Reliability

Some printers are designed to have a short lifespan. Some brands of printers are more reliable than others. In general, it makes sense to spend a bit more upfront and have a more durable printer. When considering a printer brand, examine the construction. Is the cartridge attached to the print head? Replacing a print head is much more expensive than replacing a print cartridge. Try to determine the ease of replacing parts and the availability of these parts.

Testing the Printer

Never buy a printer without testing it first. Read the printer's specifications, and see how the printer measures up to those specifications when it is used. Observe how the printer prints both a page of text and a page of graphics/photos; many printers cannot do both well. If you are considering a color ink jet printer, pay particular attention to the sharpness of the text and images; some ink jets do a poor job with sharp lines.

Cost of Ownership

It is important to check the related costs of the cartridges, toner, replacement parts, printing paper, and so on. What is the frequency of replacement, and how much of each is required to run the printer yearly or per business cycle? These are issues that account for the running cost and the total cost of ownership (TCO). Supplies for the ink jet and laser printers are shown in Figure 10-9.

To print true black, most ink jets must have a separate black cartridge. Check for ink jet printers that have separate cartridges for each color. It is much cheaper to replace just the color that is empty than to replace a multicolor cartridge. Note that replacing a color laser's toner cartridge is much more expensive than replacing an ink jet cartridge, but printing with a color laser typically costs less per page.

Figure 10-9 Printer Supplies for the Ink Jet Printer and Laser Printer

Laser Versus Ink Jet Printers

A laser printer is different from an ink jet printer in several ways. In addition to the cost difference when purchasing these printers, the following list details additional considerations:

- The toner or ink in a laser printer is dry; in an ink jet, it is wet.
- An ink jet printer is about ten times more expensive to operate, over time, than a laser printer because ink needs to be replenished more frequently.
- If wet, the printed paper from an ink jet printer might smear, but a laser-printed document will not.
- If printing needs are minimal, an ink jet printer is sufficient, but if printing volume is high, a laser printer would be a better choice.

In terms of similarities, both ink jet and laser printers operate quietly and allow you to add fonts by using font cartridges or by installing soft fonts.

Connecting a Printer

This section includes the following topics:

- Serial, parallel, USB, SCSI, and network communication types
- Page description languages
- Installing and updating printer drivers

- Installing and replacing ink and toner
- Installing and adjusting print media
- Installing additional printer memory
- Adding a local printer
- Printing a test page

Serial, Parallel, USB, SCSI, and Network Communication Types

Printers require a method of communicating with the computers that they serve. Communication is accomplished through the ports on both the printer and the computer (or network device) or by using wireless technologies (such as infrared signals). Most printers use serial, parallel, USB, SCSI, or network cables and ports to receive information from computers. Each of these types is described in the following sections.

Serial

Serial ports are usually found on dot matrix printers that do not require high-speed transfers of data. Serial data transfer moves single bits of information in a single cycle. Serial ports are D-shell ports that are categorized as being either male or female and by the number of pins available for each port. Popular serial cables have 9-pin connectors on both ends, 25-pin connectors on both ends, or a combination of the two. Usually, the ends of the printer cables are secured to the ports on the printer and PC with thumbscrews. The maximum length of a serial cable is 50 feet.

Parallel

Parallel printers, which use parallel communication, have faster data transfer rates than serial printers, because parallel data transfer moves multiple bits of information in a single cycle. This provides a wider path for information moving to or from the printer, as shown in Figure 10-10. IEEE 1284 is the current standard for parallel printer cables. The maximum length for IEEE 1284 cables is 15 feet. Other standards such as enhanced parallel port (EPP) and enhanced capabilities port (ECP) allow bidirectional communication across the parallel cable.

Parallel printer cables have two unique ends. Figure 10-11 shows a 1284 Type A 25-pin DB-25 connector. The Type A connector attaches to the PC (or daisy-chained peripheral) and has two screws that should be hand-tightened. Figure 10-12 shows a 36-conductor Centronics connector. This connector attaches to the printer with the port's clips.

Figure 10-10   A Comparison of Serial and Parallel Data Transfer

Parallel Connector (25 Pin Male)

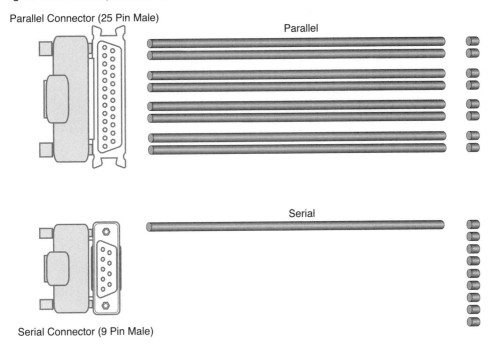

Parallel

Serial

Serial Connector (9 Pin Male)

Figure 10-11   The DB-25 Parallel Cable Connector

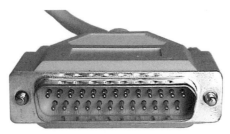

Figure 10-12   The Centronics Parallel Cable Connector

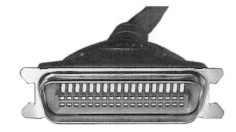

Universal Serial Bus

Universal serial bus (USB) is a popular communication type, not only for printers but also for other devices, due to its speed and ease of setup. Newer operating systems offer Plug and Play USB support. When a device is added to a computer system using a USB port, the device is automatically detected, and the driver-installation process begins. A USB cable is a four-wire cable that has two unique ends, as shown in Figure 10-13. The slimmer end connects to the PC, and the wider end, which is square, connects to the printer. These ends are keyed so that they only fit one way into each port.

Figure 10-13 USB Cable and Connectors

Small Computer System Interface

Small computer system interface (SCSI) is a type of interface that uses parallel communication technology to achieve high data transfer rates. There are many SCSI types; the most popular are SCSI 1 (plain SCSI), SCSI 2 (wide SCSI), and SCSI 3 (fast SCSI). SCSI printers and computers require the proper cabling for the ports. These ports can be DB-50 (male or female), Mini-DB-50 (male or female), and DB-68 (male or female).

FireWire

FireWire, also known as i.LINK or IEEE 1394, is a high-speed, platform-independent communication bus that interconnects digital devices such as printers, scanners, cameras, hard drives, and so on. Figure 10-14 shows an example of FireWire. Developed by Apple, FireWire was designed to allow peripherals to seamlessly plug into a computer. It also allows a device such as printer to be hot-plugged. FireWire provides a single plug-and-socket connection on which up to 63 devices can be attached, with data transfer speeds up to 400 Mbps. IEEE 1394 implementations are envisioned to replace and consolidate today's serial and parallel interfaces, such as Centronics parallel, RS-232C, and SCSI. The first printers to be introduced with FireWire are just beginning to come on the market.

Figure 10-14 FireWire Cable and Connectors

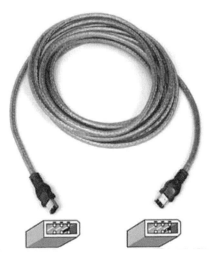

Network

Network printers are popular in today's workplace because they act as shared resources for all users on the network. Each user is not required to have his or her own printer. These printers offer many options (such as LAN fax, duplex, and finishers) and have high-speed outputs. Connecting a printer to the network requires a type of cabling that is compatible with the existing network. Most network printers ship with an RJ-45 interface for connection to an Ethernet network. Other connection options include Bayonet Neill-Concelman or British Naval Connectors (BNC) and Token Ring ports. The maximum length of a Category 5 cable used to connect a printer to a network is 100 meters.

Infrared

Current wireless printing technology is built on *infrared technology*, which uses a spectrum of light that is invisible to the human eye. For infrared communication to take place between a printer and a computer, transmitters and receivers are required on both devices. When setting up an infrared printer, there must be a clear line of sight between the transmitters and receivers on both devices, with a maximum distance of three meters.

Page Description Languages

Page description language (PDL) is a code that describes the contents of a document in a language that a printer can understand. These contents include text, graphics, and the overall formatting of the document. PDLs are used by software applications to send what-you-see-is-what-you-get (WYSIWYG) images to the printer so that the printer's output mirrors the document shown on the screen. PDLs also speed the printing process by sending larger amounts of data to the printer at a time. Finally, PDLs handle fonts that are used by the printer. *Fonts* are sets of formatted text types that can be scaled to various sizes and weights without deteriorating the quality. Fonts are either raster-based (consisting of multiple dots) or vector-based (complicated, outline-oriented fonts). Some of today's popular PDLs are as follows:

- **Printer control language (PCL)**—Developed by Hewlett-Packard to allow software applications to communicate with HP and HP-compatible laser printers, ink jet printers, and plotters. It is the standard PDL on which many others are based.

- **PostScript (PS)**—Developed by Adobe Systems to allow fonts (text types) to share the same characteristics on-screen as well as on paper.

- **Interpress**—Developed by Xerox to handle its line of high-speed laser printers.

Most current printers can understand multiple PDLs (such as PCL and PS) and can use any of the available languages if the proper printer driver is installed.

Installing and Updating Printer Drivers

Printer drivers are software programs that allow the computer and printer to communicate. These programs also provide the user with an interface to configure the printer's options. Every printer model has a unique driver program. Printer manufacturers frequently update drivers to increase the performance of the printer, to add new and improved printer options, and to address general compatibility issues. These drivers can be downloaded from the printer manufacturer's website. Use the following steps to install and update a printer driver:

Step 1 Determine the version of the installed printer driver—All printer manufacturers use version numbers to uniquely identify print driver software. In general, the higher the version number, the newer the printer driver software. It is important to know the version of the currently installed printer driver to ensure that you do not replace it with an earlier version.

Step 2   Check to see if a newer, more compatible driver is available—Use a web browser to visit the printer manufacturer's website. The URL for the site is usually www.manufacturer's_name.com. If this is not the case, use a search engine to find the manufacturer's site. Because driver updates are fairly common, most websites have a link from the main page to the drivers' (or support) page. Once the driver page is found and a newer version of the printer driver is located, research the printer driver to ensure that it is compatible with your system. Compatibility issues include required operating system, system hardware specifications (such as RAM, hard drive space, etc.), application issues, and communication cabling.

Step 3   Download the driver—After you determine that the driver is compatible with the system, download the printer driver file(s) to the local machine. Be sure to download all necessary files as well as any documentation for installing the newer software. These items should be downloaded and saved to a unique folder on the computer.

Step 4   Install the downloaded driver—The downloaded driver can be installed automatically or manually. Most printer drivers are packaged with extra software that, when executed, automatically searches the system for an older driver and replaces that driver with the new one. Manual printer driver installation is accomplished by moving or copying files to certain locations on the computer, and letting the operating system know of the changes.

Step 5   Test the newly installed printer driver—You should run multiple tests to ensure printer driver compatibility. These tests include using applications to print different types of documents, changing and trying each printer option, and noting any problems that occur. If there are problems once the new driver software is installed, restart the computer and printer, and run the tests again. If the problems still exist, contact the printer manufacturer or visit the manufacturer's website to report any bugs.

Installing and Replacing Ink and Toner

Follow the manufacturer's specifications to install the printer's ink cartridges, toner units, and ribbons. Some ink jet printers must be powered on before installing ink cartridges. An example of a replacement cartridge for a laser printer is shown in Figure 10-15, and a replacement ink jet cartridge is shown in Figure 10-16.

Figure 10-15 Laser Cartridge

Figure 10-16 Ink Jet Cartridge

In general, laser and dot matrix printers should not be powered on when installing the toner unit or print ribbon. The following precautions should always be taken when installing toner units, ink cartridges, or ribbons:

- Laser printer toner units should be shaken vigorously in a side-to-side manner to evenly distribute the toner inside the hopper. If toner spills out of the cartridge, it can be wiped up with a damp cloth.

- Ink jet printer cartridges can be fragile. Be sure to handle them with care, and do not touch the print head or foil contacts. This could clog the nozzles and cause erratic output. Also, be sure to install the correct color cartridge in the appropriate slot in the printer.

- Printer ribbons should be handled by the plastic ends only. Never touch the ribbon.

- Recycle ink cartridges, toner units, and ribbons according to environmental recommendations. Manufacturers typically include the packing material in which you can return the toner units.

Installing and Adjusting Print Media

Print media are the materials on which the final output is to be placed. Traditionally, this medium has been paper, but recent advances in printer technology allow other materials, such as transparency media, slides, card stock, etc., to be printed upon. Before installing any print medium, be sure that it meets the specification of the printer. Size, weight, texture, and absorbency should all be taken into consideration.

Use the following steps when installing print media:

Step 1   **Adjust the appropriate media tray**—Most printers can handle multiple media types and provide different media trays and feed options. Identify the proper media-handling input tray first. For example, HP ink jet printers require users to place regular, 20-lb bond paper into the lower media tray, while heavier stock is fed in single sheets at a different location.

After you identify the tray, adjust it so that the media fits correctly. Most media trays have adjustable guides, as shown in Figure 10-17, that keep the medium aligned as it enters the printer. Adjust these guides carefully; too much slack can cause a misfeed, while too much pressure can cause a jam. Also, determine if the printer has a media selection lever near the input tray(s). This lever (or button) sets the height of the rollers used to pull the media from the tray.

Figure 10-17 An Ink Jet Printer Media Tray and Guide

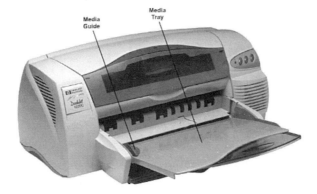

Step 2   **Prepare the media**—When using a stack of media, be sure to fan the media to negate the effect of static electricity. Static electricity can cause sheets to cling to one another, causing a printer jam. Also, the print surface of the media must be properly oriented. Most transparencies and

many types of paper have a special printing surface that is indicated on the media packaging. Failure to print on the correct surface can cause poor output and could harm the printer.

Step 3   **Make any other adjustments to the printer**—Many of today's printers have multiple media output options. For example, printed plain paper might fall into a catch tray, while printed envelopes are held at the end of the output path for the user to retrieve one at a time. If a printer has these capabilities, it usually has a switch with which to select output paths. (This can be the same as an input switch.) If the printer's output is to be placed into an output tray, be sure to adjust the guides on that tray for the intended media.

Step 4   **Configure the print driver for the proper media**—This is accomplished on the computer using the print setup option. In print setup, the user can inform the printer of the specifics of the media: size, weight, texture, absorbency, input tray, and output path. Bypassing this important step can lead to printer errors.

Installing Additional Printer Memory

The main method of speeding up a printer and allowing it to handle more complex print jobs is to upgrade the printer's memory. All today's printers have at least a small amount of RAM. Generally, the more memory a printer has, the more efficiently it works, and the requirements for the computer's resources (CPU cycles and RAM) become smaller. This printer memory is used for tasks such as buffering or page creation (drawing). *Print job buffering* is the ability of the printer to capture as much of the print job into its internal memory as possible. This allows the computer to focus on other tasks instead of waiting to send the remaining data for the print job to the printer. Buffering is common in laser printers and plotters as well as in higher-end ink jet and dot matrix printers.

Page creation is the process of recreating an entire page of a document before output. This allows the printer to output an entire page at one time while drawing the next page to be printed. This is a key component of laser printers, as these pages are drawn onto the drum and then transferred to paper. The following are important guidelines for printer memory installation:

1. Determine the type of memory used by the printer (standard or proprietary).

2. Determine the number and type of memory slots available and how they are populated.

3. Know the proper procedures for installing printer memory.

The first step in installing additional printer memory is to consult the printer's documentation. Determine the memory type used, the current memory population and availability, and the proper procedures for memory upgrades.

- **Memory type**—Memory specifications include the physical type of memory, speed, and capacity. Some printer manufacturers use standard types of memory in their printers, as shown in Figure 10-18, while others require the use of special or proprietary memory.

- **Memory population and availability**—If a printer has multiple memory upgrade options or slots, determine how many slots are used and how many are available. This might require opening a compartment on the printer to check RAM population.

- **Proper procedures**—Each printer manufacturer has a unique set of procedures for memory upgrades. The procedure list should include the steps for physically accessing the memory area of the printer, the removal and installation of the memory, and an initialization process as well as any other software/driver changes that must be made before use.

Figure 10-18 A SIMM

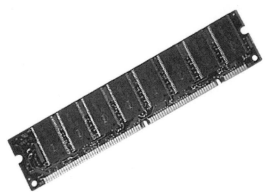

Adding a Local Printer

Adding a local printer is a relatively easy process. In Windows 2000, choose **Start, Settings, Printers**. Figure 10-19 shows the printers window. Select the Add Printer button. This launches the Add Printer wizard, as shown in Figure 10-20. Windows then asks if the printer being added is local or part of a network. If the user is the only one who will be using the printer, choose Local, as shown in Figure 10-21. Connecting a network printer is discussed in the next section.

Figure 10-19 The Printers Window

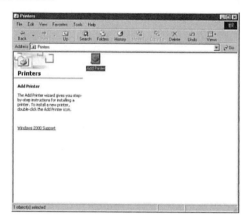

Figure 10-20 The Add Printer Wizard

Figure 10-21 Adding a Local Printer

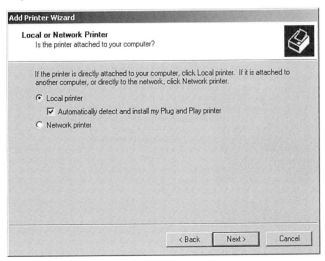

Choose the port to be assigned. Figure 10-22 shows the most common port for local printers: LPT1. The printer manufacturer and model type must be provided. Choose the correct model from the list. If the model does not display, check the printer's user guide or choose a model from the same manufacturer with a similar name. For example, if the printer is an HP DeskJet 550 and that model is not listed in the Add Printer wizard, choose the HP DeskJet 500.

Figure 10-22 Selecting a Printer Port

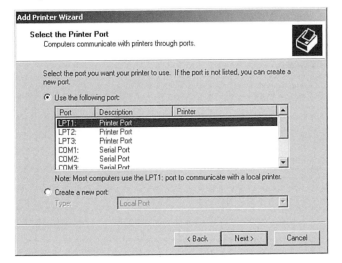

After a printer is chosen, the wizard notifies the user that the printer is ready to use, as shown in Figure 10-23. However, this does not necessarily mean that the printer and computer are communicating properly. To verify this, print a test page.

Figure 10-23 Completing the Add Printer Wizard

 Lab Activity 10.3.8 Adding an Ink Jet Printer to Your Computer

In this lab, you install the correct printer driver and verify computer/printer communication by printing a test page.

Printing a Test Page

Printing a test page is the final step when connecting a printer. This ensures that the printer is functioning properly, the driver software is installed and working correctly, and the printer and computer are communicating.

The following list describes several ways of printing a test page:

- **Use the Print Test Page option from the Printer Properties dialog box**—After adding a new printer to a computer, the user is given the option of printing a test page. Figure 10-24 shows the screen that displays. If this step is skipped or a change has been made and the user would like to print another test page, this option can be accessed using the next method.

Figure 10-24 Printing a Test Page

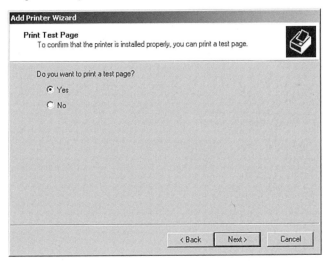

- **Access the Print Test Page option in Windows.** Choose **Start, Settings, Printers**—Alternatively, double-click to open My Computer and then open the Printers folder. Right-click the icon of the desired printer, and choose Properties. This opens a dialog box that contains most of the customizable features of that printer. Near the bottom of the General tab, locate the Print Test Page button. Clicking this button initiates the printing of a test page, which is followed by another dialog box that asks the user if the page printed correctly. If it did not, access the built-in help files to obtain troubleshooting steps.

- **Use an application to print a test page**—All computers have a basic text application installed. In Windows, a good application to use is a text editor such as Notepad or WordPad. Start the text editor by choosing **Start, Programs, Accessories, Notepad** (or **WordPad**). After typing a few lines of text, choose **File, Print**. If the printer is installed and configured correctly, it should print the text that is on the screen. To test the graphics (or color) capabilities of the printer, start a drawing application, such as Paint, and print a test page. If a file has been created and saved, the user can right-click the file in Windows Explorer and select Print from the menu of options. This causes Windows to open the file in the associated application and print it automatically.

- **Send a file directly to a parallel port printer using the command line**—When older command-line–oriented operating systems, such as MS-DOS, were used, this was a popular method for testing the printer as well as for printing documents. Only ASCII files (such as txt and bat files) can be printed from the command line. To begin a command-line session in Windows, choose **Start, Run,** type **COMMAND.COM,** and click **OK.** This opens a shell session. At the command line, type the following command:

TYPE THEFILE.TXT > PRN

In this command, each element is described as follows:

— **TYPE:** This sends the file to an output device.

— **THEFILE.TXT:** This is the ASCII file that is to be printed.

— **>:** This symbol redirects the file to a specific output device.

— **PRN:** This sets the printer to be the output device.

If an ASCII file is not available, the current directory can be printed using the following command:

DIR > PRN

Sharing a Printer

This section includes the following topics:

- Host-based printing technology
- Printer switches
- Printer built-in fonts and font cards
- Configuring printer sharing
- Adding a network printer
- Installing print services
- Network print servers
- Printer network interface cards

Host-Based Printing Technology

When a computer sends a document to a printer for output, the information must be translated from the operating system's format to the PDL of the printer. The PDL then creates a raster (bitmap) image of the document, and the printer outputs the image. These language translations and the drawing of the raster image can be time-consuming. A method of speeding print jobs is known as host-based printing.

Host-based printing, also known as *graphical device interface (GDI) printing*, is a technology in which the operating system communicates directly with the printer and sends the printer an image that is ready to print. Because no translations are needed and because the computer sends the data to the printer at the rate they are printed out, the speed of the printing process is significantly increased. Printers that take advantage of host-based printing technology are usually less expensive than traditional PDL-based printers. Because the computer's CPU and memory are doing all the work, manufacturers no longer have to place complicated processors or memory buffers in their printers. Therefore, host-based printing technology takes advantage of the power of the computer and the efficiency of the operating system. To increase the performance of the printer, users can upgrade the PC and update the printer driver.

There are some drawbacks with host-based printing technology. A printer-specific driver must be installed. Many PDL-based printers can use generic drivers, while GDI printer drivers are printer-specific so that the operating system knows how to communicate with the printer. Also, host-based printers placed on a network require a direct connection to a host and require that printer sharing is configured. This host then becomes a print server, which can limit the role that the computer can perform.

Printer Switches

It is often desirable to have multiple printers available to handle different types of print jobs. Standard black-and-white laser printers are fast and can produce crisp text output, while ink jet printers turn out photo-realistic prints on various media. Generally, if multiple printers are to be connected to a single host PC and the user needs to connect/disconnect the desired printer on demand, the printers must connect to different ports (parallel and USB, multiple USBs, etc.). The alternative is to use a printer switch.

A *printer switch* is a piece of hardware that is used to take data input from one or more devices and route the input to one or more output devices. Figure 10-25 shows the front and rear view of a printer switch. Also known as an *A/B switch* or *data switch*, these devices allow a host to access two or more output devices by simply flipping a switch. In addition to printers, these output devices can be Zip drives, scanners, or CD-R drives.

Figure 10-25 A Printer Switch

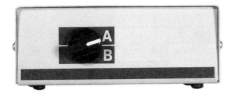 

The parallel port is still the standard printer interface port on the PC. Most PCs are assembled with only one parallel port. Although it is possible to install and configure a second parallel port, the most feasible method of having access to multiple printers on a single host is through the use of a parallel printer switch. The switch connects to a host's parallel port and gives the host access to two (or more) user-selectable parallel ports. The port that the host connects to is labeled Input or Host, and the output ports are usually labeled A and B. Inside the printer switch is mechanical or digital circuitry that performs the switching when the user selects the port connected to the desired output device. The user selects the device by turning a knob, flipping a switch, or pressing a button.

A printer switch is a useful device that is simple to set up and use, but several rules should be followed before installation:

- A printer switch can only output to one device at a time.
- Each printer (or other device connected to the switch) must be installed and configured properly on the host. The correct printer and device drivers are still needed for printer operation.
- Be sure to choose the correct printer for each print job, and check to see that the printer switch is pointing to that printer.
- Read the printer switch and printer manual to ensure that the two devices are compatible. Many printers require precise bidirectional signaling from the host, so the printer switch must be able to handle this.
- Consider using electronic rather than mechanical switch boxes for laser printers, because these printers do not operate reliably with mechanical switches.

Printer Built-In Fonts and Font Cards

A *font* is a complete set of characters of a particular typeface used for display and printing purposes. These characters include letters, numbers, and other symbols that share a common theme or look. Fonts can be modified by size, weight, and style. Groups of fonts with differing styles are called *font families*. Display fonts are used for screen output, and print fonts are used for hard copy output. Display fonts and print fonts try to match one another as closely as possible to ensure that the user has true WYSIWYG output. When using host-based printing technology, virtually any font that can be displayed on-screen can be output to the printer, but using true print fonts can speed the printing process even more.

Print fonts come in two varieties: printer built-in fonts and font cards. Both are described in the following sections.

Printer Built-In Fonts

Printer built-in fonts are also known as *resident fonts*. These character sets are part of the firmware (ROM that includes software) that is built into the printer. These are usually common fonts of serif and sans serif types. Upgrading a printer's built-in fonts is limited by the specifications of the printer. Many printers require a firmware change for an upgrade, which can be a costly and difficult task. Other printers allow users to download fonts (sometimes referred to as *soft fonts*) directly to the printer, where the firmware can be flash upgraded or the fonts can be saved to another part of the printer's memory.

Font Cards

Many printers (especially laser printers) have expansion slots similar to those in personal computers. These slots allow memory upgrades, different printer interfaces, and font upgrades. Font upgrades are accomplished through the use of *font cards*, which are hardware cards that contain firmware housing other print fonts. Font cards can be purchased with single or multiple font families and are easy to install and configure. Users can also swap font cards for use in particular print jobs. These cards must be purchased for specific printers, because printer expansion slots vary by manufacturer.

Configuring Printer Sharing

Printer sharing allows multiple users, or clients, to access a printer that is directly connected to a single computer, the *print server*. Sharing resources, like printers, was one of the reasons that networks were developed. Having a group of users share a single printer is far more economical than buying each user a printer.

For print sharing to work, special software must be installed and configured on the print server. Then, the clients must be configured to be able to access the printer that is located on the print server. While third-party software applications are available, most personal computer operating systems have built-in printer-sharing capability.

In Windows, this option is called *file and print sharing*. While Windows 2000 installs this component automatically, the component is easily added to the rest of the Windows operating systems. To install file and print sharing or to verify that it is installed on a Windows 9X computer, right-click My Network Places (in Windows Me) or Network Neighborhood (in Windows 95/98) and choose Properties. The dialog box shown in Figure 10-26 displays. The user can then verify if File and Printer Sharing for Microsoft Networks is installed. If it is not installed, click the File and print sharing button. Remember that the printer must be installed and configured on the print server before printer sharing can work.

Figure 10-26 File and Print Sharing Properties Dialog Box

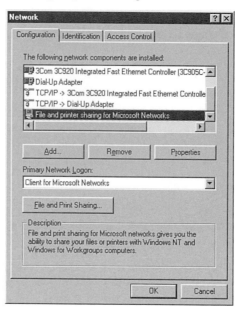

After verifying that the printer sharing software is installed, the server must know which printer it is going to share. In the Printers folder, right-click the printer to share, choose Properties, and select the Sharing tab. Choose the option to share the printer, and assign it a unique name.

NOTE

In a mixed operating system environment, compatible printers for each operating system are needed on the print server. Additionally, if there are different printers, the drivers for each printer must be installed on the server.

Finally, each client computer that is to access the printer must have the correct printer drivers installed. Begin the Add a Printer wizard to find and install the shared printer. If configured properly, the client automatically downloads the driver information from the server.

Lab Activity 10.4.4   Setting Up Print Sharing Capabilities

Upon completion of this lab, you will be able to verify communication between the server and the client, set up the print server, configure the client, and test the client's print capability.

Adding a Network Printer

There are two basic types of computer networks: peer-to-peer and client/server. Peer-to-peer networks are small computer networks in which each computer has an equal responsibility. Client/server networks can be of various sizes and are made up of client computers and servers. A client computer is a workstation that makes the request of the server, such as application information, e-mail, web pages, and printer services. A client/server network with a printer is illustrated in Figure 10-27.

Figure 10-27 A Client/Server Network Printer

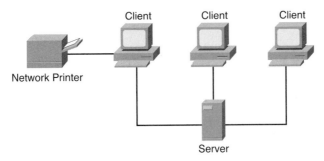

A *network printer* is attached directly to the network as are the client workstations. The network server manages all requests by the workstations to use the printer.

Configuring a printer to print over a network involves a method that is similar to accessing a server resource or drive on the network. The network operating system has utilities that allow network printing to be set up and managed.

The following steps are involved in setting up network printing:

Step 1   The application formats the document to be printed into data that the printer can understand and sends the data out.

Step 2   The redirector in the computer sends the data out on the network, and the data then travel to the print server.

Step 3   The print spooler in the software on the print server places the data in a print queue (print jobs waiting to be processed). A *print spooler* is a collection of dynamic link libraries (DLLs) that are used to acquire, process, catalog, and dispense print jobs to the printer.

Step 4   The print data are held in the print queue until the printer is ready to print them.

Installing Print Services

Depending on the network operating system used, this installation procedure varies. However, the following basic procedures are common to most networks:

- Printer drivers must be installed to allow the printer to communicate with the print server.
- A name must be assigned to the printer so that users on the network can find and share the printer.

- The output destination information must be supplied so that the print director knows where to send the print job.

- Setting information and output format details must be identified so that the network knows how to process the print job.

- Most network operating systems have their own utilities to set up printers with the previously listed information. This is called the Print Manager in most Windows operating systems.

Network Print Servers

A *network print server* is a computer dedicated to handling client print jobs in the most efficient manner. Because it handles requests from multiple clients, a print server is usually one of the most powerful computers on the network. A print server should have the following components:

- **A powerful processor**—Because the print server uses its processor to manage and route printing information, the server must be fast enough to handle all incoming requests.

- **Adequate hard disk space**—Print servers capture print jobs from clients, place them in a print queue, and feed them to the printer in a timely fashion. This requires the computer to have enough storage space to hold these jobs until completed.

- **Adequate memory**—The server's processor and random-access memory (RAM) handle feeding print jobs to a printer. If a server has too little memory to handle an entire print job, the job must be fed from the hard drive, which is much slower.

The role of a print server is twofold: to provide client access to print resources and to provide feedback to the users. When using printers that connect directly to the network, the print server routes print jobs to the proper printer, as shown in Figure 10-28. With host-based printing technology, the print server acts as the interpreter between the client and the printer to which it is directly connected. This is illustrated in Figure 10-29. If configured properly, the print server can also send clients the printer driver software needed to access the printer.

Because print servers manage print jobs through a print queue, the servers can also provide feedback about the printers to the users on the network. This feedback can include a confirmation message that a print job has been completed and an estimated time of print job completion as well as any errors that might have been encountered in the printing process. These errors include printer out of paper, wrong paper type, paper jam, printer out of toner/ink, etc.

Figure 10-28 Printers that Connect Directly to the Network

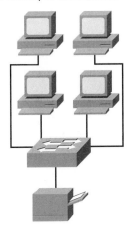

Figure 10-29 The Print Server Using Printer Sharing

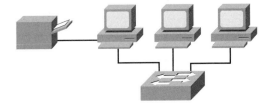

Printer Network Interface Cards

For a printer to connect directly to a computer network, the printer must have the proper type of port for network connection. A *printer network interface card (NIC)* is an adapter that the printer uses to access the network media. This NIC can be built into the printer or can come in the form of an expansion card. Currently, the most popular printer NICs have RJ-45 ports to connect to copper-based Ethernet networks, as shown in Figure 10-30. Usually, connecting the printer NIC to a network hub or switch with a Category 5 cable provides the connection. Other printer NIC types include BNC, RJ-11 (four-wire telephone cabling), and wireless (infrared or radio frequency).

Figure 10-30 A Printer NIC

Managing a Printer

This section includes the following topics:

- Using the printer queue to manage print jobs
- Setting print times for large or less important documents
- Selecting a default printer
- Configuring individual printer options

Using the Printer Queue to Manage Print Jobs

The purpose for sharing a printer or using a network printer is to make the printer available for multiple users. Regardless of how advanced these printers are, they can only process one print job at a time. When a print job is sent to a printer while the printer is busy, that print job is held in the printer queue, as shown in Figure 10-31.

A *printer queue* is a temporary holding area for print jobs that are later fed to the printer when it is ready for the next job. This queue is an area of memory that is set aside on the print server for managing print jobs. When a user decides to print a document, the document is immediately sent to the printer queue. If there are no other jobs in the queue, the job is processed at once. Printer queues, by default, use the first-in, first-out (FIFO) rule. With this rule, the print job that reaches the queue first receives the highest priority and is output before all other jobs.

Figure 10-31 The Windows Printer Queue

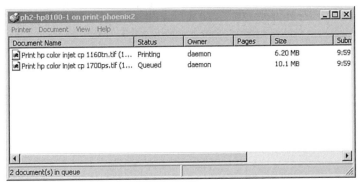

The printer queue is also a management tool that can be used to view and manipulate print jobs. The queue can show information about each print job and the progress of the job as it is being fed to the printer. This information includes the user's identification, job start time, and current status of the print job. Some print job manipulation tasks that can be performed in the printer queue are as follows:

- **Deleting print jobs**—The printer queue can be used to delete single, multiple, or all the print jobs currently being held in the queue. This is useful if an error occurs or multiple copies of a document are accidentally sent to the printer.

- **Rearranging print jobs**—Even though the printer queue uses the FIFO rule, the order in which jobs are processed can be changed. Higher-priority print jobs can be placed closer to the top of the queue while low-priority jobs can be moved to the bottom of the list.

- **Pausing the printer**—Sometimes, it is beneficial to temporarily pause the entire printing process. Choosing to pause printing puts the queue in a wait state. During this pause time, changes can be made within the queue (such as deletions or rearrangements) and changes can be made to the printer (such as changing media type, ink, or toner). "Unpause" the printer queue to resume processing the print jobs.

Managing the printer queue must be restricted to a few individuals such as the network administrator and print server administrator. The network administrator can then determine the priority of users and print jobs.

 Lab Activity 10.5.4   Managing Files in a Printer Queue

In this lab, you open the printer queue, add jobs, delete a job, rearrange jobs, and then purge all jobs held in the queue.

Setting Print Times for Large or Less Important Documents

In busy, high-print-volume environments where multiple users share access to printers, a large print job can tie up a printer for a significant amount of time. This can reduce the efficiency of those requiring services of the printer. In these situations, it is beneficial to be able to set print times for large or less important documents. If not needed immediately, a large document can be set to print after business hours or during a lunch break.

Selecting a Default Printer

A *default printer* is the printer to which all print jobs are sent if another printer is not selected. With simple applications like Notepad, selecting the Print option sends the document to the default printer. Other applications allow the user to choose any of the installed printers, but these applications list the default printer as the first option.

Any computer with a printer installed has a default printer. If a single printer is installed, it becomes the default printer. As other printers are installed, the user must decide which printer should be the default printer.

Choosing or changing the default printer on a computer can be done in the following ways:

- **During printer installation**—Each time a printer is installed on a computer, the user is given the opportunity to designate that printer as the default printer.
- **Using manual selection**—Opening the Printers folder in Windows allows the user to see icons that represent all the installed printers. A list of installed printer icons can be seen by choosing **Start**, **Settings** and then choosing the Printer folder or by opening the Control Panel from the Windows 9X desktop. The current default printer has a small checkmark in a dark circle in its icon, as shown in Figure 10-32. Designating a new default printer can be done by right-clicking the desired printer's icon and choosing Set as Default. Figure 10-33 shows setting the default printer option.
- **Using the printer queue**—When viewing the queue of a particular printer, that printer can be designated as the default printer by choosing Printer from the menu bar and selecting Set as Default.

Figure 10-32 The Windows Default Printer

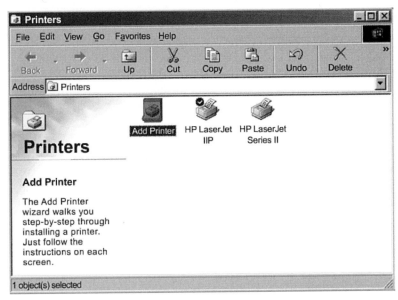

Figure 10-33 Set as Default Printer

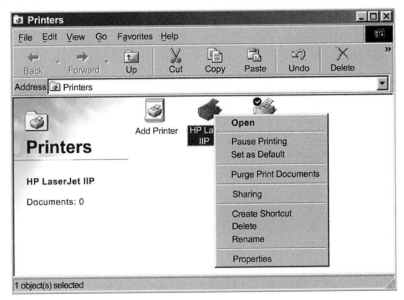

Configuring Individual Printer Options

Each model of printer can have its own set of user-selectable options. The two main categories of printer options are media handling and printer output. In general, *media handling options* are used to set the way that a printer handles the media. This can include input paper tray selection, output path selection, and media size and orientation as well as paper weight selection. *Printer output options* deal with how the ink or toner is placed on the media. Color management, print quality, and print speed are common printer output options.

While some printer options can be selected through switches located on the printer, most of today's printer options are configured through the printer driver. Two methods of selecting individual printer options are described in the following sections.

Global Method

The global method refers to printer options that are set for all documents. Each time a document is printed, the global options are used (unless overridden by per-document selections). Global printer configuration changes are made by choosing **Start**, **Settings** and selecting the Printer folder. Right-click the individual printer, and choose Properties. The Printer Properties dialog box displays all the printer options. At this point, configuration changes must be applied to the printer to become the default printer settings. For example, if a user prefers not to use the color capabilities of an ink jet printer, he or she can select to print in black only. Although these settings become the defaults, they can be overridden using the per-document method of configuring printer options.

Per-Document Method

Most of today's users print many different types of documents. Letters, spreadsheets, and digital images are common document types that can require different settings to be configured on the printer before output. Most computer applications allow the user to override any globally selected printer options through the use of *per-document printer settings*. Within the application used to create the document, a user can select Print Setup from the File menu to access printer options. The default settings appear but can be changed for the specific document to be printed. A user that has been writing letters using a word processor might want to change the color- and print-quality options of a particular printer before printing a full-color photograph.

Dealing with Paper Problems

This section includes the following topics:

- Obstructions in the paper path
- Stripped and broken drive gears
- Stepper motor problems
- Defective registration roller and other feed rollers
- Wrong paper type
- High humidity
- Paper dusting

Obstructions in the Paper Path

The large majority of printer problems are paper jams. Many problems are related to the paper itself. Fragments of paper that are torn in the printing process must often be removed from the paper path. This usually involves understanding the path that the paper travels from the registration roller to the output roller. An intense visual check of this path usually discloses the location of the fragment. Use care to not damage the printer while removing the obstruction.

Parts that drive paper movement can fail, causing paper to crumple or z-fold in the process of moving through the path. This problem shuts the printer down and requires removal of any trapped paper. Again, care in removal is emphasized. Never clear a paper jam by pulling the paper in the opposite of its intended direction. Doing this can damage the printer gears. Clear such jams by pulling the paper out in the same direction that it goes through the printer.

A paper jam can occur when the wrong type of paper is used. This can cause more than one page to enter the registration rollers and is called *paper clumping*. A defective separator pad can also cause clumping. The defective separator pad should be replaced if it is the cause.

Most of the problems in laser printers that require service are rooted in the paper dust that is accumulated in the paper path. This paper dust requires regular removal to prevent costly service at a later date. However, it is difficult to clean something that is not easily seen. The technician must open or take apart the printer and clean all the places where the dust accumulates. The technician must know where to clean and understand the proper cleaning method. The technician should consult service information on any printer that he or she is not familiar with. Because there are static charges present in the laser-printing process, dust also accumulates outside the paper path. At some point, this dust falls back into the paper path, causing jams.

Replacing toner units and pulling out paper jams can release toner that has not been fused to the paper. Use compressed air or a toner vacuum to remove excess toner. If toner leaves a smear on the printer, use an approved solvent to clean the affected area.

Stripped and Broken Drive Gears

When clumping or other jam failures occur, the drive system can overload. This can result in teeth being stripped from a gear or result in a broken gear. The only solution is to replace the gear. Use care due to the timing of the paper movement. Service instructions are necessary even for skilled technicians to perform this repair properly.

Stepper Motor Problems

Stepper motors are used in printers to position the head as well as to move paper through the printer, as shown in Figure 10-34. Stepper motors are usually trouble-free. However, overloading can damage the motor. In this situation, the motor must be replaced. Timing of the print process must be observed; follow the manufacturer's procedure. Improper solder connections on stepper motors can cause intermittent operations. Properly resoldering these connections can correct this condition.

Figure 10-34 A Stepper Motor

 Worksheet 10.6.1 Paper Jams

This true/false worksheet tests your knowledge of clearing paper jams.

Defective Registration Roller and Other Feed Rollers

The rubber used on feed rollers becomes hardened over time. Paper slippage on these rollers can cause jams. Solutions that clean and soften rubber are available as a remedy for this problem. If this does not correct the problem, the rollers should be replaced.

Wrong Paper Type

Most printers are designed for a specific type of paper and a certain weight of paper. When problems occur, such as clumping or folding, check the type of paper to determine if it is in compliance with the manufacturer's recommendations.

High Humidity

A majority of the printers that are used today print on cut sheets of paper. As a result, paper-handling problems are much more likely to occur with these printers than with older printers that used tractor-fed sheets of paper. Problems include jams and paper clumping. One of the primary reasons for these problems is damp paper. Paper has a tendency to absorb moisture when it is stored. A cool dry location is the best place to store paper; high-humidity areas should be avoided. The paper package should not be opened until it is ready to be used. It is good to riffle, or fan, the edges of the paper before putting it into the printer.

Paper Dusting

Paper should be kept in its original wrapper until needed. This keeps the paper clean and ready for use. In extreme cases, compressed air can be used to dust the paper before inserting it in the printer. This is especially useful if the printer is in a dusty environment or has experienced dust-related problems.

Summary

This chapter discussed the basics of printers and printing. Important concepts to retain from this chapter are as follows:

- Printer types used today include laser, ink jet, and dot matrix. Of the three, the laser printer has the most complicated operation, and the purchase price is generally higher. High resolution, superior operation, and speed make it the preferred printer.

- The following steps comprise the laser-printer process: Cleaning removes toner from the drum, conditioning removes the old image and prepares the drum for a new image, writing scans the photosensitive drum with a laser beam, developing is where the toner is applied to the latent image, transferring is where the toner that is attached to the latent image is transferred to the paper, and fusing is where the printed paper is rolled between heated rollers.

- Considerations when purchasing a printer include the print capacity or the amount of printing a printer can handle, the speed of the printer, the quality of the print produced, the resolution that the printer is capable of, and the cost of ownership. The cost of ownership includes the type of paper the printer uses, the cost of ink replacement cartridges or toner units, and the warranty.

- A printer communicates by using cables that connect to ports on the computer and the printer or by using wireless technologies such as infrared signals. The type of printer used determines if a serial, parallel, SCSI, USB, or FireWire port is used. The parallel port is the standard printer interface on the PC.

- Networked printers are used to save resources. For an Ethernet connection, the RJ-45 connector is used. Other connection options include BNC and Token Ring ports. The maximum length of a Category 5 cable, used to connect a printer to the network, is 100 meters.

- A document must be translated from the operating system format to the page description language, or PDL, of the printer. A raster or bitmap image of the document is then created, and the printer outputs the image. This method is sped up with the use of host-based printing, which allows the operating system to communicate directly with the printer.

- A hardware device that allows a computer to route data to two printers or devices is called a printer switch, A/B switch, or data switch.

- A network print server is a computer that is dedicated to handling multiple print requests from multiple clients. It should provide access to print services and provide feedback to the users. A network print server should have a powerful processor, adequate hard disk space, and sufficient memory.

- The print queue in Windows is a temporary holding area for print jobs that are sent to the printer. In the queue, the network administrator can manage print jobs and pause, delete, or rearrange the jobs waiting to be processed.

- Preventive maintenance for printers includes keeping the printer clear of obstructions that can cause a paper jam, using the proper paper, keeping dust to a minimum, and keeping humidity levels low.

The next chapter provides information on proper preventive maintenance. It discusses hardware and software preventive maintenance, electrostatic discharge (ESD), and power issues.

Check Your Understanding

The following are review questions for the A+ exam. Answers can be found in Appendix B, "Answers to Check Your Understanding Review Questions."

1. What is the name of coils of wire that form electromagnets in a dot matrix printer?

   A. Rollers

   B. Solenoids

   C. Platens

   D. Energizers

2. How many pins are in dot matrix printer print heads?

   A. 9 or 24

   B. 9 or 28

   C. 7 or 24

   D. 7 or 28

3. Which part of a dot matrix printer produces a burn if touched?

   A. The platen

   B. The rollers

   C. The print head cable

   D. The print head

4. Which of the following is a nonimpact printer?

   A. Dot matrix

   B. Ink jet

   C. Daisy wheel

   D. Feed

5. What type of printer forces ink through a nozzle when heated by an electrical current?

   A. Laser

   B. Dot matrix

   C. Ink jet

   D. A plotter

6. When an ink jet printer has completed a print job, which of the following describes the paper?

   A. Is often still wet

   B. Is very hot

   C. Is charged with electrostatic particles

   D. Has a uniform positive charge

7. How is the quality of print for an ink jet printer measured?

   A. rpm

   B. dpi

   C. kps

   D. lpi

8. To fix the toner to the paper, the top fuser roller in a laser printer is heated to about what temperature?

   A. 250°F

   B. 350°F

   C. 150°F

   D. 450°F

9. What is the primary corona wire of a laser printer?

   A. A device used to apply the toner

   B. The voltage device that is used to erase the drum

   C. A negative voltage device that scans the drum

   D. A positive voltage device that scans the drum

10. In which laser-printing step is the toner applied to the latent image?

    A. Developing

    B. Conditioning

    C. Redeveloping

    D. Transferring

11. What comes between the conditioning phase and the developing phase in the laser-printing process?

    A. Charging phase

    B. Writing phase

    C. Fusing phase

    D. Cleaning phase

12. What command and control languages are most commonly associated with printers?

    A. PCL and PostScript

    B. PPP and PC Script

    C. Electrophotographic and PCL

    D. PCL and PPP

13. What type of data transfer moves multiple bits of information in a single cycle?

    A. Ethernet

    B. Serial

    C. Parallel

    D. Infrared

14. What is a printer driver?

   A. A hardware device that enables color printing

   B. Software programs that allow the computer and the printer to communicate

   C. Software that installs fonts for the printer

   D. A part of the solenoid

15. How do you open the print queue in Windows 2000?

   A. Click the printer PostScript icon.

   B. Choose **Start, Settings, Printers** and double-click the printer.

   C. Choose File where the document was created.

   D. Click the desired printer in the Printer folder.

16. How do you reorder a print job in a print queue in Windows 2000?

   A. Drag and drop it to the **Start, Print, Top Queue** icon.

   B. It is not possible.

   C. Drag and drop it to the desired position in the queue.

   D. Use the Print Order menu in My Computer.

17. What is the first thing you should do when troubleshooting a printer problem?

   A. Check the power and paper.

   B. Check for IRQ conflicts.

   C. Reinstall the print driver.

   D. Remove the ink cartridge or toner cartridge and reinstall.

18. What does Windows 2000 use to make the printer setup easier?

   A. Queue support

   B. Plug and Play support

   C. Updated printer support

   D. Port support

19. What causes the majority of printer problems?

   A. Paper jams

   B. Toner units

   C. Stripped gears

   D. Defective rollers

Key Terms

built-in fonts   Resident fonts that are part of ROM and built into the printer.

cleaning   The first step in the laser-printing process that removes toner from the drum.

color ink jet printer   Type of printer that uses liquid ink-filled cartridges that spray ink to form an image on the paper.

conditioning   The second step in the laser-printing process that prepares the drum for a new image.

default printer   The printer that all print jobs are sent to automatically.

developing   The fourth step in the laser-printing process that applies toner to the latent image.

dot matrix printer   A printer that works by impacting the ribbon onto the paper.

dots per inch (dpi)   How the quality of print is measured on a dot matrix printer.

FireWire   High-speed, platform-independent communication bus that interconnects digital printers and other devices.

font   A complete set of characters of a particular typeface used for display and printing purposes.

font card   Expansion slot that allows memory upgrades, different printer interfaces, and font upgrades.

fusing   The sixth step in the laser-printing process that rolls the paper between a heated roller and a pressure roller.

global method   Allows a printer to be selected and used for all applications.

host-based printing   Technology in which the operating system communicates directly with the printer and sends the printer an image that is ready to print.

impact printer   Class of printer that includes dot matrix and daisy wheel.

infrared   Type of communication that uses a spectrum of light to transmit and receive.

Interpress   PDL developed by Xerox to handle the Xerox line of high-speed printers.

laser printer   Type of printer that uses static electricity and a laser to form the image to the paper.

latent image   In laser printers, the undeveloped image.

media handling option   The way a printer handles media, such as paper.

near letter quality (NLQ)   The highest quality of print that is produced by the dot matrix printer.

network printer   Printer set up to be shared by multiple users.

Page Description Language (PDL)   Code that describes the contents of a document in a language that the printer can understand.

pages per minute (ppm)   How the print speed is measured on a dot matrix printer.

parallel printer   Transfers multiple bits of information in a single cycle.

per-document setting method   Allows global settings to be overridden for an individual document.

platen   The large roller in a dot matrix printer.

PostScript (PS)   Developed by Adobe Systems to allow fonts to share the same characteristics on-screen and on paper.

primary corona wire   Also called the grid or conditioning roller, it is the voltage device that is used to erase the drum.

print resolution   The number of dots that the print head is capable of fitting per inch when forming an image.

print sharing   Allows multiple users or clients to access a printer that is directly connected to a single computer, the print server.

Printer Control Language (PCL)   Developed by Hewlett-Packard to allow software applications to communicate with HP and HP-compatible laser printers.

printer driver   Software that must be installed on the PC so that the printer can communicate and coordinate the printing process.

printer network interface card (NIC)   An adapter that the printer uses to access the network media.

printer output option   Determines how the ink or toner is transferred to the paper.

printer switch   Also known as an A/B switch, it is hardware that routes data input from one device to another.

serial port   Transmits data to the printer one character at a time.

Small Computer System Interface (SCSI)   Type of interface that uses parallel communication technology to achieve high data transfer rates.

solenoids   Coils of wires that form electromagnets used in the dot matrix printer.

transferring   The fifth step in the laser-printing process where toner is attached to the latent image and transferred to the paper.

Universal Serial Bus (USB)   Type of interface for printers and other devices that use Plug and Play.

writing   The third step in the laser-printing process where the photosensitive drum is scanned with the laser beam.

WYSIWYG   What-you-see-is-what-you-get.

Objectives

Upon completion of this chapter, you will be able to perform the following tasks:

- Document the procedures for preventive maintenance and keep the maintenance log
- Follow the environmental guidelines set for the disposal of computer components
- Protect against electrostatic discharge
- Perform preventive maintenance on computer components
- Run software and antivirus utilities to maintain system integrity
- Understand the power issues that affect computer systems

Chapter 11

Preventive Maintenance

Introduction

Avoiding costly computer repairs is the goal of an effective preventive maintenance program. This chapter stresses the importance of preventive maintenance and the tools that are necessary. Also discussed are the safety issues to consider when working on the computer and when disposing of components. Using proper maintenance helps to prolong the life of the hardware. Running software utilities on a regular basis can make the computer system run faster and more efficiently.

Preventive Maintenance and the Technician

This section includes the following topics:

- Elements of a preventive maintenance program
- Tools and equipment
- General environmental guidelines
- Environmental guidelines for a server room
- Disposal of hazardous materials
- Material safety data sheets

Elements of a Preventive Maintenance Program

The main goal of a preventive maintenance program is to prevent problems before they happen. Three questions need to be addressed when developing a preventive maintenance program: when, why, and how.

- **When is the best time to prevent problems from happening?** A schedule should be created for specific tasks to be completed at certain times of the day, week, and month.

- **Why is this maintenance being done now?** Every time a maintenance task is done on a computer system, the task should be noted in a preventive maintenance log. Items that should be listed with each entry are the date, time, technician's name, and computer system on which the maintenance was done.

- **How is this system to be maintained?** Keeping the work area clean and dust-free prevents many problems. Using common sense also aids in keeping a system running smoothly. Documentation, such as logs to track periodic changes, can be of great help in future diagnostics and troubleshooting.

Details on how to maintain specific components of a computer system are covered in the following sections.

Tools and Equipment

Every technician's toolbox should contain the basic tools that are shown in Figure 11-1.

Figure 11-1 A Typical Technician's Tool Set

In addition, a tool kit should include the following:

- Flat-head screwdriver
- Phillips-head screwdriver
- Nut driver
- Needle-nose pliers
- Diagonal or crosscut pliers
- Mirror
- Digital multimeter
- Flashlight

A wide variety of flat-head and Phillips-head screwdrivers should be carried in a technician's tool set. Technicians can expect to encounter a variety of screws and nuts. Also, the position of certain screws might require different lengths of screwdrivers.

Technicians work with wiring and cabling on a daily basis. Sometimes, a wire or cable must be cut. Diagonal or crosscut pliers allow the technician to precisely cut wires and cabling to the proper specifications.

A good tool set should include a socket set. Most screws in computers fit hex-style sockets, and the technician can use a nut driver to loosen or tighten hex-style screws. Also, a mirror helps the technician to see into tight spots or corners.

Other items, such as an antistatic vacuum cleaner, canned air, various solvents, and lint-free cloths, should be available. Antistatic vacuum cleaners should be used whenever vacuuming computer components because normal vacuum cleaners generate static. This means that only a vacuum cleaner that is certified for use with a computer should be used. To clean toner from a laser cartridge, a standard vacuum cleaner should not be used due to the fine consistency of the toner particles. In these cases, a vacuum cleaner with a higher level of filtration is necessary.

Canned (pressurized) air is one of the most useful tools for computer components. If the inside of a computer needs to be cleaned, a quick pass with a can of air removes the dust without creating static. If the outside of a computer case or a component needs to be cleaned, a lint-free cloth with some water and mild soap can make it look as good as new.

Digital Multimeter

The tool set should include a multimeter, which is a measuring device. A *digital multimeter (DMM)*, as shown in Figure 11-2, combines the functionality of a voltmeter, ohmmeter, and ampmeter into one easy-to-use device. A DMM can measure voltage, amps, and ohms in both alternating and direct current. A DMM can be used to test power supplies, DC/AC voltage and polarity, resistance (ohms), diodes, continuity, coaxial cable, fuses, and batteries.

NOTE

Before using a DMM for testing, verify that it is set to the proper function. For example, if you need to test DC readings for the motherboard, verify that the DMM is set to the DC voltage function.

It is important to know the range of expected results before performing a test. For example, before performing a motherboard test for DC voltage, expected results are +12V, –12V, +5V, or –5V. Technicians can expect these voltage readings on the motherboard to vary by plus or minus 5 percent.

When using a DMM to measure a device with unknown voltage, set the DMM to its highest voltage setting or range.

Figure 11-2 A Digital Multimeter

Today, most technicians carry a digital multimeter (DMM) in the field. Table 11-1 lists important terms of a DMM.

Table 11-1 Digital Multimeter Terms

Voltage (V)	Voltage is the electrical potential difference between two points in a wire. Voltage is measured in volts (abbreviated V). In North America, wall outlets supply 120V, but in Europe, wall outlets supply 240V.
Current (Amps or A)	Current is the flow of electricity through the wire. Current is measured in amperes (or amps, abbreviated A).
Watts (W)	A watt is a measure of power. Power is derived from voltage multiplied by current, as follows: Power (W) = V × A
Resistance (Ohms or R)	Resistance is the opposition to the flow of electricity through a substance.
Capacitors	Capacitors store electrons (electricity) for a short period of time.

The *DC voltage test* is used to test live DC circuits. This test is most often performed on motherboard circuits. The test should be conducted in parallel with the device that you are testing. A parallel test is performed on the device by connecting it to the red (measuring) lead of the DMM and connecting the black (reference) lead to ground.

A *continuity test* is performed by a DMM to verify that a device or conductor makes a complete circuit or path. For example, resistance tests are performed to test fuses. Disconnect one end of the fuse from the system. Set the DMM at 1 ohm; a good fuse should read close to 0 ohms. If the fuse is defective, the reading will be infinite.

A resistance test should never be conducted when the power is turned on. Serious damage to the technician and the DMM can occur if the system is receiving power. Also, before resistance testing can be conducted on a circuit, the circuit must be removed from the system. Isolating a component from the system board can be accomplished by unsoldering one or both leads.

Another common use of the DMM is to set it to produce a sound when no resistance is detected (continuity exists). This is typically used to test continuity in suspect RAM modules. Unplug the module from the motherboard, set the DMM to make a sound when it detects no resistance, and then, using the red and black leads, touch the leads to both end pins of the module simultaneously and listen. If you hear a sound, there is continuity; if there is no sound, the chip is most likely defective.

The *AC voltage test* is used to check system components. Testing power supplies is the main use of the AC voltage test. Use extreme caution when testing power supplies. The electrical current supplied by a power supply unit can be dangerous to the technician. Also, voltage from the DC output can be tested with the AC voltage function.

 Lab Activity 11.1.2   Using a Digital Multimeter

In this lab, you identify and record power supply specifications and connecter types. You will also focus on the use of a multimeter to safely test and record voltage readings.

Loopback Plugs

Loopback plugs can provide important diagnostic information while troubleshooting serial and parallel ports. Loopback testing works by sending signals out and verifying if the correct input is sent back (received). Diagnostic information can be gained from individual pins, ports, controllers, and printer output. Figure 11-3 shows an example of a loopback plug.

NOTE

By design, the PC power supply must have a load on it before making any output tests on the leads. This means some component, such as the hard drive, must be running and drawing power before the power supply can produce DC output. This is called a *switched power supply*.

Figure 11-3 A Loopback Plug

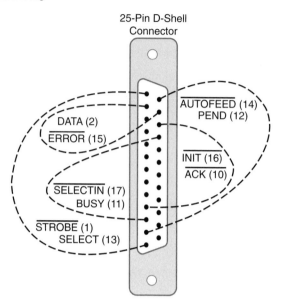

General Environmental Guidelines

As with other devices, a computer eventually reaches the end of its life. This normally happens for one or more of the following reasons:

- Parts or components begin to fail more frequently because the machine is too old and uneconomical to keep.
- The computer becomes obsolete for the application for which it was originally intended.
- Newer machines, often with improved features, arise to replace earlier models.

Eventually, the question arises: What do you do with the old computers or parts? Can they simply be placed in the garbage bin and hauled to a landfill?

Computers and peripherals contain environmentally unfriendly materials. Most computer components are either environmentally hazardous or contain some level of hazardous substances. Waste materials are listed as hazardous because they are known to be harmful to human health and the environment when not managed properly. Also known as toxic waste, hazardous materials typically contain high concentrations of heavy metals, such as cadmium, lead, or mercury. Computer printed circuit boards consist of plastics, precious metals, fiberglass, arsenic, silicon, gallium, and lead. Cathode ray tubes (CRTs) or monitors contain glass, metal, plastics, lead, barium, and rare-earth metals. Batteries from portable systems can contain lead, cadmium, lithium, alkaline manganese, and mercury.

In addition to the computer parts that are hazardous materials, many of the cleaning substances used on computer equipment can be classified as hazardous materials. Although these cleaning materials are classified as hazardous, there are currently no widely accepted regulations for their disposal.

The rest of this section focuses on those items that require special disposal procedures to comply with environmental guidelines. Examples include batteries, CRTs, chemical solvents/cans, and toner kits/cartridges from printers. Finally, the material safety data sheet (MSDS) is discussed.

Environmental Guidelines for a Server Room

In the server room, temperature is important. Never put the server against ductwork or next to the air conditioner. Be aware of items that can cause interference with electrical pull (motors, microwaves, etc.) and electromagnetic interference (EMI), and try to utilize only isolated grounding circuits.

The area around the server should be kept free of debris and clutter. Ideally, the server should be in a locked closet with limited access and with no likelihood of being bumped, jostled, or accessed by nonadministrators.

The space above a dropped ceiling (the area between the ceiling and the floor of a building's next level) is significant to both network administrators and fire marshals. This space, called the *plenum*, is a convenient place to run network cables through a building. The plenum, however, is typically an open space in which air circulates freely, and consequently, fire marshals pay special attention to it.

The most common outer covering for coaxial cabling is polyvinyl chloride (PVC). PVC cabling gives off poisonous fumes when it burns. For that reason, fire codes prohibit PVC cabling in the plenum because of the potential for poisonous fumes.

Plenum-grade coaxial cabling is designed to be used without conduit in plenums, walls, and other areas where fire codes prohibit PVC cabling. Plenum-grade cabling is less flexible and more expensive than PVC cabling, so it is only used where PVC cabling cannot be used.

Temperature

As in many homes, heating and cooling systems control the temperature of the computing environment. During cold weather, the heating system maintains the temperature at a comfortable level. Heat is used in the open-office and server-room environments. However, enterprise data centers are usually air conditioned year round, due to the heat that is generated by the equipment. In all conditions, the server must be maintained below its maximum operating temperature.

Whenever you are implementing a new server, determine the number of British thermal units (BTUs) that your server emits. This can be difficult to determine, because BTU specifications are often not provided. Make sure that the aggregate number of BTUs can be cooled by your air conditioning unit. If the server is to be rack-mounted, you also make sure that the rack is well ventilated and, if possible, contains some type of airflow management (such as a fan).

Liebert (www.liebert.com) is a manufacturer of precision air conditioning systems for use in critical environments such as data centers. Liebert's enterprise air conditioners measure their cooling capacity based on the volume of air in the data center. Visit the Liebert website to find more information on data center environmental controls; Liebert offers systems ranging from 6 to 60 tons in capacity.

Know the designed operating temperature for your equipment. A typical server operates in the following ranges:

- Operating temperature: 50°F to 95°F
- Storage temperature: −40°F to 105°F
- Maximum heat dissipation: 10,000 BTU/hour

Humidity

Humidity is another environmental variable that is critical to the proper functioning of your server. Excessive moisture in the air can damage your server's electronic components. Excessive dryness can subject the server to electrostatic discharge (ESD), which is discussed later in this chapter.

If your server is in a controlled environment (an air conditioned office area, server room, or data center), the humidity control is usually a function of the air conditioning and heating units. In an environment where humidity is not controlled, a dehumidifier or humidifier should not be used because they are unreliable for the immediate server area. A humidifier or dehumidifier also introduces a water source that could potentially cause severe problems. An investment in a network server should include a climate-controlled room that maintains relative humidity in the range of 20 to 50 percent.

Air Quality

Air quality is generally not an issue in a data center environment, but it can be an issue when servers are placed in areas with dust and debris in the air. The server fans can pull much of the dust in the air through the system and deposit the dust on components. Over time, this can cause components to become caked in dust, and they will overheat and fail in a much shorter time than they should. If your equipment is in an area where the air quality is questionable, you should schedule weekly or monthly maintenance to clean the system using a computer vacuum cleaner or canned air.

Fire Suppression

You might be asked to install servers in several different environments. Be aware of the fire-suppression considerations in these areas.

A data center environment generally has an inert gas–based fire-suppression system that works by driving all the oxygen out of the air. Halon was a favorite for many years, but is being phased out in favor of more environmentally friendly gases, such as carbon dioxide. Table 11-2 provides common clean replacement chemicals for Halon.

Table 11-2 Halon Replacement Chemicals

Chemical Name	Trade Name	Manufacturer
FC-3-1-10	CEA-410	3M Specialty Chemicals
HFC-23	FE 13	DuPont
HFC-27ea	FM-200	Great Lakes Chemical
IG-541	Inergen	Ansul Fire Protection
CO_2	—	Various, including Kidde, Fike Protection Systems, and Ansul Fire Protection

Carbon dioxide extinguishes a fire by reducing the oxygen content of the protected area below the point where the area can support combustion. DuPont originally developed FE 13 as a chemical refrigerant; FE 13 also suppresses fire by absorbing heat until the atmosphere can no longer support the fire.

Another fire-suppression material is foam. Foam fire-suppression systems work by separating the fire from the oxygen in the air. Depending on the type of foam system, this separation can be done by using the foam to blanket the fuel surface, smothering the fire by cooling the fuel with the water content of the foam, or by suppressing the release of flammable vapors that can mix with the air and burn.

If the server room is part of a building's sprinkler system, make sure that the sprinkler system can be properly disconnected or disabled by a qualified electrician. Any type of fire or smoke would trigger the system, and the water damage to the server components would be irreversible.

In a shared office environment, it is generally not practical to disable the sprinklers. In this case, try to shield the server from any possible water from the sprinklers. This can be done by placing the server under a desk, enclosing the server in a sealed rack, or otherwise shielding it from moisture.

A good ABC or BC fire extinguisher is essential equipment in the server room. Anyone with access to the server room should be trained to use the fire extinguisher safely. Table 11-3 describes fire extinguisher letter ratings.

Table 11-3 Fire Extinguisher Ratings

Letter Rating	Treatment
A	Fires of ordinary combustibles, such as wood, cloth, and paper
B	Fires of flammable liquids, oils, and grease
C	Fires in live electrical equipment
D	Fires containing combustible metals, such as magnesium, potassium, and sodium

Mount the fire extinguisher prominently either directly inside or on the wall outside the door to your server room.

Flooding

Flooding is a critical problem for computers and especially servers. In most cases, if you are unable to save the equipment before the flood, it will most likely be unrecoverable. In the event of an impending flood, take the following precautions:

- Remove all removable media and backup tapes from the premises. Ensure that they are stored in waterproof containers.
- Power off all servers and move them to the highest location in the building. If possible, remove them from the building and store them on high ground. In many instances, the power shuts down before the flooding damages the servers.
- In the event of flooding, immediately remove any hot-swap drives from the servers and move them to a dry location.

- If the servers have been flooded, they are probably not going to be dependable. If you want to try to recover them, remove all components and dry them as quickly as possible. Allow the components to air dry for at least 48 hours before cleaning and testing them. Corrosion is one area of concern, and moisture on the components is another. If you apply electric current to a motherboard that still has droplets of water on it, there could be extensive damage to the electrical components.

A disaster-recovery plan is crucial for situations such as flooding. Backing up data and saving the data in a separate location allow a system to be restored after damage from a flood.

Monitoring the Server State

You have already learned about the environmental factors that can adversely affect the server. To keep these factors from affecting the server, you must monitor the temperature, line voltage, and other environmental operating factors of your server. There are several ways to measure the server's temperature, including the basic thermometer. In addition, a new generation of add-on server cards can give you detailed information on the environmental state of your server.

The best way to monitor your servers is to add a hardware remote-management card. This card provides detailed information on the internal environment of the server. You can usually get information on the hardware components (for example, active hard drives and processor utilization), and sometimes you can obtain operating system statistics. From an environmental perspective, you can also get information such as system temperature and line voltage. With many remote-management cards, you can set temperature thresholds to alert the technician if the server temperature is out of the operating range.

 Worksheet 11.1.3   Environmental Considerations

This worksheet reviews important considerations regarding hazardous materials and the environment.

Disposal of Hazardous Materials

The list of substances identified as hazardous in the workplace is constantly growing. Some substances, such as adhesives, solvents, and abrasives, present fairly obvious hazards to humans and the environment. Others, such as the toner in office copiers and printers or some cleaning and disinfecting products, might not be as obvious. Proper disposal is therefore a matter of safety as well as the law. Check regulations concerning disposal of hazardous materials to ensure that you are in compliance.

Proper Disposal of Batteries

Batteries often contain rare-earth metals that can be harmful to the environment. Typically, batteries from portable computer systems contain lead, cadmium, lithium, alkaline manganese, and mercury. These metals do not decay and remain in the environment for many years if not carefully disposed of. Mercury, one of the elements commonly used in manufacturing batteries, is toxic (harmful) to humans. Lead and the other metals, although not as harmful as mercury, can still cause problems to the environment.

Because of these metals, depleted batteries are classified as hazardous materials. The disposal of batteries is, therefore, tightly controlled, at the national and the state or local levels. In addition to the federal guidelines on disposal of batteries and other potentially harmful materials into the environment, most states and local communities in the United States have enacted laws that are designed to control where and how batteries can be disposed.

The desired method for the proper disposal of batteries is to recycle them. Additionally, all batteries, including lithium-ion, nickel-cadmium, nickel-metal hydride, and lead-acid, are subject to special disposal procedures that comply with existing environmental guidelines. However, because the regulations vary from state to state and from country to country, contact your local disposal service for more information.

Proper Disposal of Monitors or CRTs

CRTs that have reached the end of life must be handled with care due to the potentially lethal voltage that is maintained even after the unit is disconnected from power. Additionally, CRTs contain glass, metal, plastics, lead, barium, and rare-earth metals. According to the U.S. Environmental Protection Agency (EPA), CRT monitors contain 4 pounds of lead on average. Lead and many of the other metals, as mentioned in the previous section, have been cited as toxic; therefore, they are harmful to the environment and humans.

As with batteries, all or most of the components of end-of-life CRTs can be salvaged or recycled. Monitors must be disposed of in compliance with environmental regulations. Consult your local waste collection agent or recycling company for information on how to best deal with end-of-life CRTs.

Proper Disposal of Toner Kits, Cartridges, and Developers

Used toner kits, cartridges, and developers from printers can be destructive to the environment, and their sheer volume necessitates caution in the way that they are handled and disposed of.

Laser printer toner cartridges can be refilled and recycled. Ink cartridges from ink jet printers can also be refilled and reused. Most of the time, when a new toner cartridge is purchased, the old cartridge can be exchanged for a small credit from the supplier. The vendor should at least accept the old cartridges for processing at no charge. This is the preferred method for disposing of cartridges. The cartridges are eventually returned to the manufacturer to be recycled and reloaded with toner and developer.

Proper Disposal of Chemical Solvents and Aerosol Cans

The chemicals and solvents that are used to clean computers are another source of environmental problems. When leached (drained or evaporated) into the environment, these chemicals can cause significant damage. Therefore, contact your local waste collection company for guidelines on how to dispose of these chemicals and solvents, as well as their containers. Never pour them down the sink or dispose of them in a drain that connects to a public sewer.

Free liquids are those substances that can pass through a standard paint filter. Many dump sites do not handle free liquids, and they cannot be disposed of in a landfill. Therefore, solvents and other liquid cleaning materials must be properly categorized and disposed of at an appropriate disposal center.

Additionally, any cans or bottles that contained the solvents and other cleaning supplies must also be specially treated. Make sure that they are identified and treated as hazardous waste. Some aerosol cans whose contents are not completely used can explode when exposed to heat.

Material Safety Data Sheets

A *material safety data sheet (MSDS)* is a fact sheet that summarizes information about material identification. This includes hazardous ingredients that can affect a person's health, fire hazards involved in using the material, and first aid requirements. The chemical reactivity and incompatibilities include spill, leak, and disposal procedures and protective measures required for safe handling and storage of materials. To determine if a material used in PC repairs or preventive maintenance is classified as hazardous, consult the manufacturer's MSDS. The Occupational Safety and Health Administration (OSHA) developed these data sheets on hazardous materials, indicating their hazards and handling. All hazardous materials are required to have MSDSs that accompany them when they change hands. This means that some of the products purchased for computer repairs or maintenance come with relevant MSDS information in the user's manual. If the MSDS is not available, visit www.msdssearch.com for current information.

OSHA requires that MSDSs are posted prominently in organizations that work directly with these materials. MSDSs are a valuable source of information and typically contain the following information:

- The name of the material
- The physical properties of the material
- Any hazardous ingredients within the material
- Reactivity data, including fire and explosion data
- Spill or leak procedures
- Special precaution information
- Health hazard information
- Special protection information

An MSDS is used to inform workers and management about hazards associated with the products and how to handle the products safely. The MSDS is valuable in determining how to dispose of any potentially hazardous material. Check local regulations concerning acceptable disposal methods for computer-related components before disposing of any electronic equipment.

Preventive Maintenance and Electrostatic Discharge

This section includes the following topics:

- Electrostatic discharge overview
- Antistatic bags
- Grounding wrist straps
- Compressed air
- Grounded workbenches
- Avoiding ESD

Electrostatic Discharge Overview

Have you ever gotten zapped by touching a doorknob in a carpeted room? That pulse is static electricity, the buildup of an electric charge resting on a surface. That zap is formally known as an *electrostatic discharge (ESD)*. ESD is the worst enemy of the fine electronics found in computer systems; that is why it is discussed in almost every chapter of this text.

In order for a person to feel an ESD, there must be a buildup of at least 3000 volts. If the discharge causes pain or makes a noise, then the charge was most likely above

10,000 volts. Most computer chips run on less than 5 volts of electricity. If less than 3000 volts of static electricity have built up, a computer component could be damaged without the technician knowing or feeling it. Table 11-4 summarizes the important dos and don'ts of static electricity.

Worksheet 11.2.1 Electrostatic Discharge

This worksheet provides a review of electrostatic discharge (ESD) and how it can be avoided.

Table 11-4 Dos and Don'ts of Static Electricity

Do	Don't
Work at an antistatic workstation equipped with tiled floors, a grounding strap, and a grounding mat.	Walk across the room and then handle an electronic component without grounding yourself.
If possible, make sure that the relative humidity is greater than 50 percent.	Touch pins or leads on a circuit board.

Antistatic Bags

When purchasing components to assemble a computer, special packing materials are used with microchips and printed circuit boards (PCBs). These packing materials range from special molded plastics and foams for microchips to antistatic bags for PCBs. Do not remove a component from special packaging until it is ready to be installed. Figure 11-4 shows an *antistatic bag*, which can be used to temporarily store parts and components when disassembling a computer for cleaning or other preventive maintenance actions.

Figure 11-4 An Antistatic Bag

Grounding Wrist Straps

When working on a computer or the individual components, certain tools should be used to reduce the risk of ESD. A *grounding wrist strap*, as shown in Figure 11-5, provides a place for the static to go before it attacks a sensitive computer component.

Figure 11-5 A Grounding Wrist Strap

Compressed Air

Another item that can be used when working on computers is *compressed air* or *anti-static spray*, as shown in Figure 11-6. These sprays or solutions can be used on floors, desks, and in some cases, on the equipment itself. Make sure to follow the safety instructions when using these items.

Figure 11-6 Compressed Air

Grounded Workbenches

Grounding the workbench, discussed in an earlier chapter, is also a common practice in some lab or work environments. Figure 11-7 illustrates a typical workbench. With the surface grounded, there is no need for a grounding mat when computers and other electronic devices requiring grounding are placed on the workbench during repairs.

Figure 11-7 A Grounded Workbench

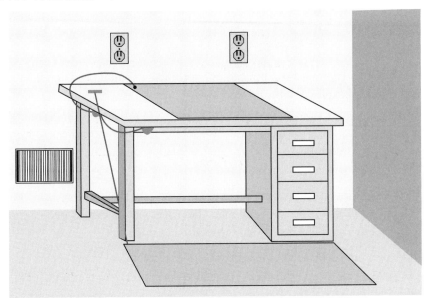

Avoiding ESD

To avoid ESD, you should know the conditions in which it is most likely to occur. When the humidity is low, the potential for ESD increases. Also, if the temperature is low or if there is carpeting on the floor, the potential for static electricity increases. Table 11-5 demonstrates the different conditions that can cause static buildup.

Table 11-5 Conditions that Cause Static Buildup

Causes of Static Generation	Voltage Generated at 10%–25% Relative Humidity	Voltage Generated at 65%–90% Relative Humidity
Walking on carpet	35,000	1,500
Walking on vinyl tile	12,000	250
Working at a bench	6,000	100
Using a poly bag picked up from the bench	20,000	1,200
Moving a chair with urethane foam	18,000	1,500

A few key elements to a good working area include antistatic tile on the floors, grounded workbenches with antistatic mats, and wrist straps. The area should be clean and well lit, and the humidity level should be maintained between 20 and 50 percent. If all these elements are in place, the risk of ESD is significantly reduced.

After the computer case has been opened, the technician should be grounded to the case by touching an exposed part of the computer case. If just a painted part of the case is touched, it might not release static buildup. Once any static buildup has been discharged onto the exposed case, attach the grounding wrist strap to the case to help prevent additional buildup. An ESD-free environment is crucial to preventive maintenance that involves opening the computer case.

Many things can cause a computer system to fail. The most common are dust buildup, extreme temperatures, and rough handling. The placement of the PC (whether in a clean or dusty environment) determines how often it needs to be cleaned.

If a computer is not regularly cleaned, dust can build up on the components inside the computer, such as the fan bearings or the printed circuit boards. If a large amount of dust builds up on a fan, it could cease operation, causing the system to overheat. This is especially true with newer CPUs. If the processor fan stops working, the computer either malfunctions or shuts down, and the processor can be damaged.

For these reasons, keeping the inside of the computer clean is important. To properly clean the inside the computer case, unplug the unit and move it away from other equipment. Use a can of compressed air, making sure to follow the directions carefully, to blow out all the dust within the case. This simple process should be done at least once a year in relatively clean environments and two to three times a year in dusty areas. This process serves two purposes. By removing the dust, the motorized components work more efficiently for a longer period of time. The cleanout also keeps dust from building up, which reduces the chances of an ESD from the dust.

Extreme Temperatures

Another hazard to computers is extreme temperatures. If a computer system overheats, several problems can occur, such as a system malfunction and data loss. To prevent this, make sure that the ventilation mechanisms of the case are properly functioning and that the room is at a comfortable temperature.

A final item that could cause damage to a computer is rough handling. When moving the system, take care not to loosen internal components. If a component becomes loose while the machine is turned off, it could be damaged when the unit is restarted.

Preventive Maintenance for Computer Peripherals

This section includes the following topics:

- Monitors
- Mice
- Keyboards
- Printers
- Scanners

Monitors

Because the display unit, as shown in Figure 11-8, is the most visible piece of equipment, it should be kept clean for both appearance and functionality. The following concepts apply both to CRT and LCD screen types.

Figure 11-8 A Monitor

Make sure that the device is unplugged from the wall to prevent damage should water get inside. Using a damp cloth with a mild detergent, wipe down the entire display unit to remove any dust buildup. To remove any cleaner residue, run another cloth, damp with water only, over the surface of the monitor. Do not use so much water that it drips. Once the display has been cleaned, a dry cloth can be used to promptly finish the job. Use care when cleaning the screen portion of the monitor so as not to scratch it. After cleaning the monitor, make sure that the power cord is plugged back in securely.

Mice

There are two different types of mice: mechanical and optical. Both are shown in Figure 11-9. A mechanical mouse can act erratically if it gets dirty. To keep a mechanical mouse working smoothly, a few simple cleaning methods are used. As dust settles on the mouse pad, it gets swept up into the moving parts of the mouse when it is used. This causes a buildup of a crusty residue on the rollers inside the mouse. The fastest way to clean this residue is to remove the plate on the bottom of the mouse, remove the mouse ball, and then gently scrape the dust buildup from the rollers with your fingernail or other gentle scraping tool. You can also use isopropyl alcohol or methanol with a cotton swab.

Figure 11-9 A Mechanical and an Optical Mouse

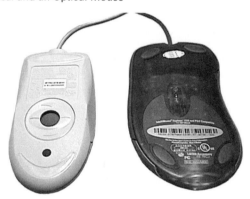

Use a damp cloth on the optical sensor surface of an optical mouse. However, this could cause damage and should only be done if absolutely necessary. Be sure to unplug the optical mouse when cleaning. Do not to expose your eye to its laser.

Keyboards

A keyboard takes the most abuse of any computer component. Keyboards are also open to the environment, which allows dust to build up over time. Periodic cleaning of the keyboard prolongs its life and prevents malfunction. The keys on a keyboard can be removed, as shown in Figure 11-10; this allows easy access to the areas where dust collects.

A soft brush or cotton swab can be used to remove dirt from below the keys. You can also use compressed air to blow out dust from below the keys. However, you must hold the keyboard vertically or in an inclined position and direct the blasts of air across the keyboard so that the dirt and dust are knocked off and out of the keyboard. Otherwise, larger dirt or dust particles can be blown into the interior corners or other areas associated with the springs or foam material that controls the keys.

Figure 11-10 Keyboard with Keys Removed

Printers

Because printers have many moving parts, a higher level of maintenance is needed. Printers produce impurities that collect on the internal components. Over time, these impurities must be removed; otherwise, they can cause the printer to malfunction.

When working with dot matrix printers, clean the roller surfaces with a damp cloth. Make sure to observe safety procedures by first unplugging the power cord before applying a damp cloth.

When cleaning an ink jet printer, the paper-handling mechanism most often requires cleaning. Over time, as paper passes through, particles of paper build up. These particles can be removed with a damp cloth when the unit is unplugged. In addition, the proper handling of ink cartridges keeps the printer output from smearing. Open the cover, as shown in Figure 11-11, and replace the ink cartridges according to the manufacturer's recommendations.

Figure 11-11 An Ink Jet Printer

Laser printers usually require little maintenance unless they are in a dusty area or are older units. Remember two things when cleaning a laser printer. First, to clean a toner spill, use a vacuum cleaner designed specifically for this purpose. If a household vacuum cleaner is used to remove toner, the particles will pass through the filtration system and into the air. Second, unplug the unit before cleaning it due to the high amounts of voltage within the laser printer.

Using the right paper for the printer and the proper toner, ink, or ribbon goes a long way toward keep a printer working smoothly. The following items clarify these considerations:

- **Paper selection**—Choosing the right type of paper helps the printer last longer and print more efficiently. In most computer supply stores, several types of paper are available. Each type is clearly labeled for the type of printer for which it is intended: ink jet printer paper, laser printer paper, etc. The printer manufacturer usually recommends a certain type of paper in its user's manual.
- **Ink selection**—When choosing ink, consult the printer's manual to determine the manufacturer's recommendation. The printer will either malfunction or print poorly if the wrong type of ink is installed. Refilling the ink cartridges is recommended because the ink can leak during the process. Always buy the vendor-recommended ink cartridges.

Scanners

The most important thing to remember when using a scanner, as shown in Figure 11-12, is to keep the scanner surface clean. If dust or a foreign item makes the glass dirty, consult the user's guide for the manufacturer's cleaning recommendations. If the manual does not make a recommendation, try using glass cleaner and a soft cloth so that the glass does not get scratched.

Figure 11-12 A Scanner

If the underside of the glass becomes dirty, refer to the manual for instructions on opening the unit or removing the glass from the scanner. If glass removal is possible, thoroughly clean both sides, and replace the glass the same way that it was originally set in the scanner.

Lab Activity 11.3.5   Cleaning Computer Components

In this lab, you learn the proper procedures for cleaning components.

Worksheet 11.3.5   Preventive Maintenance for Components

This worksheet tests your knowledge of computer components and proper maintenance.

Preventive Maintenance for the End User

- Software utilities
- User responsibilities
- Antivirus applications
- Power issues
- Using a UPS in a server environment

Software Utilities

Several utilities are included with DOS and Windows that help maintain system integrity. If run on a regular basis, the following utilities can make the system run faster and more efficiently:

- **ScanDisk**—This utility is included with both DOS and Windows. It is used to check the integrity of files and folders or to do a more thorough check of the system by scanning the disk for physical errors. ScanDisk can be used on any formatted disk that is readable by the operating system. Run this program whenever the system is not shut down properly or at least once a month. Figure 11-13 shows ScanDisk in progress on drive C.

Figure 11-13 ScanDisk

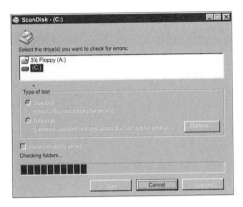

- **Disk Defragmenter**—When a program in installed on a computer, it can become located in various portions of the hard drive. This is known as *fragmentation*. The performance of a fragmented drive is reduced. The Disk Defragmenter utility was created to optimize space on the hard drive so that programs execute faster. Technicians often run this utility after running the ScanDisk utility. Figure 11-14 shows the Disk Defragmenter utility in progress.

Figure 11-14 Disk Defragmenter

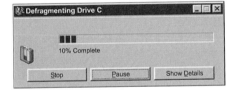

- **CHKDSK /f**—A DOS application that runs on the command line, this command is used to check the file system for errors. It can be compared to ScanDisk for Windows 2000/XP. The command is shown in Figure 11-15.

Figure 11-15 CHKDSK /f

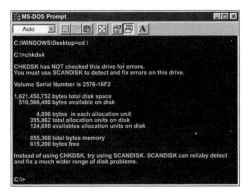

■ **REGEDIT**—The registry is a database that holds configuration data about the hardware and environment of the PC. REGEDIT is a command for advanced technicians. It provides access to the Registry in a view similar to Windows Explorer. However, if a change is made in the Registry, there is no undo command. System errors or malfunctions can result. Extreme caution is advised when using this program. The Registry Editor is shown in Figure 11-16.

Figure 11-16 The Registry Editor

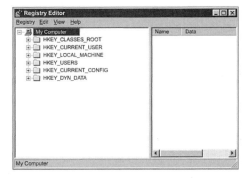

User Responsibilities

A computer's end user can do several things to make the system work properly. Using the system utilities is one way to make a system run more smoothly. The following list offers additional ways to manage files and programs to improve performance:

■ **Managing applications**—When installing applications, use the Add/Remove Programs dialog box, which is accessed in the Control Panel. Certain applications might not use an install shield, and if the setup program crashes during the installation, it could cause the system to fail. Also, use the Add/Remove Programs utility to uninstall programs. Simply deleting the folder where the application resides does not remove the application from the system.

■ **Managing files and folders**—The file-management system of an operating system is designed to keep data in a hierarchical tree. Much like a physical filing cabinet, the hard drives should be organized so that data files are in one location and programs are in another. This makes the various files easier to find and back up.

■ **Backing up your work**—When working with files and folders, remember that computers can fail. Your personal files should be backed up regularly. The best way to back up data is to make a copy on a form of removable media (floppy disk, CD, or Zip disk) and then store that media away from the computer, preferably in a different building. Do not use the same disk repeatedly. Use multiple disks, and create multiple copies of the same data, in case one disk fails.

Lab Activity 11.4.1   Using the Scandisk Utilities

This lab covers Scandisk and Defrag utilities to help maintain system integrity.

Antivirus Applications

Computer viruses are programs that have been written by people with malicious intent. Once a computer has been infected, the virus can be spread to other machines by way of a network connection or by removable media.

To prevent a virus from infecting the system, the best defense is an *antivirus application.* Antivirus programs, once installed, can run in the background to make sure that a virus is not infecting the computer. They can also be run on command; they can scan the entire computer or just a specific file for viruses. If a virus is found, the antivirus software can perform one of two actions. It can clean the infected file, or if the software cannot clean the file, it can isolate the file. If a file becomes isolated, or quarantined, the user cannot open it. Remember to update your antivirus program often (or use an auto-update function).

A good defense against viruses is common sense. Viruses are typically sent as e-mail attachments. Once the attachment is opened, the virus can infect the computer and reproduce itself using e-mail addresses found in programs such as Microsoft Outlook. Other users might assume that the e-mail is legitimate, opening the attachment and allowing the virus to spread. Be suspicious of e-mail attachments with exe extensions. When in doubt, contact the sender before opening an attachment.

Types of Viruses

Part of defending against a virus is knowing the different types of viruses and what they do. The following is a list of the most common forms of viruses:

- **File virus**—One of the most common forms of viruses, file viruses modify an existing program so that upon execution of a seemingly safe program, the malicious intent of the virus is carried out.

- **Boot sector virus**—This kind of virus targets the boot sector of a floppy or hard disk. If the boot sector of the primary hard drive is infected, the virus runs every time that the computer is started.

- **Macro virus**—This type of virus takes advantage of built-in macro programming languages in word processors. Macros automate the formatting of documents and can be quite useful. However, macros can also be written to do damaging things.

If a computer system is behaving strangely and the hardware is functioning properly, do not immediately rule out a virus, which can act like a hardware failure. If antivirus software is installed, run it immediately to verify the integrity of the system. Additionally, schedule antivirus software to run on a regular basis.

Power Issues

Computer components are vulnerable to electrical fluctuations and can be damaged by electrical discharges because of the delicate nature of the internal components. Computers can be damaged or destroyed by high levels (lighting strikes) or low levels (static electricity) of electrical releases. Blackouts, brownouts, noise, spikes, and surges are examples of power interruptions that can cause system malfunctions or failures. These are explained in more detail in the following list:

- **Blackout**—This is a complete loss of power for any amount of time. It is usually the result of a strong weather event, such as high winds, lightning, or earthquakes.

- **Brownout/sag**—Sags and brownouts are reductions in power. A sag is a brownout that lasts less than a second. These incidents occur when voltage on the power line falls below 80 percent of the normal value. Overloaded circuits can cause them. Brownouts can also be caused intentionally by utility companies seeking to reduce the power drawn by users during peak demand periods. Like surges, sags and brownouts account for a large proportion of the power problems that affect networks and the computing devices that are attached to them.

- **Noise**—Noise is caused by interference from radio broadcasts and generators, and by lightning. The ultimate effect is unclean power, which can cause errors in a computer system.

- **Power surge**—Also known as transient voltage, a power surge is a dramatic increase in voltage above the normal level. For example, a standard wall outlet in the U.S. increasing from 120V to 250V represents a power surge. A power surge lasts more than 3 nanoseconds (billionths of a second). This voltage increase is enough to overwhelm the delicate components of a computer. However, surge suppressors can help defend computer components against power surges.

- **Spikes**—Are sudden increases in voltage that are much higher than normal levels. If a power surge lasts one or two seconds, it is called a *spike*. Spikes are usually caused by lightning strikes but can also occur when the utility system comes back online after a blackout.

By understanding the types of power issues that can cause problems with computer systems, you are better prepared to prevent these problems from occurring. The next section discusses the different types of equipment that can be used to protect equipment from power events.

Surge Suppressors

A *surge suppressor* is also known as surge protector. It can help guard against electrical surges and spikes. A surge suppressor, as shown in Figure 11-17, works by diverting the extra voltage to the ground. Surge suppressors use a component called a metal oxide varistor (MOV) to divert the over-voltage. A clamping voltage triggers the MOV. If the voltage is above the minimum for the clamping voltage, it is diverted to the MOV. If this occurs, the over-voltage bypasses the computer components.

Figure 11-17 A Surge Suppressor

Surge suppressors make sure that the voltage going to a device stays below a certain level. They are mainly used to stop spikes from damaging the hardware, but they also prevent surges that are high enough to do damage. Surge suppressors usually have a built-in fuse that stops excess power from flowing through the unit. However, a surge suppressor is useless during brownouts or blackouts.

Standby Power Supplies

A *standby power supply (SPS)*, as shown in Figure 11-18, is equipped with a backup battery to supply power when the incoming voltage drops below the normal level. The battery is on standby during this unit's normal operation. When the voltage decreases, the battery kicks in to provide DC power to a power inverter, which converts it to AC power for the computer. A problem with this device is the time it takes to switch to battery power. If the switching device fails, the battery is not able to supply power to the computer.

Figure 11-18   A Standby Power Supply

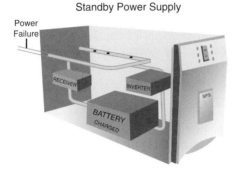

Uninterruptible Power Supplies

An *uninterruptible power supply (UPS)* is comparable to a standby power supply; however, a UPS runs on battery power whenever it is in use, as shown in Figure 11-19. The AC power coming into the unit recharges the batteries while they are in use. The power from the battery is sent to an inverter, which sends AC power to the computer.

Figure 11-19   An Uninterruptible Power Supply

A UPS provides a limited supply of power in the event of a power failure. A UPS is designed to provide enough time to save your data and exit the system before a lack of power shuts down the machine. A UPS can also help guard against power sags or brownouts. Many people choose a UPS over an SPS because of the switching time involved with an SPS. A UPS provides a steady stream of power with no delay.

Overall, the best solution for power events is to have a properly grounded building as well as to have enough battery power to run the equipment for a short time in case of a power outage.

UPSs in a Server Environment

The UPS might be a freestanding unit next to the server, as shown in Figure 11-20, or a rack-mounted unit, as shown in Figure 11-21. The UPS is plugged directly into the power source. The server and its components are then plugged into the UPS. A serial or USB cable that runs from the UPS to a port on the server gives the network operating system the capability to monitor the UPS. In this way, the server knows when the power has failed and the UPS is providing battery power. If the UPS is installed in the sever rack, it is generally installed as the lowest device in the rack.

Configuring the UPS

After you install the UPS-monitoring software, you must configure the following parameters:

- **Time to wait before sending a warning to clients that the server is running on battery power**—This time period is generally a few seconds. It allows time for power to be restored before sending a message. This prevents warning messages from being sent to clients when there is only a momentary loss of power.
- **Time to wait before beginning a shutdown of the network server**—This time period is generally a few minutes.
- **Name of a program or group of commands to run as part of the shutdown process**—This can be simply the name of the server shutdown command, but it can also include programs to send a message to the network server's administrator's pager along with the network server shutdown command.

The UPS-monitoring software enables you to check the status of the UPS. Status items include the level of voltage entering the UPS as well as the level leaving the UPS. Some UPS manufacturers go beyond the simple functions and offer sophisticated software so that you can remotely manage your UPS over the Internet.

Figure 11-20   A Freestanding UPS

Figure 11-21   A Rack-Mounted UPS

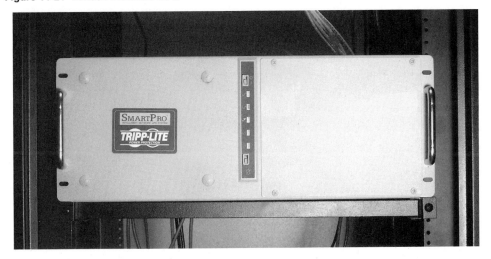

Upgrading the UPS

Upgrading a UPS could mean replacing the UPS battery (which can be a hot-swap operation) or installing a UPS with a higher voltage rating in place of a smaller UPS. A UPS upgrade could be required for any of the following reasons:

- The existing UPS does not provide power for a time period that is long enough to allow the network server to properly shut down.

- The network server's power requirements have increased because of the addition of power-consuming hardware to the network server (for example, additional internal hard disk drives).

- The amount of equipment (such as external hard disk drives) that must be supported by the UPS during a power failure has increased, thus increasing the load on the UPS.

To replace a UPS with a `higher voltage rating`, you must shut down the network server. Use the following checklist for upgrading or replacing the UPS:

1. Shut down the network server and other devices that are connected to the UPS.

2. Turn off the existing UPS.

3. Disconnect all power cords from the existing UPS.

4. Disconnect the existing UPS power cord from the power source.

5. Disconnect the existing UPS-monitoring cable.

6. If the UPS is rack-mounted, remove the UPS from the server rack.

7. Install the new (fully charged) UPS.

8. Plug the new UPS into the power source.

9. Plug the power cords of the devices to be supported by the UPS into the UPS.

10. Connect the UPS-monitoring cable.

11. Turn on the new UPS.

12. Power up the network server and other devices that are plugged into the UPS.

13. Upgrade and reconfigure the UPS-monitoring software on the network server.

Before installing the new UPS, plug it into a power source to charge its batteries. The initial charge time is usually 12 hours or more. Follow the manufacturer's instructions for unpacking the UPS and preparing it for use.

Check the following items of the new UPS:

- Is the existing power source adequate?

- Is the existing power source the correct amperage?

- Does the new UPS use the same type of power plug as the existing UPS?
- Does the new UPS use the same type of monitoring cable as the existing UPS (serial port, USB port)?
- Does the new UPS need updated or different UPS-monitoring software installed on the network server?
- Does the new UPS fit into the space occupied by the existing UPS?

Although rechargeable, UPS batteries do not last indefinitely. At some point, you must replace the UPS battery. To replace the battery, consult the UPS manufacturer's instructions. You can perform some UPS battery replacements while the network server is running and the UPS is supplying power to the network server. This would be considered a *hot-swap battery*. However, when replacing the battery, the UPS may have to be turned off. If this is the case, you must shut down the network server before replacing the UPS battery.

Summary

This chapter discussed preventive maintenance and the importance of keeping computer hardware in good working condition to avoid costly repairs. Important concepts to retain from this chapter are as follows:

- Three questions are addressed when developing a preventive maintenance program: when, why, and how. Preventive maintenance should be done on a regular basis, and each task should be recorded in a maintenance log. Documentation should be developed that details how maintenance is carried out so that it is consistent and thorough.

- The tools and equipment required to safely maintain computer components include a basic tool kit and items such as an antistatic vacuum, canned air, lint-free cloths, etc.

- Environmental guidelines must be followed regarding the proper disposal or recycling of CRTs, batteries, printing supplies, etc. MSDSs are used to detail specific hazards and special handling procedures.

- Using electrostatic discharge (ESD) protection devices and creating an ESD-free environment are important to prevent problems. Use a wrist strap when working on the system with either an antistatic mat or a grounded workbench to prevent ESD.

- Individual computer components must be cleaned on a regular basis. Be sure to unplug these components when cleaning them.

- Software utilities, including ScanDisk and Disk Defragmenter, manage applications and files to keep the system running smoothly.

- Protect your system against computer viruses. Virus types including viruses that attack program files, boot sector viruses that infect the hard drive, and macro viruses that can automatically damage one system or an entire network.

- Identify power interruptions that can cause malfunctions, and know the devices that are used to protect sensitive equipment.

The next chapter details troubleshooting basics for computer hardware. The steps used to determine the cause of specific problems and the steps to follow to resolve hardware problems are detailed.

Check Your Understanding

The following are review questions for the A+ exam. Answers can be found in Appendix B, "Answers to Check Your Understanding Review Questions."

1. Which equipment is not used to clean computer components?

   A. Canned air

   B. Lint-free cloths

   C. Soap and water

   D. A regular vacuum cleaner

2. What is the proper way to dispose of batteries used in portable computers?

   A. Recycling

   B. Recharging

   C. Designated landfill

   D. Special disposal is not required

3. What does MSDS stand for?

   A. Maintenance standard data specifications

   B. Material safety data sheet

   C. Material standard distribution sheet

   D. Maintenance safety data specifications

4. What substances can pass through a standard paint filter?

   A. Free liquids

   B. Micro liquids

   C. Municipal liquids

   D. Macro liquids

5. What does ESD stand for?

   A. Electrostandard discharge

   B. Electric static disarray

   C. Electrostatic discharge

   D. Electrostandard direct

6. How many volts must be built up in order for a person to feel an ESD?

   A. 3000

   B. 300

   C. 10,000

   D. 1000

7. Once a computer case has been opened, what should a technician do?

   A. Work quickly

   B. Wear a grounding wrist strap

   C. Increase the humidity

   D. Work on carpet

8. What is the first thing to do if a new monitor is not working?

   A. Adjust the brightness and contrast

   B. Check the monitor for broken parts

   C. Measure the voltage inside the monitor

   D. Make sure that the power cord is firmly plugged in

9. What is a common cause of erratic mouse movement?

   A. One of the potentiometers has failed

   B. Corrupt mouse driver

   C. The mouse is plugged into the wrong port

   D. The mouse needs to be cleaned

10. What utility is used to check the integrity of files and folders?

    A. ScanDisk

    B. Disk Defragmenter

    C. CHKDSK

    D. REGEDIT

11. What utility reorganizes files on a hard drive?

    A. ScanDisk

    B. Disk Defragmenter

    C. CHKDSK

    D. REGEDIT

12. What is the term for a complete loss of power?

    A. Blackout

    B. Brownout

    C. Spike

    D. Sag

13. What is the term for a drop in power?

    A. Blackout

    B. Brownout

    C. Spike

    D. Surge

14. What is the term for a sudden increase in voltage that is higher than normal levels?

    A. Blackout

    B. Brownout

    C. Spike

    D. Sag

15. What usually causes a brief increase in voltage?

    A. Blackout

    B. Surge

    C. Spike

    D. Sag

16. When should antivirus software be run?

    A. When you are notified of a potential virus

    B. On a regular basis

    C. When the system is acting strangely

    D. All of the above

17. What system runs off of a battery that is constantly charged?

    A. Uninterruptible power supply (UPS)

    B. Standby power supply (SPS)

    C. Uninterruptible power plug (UPP)

    D. Uninterruptible power unit (UPU)

18. How is a surge suppressor used?

    A. During brownouts

    B. To keeps voltage below a certain level

    C. To cause a spike

    D. To work with software to even out voltage levels

19. In what system is a battery engaged when power is called for?

    A. Uninterruptible power supply (UPS)

    B. Standby power supply (SPS)

    C. Uninterruptible power plug (UPP)

    D. Uninterruptible power unit (UPU)

Key Terms

antistatic bag   Special packaging material that protects components from ESD.

antivirus application   A program that is installed on the system to prevent computer viruses from infecting the computer.

blackout   A complete loss of power.

boot sector virus   Virus that targets the boot sector of the system so that the virus is run when the computer starts.

brownout   A temporary drop in power.

CHKDSK /f   DOS utility that checks the system for errors.

compressed air   Also called canned air, it is compressed air in a can that is used to blow dust off of computer components without creating static.

Disk Defragmenter   Utility that optimizes space on the hard drive.

electrostatic discharge (ESD)   The buildup of an electric charge resting on a surface.

file virus   Virus that modifies an existing program so that, upon execution, it carries out a malicious intent.

free liquids   Substances that can pass through a standard paint filter. Many dump sites do not handle free liquids.

grounding wrist strap   Device that attaches to a technician's wrist and the computer case that dissipates ESD.

macro virus   Virus that takes advantage of programming languages to attack a system.

material safety data sheet (MSDS)   A fact sheet that identifies hazardous materials.

noise   Interference that causes unclean power.

REGEDIT   A utility used to edit the Registry.

sag   *See* brownout.

ScanDisk   Utility that checks the integrity of files and folders on the hard drive.

spike   A sudden increase in voltage usually caused by lightning strikes.

standby power supply (SPS)   Battery backup that kicks in when voltage levels fall below normal.

surge   A brief increase in voltage usually caused by high demands on the power grid in a local area.

surge suppressor   Device that ensures that the voltage going to another device stays below a certain level.

uninterruptible power supply (UPS)   Power supplied by a battery that is constantly recharged by a regular power source.

virus   Program written with malicious intent.

Objectives

Upon completion of this chapter, you will be able to perform the following tasks:

- Use the steps in the troubleshooting cycle
- Gather correct data from the end user to properly troubleshoot the computer problem
- Isolate hardware problems from software problems
- Troubleshoot hardware components
- Identify the most common failure points in computer components
- Identify common field-replaceable units

Chapter 12

Troubleshooting PC Hardware

Introduction

This chapter details the troubleshooting process for computer hardware components. The troubleshooting cycle details the techniques used to diagnose computer problems and implement the solution. You learn the steps to take when errors are encountered and the specific solutions for hardware, peripheral, Internet, and network access device problems.

Troubleshooting Basics

This section includes the following topics:

- What is troubleshooting?
- Troubleshooting steps.
- Troubleshooting tools.
- Diagnostic software.
- Disposal actions.

What Is Troubleshooting?

Effective *troubleshooting* uses techniques to diagnose and then fix computer problems. A series of logical steps speeds the troubleshooting process. Rarely does simple guessing provide solutions for a problem. It is best to use the troubleshooting steps.

Troubleshooting is a cycle. It starts with identifying (stating) the problem. After the problem is identified, information must be gathered to begin defining the causes. Next, a solution is developed and implemented. Finally, you must verify that the solution worked. If the problem is resolved, the troubleshooting cycle ends with documenting the solution. If the problem is not resolved, the cycle starts over, and the process is repeated until a solution is found.

Troubleshooting Steps

There are six steps in the troubleshooting cycle:

Step 1   Identify the problem.

Step 2   Gather the information.

Step 3   Develop a solution.

Step 4   Implement the solution.

Step 5   Verify that the problem is resolved.

Step 6   Document the solution.

Each step is detailed in the following sections.

Step 1: Identify the Problem

In this step, the problem is identified. This includes defining the general symptoms so the possible causes can be narrowed down. The outcome is a detailed statement that clearly describes the problem. Without a clear understanding of what the problem is, the technician cannot gather the right information to develop an appropriate solution.

There are many different ways to organize your information. Technicians develop individual methods of documentation.

Step 2: Gather the Information

After the problem is identified, the next step is to begin gathering information so a solution can be developed. A technician can make better decisions when the problem has been accurately described. Having the wrong information can make troubleshooting a long and frustrating process.

Fast and efficient troubleshooting involves gathering all the correct information that is necessary to develop an accurate solution.

Computer problems can range from simple to extremely complex. However, computer problems can become increasingly complicated if the technician does not have the correct information.

Today, technicians have many resources available to help them to diagnose the problem. Technicians can use digital multimeters (DMMs), use software-based diagnostic tools, and speak to the end user to gain information. Technicians can also inspect the system, looking for broken components and listening for evidence of a problem.

Gathering Information from the End User

One of the best resources of information is the end user or customer. The end user can provide insights into how the computer was operating before the system had problems.

Most likely, the end user was the last person to see the computer system operating correctly. The technician and the end user can backtrack to the last functioning configuration. While backtracking, the technician should listen for any changes that were made by the end user that might have adversely affected the system. The end user can describe any changes to the system, errors that were received, and system performance leading up to the problem. All this information helps the technician accurately define and quickly resolve the problem. From this information, the technician can begin the process of isolating and fixing the problem.

Common Questions to Ask the Customer

Because the customer is an important troubleshooting asset, the technician needs to know how to properly question the end user. Listed below are typical questions that the technician can ask while gathering information. Be sure to document this information. It will be important throughout the troubleshooting process.

Can You Describe the Error?   This question gives the technician an introduction to the problem. It is important to allow the end user to describe the problem. The end user can supply relevant information to help the technician solve the problem. Document the description of the problem.

Did You Receive an Error Message?   Computers are manufactured with self-diagnostic tools. If the computer fails one of the self-diagnostics tests, it typically generates an error message. These computer-generated error messages help technicians isolate the problem. Have the end user recall the error message or re-create it. In the case of a POST error, ask the customer for the number of beeps heard.

Is This the First Time You Have Had This Error/Problem?   Try to establish a timeline for the event. Is the problem a sudden crash or is it reoccurring? If the problem has happened before, what, if any, changes were made to the system? How was it resolved? A timeline helps to highlight potential causes of the event.

Have There Been Any Changes to the System?   Identifying recent changes to the hardware or software can help the technician isolate the problem. Changes made to attempt to correct previous problems can be the source of the current problem. Also, adding or removing hardware and/or software can create unforeseen problems with system resources.

For example, the end user or customer might report a failure with the video display. One of the first questions the technician should ask is whether there have been any changes to the computer system. The end user might report that the video card has been replaced and he or she is now having video display problems. The technician can now focus on correcting a bad installation of the video card.

Always approach the end user in a respectful and polite manner. Some end users might hesitate to admit what they have done to the system. A professional approach establishes the required trust that enables the end user to discuss any changes.

The end user often does not have technical experience with computers and can overlook seemingly small changes. Even the smallest changes can have major effects on a computer.

Can You Reproduce the Error?   Reproducing the problem allows the end user to concisely describe the error. An on-site technician can then experience the problem firsthand. Reproducing the error exhibits the circumstances under which the computer fails. These circumstances include when the problem occurred, what sequence of events leads to the error, and how the system responds.

However, use caution when reproducing the system error. Do not reproduce the error if it might adversely affect the computer components. For example, do not reproduce a problem such as an arcing power supply.

Is the Problem Hardware or Software Related?   After asking all the necessary questions, obtaining answers, and assessing the answers, the problem should be isolated as being either hardware or software related. The problem can then be isolated to a specific component or part of the system. Once this happens, the technician can then proceed with developing a solution to the problem, as outlined in the next section.

Network Server Problem-Solving

Ask the following questions when diagnosing a problem with a network server:

- When was the last time that the network server was operational?
- What has changed since the last time the network server was operational?
- What hardware or software has been recently added to the network server?
- Who first reported the problem with the network server?
- Where is the network server logbook?
- How is the failure of the network server affecting the operation of the corporation?

Questions Answered by Using Your Senses

A good troubleshooter uses his or her senses to help find problems. The following questions can be answered by using your senses:

- Is the server room too hot?
- Is the server room too humid (that is, above the maximum operating humidity for the equipment)?
- Is there the smell of something burning in the server room?

NOTE

End users have varying levels of expertise with computers. It is important to approach the end user calmly and professionally when problems arise. Computer end users should never feel guilty when a problem occurs. However, a high percentage of computer problems can be directly related to the end user. Computer malfunctions will happen, and it is the technician's job to define and correct the problem. End users are a good resource when gathering information, so it is important to treat them with respect.

- Is smoke visible in the server room?
- Are server alarms sounding?
- Are UPS alarms sounding?
- Are error lights flashing on disk drives?
- Are any of the network server components hot to the touch?
- Are power cords disconnected from any of the components?
- Are network cables disconnected from any of the network devices, including the servers?
- Are all external SCSI cables properly connected?

Using your senses to answer these basic questions is an integral part of troubleshooting. Also important is the use of hardware/software tools and utilities.

Step 3: Develop a Solution

The technician should assess the gathered data and their definition, using experience, logic, reasoning, and common sense to develop a solution.

Step 4: Implement the Solution

This step involves the technician working on the computer. The technician attempts a solution through hands-on manipulation of the computer components, which can be hardware and/or software. Remember the following items when implementing a solution to a problem:

- Back up critical data before making any changes that have the potential to corrupt data stored on the computer.
- Start with the simplest things first.
- Change only one thing at a time, and evaluate its effect on the computer.
- Reverse any changes that make the problem worse or cause further harm to the system.

Step 5: Verify that the Problem Is Resolved

After the technician implements the solution, he or she is responsible for verifying that the system is operating correctly. The technician can run diagnostic tests, visually inspect, and listen to verify that the system is running properly. Then, the technician must verify with the end user that the problem has been fixed. The first goal of a service technician is to ensure that the end user is satisfied.

If the system is operating properly, the troubleshooting cycle is nearly complete. If the system is not running correctly, the troubleshooting cycle continues. The technician

NOTE

Troubleshooting is an acquired skill that improves with time and experience. The initial diagnosis often proves to be incorrect, and the strategy must be revised.

must undo any changes made to the system and return to the beginning of the trouble-shooting cycle. The technician has the freedom to return to the troubleshooting cycle at any step. Each circumstance dictates to which step the technician needs to return. If the technician needs more information, return to Step 1, identifying the problem.

Step 6: Document the Solution

It is important to always document all the changes that were introduced to the system as a result of solving a problem. This record can be the starting point for troubleshooting future problems. In some cases, solving one problem can introduce another problem. Documentation is a useful record because it can lead to the elimination of an entire set of suspect problems. Over time, documentation tracks all the changes or modifications made to a system. If the next system problem is evaluated by a different technician, as often happens in large corporate environments, records of previous repairs are invaluable troubleshooting tools; they educate the technician on the previous state of the machine.

Lab Activity 12.1.7   Steps of the Troubleshooting Process

Upon completion of this lab, you will be able to describe the importance of and identify the steps in the troubleshooting process.

Troubleshooting Tools

Every technician should have a good tool set. To correctly troubleshoot hardware problems, technicians must be equipped with the right tools. Solving the average computer problem does not require the use of sophisticated tools. Usually, a screwdriver and nut driver are the only tools required. However, technicians should be prepared for a wide range of circumstances. Items in a good tool set include both mechanical and digital tools. Technicians should plan ahead if they are going to work away from their tech bench and bring the necessary tools. Specific tools used by the technician were covered in Chapter 11, "Preventive Maintenance."

Diagnostic Software

Many commercial software products are available to assist in troubleshooting computer problems. These products, referred to as *diagnostic software*, are also helpful in preventing potential system failures. Some of the more popular programs are as follows:

- SpinRite: http://grc.com/default.htm/
- Checkit: www.hallogram.com/

- PC Technician: www.windsortech.com/
- AMI Diags: www.ami.com/
- SiSoft Sandra (freeware): www.3bsoftware.com/

SpinRite

SpinRite is a program used to recover data from a crashed hard drive. It has gained market recognition and can recover data from some of the worst crashes. SpinRite is a standalone application that is capable of booting independent of DOS. SpinRite can help prevent hard drive failures as well. If loaded before a failure, it can warn users of a potential problem and can prevent a crash by isolating problem areas of the hard drive. These defective areas are designated as being corrupt. If an area has been corrupted, it cannot be used for reading or writing data.

Checkit

Checkit performs system analysis and testing. It can provide the technician with performance reports for the hardware components. Checkit can perform loopback testing using loopback plugs. It can also verify proper operation of the CPU, PCI slots, DMA, CMOS, cache, keyboard, and the first 64 MB of video RAM.

PC Technician

PC Technician is a standalone diagnostic tool that operates independent of DOS. PC Technician can perform diagnostic tests on parallel ports, serial ports, hard drives, keyboards, video adapters, and RAM.

AMI Diags

AMI Diags provides advanced diagnostic system testing. AMI Diags can provide reports on memory, serial ports, parallel ports, modems, hard drives, keyboards, the BIOS, and video adapters.

SiSoft Sandra

SiSoft Sandra (system analyzer, diagnostic and reporting assistant) is a freeware program that provides a set of diagnostic tools to aid in troubleshooting and benchmarking computer components. SiSoft Sandra can test the performance of the CPU, modem, video card, memory, BIOS, and hard drives.

Disposal Actions

Proper practices should be followed when disposing of hazardous materials. Technicians should be knowledgeable of local regulations for disposing of computer components. Chemicals, batteries, CRTs, and printer cartridges all must be disposed of properly. Information for disposing computer components was covered in Chapter 11.

Worksheet 12.1.2   Troubleshooting Basics

This worksheet tests your knowledge of basic troubleshooting concepts, including the steps used to solve a problem.

Troubleshooting the Hardware Box

This section includes the following topics:

- Overview of field-replaceable units
- POST errors
- CMOS/BIOS errors
- Motherboard-related errors
- CPU issues
- RAM issues
- Cable issues
- Port issues
- The video system
- Secondary storage devices
- Sound cards
- Power supply issues
- Box cooling issues

Overview of Field-Replaceable Units

Devices that can be replaced or added in the field are called *field-replaceable units (FRUs)*. Some of the common FRUs are illustrated in Figure 12-1. FRUs do not require soldering and are easy to remove and install. For example, a PCI sound card is considered an FRU because removing it requires no special tools. FRUs include the following items:

- Monitors
- Keyboards and mice

- Modular expansion cards
- Most microprocessors
- Power supplies
- RAM: DIMMs, SIMMs, RIMMs, etc.
- Floppy and fixed disk drives
- Motherboards

Figure 12-1 Common Field-Replaceable Units

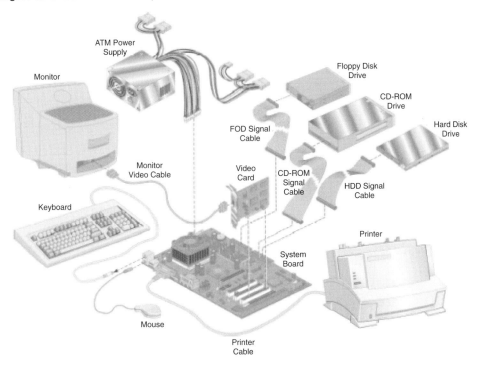

Power-On Self Test Errors

Every time the computer is turned on, it runs through a *power-on self test (POST)*. The POST is a series of self-diagnostic tests that the computer runs to test the major hardware. It is the first task run by the computer's basic input/output system (BIOS). The POST performs basic test routines on the motherboard and major hardware devices. It does not perform in-depth testing on the computer system. The POST can only detect major problems that can stop the bootup process.

The POST is stored in the computer's ROM BIOS. As the computer is turned on, the POST function is passed to the first bank of RAM. For example, the computer checks for a properly functioning system timer, CPU, video card, memory, and keyboard during the POST. If an error occurs, the BIOS has predefined error codes that are reported to the user. These errors can be reported visually or through a series of beep codes.

The *beep code error messages* are a useful troubleshooting aid. If, while running the POST routine, the BIOS encounters hardware errors, it issues a series of beeps. These beep codes indicate and/or confirm that there is a problem with the computer's hardware. Beep codes are produced with a combination of short and long tones.

AMI BIOS beep codes are described in Table 12-1, and common visual display errors are illustrated in Table 12-2. Note that these error codes or messages are BIOS dependent, that is, they depend on the specific BIOS that the system is using.

NOTE

The error reports generated by the POST vary slightly depending on the BIOS that is installed on the computer. For specific information about POST errors, refer to your BIOS documentation or the manufacturer's website. The error messages shown in the following table apply only to the referenced BIOS.

Table 12-1 AMI BIOS POST Errors

Audible Beep	Error Message	Description
No sound	Not plugged in or bad power supply	The power supply is either bad or is not plugged in.
1 short beep	DRAM refresh failure	The programmable interrupt timer or controller could be defective.
2 short beeps	Memory parity error	A memory parity failure has occurred with the first 64 KB of RAM.
3 short beeps	Base 64-KB RAM error	A memory failure has occurred in the first 64 KB of RAM.
4 short beeps	System timer error	There is a failure with the system timer or with the first bank of memory.
5 short beeps	Microprocessor error	There is a failure with the CPU.
6 short beeps	Keyboard/Gate A20 failure	There is a failure with the keyboard.
7 short beeps	Virtual mode exception error	There is a failure with the motherboard or CPU.
8 short beeps	Video display memory error	There is a failure with the video adapter.
9 short beeps	ROM BIOS checksum failure	There is a failure with the BIOS chip.
10 short beeps	CMOS shutdown register read/write error	The CMOS shutdown has failed.

Table 12-1 AMI BIOS POST Errors (Continued)

Audible Beep	Error Message	Description
1 long beep, 2 short beeps	Failure is in video system	There is a failure of the video display or the cable is not attached.
1 long beep	Normal operation	The computer has passed the POST and is performing normally.

Table 12-2 Display Errors

Error Message	Description
CMOS BATTERY LOW	There is a failure with the CMOS battery or the checksum test.
CMOS SYSTEM OPTION NOT SET	There is a failure with the CMOS battery or the checksum test.
CMOS CHECKSUM FAILURE	The checksum test failed or the CMOS battery is low.
CMOS DISPLAY MISMATCH	There is a display-type verification failure.
CMOS MEMORY SIZE MISMATCH	There is a setup and system configuration failure.
CMOS TIMER AND DATE NOT SET	There is a setup and system configuration failure with the timer circuitry.
Nonfatal errors without setup option	
KEYBOARD ERROR	There is a keyboard failure.
KEYBOARD LOCKED	There is a keyboard failure.
CH-X TIMER ERROR	There is a Channel X (0, 1, or 2) timer failure.
DISPLAY SWITCH SETTING NOT PROPER	There is a display-type error.
FDD CONTROLLER ERROR	There is a floppy drive setup failure.
HDD CONTROLLER ERROR	There is a hard drive setup failure.
C: DRIVE ERROR	There is a hard drive setup failure.

continues

Table 12-2 Display Errors (Continued)

Error Message	Description
D: DRIVE ERROR	There is a hard drive setup failure.
System-Halted Errors	
INVALID SWITCH MEMORY FAILURE	There is an error with real/protected mode changeover.
8042 GATE A20 ERROR	The Gate A20 portion of the keyboard controller has failed.
CMOS INOPERATIONAL	The CMOS shutdown register test has failed.
DMA ERROR	There is a failure with the DMA on the motherboard.
DMA #1 ERROR	There is a failure with the first DMA on the motherboard.
DMA #2 ERROR	There is a failure with the second DMA on the motherboard.

POST Card Error Indicators

A *POST card* is a device that helps troubleshoot computer problems that occur before the BIOS can report an error. A computer can fail before a BIOS error can be reported. In this case, a POST card is useful because it provides the technician with a digital readout of POST errors. POST cards are useful for troubleshooting power supply voltages, IRQ/DMA conflicts, and motherboard timers. Also, POST cards are compatible with either ISA or PCI slots.

For example, the computer might crash before the video card can be initialized. A POST card has the ability to decipher the POST error, and it reports the error in hexadecimal code. Each code represents a particular error message. POST card error messages are displayed on the card itself; no video display is necessary to read the error message. Figure 12-2 shows a picture of a POST card; notice the LCD and hexadecimal BIOS code.

Figure 12-2 A POST Card

Lab Activity 12.2.3   Identifying POST Errors

Upon completion of this lab, you will be able to identify common POST errors.

Complementary Metal Oxide Semiconductor/BIOS Errors

The *complementary metal oxide semiconductor (CMOS)* or *nonvolatile random access memory (NVRAM)* stores the systems startup configurations and parameters. Common errors associated with the BIOS include CMOS checksum errors, IRQ/DMA conflicts, hard drive errors, memory errors, and CPU problems. Table 12-3 provides common errors that can be received by the computer's operator.

Table 12-3 CMOS/BIOS-Related Errors

Symptom/Error	Problem	Solution
CMOS battery is low.	Indicates a low CMOS battery, either internal or external.	For internal batteries, leave computer on to recharge the batteries. For external batteries, buy a replacement. If the problem remains, the CMOS chip might have to be replaced. The CMOS chip is usually soldered onto most motherboards. Consider the option of replacing the board or resoldering a new CMOS chip.
CMOS checksum error.	CMOS battery failure.	Replace the CMOS battery.

continues

Table 12-3 CMOS/BIOS-Related Errors (Continued)

Symptom/Error	Problem	Solution
Incorrect CPU speed shown.	CPU speed mismatch.	Reset or update the BIOS. Also, verify the jumper settings on the motherboard.
Inaccessible boot device.	Hard drive is not valid.	Verify the boot order in the BIOS, and verify the jumper settings.
Incorrect memory size.	Memory mismatch.	Verify the compatibility of the memory, and replace the existing memory with known good memory.

The BIOS is a good place in which to start diagnosing hardware problems. The BIOS features provide technicians with low-level hardware and software configuration information. Although the BIOS provides low-level information, it is extremely useful when troubleshooting computer hardware. The average computer/server problem is easy to solve. Most end users do not know how to interpret BIOS information on a desktop computer, so this information is rarely used effectively while troubleshooting.

Checking the System BIOS

When a computer or network server is powered up, the version number of the system BIOS usually displays. Check the vendor's website to determine whether the installed version of the system BIOS is the latest BIOS available for the computer model that you are evaluating. If a newer version of the system BIOS is available on the vendor's website, download the upgrade and follow the vendor's instructions to update the system BIOS on the computer or network server. Most network servers and computers have a *flashable BIOS*, that is, the BIOS can be easily erased and updated using software.

Accessing the CMOS

To access the CMOS setup utility, press the setup key during the boot process. The setup key must be pressed early in the boot process, or the system will load the installed OS. The CMOS setup key is usually F1, F2, or Delete. However, there is no standard, so verify the setup key with the proper documentation. If the video display is functional, a prompt to enter the Setup menu by pressing a certain key is usually displayed. Figure 12-3 shows a typical CMOS setup utility screen.

Figure 12-3 CMOS Setup Utility Screen

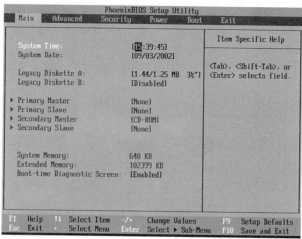

Identifying the Faulty/Incorrect CMOS Setting

One way to help resolve CMOS-related errors is to reset the defaults to the CMOS settings. Resetting the CMOS clears the memory and all potentially corrupted data. Clearing the CMOS memory is useful when the computer does not boot. There are two ways to clear the CMOS memory. The easiest way is to remove the CMOS battery (the small round battery on the motherboard, as shown in Figure 12-4). Use the following steps:

Step 1   Turn off the computer.

Step 2   Remove the CMOS battery from the motherboard.

Step 3   Short (connect) the negative and positive connections (terminals) of the battery holder on the motherboard, using any conducting material (wire, screwdriver head, etc.). Shorting removes any residual capacitance (accumulated charges).

Step 4   Replace the CMOS battery in its original position on the motherboard.

Step 5   Turn on the computer.

Figure 12-4 shows the location of the CMOS battery on the motherboard.

If the just described procedure fails to clear the CMOS memory, you must move the motherboard jumpers manually to the "Clear CMOS position" for a few seconds. To locate these jumpers, refer to the motherboard documentation provided by the manufacturer.

Figure 12-4 The CMOS Battery

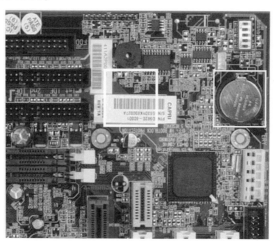

Upgrading the BIOS

A BIOS upgrade can include patches, fixes, additional features, and additional support for the latest devices. However, you should not upgrade the BIOS if problems do not exist. If the system is operational, BIOS upgrades are risky and should be avoided. If the BIOS is updated incorrectly, it could damage the motherboard and peripheral devices.

Special consideration is required when upgrading the BIOS. The motherboard must have a flashable BIOS, and the motherboard must support the upgraded version. The BIOS chip also needs to support the upgrade version number. Only when these criteria are met can the BIOS be successfully updated. Always obtain this information before attempting a flash BIOS upgrade.

Generally, if the motherboard has PCI slots, it has a flashable BIOS. The BIOS revision number should display during startup. It will be in the format #401A0-1234. In this example, the revision number is 1234. The motherboard revision number is printed on the motherboard. On newer motherboards, the revision number is located near the CPU or the center of the motherboard.

To upgrade a flashable BIOS, follow these general steps:

Step 1 Obtain the latest BIOS program from the BIOS vendor (generally from the vendor's website).

Step 2 Follow the vendor's instructions as you load the BIOS upgrade program onto a floppy disk.

Step 3   Shut down and reboot the computer or server from the floppy disk that contains the BIOS upgrade program and the latest BIOS.

Step 4   Follow the on-screen instructions as you perform the BIOS upgrade.

Step 5   Never interrupt the flash BIOS upgrade process, because doing so could result in a computer or network server that cannot be booted.

Upgrading Adapters

Upgrading the BIOS or firmware on certain adapters (for example, SCSI adapters and RAID controllers) follows a procedure that is similar to upgrading the system BIOS. The following general steps apply:

Step 1   Locate the latest BIOS or firmware at the adapter vendor's website.

Step 2   Download the BIOS or firmware upgrade, and follow the vendor's instructions to install the upgrade.

Motherboard-Related Errors

The motherboard coordinates the functioning of the system components. It allows devices to communicate and work in harmony with each other. Troubleshooting a "dead" computer system is a process of elimination. The technician should start from the outside and work in to the motherboard. If the motherboard is malfunctioning or defective, it must be replaced. The following scenarios illustrate problems that can occur and the outline the procedures used to resolve these problems.

Scenario 1

The computer does not boot and appears to be "dead." The first device to check is the external power supply. Verify that the wall electrical outlet is working and that the power cable is properly connected to the computer. If computer still does not operate, move your focus to the inside of the computer case. Visually inspect the cabling. Make sure that the motherboard and drives are connected to the internal power supply. Inspect the motherboard mounting. The motherboard should not be touching the metal case. The motherboard must be separated from the case by rubber buffers at each mount point. If these rubber buffers are not properly installed, the motherboard can short.

If the problem still exists, the next step is to remove the expansion cards. Remove one card at a time, and then try to reboot the system. If the computer boots, the expansion card that was removed is faulty. Next, check the drive controllers. Remove them and try to boot the computer. If the system boots, the problem can be isolated to one of the drives. If the computer still does not operate, remove any modular video cards. If the computer boots, replace the video card with a known good video card and reboot. If the computer still does not start, replace the first bank of RAM with a known good bank. If none of these solutions work, the motherboard most likely needs to be replaced.

Scenario 2

On the surface of most motherboards are dip switches and jumpers. While troubleshooting, these settings can be reconfigured. For example, on some motherboards, the CMOS startup utility can be entered by a particular placement of the jumpers. If these jumpers are not returned to their original configuration, the computer will not operate correctly. To verify a motherboard's jumper settings, consult the motherboard documentation or the manufacturer's website.

Scenario 3

An end user receives the message "BIOS ROM checksum error." During the POST routines, the POST checks the compatibility of the ROM chip and the motherboard. If the POST fails, the end user receives the BIOS ROM checksum error message. This message signifies that the ROM chip and motherboard are not compatible. The ROM chip must be replaced with a chip that is compatible with the motherboard.

CPU Issues

Symptoms of a processor error can include slow performance, POST beep errors, or improper system performance. These errors usually indicate that an internal error has occurred. Internal errors can also cause failures to be intermittent. The CPU might begin a task and then fail. If the system continuously counts RAM or freezes while counting the RAM, the CPU is creating the errors and might need to be replaced. Requirements for a CPU to work with a motherboard include the correct voltage, socket type, and clock speed.

Cooling Issues

Most CPUs have an onboard fan. Figure 12-5 shows a fan, and Figure 12-6 shows the fan attached to a heat sink. The heat sink provides cooling directly to the CPU. If the system freezes after being on for a while or is overheating, the CPU fan might be malfunctioning.

Proper maintenance of internal components can help prevent costly repairs to the CPU. Keep the computer in a well-ventilated area, clean the vents, ensure that case slots are replaced, and dust the inside of computer. The proper cooling fan for the specific CPU is also required.

Figure 12-5 A CPU Fan

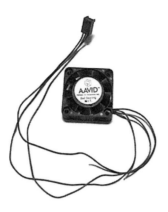

Figure 12-6 Heat Sink with the CPU Fan

CPUs can also become loose due to the expansion and contraction of metals when heated and cooled. Metal fluctuation eventually causes the CPU to become unstable and affects performance. Inspect the CPU, and if it appears to be loose, push it firmly back into place.

Voltage Supply Issues

CPUs must be set to receive the correct voltages to run properly. Motherboards that use Socket 5, Socket 7, or Super Socket 7 chips need to use voltage regulators. Those that use Socket 370, Slot 1, Slot A, or Socket A use an automatic voltage regulation feature. This capability allows the CPU to determine the voltage setting automatically. Typically, the voltage regulators are built into the board. They must be set at the proper voltage, or the CPU can be damaged. Inspect and examine the motherboard and CPU chip, and review the motherboard documentation to find the correct CPU voltage. Figure 12-7 shows the different types of CPU designs.

Figure 12-7 CPU Types

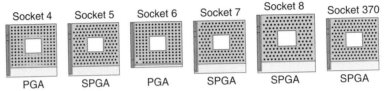

RAM Issues

Today, most RAM implementations are synchronous dynamic RAM (SDRAM) and Rambus DRAM (RDRAM). SDRAM modules with 168-pin DIMMs (described later in this section) are the most common modules. Before SDRAM and RDRAM, there was dynamic RAM (DRAM). Older Pentium computers used fast page mode (FPM) and extended data-out (EDO) RAM. FPM and EDO RAM are 72-pin memory modules. Various memory terms are defined as follows:

- **Dynamic RAM (DRAM)**—A classic form of RAM and has since been replaced by the faster and less expensive SDRAM. DRAM works by storing data electrically in a storage cell, and every few milliseconds, the storage cell is refreshed.

- **Extended data-out RAM (EDO RAM)**—Faster than DRAM. EDO RAM has also been replaced by SDRAM. EDO RAM was an improvement over DRAM because it has advanced timing features. EDO RAM extends the amount of time that data are stored and has a reduced refresh rate. This alleviates the CPU and RAM from timing constraints and improves performance.

- **Synchronous DRAM (SDRAM)**—Replaced DRAM, FPM RAM, and EDO RAM. SDRAM was an improvement because it synchronized data transfer between the CPU and memory. SDRAM allows the CPU to process data while another process is being queued.

- **Double data rate SDRAM (DDR SDRAM)**—A newer form of SDRAM that can theoretically improve memory clock speed to at least 200 MHz.

- **Single inline memory module (SIMM)**—A memory module with 30 or 72 pins, as shown in Figures 12-8 and 12-9. SIMMs are considered legacy components and can be found in older machines. SIMMs with 72 pins can support 32-bit transfer rates, and 32-pin SIMMs can support 16-bit transfer rates.

- **Dual inline memory module (DIMM)**—A memory module with 168 pins, as shown in Figure 12-10. DIMMs are widely used today and support 64-bit transfer.

- **Rambus inline memory module (RIMM)**—A 184-pin memory module that uses only RDRAM as illustrated in Figure 12-11. Smaller RIMMs, called SO-RIMMs, have a 160-pin connector. Some systems require RIMMs to be added in identical pairs, and others allow single RIMMs to be installed.

Figure 12-8 A 30-Pin SIMM

Figure 12-9 A 72-Pin SIMM

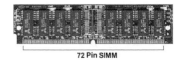

Figure 12-10 A 168-Pin DIMM

Figure 12-11 A 184-Pin RDRAM

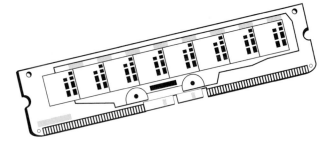

More information about specific memory types can be obtained from the manufacturers' websites.

Troubleshooting RAM Issues

RAM failures come in two forms: sudden or intermittent. Overused or defective memory can cause the system to fail at any time. A good indication of the state of memory is the performance of the system. If the system is running smoothly and applications rarely stall, the RAM workload is well within specifications, and the RAM is functioning correctly. If the computer is multitasking and frequently freezes, the RAM is probably insufficient for the workload and should be upgraded.

Troubleshooting RAM modules is straightforward. Today, RAM is inexpensive and easy to replace. Technicians can easily remove the defective memory and add a known good module. If the problem is resolved, the technician should infer that the RAM module is defective and discard the old module. If the memory problem remains, consult the motherboard documentation. Some motherboards require memory modules to be installed in a particular slot order, or require jumpers to be set. Figures 12-12, 12-13, and 12-14 show the correct way to install SIMMs, DIMMs, and RIMMs.

Figure 12-12 Installing a SIMM

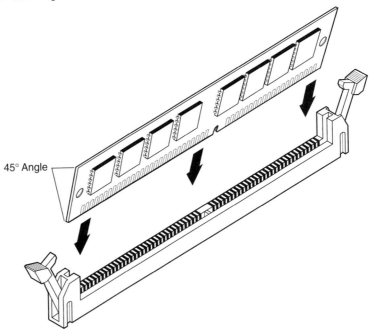

45° Angle

Figure 12-13 Installing a DIMM

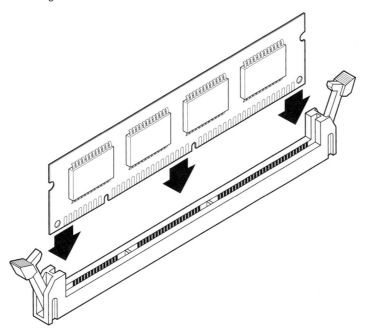

Figure 12-14 Installing a RIMM

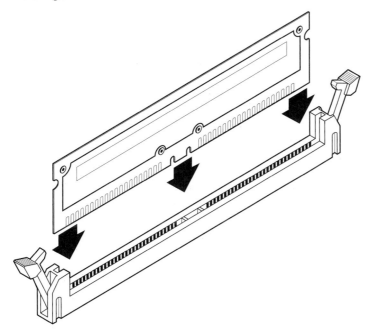

Also, verify that the module has been installed correctly. Memory modules are notched and are inserted only one way. If you suspect an improper installation, remove the module and inspect the module socket. Check for debris, dust, or dirt. Remove any debris and reset the memory module.

Today, computers run software applications that are memory intensive. These programs continually put stress on the memory modules, potentially causing them to fail. The most common symptoms for failed memory are as follows:

- HIMEM.SYS has problems loading.
- The computer does not boot.
- Windows is unstable or programs are freezing.
- There are POST errors.
- There is no video display.

RAM Compatibility Issues

SDRAM memory modules come in various speeds. The most common SDRAM speeds are PC-66, PC-100, and PC-133. The speed of SDRAM is measured in megahertz (MHz). A higher MHz rating indicates a higher-performing memory module. SDRAM could have compatibility issues with the bus on the motherboard. The speed of the SDRAM module must match the speed of the bus. Common bus speeds are PC-100 or PC-133. When purchasing RAM modules, verify your bus speed and buy a compatible RAM module.

The speed of EDO and FPM memory modules is measured in nanoseconds (ns). The memory module with the lowest ns rating is the fastest. EDO and FPM modules can also have compatibility issues with the system bus.

Faster DRAM can be installed on a slower system bus and not affect performance. The system operates at the designated bus speed, even if faster memory is installed. However, a slower or mixed DRAM module cannot be installed on a system with faster DRAM requirements or differently clocked DRAM.

Legacy machines might require parity RAM. *Parity RAM* performs error-checking calculations for every eighth bit of data stored. Today, RAM is nonparity and does not perform parity calculations on data. Never mix parity and nonparity SIMMs. For older systems, the setup utility has an option for enabling or disabling RAM parity checking. Also, error correction code (ECC) and non-ECC RAM cannot be mixed. ECC RAM has the ability to correct data errors and is typically found in file servers. The following scenario helps to illustrate a RAM issue.

Scenario

After a recent update, the computer does not boot; the memory is not being correctly recognized. This error usually occurs when there is a clocking issue with SDRAM. Computers require SDRAM to be either 2-clock or 4-clock. Legacy equipment usually requires 2-clock SDRAM. Newer computers usually require 4-clock SDRAM. Different clock rates are not compatible and cannot be mixed. In this case, the clock rating is most likely not compatible with the motherboard specifications and cannot be used. Consult the motherboard documentation to find the compatible clock rating for SDRAM modules.

Cable Issues

Many cabling issues are obvious because they are usually caused by faulty connections. Reconnecting cables can resolve many of these problems.

Another common cable issue is mismatched interfaces. Different cables look similar. Always verify that the proper cable is being used with the proper interface. The best way to verify that the proper cabling is being used is to check the writing on the cable. Most cables have a written description on the side that details the cable type.

Also, placing cable near an electrical source can cause signaling problems. Electromagnetic energy can pass through the cable and interfere with the data being transmitted by that cable. The concept of signal distortion is illustrated in Figure 12-15.

Figure 12-15 Signal Distortion

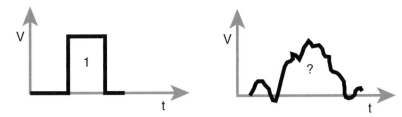

Port Issues

Port problems are typically apparent with a slow-performing or inoperative peripheral device. Common symptoms include the following:

- An inoperative port
- A "Device not found" error message
- A slow or poorly performing peripheral device

Port problems can generally be attributed to the one or more of the following items:

- A bad cable connection
- A peripheral device that is inoperative
- Software problems
- Outdated or missing drivers
- A defective port

NOTE

Some computers have two video cards. If this is the case, try connecting the video cable to each video card. If the video problem still exists, one of the cards must be disabled and the other card enabled. This is usually required when the video card is integrated into the motherboard. The onboard video card can be auto-detected and reinstalled as new hardware at each startup. If this is the case, the onboard video card is the operational card.

Plugging the monitor into the onboard video card can provide access to the CMOS setup. Change the video settings, and exit and save the changes. Plug the monitor into the modular video card, and start the system.

Common port/connection problems are usually found on the following ports:

- Parallel (IEEE 1284)
- Serial
- USB
- FireWire (IEEE 1394)
- AGP video

These ports are discussed in Chapter 2, "How Computers Work," and Chapter 3, "Assembling a Computer."

The Video System

Typically, when a computer is having video display errors, the system might boot normally, but there is no video display on the monitor. Troubleshooting the video display should start outside the computer case. The technician should begin by verifying that the monitor is turned on and plugged into a functional wall outlet. Test the wall socket by plugging in a known good device. After the connection has been verified, check the connections to the computer case. The female DB-15 jack, located on the back of computer case, is the most common monitor connection. Figure 12-16 shows the female DB-15 connection circled on a motherboard with integrated video.

Figure 12-16 A Female DB-15 Connection

After all the connections have been correctly attached, move inside the computer to troubleshoot the problem. Open the case and verify that the video card is properly inserted. It might have to be removed and reseated to verify the installation. If the video card is in a PCI slot, install the video card in another slot. Some video cards need to be inserted into a particular PCI slot to work properly.

Video cards can also have software-related problems. Always verify that the latest video card driver is installed. Use the disks that came with the card, or visit the manufacturer's website.

Video Monitor

The problems associated with the video monitor are usually caused by the configurations of the video card. High-performance video cards can overload a lower-performing monitor. Overloading the monitor can cause damage to its circuitry. If the monitor is being overloaded by the output of the video card, set the monitor to the standard VGA settings of 640×480 pixels. Troubleshoot the monitor's settings if the problem remains. If advanced monitor settings are incorrect, they can adversely affect the video display.

Secondary Storage Devices

Some computers are configured with two hard drives. Configuring a computer with two hard drives increases disk space for backups and for storing data. If two hard drives are configured on the same ribbon cable, they must have a master/slave relationship. During normal operation, the computer boots from the OS that is loaded on the master hard drive. The master drive manages the slave drive (the drive with the jumper set to slave) once the computer boots up.

When two drives are installed, the majority of problems result from improperly set jumpers or incorrect BIOS settings. Hard drive manufacturers determine the jumper settings, so the technician must consult the hard drive manual or the manufacturer's website for specific details. However, each drive must be set to master or slave, or cable select (see next paragraph). The hard drive that contains the OS must have its jumpers set to master. The secondary drive is then set to slave.

Cable select (CSEL) is an option that decides master/slave hard drive relationships based on the position of the drive on the IDE cable. In order for cable select to work properly, each device must have its jumpers set to CSEL, CSEL cabling must be used, and the host interface connector must support CSEL. Figure 12-17 shows a typical hard drive with the available configuration jumper settings, and the cables used to connect it as described.

If there are problems with a dual hard drive system, verify that the jumper settings are correctly set. Devices need to be set to master or slave, or both set to CSEL.

WARNING

Troubleshooting monitors can be fatal. The cathode ray tube (CRT) contains a capacitor and can store 25,000 volts. This voltage can be stored long after the monitor has been disconnected. Never assume that this voltage is not present. Only experienced technicians should troubleshoot the internal components of a monitor.

Figure 12-17 Hard Drive with Cables

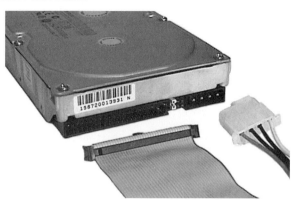

Sound Cards

Legacy sound cards had well-documented interrupt conflicts with other devices, typically peripheral devices. Hardware errors can be caused by a physically damaged sound card and by improperly set jumpers. Today, most sound cards are Plug and Play (PnP) compatible. Installation includes inserting the sound card into the appropriate expansion slot, booting the computer, and loading the driver. Check the manufacturer's website for recent driver updates. If the sound card problem is widespread, check the manufacturer's website for an updated driver to fix the problem.

If an end user is experiencing sound card problems, start outside the computer case and then move inside the case. Verify that the speakers are turned on and attached to the correct speaker port. A common error is plugging the speaker jack into the microphone port. If the problem is related to balancing the sound output, this can easily be corrected. Access the volume controls by double-clicking the speaker icon on the toolbar or by choosing **Start, Programs, Accessories, Entertainment, Volume Control**. Verify that the balance is correct and that the sound is not muted. Figure 12-18 shows the sound card volume controls.

Figure 12-18 Sound Card Volume Controls

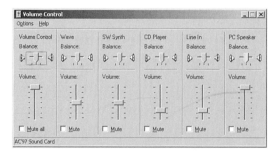

Intermittent problems or a nonoperational sound card usually indicates resource conflicts. If the sound card is in conflict with another device, it might operate sporadically. For example, if the sound card does not work when a document is being printed, this would indicate that resources are conflicting. The sound card and printer might have been configured to use the same IRQ channel.

To troubleshoot these conflicts, first verify the hardware and software configurations. The majority of these problems are caused by uninstalled/outdated drivers and resource conflicts. Software diagnostic tools can help reveal interrupt conflicts. Most diagnostic tools include some tests for the sound card. Running these tests helps you gain information on the computer's multimedia performance.

The Windows OS also has management features to diagnose problems. In Windows 98/2000, right-click My Computer and select Properties. The System Properties dialog box should appear. Press the Hardware tab, and then select the Device Manager button. The Device Manager dialog box opens. Select "Sound, video and game controller list." If the system detects a conflict, it places a yellow question mark next to the device. Figure 12-19 shows an example of a conflict in the Device Manager in Other Devices.

Figure 12-19 Device Manager

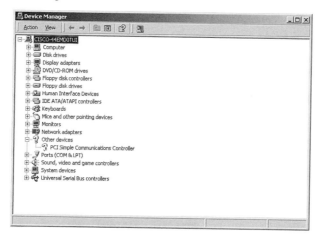

A yellow question mark next to a device indicates that there is an error. Right-click the device and select Properties to view the resource and other information regarding the conflicting device. Figure 12-20 shows the Resource tab in the Device Properties dialog box.

TEST TIP

The Windows Device Manager uses the following symbols:

- A yellow question mark indicates that the device has a problem.

- A yellow exclamation point indicates that the device has a conflict.

- A red *X* indicates that the device is disabled.

- A blue *i* (for information) indicates that the device has forced resource configurations. This icon is seen only in the two resource views.

Figure 12-20 The Resource Tab

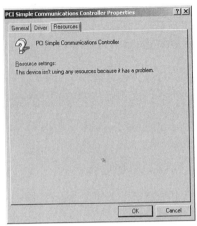

Also check the Control Panel's Device Manager to see that the correct audio driver is installed and to verify that the settings match those recommended by the sound card manufacturer. If the drivers are missing or incorrect, they must be added to the system using the Control Panel's Add/Remove Hardware wizard. Figure 12-21 shows the screen that displays when new hardware is found.

Figure 12-21 Add/Remove Hardware Wizard

Power Supply Issues

The power supply plays a vital role in the operation of a computer system. If the power supply is not working properly, the computer components can be receiving the wrong voltages and might not operate correctly. The power supply converts the current coming from the wall outlet from alternating current (AC) to direct current (DC).

As shown in Figure 12-22, the AC from the wall outlet is 120V or 240V, depending on the country or region that supplies it.

Figure 12-22   Alternating Current Entering the Power Supply

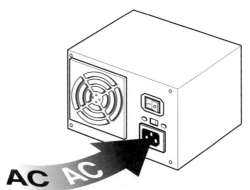

TEST TIP

When a PC randomly reboots or locks up after running for a time, a faulty power supply could be the cause.

AC is converted into DC +/–5V and +/–12V. After the current is converted from AC to DC, the power supply provides two important functions to the computer:

- **Supplies power**—The power supply is responsible for delivering the correct amount of DC to the system components. All the system components, including the microprocessor, modular cards, RAM, and drives, are powered by the power supply.

- **Acts as a cooling mechanism**—This is a less-obvious function of the power supply. However, do not overlook this functionality because it plays an important role in system performance. Computer systems perform better if they are properly ventilated and cooled. An onboard fan attached to most power supplies cools the power supply and internal components, as shown in Figure 12-23.

Box Cooling Issues

Computer components are susceptible to heat. These components operate at high speeds and in tight spaces. For example, hard drives operate at 7200 rpm and can be located centimeters from one another. This environment is conducive to heat buildup, which is an enemy to the components. Every computer case needs proper airflow for the components to perform at their optimal levels. The design of the computer case should maximize the airflow.

Figure 12-23 Power Supply Airflow

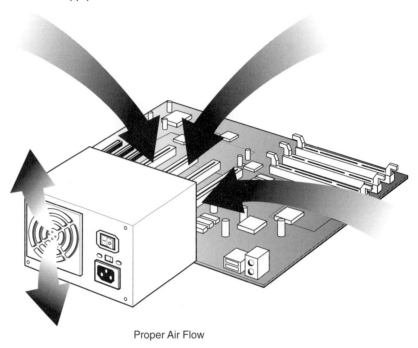

Proper Air Flow

The power supply usually generates the majority of the airflow. The fan on a power supply cools the power supply unit and other internal components of the system. The fan pulls ambient air in over the internal components, motherboard, chip, and modular cards and exhausts hot air out the back of the computer case. This is typically the case with the newer ATX form factors. With the older AT systems, the fan pulls air from the outside and sends it directly over the motherboard components. Today, most processors have an attached fan; the onboard fan cools the CPU. Verify that the fans are working by listening for fan noise. The fan should quietly run in the background but should not make loud or excessive noise.

The computer case plays an important role in cooling the internal components and is designed with cooling features. Computer cases have air intake vents, which are usually cut into the sides or front of the cases. In the back of the case is located an air output vent, which is the exit point of the airflow. Ambient air enters the front of the case (pulled in by the system fan located at the front), flows across the components, and exits at the back of the case as hot air. (The power supply fan helps the air circulation.) Figure 12-24 shows the airflow through a typical computer.

Figure 12-24 Airflow Through the Computer Case

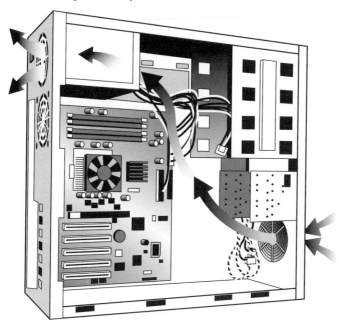

It is important to keep the air vents free of any debris. These vents attract a considerable amount of dirt and dust. Airflow can be limited if the vent is covered with dust. The air vents should be cleaned frequently to ensure unrestricted airflow. A vacuum or a damp cloth can be used to clean the vents. Use only a vacuum that is specially certified for computer cleaning.

Additional cooling fans can be added for computers that are used for long periods of time or are located in warmer environments. Computer systems that run cooler last longer and perform better.

Adding cooling fans is an example of proactive management. Proactive management involves a technician looking for potential problems before they become serious issues.

Troubleshooting Peripheral Devices

This section includes the following topics:

- Input devices
- Output devices
- SCSI interface issues
- Internet/network access devices

Input Devices

Input devices, such as a keyboard, mouse, scanner, or digital camera, transfer data to the computer. Most input devices are detected at startup.

When troubleshooting input devices, always start with the simple solutions. Ensure that the device is properly connected. Verify that the power cable is in good condition and is not frayed. As with any hardware problem, start from the outside of the box.

After checking the connections of the input device, try rebooting the computer. Sometimes, an input device can be disconnected while being used, and a reboot is required. Note any errors that display during startup. The errors are indicated as either a text error on the video display or as a POST beep code. For example, if a keyboard is not properly connected, the user might get a beep code or a "301 error message."

Two common errors with input devices are incorrect character input and unrecognized devices. Both of these errors can result from a defective or outdated device driver. Always check the manufacturer's website for updated device drivers. Input devices need the right driver to work correctly.

Keyboards

Keyboards are heavily used input devices. Due to the heavy workload and numerous movable components, keyboard failures are frequent. The best protection against keyboard errors is proactive maintenance. Table 12-4 lists some of the most common errors associated with the keyboard.

Table 12-4 Common Keyboard Errors

Problem/Error	Solution
Keyboard is running on legacy equipment and isn't supported.	Keyboards are either AT or XT compliant. However, an AT keyboard does not work with an XT-compliant keyboard, and vice versa. (An AT-compliant keyboard is used in an 80286 or higher system, for this discussion.) However, some keyboards can be configured for either AT or XT with a dip switch or a slider switch located on the bottom of the keyboard. Determine if these switches are set properly when troubleshooting keyboards.
Gate A20 failure.	This indicates that an 80286 or higher system must switch to protected mode to use more than 1 MB of RAM. Verify whether the system is an AT or XT configuration, and replace the keyboard. If the error message remains, replace the motherboard.

Table 12-4 Common Keyboard Errors (Continued)

Problem/Error	Solution
Voltage issue.	Troubleshoot the keyboard connections to the motherboard. Check the voltage. The clock pin should read between +2.0 V and +5.5 V. The power Pin should read between +2.0 V and +5.5 V. The data Pin should read between +4.8 V and +5.5 V.
Keyboard is not properly connected (301 error message or keyboard error).	There might be stuck keys. Remove the keys and clean the keyboard (using distilled water), reboot the computer, and verify the connection. If the error message remains, replace the keyboard.

Mouse

The mouse is also a heavily used input device. Mice are prone to performance problems mainly because dust and dirt can get into the components. Maintain a clean environment, and clean the mouse frequently for optimal performance. Table 12-5 lists common mouse errors.

Table 12-5 Common Mouse Problems

Problem/Error	Solution
Unrecognized or malfunctioning mouse	This can be caused by an uninstalled or outdated device driver. Visit the mouse manufacturer's website, and download and install the latest driver. Also, make sure that the mouse is properly connected.
Erratic movement of the cursor	Clean the ball located on the bottom of the mouse. Also, try reconfiguring the mouse settings. (This is done through the Control Panel.) If the problem remains, replace the mouse.

Scanners

Most scanner errors are the result of an improper software installation or an improperly connected device. Table 12-6 lists common errors associated with scanners.

Table 12-6 Common Scanner Problems

Problem/Error	Solution
Improper software installation; device is not recognized.	Reinstall the software and the necessary drivers.
Low-quality image on the monitor.	Scanners use 24-bit color (with 16 million color variations), and the monitor resolution might be set too low. Change the monitor settings to display true color (24-bit color).
Slow or poor performance.	Two devices might be daisy-chained (the devices are connected on one cable). To access more than one peripheral on a parallel port, use a switch box. This is a device that switches between the two peripherals, allowing the use of each device independent of the other.
Vertical streak on the image.	Scanners can pick up dust or smudges on the glass. Use a damp cloth to clean the glass.

Parallel Ports

Parallel ports rarely fail. However, a more common problem is slow performance from a parallel device. Common errors associated with parallel ports are listed in Table 12-7.

Table 12-7 Common Parallel Port Errors

Problem/Error	Solution
Cable cannot supply the necessary data transfer rates.	Troubleshoot with a cable that has been verified to work.
Legacy equipment does not support new product requirements, or there is a hardware defect.	Upgrade the ports.
Outdated or defective drivers.	Update or reload the drivers.
IRQ conflict: two devices sharing same device.	Remove a conflicting device (ISA cards are often the problem; IRQ 5 conflicts with LPT2, or IRQ 7 conflicts with LPT1).
Wrong mode is selected (EPP, ECP, or EPP/ECP)	Use an IEEE 1284–compatible cable, which supports all parallel port modes.

Universal Serial Bus Ports

Most new computers are equipped with a *universal serial bus (USB) port.* USB ports are replacing the serial ports found on most older computers. USB devices are based on Plug and Play technology. This means that USB devices should install and operate with minimal configuration. However, USB devices are not free from errors. The most common failures with USB devices are caused by the following items:

- Missing or outdated driver
- Wrong cabling
- Defective hardware
- Resource conflicts

USB devices should load automatically in most versions of Windows. Windows 95 OSR2, Windows 98, Windows Me, Windows 2000, and Windows XP support USB ports. However, Windows NT does not support the USB standard. While installing a USB device, Windows might prompt the user for the location of a USB device driver. In such cases, the technician must find a suitable USB device driver. Most USB devices are packaged with a disk that contains the device driver; otherwise, visit the manufacturer's website to obtain the latest driver.

USB devices connect using *USB cables.* The USB device and cable must be the same speed to function properly. USB cables come in two speeds, low and high. If a faster device is connected to a slower cable, the signal can become corrupted over long distances. If a cable problem is suspected, replace the cable with a faster cable. Additionally, USB devices require an IRQ channel to work properly. IRQ conflicts can be viewed in the Device Manager dialog box.

To access the Device Manager in Windows, right-click My Computer, select Properties, and choose the Hardware tab. Click the Device Manager button. The Device Manger then opens, displaying the computer's hardware devices. The Device Manager indicates device conflicts with an exclamation mark highlighted in a yellow circle. If an IRQ conflict exists, verify that the device is properly installed and that the system resources have been correctly allocated.

Output Devices

An *output device* displays or prints data processed by the computer. The computer communicates with an output device, for example, the printer, when the user sends the request. Printers are heavily used, and problems can arise due to this constant use. Proper cleaning of the printer can reduce downtime, productivity loss, and repair costs.

The length of time between cleanings depends on the printer's usage. Printer maintenance involves inspecting the unit for debris that might hinder the performance of the its components. The technician should look for dirt, dust, and paper jams during the visual inspection of the printer. Preventive maintenance does not prevent all printer errors. Printers are intricate, delicate devices. There are numerous moving parts, and each can potentially cause a problem. Printers can fail in a number of ways.

A convenient troubleshooting and diagnostic tool is the printer's self-test capability. Printing a test page can help the technician isolate the location of the printer error. If a page does not print, determine if the connections are correct, the printer is turned on, the paper has been loaded properly, and the printer is online. Also, verify that the printer is the default printer in the Control Panel. Selecting the default printer is covered more thoroughly in Chapter 11, "Preventive Maintenance."

Common Printer Errors

The most common causes of printer problems are broken parts, cabling issues, parallel port errors, and outdated or defective drivers. If the printer completes the self-test or prints double-spaced but not single-spaced, there might be a problem with the dip switch setting, driver, or cable. If the dip switch settings are to be changed, make sure that the power is turned off. The circuitry can be damaged if the power is left on.

If the printer shuts off intermittently, there could be a problem with its thermistor. A thermistor is used to keep the printer from overheating. The only way to repair this problem is to replace the thermistor.

Troubleshooting paper jams is a common task for most technicians. The usual symptom is an error message or the fact that the paper is not advancing. Check the paper loader for jammed paper or an overloaded paper tray. Clean any jammed paper and inspect the paper path for obstructions. The printer could also be configured for the wrong paper tray. Verify that it is set to correct tray. In rare cases, the paper feed motor can be defective, in which case a new feed motor is required.

Troubleshooting Ink Jet Printers

If an ink jet printer is not printing clearly or correctly, it might be experiencing problems with the print heads. The print heads work by spraying ink through tiny nozzles. When the print heads are clogged, they do not print correctly. Inspect the print heads for any debris that is restricting the flow of ink. If the print head looks clogged, it must be cleaned. Print heads can be cleaned by using the printer's software (if available) or by manual cleaning by the technician.

If the ink jet printer indicates that it is offline but is connected, verify that the cables are properly connected.

The printer software might be capable of running a series of cleaning events. Right-click the printer icon in the Control Panel to determine if the printer can perform a self-cleaning test. Manual cleaning varies among manufacturers. Refer to the printer manual for instructions on how to clean an ink jet printer.

Troubleshooting Dot Matrix Printers

Dot matrix printers use a series of pins, which are located on the print head, to transfer ink to the paper. These pins repeatedly strike the paper and over time can become clogged. Dust and ink can prevent the pins from functioning correctly. To resolve this problem, first unplug the printer. Carefully remove the print head from the ribbon cable. While removing the print head, pay attention to how it is installed so that it can be reinstalled properly. Soak the print head in denatured alcohol. Also, place the pins in the alcohol and let them stand for two to three minutes. Allow the print head to dry, and reinstall it. Run the printer's self-test without the ribbon attached to the print head. This allows excess or residual ink to be removed from the pins. Replace the ribbon after the pins are free of excess ink.

If the printed characters are not properly aligned on the page, the ribbon cable might be misaligned with the print head. Verify that the ribbon cable and print head are properly spaced. Also, verify that the ribbon is advancing properly. If the problem still exists, the printer might be out of ink. If, after replacing the ink, the problem still exists, consult the printer manual to verify the proper printer control settings.

Troubleshooting Laser Printers

To efficiently troubleshoot laser printers, technicians must understand the components of these printers. Table 12-8 describes common laser printer problems.

Table 12-8 Common Laser Printer Problems

Problem/Error	Solution
Printer is online and properly connected but does not print.	The toner cartridge might be empty. If so, replace it.
Printer is printing vertical lines.	The toner cartridge is most likely broken and needs to be replaced.
Pages are dirty.	The toner cartridge is most likely broken and needs to be replaced.
Paper is not feeding correctly.	This could be caused by a paper jam. Manually feed the paper, or change the software configuration.

Refer to Chapter 10, "Printers and Printing," for more information.

Worksheet 12.3.2   Troubleshooting Printers

Test your knowledge on dot matrix, ink jet, and laser printers by completing this true/false worksheet.

SCSI Interface Issues

SCSI drives require a controller that is separate from the IDE controller. The SCSI controller operates with ROM BIOS under DOS and Windows. The ROM BIOS contains management, surface verification, and low-level format applications. SCSI BIOS is accessed during the bootup process by pressing the setup key.

The SCSI bus operation and the transfer rate are controlled by adapter settings. If there is a transfer speed mismatch among the SCSI controllers, the drive could have input/output (I/O) errors. I/O errors are fatal to the computer. As a rule, attach the SCSI controller set to the last SCSI ID, which is SCSI ID 7. I/O errors might result if the SCSI ID is not set to 7. Also, to ensure optimal performance, enable parity checking and host adapter termination.

SCSI devices must have unique SCSI IDs. SCSI devices cannot share ID numbers. The location of the SCSI ID on the bus is not important. The SCSI IDs do not need to be placed sequentially on the bus. Be sure that devices do not share the same ID numbers. If SCSI device share IDs, errors will occur.

With SCSI IDs, the higher the ID, the higher the priority. The ID priority is 7, 6, 5, 4, 3, 2, 1, 0, 15, 14, 13, 12, 11, 10, 9, 8. The SCSI host controller should be set to ID 7. This gives the SCSI host controller the highest priority. Hard drives should be set with lower IDs. Hard drives have the potential to consume a large amount of the bus speed. Setting the hard drives to a lower priority allows time-sensitive information to have a higher priority. Use IDs 6, 5, and 4 for CD-RW drives and other streaming media drives. SCSI controllers are configured with the following parameters:

- Sync negotiation
- Transfer rate
- BIOS scan
- Send start unit command

SCSI fixed disk I/O errors occur if the SCSI parameters are incorrectly configured. SCSI controllers allow drive configuration for larger SCSI drives. If these parameters are not set correctly, the drive might be inaccessible. This error can be fixed if the configuration parameters for the SCSI controllers are correctly set.

A SCSI drive can have built-in or external termination that can be enabled or disabled. The SCSI bus must be terminated at both ends of the controller and must have two termination points, one at the beginning and one at the end of the SCSI bus. The ending termination point must also be within four inches of the ending points of the bus. The drives on the SCSI bus must also run sequentially: drive A to B, B to C, C to D, and so on. Also, the SCSI bus must not contain a Y-shaped drive configuration.

SCSI Interface Levels

Most modern personal computers have built-in SCSI ports. SCSI ports are supported by all major operating systems. There are several levels of SCSI, including SCSI-1, which evolved into SCSI-2 and SCSI-3 (all three are mostly outdated); Ultra-SCSI (a widely implemented SCSI standard); and Ultra-3, which is the latest SCSI standard. Although not all devices support all levels of SCSI, the evolving SCSI standards are generally backward-compatible.

All the SCSI standards have different speeds. When installing SCSI drives and other devices, it is important to consider the cabling. The cable length specifications for the various SCSI types are summarized in Table 12-9. SCSI devices can malfunction if these specifications are ignored when installing and configuring these devices.

Table 12-9 SCSI Interfaces

SCSI Type	Maximum Cable Length (Meters)	Maximum Speed (MBps)	Maximum Number of Devices
SCSI-1	6	5	8
SCSI-2	6	5–10	8 or 16
Ultra SCSI-3, 8-/16-bit	1.5	20/40	8/16
Ultra-2 SCSI	12	40	8
Wide Ultra-2 SCSI	12	80	16
Ultra-3 (Ultra-160/m) SCSI	12	160	16

Internet/Network Access Devices

Troubleshooting network problems can range from an unattached Category 5 cable to advanced protocol issues. Discussing advanced network problems is beyond the scope of this chapter. However, basic techniques for troubleshooting common network problems are presented.

Begin network troubleshooting by determining if there has been a recent change to the system. If there has been a change to the system, the change might be causing the problem. Reverse the changes, and determine if the problem is resolved.

If there have been no changes, the next area to troubleshoot is the physical layer. Start outside the computer case with the cabling. Verify that the cabling is attached to the back of the computer. The cabling should run from the wall jack to the back of the computer or external modem. Verify that the cable is attached to the correct wall jack and/or port and that the cable is in good condition. The NIC and modem provide basic troubleshooting information by using onboard lights. Most NICs have a green blinking light that signifies that data are being processed. However, this does not mean that the computer has established a network connection. The blinking green light tells the technician that the NIC is recognized and properly set in its slot. Figure 12-25 shows the troubleshooting lights on a NIC.

Figure 12-25 NIC Lights

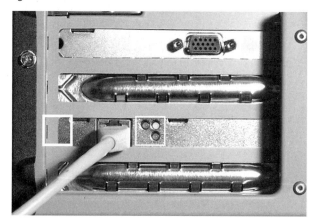

Modems typically have indicator lights that can be used to diagnose a problem. Each modem manufacturer has a different set of lights, but generally there are power, status, and activity lights. These lights can help isolate the problem. For example, the status light can indicate if the modem is offline. The technician can then refresh the IP address to get the modem back online.

If the problem still exists after all the connections have been verified, move inside the computer box. Make sure that the NIC or modem is properly inserted into the expansion slot. Remove and reinstall the device if you feel the card has been improperly installed.

Most network adapter problems involve conflicting resources and configuration settings. Common resource problems are conflicting IRQs, I/O addresses, and memory. Common configuration errors include adapter card speed mismatch and defective drivers.

 Worksheet 12.3.4   Troubleshooting Hardware

Use this worksheet to test your knowledge of the basic terms and procedures used when troubleshooting hardware.

Summary

This chapter discussed troubleshooting methods, including tips and tricks used to solve computer problems. The following items were covered:

- Understand the six steps in the troubleshooting process. They include identifying the problem, gathering the information, developing the solution, implementing the solution, verifying that the problem is resolved, and documenting the solution.

- Diagnostic software is available. SpinRite is used to recover data from a crashed hard drive, and Checkit, PC Technician, AMI Diags, and SiSoft Sandra are used to perform system analysis and testing to aid in the troubleshooting process.

- Field-replaceable units are components that can easily be replaced without special tools. These components include monitors, keyboards, expansion cards, and memory upgrades.

- The POST is a series of self-diagnostic tests that a computer runs to test the major hardware. Any errors are reported visually or as a series of beep codes that indicate the specific problems. Beep codes are BIOS specific and are helpful in the troubleshooting process.

- The BIOS features provide technicians with low-level hardware and software configuration information. Upgrading the BIOS includes patches, fixes, additional features, and additional support for devices to resolve problems.

- RAM failures come in two forms: sudden and intermittent. RAM is inexpensive and easy to replace. Make sure that memory is installed correctly when there is a problem or when upgrading.

- The power supply provides two functions in a computer system. It is responsible for delivering the appropriate amount of current to the components in a computer, and it cools the system with an onboard fan. A faulty power supply could be the problem when a computer randomly reboots or locks up after running for a time.

- Troubleshooting peripheral devices should always start by working from outside the computer and moving in. Check cables, device drivers, IRQ conflicts, and mode selection.

- Internet access and network access problems range from simple cabling issues to advanced protocol issues. The first step in resolving these problems is to check any changes that have been made to the system. Most NICs have a blinking green light, which indicates that the connection is recognized and properly set.

The next chapter details troubleshooting basics for computer software. The steps to determine the cause of specific problems and the steps to follow to resolve hardware problems are detailed.

Check Your Understanding

The following are review questions for the A+ exam. Answers can be found in Appendix B, "Answers to Check Your Understanding Review Questions."

1. What is the first step in troubleshooting a PC problem?

   A. Remove the cover

   B. Unplug all the cords from the computer

   C. Remove all optional equipment from the system

   D. Eliminate the user as the source

2. What range should the multimeter be set to when checking a power supply unit?

   A. AC voltage

   B. DC voltage

   C. Ohms

   D. Amps

3. How many changes should you make at one time when troubleshooting a PC?

   A. One

   B. Two

   C. Three

   D. It doesn't matter

4. What is the most likely cause for a shaky video display?

   A. Faulty monitor

   B. Faulty cables

   C. Faulty video adapter

   D. Incorrect settings

5. What is the first thing to do if a new monitor is not working?

   A. Adjust the brightness and contrast

   B. Check the monitor for broken parts

   C. Measure the voltage inside the monitor

   D. Make sure that the power cord is firmly plugged in

6. What would cause a monitor to fade?

   A. Electron guns clog up with electrons.

   B. Phosphor coatings wear away.

   C. Brightness controls fail over time.

   D. Fluorescent tubing interferes with monitors.

7. What problem is indicated with one long beep and two short beeps during the bootup process?

   A. Video controller

   B. Floppy drive

   C. Hard drive

   D. Mouse

8. If a power supply fan is running and the hard drive spins but the system seems dead, what might be the problem?

   A. The monitor is turned off.

   B. A faulty expansion card has disabled the system.

   C. The hard drive is defective.

   D. The system board is defective.

9. What component might need to be replaced in a PC that randomly reboots or locks up after running for a time?

   A. Sound card.

   B. Nothing; it is a DMA conflict.

   C. Keyboard.

   D. Power supply.

10. What is the problem if the system time resets when you turn off the computer?

    A. Defective CMOS battery

    B. Defective BIOS chip

    C. Faulty power cord

    D. Faulty motherboard

11. A new mouse has been installed but does not work. What is the problem?

  A. It is plugged into the wrong port.

  B. It requires a new driver.

  C. The operating system needs to be reinstalled.

  D. It is a faulty mouse.

12. What is the most likely cause of an erratic mouse?

  A. One of the potentiometers has failed.

  B. There is a corrupt mouse driver.

  C. The mouse is plugged into the wrong port.

  D. The mouse needs cleaning.

13. What can create a memory problem?

  A. Installing different-speed memory modules

  B. Skipping over an empty memory socket

  C. Not installing memory in pairs

  D. Using memory from different manufacturers

14. One of your memory modules is hot. What does this indicate?

  A. It is normal.

  B. It needs a new cooling fan.

  C. The voltage to the memory is insufficient.

  D. It is defective or becoming defective.

15. What symbol is typically used in Windows to indicate a disabled hardware device?

  A. A yellow question mark on the hardware icon

  B. A circled exclamation point on the hardware icon

  C. An upside-down question mark

  D. A red X

16. What symbol is typically used in the Windows Device Manager to indicate that a device has a problem?

  A. A question mark on the hardware icon

  B. A yellow exclamation point

  C. An upside-down question mark

  D. A blinking red X

17. What is a good way to test a problem with RAM?

    A. Use the POST.

    B. Use mem.exe.

    C. Use memmaker.exe.

    D. Replace the module to see if the problem reoccurs.

18. The computer fails to start after installing a new sound card. What is the most likely cause of this problem?

    A. The sound card is not compatible.

    B. There is not enough memory present in the system.

    C. There is an interrupt conflict between the sound card and another device.

    D. The sound card needs a different DMA setting.

19. A computer powers up but does not attach to the network. After rebooting, the problem still persists. What is a possible solution?

    A. Reinstall the NIC.

    B. Check the Device Manager for network adapter conflicts.

    C. Check for a new driver.

    D. Perform diagnostic tests on the server.

20. What is the best source for troubleshooting information?

    A. The user

    B. The manufacturer's website

    C. Other technicians

    D. All of the above

Key Terms

AMI Diags   Program that provides advanced system testing and reports on memory, serial ports, parallel ports, modems, hard drives, keyboards, the BIOS, and video adapters.

beep code error messages   The audible reporting of errors found by the BIOS during the POST.

cable select (CSEL)   An option that decides master/slave hard drive relationships based on the position of the drive on the IDE cable.

Checkit   Program that performs system analysis and testing.

CMOS (complementary metal oxide semiconductor)   Stores the system startup configurations and parameters.

diagnostic software   Programs used to assist in the troubleshooting process.

double data rate SDRAM   New synchronous dynamic RAM that increases memory clock speed to at least 200 MHz.

DRAM (Dynamic RAM)   Works by storing data electrically in a storage cell and refreshing the storage every few milliseconds.

dual inline memory module (DIMM)   Memory module with 168 pins that supports 64-bit transfers.

EDO RAM (extended data-out RAM)   Extends the amount of time that data are stored and has a reduced refresh rate.

field-replaceable unit (FRU)   Computer component that can be easily replaced.

input device   A device that transfers data into the computer, including a keyboard, mouse, scanner, etc.

NVRAM (nonvolatile random access memory)   Stores the system startup configurations and parameters.

output device   Displays or prints data processed by the computer.

PC technician   Program that operates independent of DOS to perform diagnostic tests on parallel ports, serial ports, hard drives, keyboards, video adapters, and RAM.

POST (power-on self test)   A series of self-diagnostic tests that the computer performs to test the major hardware.

POST card   A device that digitally reports errors in the event the computer fails before a BIOS error can be generated.

rambus inline memory module (RIMM)   Memory module with 184 pins that uses only RDRAM.

single inline memory module (SIMM)   Memory module with 72 or 30 pins.

SiSoft Sandra   System analyzer, diagnostic, and reporting assistant. It is a freeware program that can aid in troubleshooting and benchmarking computer components.

SpinRite   Program used for recovering data from a crashed hard drive.

synchronous DRAM   Allows the CPU to process data while another process is being queued.

troubleshooting   A series of logical steps used to diagnose a computer problem.

universal serial bus (USB)   Based on Plug and Play, USB devices are installed with minimal configuration.

USB cable   Used to connect a USB device to the computer. The device and cable must be the same speed.

Objectives

Upon completion of this chapter, you will be able to perform the following tasks:

- Communicate with the end user to determine the cause of system problems
- Create a bootable disk that enables you to access the system when it does not boot
- Recognize DOS error messages, what causes them, and how to address them
- Understand startup modes, including normal, and the different safe modes used for troubleshooting
- Troubleshoot Windows installation problems, memory usage problems, and system lockup errors
- Use Windows system tools, the Device Manager, and system editors to diagnose and fix computer errors
- Understand the Registry structure, the key for every process that is running on the system
- Know the different types of backup procedures to make sure that the system can be restored

Chapter 13

Troubleshooting Software

Introduction

This chapter provides information on general troubleshooting procedures relating to software. It also describes various tips and tricks that can help gather the information necessary to diagnose and repair common computer problems. Unlike the previous chapter, which emphasized troubleshooting the hardware, this chapter emphasizes troubleshooting software and operating system–related issues.

The Troubleshooting Process

This section includes the following topics:

- Overview of the troubleshooting process
- Eliciting information from the end user regarding the problem
- Reproducing the error symptoms
- Identifying recent user changes to the software environment
- Determining whether the problem is hardware or software related
- Fixing the software

Overview of the Troubleshooting Process

The troubleshooting process usually begins with the end user, because he or she has the most valuable information. The end user's input can help narrow the search for the problem that is affecting the computer. Regardless of whether the end user (or customer) is a direct cause of the problem, the main goal of troubleshooting is to get the end user's system operational. The process starts when the end user calls for support, as illustrated in Figure 13-1.

Figure 13-1 End User Calling for Support

Eliciting Information from the End User Regarding the Problem

Before evaluating the computer to begin the troubleshooting steps, talk to the end user to elicit information regarding the problem. As the previous chapter mentioned, this can be a delicate process and should not be overlooked. Sometimes, the end user can give an idea of what might have been done to cause the problem. Establish what the end user was doing at the time the problem began. For example, find out what application was being used or if there was an attempt to install or uninstall a piece of hardware or software. Finding out this information first gives you a better idea of where to start troubleshooting the computer as well as what area to begin examining.

As stated before, eliciting information from the end user can be a tricky process. Each end user who calls for help will be different. Some end users are easy to deal with and answer all questions honestly; others do not. In a working environment, end users are limited in what they are allowed to do to their computers. The administrator determines the level of access they are granted, and some end users do not like this constraint. Unfortunately, many of the troubleshooting calls are a result of an end user trying to do something he or she is not supposed to be doing, such as installing software or downloading files from the Internet. Obviously, if their systems are not working as a result of these actions, they are less likely to say exactly what is wrong.

Another source of difficulty is the fact that administrators or service technicians usually have more knowledge about computers than the typical end user. For this reason, be patient with the end user, and do not get frustrated. A seemingly trivial problem that might be obvious to the administrator could be something that the end user does not understand. It is always important to be polite and courteous when eliciting information from an end user.

Reproducing the Error Symptoms

After talking to the end user to find out what he or she was doing and what application was being used when the problem began, start by trying to reproduce the error symptoms. This is another reason why eliciting information from the end user is so important. Reproducing the error symptoms is helpful because knowing at what point the error occurs in the process can help identify the area in which to begin the search for the problem.

For example, the previous chapters discussed the boot process. A call from an end user states that when he boots up his computer, it stops, and he gets an error message. In this case, reproduce the error symptoms by rebooting the computer. This determines at what point in the boot process the computer stops.

Identifying Recent User Changes to the Software Environment

Identifying any changes that the end user has made to the software environment is another important step that can make the troubleshooting process easier. Troubleshooting calls are often a result of an end user installing or uninstalling software. The end user could have deleted a critical folder or file by accident. Again, eliciting information from the customer can be of great help.

The customer might have installed software that is incompatible with the operating system, or the software that the end user installed could have overwritten or deleted files. Sometimes an end user uninstalls software and accidentally deletes files that are critical to the operating system.

Determining Whether the Problem Is Hardware or Software Related

The two essential parts of a computer are the *hardware*, or the physical components of the computer such as the case, floppy disk drives, keyboard, monitor, cables, speakers, and printers, and the *software*, which is the programs that are used to operate the computer system. Computer hardware and software are closely related. Because both work with each other, problem-solving can be difficult. Thus, it is important to determine whether the problem is a hardware failure or corrupt programming in the software.

Hardware Issues

To begin separating the hardware and software, first look at the boot sequence. When the computer boots up, the user should hear a single beep that occurs after the POST and just before the boot process begins. If there are hardware issues with the computer, these issues will occur or will be displayed before this beep. This is because the operating system or software side of the system does not start until after this beep is sounded; only the BIOS and basic system hardware have been active before the beep is heard.

Hardware-related issues are either configuration errors or hardware failures. A *hardware failure* is the malfunction of a component. It is typically identified by the operating system being unable to load. After the BIOS and basic system hardware have been checked and passed, the operating system starts to load, as shown in Figure 13-2.

Figure 13-2 The Boot Process

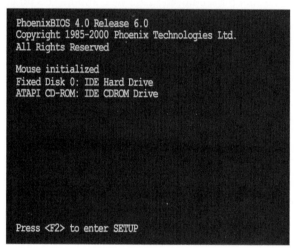

If the hardware is unable to load, this is a good indication that a component has failed. If the problem appears to be a hardware failure, you must determine what has failed, replace the component, and retry the boot process. *Configuration errors* occur as a result of a mismatch between the system's programmed configuration and the equipment that is installed in the system. For example, if the end user installs software, he might enter some parameters into the programs to match the program's capabilities to the configuration of the computer. If these configuration parameters are set incorrectly, the software is unable to detect the system's hardware properly, and an error results. Hardware-specific troubleshooting issues were covered in Chapter 12, "Troubleshooting PC Hardware."

Fixing the Software

After determining what the problem is and where the problem exists, it is time to fix the software. Fixing the software depends on what problem was preventing it from working. It might be necessary to copy some files from the installation CD of the operating system or an application CD to the hard drive. You may need to change some shortcut paths to correctly point to the executable file of the application that is installed. Sometimes, simply reinstalling the software resolves the problem. This chapter discusses many of these techniques, including various troubleshooting aids for software-related problems.

DOS Troubleshooting Issues

This section includes the following topics:

- System boot problems
- DOS error messages
- Invalid directory errors

System Boot Problems

The bootup procedure that starts the computer system reveals much about the health of the system. The possible causes of errors can be eliminated or determined during bootup. The boot process has been discussed in previous chapters. If the problem lies in the boot process, the operating system does not load. Knowing the details of each step of the boot process helps determine what section failed if the system does not boot past a given step. For example, if the system boots up to the point where it is checking the floppy drive, and the floppy drive light does not come on, the problem exists in the floppy drive.

The Bootable Disk

Every system administrator should have a bootable disk. Systems often have issues that cannot be resolved, or the operating system has become so corrupt that despite all efforts, the system does not start up. A *bootable disk* allows administrators and service technicians to boot from a floppy disk instead of the hard drive. This disk can be used to fix problems that arise during the life of the computer. If a system is unable to boot, simply insert the disk into the floppy drive and restart the computer, making sure that the BIOS is set to boot from the floppy drive.

Figure 13-3 shows the BIOS settings for booting to the floppy drive. The disk contains the files that are required to boot the system, bypassing the operating system files on the hard drive that is corrupted. Booting from a bootable disk brings up a DOS prompt to allow the administrator to recopy files, inspect the hard drive's partition, or reformat the drive. The bootable disk enables the administrator to navigate through the files on the hard drive for problem inspection.

Figure 13-3   BIOS Settings: Booting to a Floppy Disk

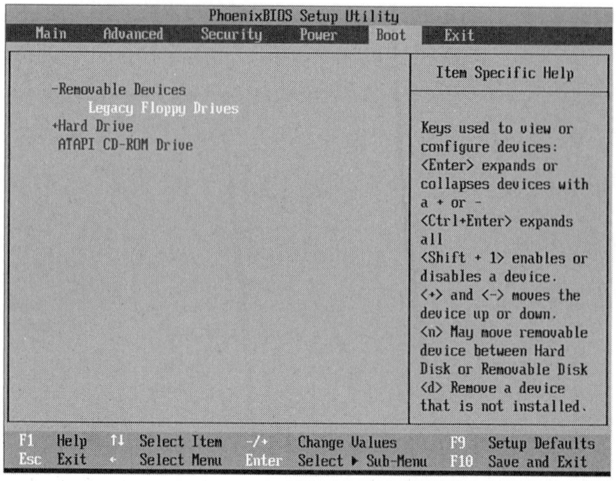

Hidden Files

A *hidden file* is a file that is tagged with a special hidden attribute, and the file is not normally visible to users. For example, hidden files are not listed when the DOS DIR command is executed. However, most file-management utilities allow the viewing of hidden files.

DOS hides some files, such as msdos.sys and io.sys, so that users do not corrupt them. These are two special files in the operating system boot record. Without them, the system cannot boot successfully. Any file can be marked as hidden, making it invisible to casual viewers. The ATTRIB command is used to view and change file attributes.

The Command Interpreter

The *command interpreter* program is known as *command.com*. It is the most important system file, because the computer cannot boot without it. The command.com file contains the operating system's most commonly used commands. For example, when a DOS command is entered at the DOS prompt, command.com first examines it to see if it is an internal or external DOS command. Internal commands are understood by the command.com program and are executed immediately. External commands are stored in the C:\DOS directory, and the command.com file must browse through this directory to find the command program.

When DOS runs an application, command.com finds the program and loads it and then gives it control of the system. When the program is shut down, it passes control back to the command interpreter. The command.com file is used in Windows 95/98; cmd.exe is used in Windows NT/2000.

DOS Switches

Many of the common DOS switches were discussed in Chapter 4, "Operating System Fundamentals." In this chapter, more switches, which are useful in troubleshooting software problems, are added to the list. DOS switches are used to configure DOS commands to perform specific functions. For example, DOS switches are used in the config.sys file to tell DOS to emulate different hardware configurations. The SWITCHES command is helpful when using older applications with a newer, enhanced keyboard that is incompatible with the operating system. Entering the following line in the config.sys file configures the keyboard to act like a standard keyboard:

SWITCHES=/K

These switches can be helpful when troubleshooting computer systems, and they are important to remember because they can be used to manipulate the DOS commands.

Examples of common switches are as follows:

- /K—Causes an enhanced keyboard to act as though it were an older, standard keyboard.
- /F—Removes the 2-second delay that occurs when the message "Starting MS-DOS" is displayed on the screen (DOS version 6 only).
- /N—Disables the F5 and F8 keys during system startup (DOS version 6 only).
- /W—Tells DOS that the wina20.386 file has been moved to a directory other than the root directory.

Bootable Disk Utility Files

A DOS boot disk, as detailed in Chapter 4, can be used to boot the system to the DOS prompt. This allows a system with boot problems to start so that troubleshooting can begin. In this regard, two useful utility files, format.exe and fdisk.exe, should be added to the boot disk. The significance of these utilities is discussed next.

The format.exe File

In the event that the operating system becomes so corrupted that it is beyond repair, the *FORMAT command* can be used to erase the disk and reformat it. The boot disk allows the administrator to boot the computer to a DOS prompt, and the format.exe utility allows the hard drive to be reformatted. This command is also used to prepare a new disk for use with an operating system. However, not all the information on the hard drive is erased.

The fdisk.exe File

FDISK is one of the most commonly used MS-DOS commands, even with newer operating systems such as Windows 98, 2000, and XP. *FDISK* allows the technician to delete and create partitions on the hard drive. This is another useful tool for troubleshooting a computer system. The boot disk allows the technician to boot to a DOS prompt. Once this is completed, type **FDISK** to enter the FDISK screen. Figure 13-4 shows the FDISK options that allow changes to be made to the system's hard disk partitions.

Figure 13-4 FDISK Options

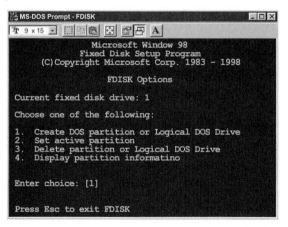

The /MBR Switch

Sometimes during troubleshooting, the computer is unable to boot. This typically means that the master boot record (MBR) has been corrupted in some way. A virus can cause this, or the files could have been deleted. The MBR is a program that is executed when a computer boots up. Typically, the MBR resides on the first sector of the hard drive. The program begins the boot process by looking up the partition table to determine which partition to use for booting. The program then transfers program control to the boot sector of that partition, which continues the boot process. In DOS and Windows systems, the MBR is created with the *FDISK/MBR command*. This command is used to rewrite the master boot record so that the system can again boot up.

Bootable Configuration Files

The two main configuration files that a computer uses during boot up are config.sys and autoexec.bat. The *config.sys file*, as shown in Figure 13-5, contains setup or configuration instructions for the computer system. The commands in this file configure the DOS program for use with devices and applications in the system and set up the memory managers in the system. Once the commands in config.sys have been carried out, DOS begins searching for the *autoexec.bat file*. This file, as shown in Figure 13-6, contains a list of DOS commands that are automatically executed when DOS is loaded into the system.

Figure 13-5 The config.sys File

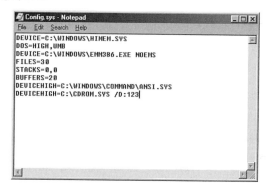

Figure 13-6 The autoexec.bat File

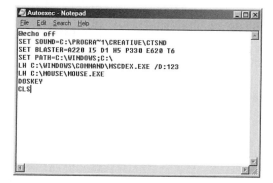

Without these files, or if these files are corrupted, the system can still boot. However, these files are essential for the complete bootup process to occur with the DOS operating system. They contain information that is used for operations such as changing the operating system for personal preferences. They also contain the requirements of different software applications. A troubleshooting call would result if either of these two files becomes damaged.

DOS Error Messages

Another common operating system troubleshooting issue is error messages. Many things can cause these error messages to display. As a technician's experience with troubleshooting computer systems increases, these messages become easier to recognize. Technicians eventually learn the causes of the various error messages and know how to address them. Error messages are usually displayed when the operating system identifies a problem or when an end user attempts to run an application that the operating system cannot recognize.

Bad or Missing command.com File

In the DOS environment, the "Bad or Missing COMMAND.COM" error message is common. The command.com file and the role it plays in the operating system were previously discussed, and the system cannot boot without this file. Several things can cause this error message to appear. The first is if the command.com file cannot be found on the hard drive. The second condition is if the command.com file is not located in the hard drive's root directory. This usually occurs when a new hard drive or operating system is installed. The last scenario that can cause this message to appear is if the end user accidentally erases the command.com file from the root directory of the hard drive.

If this error message appears, it does not mean that the operating system has been corrupted and must be reinstalled. Instead, use the bootable disk to boot the system to a DOS prompt, and then type the following command:

SYS C:

The SYS command copies the io.sys, msdos.sys, and command.com system files from the boot disk to the hard drive. Remove the bootable disk and reboot the system.

Configuration File Errors

The previous section discussed the role of the autoexec.bat and config.sys files in the boot process. Again, these files are not critical to booting the operating system, but some of the applications will most likely not work properly without them.

Other common error messages are associated with the config.sys and the autoexec.bat files. Errors in these two files produce the "Error in CONFIG.SYS Line *XX*" or "Error in AUTOEXEC.BAT Line *XX*" messages. The line specified by the *XX* in the error message contains a syntax error that prevents these files from running. This means that, somewhere in the file, a spelling, punctuation, or usage error is preventing the file from running. These types of errors can also produce an "Unrecognized command" error as well. There can be missing or corrupted lines in the config.sys and autoexec.bat files. To correct these files, use a text editor to correct the required line(s). Reload the indicated file, and restart the computer.

REM Statements

Editing the config.sys or the autoexec.bat file requires that the administrator be familiar with the various REM statements that are contained in these files. These REM
statements prevent a line from being read, or executed, when the config.sys and
autoexec.bat files are being executed. For example, if Windows 98 is running and there
are problems booting up because some DOS-based applications are causing the system
to stall, reboot the computer and press F8 when the message Starting Windows 98
displays. Choose to restart in MS-DOS mode, and edit the autoexec.bat file from this
point. Place a REM statement (type **REM**) at the beginning of any suspect application
statements (in autoexec.bat) that could be preventing the system from booting. When
the system is restarted, the lines that begin with REM are not be executed in the
bootup process, and the system should start up normally. Figure 13-7 shows the
autoexec.bat file with the REM statement added.

Figure 13-7 The REM Statement

A REM statement might also be used is in the config.sys file. Remember that this file
contains configuration information about the system hardware and devices. For example, a device driver might be preventing the system from booting up properly. Edit the
config.sys file by placing a REM statement at the beginning of the line that configures
the device driver. Temporarily prevent the device from running when the config.sys file
is loaded.

Extended Memory Access

DOS 4.0 versions and above have a memory-management program called *himem.sys*
that manages the extended memory, that memory above 1024 KB. When this utility is
loaded into memory, it shifts most of the operating system functions into the high

memory area of extended memory. Add the following line to the config.sys file to activate this function:

DEVICE=C:\DOS\HIMEM.SYS

This command loads the DOS extended memory manager (XMS) driver. This causes himem.sys to be executed automatically when the computer is started.

When troubleshooting a himem.sys error, use the System Editor to determine if the correct entry is present in the config.sys file. In Windows 98, the himem.sys statement must be present and correct for the operating system to run. Also, be sure that the himem.sys file is the correct version and that it is in the correct location.

Expanded Memory Access

The *emm386.exe file* is another memory-management program that provides the system with access to the upper memory area (UMA) of RAM. This program operates together with the himem.sys utility and provides the system with the capability to conserve conventional memory by moving device drivers and memory-resident programs into the UMA.

Some common troubleshooting issues with this program occur when conflicts exist in the allocation of the upper memory blocks. This can happen if there is a missing or incorrect himem.sys file or if there are conflicting third-party drivers. To detect this type of memory conflict, start Windows at the DOS prompt by entering the following command:

WIN /D:X

This command avoids the upper memory portion in the bootup process. If Windows starts successfully using this switch, it has identified that an upper memory block conflict exists and needs to be resolved. To resolve the conflicting driver issue, run the msd.exe diagnostic tool to examine the drivers that are using the upper memory block. If a conflicting driver is located, add the following line to the [386Enh] section of the system.ini file.

EMMEXCLUDE=

Adding this statement to the system.ini file prevents Windows from trying to use the space to establish buffers. Figure 13-8 summarizes information about the MS-DOS memory layout.

Figure 13-8 The MS-DOS Memory Layout

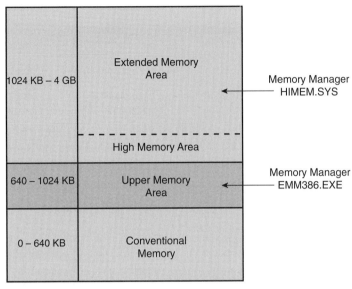

LASTDRIVE Errors

The *LASTDRIVE= command* is contained in the config.sys file and specifies the maximum number of drives the system can access. Common troubleshooting issues with this command can be easily fixed by editing config.sys. Usually, the parameter that indicates the number of drives is incorrect. After correcting this value, restart the system, and see if it boots properly. If the available disk drives are set to a letter value that is lower than what is required of the existing system, DOS automatically overrides the letter value to accommodate the drives installed in the system. Only increase the number of drives if additional drives are going to be used, because each drive letter above E decreases the amount of RAM that is available for other purposes.

DEVICEHIGH Errors

The previous section mentioned that the device driver configurations are stored in the config.sys file. Edit the file to change entries, or use a REM statement to prevent devices from running when the system is booting up. The *DEVICEHIGH= command* is used to load drivers into the UMA instead of loading them into conventional memory. Errors can occur when this command attempts to load a device driver file that is too large to fit in the buffer space that is available in a block of the UMA. If this happens, the system can lock up. Access the command prompt and run the MEM /D command to determine the size of the file, and then edit this value by modifying the entry in the config.sys file. This modifies the DEVICEHIGH= line to use only the buffer size that is needed.

Invalid Directory Errors

In some cases, invalid directory errors appear. These occur while attempting to navigate through the file system in DOS. For example, a hard drive contains two partitions; the first partition has been formatted but the second partition has not. Attempting to access this second partition's drive letter results in an "Invalid directory error" message, as shown in Figure 13-9. This error also appears when trying to access a directory that has been deleted or damaged. If the system has been backed up, recopy the directory to the hard drive and access it again.

Figure 13-9 Invalid Directory Error Message

Common Windows Operating System Problems

This section includes the following topics:

- Setup (installation) problems
- Startup (booting) problems
- Windows memory usage problems
- Windows OS missing/corrupt dll or vxd files
- System lockup errors
- Shutdown problems

Setup (Installation) Problems

Most setup problems are errors that occur during the installation phase of the operating system. The early versions of DOS offered simple installations. However, with the latest versions of Windows, setup procedures have become a complex issue that requires running an installation or setup program. Therefore, technicians spend increasingly more time troubleshooting setup problems.

A common type of installation problem occurs while attempting to install the operating system on the hard drive. The error message states, "The system's hard drive does not have enough space to carry out the installation process," as shown in Figure 13-10. When this happens, either delete obsolete files until there is enough space or add another hard drive to the system to increase the available space.

Figure 13-10 Insufficient Disk Space Message

```
Hard Disk is Low on Disk Space
You are running out of disk space on drive C.
To free space on this drive by deleting old or
unnecessary files, click Disk Cleanup.
```

Other common installation issues are hardware issues. These are identified by "Insufficient memory" and "Incompatible device driver" errors. The best way to resolve hardware problems is to consult the Microsoft website to determine if the hardware is compatible with the operating system that is being installed. If the hardware is no longer supported, it should be replaced.

Startup (Booting) Problems

Startup issues typically involve problems with hardware, configuration, and boot or operating systems. Some of these problems simply prevent activity from appearing in the system, while others produce error messages that make it easy to find the cause.

If the system produces an error message or a beep-coded error signal before the beep signaling that the BIOS has passed and the operating system is about to load, then the problem is most likely hardware related. If the error message or beep-coded error message occurs after the beep signaling that the BIOS has passed and the operating system is about to load, then the problem is most likely in the operating system or is software related.

Creating a Windows 9X Startup Disk

A startup or boot disk is necessary to start the computer when it does not normally start, and it also allows diagnostic programs to be run to determine the cause of the problem. Use the following steps to create a Windows 98 startup disk:

Step 1   Take a blank floppy disk, and label it Windows 98 Startup Disk.

Step 2   Choose **Start, Settings, Control Panel**.

Step 3   Double-click the Add/Remove Programs icon.

Step 4   Click the Startup Disk tab, and then click Create Disk, as shown in Figure 13-11.

Step 5   Insert the blank disk into the floppy disk drive, and click OK.

Figure 13-11   Creating a Startup Disk

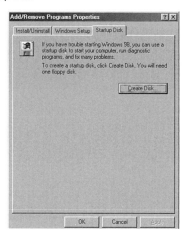

Using the Windows 9X Startup Disk

TEST TIP

A boot disk contains the basic files (config.sys, io.sys, and msdos.sys) needed to start the computer, and a startup disk contains those files plus additional files that enable a technician to troubleshoot problems with the system. Know how to create and use a startup disk.

One of the most important tools for a technician is a boot disk. The Windows 9X startup disk (boot disk) allows access to the system when the OS has become corrupted. To use the disk, insert it into the floppy drive and restart the system. Make sure that the BIOS is set to boot from the floppy drive. The system then boots with only minimal files and drivers. Use the Windows 9X startup disk to gain access to the operating system's files, and use the built-in troubleshooting tools on the disk to identify the cause of the problem.

In addition to providing the system files that are needed to start the system in a minimal or DOS mode, the Windows 9X startup disk provides many diagnostic programs and CD-ROM drivers. The startup disk also contains a RAM drive and an extract.exe file that can be used to copy cab files from the Windows 98 CD.

Using Windows' System Tools to Troubleshoot Startup Problems

The Windows operating system provides many other troubleshooting tools. These tools are referred to as *system troubleshooting tools*. They can be used to isolate and correct issues and can be helpful when troubleshooting a system. Load the system tools configuration utility from the command line by typing **MSCONFIG.EXE**. Figure 13-12 shows the screen that displays. This is a troubleshooting tool that can interactively load device drivers and software options. This utility can be used to systematically go through a step-by-step process of viewing the lines of the config.sys and the autoexec.bat files. It can enable or disable items until all the problems are identified.

Figure 13-12   The MSCONFIG Display

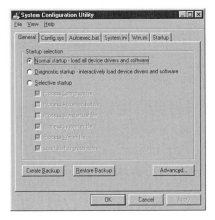

If inspecting the config.sys and autoexec.bat files does not solve the problem, the System Tools utility provides other options. Lower-level configuration settings, such as real-mode disk access and VGA standard video settings, can be inspected. The Device Manager can also be started from the MSCONFIG View option, allowing technicians to troubleshoot protected-mode device drivers. You can also verify that system files are not missing or corrupted. Other items that can be inspected are corrupted Registry entries, viruses, and possible hardware conflicts.

Windows Memory Usage Problems

Memory usage errors occur when the operating system or an application attempts to access a memory location that is unallocated. When this type of conflict occurs, the unallocated memory location becomes corrupted; this usually results in the operating system crashing. This could occur if a user is running more than one application at a time and one of the applications attempts to use another application's memory space. When this happens, the operating system generates an error message or locks up. The typical error message is "This operation has performed an illegal operation and is about to be shut down."

Some memory usage errors are nonfatal, meaning that they do not lock up the application or cause the system to lock up. These types of memory usage errors provide an option to continue working or to shut down the application. If a nonfatal error occurs, save your data and exit the application, because the application has most likely become unstable and could soon lock up.

In the event that a Windows memory error affects the Windows core files (krnlxxx.exe, gdi.exe, or user.exe), restart the Windows operating system.

Windows Resources Low Issues

You should know the level of the operating system resources. When the Windows resource level gets too low, it can cause the applications or the operating system to lock up. This type of error indicates that the operating system is running out of real and virtual memory. In general, it becomes obvious that Windows resources are getting low when the system's performance begins to degrade. This usually occurs when many applications are running at the same time or when the system has not been restarted in a long time. The system tray in the lower-right corner of the screen displays programs that are running in the background. Because these programs are active, they use system resources. Disable or remove unneeded icons in the system tray to free more resources for other applications.

General Protection Faults Problems

A *general protection fault (GPF)* occurs when one of the operating system applications attempts to access an unallocated memory location. Figure 13-13 shows the screen that displays. General protection faults are usually the result of programs that use illegal instructions to access areas of memory that have been protected. In earlier versions of Windows, a GPF would crash the system and require the system to be rebooted, thus losing unsaved data. The latest versions of Windows remains stable after a GPF so that users can close the error message and save their data before closing the application or restarting the system.

Figure 13-13 General Protection Fault Problems

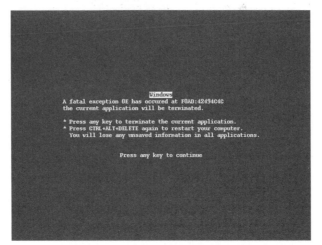

Typical causes of general protection faults include running applications that are not written for the Windows operating system, selecting the wrong machine or network during installation, or using incorrect versions of DOS in the system. The config.sys and autoexec.bat file that contains the incompatible or unsupported programs or drivers could also be a cause.

Windows OS Missing/Corrupt dll or vxd Files

Two important types of files associated with the operating system are vxd and dll files. It is important to learn what these files do and how to repair them because they are critical to the health of the system. If these files get deleted or become corrupt, the system will no longer run properly.

A *vxd file* is a virtual device driver and is only found in Windows 9X and 2000. These vxd files take the place of the DEVICE= and LOADHIGH= commands for devices that are in versions of DOS. The vxd files are protected-mode drivers that allow multiple applications to access a system hardware or software resource. The *x* in vxd stands for a particular type of driver. For example, vdd is a display adapter driver and vpd is a printer driver. If these vxd files are missing or corrupt, many devices can fail. This can result in the system not being able to boot. If this happens, try reloading the driver that came with the hardware or try to update the driver by downloading it from the manufacturer's website.

Another file, called a *dynamic link library (dll) file*, can communicate with the Windows core directly. These small files store subroutines that either come with the application or are made by the programmer. Loss or corruption of dll files causes an application to lock up or prevents it from loading. Windows 95, 98, and 2000 applications use the operating system as a pool of resources (for memory, modem, video, and printer). Programs or dlls make calls to these resources when the program or dll needs to place something on the screen, to check the status of the mouse, to use memory, or to gain access to other items. Problems arise when a new application is installed and updates one of the shared dlls, thereby creating a dll conflict. As a result of this conflict, older applications might not be able to handle the updated file and can fail to work.

SFC Utility

The Windows operating system includes many tools to help make it stable and dependable. One such tool is called the *System File Checker (SFC)*. The SFC is a command-line utility that scans the operating system files to ensure that they are the correct (original Microsoft) ones. Some applications can replace system files (for example, vxd or dll files) with different files of the same name, although this is less common with modern software. This quickly brings a computer system to halt. The operating system is no longer stable and has difficulty booting after installing or uninstalling some applications or utilities.

The SFC is a tool that allows users to scan their system and verify that the versions of protected system files are up to date. If a protected system file has moved or has been removed, the SFC automatically replaces the file with the correct version from the dll cache folder.

Locating/Replacing Missing or Corrupt dll or vxd Files

The SFC utility scans the hard drive for damaged and missing Windows files and corrects many problems. This requires an available operating system CD so that missing files can be restored from the CD to the proper system location. This utility is available in Windows 98 and Windows 2000. In Windows 2000, type the following at a command prompt to execute this command:

    SFC /SCANNOW

To return to the default Windows file protection operation, type the following command:

    SFC /ENABLE

In this mode, SFC automatically prompts the user to restore the correct system file version when it detects that an application has overwritten a file. Remember to enable this option before exiting the command-prompt window.

Although running the SFC utility solves most problems, many programs load their own restore file in their own folder, causing the problem. In this case, there are several choices.

One example would be an error with the mfc42.dll files. First, rename any mfc42.dll files that can be found, other than those in the system and cabs folders, from mfc42.dll to mfc42.old, and reboot the computer. This can only be done from a true DOS prompt and not from Windows. If the problem is resolved, the filename can always be changed back to the original. Do this one file at a time. If three mfc42.dll files are found, rename only the first. Reboot, and if the problem remains, rename the next, and so on. Eventually you should only have one copy of this file in the system folder and one in the cabs folder.

If this does approach does not fix the problem, rename the mfc42.dll file in the system folder to mfc42.old. Then, one file at a time, copy one of the other mfc42.dll files that were found in the other folders to the system folder, and rename it mfc42.dll. The object is to use the other versions and see if they work. This usually solves the problem of missing or corrupt dll files.

System Lockup Errors

As previously discussed in this chapter, the majority of system lockup errors occur when a memory allocation error exists or when system resources are low. Some system lockup problems can be prevented by running only one or two applications at a time. Figure 13-14 shows the screen that displays when a program has locked up and is no longer responding. A more permanent solution is to add system resources; for example, the processor could be upgraded or memory can be added.

Figure 13-14 System Lockup Errors

Shutdown Problems

Sometimes, technicians receive troubleshooting calls from end users whose systems do not shut down. Usually, this is caused by an application that remains running in the background. This application might have encountered an error, and the application's processes might be hanging up the system and preventing it from shutting down. If this occurs, one solution is to press Ctrl-Alt-Del. A screen, similar to the one shown in Figure 13-15, then displays. The application's processes can be shut down manually, and then the system can be shut down normally. Further troubleshooting steps should be taken to see what caused the application to hang up in the first place.

Figure 13-15 Troubleshooting Shutdown Problems

Windows 9*X* Troubleshooting Problems

This section includes the following topics:

- Upgrade issues
- Error codes and startup messages
- Windows 9*X* startup modes
- Windows 9*X* error log files
- Windows virtual memory errors

Upgrade Issues

Problems encountered during upgrades to Windows 9X can be related to hardware, software, or both. Before an upgrade is started, consult the Microsoft website to see if the hardware your compatible. Check with the manufacturers of the hardware components and the software publishers to determine if updated drivers are needed for the upgrade.

Prior to doing an upgrade, determine if your hardware meets the minimum system recommendations for the upgrade.

The minimum system requirements for Windows 98 are as follows:

- 486DX 66-MHz or faster processor
- 16 MB of memory
- 225 MB of free hard disk space for a full installation on a FAT16 drive (175 MB on a FAT32 drive)
- VGA or higher resolution monitor
- Keyboard
- CD-ROM drive (optional but recommended)
- High-density 3-1/2-inch floppy disk drive (if no bootable CD-ROM drive is available)

Visit the Microsoft website for information that identifies the type of processor and amount of RAM required to run the selected operating system.

Error Codes and Startup Messages

Error codes that are generated at system startup usually indicate hardware problems, configuration problems, or bootup problems that are associated with the operating system. Any errors that occur in these areas can result in a startup failure. If one of the errors shown in the subsequent sections appears, use the emergency boot disk to start the system and begin the troubleshooting process.

Error: No Operating System Found

If the "No operating system found" error message appears during startup, as shown in Figure 13-16, the most likely culprits are either a failed hard drive or a damaged or corrupted MBR. This error message can also appear if the command interpreter (command.com) file is missing. To troubleshoot the problem, first make sure that the hard drive is properly installed and that all the cables are properly connected. If the problem persists, start the system from a boot disk containing fdisk.exe, and then use the FDISK.EXE /MBR command to fix the master boot record on the hard drive. At this point, you might need to run diagnostics on the hard drive to determine if it has failed.

Figure 13-16 Error Message: No Operating System Found

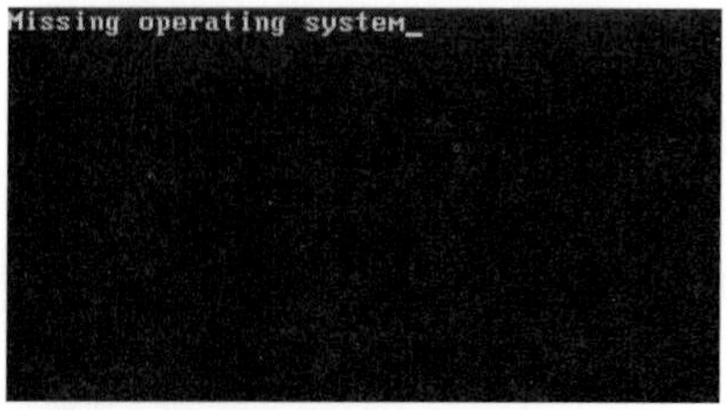

Error: Windows Protection Error

The "Windows protection error" error message can occur when a computer loads or unloads a virtual device driver (vxd). In many cases, the vxd that did not load or unload is mentioned in the error message. In other cases, you might not be able to determine which vxd caused the behavior. Windows protection error messages can occur under the following conditions:

- A real-mode driver and a protected-mode driver are in conflict.
- The Registry is damaged.
- The win.com file or the command.com file is infected with a virus, or is damaged.
- A protected-mode driver is loaded from the system.ini file, and the driver is already initialized.
- There is an I/O address conflict or a RAM address conflict.
- There are incorrect CMOS settings for a built-in peripheral device (such as cache settings, CPU timing settings, hard disk settings, and so on).
- The Plug and Play feature of the computer's BIOS is not working correctly.
- The computer contains a malfunctioning cache or malfunctioning memory.
- The computer motherboard is not working properly.

Error: Illegal Operation

The "Illegal operation" error message means that the current program is having a problem. This error designation covers a wide range of errors. It can take some time, patience, and troubleshooting to pinpoint the cause. The most common causes of an illegal operation include problems between the running program and a software driver in the operating system, or memory-management problems between the running program and a program that is open in the background. Problems and conflicts with different dynamic link library (dll) files, which are added to the system when software programs are installed, can also cause illegal operation errors. Furthermore, hardware conflicts, defective RAM chips, and program bugs can cause the error.

To pinpoint the cause, ask the following questions: Has this program always worked but is now crashing unexpectedly? Has anything, such as new hardware devices or software, been added lately? Tracing the advent of the problem to a specific event can help narrow the list of likely suspects. The "Illegal operation" error can be generated due to an incompatibility of a printer driver as well, even if this error is not generated when printing.

Error: A Device Referenced in SYSTEM.INI, WIN.INI, or Registry Is Not Found

The win.ini file contains parameters that can be altered to change the Windows environment and the software settings to the user's preferences. The win.ini file is a software initialization file for Windows. It contains information about some Windows defaults, the placement of windows, color settings for the screen, and available ports, printers, fonts, and software applications. The system.ini file contains hardware-setting information for the drivers that Windows uses for configuration. When the "A device referenced in SYSTEM.INI, WIN.INI, or Registry is not found" error message displays, it usually means that these files contain an entry that is no longer installed in the system. To fix this error, edit these files to remove the lines that reference the omitted hardware or software.

Error: Failure to Start GUI

The operating system files that control the graphical user interface (GUI) can become corrupted and generate the "Failure to start GUI" error message. If this happens, choose to start the operating system from the DOS prompt or command line. From the DOS prompt, troubleshoot the operating system to repair the files that start the GUI.

Windows 9X Startup Modes

Access the Windows 9X startup modes by pressing F8 when the "Starting Windows 9X" screen is displayed. The Startup menu offers several startup options, including Normal, Logged, Safe Mode, Step-by-Step Confirmation, and DOS Modes, as shown in Figure 13-17. These startup modes can help in troubleshooting startup issues. In Normal mode, the system boots up as it normally would, with all the proper drivers and Registry files. The Logged mode boots up just like the Normal mode, but Windows creates an error log that contains the performed steps and their outcomes.

Figure 13-17 Windows 9*X* Startup Modes

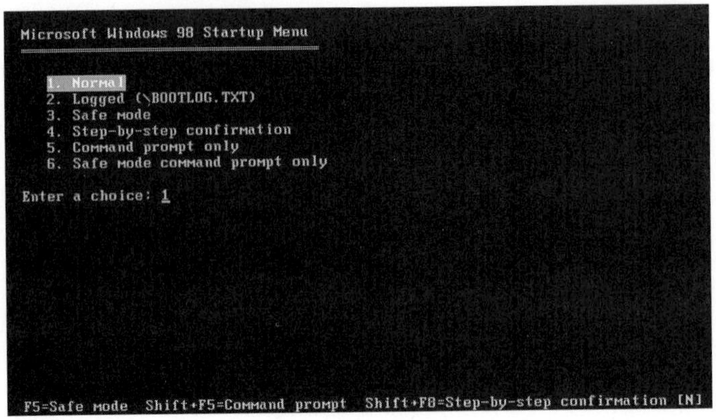
Microsoft Windows 98 Startup Menu
1. Normal
2. Logged (\BOOTLOG.TXT)
3. Safe mode
4. Step-by-step confirmation
5. Command prompt only
6. Safe mode command prompt only
Enter a choice: 1
F5=Safe mode Shift+F5=Command prompt Shift+F8=Step-by-step confirmation [N]

Safe Mode

Safe mode is a troubleshooting tool for Windows. It works much like the command-line switches for Windows 3.*X*. Safe mode allows access into Windows using only the most basic drivers. The following items are not loaded:

- The autoexec.bat and config.sys files
- The main portion of the Registry
- The load= and run= lines in win.ini
- The [Boot] and [386Enh] sections in system.ini

TEST TIP

Know what Safe mode is and why it is used.

Starting Windows 9*X* in Safe mode bypasses the current real-mode configuration and loads a minimal protected-mode configuration, disabling Windows 95 device drivers and using the standard VGA display adapter. If the given problem does not occur in Safe mode, the problem might be a conflict with hardware settings or could be real-mode configuration issues, incompatibilities with legacy Windows programs or drivers, or Registry damage.

While Windows is in Safe mode, check the Device Manager for any hardware device conflicts. If conflicts exist, you may need to change IRQ or DMA settings. If no conflicts exist, the problem is probably software related.

Safe mode is the best troubleshooting tool in Windows, but Safe mode does not state where the problem is occurring. Common Safe mode actions are as follows:

- Switch hardware acceleration (**Start, Settings, Control Panel, System, Performance tab, Graphics**) to None.
- Switch read-ahead (**Start, Settings, Control Panel, System, Performance tab, File System**) to None.

- Change the video driver (**Start, Settings, Control Panel, Display, Settings tab, Change Display Type**) to Standard VGA.
- Restart the computer and boot to Normal mode each time something is changed.

If you determine that the problem is software related, consider editing the win.ini file. Only two lines in win.ini do not load in Safe mode: the run= and the load= lines. Stop these lines from being read by placing a semicolon in front of them, and then start the computer. If this solves the problem, something that is being loaded by these lines is causing the problem.

If you determine that the problem is hardware related, consider editing the system.ini file. Examine the [Boot] and [386Enh] sections in this file. These are the only two sections that are not loaded when booting to Safe mode. In general, any line that has an exe extension represents a program that is loading. Stop these lines from being read by placing a semicolon in front of them. Also, look for lines that access files with a 386 in them. These lines load old legacy drivers and might need to be marked with a semicolon.

Command Prompt Only Mode

Depending on the configuration of the system, starting the system in DOS mode to troubleshoot issues is also possible. Enter DOS mode by selecting the "Command Prompt Only Mode" option. Starting the system in this mode gives you the ability to troubleshoot the operating system from the command-line interface. Command-line tools and DOS editors are available. Loading the himem.sys and ifshlp.sys files or any of the Windows 9X files can also be avoided. Choose this startup option if the system fails to boot in Safe mode.

WIN Switches

The *WIN switches* provide the ability to start Windows from the command line. Use the WIN /D command to troubleshoot and isolate a number of problems with the operating system. Do this by modifying the /D switch to start Windows in a number of different configurations, and then use these configurations to start Windows with different options to troubleshoot specific areas of the operating system when it is not starting up properly. The following are examples of how these switches work:

- WIN /D:F—Use the /D:F switch to disable 32-bit disk access.
- WIN /D:M—Use the /D:M switch to start Windows in Safe mode or Safe mode with Networking.
- WIN /D:S—Use the /D:S switch to prohibit Windows from using the address space between F000h and FFFFFh.
- WIN /D:V—Use the /D:V switch to prevent Windows from controlling disk transfers; instead, the hard drive disk transfers are handled by the BIOS.

Windows 9X Error Log Files

When troubleshooting a computer system, it can be difficult to pinpoint the error or to determine what caused the error. The problem might be recognized immediately, and the solution might be obvious, but it is important to know what caused that error. Fixing the problem without fixing the cause does not prevent the problem from reoccurring. Windows 9X maintains error log files of system operations that show which events led to the error. The names of these log files indicate the type of information that they track. These log files are discussed in the following sections. Table 13-1 details the function and location of each log file and indicates when each log file is created.

Table 13-1 Summary of Log Files

Filename	When Created	Function	Location
Bootlog.txt	As the system is booting up	It is used to debug windows startup problems. It is not updated automatically. To update, press F8 during startup or start Windows with the WIN /B command.	This file is stored in the Windows Directory. It is created during the Windows installation process.
setuplog.txt	When Setup fails before hardware detection.	Windows 98 recovers by reading this file. This file can also be used for troubleshooting errors that occur during installation.	This file is located in the root directory. It determines where the system stalled, what to redo, and what to skip.
detcrash.log	When Setup fails during hardware detection.	This file records information about the detection module that was running and the memory resources or I/O port that Windows was accessing when Setup failed.	This file can only be read by Setup. If the detection process is completed successfully, this file is deleted.
detlog.txt	Every time that the detection process runs.	This file contains a record of specific hardware device(s) that were detected and identifies the parameters for the detected device(s).	This file is located in the root directory once Windows 98 is installed. The file indicates the start of a detection test and indicates if the test was completed.

The bootlog.txt File

The *bootlog.txt file* contains the system information that is collected as the system is booting up. The file is created during the Windows installation process. It is not updated automatically each time the system boots. The file can be updated by pressing F8 during startup or by starting Windows with the WIN /B command.

The log information is recorded in the following five steps:

Step 1   **Loading real-mode drivers**—The system attempts to load the real-mode drivers, but if it is unsuccessful in doing so, it reports an error in the log.

Step 2   **Loading virtual device drivers (vxds)**—The system attempts to load the vxds but marks the log if it is unsuccessful in doing so.

Step 3   **Initialization of critical vxds**—Check this section to verify that system-critical vxds have been initialized.

Step 4   **Device initialization of vxds**—This log shows all the vxds that have been initialized. In this section, a success or failure report for each device is generated.

Step 5   **Successful initialization of vxds**—This section verifies the successful initialization of the system vxds.

The setuplog.txt File

The *setuplog.txt file* is also created during the installation process and contains the system setup information. It can be used for safe-recovery situations and is stored in the system root directory. The entries in this file are displayed in a step-by-step list in the order that they occurred during the startup process. This can be helpful when troubleshooting, because this order can show where the error occurred.

The detcrash.log File

If the system crashes during the hardware detection phase of the startup process, the *detcrash.log file* is created. This file contains information about the processes that were running when the crash occurred. This file cannot be read directly because it is in binary form. To read this file, use the detlog.txt file.

The detlog.txt File

The *detlog.txt file* is used to read the information that is generated when the detcrash.log file is created. It indicates which components have been detected by the system and which ones have not. This file is a detailed report of the hardware detection phase of the system's Plug and Play operation.

Windows Virtual Memory Errors

Computers need an operating system, and these operating systems usually require more memory than is onboard in the system RAM. Windows is no exception to this rule. Even if there is sufficient memory to run Windows itself, Windows applications require even more memory. Without virtual memory, it might be impossible to run these applications.

Virtual memory is the part of the hard drive that is reserved for the operating system to do *paging*. Data are stored in memory in pages, and only a certain number of these pages can fit in RAM at a given time. Therefore, the operating system takes some of these pages and moves them out to virtual memory so that the more-current pages (usually the ones for the program currently being used) can be kept in RAM, which is faster. This process is often referred to as *swapping*, hence the term swap file. The *swap file* is a huge file that often contains thousands of these pages on a reserved portion of the hard drive.

Virtual Memory Settings

The default paging file size is 2 MB. The recommended paging file size for Windows 2000 is 1.5 times the amount of RAM. Windows sets a default paging file size during installation. Figure 13-18 shows the virtual memory window. In some circumstances, such as when a large number of applications are running simultaneously, using a larger paging file or multiple paging files can be beneficial. Unused space in the paging file remains available to the internal Windows Virtual Memory Manager.

Figure 13-18 Virtual Memory Settings

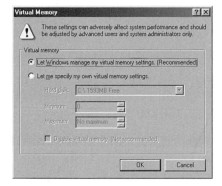

If Windows detects that the Windows paging file is set too low, the "Virtual memory minimum too low" error message appears after logon. The message indicates that Windows is increasing the size of the paging file. While this occurs, any programs that are running might run more slowly, or they could pause because memory requests by those applications might be denied.

Swap File Errors

In some instances, swap file errors or the "Swap file corrupt" error message can display, indicating that the permanent swap file that was created for Windows has become corrupt. The most common reason for swap file errors is that you are running out of hard drive space. This error can also appear when disk-management functions such as FORMAT and FDISK are running. The swap file can also be overwritten or become corrupt. If the swap file becomes corrupt or if it is disabled, you must reinstall the operating system.

Worksheet 13.4.5   Troubleshooting Software

This worksheet tests your knowledge of troubleshooting software by having you match the terms with the correct descriptions.

Using System Tools and System Editors to Troubleshoot Windows 9*X*/2000

This section includes the following topics:

- Using system tools
- Using the Windows Device Manager to troubleshoot
- Using the Windows system editors

Using System Tools

Both Windows 9X and 2000 have many system tools that are helpful when troubleshooting. These tools can provide a number of administrative and diagnostic tools to help fix computer problems.

Event Viewer

The *Event Viewer*, as shown in Figure 13-19, is used to monitor system events, application events, and security events in Windows 9X. System events include successful and failed Windows component startups. Application events store information about the system applications and their performance. Security events store events related to system security, such as logons and logoffs, file and folder access, and the creation of a new active directory.

TEST TIP

Know what the system tools are and understand how to access them in Windows.

Figure 13-19 The Event Viewer

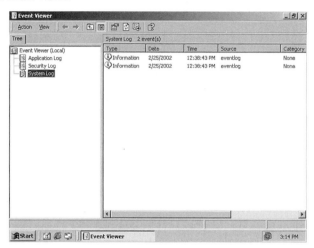

The Event Viewer also creates categories of system and application events. Information events indicate that an application, service, or driver has loaded successfully. Warning events warn about items that might be harmful in the future. Error events indicate that an application, service, or driver has failed to load. Because the security log is limited in size, and because a large number of routine audit records can make it difficult to find records that suggest a security problem, carefully consider how to audit object access. Generating too many audit records requires that the security log be reviewed and cleared more often than is practical. This can generate the "Event log is full" error message. When this happens, open the event log and delete some of the entries.

Dr. Watson Utility

The *Dr. Watson utility* is used to isolate and correct general protection faults (GPFs). When the cause of the GPF cannot be traced to the operating system, the GPF is usually caused by an application. The Dr. Watson utility can be started to run in the background as an application runs. The utility monitors application operations and logs the key events in the drwatson.log file. This log provides details about the events that caused the GPF. If the error repeats in the same application, you might need to install a software patch.

The scanreg.exe File

The *scanreg.exe file* is used to scan the Registry for corruption. Run SCANREG if system troubleshooting indicates that an error is caused by a corrupted Registry entry.

Figure 13-20 shows the Windows Registry being scanned. If the scan finds corrupted files, try to repair them by inserting the installation CD and choosing the repair installation option.

Figure 13-20 Running SCANREG

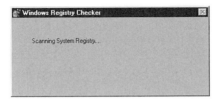

The defrag.exe File

System performance can be degraded when files become fragmented on the hard drive. Over time, files are added and deleted from the hard drive, and pieces of files become scattered throughout the hard drive. This degrades performance and can cause the system or applications to lock up. Run the *defrag.exe file* to start the DEFRAG utility. Figure 13-21 shows the DEFRAG utility running. This utility rewrites all the files on the hard drive contiguously, making it easier and faster for the hard drive to retrieve the information.

Figure 13-21 Running DEFRAG

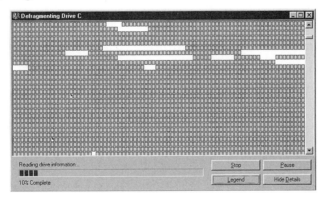

The chkdsk.exe File

The *chkdsk.exe* file is a command-line tool that is used to recover lost allocation units from the hard drive. The lost allocation units are generated when an application terminates unexpectedly. Over time, lost allocation units can accumulate and occupy large amounts of disk space. By adding the /F switch to the CHKDSK command, the lost allocation units can be converted into files so they can be viewed and deleted if necessary. This utility is used to optimize disk storage space by locating and removing files that have been corrupted.

The scandskw.exe File

The ScanDisk for Windows (*scandskw.exe file*) disk-checking and repair-tool checks the integrity of the media (which includes hard disks and floppy disks) and can repair problems that occur.

Windows 98, Windows 98 Second Edition, and Windows Me start ScanDisk automatically when the operating system is shut down improperly or if the hard disk contains a critical error.

The msconfig.exe File

Load the system tools configuration utility from the command line by typing **MSCONFIG**. This troubleshooting tool is used to interactively load device drivers and software options. With this utility, you can systematically view the lines of the config.sys and autoexec.bat files, and decide whether to load each line. Items can be enabled or disabled until all the problems are identified.

The edit.com File

The *edit.com file* is a Windows troubleshooting tool that can view and edit configuration (text) files such as autoexec.bat, config.sys, ini files, and other files.

Using the Windows Device Manager to Troubleshoot

The Windows Device Manager provides a way to view the hardware on the system in a graphical interface while also helping to manage and troubleshoot. The *Device Manager*, as shown in Figure 13-22, is used to disable, uninstall, and update device drivers. The Device Manager helps to determine whether the hardware on the computer is working properly and if the correct drivers are installed for the hardware. It also lists the devices with problems. Each problem device is labeled so the hardware that is not installed properly can be easily identified.

When manually changing device configurations, the Device Manager can help avoid problems. The Device Manager is used to identify free resources and assign a device to that resource, disable devices to free resources, and reallocate resources used by devices to free a required resource. In Windows 2000, users must be logged on as a member of the Administrators group to change resource settings. Even if a user is logged on as administrator, if the computer is connected to a network, policy settings on the network might prevent the user from changing resources.

Figure 13-22   The Device Manager

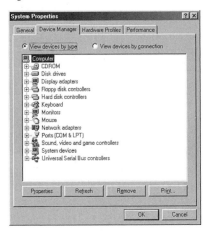

Using the Windows System Editors

The Windows operating systems contain important editors. These editors allow Windows settings to be customized to the policy that the system administrator desires. A system administrator can use the sysedit.exe and poledit.exe editors to edit configuration settings to the user interface. In Windows 2000, the Group Policy Editor (GPE) allows the administrator to edit a policy for an entire group of users at one time.

The System Editor

The *System Editor (sysedit.exe)* is accessed by choosing **Start, Run** and typing **SYSEDIT**. The SYSEDIT utility is used to modify text files such as the system ini files as well as the config.sys and autoexec.bat files. The SYSEDIT commands are similar to those for other Windows-based text-editing programs. Figure 13-23 shows the system configuration editor.

Figure 13-23 The System Configuration Editor

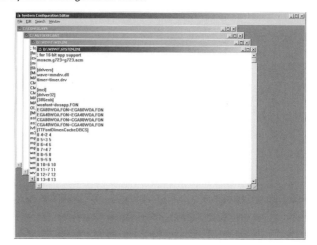

The System Policy Editor

Use the *System Policy Editor (poledit.exe)* to set up different security restrictions for different users. You can set one policy for a whole group, configure desktops for roving users so that any computer they use has the same look, or protect a computer if it is unplugged from the network.

The System Policy Editor is a powerful tool that is used to create and edit local Registry values to standardize desktop settings, to prevent users from modifying hardware and environment settings, and to control or restrict user actions.

The System Policy Editor also prevents security problems such as file-tampering, loss of data as a result of accidental system software changes, or users being locked out of their computers.

The Group Policy Editor

Group policies provide a means for further refining and centralizing the management of an end user's desktop environment. Group policies can be used to control the programs that are available to users, the programs that appear on a user's desktop, and the Start menu options.

The *Group Policy Editor (GPE)*, available in Windows 2000, is used to set group policies. These policies are a group of configuration settings that a system administrator can apply to one or more objects in the active directory database. A group policy is used to control the work environments of users in a domain. Group policies can also control the work environment of accounts that are located in a specific organizational unit. In addition, group policies can be set at the site level, using the Active Directory Sites and Services snap-in.

A group policy consists of the settings that govern how an object and the subobjects behave. Group policies allow a group policy administrator to provide users with a fully populated desktop environment. This environment can include a customized Start menu and applications that are automatically set up, and can restrict access to files, folders, and Windows 2000 system settings. Group policies can also affect the rights that are granted to user accounts and groups.

Windows 9*X*/2000 Registry Problems

This section includes the following topics:

- Registry files
- Registry structure
- Editing the Registry
- Cleaning the Registry

Registry Files

The Registry files contain all the system configuration information. This includes the local hardware configuration, network environment, file associations, and user configurations. The user.dat and system.dat files are the Registry files that contain the contents in the Registry. These files, as well as additional related files, as described as follows:

- **user.dat**—This file contains all the information that is specific to the user. For example, this file maintains user profiles, such as mouse speed, wallpaper, and color scheme.
- **user.da0**—When Windows successfully boots, this file, a backup of user.dat, is created. If the user.dat file gets corrupted or is erased, rename the user.da0 file to user.dat, and the Registry can be restored.
- **system.dat**—This file holds hardware profiles, computer-specific profiles, and settings information. For example, when a new piece of hardware, such as a video card, is installed, the system.dat file is updated.
- **system.da0**—Like the user.da0 file, the system.da0 file is also created when Windows successfully boots. This file is a backup of the system.dat file. If the system.dat file gets corrupted or is erased, rename the system.da0 file to system.dat, and the Registry can be restored.

NOTE

The *win.com file* is another Registry file. It controls the initial environment checks and loads operating system core components when Windows 95 is loading.

TEST TIP

Know how to access the Registry Editor and the files that are associated with the Registry.

- **system.ini**—This file contains hardware-setting information for the Windows configuration drivers. When the operating system needs to reference information about the hardware, it uses the system.ini file.

- **win.ini**—This file contains parameters that can be altered to change the Windows environment or the software settings to suit the user's preferences. The win.ini file is a software initialization file for Windows. It contains information about some Windows defaults, the placement of windows, the color settings for the screen, and the available ports, printers, fonts, and software applications.

Registry Structure

TEST TIP

Know each HKEY, and understand what it does in the Registry.

Becoming familiar with the Registry structure subtrees and understanding the purpose of these subtrees can help you troubleshoot and maintain the computer. There is a key in the Registry Editor for every process that is running on the system, as shown in Figure 13-24. Five subtrees, or subtree keys, are displayed in the Registry Editor window. The Registry HKEY notation is as follows:

- **HKEY_USERS**—Contains the system default settings that are used to control individual user profiles and environments such as desktop settings, Windows environment, and custom software settings.

- **HKEY_CURRENT_CONFIG**—Contains data on the active hardware profile that is selected during the boot process. This information is used to configure settings for the device drivers to load and for the display resolution to use.

- **HKEY_CLASSES_ROOT**—Contains software configuration data of all the software that is installed on the computer.

- **HKEY_CURRENT_USER**—Contains data about the user who is currently logged on to the computer. This key retrieves a copy of each user account that is used to log on to the computer and stores it in the Registry.

- **HKEY_LOCAL_MACHINE**—Contains all configuration data for the local computer, including hardware and operating system data such as bus type, system memory, device drivers, and startup control data. Applications, device drivers, and the operating system use these data to set the computer configuration. The data in this subtree remain constant, regardless of the user.

Editing the Registry

End users typically do not need to edit the Registry. However, a technician can edit the Registry for troubleshooting purposes; activities include viewing, editing, backing up, and restoring the Registry. The contents of the Registry can be edited and viewed through the Registry Editors. Access the Registry Editors by choosing **Start, Run** and typing **REGEDIT** or **REGEDT32**. When these commands are typed, the Registry subtrees window is displayed, allowing the search of all Registry values. This allows the manual changing of any Registry values.

The regedit.exe and regedt32.exe Files

The *regedit.exe file*, as shown in Figure 13-24, is the registration editor for 16-bit Windows; this file is used to modify the Windows registration database. The database is located in the Windows directory as reg.dat and contains information about 16-bit applications. Regedit.exe is used by the File Manager for opening and printing files. It is also used by applications that support object linking and embedding (OLE). The regedit.exe file is automatically installed in the systemroot folder.

Figure 13-24 The regedit.exe File

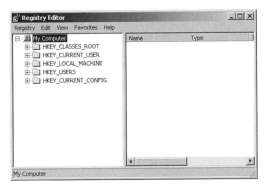

The configuration editor for Windows NT is *regedt32.exe*. This file allows you to view or modify the Windows NT Registry. The editor provides views of windows that represent sections of the Registry, called *hives*. Each window displays two sections. On the left side, the folders represent Registry keys. On the right side are the values associated with the selected Registry key. The regedt32.exe file is automatically installed in the systemroot\System32 folder. Figure 13-25 shows the regedt32.exe file.

Third-Party Registry-Editing Tools

Navigating and editing the Windows Registry can be difficult and confusing, even for the most experienced technician. You can damage the operating system beyond repair if the wrong value is edited or deleted. To make editing the Registry an easier and safer task, purchase third-party Registry-editing tools. Some examples of popular third-party editing tools are Norton's WINDOCTOR, McAffee's Registry Wizard, and PC Doctor OnCall. These tools provide an interface that is easier to use and navigate than that of the standard Windows Registry Editors.

Figure 13-25 The regedt32.exe File

Cleaning the Registry

An important part of maintaining a healthy computer is cleaning the Registry. As the system is used and applications are installed and uninstalled, values can be left behind in the Registry. These values remain even if they were uninstalled with the Add/Remove Programs wizard. If the Registry becomes too cluttered with old files and application entries, it can degrade system performance.

Third-Party Registry-Cleaning Tools

Third-party Registry-cleaning tools are recommended to edit the Registry. Popular third-party cleaning tools are Norton's WINDOCTOR and Microsoft's RegCleaner.

Windows NT/2000 Troubleshooting Problems

This section includes the following topics:

- Windows NT/2000 installation problems (review)
- Windows NT/2000 upgrade issues
- Windows NT startup modes
- Windows 2000 startup modes
- Windows 2000 Recovery Console

Windows NT/2000 Installation Problems (Review)

The most common types of installation problems that occur when installing Windows NT or 2000 are hardware and software compatibility issues. Before installing Windows 2000, make sure that the hardware is capable of running Windows 2000. The processor must be at least in the Pentium class, and the system must have at least 64 MB of RAM. The hard drive or partition that the operating system files are to be installed on must be at least 2 GB in size. A VGA monitor and a CD-ROM drive that is capable of reading at a 12X or higher speed are also required. Windows 2000 is a network operating system, and to enable networking, a network card is required.

Microsoft's Hardware Compatibility List (HCL) can be used before installing Windows 2000 to verify that the hardware will work with Windows 2000. Microsoft provides tested drivers for only those devices that are included on this list. Using hardware that is not listed on the HCL can cause problems during and after installation. View the HCL by opening the hcl.txt file, which is located in the Support folder on the Windows 2000 Professional CD.

Windows NT/2000 Upgrade Issues

The issues that can occur when upgrading to Windows NT and 2000 are similar to the issues that occur when performing Windows 9X upgrades. As with Windows 9X, Windows NT and 2000 upgrade problems are either hardware or software related; sometimes problems occur with both. Before beginning an upgrade, consult the Microsoft website to determine if the hardware is compatible. Check with the manufacturers of the hardware components and software to determine if they have updated drivers that are necessary for the upgrade. The following are system requirements for Windows 2000:

TEST TIP

Know the minimum requirements for installing Windows 2000 Professional.

- 166-MHz Pentium or higher microprocessor
- 32 MB of RAM (64 MB is recommended)
- 2 GB of hard disk space, with a minimum of 650 MB free space
- VGA or higher resolution monitor
- Keyboard
- Mouse
- CD-ROM drive
- High-density 3-1/2-inch floppy disk drive (if no bootable CD-ROM drive is available)

Hardware should be checked to verify that it meets the minimum recommendations for the upgrade. Microsoft maintains a list of recommendations on its website for types of processors and amount of RAM needed to run the selected operating system, as well as recommendations for other hardware components.

Windows NT Startup Modes

Startup mode options are available in Windows NT, just as in Windows 9X. However, the startup process for Windows NT is slightly different. The Windows NT startup depends on the boot loader file (boot.ini). The NTLDR (pronounced NT loader) program uses this file to generate a boot loader menu. This menu displays to allow you to select which operating system to use. From this menu, choose to start the system normally, start in VGA mode, or start in the last known good hardware configuration mode. The VGA mode and last known good hardware configuration mode are explained in the next section, because these startup modes are included with Windows 2000 as well.

Windows 2000 Startup Modes

The Windows 2000 operating system provides a choice of startup modes, just as the Windows 9X operating systems. However, Windows 2000 provides an advanced options menu that provides features in addition to the Safe mode options. Figure 13-26 shows the options available to enable boot logging and enable VGA mode, last known good configuration mode, and debugging mode.

Figure 13-26 Windows 2000 Advanced Options Menu

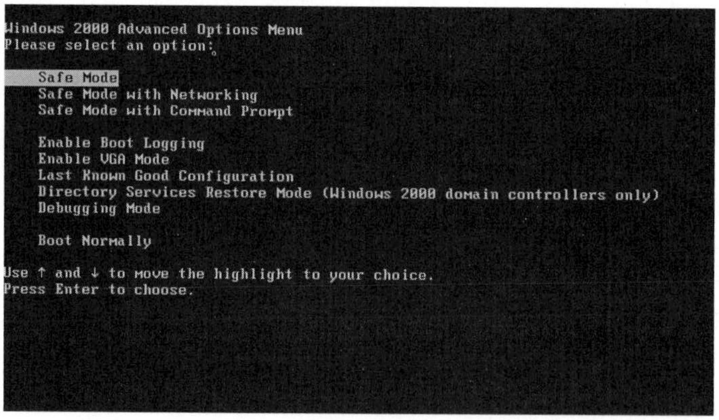

Normal and Safe Mode Boot Modes

Windows 2000 allows you to boot normally or boot to Safe mode, Safe mode with Networking, or Safe mode with Command Prompt. As with Windows 9X, Windows

2000 provides a means of booting the system into Safe mode with minimal drivers to allow troubleshooting.

Enable Boot Logging

If the Enable Boot Logging startup mode is chosen, an ntbtlog.txt file is created. This works similarly to the bootlog.txt file, as it contains a listing of all the drivers and services that the system attempts to load during the bootup process. Use this startup mode to determine what device or service is causing the system to fail.

Enable VGA Mode

Use the Enable VGA Mode startup mode if you experience display problems while booting up. This mode loads the standard VGA driver instead of the driver for your video card. Reconfigure your display settings while in this mode.

Last Known Good Configuration Mode

If a new device driver is loaded into the system and the system then fails to boot, use the Last Known Good Configuration Mode startup mode option. This enables the system to start from the point of the last successful user logon, without the new device driver.

Debugging Mode

The Debugging Mode startup mode enables the use of special debugger utilities to access the kernel for troubleshooting and analysis by starting the operating system in a kernel debug mode.

Lab Activity 13.7.4   Booting into Safe Mode

In this lab, you boot the computer and use the advanced troubleshooting options of Windows 2000.

Windows 2000 Recovery Console

The *Windows 2000 Recovery Console* is a command-line interface that is used to perform a variety of troubleshooting and recovery tasks. These tasks include starting and stopping services, reading and writing data on a local drive (including drives that are formatted with the NT file system), and formatting hard disks. Figure 13-27 shows the startup screen with the Recovery Console option. Once the recovery console has been started, use the commands from the command line to remove, replace, or copy corrupt files.

TEST TIP

Know how to use the Windows 2000 Recovery Console.

Figure 13-27 Windows 2000 Recovery Console

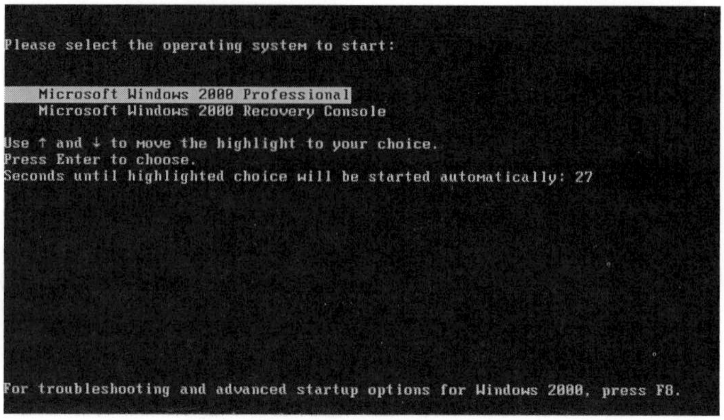

There is more than one way to start the Recovery Console. The first way is to insert the Windows 2000 CD into the CD-ROM drive and wait for the Microsoft Windows 2000 dialog box to open. If it does not start, choose **Start, Run** and type **CMD**. This displays the command-prompt window. Change to the drive letter of the CD-ROM drive and then to the I386 folder, and issue the following command:

WINNT32 /CMDCONS

After the Recovery Console is installed, access it from the "Please select operating system to start" menu. The Recovery Console can also be started by starting the system with the Windows 2000 setup disks or the CD, and by selecting the Recovery Console option when prompted.

Lab Activity 13.7.5 Using the Windows 2000 Recovery Console

In this lab, you use the Windows 2000 Recovery Console to repair a damaged file.

The FIXMBR and FIXBOOT Commands

The *FIXMBR command* can be used with the Recovery Console to fix hard drive problems. This command repairs a master boot record (MBR). The syntax for this command is as follows:

FIXMBR [device name]

If the [device name] parameter is omitted, FIXMBR rewrites the MBR on the boot device. A device name can be specified to write an MBR to a different drive (such as a floppy disk drive or secondary hard drive). Use the MAP command to retrieve a list of device names. An example is as follows:

MAP \Device\HardDisk0

The *FIXBOOT command* writes a new boot sector to the system partition. The syntax for this command is as follows:

FIXBOOT [drive:]

Note that if the [drive:] option is not specified, FIXBOOT writes the boot sector to the default boot partition. Specify a different drive if a boot sector is to be written to a volume other than the default boot partition.

Troubleshooting Applications

This section includes the following topics:

- Troubleshooting DOS applications
- Troubleshooting Windows NT/2000 applications

Troubleshooting DOS Applications

Successfully troubleshooting the Windows operating system includes being able to troubleshoot the applications that are installed on the operating system. At least half of all troubleshooting calls are concerned with troubleshooting applications.

Windows Application Missing/Corrupt xx.dll or xx.vxd Files

Two important types of files are associated with the operating system and its applications: dll and vxd files. As previously discussed, knowing what these files do and knowing how to repair them are critical to the health of the system. If these files get deleted or become corrupt, the system applications no longer run properly, and the system might not be able to boot.

Another important set of files, called the dynamic link library (dll) files, was also previously mentioned. These small files store subroutines that either come with the application or are made by the programmer. The loss or corruption of dll files causes an application to lock up or prevents it from loading. Problems arise when a new application is installed and updates the shared dlls, creating a dll conflict. As a result of this conflict, older applications might not be able to handle the updated dll file and can fail to run.

System File Checker

The System File Checker (SFC) was also discussed earlier in this chapter. Figure 13-28 shows the SFC in DOS. The command-line utility can be used to scan the operating system files to ensure that they are the correct (original Microsoft) ones. Some applications can replace system files (for example, vxd or dll files) with different files of the same name, although this is less common with modern software. The result is an operating system that is no longer stable and might not boot after installing or uninstalling certain applications.

Figure 13-28 System File Checker

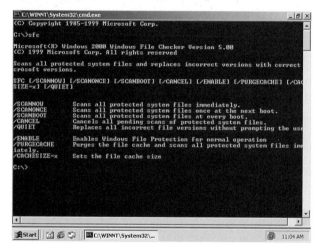

The SFC is a tool that allows users to scan their system and verify that versions of the protected system files are up to date. If a protected system file has moved or has been deleted, the SFC automatically replaces the file with the correct version from the dll cache folder. When the SFC utility is run and the copy in the system folder is replaced, the problem usually goes away. Unfortunately, many programs load their own copy in their own folder, thereby causing the problem.

Troubleshooting Windows NT/2000 Applications

Windows NT and 2000 often display application errors that are similar to those in the Windows 9X operating systems. For example, the application's properties might be incorrect, the Registry entries might be missing or corrupt, or the dll files might be corrupt. However, the Windows NT/2000 operating systems are usually part of an integrated network. This means that a host of new problems associated with the applications can occur. Users might not be able to gain access to folders, permissions that are set on files or folders might be too restrictive for the end user trying to access them, or the permissions might not be restrictive enough. The end users then might not be able to set NTFS permissions on the files or the folders containing the files.

Windows 2000 Task Manager

The *Windows 2000 Task Manager* is a tool that is used for troubleshooting applications. Access the Task Manager by pressing Ctrl-Alt-Del, and then click the Task Manager tab. As shown in Figure 13-29, the Task Manager displays a list of active applications and helps to identify the applications that are currently not responding. The Task Manager can switch to a particular application to troubleshoot it. Alternatively, you can choose to end the application.

Figure 13-29 Windows 2000 Task Manager

The Process tab provides information that is used to identify applications that can slow system operations. When an application crashes, it can hang up the system processor as well. This causes the rest of the system to lock up or slow to a state that makes it unusable. The Process tab indicates the percentage of CPU resources that a particular application is using. If an application is not responding and taking many CPU resources, shut down the application and see if the system returns to normal.

The Performance tab allows users to view a graphical interface that shows the processor performance and memory usage. Past and current usage can be viewed to obtain information about the applications that were running and at what point these applications caused the system to lock up.

Windows Data Backup and Recovery

This section includes the following topics:

- Windows Registry backup and recovery tools
- Windows data and application backup and recovery tools
- Types of data backup procedures

Windows Registry Backup and Recovery Tools

The technician can encounter Windows blue screens (also referred to as the blue screen of death), pop-up boxes that report errors, and other messages that report the Registry is corrupt or cannot load a device. The only solution is to reinstall Windows, because the database or Registry has become corrupted. With proper backup and recovery tools, the operating system can be reinstalled and user data loss can be minimized. The method for backing up the Registry depends on the operating system being used.

Windows 95

Previous sections of this chapter discussed the system.dat and user.dat files. Typically, Windows 95 creates a backup copy of the Registry each time the operating system is started, whether successfully or unsuccessfully. It copies system.dat to system.da0 and user.dat to user.da0. If Windows 95 has not replaced either backup file with a corrupt Registry, these files can be restored. This would be the case if Windows 95 has not been restarted since the Registry became corrupt. Copy system.da0 to system.dat and user.da0 to user.dat to recover the last copy of the uncorrupted Registry files.

Windows 98/Me

Windows 98 does not copy the Registry to da0 files when the operating system starts. Instead, it provides a program called the Registry Checker. Once each day, the Registry Checker, SCANREGW, backs up the Registry to a cab file that it puts in C:\WINDOWS\ SYSBCKUP, which is a hidden folder. The first backup is named rb000.cab, the second backup is rb001.cab, and so on. The file with the most recent date is the latest backup.

The Registry Checker can also be forced to make additional backup copies of the Registry even if it has already made its daily copy. Find scanregw.exe in C:\WINDOWS, or start it quickly by choosing **Start, Run** and typing **SCANREGW** in the dialog box. After scanning the Registry for errors, SCANREGW asks if you want to make another backup of the Registry. Click Yes, and the Windows Registry Checker backs up the Registry to another cab file and displays a dialog box stating that it is finished. Click OK to close the Windows Registry Checker.

Windows NT 4.0

Windows NT 4.0 offers several ways to back up and recover the Registry or the individual hives in the Registry. A *hive* is a discrete body of Registry keys, subkeys, and values that are stored in a file. The easiest way to back up is to use the Emergency Repair Disk (ERD). The ERD copies local hive files found in %SYSTEMROOT%\ SYSTEM32\CONFIG to %SYSTEMROOT%\REPAIR. You have an option to copy them to a floppy disk as well. Use the Windows NT Resource Kit backup utilities or a third-party backup program to copy the hive files to tape.

When running the ERD from the Windows NT Backup utility, you have an option to back up current Registry hives to the repair directory on the system hard drive prior to creating the ERD floppy disk. If you choose this option, all Registry hives are copied to a directory called regback in %SYSTEMROOT%\REPAIR. This option also copies the current user's ntuser.dat file to this folder as well as the user-specific COM Classes portion of the user profile (to a file called usrclass.dat). This is equivalent to Windows NT 4.0 running rdisk.exe (recovery disk program) with the option to create the files on the hard drive instead of a floppy disk. If required, these saved Registry hives can be used during a system repair process.

Windows 2000

The Registry backup is included as part of the System State backup, which also includes critical boot files and, on domain controllers, the active directory database. To start the Windows 2000 Backup utility, choose **Start, Programs, Accessories, System Tools, Backup,** or choose **Start, Run** and type **NTBACKUP** in the dialog box. Figure 13-30 shows the screen that displays. When the Windows 2000 backup starts, the welcome page displays, along with wizards for automating the backup and restoration processes.

Figure 13-30 Windows 2000 Backup and Recovery

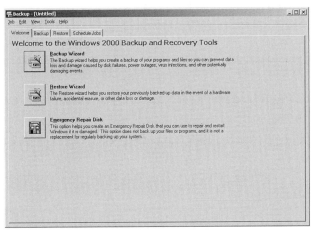

To back up the Registry using Windows 2000 Backup Utility, choose the Backup wizard or select the Backup tab. If the wizard is used, the next prompt asks you what to back up. If Windows 2000 Backup is running on a Windows 2000 domain controller, back up the active directory as well as the Registry and data by selecting the option to back up System State data, as shown in Figure 13-31.

Figure 13-31 Windows 2000 Backup System State

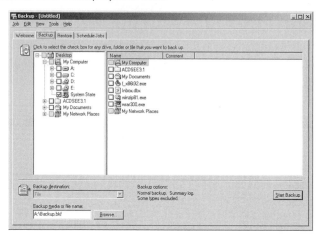

After choosing to back up the System State, select the media. Choose a disk, file, or tape. The Windows 2000 Backup utility backs up all the hives of interest in %SYSTEMROOT%\SYSTEM32\CONFIG, including Default, Software, System, SAM, and Security. However, it also backs up system files, user profiles, and any part of the system that is required to do a complete system restoration. This can potentially mean backing up a lot of data, depending on the size of the user profiles and Registry hive files that are stored on your machine. To perform a selected backup of the Registry hive files only, use a tool from the Resource Kit, such as REGBACK.

Lab Activity 13.9.3   Windows Registry Backup and Recovery

In this lab, you learn how to back up and recover the registry.

The option to create an ERD is available in the Windows 2000 backup utility. It backs up only three files: autoexec.nt, config.nt, and setup.log. The setup.log file is a list of the system files on the machine, and it includes a checksum value that indicates the correct version of the file. Use setup.log to restore corrupt system files when booting from a Windows 2000 CD, and choose the repair option.

Windows Data and Application Backup and Recovery Tools

There are many ways to back up data and applications. Windows backup utilities are installed with the operating system; third-party utilities can also be purchased to backup data and applications. The chosen backup method depends on the type and amount of data that are being backed up. In Windows 2000, use the Backup wizard that was described in the previous section by executing the NTBACKUP tool. With this tool, the first phase is to specify what to back up by choosing one of the following options:

- **Back up everything on my computer**—Backs up all files on the computer except the files that the Backup wizard excludes by default, such as certain power-management files.
- **Back up selected files, drives, or network data**—Backs up selected files and folders. When this option is chosen, the Backup wizard provides a hierarchical view of the computer and the network (through My Network Places).
- **Only back up the System State data**—Backs up important system components, such as the Registry and the boot files of the computer.

If Windows 9X is being used, use the BACKUP and RESTORE commands to back up data. The backup command, *backup.exe*, can be executed to begin the backup process. However, this program is not installed automatically when Windows 9X is installed. Install it by choosing **Start, Settings, Control Panel, Add/Remove Programs** and selecting the Windows Setup tab. When this backup program is executed, you are prompted to create a new backup job, open an existing backup job, or restore backed up files.

Types of Data Backup Procedures

Backup and restore operations can take various forms. In this section, some common examples, including normal, incremental, differential, and daily backup, are discussed. The first three backup procedures are the most widely used. Figure 13-32 shows the available backup types.

Normal Backup

Normal backup is also known as *full backup*. With normal backup, all files on the disk are stored to tape (or other backup medium), and the archive bit for all files is set to off or cleared.

It is impractical to run a full backup each day because of the time required to do so. Neither copy backup (discussed later) nor daily backup (discussed later) resets the archive bit, and both are used for backup of selected files.

Figure 13-32 Windows 2000 Backup Types

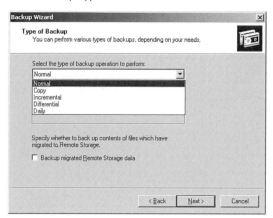

Incremental Backup

An *incremental backup* backs up all the files that have been created or modified since the last full backup. It is important to remember two things about an incremental backup: First, it works only in conjunction with a full (normal) backup, and second, any file that was created or modified has its archive bit turned back on so that it is saved to tape during the next incremental backup.

To perform an incremental backup, first do a full backup (for example, on Monday). This resets all the archive bits on the files. The following day, perform an incremental backup to a separate tape. This stores all the files modified on that day to tape and resets their archive bit to off. This process is repeated for all the other days of the week, each with a separate tape. You now have a complete backup of all files modified during that week. On the following Monday, start the process over again. Consider the following advantage and disadvantage:

- **Advantage**—This type of backup scheme requires the least amount of time per day to do the backup, so it has the least impact on the network resources in a networked environment.
- **Disadvantage**—If you need to restore a complete system backup, you must first restore the full backup from tape and then restore all the incremental backup tapes in order; this can take a great deal of time. In addition, if one of the tapes is bad, you lose that day's information.

Differential Backup

A *differential backup* backs up all the files that have been created or modified since the last full backup. This appears to be the same as an incremental backup, but in a differential backup, even though a file is saved to tape, the archive bit is not reset. This means that each time a differential backup is performed, all files that were modified or created since the last full backup are backed up.

To do a differential backup, first do a full backup (for example, on Monday) to reset all the archive bits on the files. The next day, a differential backup would be performed to a separate tape. This stores all the files modified on that day to tape, but it does not reset their archive bits. This process is repeated for all the other days of the week, each with the same tape. This process also provides a complete backup of network data in a networked environment. Consider the following advantage and disadvantage:

- **Advantage**—The differential backup requires only two tapes to make and restore the backup, if necessary.
- **Disadvantage**—The files that were backed up on previous days are stored again; this takes more of the network resources per day. Also, if the deferential backup tape is damaged and the restore was attempted on Friday, for example, four days' worth of data are lost.

Copy Backup

A *copy backup* backs up user-selected files to tape. This backup also does not reset the archive bit to off.

TEST TIP

Know the different types of backup options and how they are used.

Daily Backup

A *daily backup* backs up only the files that are modified on the day of the backup. This backup also does not reset the archive bit to off.

Windows-Specific Printer Software Troubleshooting

This section includes the following topics:

- Print spoolers
- Print queues
- Incorrect/incompatible printer drivers

Print Spoolers

Spooling is an acronym for simultaneous peripheral operations online. It refers to the process of loading documents into a buffer (usually an area on the hard drive) until the printer is ready. This allows users to place multiple print jobs into a queue and print them in the background instead of waiting for each job to finish. The Print Spooler is the printer managing function, and its support components are integrated into a single print-processing architecture.

Configuring the Print Spooler

The Print Spooler is installed in Windows when the printing services and printer are installed. The Print Spooler sends print data to the printer. The data are only moved to the printer at the appropriate time. Spooler settings can be changed by using the My Computer icon on the desktop or by choosing, **Start**, **Settings**, **Printers**.

Print Queues

The purpose of sharing a printer or using a network printer is to make the printer available for multiple users. However, the printer can only process one print job at a time. When a print job is sent to a printer while it is busy, that print job is held in the print queue, as shown in Figure 13-33.

Figure 13-33 The Print Queue

A *print queue* is a temporary holding area for print jobs that are fed to the printer only when it is ready for the next job. This queue is an area of memory that is set aside on the print server for managing print jobs. When a user decides to print a document, it is immediately sent to the print queue. If there are no other jobs in the queue, the job is processed immediately. Print queues, by default, use the first in, first out (FIFO) rule. This means that the print job that reaches the queue first receives the highest priority and is output before other jobs.

Configuring the Print Queue

The print queue is automatically set up and configured when the printer is installed. During printer installation, a queue is created so that the jobs being sent to the printer are temporarily held until the printer is ready to accept each job. Configure the print queue in the Properties page of the printer's dialog box. The size of the queue can be specified. Printing priorities can also be set so that high-priority jobs are printed before other jobs.

Clearing Print Jobs

The print queue is also a management tool that can be used to view and manipulate print jobs. The queue can show information about each print job and the progress of that job as it is being fed to the printer. This information includes the user's identification, job start time, and current status of the print job. The following print-job manipulation tasks can be performed in the print queue:

- **Delete print jobs**—The print queue can be used to delete single, multiple, or all the print jobs currently being held in the queue. This is useful if an error occurs or if multiple copies of a document are accidentally sent to the printer.

- **Rearrange print jobs**—Even though the print queue uses the FIFO rule, the order in which jobs are processed can be changed. Higher-priority print jobs can be placed closer to the top of the queue, while lower-priority jobs can be printed later.

- **Pause the printer**—It can be beneficial to temporarily pause the printing process. Choosing to pause printing puts the queue in a wait state. During this pause time, changes can be made within the queue (such as deletions or rearrangements), and changes can be made to the printer (such as changing the media type, ink, or toner). You can then "unpause" the print queue to resume processing the print jobs.

Redirecting Print Jobs

Print documents can be redirected to a different printer. For example, if a printer is connected to a faulty print device, the documents can be redirected so that users do not need to resubmit them. All print jobs for a printer can be redirected, but specific documents cannot. The new printer must use the same printer driver as the current printer.

Redirect documents to a different printer using the following steps:

Step 1   Open the Printers window, right-click the printer, and then click Properties.

Step 2   In the Properties dialog box, click the Ports tab, and then click Add Port.

Step 3   In the Available Port Types list, click Local Port, and then click the New Port button.

Step 4   In the Port Name dialog box, in the Enter A Port Name box, type the unique name for the printer to which the documents are being redirected (for example, \\prntsrv9\HPLaser4XL). Click OK to close the Port Name dialog box.

Step 5   Close the Printer Ports dialog box and the Printer Properties dialog box.

Incorrect/Incompatible Printer Drivers

A printer can only function properly if you have installed the proper printer driver. Drivers are used by the operating system to communicate with the system hardware. Without having the proper drivers installed, the system cannot print. Error messages usually appear, stating that the incorrect driver has been installed and that the operating system is unable to find the printer.

Incorrect Printer Drivers

Drivers are usually included with the purchase of a printer. However, these might not be the correct drivers. The current operating system might not accept the prepackaged drivers. Most manufacturers maintain a website that contains downloadable printer drivers for various operating systems.

In some cases, you might have the correct printer drivers and the printer still does not work. This usually means that the printer hardware is not compatible with the system hardware or with the system operating system.

Incorrect Printer Software Parameter Settings/Switches

TEST TIP

Understand the common printers problems that occur and know how to fix them.

In some instances, the correct driver might have been installed, but the printer still does not function. Some printers and printer drivers have numerous software and parameter settings or switches. In these instances, check the printer software and parameter settings. After installing the drivers, these settings or switches must sometimes be reconfigured to allow the printer to work properly. For example, there could be a nonstandard-size paper in the printer. The current settings might not recognize the paper size; therefore, the printer settings must be changed to recognize that size.

Windows-Specific Networking Software Connection Troubleshooting

This section includes the following topics:

- Error messages
- Incorrect parameter settings/switches
- Incorrect protocols or protocol properties
- Incorrect client or client properties
- Missing or incorrect bindings
- Incorrect service selection

- Incorrect primary network logon settings
- Incorrect computer name or workgroup name
- Network troubleshooting software utilities

Error Messages

This chapter has discussed troubleshooting the various error messages that display due to operating system issues, application issues, and driver issues. The technician is also called to troubleshoot software issues with networking.

Error: Cannot Log onto Network—NIC Not Functioning

One error that is typically related to networking issues is the "Cannot log onto Network—NIC not functioning" error message. This can be caused by several issues. The network interface card (NIC) might be defective or malfunctioning. In this case, open the system case and replace the NIC. Check the NIC on the back of the system, and verify that the NIC LED is illuminated. A green light usually means that the card is good and most likely does not need to be replaced.

Ping the card with its local loopback address, which is 127.0.0.1. (See the section, "The ping.exe Utility," later in this chapter.) This sends a packet out to the NIC and back to see if it is functioning properly. If a message displays stating that the packet was not received, the NIC is defective and must be replaced. If there is a reply to the ping, the NIC is working properly.

NIC Driver Software Issues

NIC driver software issues most likely include incorrect versions of the drivers, corrupt drivers, or incompatible drivers. In the event of an incorrect driver, contact the manufacturer to obtain the correct one. The correct driver can usually be downloaded from the manufacturer's website. Figure 13-34 shows the HP download site with the drivers that are available.

Most manufacturers have similar websites. If the driver is corrupt, get a clean version from the website. If there are other conflicts or errors with the operating system that produce an error, repair the cause of the conflict or error, and the driver might work properly. In the event of an incompatible driver error message, determine what version of the driver is installed, and update the driver to match the version that is required by the operating system.

TEST TIP

Know how to trouble-shoot a NIC.

Figure 13-34 The HP Driver Download Site

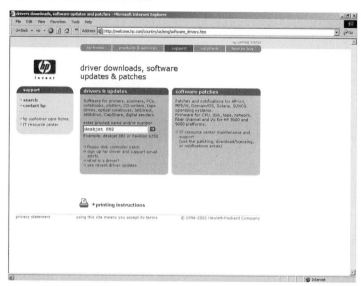

Incorrect Parameter Settings/Switches

Incorrect parameter settings/switches on the printer drivers applies in this case to NIC drivers. In some instances, NICs and NIC drivers are installed that have numerous amounts of configuration software and parameter settings or switches. The correct driver might have been installed, but the NIC might still not be functioning. In these instances, check the software settings that were provided. After installing the drivers, specific settings or switches must sometimes be reconfigured to allow the NIC to work properly. Figure 13-35 shows the advanced settings for a NIC.

Figure 13-35 Advanced NIC Settings

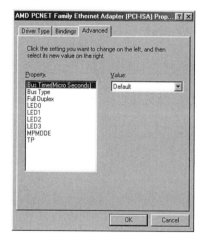

Incorrect Protocols or Protocol Properties

In order for the system to successfully log on to the network, the protocols must be set correctly. If they are not, the user cannot see the other computers on the network and cannot access the network resources. First, determine what type of protocol the network is using; it could be TCP/IP, IPX/SPX, or another protocol. Then access the Properties page of the network settings, as shown in Figure 13-36. Determine what protocol is installed, and decide if it is the correct one. Check the protocol properties to see if they are configured properly. For example, the correct protocol might be installed but the IP address settings might be wrong. These both must be correct to access the network.

Figure 13-36 The Network Properties Page

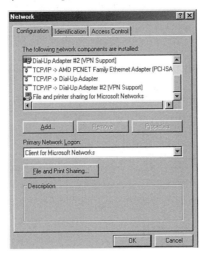

Incorrect Client or Client Properties

The proper client and/or client properties must also be installed. For example, if Novell NetWare Servers is running and the system needs to connect to resources on the Novell servers, the client for Novell networks must be installed on the Windows operating system. Without having the proper clients installed, users cannot access the resources on the servers. Figure 13-37 shows the screen for Microsoft client settings.

Figure 13-37 Microsoft Client Settings

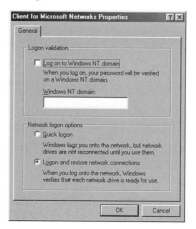

Missing or Incorrect Bindings

The technician must understand network bindings and know how they affect the networked computers. For example, to run two different protocols on two different network adapters in the server, network bindings must be manipulated. Also, to optimize network performance, change the order of bindings for the most efficient operation. Transport protocols are assigned to run on specific network adapters. When a protocol runs on a specific network adapter, the protocol and adapter are bound to each other. Typically, the most frequently used protocol is listed first in the protocol binding on the NIC. The act of creating this association between protocols and adapters is called *binding*. If the bindings are missing or incorrect, the NIC cannot function and the user cannot receive network access. The bindings screen is shown in Figure 13-38.

Figure 13-38 The Bindings Screen

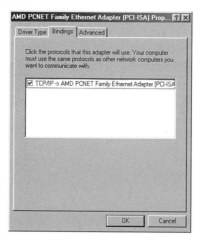

Incorrect Service Selection

Network services provide added features to clients on the network. For example, file and print sharing services are popular and are included in most networks. If these services are not installed, files or printers cannot be shared on the network. Figure 13-39 shows the screen that enables print sharing.

Figure 13-39 File and Print Sharing Services

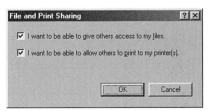

Incorrect Primary Network Logon Settings

Accessing the network starts with the logon feature, as shown in Figure 13-40. If a user cannot log on, he or she cannot access the desktop or the network resources. If this happens, log on with the administrator account and determine if the account settings are correct. Check the password setting, and make sure that the password has not expired or been locked out.

Figure 13-40 Primary Network Logon

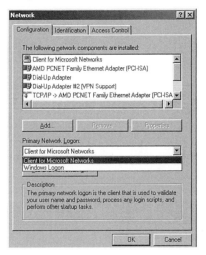

Incorrect Computer Name or Workgroup Name

Another problem that can keep the system from accessing the network is an incorrect computer name or workgroup name. Figure 13-41 shows the identification window. Common error messages that can display are as follows:

- User cannot see any other computers on the local network.
- User cannot see any other computers on different networks.
- Clients cannot see the DHCP server, but do have an IP address.

Figure 13-41   Network Identification Window

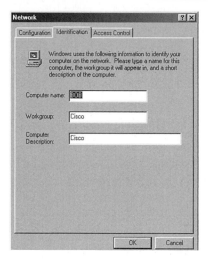

When a computer is added to the domain or network, an account is created in the domain to allow the computer to access resources in that domain. The computer name is registered, and if that name changes, the domain controller cannot recognize it and denies it access. The same rule applies to the workgroup name. The computer can be a part of a particular workgroup, and if it has an incorrect workgroup name, it is denied network access. Administrators can change the computer name and then recreate an account in the domain for the new name in case they forget the name of the computer.

Network Troubleshooting Software Utilities

To help troubleshoot network issues, Windows provides several tools to identify why an end user is unable to access the network. Some of more common tools were mentioned in Chapter 9, "Networking Fundamentals." Use these tools to test connections and settings, and to trace the route through which the packets are being sent on the network to identify where the problem lies.

The ping.exe Utility

The *ping.exe utility* is short for packet Internet groper utility. It is used to determine whether a specific IP address is accessible. The utility works by sending a packet to the specified address and waiting for a reply. PING is used primarily to troubleshoot Internet and network connections. Figure 13-42 shows the PING command.

Figure 13-42 The PING Command

Figure 13-43 shows an illustration of how the ping command works.

Figure 13-43 Ping Operation

Ping

The tracert.exe Utility

The *tracert.exe utility* traces a packet from the computer to an Internet host. It shows how many hops the packet requires to reach the host and how long each hop takes. If website pages are appearing slowly, use tracert.exe to identify where the longest delays are occurring. Figure 13-44 shows the TRACERT command.

The tracert.exe utility works by sending packets with time-to-live (TTL) fields. The TTL value specifies how many hops the packet is allowed before it is returned. When a packet cannot reach its destination because the TTL value is too low, the last host returns the packet and identifies itself. By sending a series of packets and increasing the TTL value with each successive packet, tracert.exe determines all the intermediary hosts.

Figure 13-44 The TRACERT Command

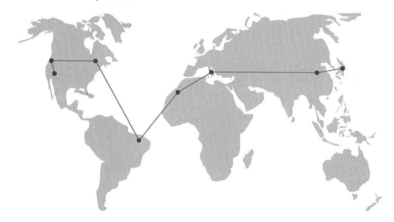

Figure 13-45 illustrates how the trace route command works.

Figure 13-45 Trace Route Operation

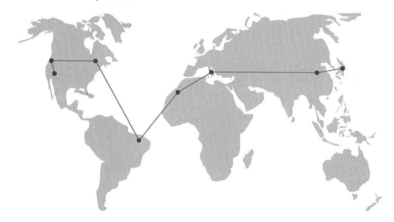

The winipcfg.exe Utility

The *winipcfg.exe utility* is short for Windows IP configuration. It is a tool that allows the technician to view the basic IP networking settings of a Windows 95, Windows 98, or Windows Me computer. This utility does not work on Windows NT or 2000 systems; technicians must use ipconfig.exe on these systems. IP addresses are allocated and assigned by the dynamic host configuration protocol (DHCP). (Each computer must have an IP address to interact with the Internet.) When the system boots up, it sends a request for an IP address to the DHCP servers. A DHCP server finds an address that is not in use and assigns it to the computer. Figure 13-44 shows the IP configuration from the WINIPCFG utility.

Figure 13-46   The WINIPCFG Utility

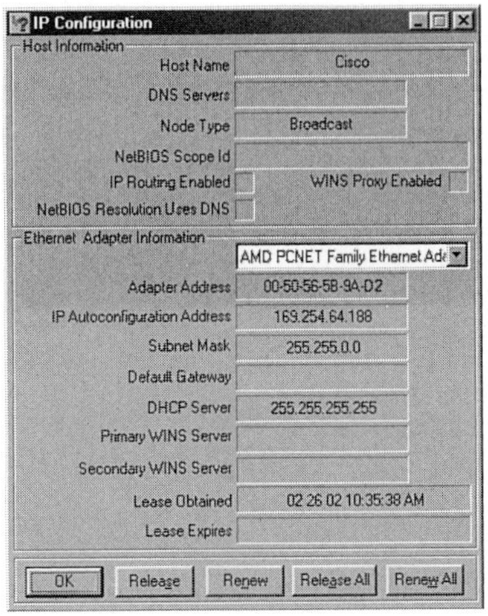

The WINIPCFG utility lets the technician obtain new IP information (such as an address, mask, and gateway) without rebooting. Select the Release button, which releases the IP information. Then select the Renew button to assign the computer a new IP address from the DHCP server. Again, this can be done without rebooting the system. Frequently, requesting new information can help with IP-related problems.

To run WINIPCFG, choose **Start, Run** and type **WINIPCFG** in the dialog box. This utility can also be run from a DOS prompt.

The ipconfig.exe Utility

The *ipconfig.exe utility* is the Windows NT/2000 equivalent of the winipcfg.exe utility in Windows 95, 98, and Me. The ipconfig.exe utility performs the same functions in that it allows users to view all the IP address information as well as the WINS server addresses, DNS server addresses, and the DHCP server addresses. Use the /RELEASE and the /RENEW switches to obtain new IP addresses. The main difference is that the IPCONFIG command must run from the DOS prompt. It cannot be typed in the Start menu's Run dialog box. Figure 13-47 shows the IPCONFIG utility run from the DOS prompt.

Figure 13-47 The IPCONFIG Utility

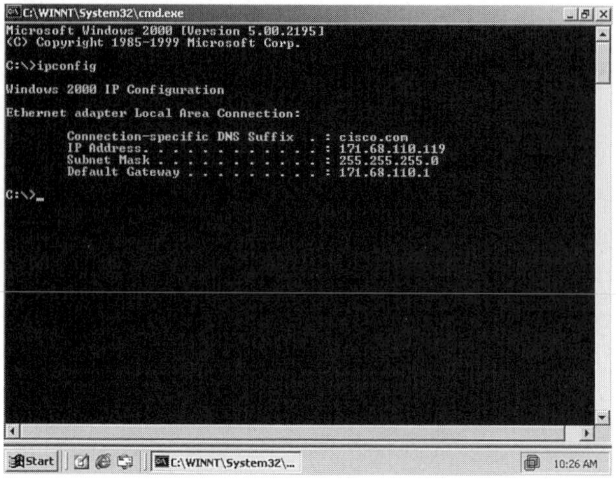

The Net View Command

The *Net View command* displays a list of domains, a list of computers, and a list of resources for a computer. This command, typed at the DOS prompt, performs all the browsing functions that are available in Network Neighborhood or My Computer, except that a user cannot view a list of workgroups.

The syntax for the Net View command is as follows:

net view [\\computername | /domain[:domainname]]

Typing **net view** with no parameters displays a list of computers in the domain. Other components of the command are as follows:

- \\computername is the computer name whose resources (shares) are to be displayed.
- /domain[:domainname] is the domain whose computer names are to be viewed.

Using the /domain switch displays all domain names on the network.

The netstat.exe Utility

TEST TIP

Know the utilities that are used to troubleshoot a network.

The ***netstat.exe utility*** (short for network statistics) displays the current TCP/IP network connections and protocol information for the computer. The NETSTAT command symbolically displays the contents of various network-related data structures. There are a number of output formats, depending on the options for the information presented. For example, this command can be used to display a list of active sockets for each protocol being used. It can present the contents of other network data structures according to the option selected. The NETSTAT utility can also continuously display information regarding packet traffic on the configured network interfaces. Figure 13-48 shows the NETSTAT command, which is run from the DOS prompt.

Figure 13-48 The NETSTAT Command

Windows 9X/NT/2000 Help

This section includes the following topics:

- Help and troubleshooting files
- Troubleshooting and information resources

Help and Troubleshooting Files

All the Windows 9X, NT, and 2000/XP operating systems come with built-in help files that provide assistance with basic system troubleshooting tasks. The Windows 9X and 2000/XP help files are more comprehensive than the Windows NT help files. Access the Help Files utility from the Start menu or from the Help icon located on the main Toolbar. The help and troubleshooting files contain several entries regarding common Windows issues.

The Windows 98 and higher operating systems have increased the help file database and tools as well as incorporated an integrated web browser to access online help. The online access provides a vast amount of online resources from Microsoft and other sources. Figure 13-49 shows the help screen.

Figure 13-49   Windows Help Screen

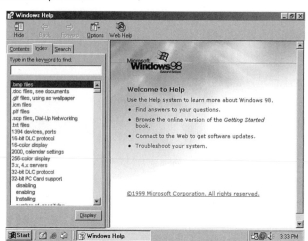

Troubleshooting and Information Resources

Along with the help and troubleshooting files that come with the operating system, other resources are available. For issues not found in the help and troubleshooting files, consult the Windows 9X/NT/2000 Resource Kits and the various Internet help URLs.

Windows 9X/NT/2000 Resource Kits

The Windows 9X/NT/2000 Resource Kits provide a solution for most troubleshooting issues. They provide CDs and textbooks with thousands of pages of in-depth technical information that provide reference material when researching a problem. As well as the information that the resource kits contain, These kits also provide many added features and troubleshooting tools that can be installed on computer systems. For example, they provide hundreds of additional utilities that are used to troubleshoot and maintain a network. These Resource Kits usually must be bought separately, because they are not included with the operating system installation CD.

Internet Help URLs

Additional help and troubleshooting aids are found on the Internet. Many websites provide information and topics regarding common Windows operating system issues. For example, the Microsoft website maintains *Microsoft TechNet*, a large database of troubleshooting pages. Other websites dedicated to troubleshooting and providing help for common operating system issues can be found by using the search feature in your browser.

Summary

This chapter discussed troubleshooting software. Important concepts to retain from this chapter are as follows:

- Take specific steps to determine the source of an error. These steps include defining whether the issue is hardware or software related, soliciting the end user, reproducing the error, and identifying changes to the system.

- When dealing with system boot problems, an important tool to use is the bootable disk. Booting to a floppy disk allows the technician to recopy files, inspect the hard drive partitions, or reformat the hard drive. It also provides the ability to navigate through the files on the disk.

- The MBR resides on the first sector of the hard drive, and if it has been damaged, the computer cannot boot. The FDISK /MBR command is used to rewrite the MBR so that the system can boot.

- DOS error messages typically occur when the operating system identifies a problem or when an end user attempts to run an application that the operating system cannot recognize. Error messages include bad or missing commands, configuration files errors, and memory errors.

- A startup disk is created to start the computer when the operating system has become corrupt. Shutdown problems are usually caused by an application that remains running in the background. Press Ctrl-Alt-Del to open the Task Manager, which allows the user to end an application that has stopped working or to restart the computer.

- A GPF occurs when one of the operating system applications attempts to access an unallocated memory location. Running applications that are not written for the Windows operating system, selecting the wrong machine or network during installation, or using incorrect versions of DOS in the system can cause a GPF.

- Safe mode is a Windows troubleshooting tool. This mode allows the technician to access the Device Manager and run system utilities. In Safe mode, autoexec.bat and config.sys are not loaded; the Registry, load=, and run= lines are not loaded in win.ini; and the [Boot] and [386Enh] sections are not loaded in system.ini.

- The Registry Editor is accessed by typing **REGEDIT** or **REGEDT32** in the Run dialog box. Six Registry files contain all the system configuration information. Understanding the Registry subtree keys helps you to troubleshoot and maintain the computer. Using Registry editing tools cleans the Registry of unused files that can cause problems and degrade the system performance.

- One of the most important tasks to perform is a regular backup. Backups include normal or full backup, which stores all files, and incremental backup, which saves the files that have been created or modified since the last full backup. A differential backup is the same as an incremental backup except that the archive bit is not reset. Copy backup backs up user-selected files but does not reset the archive bit to off.

- Device drivers are key for computer components such as the NIC, printer, etc. The manufacturer's website is the most reliable place to find a current device driver. Download the driver from the website, and install it in your computer.

- Windows provides help files. Help is available as part of the operating system and can be accessed from the Start menu. You can also find help information on the Microsoft website as well as from various independent websites.

Check Your Understanding

The following are review questions for the A+ exam. Answers can be found in Appendix B, "Answers to Check Your Understanding Review Questions."

1. What the three things make a successful technician?

   A. Communication skills, local employees, and smart dresser

   B. Communication skills, technical skills, and troubleshooting skills

   C. Sense of humor, large inventory of parts, and resource kits

   D. Location, location, location

2. When troubleshooting an end user's computer, which item should not be explored?

   A. When the problem occurred

   B. If the problem occurs often

   C. If the problem can be resolved by rebooting

   D. The user's knowledge of computers

3. When isolating a problem during the troubleshooting process, which item should not be performed?

   A. Reproduce the problem

   B. Classify the problem

   C. Reconfirm the problem

   D. Remove all the internal components before doing anything else

4. What is the name of the MS-DOS–based automated memory optimizer?

   A. MEM

   B. Memmaker

   C. REM

   D. MSD

5. Which key is pressed to skip autoexec.bat and config.sys when the message "Starting MS-DOS" displays?

   A. F5

   B. F6

   C. F7

   D. F8

6. Which of the following utilities can recover files from damaged disks?

   A. Recover and FDISK

   B. Recover and Unformat

   C. ScanDisk and Unformat

   D. ScanDisk and CHKDSK

7. If you have ScanDisk, you do not need to run which utility?

   A. FORMAT

   B. CHKDSK

   C. FDISK

   D. Volume

8. Which utility can be used to increase access speed by rearranging files and directories on the hard drive?

   A. Sort

   B. ScanDisk

   C. Disk Defragmenter

   D. FORMAT

9. An "Insufficient memory to run this application" error message displays. What should you do?

    A. Install a hard drive with more space.

    B. Increase the size of the swap file.

    C. Buy more ROM chips.

    D. Buy a new computer.

10. Which of the following software problems does not corrupt files?

    A. Faulty hard drive

    B. Downloading problems

    C. Defective writes during a copy

    D. Disk Defragmenter problems

11. What is the most common symptom of a corrupt file?

    A. Overheating

    B. Inconsistent lockups

    C. Consistent lockups

    D. Unable to start computer

12. What command allows you to access the Registry from the Start, Run dialog box?

    A. Registry

    B. REGEDIT

    C. SYSEDIT

    D. SYSTEM

13. What is the first utility you should run if a computer locks up?

    A. Registry

    B. ScanDisk

    C. FORMAT

    D. Unlock

14. Why does a GPF occur?

    A. The hard disk cannot store any more data.

    B. An application is using too many system resources.

    C. An application is trying to write to a memory space that is occupied by another application.

    D. A memory module in the computer is defective.

15. What causes a page fault in Windows 98?

    A. Corrupt device drivers

    B. Poorly written applications

    C. Faulty hard drives

    D. All of the above

16. A NIC was working properly but is now causing connectivity problems. What do you check first?

    A. Just install a new NIC

    B. Upgrade the NIC driver

    C. Contact the vendor for any updates and patches

    D. Verify that the NIC is installed and seated properly

17. Which two files do not load in Safe mode?

    A. autoexec.bat and config.sys

    B. system.ini and autoexec.bat

    C. config.sys and Memmaker

    D. autoexec.ini and Memmaker

18. Which item is not displayed in the resource window for a device in the Device Manager?

    A. IRQ

    B. I/O address

    C. Settings button

    D. Delete settings button

19. Which utility is used to determine whether a specific IP address is accessible?

    A. tracert.exe

    B. winipcfg.exe

    C. ping.exe

    D. netstat.com

20. Which utility traces a packet from the computer to an Internet host?

    A. tracert.exe

    B. winipcfg.exe

    C. ping.exe

    D. netstat.com

Key Terms

autoexec.bat   Contains a list of DOS commands that are automatically executed when DOS is loaded into the system.

backup.exe   Used to start the backup process.

bootable disk   Troubleshooting tool that allows the computer to boot from a disk when the hard drive does not boot.

bootlog.txt   A file that contains the system information that is collected as the system is booting up.

chkdsk.exe   A command-line tool that is used to recover lost allocation units from the hard drive.

command interpreter   Also known as command.com in Windows 95/98 and cmd.exe in Windows NT/2000, it displays the DOS prompt and executes the commands typed in.

config.sys   A file that contains setup or configuration instructions for the computer system.

copy backup   Backs up user-selected files. It does not reset the archive bit.

daily backup   Backs up only the files that are modified on the day of the backup. It does not reset the archive bit.

defrag.exe   Used to rewrite all the files on the hard drive contiguously, making it easier and faster for the hard drive to retrieve data.

detcrash.log   A file that is created if the system crashes during the hardware-detection phase of the startup process.

detlog.txt   Used to read the information that is generated when the detcrash.log file is created.

DEVICEHIGH=   Command used to load drivers into the upper memory area instead of loading them into conventional memory.

Device Manager   Used to disable, uninstall, and update device drivers.

differential backup   Backs up all the files that have been created or modified since the last full backup. It does not rest the archive bit.

Dr. Watson utility   Used to isolate and correct GPFs.

dynamic link library (dll) file   A small files that store subroutines for a program.

edit.com   A Windows troubleshooting tool that can view and edit configuration files such as autoexec.bat and config.sys and ini files.

emm386.exe   Memory-management program that provides the system with access to the upper memory area of RAM.

Event Viewer   Used to monitor system events, application events, and security events in Windows 9X.

fdisk.exe   Used to delete and create partitions on the hard drive.

FDISK /MBR   Command used to create or rewrite the MBR so that the system can boot.

FIXBOOT   Command that writes a new boot sector to the system partition.

FIXMBR   Command used with the Recovery Console to fix hard drive problems.

format.exe   Used to erase a hard drive.

full backup   Also called a normal backup, it backs up all files on a disk.

general protection fault (GPF)   An error that occurs when one of the operating system applications attempts to access an unallocated memory location.

Group Policy Editor (GPE)   Used to edit the configuration settings in a network environment.

hardware   The physical components of the computer.

hardware failure   A malfunction of a computer component.

hidden file   An attribute that can be applied so that a file cannot be seen by users.

himem.sys   Memory-management program that manages the extended memory above 1024 KB.

HKEY_CLASSES_ROOT   Contains software configuration data of all the software that is installed on the computer.

HKEY_CURRENT_CONFIG   Contains data on the active hardware profile that is selected during the boot process. This information is used to configure settings for the device drivers to load and for the display resolution to use.

HKEY_CURRENT_USER   Contains data about the user who is currently logged on to the computer. Retrieves a copy of each user account that is used to log on to the computer and stores it in the Registry.

HKEY_LOCAL_MACHINE   Contains all configuration data for the local computer, including hardware and operating system data such as bus type, system memory, device drivers, and startup control data. Applications, device drivers, and the operating system use these data to set the computer configuration. The data in this subtree remain constant, regardless of the user.

HKEY_USERS   Contains the system default settings that are used to control individual user profiles and environments such as desktop settings, the Windows environment, and custom software settings.

illegal operation   Error message in Windows that indicates that the system has encountered an problem.

incremental backup   Backs up all the files that have been created or modified since the last full backup.

ipconfig.exe   A utility that is the Windows NT/2000 equivalent of the winipcfg.exe utility found in Windows 95, 98, and Me. It performs the same functions as the winipcfg.exe utility in that it allows users to view all the IP address information as well as the WINS server addresses, DNS server addresses, and the DHCP server addresses.

LASTDRIVE=   Command contained in the config.sys file. It specifies the maximum number of drives the system can access.

master boot record (MBR)   The program responsible for starting the boot process. It determines which partition is used for booting the system and transfers control to the boot sector of that partition, which continues the boot process.

Microsoft TechNet   A large database of troubleshooting pages found on the Microsoft website.

msconfig.exe   A command-line tool that is used to interactively load device drivers and software options.

netstat.exe (network statistics)   A utility that displays the current TCP/IP network connections and protocol information for the computer.

Net View   A command that displays a list of domains, a list of computers, and a list of resources for a computer.

ping.exe (packet Internet groper)   A utility used to determine whether a specific IP address is accessible.

poledit.exe   Used to set up different security restrictions for different users.

print queue   A temporary holding area for print jobs that are waiting to be fed to the printer.

Recovery Console   A command-line interface used to perform a variety of troubleshooting and recovery tasks in Windows 2000.

scandskw.exe   ScanDisk for Windows checks the integrity of the media to repair problems that occur.

scanreg.exe   Used to scan the Registry for corruption.

setuplog.txt   A file that is created during the installation process and contains the system setup information.

software   The operating system and programs that run on the computer.

spooling   An acronym for simultaneous peripheral operations online, it refers to the process of loading print jobs into a buffer (usually an area on a hard drive) until the printer is ready for a job.

sysedit.exe   Used to modify text files such as the system ini files as well as config.sys and autoexec.bat.

system.da0   Created when Windows successfully boots. This file is a backup of the system.dat file. If the system.dat file gets corrupted or deleted, rename the system.da0 file to system.dat to restore the Registry.

system.dat   A file that holds hardware, computer-specific profiles, and setting information.

system.ini   A file that contains hardware-setting information for the Windows configuration drivers. When the operating system needs to reference information about the hardware, it uses the system.ini file.

System File Checker (SFC)   A command-line utility that scans the operating system files to ensure that they are the correct ones.

Task Manager   Displays active applications and identifies those applications that are not responding so that they can be shut down.

tracert.exe   A utility that traces a packet from the computer to an Internet host.

user.da0   Created when Windows successfully boots. This file is a backup of the user.dat file. If the user.dat file gets corrupted or deleted, rename the user.da0 file to user.dat to restore the Registry.

user.dat   File that contains all the user-specific information.

virtual device driver (vxd) file   A file that takes the place of the DEVICE= and LOADHIGH= commands.

win.com   A Registry file that controls the initial environment checks and loads Windows 95 core components.

win.ini   A file that contains parameters that can be altered to change the Windows environment or software settings to suit the user's preferences. This file is a software initialization file for Windows. It contains information about some Windows defaults, the placement of windows, the color settings for the screen, and available ports, print-ers, fonts, and software applications.

winipcfg.exe (Windows IP configuration)   A tool that allows the technician to view the basic IP networking settings of a Windows 95, Windows 98, or Windows Me computer.

WIN switch   Allows the technician to start Windows from the command line.

Appendix A

The Information Technology Professional

The Cisco Networking Academy Program has driven great change in the information technology (IT) workforce in the last five years. To a significant extent, the Networking Academy Program enables students to enter the IT workforce with a good salary by pursuing a series of certifications within certain IT career tracks. IT careers can be classified as software, hardware, and nontechnical. There can be overlaps, but the categories in the matrix below are fairly representative—most IT jobs fit into one of these categories. Some careers are inherently hybrid, such as that of the network engineer and the network administrator.

What Is IT

IT touches almost every aspect of the modern-day work world. Computers are now used in almost every occupation imaginable. If IT is defined as any job that uses computers or electronic devices, this would mean that IT encompasses almost all jobs! A more accurate interpretation of IT includes only those jobs where the primary focus of the job is the computer itself, the computer software, or the electronic devices. A career in IT is one where the product of the work is an electronic device, a software program, or information. An IT career might also be a parallel effort, such as sales or marketing of the computer-related product.

For the purposes of this book, the term *information technology* means "that which concerns the advance of computer science and technology, and the design, development, installation, and implementation of information systems and applications."

Careers in IT and Setting Career Goals

The range of careers in IT is very broad. Something can be found for every personality in a wide salary range. Do you want to be a computer programmer? A system administrator? A hardware designer? A network engineer? A project manager? These are just a sample of the careers in the IT industry.

All IT careers have a technical component in common. But keep in mind that companies employing IT workers also offer a wide range of jobs that are not directly technical in nature, for example, sales and marketing professionals, accountants, financial analysts, attorneys, managers, and executives.

IT professionals usually have a strong technical ability, but this doesn't necessarily imply a college or university education. Various career tracks, such as MCSE and CCNA/CCNP/CCIE certifications, are options that you can pursue as a means of entering the IT industry. However, it is often helpful to have a college degree when entering this field, especially in software development, engineering, and management positions.

Some IT job titles can be misleading. For example, a person can become a network engineer or system engineer for some companies without having a college degree if he or she has the appropriate certifications and experience. Other types of engineering careers, such as computer, electrical, mechanical, and civil engineering, require bachelor's, master's, or doctor's degrees. Knowing your personal strengths and interests makes it easier to plan a career in the IT world. It's easiest to enter the IT industry as a young person with a college education or a set of appropriate certifications, but many people have successfully entered the field later in life. Those who choose to make the transition from careers unrelated to IT often take specialized training in colleges or technical schools. If you're still in school, prepare for a career in the IT industry by focusing on math and the sciences as much as possible. The analytical thinking that is required in math and science is exactly the type of thinking that is required for the troubleshooting and problem-solving that are common in IT jobs.

Communication skills are also very important in the IT world, just as they are in most professions. These skills include one-on-one communication, interviewing skills, and public speaking. They are learned by practice and in courses in English and communications.

Career Paths in IT

The job market in the IT sector continues to grow rapidly (see *www.itprc.com/jobs.htm*). The U.S. government's projections show that the fastest-growing occupations in the IT sector are as follows (see *http://stats.bls.gov/news.release/ecopro.t06.htm*):

- Computer software engineers, applications
- Computer support specialists
- Computer software engineers, systems software
- Network and computer systems administrators
- Network systems and data communications analysts
- Desktop publishers
- Database administrators
- Computer systems analysts

The following list, taken from the University of Washington's IT career page, is a sample of careers in information technology (see *www.washington.edu/students/it/careers.htm*):

- Computer engineer
- Computer programmer
- Computer scientist
- Computer user
- Database administrator
- Database specialist
- Interface designer
- Network specialist
- Software engineer
- Statistician
- Systems analyst
- Technical communicator
- Web designer

Nontechnical IT careers include accounting, sales, marketing, law, and project management; however, the focus in this book is on technically oriented IT careers.

The most popular software jobs include networking, Internet/intranet and e-commerce development, network security, and database administration.

The sections that follow provide brief descriptions of some key IT careers in software.

Programmers

Computer programmers write computer code that makes the computer perform various functions. This requires much attention to detail and a strong technical aptitude. Programmers write software according to the specifications determined by systems analysts.

Systems Analysts and Software Engineers

Systems analysts produce specifications for adapting existing systems or creating new ones. The design process is generally lengthy and complex. Note that a system analyst can be involved with overseeing the development of hardware devices, if this is part of the overall system.

Technical Writers

Technical writers produce a variety of technical publications, including instructional materials, technical manuals, product documentation, and so on. They might produce materials to assist end users with hardware devices and software applications, such as online help, user's manuals, installation manuals, guided tours, and tutorials.

Multimedia Developers

Multimedia developers have the skills of the computer programmer and the artist. They produce multimedia documents that can contain graphics, text, and digital audio and video with interactivity.

Multimedia development is a rapidly changing field. New advances in hardware and software continue to improve the functionality of multimedia development tools.

Multimedia is still in its infancy. The people who are making multimedia work are taking newly created tools and inventing the ways in which the tools are used.

Those who work as multimedia developers probably started in other careers. They could have been graphic designers, software engineers, writers, publishers, or educators, or might have worked in one of the many other fields that contribute to what we think of as multimedia.

Interface Designers

Human–computer interaction is a relatively new field of research in computer science that addresses ergonomic and interaction issues in computing. Interface designers use human factor analysis, graphic design theory, and other methodologies to design the user interface of a computer system. The user interface—the communication system between the user and the computer—determines how a user is led through a program or process, providing a likely path or paths for the user to navigate. The interface also provides a conceptual structure for organizing large amounts of information. Furthermore, the user interface offers tools for filtering information and then retrieving it at a later point, according to a predetermined set of criteria.

Web Developers

Web developers design, produce, build, and support websites and e-commerce sites. Web development isn't a single function but rather a series of functions. Some functions overlap, for example, programming and database administration. Other functions, such as web design and content management, generally don't overlap, but those responsible for either function need to work closely together.

Because of the variety of skills brought to bear on building and maintaining a website, web development is a difficult job to define. The functions performed by a web developer vary widely. They include website design, database administration, software programming, content management, e-marketing, information architecture, and production management.

Web developers are charged with designing, building, programming, populating with content, marketing, supporting, and managing a website. Developers manage server migrations, download times, and site crashes, in a virtual space driven by databases where user experience (measured in page views, site traffic, time spent surfing, and conversion to membership or paying customer) is the key to a website's success.

Database Developers

Database developers follow a product development cycle that is similar to that of software engineers. In general the development cycle of a database is as follows:

1. **Gather user requirements**—At the beginning of the cycle, a database developer interviews the people who will be using the database to find out what kinds of queries and reports the users need.

2. **Design the database**—A web designer or graphics designer might work with the database developer to create a storyboard, that is, a series of pictures showing how users will access the computer database and what kinds of answers they expect from a query. This storyboard is shown to users for feedback.

3. **Build the database**—The database developer builds the database, and a data entry person puts all the information into the database.

4. **Gather feedback**—Once the database is ready to use, the database developer requests feedback on how it works.

5. **Modify the database**—Depending on the feedback received, the database developer can make modifications to the database.

6. **Maintain the database**—Eventually, when the database is in production, a database administrator takes over. This person is responsible for making sure that the database runs smoothly, is backed up regularly, and is kept up to date.

Related IT Careers

The software careers described typically require a college education, with the possible exception of multimedia and web development. Courses or degrees in math or computer science are recommended for these careers.

Many IT careers are related to electrical and computer engineering. Computer engineers and electrical engineers design, build, test, and evaluate new computer chips, circuit boards, computer systems, and peripheral devices. The goal of computer engineering is to produce computing devices that run reliably, efficiently, and economically.

Different kinds of engineers handle different aspects of the production process. Development engineers often work in research and development departments of computer firms, and conceive of new product ideas. Design engineers work with development engineers to design the product. Production engineers supervise the production process (and associated staff) in manufacturing the product once it has been designed. Quality assurance engineers control the production process, making sure that the product is manufactured properly and that no flaws occur in production.

Device development engineers develop electronic components, such as transistors, integrated circuits, Application-Specific Integrated Circuits (ASIC), etc. Most circuits are built on silicon chips, making the circuitry microscopic. Chip designers, integrated circuit designers, and logic designers are all involved in circuit design. Computer hardware is designed by combining circuitry so that the various functions of the component circuits work together to perform larger functions. Much of computer engineering takes place on the level of microprocessors and other specialized boards (for example, graphics, audio, and networking boards) that add functionality to a computer. The first task of a design engineer is to determine the precise function of the planned device. Having established the project specifications, the engineer (or more likely, the team of engineers and other personnel) designs the components, assembles them, tests the new device, and evaluates the design for its overall effectiveness, cost, reliability, and safety. This process applies regardless of the end product.

Engineers often use computer-aided design (CAD) software to produce and analyze designs. CAD software is powerful design software that automates the drafting and design process for mechanical and electronic applications. With CAD software, engineers can create three-dimensional models of objects that can then be manipulated by computer. This allows the engineer to experiment with different designs that would be too costly to produce as prototypes.

Computer and electrical engineers design computers of all descriptions, but they also design industrial robots, industrial automated systems, and artificial intelligence–based hardware systems. These engineering jobs require bachelor's degrees or graduate (master's or doctor's) degrees.

With the rapid change in technology, job titles come and go. Some careers in the IT industry don't lend themselves to categorization. Many of these jobs are hybrid jobs; they are not only difficult to classify, but they also have no prescribed mechanism for entry into the field. Many of these careers do not require a college education and can be entered through the training and certification process. However, a college education is always an advantage in getting a job and usually commands a higher salary.

One hybrid career is that of the network engineer. A network engineer is responsible, either as a consultant or as a corporate employee, for troubleshooting and maintaining computer networks. This involves configuring networking equipment such as routers and switches. A network engineer or system engineer can also play a critical role in the design process of a computer network for a company that is upgrading or expanding its network. Most of the work of a network engineer is software based, but the software is integrated into various types of network hardware with which the network engineer must also be familiar.

Whereas a network administrator usually works at a single location with the responsibility for a single network or internetwork, the network engineer has wider responsibilities and can work across several sites with more than one company.

Another hybrid career is that of system administrator. A system administrator is responsible for maintaining a multiuser computer system, including a local-area network (LAN). Typical duties are as follows:

- Adding and configuring new workstations
- Setting up user accounts
- Installing system-wide software
- Performing procedures to prevent the spread of viruses
- Allocating mass storage space

The system administrator is sometimes called the *sys admin*. Small organizations might have just one sys admin, while larger enterprises usually have a team of system administrators. The sys admin might work on several operating systems or platforms, such as Windows 2000 Server and Solaris.

Another category of IT careers involves the support of products that have already been released. Desktop support, technical support, and help desk positions are closely related and sometimes interchangeable. When an end user has problems, it is the job of the technical support personnel to help that person. Technical support and help desk positions are often a "foot in the door" to an IT company, and they can lead to more challenging, higher-paying positions.

Software testing, another key IT job, is critical for the success of a software program. In this area, software bugs are discovered and eliminated before the product is released to the end user. Many careers are available in software testing.

Working as a technical assistant to an engineer or project manager is an excellent means of entry into the IT industry. This type of position often leads to better opportunities, so it is wise to take such a position when entering the IT field.

A technical trainer is highly valued, because someone has to teach all these IT experts and keep them up to date with the latest technologies! Becoming a trainer in the IT field usually involves some college education, a set of required certifications, and verification of one's teaching ability.

This list of IT careers is far from complete, but the major categories have been covered. You should have a good idea of the types of jobs that are available, and perhaps have enough information to decide which IT career is best for you.

In many cases, there is a strong association between careers and personality types. (See *www.haleonline.com/psych/* or *www.ibiblio.org/pub/academic/psychology/ alt.psychology.personality/profiles/*.) Understanding your personality type can help you choose a career, but don't take this too seriously—there's always room for change.

Try to avoid locking yourself into a particular career just because you think that's what you're supposed to do. It helps to remain open to the idea of changing careers as you move through your work life. Changing careers has become common. The U.S. Department of Labor (DOL) has determined that workers will have 8 to 10 jobs on average prior to their retirement. The DOL also notes that job changing declines with age and work experience. (See "Report on the American Workforce" at *http:// stats.bls.gov/opub/rtaw/rtawhome.htm*.)

Degree Programs in IT

Traditionally, colleges or universities were the only avenues to a professional career. For some careers, such as medicine, law, or academia, this is still true. However, the IT explosion over the last few decades has changed many traditions. For example, it is now fairly common for colleges and universities to accept work experience for college credit.

It is now possible for an individual to become an IT professional and command a relatively high salary without having a formal postsecondary education. (Remember that a college education always improves your opportunities in the IT world and in other careers.)

If you pursue a career in engineering (for example, as an electrical or computer engineer), you must complete a four-year degree in the appropriate field. To become a software developer, programmer, or systems analyst, you are almost always required to have at least a four-year degree in computer science or information systems. To become an IT project manager, you often need a four-year degree in business administration. However, project managers come from a broad range of backgrounds, so the degree requirements are somewhat flexible.

Just as it improves your opportunities in general to get a college degree, the more advanced your degree, the better your chances of getting a job in the field of your choice with the salary range you desire. Unfortunately, nothing is certain. However, you improve your chances of doing what you want to do and getting paid what you want to earn by obtaining an advanced degree.

Many two-year college programs are available for entry into the IT workforce. Community colleges and junior colleges have IT programs that are designed solely to teach you to work in the IT world. These schools often have placement services to help you find a job after graduation. These colleges also have internships with local companies that are part of earning your degree. These internships can open the door to a new career.

Certification Tracks in IT

Certification programs, such as MCSE and CCNA/CCNP/CCIE, have driven the greatest change in the IT workforce in the last 20 years. To a significant extent, these certification options have replaced college education and have forced colleges to rethink the way they deliver education.

It is now possible to enter the IT workforce with a good salary by pursuing a series of certifications. Companies such as Cisco Systems, Microsoft, Novell, and Sun Microsystems create these certifications. These corporations create training programs and exams that map to specific courses. The exams test the mastery of subject matter related to specific software or hardware.

The courses associated with the certifications are not inexpensive, and the high cost is often a hurdle to obtaining the required training. Many corporate and government programs subsidize a portion of the cost of these courses, so it's important to do some research to see what options are available to you. It might cost you US$ 10,000 to US$ 15,000 to receive the required training and practice for the MCSE 2000 certification. For the prestigious CCIE certification, it is common for an individual to invest US$ 20,000 to US$ 40,000 over several years.

Programs such as the Cisco Networking Academy Program, begun in 1997, are integrated into high school, two-year college, and four-year college programs. These are relatively new options for students that allow exposure to the same material and training as in the costly certification programs, but for a much lower financial investment. However, you must be enrolled in one of these educational institutions to receive the training; this often means going to college. With the notable exception of the CCIE, all the major certifications can be obtained strictly by reading books, memorizing facts, and practicing exam questions found on the Internet. However, if you don't perform hands-on labs to internalize the concepts laid out in the certification books, you aren't particularly useful to a company. Employers are aware that these certifications can be obtained without mastery of the hands-on skills required to work in industry. However, employers are interested in your ability to create software, configure servers, or configure networking hardware for their enterprise, not in the paper certifications that you might have.

The hundreds of hours of hands-on practice that are needed to reinforce a theoretical knowledge base are difficult to complete and might require some investment in equipment. Most veterans of the IT industry say that it is a worthwhile investment. There is no sure path to success in the IT world. You must have the desire to pursue an IT career. It's important to enjoy what you're doing; if not, you're probably pursuing the wrong career goal. A successful pursuit of your goals requires much hard work. But if you enjoy what you're doing, the hard work can add to the enjoyment and sense of satisfaction.

Summary

This appendix described the various careers that are available in information technology and the educational paths that lead to these careers. You need to have fairly strong technical skills to succeed in the world of information technology. This means taking math and science courses to build these skills. If information technology courses are available at the school you are attending, take advantage by enrolling in these courses. Courses in system administration, computer programming, database administration, electronics, and operating systems can all aid your success in IT.

The world of IT is diverse, and there's no end to the opportunities. If you choose to pursue a career in IT, you've chosen a field that has a great range of possibilities and potential for growth. The most common ingredient to success in IT is the desire to learn more and keep current about the latest information in the field. If you don't like change, this is not the field for you, because your IT career is guaranteed to involve constant change.

Information Technology Industry's Certifications Outline

I. 3Com

1. 3Com Certified Solutions Associate—Designed to provide networking professionals with introductory technology, product, and solutions knowledge. Primarily aimed at employees working in nontechnical capacities such as sales, marketing, and management who require fundamental knowledge of network technologies, product options, and recommended business solutions.

2. 3Com Certified Solutions Expert—Designed for systems engineers and other technical professionals with a need to identify customers' needs and to recommend, design, and install 3Com solutions. Developed for IT/MIS staff with focus on determining customer needs, designing and installing custom solutions, and maintaining client systems after installations.

3. Focused specializations such as network telephony can be obtained to recognize expertise above and beyond Solutions Expert.

II. Adobe

1. ACE: Adobe Certified Expert—For graphic designers, web designers, developers, and business professionals who wish to be recognized experts using Adobe products. Adobe product proficiency exam must be passed for a specific Adobe software product to be shown as a highly skilled, expert-level user.

III. Adaptec

1. ACSP: Adaptec Certified Storage Professional—Program for IT professionals and resellers teaching complex storage technologies and the implementation and support for storage solutions based on these technologies. Provides a training platform to allow IT professionals to build technical expertise using basic to advanced storage solutions. ACSP for RAID provides in-depth knowledge of Adaptec RAID products, server technologies, implementation, and troubleshooting techniques for increased array performance.

IV. Allaire

1. Certified ColdFusion Developer—Designed for any IT professional that desires recognition of expert-level knowledge of CFML, with exceptional handling skills, and the ability to manage user sessions. Scoring 80 percent

or better on the exam gains Advanced ColdFusion Developer status. This entitles a person to use logos and letterheads, as well as to have a listing in the Macromedia directory.

2. Certified Website Developer—Proof to employers and potential clients of expertise in web page design and authoring skills. This certification represents a thorough understanding of web page design, web page authoring, and supporting technologies at a professional level.

V. **Check Point**

1. CCSA: Check Point Certified Security Administrator—This is the foundation-level certification for individuals who wish to manage basic installations of Check Point's VPN-1/FireWall-1. The designation indicates the ability to install, configure, and use the VPN-1 and FireWall-1, apply NAT (Network Address Translation) rules in firewall configurations, and authenticate users in the environment.

2. CCSE: Check Point Certified Security Expert—Demonstrates in-depth knowledge for establishing, managing, and implementing complex installations of VPN-1/FireWall-1. This advanced certification also teaches content security, encryption schemes, remote access using a VPN, server load balancing, modifying attack detection parameters, and setting up tracking within VPN-1/FireWall-1.

3. CCAE: Check Point Certified Addressing Engineer—Focused certification for managing Check Point's Meta IP. Program teaches security specialists how to configure policy-based network management for user-centric networks, installing Meta IP or upgrading to Meta IP, configuring Meta IP, and structuring automated IP address allocation as well as load balancing and troubleshooting.

4. CCQE: Check Point Certified Quality of Service Engineer—Provides the skills and knowledge required to implement and manage Check Point's FloodGate-1. This certification proves knowledge of installation and navigation of FloodGate-1, integration of FloodGate-1 with VPN-1/FireWall-1, creation and configuration of standard and bandwidth policies, use of network objects, services, and resources managers.

VI. **Cisco Systems**

A. *Network Installation and Support*

1. CCNA: Cisco Certified Network Associate—Certification in the fundamentals of networking for the small office/home office market. Provides the knowledge to install, configure, operate LAN, WAN, and dialup

services for small networks of 100 nodes or fewer using numerous protocols.

2. CCNA WAN Switching—CCNA concentrating on the apprentice knowledge of WAN switched networks and the installation of WAN switches: IPX, IGX, BPX, AXIS, Shelf, and modems.

3. CCNP: Cisco Certified Network Professional—Provides advanced knowledge concerning the installation, configuration, operation of LAN and WAN, and dial access services for organizations with networks with 100 to more than 500 nodes using many different protocols.

4. CCNP WAN Switching—Advanced certification indicating journeyman knowledge of WAN switched networks. Provides the knowledge to configure, operate, troubleshoot, and manage WAN switched networks.

5. CCIE Routing and Switching: Cisco Certified Internetwork Expert—Certification for the high-level network professional concentrating on IP and IP routing, non-IP desktop protocols such as IPX, and bridge and switch related technologies.

B. *Network Engineering and Design*

1. CCDA: Cisco Certified Design Associate—Fundamental certification indicating apprentice knowledge of network design for the small office/home office market. Shows ability to design routed and switched networks involving LAN, WAN, and dial access services for organizations with 100 or fewer nodes.

2. CCDP: Cisco Certified Design Professional—Indicates advanced knowledge of designing routed and switched networks involving LAN, WAN, and dial access services for organizations with 100 to over 500 nodes.

3. CCDP WAN Switching—Advanced certification concentrating on designing and implementing an ATM network (with CBR, ABR, and VBR traffic) and a Frame Relay network (with CIR and MIR traffic parameters); troubleshooting a WAN switched network; and managing traffic and voice technologies.

C. *Communications and Services*

1. CCIP: Cisco Certified Internetwork Professional—Shows competency in infrastructure or access solutions in a Cisco end-to-end environment. Indicates detailed understanding of diverse telecommunications technologies including IP routing, IP multicast, cable, DSL, content networking, or IP telephony.

2. CCIE Communications and Services: Cisco Certified Internetwork Expert—Shows mastery of IP and IP routing, optical, DSL, dial, cable, wireless, WAN switching, content networking, and voice.

D. *Cisco Qualified Specialist*

1. Cable—Provides the knowledge and skills required to support and deploy Cisco cable two-way data services including proficiency in DOCSIS, DVB, RF, and Cisco IOS.

2. Security—Designation focusing on the design, installation, and support of Cisco security solutions in the network security market.

3. Internet Solutions—Targets individuals involved in e-business solutions, and designing and delivering the underlying network architectures. Emphasizes the skills and knowledge in the areas of applications, tools, operating systems, and networks pertaining to systems planning to bring together Cisco services with Internet business solutions.

4. SNA/IP Design or Support Specialist—Designation to show knowledge and proficiency in the design, installation, and support of Cisco SNA/IP integration solutions.

VII. Citrix

1. CCA: Citrix Certified Administrator—For system administrators and resellers who wish to show a thorough knowledge of Citrix products for Windows and UNIX.

2. CCEA: Citrix Certified Enterprise Administrator—An advanced technical certification building on the CCA program. This certification shows expanded knowledge of Citrix products and provides more extensive education of the installation and administration of Citrix Management Services, Load Balancing Services, Program Neighborhood, and NFuse.

3. CCSP: Citrix Certified Sales Professional—A continued certification designed for individuals who wish to expand their customer base by acquiring advanced knowledge of Citrix technology, products, services and know how to sell and market them.

4. CCI: Citrix Certified Instructor—Demonstrates exceptional knowledge of the MetaFrame and WinFrame product lines and their underlying operating systems. Ensures the highest level of instruction on Citrix products.

VIII. Cognos, Inc.

1. CCPP—Cognos Certified Professional Program.

2. BI Author—Foundation knowledge and skills concerning understanding of client tools from the user and administrator perspective.

3. BI Administrator—Addresses advanced techniques and troubleshooting skills.

4. BI Architect—Focusing on data modeling, data mart creation, and meta-data delivery.

5. BI Engagement Manager—Ensures the ability to define and promote successful enterprise BI application deployment.

IX. Compaq

1. APS: Accredited Platform Specialist—Certifies warranty-level support skills and remedial maintenance for warranty-trained technicians. Pre-dominantly hardware focused, the certification provides knowledge of diagnostic tools, troubleshooting methodologies, FRU call out and replacement, hardware and driver configuration, installation, and upgrade.

2. API: Accredited Platform Integrator—Designed to provide certification of basic networking, system integration and support skills for Compaq customers, resellers, and service support staff. Accreditation focuses on system architecture, product specification, implementation, optimization, and hardware-OS management and administration.

3. ASE: Accredited Systems Engineer—Certifies advanced networking, systems integration and support skills for systems engineering specialists and advanced integration of hardware and operating system. Courseware includes advanced systems architecture, challenging implementations, and advanced troubleshooting.

4. Master ASE: Master Accredited Systems Engineer—Building on the ASE certification, the Master ASE demonstrates design and integration of solutions based upon customer business needs. Courseware includes advanced management, solutions planning, and system, network and application architectures.

X. CompTIA

1. A+ Service Technician Certification—Covering a broad range of hardware and software technologies, the certification acknowledges competency of entry-level (6 months experience) computer service technicians. CompTIA A+ program is backed by major computer hardware and software vendors and defines basic computer technical and safety standards.

2. CDIA: Certified Document Imaging Architect—Acknowledges competency and professionalism in the document imaging industry. The CDIA shows critical knowledge of planning, designing, and specifying all major areas of an imaging system.

3. EBiz+—Shows the knowledge surrounding basic concepts, key issues, and critical technologies of e-business. This certification is designed for anyone working in an e-business environment.

4. INet+—Targets IT professionals who wish to demonstrate a baseline of technical knowledge in a variety of Internet-related careers. Covering Internet basics, Internet development, networking, security, Internet, intranet, and extranet technologies. This certification helps managers determine a prospective employee's knowledge and skill level.

5. IT Project+—An industry-recognized certification that shows competency and professionalism in IT project management. Courseware includes basic business knowledge, interpersonal skills, and project management processes needed to manage IT projects.

6. Linux+—Credential measuring Linux knowledge and skills. This certification is a fundamental building block for any individual interested in an entry-level job using Linux such as help desk, sales/marketing, or application developers.

7. Network+—Shows knowledge of networking professionals with 18–24 months of experience in the IT industry. Courseware covers a wide range of networking technologies to prepare candidates for a variety of networking roles.

8. Server+—Shows competency dealing with advanced PC hardware issues such as RAID, SCSI, multiple-CPU PCs, and SANs, to name a few.

9. CTT+: Certified Technical Trainer—A cross-industry credential certifying an instructor who has achieved a standard of excellence in the technical training industry. Although this certification is endorsed by the computer industry, it can be applied to any industry that provides technical training and education.

XI. **Computer Associates**

A. *CACP—Computer Associates Certified Professional Program*

1. Project Engineer Certification—For individuals who have successfully demonstrated the effective utilization of Project Engineer for planning and monitoring projects. Signifies a deep understanding of Project Engineer's functionality and ability to assist others with the utilization of Project Engineer.

2. Process Continuum/Process Engineer Specialist—Demonstrates skills to manage the Process Continuum libraries and development of custom processes to fulfill the business mission of an organization.

3. ERwin Logical Modeling Specialist—Teaches a solid understanding of logical data modeling in ERwin, ability to explain data modeling theory for IDEF1x and IE methodologies, and development of logical data models using ERwin.

4. ERwin Physical Modeling Specialist—Demonstrates understanding of physical model creation from a script file, ability to modify the resulting physical model to implement additional requirements, and understanding the implementation of ERwin for model-based maintenance of the DBMS.

5. BPwin Business Modeling Specialist—Certification demonstrating ability to successfully collect information necessary for construction business models and translating them into valid diagrams, linking BPwin business models with ERwin data models, and understanding and developing business process models using BPwin.

6. CACP Network Specialist—Qualifies an individual to safeguard service levels by monitoring network performance and utilization, increase productivity by maximizing response times, solve problems with virtual LANs, troubleshoot problems with network devices, and plan effectively for the future of the network.

7. CACP Help Desk Specialist—Provides the ability to respond more quickly by integrating the help desk with Unicenter TNG event monitoring, reduce user downtime by reusing proven solutions, and improve users' access to solutions by creating self-service help environments.

8. CACP Storage Specialist—Teaches the skills to optimize backup performance by diagnosing system components to isolate bottlenecks, streamline administrative by automating a series of tasks, restoring a single file or multiple files or server, protecting data on local and remote servers from one central location, and preparing an airtight strategy for critical data recovery.

9. CACP Desktop Specialist—Qualifies an IT professional to be able to reduce total cost of ownership for desktop environments by automating software delivery, streamline day-to-day operations by monitoring and troubleshooting desktop hardware and software configurations, control software cost by metering usage, and improve productivity by delivering software according to predefined policies.

10. CACP Security Specialist—Provides the knowledge to verify security measures by centrally auditing data integrity, design and implement an architecture to utilize and optimize Unicenter TNG security, streamline administration by establishing one security architecture for multiple platforms, and control access to data by user, user group, and asset group.

11. CUE: Certified Unicenter Engineer—The standard for enterprise management software; CUE certification is a multifaceted education program providing training for engineers deploying CA's Unicenter TNG enterprise management solution. CUEs demonstrate in-depth knowledge of Unicenter TNG architecture and enterprise management tools, and can effectively plan and execute the deployment of Unicenter TNG.

12. CUA: Certified Unicenter Administrator—This certifies technical professionals with the ability to monitor the performance of a company's IT resources, maintain policies for Unicenter TNG throughout the network, leverage Unicenter TNG's security features to enhance existing operating system security, and analyze problems within the enterprise and resolve them with Agent technology utilities.

XII. Corel Corporation

1. Corel Certified Proficient User—Indicates a proficiency in the use of CorelDRAW9, Corel PHOTO-PAINT9, WordPerfect8 and 9, QuattroPro9, and Corel Presentations9. This certification covers the basic features and functions of the applications.

2. Corel Certified Expert User—Building on the Proficient User certification, the Expert User designation indicates an expert understanding in the use of CorelDRAW9 and WordPerfect8 and 9. This certification covers the more advanced capabilities of the software.

3. CCI: Corel Certified Instructor—Qualified instructors must be able to teach users whose skills range from beginner to expert and be able to perform all tasks associated with the proficient and expert level exams. Instructors have expert-level competency with each of Corel's applications.

XIII. DRI—Disaster Recovery Institute International

1. ABCP: Associate Business Continuity Planner—Supports entry-level proficiency in business continuity planning and provides the basis for moving up to a CBCP.

2. CBCP: Certified Business Continuity Professional—For IT professionals skilled in the business continuity/disaster recovery industry. Designed for individuals with two or more years experience in the field.

3. MBCP: Master Business Continuity Professional—The highest certification designed for individuals with at least five years in the business continuity/disaster recovery industry. MBCPs must have significant demonstrated knowledge of business continuity/disaster recovery.

XIV. ETA—Electronics Technicians Association

1. CET: Certified Electronics Technician—Denotes proficiency in electronics for individuals who excel in areas of electronics equipment, service, and support. The CET consists of a four-level program from associate to journeyman to senior, and on to master level. The different levels depend on test scores and work experience and/or training in the electronics industry.

2. CSS: Customer Service Specialist—Certification specializing in the knowledge of customer and fellow worker basic human relations concepts. A CSS must have great knowledge in several human relations areas and must have at least a minimal knowledge of their company's products or services in order to express themselves.

3. FOIC: Fiber Optics Installer Certification—Provides assurance that an individual has the knowledge of the basic concepts of fiber optics safety, installation, and service.

4. CNST: Certified Network Systems Technician—Credential of knowledge of computer basic concepts which are applicable to all the various specialty areas of the computer industry. Two levels of CNST can be achieved: Journeyman CNST and Senior CNST.

5. CST: Computer Service Technician—Certifies knowledge of computer electronics basic concepts which are applicable to all the various specialty areas of the computer industry.

6. CWS: Certified Web Specialist—CWSs focus on the ability to solve problems related to the operation, maintenance, and upgrading of World Wide Web home pages. This certification is designed to provide customer service skills that allow working relationships with users that efficiently convey descriptions of difficulties, problems initiated by the user, or needs of the company.

7. CNCT: Certified Network Computer Technician—Certification focusing on computer operating systems' functions, structure, operation, hardware installation, configuration, and upgrading.

8. CECT: Certified Electronic Commerce Technician—Assures the ability of an individual to administer Windows NT Server, perform basic HTML and web design, perform basic web programming and JavaScript, plan

and implement SQL and SQL server 7, provide connectivity with active server pages and databases, and implement basic Internet security and disaster planning.

XV. Help Desk Institute

1. HDA: Help Desk Analyst—Designed for entry-level help desk analysts with 9 to 18 months' experience. This certification shows possession of all the necessary skills to handle inbound service requests, problem-solving skills, understanding of incident and call-process flows, superior customer service, and professional problem escalation and notification procedures.

2. HDSE: Help Desk Support Engineer—Designed for experienced help desk and external support-center consultants showing an understanding of technologies, processes, and key factors that optimize help desk performance.

3. HDM: Help Desk Manager—Certification for experienced help desk managers responsible for day-to-day operations of the help desk. Courseware includes management of service levels with customers and secondary-support personnel, conducting team-building techniques, measurement of customer satisfaction, and determining appropriate use of technology.

XVI. Hewlett-Packard

A. *HP STAR*

1. CSE: Certified Systems Engineer—For anyone who can properly recommend, install, configure, and manage HP NetServers. This is a professional-level certification targeted primarily at systems engineers employed by HP authorized resellers.

2. CSC: Certified Systems Consultant—Focusing on the HP Solutions area of expertise with emphasis in either the NetServer Assured Availability or Microsoft Server Cluster Solutions. This certification builds on the CSE award.

XVII. IBM Corporation

A. *Certified e-Business Professional—Designed to increase and validate the IT professional's e-business proficiency.*

1. Solution Advisor—Designed for sales representatives who demonstrate expertise in solution selling. This certification validates the ability to engage customers, develop e-business strategic visions, manage the customer relationship, and translate customer requirements into e-business opportunities.

2. Solution Designer—Proves the ability to translate customer business requirements into an e-business solution. This certification teaches how to design a secure, scalable solution utilizing the IBM framework for e-business and best practices using existing customer environments.

3. Solution Technologist—Focuses on a well-rounded perspective of e-business, and deep technical skills required to implement key IBM or qualifying e-business products. A great understanding of how to articulate e-business, issues, strategy, and methodologies is needed to receive this certification.

4. Certified Specialist—A great number of Certified Specialist certifications can be obtained for each of IBM's products including application development, DB2 Universal Database, the IBM @.server series of computers, networking software, retail store solutions, storage and storage management, among others.

B. *Certified Developer*

1. MQSeries—Certifies ability to design, code, and implement software using MQSeries.

2. XML and related technologies—Designed for developers of applications that make use of XML, this certification demonstrates a broad knowledge of XML concepts and related technology, information modeling, XML processing, rendering, and query. This certification is part of the e-Business—Solution Technologist program.

C. *Certified Solution Developer*

1. IBM VisualAge for Java—Certifies sound object-oriented analysis and design techniques based on UML, design, implementation, deployment of Java-based solutions including applications, applets, and servlets.

2. IBM Websphere Application Server—Certifies knowledge of designing and building the components needed for an Internet/intranet site and the ability to provide technical assistance for IBM Websphere Application Server components.

3. Certified Enterprise Developer—Shows the ability to design, create, and maintain Java 2 Enterprise Edition components including Enterprise Java-Beans and JavaServer Pages, deployment and configuration of these components, and support for the clients that access them. This developer has the administration skills required to tune the application to meet performance needs.

4. Certified Solutions Expert—Indicates solution development needs for numerous IBM products including CICS web enablement, DB2 Universal Database, IBM WebSphere, MQSeries, and ViaVoice, among others.

5. Certified Systems Expert—Many IBM products offer the Systems Expert certification including application development with IBM WebSphere, IBM @.server series, networking software, and OS/2 Warp, among others.

6. Certified Advanced Technical Expert—Offered to IT professionals with expert level training with AIX and IBM @.server PSeries and DB2 Universal Database for Clusters, DRDA, and DB2 Data Replication.

XVIII.   Information Systems Audit and Control Association

1. CISA: Certified Information Systems Auditor—Designed for the IS audit, control, and security professional. This certification assures an individual qualification in the skills surrounding IS audit, control, and security.

XIX.   Inprise Corp (Formerly Borland)

1. Inprise Product Certification—Demonstrates knowledge of Borland products' advanced features. This certification indicates a thorough understanding of the use of these features to create, debug, and deploy software applications.

2. Inprise Trainer Certification—Designed to ensure consistent, high-quality teaching for customers. Individuals must demonstrate thorough product knowledge and excellent teaching skills.

XX.   ISC2—International Information Systems Security Certification Consortium

1. CISSP: Certified Information Systems Security Professional—Designed for the security professional and demonstrates knowledge in access control, computer operations security, cryptography, application program security, risk management, communications security, computer architecture, systems security, physical security, policy and standards, and ethics.

XXI.   IPG—International Programmers Guild

1. Certified Programmer—The IPG's Professional Certification Program has four components: technical proficiency, analytical skill development, conformity to the Code of Ethics, and final certification by the IPG's Master Programmer. Upon fulfillment of a minimum of mandatory standards, members receive their designation as Professional Programmer.

A. *ISCET—International Society of Certified Electronics Technicians*

    1. CET: Certified Electronics Technician—Signifies the degree of theoretical knowledge and technical proficiency of practicing technicians. In the absence of governmental licensing, this certification program can help assure consumers that the person entrusted to service their electronic products possesses the knowledge, training, and experience necessary to do a good job.

XXII. **IWA—International Webmasters Association**

A. *CWP: Certified Web Professional*

    1. CWP Site Designer—Implements and maintains websites using authoring and scripting languages, content creation and management tools, and digital media.

    2. CWP Internetworking Specialist—Defines network architecture, identifies infrastructure components, and monitors and analyzes network performance. This individual also designs and manages TCP/IP networks.

    3. CWP Enterprise Developer—Builds n-tier database and legacy connectivity solutions for web applications, using Java, Java application programming interfaces, Java Database Connectivity solutions, middleware tools, and distributed object models.

    4. CWP e-Commerce Specialist—Understands the uses of secure electronic transactions, cryptography standards, certificate authorities, and electronic services. This certification shows expertise in the standards, technologies, and practices in electronic commerce.

    5. CWP Security Specialist—Implements security policies, identifies security threats and develops countermeasures using firewalls and attack-recognition technologies. This individual is an expert in transaction and payment security solutions.

    6. CWP Server Administrator—Manages and tunes e-Commerce infrastructure including web servers, FTP, news, and mail servers for midsize to large businesses. Server administrators configure, manage, and deploy e-Business solutions servers.

    7. CWP Application Developer—Builds client and server-side web applications using rapid application development tools and component technologies to implement two-tier database connectivity solutions.

    8. Master CWP—Offered to experts of Administrator, Designer, and Enterprise Developer, this certification demonstrates a much more in-depth knowledge of each designated certification and a mastery of the skill sets involved.

XXIII. **Institute for Certification of Computing Professionals**

  A. *ACP: Associate Computing Professional—Designed for new entrants into the IT field and new graduates of college or degree programs. This certification validates an individual's knowledge of the general computing industry and specific programming skills. The testing also identifies strengths within a person's area of expertise.*

  B. *CCP: Certified Computing Professional*

  1. CDP: Certificate in Data Processing—Sought after by individuals requiring proof of mastery in the area of data processing.

  2. CCP: Certified Computer Programmer—Designed for programmers who want to validate their programming skills.

  3. CSP: Certified Systems Professional—This program was developed to show expertise in the areas of system development, systems programming, core IT skills, systems security, and business information systems.

XXIV. **LPI—Linux Professional Institute**

  A. *LPIC: Linux Professional Institute Certified—There are three levels to this certification:*

  1. Level 1—Shows the ability of an individual to work at the UNIX command line, perform easy maintenance tasks, and install and configure a workstation and connect it to a network.

  2. Level 2—Moves beyond basic knowledge and proves ability to plan, implement, maintain, secure, and troubleshoot a small mixed network. The individual can also supervise assistants and advise management on automation and purchases.

  3. Level 3—This is the master level of the LPIC. Candidates should be able to design and implement complex automation solutions, initiate projects and implement them, and act as a consultant to higher management.

XXV. **Lotus**

  1. CLP: Certified Lotus Professional—Demonstrates expertise of a job function and represents a high level of technical knowledge of Lotus software. The CLP indicates a highly competent and experienced individual.

  2. CLS: Certified Lotus Specialist—Recognizes a basic level of technical expertise with Lotus Software such as Domino, Notes, cc:Mail, and SmartSuite.

3. CLI: Certified Lotus Instructor—Directed toward technical training professionals whose expertise and experience demonstrate their ability to present Lotus's courseware in a professional and understandable format.

4. CLEI: Certified Lotus End-User Instructor—Much like the CLI, this certification is geared toward training professionals who have experience presenting Lotus's end-user courseware.

XXVI. Lucent

1. LCTE: Lucent Certified Technical Expert—Designed to show a high level of knowledge and skill in networking and Lucent Technologies products, this certification is for network administrators, consultants, engineers, and any other individual interested in showing advanced technical knowledge of Lucent Technologies products.

XXVII. Marconi

1. PNE: Marconi Public Network Engineer—Verifies basic technical competency skills on Marconi's Service Provider products including ASX/TNX switches, SE-420/440, and CellPath 90 voice/data Internet Access Devices. This certification shows the ability to install, configure, and maintain Marconi Service Provider Products.

2. ENE: Marconi Enterprise Network Engineer—For systems engineers, and technical operations personnel. This certification demonstrates basic competency skills on Marconi's Enterprise products such as ASX switches, ESX/NSX switches/routers, and other ES switches.

3. PIP: Marconi Product Installation Professional—Verifies the basic installation competency skills on Marconi's entire product line. Candidates should be able to install a suite of Marconi BBSR products to satisfy a given networking scenario.

XXVIII. Microsoft

A. Technical Certifications

1. MCP: Microsoft Certified Professional—Numerous MCP certifications are available for individuals who have the skills to successfully implement a Microsoft product or technology as part of a business solution in an organization.

2. MCP + Internet—A credential for professionals who install and configure server products, manage server resources, plan security, and troubleshoot problems. This certification is designed for network administrators and website server managers.

3. MCP + Site Building—For IT professionals who plan, build, maintain, and manage websites using Microsoft technologies and products. This credential is for individuals who manage sophisticated, interactive websites with database connectivity, multimedia, and searchable content.

4. MCSD: Microsoft Certified Solution Developer—The premier certification for individuals who design and develop business solutions with Microsoft technologies. MCSDs are able to develop desktop applications and multiuser, web-based, and transaction-based applications. These professionals analyze business requirements and maintain solutions.

5. MCSE: Microsoft Certified Systems Engineer—For professionals who analyze the business requirements and design and implement the infrastructure for business solutions based on the Windows 2000 platform and Microsoft server software. MCSEs are able to install, configure, and troubleshoot network systems.

6. MCSE + Internet—For individuals who enhance, deploy, and manage sophisticated intranet and Internet solutions with Microsoft operating systems and server software. These professionals are also able to analyze and manage websites.

7. MCDBA: Microsoft Certified Database Administrator—Shows an individual's ability to install, configure, implement, and administer Microsoft SQL Server databases, derive physical database designs, develop logical data models, and manage and maintain databases.

8. MCT: Microsoft Certified Trainer—The exclusive product educators for Microsoft's official curriculum. These professionals are instructionally qualified and technically certified by Microsoft to deliver Microsoft courseware to IT professionals and developers.

XXIX. **Desktop Certifications**

1. MOUS: Microsoft Office User Specialist—Demonstrates desktop skills with Microsoft Office products, both Microsoft business productivity applications and Microsoft Project applications. MOUSs must prove exceptional ability to utilize the advanced functionality of these applications.

2. MOUS Master Instructor Certificate—An award given to those instructors who verify their technical expertise at the MOUS Master level in either the Microsoft Office 97 applications or Microsoft Office 2000 applications.

3. MOUS Project 2000—Offered to demonstrate an individual's advanced knowledge and skills using Microsoft Project 2000 and Microsoft Project Central. MOUS certifications are not substitutes for methodological certifications; they are a measurement of an individual's ability to productively use these tools.

XXX. Motorola

1. Colleagues Certification—This program provides a benchmark of achievement for those who sell, design, and operate Vanguard networking equipment. Four certifications are offered reflecting expertise in each area respectively: Sales Specialist, Design Specialist, and Operations Specialist. The final certification, MCNE: Motorola Certified Networking Engineer, is awarded to those who have passed each of the three specialist exams.

XXXI. Nortel

1. NNCFC: Nortel Networks Certified Field Specialist—For entry- to mid-level individuals, this certification shows a basic level of technical proficiency to install, commission, and provision equipment at a customer site.

2. NNCSS: Nortel Networks Certified Support Specialist—Demonstrates a basic level of technical proficiency to maintain a live system such as problem identification, provisioning, upgrading, operations, administration, maintenance, and troubleshooting.

3. NNCAS: Nortel Networks Certified Account Specialist—Provides a basic level of technical proficiency to support Nortel Networks solutions including the ability to analyze customer business needs in the areas of products, solutions, interoperability, and value proposition. This certification is designed for the entry-level sales representative.

4. NNCDS: Nortel Networks Certified Design Specialist—Designed for the entry- to mid-level technical sales and systems engineers. This certification shows basic levels of proficiency to support Nortel Networks solutions. Skill sets necessary include network management, functionality, interoperability, architecture, and topology.

5. NNCSE: Nortel Networks Certified Support Expert—Available to the mid- to senior-level professional; an NNCSE must demonstrate expertise with problem identification, provisioning, upgrades, configuration, operations, administration, maintenance, and troubleshooting within Nortel networks.

6. NNCDE: Nortel Networks Certified Design Expert—An NNCDE must be able to optimize customer networks using Nortel Networks solutions. Targeted to the mid- to senior-level professional, this certification incorporates an increased level and range of network components to plan and optimize network management, functionality, interoperability, service, architecture, and topology.

7. NNCA: Nortel Networks Certified Architect—Shows the ability to analyze and resolve challenging internetworking environments. NNCAs must be able to illustrate and document significant dimensions of their professional accomplishments.

XXXII.   Novell

1. CNA: Certified Novell Administrator—CNA certification gives an individual the ability to support software users in various work environments by specializing in one or more of the various Novell applications. CNAs are able to set up user workstations, manage users and resources on a network, execute network applications and shares, set up printing, and handle routine software maintenance.

2. CNE: Certified Novell Engineer—The CNE specializes in one or more of Novell's applications to support customers who have various technologies and networks. CNEs are able to integrate diverse network clients, use TCP/IP to design an internetwork, change a LAN to an intranet, centrally distribute software, configure and troubleshoot complex printing problems, design, analyze, and integrate a Novell Directory Services implementation.

3. CNI: Certified Novell Instructor—Designed for the IT educator interested in teaching individuals the technology and courseware of any of Novell's applications. The CNI is recognized worldwide.

4. CNS: Certified Novell Salesperson—This accreditation certifies the ability to position and sell business solutions from Novell.

5. MCNE: Master Certified Novell Engineer—Shows expertise in the ability to manage and troubleshoot cross-platform networks, integrate multivendor application servers with NDS, manage network databases, route and bridge applications over the LAN, manage advanced e-mail and post office services, secure WAN and LAN, and internetwork configurations.

XXXIII.   Oracle

1. OCP: Oracle Certified Professional—Consists of five areas of certification showing expertise with Oracle's applications, development, and operation.

They are: Oracle Database Administrator, Oracle Application Developer, Oracle Database Operator, Oracle Financial Applications Consultant, and Oracle Java Developer.

XXXIV. Paradyne

1. WAN A.C.E. Certification—Designed for system engineers, resellers, and distributors. This certification shows competency with the applications, functions, controls, configuration, and options of the Paradyne Analog, DDS, T1, FrameSaver, and Hotwire products.

2. FrameSaver Certification—Qualifies an IT professional to install, operate, and maintain Paradyne's 9624 and 9124 Service Level Verifier Solutions. Courseware includes how to install and configure SLVS products, how to use statistics and diagnostic tests, and how to use the performance wizard to collect data.

3. Hotwire Certification—This credential shows knowledge required to install, operate, and maintain ReachDSL, MVL, RADSL, and IDSL, and how to use Paradyne's OpenLane NMS application.

XXXV. QAI—Quality Assurance Institute

1. CQA: Certified Quality Analyst—Indicates a professional level of competence in the principles and practices of quality assurance in the IT profession. Required knowledge includes auditing and control, human resource principles, training and development, quality management, management techniques, and disaster recovery, among others.

2. CSTE: Certified Software Test Engineer—Establishes standards for initial qualification and provides direction for the testing process. Required knowledge includes test tactics, professional development, quality principles, test design, test principles and concepts, quantitative measurement, and test reporting, among others.

3. CSA: Certified SPICE Assessor—Recognizes individuals that have acquired the knowledge, skills and experience required to conduct ISO/IEC TR 15504-conformant assessment. Candidates must demonstrate knowledge and skills in ISO/IEC TR 15504, assessments experience, software engineering, communications, and human resources.

XXXVI. Red Hat

1. RHCE: Red Hat Certified Engineer—Certifies an individual at server system administration, setup of network services, and basic server security. An RHCE must show competency in the ability to install and configure

Red Hat Linux, understand limitations of hardware, configure basic networking and file systems, configure the X Window System, carry out basic diagnostics and troubleshooting, and set up common IP services.

XXXVII.   RSA Security

1. RSA/CA: RSA Certified Administrator—Designed for security professionals who demonstrate knowledge and skill in maintaining enterprise security systems that use RSA Security's products.

2. RSA/CSE: RSA Certified Engineer—For security professionals with comprehensive knowledge and skill in installing and configuring enterprise security systems that use RSA Security's products. This security professional will also have a basic understanding of security administration tasks.

3. RSA/CI: RSA Certified Instructors—Designed for professionals skilled in teaching individuals how to deploy and maintain security systems that use RSA Security's products.

XXXVIII.   Sair Linux and GNU

1. LCA: Linux Certified Administrator—Evidence of the ability to perform as a power user with the Linux OS. LCAs are able to install, configure, administer, network, and secure the operating system at a basic knowledge level.

2. LCE: Linux Certified Engineer—Requires mastery of the LCA knowledge base. The LCE has the ability to perform as a Linux System Manager.

3. MLCE: Master Linux Certified Engineer—For Senior System Managers, this achievement incorporates the LCA and LCE knowledge base to acquire in-depth knowledge of the inner workings of Linux and its associated tools.

XXXIX.   SCO

1. CUSA: SCO Certified UNIX Systems Administrator—There are two tracks to becoming CUSA certified: UnixWare7 Administration and OpenServer Release 5 Administration. CUSA is the foundation level for certification with UNIX systems.

2. ACE: SCO Advanced Certified Engineer—The ACE provides a more in-depth knowledge and understanding of UnixWare7 and OpenServer Release 5 administration.

3. Master ACE: SCO Master Advanced Certified Engineer—The top tier to the UNIX certification program. The Master ACE signifies mastery of the skills and abilities to administer UNIX operating systems.

XL.   Sniffer Technologies

1. SCP: Sniffer Certified Professional—The beginning level of the Sniffer certification model. The SCP program is designed to recognize network professionals who can demonstrate an in-depth understanding of Sniffer Technologies software.

2. SCE: Sniffer Certified Expert—The SCE designation shows expert-level knowledge of Sniffer Technologies software. An SCE must be able to implement distributed Sniffer System/RMON Pro, and understand Ethernet, WAN, ATM, Windows NT/2000, TCP/IP, and wireless LAN analysis and troubleshooting.

3. SCM: Sniffer Certified Master—The SCM must complete all SCE and SCP requirements and understand networking technologies at a master's level.

XLI.   Sun Microsystems

A.   *Java*

1. Sun Certified Programmer—Designed for the experienced programmer to demonstrate the use of basic syntax and structure of the Java programming language.

2. Sun Certified Developer—Designed for the Sun Certified Java Programmer who has a need to further apply this knowledge to develop complex, production-level applications.

3. Sun Certified Web Component Developer—For Sun Certified Java Programmers who use Java technology servlet and JavaServer Pages APIs to develop web applications.

4. Sun Certified Enterprise Architect—Developed for enterprise architects responsible for designing Enterprise Edition Java-compliant applications that are scalable, flexible, and highly secure.

B.   *Solaris*

1. Sun Certified System Administrator—Designed for system administrators who perform essential system administration procedures using Solaris. This certification shows the ability to administer a networked server running on the Solaris Operating Environment.

2. Sun Certified Network Administrator—Given to experienced system administrators capable of administering Sun systems in a networked environment including LANs and the Solaris Operating Environment.

XLII. Sybase

1. SCP: Sybase Certified Professional—The SCP is capable of designing and implementing real-world solutions using the Sybase database software including EAServer, Enterprise Portal, PowerBuilder, Adaptive Server Enterprise, Adaptive Server Anywhere, and SQL Server 11 and Adaptive Server Enterprise 11.5.

XLIII. Sysoft

1. CEP: Certified e-Business Professional—Certification offered to economy professionals, building and managing integrated e-Business architecture and process technologies. Courseware includes Internet, broadband, wireless, e-Business process improvement, customer relationship and more.

XLIV. Symantec Corp.

1. SPS: Symantec Product Specialist—Focuses on a single security product and its functionality in an overall security system.

2. SCSE: Symantec Certified Security Engineer—An SCSE is involved in the design, integration, and deployment of comprehensive enterprise security solutions. This IT security professional has product-specific training, a high-level understanding of a broad range of security solutions, and in-depth knowledge within a specific security area such as vulnerability management and intrusion detection.

3. SCSP: Symantec Certified Security Practitioner—This certifies a senior security consultant who demonstrates in-depth knowledge and expertise across the complete range of security disciplines. The SCSP has attained certification in all the security solutions categories.

XLV. TIBCO

1. TIBCO Certified Administrator—Demonstrates knowledge in the fundamentals of TIBCO's distributed system technologies and the ability to administer and configure TIB/Rendezvous, TIBCO's messaging system.

2. TIBCO Certified Developer—Qualifies an IT professional to solve the increasing complexities of enterprise application integration. Courseware includes developing applications with TIB/Rendezvous, TIB/Hawk, and TIB/Adapter SDK.

3. TIBCO Certified Solutions Administrator—Builds on the Certified Administrator certification, providing a more in-depth knowledge and mastery of the skills necessary for administrating TIBCO's distributed system technologies.

4. TIBCO Certified Solutions Developer—The second tier in the Certified Developer certification, providing a more in-depth knowledge and understanding of solution development in application integration.

5. TIBCO Certified Education Consultant—To become a Certified Education Consultant, an individual must become accredited in the Certified Solutions Administrator and Certified Solutions Developer areas at the Education Consultant level.

XLVI. TruSecure—These certifications will be available soon to enhance and improve skills specifically focused on network and computer security.

1. ICSA: ICSA Certified Security Associate

2. ICSE: ICSA Certified Security Expert

3. ICSP: ICSA Certified Security Professional

Answers to Check Your Understanding Review Questions

This appendix contains the answers to the Check Your Understanding questions that are at the end of each chapter.

Chapter 1

1. What is the name of the method that is used to connect computers?

   A. Networking

2. When was the term Internet first used?

   D. 1982

3. What does asynchronous mean?

   D. Without respect to time

4. How many nibbles are in 64 bits?

   A. 16

5. How many bytes are in 64 bits?

   C. 8

6. What type of numbering system is characterized by 0s and 1s?

   C. Binary

7. Which numbering system is based on powers of 2?

   C. Binary

8. What is the decimal number 151 in binary form?

   B. 10010111

9. What is the binary number 11011010 in decimal form?

   D. 218

10. What is the binary number 10110 decimal form?

    B. 22

11. What is the decimal number 202 in binary form?

    C. 11001010

12. What is the binary number 11101100 in decimal form?

    B. 236

13. How much time should elapse between putting on a wrist strap and touching any computer component?

    A. 15 seconds

14. How much charge (in volts) can a CRT in a monitor hold?

    D. 20,000 or more

15. What is the agreement that provides important safety information and should be signed before beginning lab exercises?

    B. Lab Safety Agreement

Chapter 2

1. What performs a quick self-diagnostic check of the system hardware early in the boot sequence?

    A. The POST, which is located in the CPU

2. What is the first thing that the POST routine does?

    B. Resets the CPU and the program counter to F000

3. What computer component is NOT tested by the POST routine?

    B. Power supply

4. During the boot process, what is the first code that is executed?

    B. BIOS

5. PC power supplies use what type of power?

    A. DC current

6. What controls the temperature of the power supply?

    C. Cooling fan

7. How do you prevent a power supply from overheating?

    B. Verify that the cooling vents are not blocked.

8. What is the main circuit board in a computer?

    D. Motherboard

9. Which of the following is not a CPU manufacturer?

    B. Cyrex

10. When powering up, where does the microprocessor find its first code?

    C. ROM

11. Pentium CPUs normally run what voltage type?

    A. VDC

12. To improve CPU access time, what do you need to upgrade?

    D. Cache

13. What does BIOS stand for?

    B. Basic input/output system

14. What is the advantage of using Flash ROM?

    A. BIOS can be upgraded without replacing the chip.

15. What is the typical size of a SIMM?

    C. 30 and 72 pins

16. What type of connector is used for a serial port connection on a PC?

    B. DB-25, male D-shell

17. Why are hardware resource conflicts more likely to be IRQ related than I/O related?

    A. There are more I/O addresses than IRQs.

18. What is a feature of EIDE?

    D. ATAPI

19. What is a common failure in SCSI devices?

    A. Improper termination

20. What type of interface has the fastest data transfer?

    B. SCSI

21. What is the minimum storage unit for an IDE hard drive?

    D. Sector

22. What is the typical CD-ROM interface?

    C. IDE

23. What are external modems usually connected to?

    C. Serial port

24. Which statement is true about IRQs?

    D. Each device on a PC must have a unique IRQ.

25. What does DMA stand for?

    A. Direct memory access

Chapter 3

1. What does ESD stand for?

    B. Electrostatic discharge

2. How do you best prevent damaging a computer with static electricity?

    D. Always wear an ESD strap when working inside a computer.

3. What type of current can kill you?

    D. AC and DC

4. Which of the following statements describes the PC power supply?

    B. It converts AC power to DC power.

5. What tool is used to check the power supply voltage at the P8 and P9 connections?

    C. Multimeter

6. What is a memory bank?

    B. The actual slot that memory goes into

7. What indicates the correct positioning when installing SIMMs?

    C. Notch on one end

8. Which method is used to install a DIMM?

    A. Line it up straight over the socket and press it in.

9. Which components reside in expansion slots on the motherboard?

    C. Network interface, sound, and SCSI cards

10. What is the purpose of expansion slots?

    D. To allow the addition of optional components

11. Care should be taken when handling an expansion card. You should not touch which component(s)?

B. Metal edge connectors

12. Which type of expansion card is configured using software instead of jumpers?

D. Plug and Play cards

13. When connecting a ribbon cable, how is the connector installed?

C. By connecting the red stripe to pin 1

14. When installing an IDE drive, which jumper settings are not a factor?

D. Secondary

15. Where do you connect an ATA CD-ROM drive in a computer with an EIDE adapter?

C. Secondary IDE

16. How should the jumpers be set on your IDE CD-ROM drive when it is attached to the primary IDE adapter with your hard drive?

B. Slave

17. Plugging in or unplugging a keyboard with the power turned on can damage which component?

C. Motherboard

18. What port does a mouse plug into?

B. Serial

19. How are PCI devices configured?

D. They are always self-configuring.

20. How many pins are in an IDE connector?

D. 40

21. What determines the length of a SCSI cable?

C. SCSI device

22. What technique loads the system BIOS from ROM into system RAM during bootup?

C. Shadowing

23. Where are basic instructions for the CPU and I/O device communication located?

D. BIOS

24. Which software or firmware routine is executed first during the computer boot up procedure?

A. BIOS

25. In which case should circuit boards or devices not be added or removed?

D. With power on

Chapter 4

1. What is the definition of an operating system?

C. A software program that controls thousands of operations, provides an interface between the user and the computer, and runs applications.

2. Which of the following is not a valid OS?

   C. LAN

3. What does DOS stand for?

   B. Disk Operating System

4. What is the maximum length of a DOS filename?

   A. 8 characters with an extension of 3 characters

5. What three files are necessary on a DOS boot disk?

   C. io.sys, msdos.sys, command.com

6. Where is the statement LOADHI or LH used?

   A. config.sys

7. What does the DOS command MEM show?

   B. Memory properties

8. Which of the following is an external DOS command?

   C. COPY

9. Which of the following is an internal DOS command?

   D. DIR

10. How do you show all the system files within a directory?

    A. DIR *.SYS

11. An ini file usually contains what type of information?

    D. Parameter information about a program

12. What does the DEVICE= statement mean in config.sys?

    D. It loads a device driver.

13. What is in conventional memory loaded right above DOS?

    B. Device drivers

14. What is the memory address from 0 to 640 KB called?

    D. Conventional memory

15. What is extended memory?

    D. All memory above 1024 KB

16. What is the first 64 KB of extended memory called?

    C. HMA

17. What is virtual memory?

    B. Simulating RAM by using a file on the hard drive

18. If the himem.sys file is corrupt or missing, what will happen?

    D. Windows 98 will not load.

19. What program is used to find and repair lost clusters?

    B. DEFRAG

20. Which program is used to set up a partition on a hard drive?

    B. FDISK

21. What file should not be edited by the user?

    D. himem.sys

22. Why would a read-only attribute be applied to a file?

A. So it cannot be changed.

23. How do you step through the startup files when DOS starts?

B. Press F8.

Chapter 5

1. What does Windows Explorer display?

C. The hierarchical structure of files, folders, and drives

2. What is the first thing that needs to be done with a new hard drive?

A. FDISK

3. What is the second thing that needs to be done with a new hard drive?

B. FORMAT

4. In Windows 98, what utilities are used to set up the hard drive?

C. FDISK and FORMAT

5. What is another name for the active partition?

A. Bootable partition

6. How many logical drives can be created by FDISK on an EIDE drive?

D. 24

7. What section of the hard drive stores the location of the operating system?

A. Boot sector

8. What is the lowest version of DOS that will allow the installation of Windows 98?

C. An existing operating system is only required when using the upgrade version.

9. What is the first thing you should try if the computer will not boot after installing the operating system?

B. Restart the computer.

10. Is it possible to upgrade a Windows 98 computer to Windows NT?

B. No

11. What does SCANDISK do?

D. Marks bad clusters

12. What program is used to edit the Registry?

D. REGEDIT

13. What should you do if the Windows 98 installation procedure fails?

B. Restart the computer using Safe mode.

14. What does the io.sys file do in Windows 98?

A. Loads the basic device drivers and sets the basic system headings

15. Where in Windows 98 can you remove or view devices and their properties?

   B. Control Panel, System, Device Manager

16. In Windows 98, how do you make an emergency startup disk?

   B. Control Panel, Add/Remove Programs, Startup Disk tab, Create Disk

17. How do you restore a file if you delete it from the Windows 98 desktop?

   C. Open the Recycle Bin.

18. By default, how much hard drive space is set aside for the Recycle Bin in Windows 98?

   A. 10 percent

19. How can you view the version of Windows that is currently installed?

   B. Right-click My Computer and select Properties.

20. How do you view the file or folder properties in Windows 98?

   B. Right-click the icon and select Properties.

21. How do you locate an object in Windows 98?

   D. Start, Find

22. What character cannot be used when naming a DOS file?

   B. > (greater-than sign)

23. If a printer is changed in DOS, what must be done?

   B. Change each application printer driver.

24. What does creating a shortcut in Windows 98 allow the user to do?

   C. Have quick access to executable files

25. Windows 98 does not support which types of applications?

   C. UNIX programs

Chapter 6

1. What does VGA stand for?

   C. Video graphic array

2. VGA describes how data are passed between which two components?

   A. Computer and the display

3. The number of bits used to describe a pixel is known as what?

   D. Bit-depth

4. The sharpness of a display image is measured in what units?

   A. Dots per inch

5. What is the resolution of super VGA?

   B. 1024×768

6. What are the basic functions of a sound card?

   A. Input, processing, and output

7. What is the major drawback of USB sound?

C. Processing power required hampers performance

8. What is required to upgrade built-in sound?

B. Disabling the built-in sound

9. What is used to select the sound card and view its properties?

A. Settings, Control Panel, System Properties, Device Manager

10. What does MIDI stand for?

C. Musical instrument digital interface

11. CDs are considered to be what type of media?

D. Optical

12. How many methods of DVD recording are currently available?

C. 4

13. What does a CD's logical standard determine?

A. Its file system structure

14. What is the physical format that defines an audio CD and specifies how songs are placed in tracks on the disc?

B. Red Book

15. What is the physical format of a recordable CD that is divided into three parts?

D. Orange Book

16. What is the standard that addresses the method of recording MPEG1 audio, video, and still graphics on a video CD (VCD)?

B. White Book

17. What is DVD 5?

A. A single-sided, single-layer DVD with a storage capacity of 4.7 GB

18. What is the storage capacity, in GB, of a DVD 18?

C. 17

19. What does the Y in YUV refer to?

A. The luminance of the signal color

20. How much throughput, in KBps, is required for full-motion video?

C. 384

Chapter 7

1. Why is a system attribute applied to a file?

D. So that the user knows it is a system file

2. What file system limits filenames to eight characters?

B. FAT 16

3. What is the largest hard drive that the FAT 32 file system can support?

A. 2048 GB

4. Which file system is capable of managing global and enterprise-level operating systems?

C. NTFS

5. Which file system is used by OS/2?

   D. HPFS

6. Which of the following is an advanced startup feature used for troubleshooting?

   B. Safe mode

7. Which of the following describes the ability to restore a disk to a consistent state with minimal data loss?

   A. Fault tolerance

8. What is the Windows Registry?

   C. A database of configuration settings

9. What does POST stand for?

   D. Power-on self test

10. What does Plug and Play do?

    A. Eliminates the need to manually configure jumpers on the hardware

11. Which of the following is a tool that provides a list of files that a user has access to?

    C. Access control list

12. Users can gain access to an encrypted file if they are assigned which of the following?

    A. Public key

13. The ntldr file uses which of the following files?

    D. ntdetect.com, boot.ini, bootsect.dos

14. What is a portion of a disk that functions as a physically separate unit of storage?

    A. Partition

15. Which of the following provides a secure set of records about the components that control the OS?

    B. Registry

16. What is a library of hardware drivers that communicate between the OS and the hardware that is installed on the system?

    A. Hardware abstraction layer

17. What is a tool, used before installing Windows 2000, that verifies the hardware will work?

    C. Hardware compatibility list

18. What is the Windows Compact installation option used for?

    A. A computer with a limited amount of hard drive space

19. Which of the Windows NT/2000/ XP system tools enables the administrator to control everything related to the local computer?

    B. Administrative tools

20. Setting up the computer to boot to Windows 2000 or Windows 98 is known as what?

    C. Dual-boot

Chapter 8

1. Which RAID level provides improved disk input/output but provides no redundancy?

   A. RAID 0

2. Which RAID level provides redundancy at the expense of 50 percent of the disk storage capacity?

   B. RAID 1

3. Which of the following RAID levels provides fault tolerance using parity information and requires a minimum of three disk drives?

   B. RAID 4 and RAID 5

4. You have a group of six 36-GB disk drives that you want to configure as a RAID 5 array. After you have configured the RAID array with the six disk drives, what is the storage capacity, in GB, of the single logical drive that is created by the RAID array?

   B. 180

5. Which of the following technologies allows a network server to run more programs than can fit into its physical RAM?

   C. Virtual memory

6. Which of the following software packages are not normally installed on a network server to support its operation?

   D. Spreadsheet software

7. Which RAID level does not provide fault tolerance?

   A. RAID 0

8. After installing a second processor in a network server, the network server boots up, and the second processor is detected by the system BIOS. However, the network server operating system does not recognize the second processor. How do you correct the situation?

   C. Upgrade the network operating system to recognize the additional processor

9. What environment variable in Windows NT and Windows 2000 is set to the number of processors in the network server?

   A. Number_of_processors

10. Which of the following must be the same on the existing processor and the processor that is to be added to a multiprocessor-capable network server?

    A. Level 2 cache and processor clock speed

11. Which memory technology requires a continuity module to be inserted into all empty memory module slots in a network server?

    C. RIMMs

12. A network server has a single EIDE disk drive configured as a master. You want to add a second EIDE disk drive to the same channel. How must the second drive be configured for both disk drives to work correctly?

    B. Slave

13. How do you upgrade an EIDE disk subsystem to a SCSI subsystem?

   A. Remove all EIDE disk drives, cables, and controllers. Add the SCSI controller, cables, and disk drives.

14. Which of the following adapters usually contain onboard memory that can be upgraded?

   C. Video adapter, RAID controller, and SCSI controller

15. In what version of Windows must the hard drive must be converted to a dynamic disk before the RAID options are available to implement?

   B. Windows 2000

16. What problem are you most likely to encounter when adding external SCSI disk drives to a SCSI bus?

   B. Exceeding the SCSI channel cable length

17. What are the proper combinations for installing memory modules into memory slots?

   D. Gold leads on memory modules, gold contacts in memory slots and tin leads on memory modules, tin contacts in memory slots

18. Which of the following limits the amount of memory that can be utilized in a network server?

   A. The control chipset on the network server motherboard

19. What is the process of replacing a SCSI disk drive with an SCA connector?

   A. Remove the old SCSI disk drive and insert the new SCSI disk drive.

Chapter 9

1. What is the name of the largest network of computers in the world?

   C. The Internet

2. When was the Internet developed?

   B. Late 1960

3. What is the term for three computers sharing communications?

   B. Network

4. How do you share a resource on the network in Windows 98 using Windows Explorer?

   D. Highlight the desired item and then right-click and select Sharing.

5. What is the problem if other computers on the network cannot see files or printers on your computer?

   D. You didn't enable file and print sharing.

6. To set up remote administration, which object would you select?

   B. Passwords

7. If you upgrade your LAN to use TCP/IP, what problem does this create?

   A. It requires large amounts of memory and lacks speed.

8. Which of the following is not a basic network architecture?

   C. Extended ring

9. What does NIC stand for?

   B. Network interface card

10. What does DNS provide?

    B. Unique alphanumeric addresses

11. When using a hub, the network topology changes from a linear bus to what?

    B. Star

12. What is the name of the standard Internet addressing scheme that creates the linkage between international subnetworks?

    B. IP address

13. If you are using a Token Ring network, when does each station transmit?

    C. Only when the station processes the token

14. How is a KVM switch used?

    B. With network servers

15. What is the name of a cable with a braided copper shield around it and only a single conductor?

    D. Coaxial

16. In a twisted-pair network, what type of conductor is used?

    C. 10BaseT

17. What should you do if you ping an IP address and cannot get a response?

    A. Use the TRACERT command.

18. How many layers does the OSI reference model have?

    B. Seven

19. Which layer of the OSI model describes the cable and how it is attached?

    D. Physical

20. Which layer of the OSI model is responsible for establishing a unique network address?

    A. Network

21. Which layer of the OSI model is responsible for the accuracy of the data transmission?

    D. Transport

22. Which layer of the OSI model translates data into an appropriate transmission format?

    C. Presentation

23. To receive access to the Internet, which network protocol is required?

    A. TCP/IP

24. Which of the following dialup protocols has the fastest connections?

    B. PPP

25. To receive a direct connection to the Internet, what is required?

    D. Only one router between the local network and the Internet

Chapter 10

1. What is the name of coils of wire that form electromagnets in a dot matrix printer?

    B. Solenoids

2. How many pins are in dot matrix printer print heads?

    A. 9 or 24

3. Which part of a dot matrix printer produces a burn if touched?

    D. The print head

4. Which of the following is a nonimpact printer?

    B. Ink jet

5. What type of printer forces ink through a nozzle when heated by an electrical current?

    C. Ink jet

6. When an ink jet printer has completed a print job, which of the following describes the paper?

    A. Is often still wet

7. How is the quality of print for an ink jet printer measured?

    B. dpi

8. To fix the toner to the paper, the top fuser roller in a laser printer is heated to about what temperature?

    B. 350°F

9. What is the primary corona wire of a laser printer?

    B. The voltage device that is used to erase the drum

10. In which laser-printing step is the toner applied to the latent image?

    A. Developing

11. What comes between the conditioning phase and the developing phase in the laser-printing process?

    B. Writing phase

12. What command and control languages are most commonly associated with printers?

    A. PCL and PostScript

13. What type of data transfer moves multiple bits of information in a single cycle?

    B. Serial

14. What is a printer driver?

    B. Software programs that allow the computer and the printer to communicate

15. How do you open the print queue in Windows 2000?

    B. Choose Start, Settings, Printers and double-click the printer.

16. How do you reorder a print job in a print queue in Windows 2000?

    C. Drag and drop it to the desired position in the queue

17. What is the first thing you should do when troubleshooting a printer problem?

    A. Check the power and paper.

18. What does Windows 2000 use to make the printer setup easier?

    B. Plug and Play support

19. What causes the majority of printer problems?

    A. Paper jams

Chapter 11

1. Which equipment is not used to clean computer components?

    D. A regular vacuum cleaner

2. What is the proper way to dispose of batteries used in portable computers?

    A. Recycling

3. What does MSDS stand for?

    B. Material safety data sheet

4. What substances can pass through a standard paint filter?

    A. Free liquids

5. What does ESD stand for?

    C. Electrostatic discharge

6. How many volts must be built up in order for a person to feel an ESD?

    A. 3000

7. Once a computer case has been opened, what should a technician do?

    B. Wear a grounding wrist strap.

8. What is the first thing to do if a new monitor is not working?

    D. Make sure that the power cord is firmly plugged in.

9. What is a common cause of erratic mouse movement?

    D. The mouse needs to be cleaned.

10. What utility is used to check the integrity of files and folders?

    A. ScanDisk

11. What utility reorganizes files on a hard drive?

    B. Disk Defragmenter

12. What is the term for a complete loss of power?

    A. Blackout

13. What is the term for a drop in power?

    B. Brownout

14. What is the term for a sudden increase in voltage that is higher than normal levels?

    C. Spike

15. What usually causes a brief increase in voltage?

    B. Surge

16. When should antivirus software be run?

    D. All of the above

17. What system runs off of a battery that is constantly charged?

    A. Uninterruptible power supply (UPS)

18. How is a surge suppressor used?

    B. To keep voltage below a certain level

19. In what system is a battery engaged when power is called for?

    B. Standby power supply (SPS)

Chapter 12

1. What is the first step in troubleshooting a PC problem?

    D. Eliminate the user as the source.

2. What range should the multimeter be set to when checking a power supply unit?

    B. DC voltage

3. How many changes should you make at one time when troubleshooting a PC?

    A. One

4. What is the most likely cause for a shaky video display?

    C. Faulty video adapter

5. What is the first thing to do if a new monitor is not working?

    D. Make sure that the power cord is firmly plugged in.

6. What would cause a monitor to fade?

    B. Phosphor coatings wear away.

7. What problem is indicated with one long beep and two short beeps during the bootup process?

    A. Video controller

8. If a power supply fan is running and the hard drive spins but the system seems dead, what might be the problem?

    D. The system board is defective.

9. What component might need to be replaced in a PC that randomly reboots or locks up after running for a time?

    D. Power supply

10. What is the problem if the system time resets when you turn off the computer?

    A. Defective CMOS battery

11. A new mouse has been installed but does not work. What is the problem?

    B. It requires a new driver.

12. What is the most likely cause of an erratic mouse?

    D. The mouse needs cleaning.

13. What can create a memory problem?

    A. Installing different-speed memory modules

14. One of your memory modules is hot. What does this indicate?

    D. It is defective or becoming defective.

15. What symbol is typically used in Windows to indicate a disabled hardware device?

    D. A red X

16. What symbol is typically used in the Windows Device Manager to indicate that a device has a problem?

B. A yellow exclamation point

17. What is a good way to test a problem with RAM?

D. Replace the module to see if the problem reoccurs.

18. The computer fails to start after installing a new sound card. What is the most likely cause of this problem?

C. There is an interrupt conflict between the sound card and another device.

19. A computer powers up but does not attach to the network. After rebooting, the problem still persists. What is a possible solution?

B. Check the Device Manager for network adapter conflicts.

20. What is the best source for troubleshooting information?

D. All of the above

Chapter 13

1. What three things make a successful technician?

B. Communication skills, technical skills, and troubleshooting skills

2. When troubleshooting an end user's computer, which item should not be explored?

D. The user's knowledge of computers

3. When isolating a problem during the troubleshooting process, which item should not be performed?

D. Remove all the internal components before doing anything else.

4. What is the name of the MS-DOS–based automated memory optimizer?

B. Memmaker

5. Which key is pressed to skip autoexec.bat and config.sys when the message "Starting MS-DOS" displays?

A. F5

6. Which of the following utilities can recover files from damaged disks?

D. ScanDisk and CHKDSK

7. If you have ScanDisk, you do not need to run which utility?

B. CHKDSK

8. Which utility can be used to increase access speed by rearranging files and directories on the hard drive?

C. Disk Defragmenter

9. An "Insufficient memory to run this application" error message displays. What should you do?

B. Increase the size of the swap file.

10. Which of the following software problems does not corrupt files?

    A. Faulty hard drive

11. What is the most common symptom of a corrupt file?

    C. Consistent lockups

12. What command allows you to access the Registry from the Start, Run dialog box?

    B. REGEDIT

13. What is the first utility you should run if a computer locks up?

    B. ScanDisk

14. Why does a GPF occur?

    C. An application is trying to write to a memory space that is occupied by another application.

15. What causes a page fault in Windows 98?

    D. All of the above

16. A NIC was working properly but is now causing connectivity problems. What do you check first?

    D. Verify that the NIC is installed and seated properly

17. Which two files do not load in Safe mode?

    A. autoexec.bat and config.sys

18. Which item is not displayed in the resource window for a device in the Device Manager?

    D. Delete settings button

19. Which utility is used to determine whether a specific IP address is accessible?

    C. ping.exe

20. Which utility traces a packet from the computer to an Internet host?

    A. tracert.exe

Glossary of Key Terms

/–Y   Switch added to the COPY command to display a confirmation prompt before overwriting an existing file.

/A   Switch added to the COPY command to copy ASCII files.

/ALL   Switch added to the SCANDISK command to check and repair all local drives at once.

/AUTOFIX   Switch added to the SCANDISK command to fix errors without further input.

/B   Switch added to the COPY command to copy binary files.

/C   Switch added to the MEM command to list programs currently loaded into memory. It shows how much conventional and upper memory each program is using.

/CHECKONLY   Switch added to the SCANDISK command to check for errors but not make repairs.

/D   Switch added to the MEM command to list the programs and internal drivers that are currently loaded into memory.

/F   Switch added to the MEM command to list the free areas of conventional and upper memory.

/P   Switch added to the MEM command to pause at each screen of information.

/Q   Switch added to the FORMAT command to perform a quick format; it does not clear the FAT.

/S   Switch added to the FORMAT command to copy system files.

/STATUS   Switch added to the FDISK command to display partition information.

/U   Switch added to the FORMAT command to perform an unconditional format.

/V   Switch added to the COPY command to verify the action.

/Y   Switch added to the COPY command to replace existing files without a confirmation prompt.

1000BaseT   Supports data transfer rates of 1 Gbps.

100BaseX   The evolution of 10BaseT. It is available in different varieties based on the type of cabling used.

10BaseT   The most popular Ethernet using the star topology with a transmission speed of 10 Mbps.

16450 UART   A two-byte buffer.

16550 UART   A FIFO (first in, first out) buffer that effectively eliminates data overrun.

3D graphics   A three-dimensional environment.

8250 UART   A one-byte buffer (temporal storage for data as it is sent out bit-by-bit out a serial line such as a phone line).

-a   Switch used with the ARP command that displays the cache.

Accelerated Graphics Port (AGP)   Developed by Intel, AGP is a dedicated high-speed bus that supports the high demands of graphical software. Expansion slot for installing the video card.

access control entry (ACE)   An entry to the ACL.

access control list (ACL)   A list managed by the administrator that displays files a user has access to and the type of access that has been granted.

access time   How quickly the data can be located.

Add Print wizard   Used to install a new printer on the system.

Add/Remove Hardware   Used to install and remove hardware on the computer.

Add/Remove Programs   Used to install and remove programs on the computer.

address bus   A unidirectional pathway, which means that information can only flow one way.

address resolution protocol (ARP)   The means by which networked computers map Internet protocol (IP) addresses to physical hardware (MAC) addresses that are recognized in a local network.

administrative tools   Utility that enables the administrator to control the computer system.

advanced accelerated graphics port (AGP)   Designed to handle the intense data throughput associated with three-dimensional graphics.

algorithm   A systematic description or method of how a series of steps is carried out.

all-points addressable displays   Displays that handle bitmaps.

AMI Diags   Program that provides advanced system testing and reports on memory, serial ports, parallel ports, modems, hard drives, keyboards, the BIOS, and video adapters.

AND gate   If either input is off, the output is off.

animation   A tool that creates sequential images that can be played in a series displaying continuous movement.

antistatic bag   Special packaging material that protects components from ESD.

antivirus application   A program that is installed on the system to prevent computer viruses from infecting the computer.

AppleTalk   A protocol suite to network Macintosh computers, comprised of a comprehensive set of protocols that span the seven layers of the OSI reference model. AppleTalk protocols were designed to run over the major LAN types, notably Ethernet and Token Ring, as well as over Apple's LAN physical topology, LocalTalk.

application layer   The fourth layer in the TCP/IP model. It is the starting point for communication sessions.

application software   Accepts input from the user and manipulates it to achieve a result, known as output.

application window   The window for a program that includes a title bar, tool bar, menu bar, status bar, and scroll bar.

application-specific integrated circuit (ASIC)   A compression chip that reduces the size of a file by removing redundant information from consecutive frames.

architecture   The overall structure of a computer or communication system.

archive   A backup copy of files.

Arithmetic/Logic Unit (ALU)   Performs both arithmetic and logical operations.

ARP cache   ARP builds and maintains a table called the ARP cache, which contains these mappings (IP address to MAC address). The ARP cache is the means by which a correlation is maintained between each MAC address and its corresponding IP address.

asd.exe   Used to skip a driver when the operating system fails during bootup.

aspect ratio   The display screen width relative to its height.

asymmetric DSL (ADSL)   Currently the most common implementation of DSL. It has speeds of 384 kbps to more than 6 Mbps downstream. The upstream speed is typically lower.

asynchronous   Does not use a clock or timing source to keep both the sender and receiver in sync.

asynchronous serial transmission   Data bits are sent without a synchronizing clock pulse. This transmission method uses a start bit at the beginning of each message. When the receiving device gets the start bit, it can synchronize its internal clock with the sender's clock.

AT commands   Modem control commands.

AT power supply   Designed to support AT compatible motherboards.

ATA-2 disk drives   A new and improved IDE.

ATTRIB   Command used to display, set, or remove one or more attributes.

attributes   A set of parameters that describe a file.

ATX   A type of motherboard.

ATX power supply   Designed according to newer ATX design specifications to support the ATX motherboard.

autoexec.bat   Configuration file used by the operating system. It contains a group of DOS commands that are automatically carried out when DOS is loaded into the system.

autoexec.bat   Contains a list of DOS commands that are automatically executed when DOS is loaded into the system.

automatic private IP addressing (APIPA)   An operating system feature that enables a computer to assign itself an address if it is unable to contact a DHCP server.

available desktop space   A consideration when choosing a computer case.

Baby AT   A type of motherboard.

background tab   Adjusts the appearance of the desktop.

backup.exe   Used to start the backup process.

Base 2   Same as binary, uses two digits to express all numerical quantities.

basic disk   A physical disk that contains the primary partition, extended partition, or logical drive.

basic disk storage   Industry standard for all versions of Windows.

Basic input/output system (BIOS)   The instructions and data in the ROM chip that control the boot process and your computer's hardware.

beep code error messages   The audible reporting of errors found by the BIOS during the POST.

bezel   Faceplate.

bidirectional   A type of parallel port used for rapid transmission over short distances.

binary   Same as Base 2, number system that uses two digits to express all numerical quantities.

BIOS   Basic input output system.

BIOS recovery   Used for recovering BIOS data from a diskette in the event of a catastrophic failure.

BIOS setup   Provides access to configure the BIOS. Allows the customization of a computer to function optimally based on the hardware and software profiles.

BIOS setup access   Enables or disables access to the Setup program.

bit   The smallest unit of data in a computer.

bit-depth   The number of bits used to describe a pixel.

bit-depth for sound   The sample size and bus size of the sound card.

bitmaps   A type of graphical image.

blackout   A complete loss of power.

block   Same as a cluster.

boot files   Used to start the system.

boot sector   Contains information about how the disk is organized.

boot sector   The first area on each logical drive.

boot sector virus   Virus that targets the boot sector of the system so that the virus is run when the computer starts.

bootable disk A disk created to boot the computer to the operating system for troubleshooting purposes. It contains the three required system files. Also known as a system disk.

bootlog.txt A file that contains the system information that is collected as the system is booting up.

Bootstrap Loader A program launched when the computer is first turned on.

boxed processors Processors that come with the fan and heat sink already attached.

bridge Connects network segments.

British Navel Connector (BNC) A connector used with coaxial cable.

brownout A temporary drop in power.

bugs Flaws in BIOS code.

built-in fonts Resident fonts that are part of ROM and built into the printer.

built-in modem Used in some notebook computers.

built-in sound An audio processor that is located on the motherboard.

bus The communication pipeline between a computer and its peripherals.

bus topology Connects all devices on a single cable.

business graphics Used in presentation applications.

byte Eight bits of data.

C drive The label for the first hard drive in a computer system.

cable modem Acts like a LAN interface by connecting a computer to the Internet. The cable modem connects a computer to the cable company's network through the same coaxial cabling that feeds cable TV (CATV) signals to a television set.

cable select (CSEL) An option that decides master/slave hard drive relationships based on the position of the drive on the IDE cable.

carrier sense multiple access/collision detection (CSMA/CD) The LAN access method used in Ethernet. A device checks to see if the network is quiet (senses the carrier). If not, it waits a random amount of time before retrying. If the network is quiet and two devices access the line at the same time, their signals collide. When a collision is detected, both devices back off and wait a random amount of time before retrying.

cascading Redirecting, in regards to IRQ.

Category 3 Primarily used in telephone connections.

Category 5   Four pairs of wires with a maximum data rate of 100 Mbps.

Category 5e   Provides more twists per foot than Category 5.

Category 6   Not yet ratified by the cabling industry. It has a plastic divider that separates the pairs of wires, preventing crosstalk.

cathode ray tube (CRT)   A type of computer display that requires a certain distance from the beam-projection device to the screen.

CD recorder   Also referred to as CD burner. Allows CD media to be recorded with data, audio, or any combination.

CD   DOS command that changes or displays the current directory on a specific drive.

CD-R   Compact disc–recordable. The CD media that can be recorded using a CD recorder.

CD-ROM   Compact disc read-only memory. Removable media for audio and data. Secondary data storage.

CD-ROM drive   A secondary storage device.

CD-ROM drive read speed   Determines the rate at which information can be pulled from the CD and sent to the communications bus.

CD-ROM library   Multiple CD-ROM drives in a tower attached to a network that can be accessed by all the users on a network.

CD-RW   Compact disc–rewritable. CD media that can be recorded multiple times.

central processing unit (CPU)   A complete computation engine that is fabricated on a single chip. It not only controls the functions of the computer, but also handles requests from many input and output devices.

Checkit   Program that performs system analysis and testing.

chipset   A group of microcircuits contained on several integrated chips or combined into one or two large scale integration (VLSI) integrated chips.

CHKDSK /f   DOS utility that checks the system for errors.

chkdsk.exe   A command-line tool that is used to recover lost allocation units from the hard drive.

Cinepak   A compression/decompression standard supported by Video for Windows.

circuit   The pathway that a data transmission takes.

circuit-switched communications network   Developed for use primarily by the telephone, it provides one physical path that is used for the duration of the transmission.

cleaning   The first step in the laser-printing process that removes toner from the drum.

clear CMOS   Used to reset the CMOS settings to the default values.

client/server network   A network where services are located in a dedicated computer that responds to client (or user) requests.

cluster   A combination of two or more sectors.

coaxial   Digital configuration that uses an RCA jack.

coaxial cable   Copper-cored cable surrounded by a heavy shielding.

cold boot   The process of starting the computer from the off position.

color depth   The number of colors that can be displayed.

color ink jet printer   Type of printer that uses liquid ink-filled cartridges that spray ink to form an image on the paper.

color space conversion   The process of converting the YUV signal into the RGB format that is acceptable to the VGA card screen memory.

colors   The number of colors that can be displayed.

command interpreter   Also known as command.com in Windows 95/98 and cmd.exe in Windows NT/2000, it displays the DOS prompt and executes the commands typed in.

command line   The main user interface in DOS.

communication circuit   Used to send the information read from the CD to the computer using the configured bus.

complementary metal oxide semiconductor (CMOS)   A battery-powered storage chip located on the system board. Stores the system startup configurations and parameters. CMOS contains software that sets and records the master configuration for all components in the system. The CMOS chip has rewritable memory since the configuration data can be changed or updated as the components or devices in the computer are changed.

compressed air   Also called canned air, it is compressed air in a can that is used to blow dust off of computer components without creating static.

compression   A tool that compresses or makes a file or folder smaller.

Compression state   Describes whether a file is compressed or uncompressed.

Computer Aided Design (CAD)   An application that performs solid modeling.

computer case   The metal chassis that houses the computer components.

computer network   Two or more devices, such as workstations printers, or servers, that are linked for the purpose of sharing information, resources, or both.

computer system   Hardware and software components.

conditioning   The second step in the laser-printing process that prepares the drum for a new image.

CONFIG   A configuration utility used in NetWare (server console) to access IP address, MAC address, subnet mask, and default gateway.

config.sys   Configuration file used by the operating system. It loads drivers and changes settings at startup.

control bus   Carries the control and timing signals needed to coordinate the activities of the entire computer.

control unit   Instructs the rest of the computer system on how to follow a program's instructions.

conventional memory   Includes all memory addresses between 0 and 640 KB. It is also known as base memory.

converter   Converts data for sound.

copper distributed data interface (CDDI)   The FDDI technology with copper cabling.

COPY   Used to copy one or more files from one location to another.

copy   Makes a duplicate of a document or file and puts it on the clipboard. The document can then be pasted to another location.

copy backup   Backs up user-selected files. It does not reset the archive bit.

Create Shortcut   Creates a link to a file or application.

cylinder   All the tracks on a hard disk with the same number.

-d   Switch used with the ARP command that deletes an entry from the ARP cache.

daily backup   Backs up only the files that are modified on the day of the backup. It does not reset the archive bit.

data bus   A bidirectional pathway for data flow, which means that information can flow in two directions.

data channel   The path over which a signal is sent.

data transfer rate   How fast data can be transferred into memory.

database   An application that organizes and manages data.

DATE   Command in autoexec.bat that causes DOS to prompt the user for the date.

date and time   Configuration data required for many types of software applications to manage data.

default gateway   The route used so that a computer on one segment can communicate with a computer on another segment.

default printer   The printer that all print jobs are sent to automatically.

defrag.exe   Used to rewrite all the files on the hard drive contiguously, making it easier and faster for the hard drive to retrieve data.

DEL   Command that removes named files.

DELTREE   DOS command that removes a directory, including all files and subdirectories.

desktop   The main display screen. It's designed to sit horizontally on the desktop.

desktop model   A type of case that sits horizontally.

Details mode   The view option that provides the most details of a file.

detcrash.log   A file that is created if the system crashes during the hardware-detection phase of the startup process.

detlog.txt   Used to read the information that is generated when the detcrash.log file is created.

developing   The fourth step in the laser-printing process that applies toner to the latent image.

device drivers   Program code for devices and internal components, which tells the operating system how to control specific devices.

Device Manager   Used to disable, uninstall, and update device drivers. Displays a list of all the hardware installed on the system.

DEVICEHIGH/LOADHIGH   Puts upper memory blocks into use once himem.sys and emm386.exe have been loaded.

DEVICEHIGH=   Command used to load drivers into the upper memory area instead of loading them into conventional memory.

diagnostic partition utility   Enables the troubleshooting of nonfunctioning hardware components.

diagnostic software   Programs used to assist in the troubleshooting process.

diagnostic tools   Utilities used to monitor the network server.

dialup networking (DUN)   When computers use the public telephone system or network to communicate. The modem must operate in the local command state or online state to enable DUN.

differential backup   Backs up all the files that have been created or modified since the last full backup. It does not rest the archive bit.

digital audio extraction (DAE)   The process of copying audio from a CD to another medium while keeping the audio in its original digital state.

digital subscriber line (DSL)   An always-on technology used to connect to the Internet.

digital versatile disc (DVD)   Removable media used primarily for movie and data storage.

digital-in port   An interface used to capture digital audio.

Dijkstra algorithm   An algorithm used to find the shortest path between a specific networking device.

DIR   Command in autoexec.bat that causes a DOS DIR command to be performed automatically.

Direct Memory Access (DMA)   Allows devices to bypass the processor and directly access the computer memory.

directories   A group of files stored in DOS.

directories and name services   Make it possible for users to find people and services on a computer network.

directory   A place to store data in the Windows file-management system.

directory tree   A graphical representation of a disk drive's directory organization.

Disk Defragmenter   Utility that optimizes space on the hard drive.

disk duplexing   Refers to a mirrored set where each disk is connected to a different disk controller.

disk management   The process of optimizing disk space.

disk mirroring   Refers to two disk drives connected to the same disk controller.

disk platter   A component of a hard drive, actual media on which data is stored in the hard disk drive.

disk quotas   Provide the ability to assign limits to the amount of hard disk space that users are allocated.

disk stripping   Also known as RAID 0, it is not fault tolerant but is used to improve disk input/output performance.

display   A computer output surface and projecting mechanism that shows text and graphic images.

display adapter   *See* video adapter.

Display utility   Allows the user to adjust the way the computer screen looks.

docking station or docking port   Allows the portable PC to operate with hardware devices associated with desktop computers.

document details   Attributes.

Documents menu   Displays the most recently accessed documents.

Domain Name System (DNS)   Translates computer names into IP addresses.

DOS (Disk Operating System)   A collection of programs and commands used to control the overall computer operation in a disk-based system.

DOS boot disk   Used to boot a computer to the DOS prompt.

DOS command   An instruction that is executed from a command line.

DOS=HIGH   Option included in config.sys to tell the operating system to move a portion of itself to the high memory area.

DOSKEY   Command in autoexec.bat that loads the DOSKEY program into memory.

dot matrix printer   A printer that works by impacting the ribbon onto the paper.

dot pitch   The size of an individual beam that gets through to light up a point of a phosphor on the screen.

dots per inch (dpi)   How the actual sharpness of a display image is measured.

double data rate SDRAM   New synchronous dynamic RAM that increases memory clock speed to at least 200 MHz.

downstream   The process of transferring data from the server to the end user.

Dr. Watson utility   Used to isolate and correct GPFs.

DRAM   Memory that is inexpensive and somewhat slow, and requires an uninterrupted power supply to maintain the data. When the power is turned off, the data is lost.

DRAM (Dynamic RAM)   Works by storing data electrically in a storage cell and refreshing the storage every few milliseconds.

Drive A: and Drive B: Configuration data identifies the types of floppy disk drives using the options available.

drive letter   Distinguishes the drives in Windows.

drive motor   Spins the CD up to the proper speed so that the laser can read the data.

dual inline memory module (DIMM)   Memory module with 168 pins that supports 64-bit transfers.

dual-boot   An option that provides the choice to boot the system to either Windows 2000 or Windows 98 if both are installed.

DVD drive   Computer drive that can play/read DVDs. A DVD drive can read CDs and DVDs, while a CD drive can only read CDs.

DVD physical formats   Define the structure of the disc and the area where the data are recorded.

DVD+RW   Similar to DVD-RW, uses variable bit-rate when encoding.

DVD-Audio   New format that includes multiple-channel audio.

DVD-R   A DVD drive that allows a DVD to be written to once.

DVD-RAM   Uses random-access memory to enable users to record DVDs multiple times.

DVD-ROM   Designed for storing computer files.

DVD-RW   Drive that allows the media to be recorded multiple times.

DVD-Video   Format used by standalone DVD players for movies and extras.

dynamic disk storage   A method of data storage using the hard drive(s) to create multidisk volumes.

dynamic host configuration protocol (DHCP)   A software utility that automatically assigns IP addresses in a large network.

dynamic link library (dll) file   Small files that store subroutines for a program.

EDIT   Command used to view or modify files.

edit.com   A Windows troubleshooting tool that can view and edit configuration files such as autoexec.bat and config.sys and ini files.

EISA configuration utility   Enables the configuration of the components of the network server.

electrically erasable programmable read-only memory (EEPROM) Flash BIOS.

electronic mail (e-mail) The ability for users to communicate over a computer network.

Electronics Industry Association (EIA) Develops standards for electronics used in the computer industry.

electrostatic discharge (ESD) The buildup of an electric charge resting on a surface.

emergency repair disk (ERD) Disk used to restore the operating system.

emm386.exe Memory-management program that provides the system with access to the upper memory area of RAM.

encryption A security feature that applies a coding to a file so that only authorized users can view the file.

encryption algorithm An algorithm that encrypts data.

encryption file system (EFS) The means to apply encryption.

end-to-end Refers to the pathway that is currently available for a telephone, for example. It is a temporary path.

enhanced IDE A new and improved IDE.

EPROM and EEPROM ROM chips that can be erased and reprogrammed.

error correcting code (ECC) Detects and corrects single-bit errors and detects double-bit errors. It is read and decoded each time data are read from the disk.

ESD discharge (ESD) Static electricity.

Ethernet architecture Based on the IEEE 802.3 standard that specifies that a network implement CSMA/CD.

Euclidean algorithm An algorithm essentially used to do long division.

Event Viewer Used to monitor system events, application events, and security events in Windows 9X.

expanded memory Memory closely related to upper memory.

expanded memory specification (EMS) Memory accessed in pages (16-KB pieces) from a 64-KB page frame, established in unused UMBs.

expansion cards Most common type of card. They plug into the motherboard expansion slots (ISA or PCI). Also called internal modems.

expansion slots Receptacles on the computer motherboard that accept printed circuit boards.

extended data-out RAM (EDO RAM)   Extends the amount of time that data are stored and has a reduced refresh rate.

extended memory   Memory above 1 MB.

extended memory specification (XMS)   Primary memory area used by Windows 9X.

extended partition   Second partition on the hard drive.

extended star topology   A star topology expanded to include additional networking devices.

external command   A command that must be executed from a file.

external modem   Used with any computer, it plugs into a serial port (COM1 or COM2) on the back of the computer. External modems are typically used for high-speed connections such as the cable modem.

external peripheral   A device that is external to the network server.

external speakers   Output devices for the sound card.

F5   Skips config.sys, including autoexec.bat files.

F8   Proceeds through the config.sys files (and autoexec.bat if needed), waiting for confirmation from the user.

faceplate   The front case panel.

Fast Ethernet   100BaseX.

FAT 16 file system   Used with DOS, Windows 3.1, and the first version of Windows 95.

FAT 32 file system   Evolved from FAT 16 and supports drives up to 2048 GB in size.

FAT32   An improved version of FAT that was introduced in Windows 98.

fault tolerance   The ability to restore a disk to a consistent state with minimal data loss.

FDDI Class A   Computers connected to the cables of both rings.

FDDI Class B   Computers connected to only one ring.

FDISK   An external DOS command used to delete and/or create partitions on the hard drive.

FDISK/MBR   DOS command used to create or rewrite the MBR so that the system can boot.

fdisk.exe   Used to delete and create partitions on the hard drive.

feature set   Additional features that include 3D audio coprocessors, device controllers, and digital output options.

Fiber Distributed Data Interface (FDDI)   A type of Token Ring used in larger LANs or MANs.

fiber-optic cable   Conducts modulated light to transmit data.

field-replaceable unit (FRU)   Computer component that can be easily replaced.

file   A block of logically related data given a single name and treated as a single unit.

file allocation table (FAT)   A table of records that includes the location of every directory, subdirectory, and file on the hard drive.

file cabinet   The hard drive in a computer where files are stored.

file extensions   Describe the file format or the type of application used to create a file.

file management   The hierarchical structure of files, folders, and drives in Windows.

file transfer protocol (FTP)   An application that provides services for file transfer and manipulation.

file virus   Virus that modifies an existing program so that, upon execution, it carries out a malicious intent.

file-management files   Enable the system to manage data.

file-management system   Used by the operating system to organize and manage files.

filename   The logical name given to a collection of data.

FireWire   High-speed, platform-independent communication bus that interconnects digital printers and other devices.

FIXBOOT   Command that writes a new boot sector to the system partition.

FIXMBR   Command used with the Recovery Console to fix hard drive problems.

Flash BIOS   Allows the upgrade of the BIOS software from a disk provided by the manufacturer without replacing the chip.

Flash ROM   Special EEPROM chips that can be reprogrammed under special software control. Upgrading BIOS by running special software is known as *flashing*.

flat-file database   Data stored in a single table.

floppy disk drive (FDD)   A device that magnetically reads and writes information onto floppy diskettes.

flux   Local magnetic direction in the media.

flux pattern   The recorded data on a track.

flux reversal   Opposite magnetic orientation in the media.

folder   A place to store data in the Windows file-management system.

font   A complete set of characters of a particular typeface used for display and printing purposes.

font card   Expansion slot that allows memory upgrades, different printer interfaces, and font upgrades.

form factor   The general layout of the computer case.

FORMAT   Command that erases all information from a computer disk or hard drive.

format.exe   Used to erase a hard drive.

formatting   Preparing a hard drive to store data.

frame-by-frame   A type of animation.

free liquids   Substances that can pass through a standard paint filter. Many dump sites do not handle free liquids.

Frequency Modulation (FM) sound card   Uses programming to create waveforms that best match the instrument that is playing.

full backup   Also called a normal backup, it backs up all files on a disk.

full duplex   Data transmission that can go two ways at the same time. An Internet connection using a DSL is an example.

fusing   The sixth step in the laser-printing process that rolls the paper between a heated roller and a pressure roller.

ganged   A way in which disks are stacked in a hard drive.

gas plasma   A type of computer display that works by lighting up display screen positions based on the voltages at different grid intersections.

gas-plasma panels   Display designed to be used in portable computers.

general protection fault (GPF)   An error that occurs when one of the operating system applications attempts to access an unallocated memory location.

Gigabit Ethernet   1000BaseT.

gigahertz (MHz)   1,000,000,000 cycles per second.

global method   Allows a printer to be selected and used for all applications.

graphical user interface (GUI; pronounced goo-ee)   Uses a visual display to represent the procedures and programs that can be executed by the computer.

graphics accelerator   An adapter that improves video.

graphics applications   An application used to create or modify graphical images.

grounding wrist strap   Device that attaches to a technician's wrist and the computer case that dissipates ESD.

Group Policy Editor (GPE)   Used to edit the configuration settings in a network environment.

half-duplex transmission   Data transmission that can go two ways but not at the same time. A telephone and two-way radio are examples.

halt on   Configuration data that allows a specific system response to errors.

hard disk drive (HDD)   The computer's main storage medium.

hard disks   Configuration data that identifies devices attached to the two IDE controllers integrated on the motherboard.

hard drive   Primary data storage.

hardware   The physical equipment of a computer system.

hardware abstraction layer (HAL)   A library of hardware drivers that communicate between the operating system and the hardware that is installed.

hardware compatibility list (HCL)   A tool used to verify that hardware is compatible with the operating system.

hardware failure   A malfunction of a computer component.

hardware profiles   Windows NT, 2000, and XP can support two or more hardware profile configurations in the Registry.

hardware-based RAID   Implements RAID using a hardware device called a RAID controller.

Hayes-compatible command set   Set of commands that most modem software uses. They are named after the Hayes Microcomputer Products Company, which first defined them.

Head Actuator Assembly   A component of the hard drive.

Help feature   Provides instructions and tips on using the computer system.

hertz (Hz)   The rate of change in the state or cycle in a sound wave, alternating current, or other cyclical waveform.

hidden file   An attribute that hides files. Primarily used to hide important files that should not be changed.

high data rate DSL (HDSL)   Provides a bandwidth of 768 kbps in both directions.

high-level format routine   Creates the logical structure on the drive that tells the system what files are on the disk and where they can be found.

high-performance file system (HPFS)   Older file system used with Windows NT 3.51.

himem.sys   Memory-management program that manages the extended memory above 1024 KB.

HKEY_CLASSES_ROOT   Contains software configuration data of all the software that is installed on the computer.

HKEY_CURRENT_CONFIG   Contains data on the active hardware profile that is selected during the boot process. This information is used to configure settings for the device drivers to load and for the display resolution to use.

HKEY_CURRENT_USER   Contains data about the user who is currently logged on to the computer. Retrieves a copy of each user account that is used to log on to the computer and stores it in the Registry.

HKEY_LOCAL_MACHINE   Contains all configuration data for the local computer, including hardware and operating system data such as bus type, system memory, device drivers, and startup control data. Applications, device drivers, and the operating system use these data to set the computer configuration. The data in this subtree remain constant, regardless of the user.

HKEY_USERS   Contains the system default settings that are used to control individual user profiles and environments such as desktop settings, the Windows environment, and custom software settings.

host-based printing   Technology in which the operating system communicates directly with the printer and sends the printer an image that is ready to print.

Hot expansion   Installing a new adapter in an empty slot while the server remains operational.

Hot replacement   Replacing an existing adapter while the server remains operational.

Hot upgrade   Upgrading an existing adapter while the server remains operational.

Hot-swappable peripherals   Peripherals that can be changed while the system is running.

hub   A device used to extend an Ethernet wire to allow more devices to communicate with each other.

hwinfo.exe   A utility that provides a detailed collection of information about the computer.

hybrid topology   A combination of one or more topologies.

HyperText Markup Language (HTML)   Page description language.

Hypertext Transfer Protocol (HTTP)   Governs how files are exchanged on the Internet.

ICMP echo request/reply   Ping works by sending an ICMP echo request to the destination computer. The receiving computer then sends back an ICMP echo reply message.

icon   An image representing an application or capability.

IEEE   Institute of Electrical and Electronics Engineers, based in New York (www.ieee.org). A membership organization that sets standards for computers and communications.

IFCONFIG   A configuration utility used in UNIX and Linux (command-line) to access IP address, MAC address, subnet mask, and default gateway.

illegal operation   Error message in Windows that indicates that the system has encountered an problem.

illustration   A tool that creates and manipulates vector based images.

image editing   A tool that creates and manipulates raster or bitmap images.

impact printer   Class of printer that includes dot matrix and daisy wheel.

incremental backup   Backs up all the files that have been created or modified since the last full backup.

Indeo   Data compression method developed by Intel.

Industry Standard Architecture (ISA)   A 16-bit expansion slot developed by IBM. It transfers data with the motherboard at 8 MHz.

information superhighway   The benefit of the Internet to business and private communications.

infrared   Type of communication that uses a spectrum of light to transmit and receive.

input   Recognizing data entered to the computer via a keyboard or mouse. As it relates to the sound card, it is the process of capturing sound from microphones, CD players, DAT players, and MIDI devices.

input device   A device that transfers data into the computer, including a keyboard, mouse, scanner, etc.

instant messaging (IM) services   The ability for users to communicate in real time, or without delay, over a computer network.

Integrated Drive Electronics (IDE)   A type of hardware interface widely used to connect hard disks, CD-ROMs, and tape drives.

internal command   A command that is built into the operating system.

internal modem   Plugs into one of the expansion slots on the motherboard. No configuration is needed for a Plug and Play (PnP) modem, which is installed on a motherboard that supports PnP.

International Organization for Standardization (ISO)   Developed the OSI model in the 1980s.

Internet   A worldwide public network forming one large web of communication.

Internet Control Message Protocol (ICMP)   Used for network testing and troubleshooting. It enables diagnostic and error messages. ICMP echo messages are used by the ping application to test if a remote device is reachable.

Internet Protocol (IP)   Provides source and destination addressing and, in conjunction with routing protocols, packet forwarding from one network to another toward a destination.

Internet service provider (ISP)   A private network that enables users to connect to the Internet.

Interpress   PDL developed by Xerox to handle the Xerox line of high-speed printers.

IPCONFIG   A configuration utility used in Windows NT and Windows 2000 (command-line) to access IP address, MAC address, subnet mask, and default gateway.

ipconfig.exe   A utility that is the Windows NT/2000 equivalent of the winipcfg.exe utility found in Windows 95, 98, and Me. It performs the same functions as the winipcfg.exe utility in that it allows users to view all the IP address information as well as the WINS server addresses, DNS server addresses, and the DHCP server addresses.

IPTRACE   A configuration utility used in NetWare NLM to trace packets on a network.

ISDN DSL (IDSL)   Has a top speed of 144 kbps but is available only in areas that do not qualify for other DSL implementations. IDSL is DSL running over ISDN lines.

Joint Photographic Experts Group (JPEG)   A compression standard used with digitized video.

kernel   The core of the operating system that loads and runs programs or processes and manages input and output.

key   Used in a database as a unique identifier.

keyboard/video/monitor (KVM) switch   A switch that allows a single keyboard, video display, and mouse to be used with all network servers.

keyframe   A type of animation.

kilobit (Kb)   1024 bits.

kilobit per second (Kbps)   Data transfer rate of about 1000 bits per second.

kilobyte (KB)   1024 bytes.

kilobytes per second (KBps)   A data transfer rate of about 1000 bytes per second.

L1 cache   A specialized computer chip that enhances memory performance located on the CPU.

L2 cache   A specialized computer chip that enhances memory performance located between the CPU and DRAM.

lands   The bumps on the surface of a CD.

laser assembly   Consists of a laser and a lens that reads the CD as it spins.

laser printer   Type of printer that uses static electricity and a laser to form the image to the paper.

LASTDRIVE=   Command contained in the config.sys file. It specifies the maximum number of drives the system can access.

latent image   In laser printers, the undeveloped image.

light-emitting diode (LED)   A type of computer display that works by lighting up display screen positions based on the voltages at different grid intersections.

line-in port   An interface used to capture audio from amplified or powered sources such as external stereos.

liquid crystal display (LCD)   A type of computer display that works by blocking light rather than creating it.

local command state   The modem is offline. It receives commands and provides status information to the host computer to which the modem is installed.

local security policy   The options selected to ensure a secure computer network.

local users   An account created that allows a user access to the network.

local-area network (LAN)   A communication network that covers a small geographical area.

logic gates   An electronic circuit that recognizes AND, OR, NOT, and NOR.

logical drives   Sections that the partition can be divided into.

logical standards   Define the way information is stored on the media.

logical topology   The paths that signals travel from one point on a network to another.

logical unit number (LUN)   A seldom-used SCSI standard that allows sub-SCSI IDs to a single SCSI ID, allowing one SCSI channel to support multiple CDs.

loopback plugs or connectors   A way of testing signaling ports.

low-level format routine   Marks off the disk into sectors and cylinders, and defines their placement on the disk.

Macintosh   Designed to be user friendly, based on the UNIX core technology.

macro virus   Virus that takes advantage of programming languages to attack a system.

mainframe   A centralized computer that allows end users to interface via "dumb terminals."

master boot record (MBR)   The program responsible for starting the boot process. It determines which partition is used for booting the system and transfers control to the boot sector of that partition, which continues the boot process.

material safety data sheet (MSDS)   A fact sheet that identifies hazardous materials.

maximize the screen   Restoring the size of the display to full screen.

media handling option   The way a printer handles media, such as paper.

medium   The communication channel or cable that enables computers to communicate over the network.

megabit per second (Mbps)   Data transfer rate of about 1,000,000 bits per second.

megabyte (MB)   1,048,576 bytes.

megabyte per second (MBps)   Data transfer rate of about 1,000,000 bytes per second.

megahertz (MHz)   1,000,000 cycles per second.

MEM   An external DOS command used to display a table showing how RAM is currently allocated.

MEMMAKER   System memory tool used to simplify the task of placing TSRs into upper memory.

mesh topology   Interconnects devices providing redundancy and fault tolerance.

metropolitan-area network (MAN)   A network that spans an area larger than a local area network typically implemented with fiber-optic cable.

microphone-in port   An interface used to connect a microphone for sound to the PC.

microsoft audio visual interface (AVI)   A popular file format for video.

Microsoft TechNet   A large database of troubleshooting pages found on the Microsoft website.

Microsoft Windows NT/2000/XP   Operating systems designed to support multiple users and to run multiple applications simultaneously.

MIDI port   A standard interface used to connect musical devices.

minijack   Configuration for the digital-in port that is physically the same as the microphone-in and line-in ports.

minimize the screen   Reducing the size of the display window.

mirrored volume   Contains two identical copies of a simple volume that stores the same data on two separate hard drives.

MKDIR   DOS command that creates a new directory or subdirectory.

modem   Stands for modulator/demodulator, a device that converts the digital data used by computers into analog signals that is suitable for transmission over a telephone line, and converts the analog signals back to a digital signal at the destination.

modulator/demodulator   *See* modem.

monitor   A device to view output. *See also* display.

MORE   DOS command that displays output one screen at a time.

motherboard location map   Shows where the major components and hardware is located on the motherboard.

Motherboard/System Board   The nerve center of the computer.

move   Relocates a file or document to a new location.

Moving Picture Experts Group (MPEG)   A compression standard used with digitized video.

msconfig.exe   A command-line tool that is used to interactively load device drivers and software options.

multimedia   The combination of text, sound, and/or motion video.

multiprocessing   Allows a computer to have two or more CPUs that programs share.

multitasking   The computer's ability to run multiple applications at the same time.

multithreading   The capability of a program to be broken into smaller parts that can be loaded as needed by the operating system.

multiuser   The ability for two or more users to run programs and share resources.

musical instrument digital interface (MIDI)   A combination of hardware and software that allows the sound card to control musical instruments and use these instruments to output the audio.

My Computer   Icon on the desktop that gives access to all the installed drives.

My Computer window   Displays the drives on the computer.

My Documents   A shortcut to personal or frequently accessed files.

name resolution   The process of name translation.

NBTSTAT   Used by Windows to display NetBIOS information.

near letter quality (NLQ)   The highest quality of print that is produced by the dot matrix printer.

Net View   A command that displays a list of domains, a list of computers, and a list of resources for a computer.

NetBIOS extended user interface (NetBEUI)   A protocol used primarily on small Windows NT networks. NetBEUI is a simple protocol that lacks many of the features that enable protocol suites such as TCP/IP to be used on networks of almost any size.

NETSTAT   A command that is used in Windows and UNIX/Linux to display TCP/IP connection and protocol information.

netstat.exe (network statistics)   A utility that displays the current TCP/IP network connections and protocol information for the computer.

network   A group of computers that are connected so the resources can be shared.

network access point (NAP)   The point at which access providers are interconnected.

network administration   The task of network administrators to maintain and upgrade a private network.

network file services   Allow documents to be shared over a network to facilitate the development of a project.

network interface card (NIC)   Used to connect a local computer to a network.

network media   The means by which signals are sent from one computer to another (either cable or wireless).

Network Neighborhood   Displays neighboring computers in a networked environment.

network operating system (NOS)   An operating system that enables the server to track multiple users and programs.

network print services   Make printers available to many users.

network printer   Printer set up to be shared by multiple users.

network protocols   The second layer in TCP/IP model. It provides internetworking for the communications session.

network server   A computer that is shared by multiple users.

network servers (also know as servers)   Computers that are capable of handling multiple users and multiple jobs.

network topology   The way computers, printers, and other devices are connected.

nibble   One half a byte, or four bits.

noise   Interference that causes unclean power.

nonvolatile random access memory (NVRAM)   Stores the system startup configurations and parameters.

NOR gate   A combination of OR and NOT, if either input is on, the output is off.

NOT gate   If the input is on, the output is off, and vice versa.

NSLOOKUP   Returns the IP address for a given host name. It can also find the host name for a specified IP address.

ntdetect.com   Used by Intel-based systems to detect hardware that is installed in a system.

NT file system (NTFS)   Designed to manage global and enterprise-level operating systems.

object based   A type of graphical image.

object-oriented programming   A type of programming that uses algorithms.

octets   Four groups of eight bits.

online state   In this state, the modem is transferring data between the host machine and a remote computer through the telephone system.

Open Systems Interconnection (OSI)   A model that was created to define the multiple layers of a network.

operating system   A program that controls thousands of operations, provides an interface between the user and the computer, and runs applications.

optical media   The method used by a CD-ROM to read and write data.

OR gate   If either input is on, the output is on.

original equipment manufacturer (OEM) processors   Boxed processors.

output   The data sent from the computer to the monitor or printer.

output device   Displays or prints data processed by the computer.

packet-switched communications network   Individual packets of data take an available route. The route does not have to be dedicated, as in circuit-switched communications.

Page Description Language (PDL)   Code that describes the contents of a document in a language that the printer can understand.

pages per minute (ppm)   How the print speed is measured on a dot matrix printer.

parallel port   A socket on the computer used to connect peripheral devices that use a parallel interface.

parallel printer   Transfers multiple bits of information in a single cycle.

partition table   Partition information created by FDISK.

partitioning and formatting   Prepare the hard drive for the installation of an operating system.

password clear   Used to clear the password if the password is forgotten.

PATH=C:\;C:\DOS;C:\Mouse   Command in autoexec.bat that creates a specific set of paths that DOS uses to search for executable files.

PC technician   Program that operates independent of DOS to perform diagnostic tests on parallel ports, serial ports, hard drives, keyboards, video adapters, and RAM.

PCMCIA card   A variation of modems that is designed for easy installation in notebook computers. Also known as PC cards, they look like credit cards and are small and portable.

peer-to-peer network   A network where computers act as equal partners.

per-document setting method   Allows global settings to be overridden for an individual document.

performance   Displays information about the system.

Peripheral Component Interconnect (PCI)   A 32-bit local bus slot developed by Intel. Because they "talk" to the motherboard at 33 MHz, the PCI bus slots offer a significant improvement over ISA or EISA expansion slots.

peripheral component interconnect (PCI)   An adapter card with an audio processor that connects to the motherboard.

peripheral device   Any device that is not part of the core computer system.

permissions   File and directory permissions used to specify which users and groups can gain access to files and folders.

personal computer   A standalone device, independent of all other computers.

Personal Computer Memory Card International association (PCMCI)   An expansion card type designed primarily to accommodate the needs of the portable computer.

physical memory (also known as system memory)   Memory that is divided into four categories: conventional, upper/expanded, high, and extended.

physical standards   Define where the information is placed on the media.

physical topology   The layout of the devices and media.

ping   A simple but highly useful command-line utility that is included in most implementations of TCP/IP. Ping can be used with either the host name or the IP address to test IP connectivity.

ping.exe (packet Internet groper)   A utility used to determine whether a specific IP address is accessible.

pits   The indentations burned on a CD.

pixels   Tiny dots that make up the light on the screen and determine the intensity of a screen image.

platen   The large roller in a dot matrix printer.

Plug and Play (PnP)   Automatically configures devices and assigns resources for new hardware.

point-to-point   Same as end-to-end.

poledit.exe   Used to set up different security restrictions for different users.

portables   System unit, input unit, and output unit into a single, lightweight package.

POST   Power-on self test is a diagnostic tool that is run when the machine boots up in order to verify and test hardware.

POST card   A device that digitally reports errors in the event the computer fails before a BIOS error can be generated.

PostScript (PS)   Developed by Adobe Systems to allow fonts to share the same characteristics on-screen and on paper.

POTS   Plain old telephone service.

power supply unit   Provides electrical power for every component inside the system unit.

power-on self-test (POST)   A diagnostic test of memory and hardware when the system is powered up.

powers of numbers   The number of times a number is multiplied by itself.

presentation applications   Organize, design, and deliver business presentations in the form of slide shows.

primary corona wire   Also called the grid or conditioning roller, it is the voltage device that is used to erase the drum.

primary partition   First partition on the hard drive.

print queue   A temporary holding area for print jobs that are waiting to be fed to the printer.

print resolution   The number of dots that the print head is capable of fitting per inch when forming an image.

print sharing   Allows multiple users or clients to access a printer that is directly connected to a single computer, the print server.

printed circuit board   A computer component.

Printer Control Language (PCL)   Developed by Hewlett-Packard to allow software applications to communicate with HP and HP-compatible laser printers.

printer driver   Software that must be installed on the PC so that the printer can communicate and coordinate the printing process.

printer network interface card (NIC)   An adapter that the printer uses to access the network media.

printer output option   Determines how the ink or toner is transferred to the paper.

printer switch   Also known as an A/B switch, it is hardware that routes data input from one device to another.

process   Manipulating data based on the user's instructions.

processor voltage   Sets the output of the onboard voltage regulator.

program   Sequence of instructions that describe how data is to be processed.

Program menu   Lists all programs installed on the computer.

PROMPT-PG   Command in autoexec.bat that causes the active drive and directory path to be displayed on the command line.

protected mode   An area of memory that has no effect on other programs.

protected-mode memory addressing   Allows one program to fail without bringing down the rest of the system.

protocol   A controlled sequence of messages that are exchanged between two or more systems to accomplish a given task.

PS/2 keyboard   A type of connection used to connect a keyboard to the computer.

PS/2 mouse port   A type of connection used to connect a mouse to the computer.

public key   Provides access to encrypted files.

public switched telephone network (PSTN)   The telephone system that allows people in every corner of the world to communicate with anyone who has access to a telephone. It is the most common example of a network.

quick-launch buttons   Shortcuts to applications.

RAID (redundant array of inexpensive disks)   Provides fault tolerance to prevent loss of data in the event of a disk drive failure on a network server.

RAID 0   An array or group of disk drives used as a single disk. Data are written in chunks or stripes to all the drives in the array.

RAID 0/1   Also known as RAID 0+1 and RAID 10, it provides the performance of RAID 0 and the redundancy of RAID 1. It requires at least four drives to implement.

RAID 1   Requires at least two disk drives and writes data to two separate locations.

RAID 2   Requires a minimum of three disk drives and uses a hamming code to create an ECC for all data.

RAID 3   Requires a minimum of three synchronized disk drives and uses bit-level parity with a single-parity disk for fault tolerance.

RAID 4   Requires a minimum of three disk drives that do not need to be synchronized because data are written to the drives in blocks.

RAID 5   Requires a minimum of three disk drives and uses block-level parity, but unlike RAID 4, it spreads the parity information among all the drives in the array.

RAID controller   A specialized controller used in a RAID array.

RAID controller onboard memory   Used as a buffer and often backed up with an onboard battery.

RAID-5 volume   Consists of three or more parts of one or more drives or three or more entire drives.

RAM drive   Setting aside a portion of RAM to emulate a drive.

rambus inline memory module (RIMM)   Memory module with 184 pins that uses only RDRAM.

random-access memory (RAM)   Computer memory that is temporary.

random-access memory digital to analog converter (RAMDAC)   A specialized form of memory designed to convert digitally encoded images into analog signals for display.

raster image   A type of graphical image.

read/write head   Used to access the media in a hard disk drive.

read-only   An attribute that allows a file to be opened but not changed.

real mode   Refers to the microprocessor chip that addresses the first 1024 KB of conventional memory by assigning real addresses to real locations in memory.

real-mode memory addressing   Software, such as DOS, that can address only the first 1024 KB of memory.

Recovery Console   A command-line interface used to perform a variety of troubleshooting and recovery tasks in Windows 2000.

Recycle Bin   Stores deleted files, folders, etc until the user is ready to empty.

redundant NIC   In a network server, it serves as a backup NIC.

refresh rate   The number of times the display is reenergized.

REGEDIT   A utility used to edit the Registry.

regedit.exe   Displays the Registry in a hierarchical format.

registered jack type 11 (RJ-11)   A connector used by the modem and the telephone.

Registry   A hierarchical database for the information used by the Windows operating system.

Registry subtrees   The hierarchical structure of the Registry.

relational database   A collection of flat-file databases or tables.

resolution   Refers to the pixels in the screen.

Reverse Address Resolution Protocol (RARP)   A protocol used to obtain IP address information based on the physical or MAC address.

ring topology   Common in Ethernet LANs, this topology connects devices in the shape of a ring. Ring topology can be single-ring, where data travel in one direction, and dual-ring, which allows data to be sent bidirectionally.

ripping   The process of digital audio extraction.

RMDIR   DOS command that removes a directory or subdirectory.

ROM BIOS   Chip that contains software that sets and records the master configuration for all components in the system.

root   The top level of a directory.

root directory   The file system's main directory.

router   A networking device that makes decisions on how to send data packets.

Routing Information Protocol (RIP)   Operates between router devices to discover paths between networks. In an intranet, routers depend on a routing protocol to build and maintain information about how to forward packets toward the destination. RIP chooses routes based on the distance or "hop count."

RS-232   A standard for serial transmissions between computers and other devices.

Run feature   An alternate method of starting a program or accessing troubleshooting applications.

-s   Switch used with the ARP command that adds a permanent IP-to-MAC mapping.

Safe mode   Advanced feature used for troubleshooting purposes.

Safe mode/Device Manager   Troubleshooting options used to check whether problems are related to device conflicts.

sag   *See* brownout.

sampling rate   The rate at which the sound card can record audio information.

SCANDISK   DOS program designed to detect and repair errors on the hard drive or floppy drive.

SCANDISK/DEFRAG   SCANDISK can locate errors, while DEFRAG pulls together different pieces of the same file scattered throughout the disk so the file can be more easily read by the system.

scandskw.exe   ScanDisk for Windows checks the integrity of the media to repair problems that occur.

scanreg.exe   Used to back up or repair the system's Registry.

Screen Saver tab   Activates a screen saver on the desktop.

screen size   The actual size of the display on the monitor.

SCSI 1   Uses two different signaling systems, known as single-ended interface and differential interface.

SCSI adapter onboard memory   Uses onboard memory as a buffer or cache between the SCSI disk drives and the network server memory.

SCSI-3   The latest standard of the SCSI family. It combines all the best features of the previous SCSI standards. It uses LVD, which uses differential signaling, and supports up to 15 devices on a single cable, which can be up to 12 meters long.

sector   Unit of storage (512 bytes) within a track.

sequenced packet exchange/internetwork packet exchange (SPX/IPX)   The protocol suite originally employed by Novell Corporation's network operating system, Net-Ware. It delivers functions similar to those included in TCP/IP.

serial port   Transmits data to the printer one character at a time, and connects devices that use a serial interface.

server   A central computer that stores resources in a network. A repository for files that can be accessed and shared across a network by many users.

server support utilities   Used for backup and virus protection in support of the network server.

SET TEMP C:\TEMP   Command in autoexec.bat that sets up a temporary data-holding area in the TEMP directory.

setting the system hardware   The process of configuring the motherboard.

Setup program   The program that is run to add new configuration data to the Registry.

setuplog.txt   A file that is created during the installation process and contains the system setup information.

shielded twisted-pair (STP)   A pair of wires that forms a circuit that can transmit data. The wires are wrapped in metallic foil to shield them from noise.

Simple Mail Transport Protocol (SMTP)   Includes messaging services of TCP/IP and supports most Internet e-mail programs.

simple volume A basic disk that contains disk space from a complete single disk and is not fault tolerant.

simplex transmission A single, one-way data transmission.

single in-line memory module (SIMM) 72-pin memory module.

SiSoft Sandra System analyzer, diagnostic, and reporting assistant. It is a freeware program that can aid in troubleshooting and benchmarking computer components.

Small Computer Systems Interface (SCSI) An advanced interface controller that is ideal for high-end computers, including network servers.

SMARTDRV.EXE 2048 1024 Command in autoexec.bat that configures the system for a 1-MB disk cache in DOS and a 2-MB cache in Windows.

Socket 7 A standard CPU interface.

software The operating system and programs that run on the computer.

solenoids Coils of wires that form electromagnets used in the dot matrix printer.

sound card Device that allows the computer to handle audio information.

sound card memory Stores samples and holds instructions for MIDI devices.

sound card output Produces sound for devices such as headphones.

sound card ports Internal and external ports for connecting to input and output devices.

sound card processor Handles the basic instructions that drive the sound card as well as the routing of audio information.

Sounds utility Allows the user to adjust the system sounds.

spanned volume Includes disk space from multiple disks (up to 32 disks). It is not fault tolerant.

spike A sudden increase in voltage usually caused by lightning strikes.

spindle motor Drives the hard disk drive.

SpinRite Program used for recovering data from a crashed hard drive.

spooling An acronym for simultaneous peripheral operations online, it refers to the process of loading print jobs into a buffer (usually an area on a hard drive) until the printer is ready for a job.

spreadsheet An application that manipulates numerical data.

SRAM   A memory type that is relatively more expensive, but is fast and holds data when the power is turned off for a brief period of time.

standard voltage   Type of voltage.

standby power supply (SPS)   Battery backup that kicks in when voltage levels fall below normal.

star topology   Common in Ethernet LANs, it is made up of a central connection point (hub, etc.) where all cabling segments meet.

Start button   Contains the access to programs, control panel, etc.

Start menu   Provides access to the programs and functions on the PC.

Startup menu   Unique security feature in the Windows 9X operating system. A multistep process is used to get to the Startup menu.

storage   An organized repository for data.

stripped volume   Also known as RAID-0. Combines areas of free space from multiple hard disks, up to 32, into one logical volume. It is not fault tolerant.

subdirectories   A directory within a directory in DOS.

subnet mask   The second group of numbers in an IP address.

Super VGA (SVGA) monitor   A monitor that can display up to 16,777,216 colors because it can process a 24-bit-long description of a pixel.

Supervisor Password   On larger networks, this password restricts the computer BIOS.

surge   A brief increase in voltage usually caused by high demands on the power grid in a local area.

surge suppressor   Device that ensures that the voltage going to another device stays below a certain level.

swap files   Implementing virtual memory by swapping files between RAM and the hard disk drive.

switch   Also know as a multiport bridge, a switch is an operation added to a command to modify the output.

Symmetric DSL (SDSL)   Provides the same speed, up to 3 Mbps, for uploads and downloads.

synchronous DRAM   Allows the CPU to process data while another process is being queued.

Synchronous serial transmission   Data bits are sent together with a synchronizing clock pulse. In this transmission method, a built-in timing mechanism coordinates the clocks of the sending and receiving devices.

sysedit.exe   Used to modify text files such as the system ini files as well as config.sys and autoexec.bat.

system bus   A parallel collection of conductors that carry data and control signals from one component to the other.

system disk   A disk created to boot the computer to the operating system for trouble-shooting purposes. It contains the three required system files. Also known as a boot disk.

system file   A file required by DOS to boot up.

System File Checker (SFC)   A command-line utility that scans the operating system files to ensure that they are the correct ones.

System Properties   A tool in the Windows Control Panel that displays information relating to the system.

system resource   The mechanisms used to interface, communicate, and control individual device adapters along with the serial, parallel, and mouse ports.

system unit   A metal and plastic case that contains the basic parts of the computer system.

system.da0   Created when Windows successfully boots. This file is a backup of the system.dat file. If the system.dat file gets corrupted or deleted, rename the system.da0 file to system.dat to restore the Registry.

system.dat   A file that holds hardware, computer-specific profiles, and setting information.

system.ini   A file that contains hardware-setting information for the Windows configuration drivers. When the operating system needs to reference information about the hardware, it uses the system.ini file.

system-monitoring agent   Vendor-specific software that monitors various aspects of the network server such as configuration, mass storage, the NIC, etc.

Task Manager   Displays active applications and identifies those applications that are not responding so that they can be shut down.

Taskbar   Contains quick launch buttons, clock, etc.

TCP/IP utilities   Most vendors implement the suite to include a variety of utilities for viewing configuration information and for troubleshooting problems.

Telnet   Enables terminal access to local or remote systems.

thin film media   Magnetically sensitive coating in the hard drive.

TIME   Command in autoexec.bat that causes DOS to prompt the user for the time and date.

token   A special signal.

Token Ring   Based on the token-passing access control method.

topology   The structure of a network. It includes the physical topology, that is, the layout of the media (or wire), and the logical topology, which is how the media are accessed by the hosts.

Toslink   A fiber-optic port developed by Toshiba for the digital-in port.

tower cases   Designed to sit vertically on the floor beneath a desk.

Tower model   A type of case that stands vertically.

TPCON   Novell uses the NLM to display TCP/IP connection and protocol information.

TRACEROUTE   A configuration utility used in UNIX/Linux to trace packets on a network.

TRACERT   A configuration utility used in Windows to trace packets on a network.

tracert.exe   A utility that traces a packet from the computer to an Internet host.

tracking mechanism   A motor and drive system that moves the lens into the correct position to access a specific area of a CD.

tracks   Magnetic area created by formatting the hard drive.

transferring   The fifth step in the laser-printing process where toner is attached to the latent image and transferred to the paper.

Transmission Control Protocol (TCP)   The primary Internet protocol for the reliable delivery of data. TCP includes facilities for end-to-end connection establishment, for error detection and recovery, and for metering the rate of data flow into the network.

Transmission Control Protocol/Internet Protocol (TCP/IP)   A suite of protocols that has become the dominant standard for internetworking.

transport layer   The third layer in the TCP/IP model. It provides end-to-end management of the communication session.

troubleshooting   A series of logical steps used to diagnose a computer problem.

true color   Also known as 24-bit bit-depth, it allows eight bits for each of the three additive primary colors: red, green, and blue.

tweening   The process of defining keyframes.

twisted pair   A pair of wires that forms a circuit that can transmit data.

Type I PCMCI card   A memory expansion unit.

Type II PCMCI card   An expansion for devices except hard drives.

Type III PCMCI card   An expansion for hard drives.

Ultra ATA disk drive   Refers to the transfer rate.

unidirectional   A type of parallel port used in older systems.

uninterruptible power supply (UPS)   Power supplied by a battery that is constantly recharged by a regular power source.

universal asynchronous receiver/transmitter (UART)   This type of chip determines the top speed at which devices can communicate using the port. It handles both synchronous and asynchronous transmissions.

universal serial bus (USB)   Based on Plug and Play, USB devices are installed with minimal configuration. A hot-swappable interface used to connect peripherals such as the USB speaker system.

UNIX   Used primarily to run and maintain computer networks.

unshielded twisted-pair (UTP)   A twisted pair of wires that relies on the cancellation effect to limit signal degradation.

upper memory blocks (UMBs)   Allocated memory in upper memory.

upper memory/expanded memory   Also known as reserved memory. It includes memory addresses between 640 KB and 1024 KB (1 MB).

upstream   The process of transferring data from the end user to the server.

USB cable   Used to connect a USB device to the computer. The device and cable must be the same speed.

user datagram protocol (UDP)   Offers a connectionless service to applications. UDP uses lower overhead than TCP and can tolerate a level of data loss.

user interface   The part of the operating system that is used to issue commands.

user password   Provides the option of setting a password that must be entered before the system will boot.

user profiles   Specific settings for all the users that log on to the computer.

user.da0   Created when Windows successfully boots. This file is a backup of the user.dat file. If the user.dat file gets corrupted or deleted, rename the user.da0 file to user.dat to restore the Registry.

user.dat   File that contains all the user-specific information.

utility files   Enable the user to manage system resources, troubleshoot the system, and configure the system settings.

utility program   Used to maintain and repair the operating system.

variable-frequency synthesizer circuit   Multiplies the clock signal so that the motherboard can support several speeds of CPUs.

vector based   A type of graphical image.

very high data rate DSL (VDSL)   Capable of bandwidths of 13–52 Mbps.

very high speed backbone network service (vBNS)   The current U.S. Internet infrastructure that consists of a commercial backbone and a high-speed service.

video   Configuration data that identifies the video adapter.

video adapter   Also called a display adapter or video board. An integrated circuit card in a computer or in some cases, a monitor that provides digital-to-analog conversion.

video adapter onboard memory   Uses memory to store the image that is displayed on the monitor.

Video BIOS   Provides the set of video functions that can be used by the software to access the video hardware.

video board   *See* video adapter.

video capture card   Converts video signals from different sources into digital signals that can be manipulated by the computer.

video capture software   Used to capture frames of television video and convert them into digital formats that can be processed by the system.

video card or adapter   The interface between the computer and monitor.

video decoder circuit   Used to convert the analog signal into a stream of digital signals.

video display terminal (VDT)   A terminal with a display and a keyboard.

video display unit (VDU)   *See* video display terminal.

Video Electronics Standards Association (VESA)   Defines how software can determine the capability of a display.

video graphics array (VGA)   How data are passed between the computer and the display.

video memory   The memory in the computer's video system.

video RAM   The memory utilized by the video.

viewability   The ability to see the screen image from different angles.

virtual device driver (vxd) file   A file that takes the place of the DEVICE= and LOADHIGH= commands.

virtual memory   Manipulating hard disk space to provide more memory than is actually installed.

virus   Program written with malicious intent.

virus scan   Checks all hard drives for viruses.

visual graphics array (VGA)   The lowest common denominator of display modes.

voice coil actuator   Positions the head actuator.

Voltage Regulator Enhanced (VRE)   Motherboard jumper to select voltage.

warm boot   Restarting the computer while it's running.

wavetable sound card   Uses digitized samples of instruments to reproduce audio.

web browser   An application used to locate and display pages from the Internet.

wide-area network (WAN)   A communication network that covers a large geographical area.

WIN switch   Allows the technician to start Windows from the command line.

win.com   A Registry file that controls the initial environment checks and loads Windows 95 core components.

win.ini   A file that contains parameters that can be altered to change the Windows environment or software settings to suit the user's preferences. This file is a software initialization file for Windows. It contains information about some Windows defaults, the placement of windows, the color settings for the screen, available ports, printers, fonts, and software applications.

Windows 98 Setup wizard   Guides the user through the installation process.

Windows Explorer   A Windows utility that represents the file-management structure.

Windows IP configuration (winipcfg.exe)   A tool that allows the technician to view the basic IP networking settings of a Windows 95, Windows 98, or Windows Me computer.

Windows NT kernel   Loads the correct device drivers in the proper order.

Windows RAM (WRAM)   Memory for video.

WINIPCFG   A configuration utility used in Windows 95, 98, and 2000 (graphical interface) to access IP address, MAC address, subnet mask, and default gateway.

word processor   An application that creates, edits, stores, and prints documents.

workstations   Individual computers in a network.

writing   The third step in the laser-printing process where the photosensitive drum is scanned with the laser beam.

wscript.exe   Allows configuration of the properties relating to the Windows scripting host.

WYSIWYG   What-you-see-is-what-you-get.

YUV   The color model used for encoding video. Y is the luminosity of the black and white signal. U and V are color difference signals. U is red minus Y (R – Y), and V is blue minus Y (B – Y).

Zero Insertion Force   A type of processor.

zones   A server's area of authority.

Index

H

J–K

L